Empowering Children

Play-Based Curriculum for Lifelong Learning

Fifth Edition

Empowering Children

Play-Based Curriculum for Lifelong Learning

Dale Shipley

NELSON

NELSON

***Empowering Children*, Fifth Edition**

by Dale Shipley

Vice President, Editorial Higher Education:
Anne Williams

Senior Acquisitions Editor:
Lenore Taylor-Atkins

Marketing Manager:
Terry Fedorkiw

Developmental Editor:
Theresa Fitzgerald

Photo Researcher:
Sheila Hall

Permissions Coordinator:
Sheila Hall

Content Production Manager:
Claire Horsnell

Production Service:
Cenveo Publisher Services

Copy Editor:
Heather Sangster at Strong Finish

Proofreader:
Jessie Coffey

Indexer:
Belle Wong

Senior Manufacturing Coordinator:
Ferial Suleman

Design Director:
Ken Phipps

Managing Designer:
Franca Amore

Cover Design:
Johanna Liburd

Compositor:
Cenveo Publisher Services

Printed and bound in Canada
9 19

For more information contact Nelson Education Ltd., 1120 Birchmount Road, Toronto, Ontario, M1K 5G4. Or you can visit our Internet site at nelson.com

Cover Image Credits:
Boy in front of trees: Ellen Senisi
Children blowing bubbles: Ariel Skelley/Getty Images
Girl with kite: Katrina Wittkamp/Getty Images
Boy in field: Ellen Senisi
Girl jumping: Biddiboo/Getty Images
Children in snow: Theresa Fitzgerald
Child by fence: Sandy Matos/Nelson Education Ltd.
Boy with snowman: Alwynn Pinard
Three children in field: Chris Tobin/Getty Images

Library and Archives Canada Cataloguing in Publication

Shipley, Carol Dale, 1945-
Empowering children: play-based curriculum for lifelong learning/Dale Shipley. —5th ed.

Includes bibliographical references and index.
ISBN 978-0-17-650223-2

1. Play. 2. Early childhood education. 3. Curriculum planning. I. Title.

LB1140.35.P55S55 2012 372.21
C2011-905345-4

ISBN-13: 978-0-17-650223-2
ISBN-10: 0-17-650223-8

Brief Contents

Contents

Preface

About the Author

Dale Shipley is an associate professor emeritus of the School of Early Childhood Education at Ryerson University and was its director from 2001 to 2006. During her career, Dale taught at all educational levels, from preschool to postsecondary. She spent several years as a professor in the early childhood education (ECE) program at Algonquin College in Ottawa and as a researcher and adviser on college academic planning. Dale was the first manager of the Ontario College University Consortium Council, a senior policy analyst for the Skills and Learning Task Force for Human Resources Development Canada, and a policy analyst on secondment to the Ontario College Standards and Accreditation Council. Dale is a graduate of McMaster University, Hamilton; Wheelock College, Boston; and Nova Southeastern University, Fort Lauderdale, where she earned a doctorate in early and middle childhood education.

Purpose of This Textbook

Empowering Children is designed to help you build a solid foundation for professional practice in early childhood education. The fifth edition continues to assume that students learn more efficiently when clear links are made between theory and practice, but this textbook does not embrace a particular model for practice. There are references to various ECE models, including Reggio Emilia, and to the approaches to curriculum described by developmentally appropriate practice and emergent curriculum. *Empowering Children* proposes, however, that an early childhood education model for Canadian programs might incorporate the best elements of many play-based models in ways that resonate with Canada's diverse population, our vast geography and climatic conditions, and particular Canadian values. We might also invent new approaches that prepare children to meet the unique challenges that today's children may face as adults. Therefore, this textbook draws upon approaches and practices derived from a number of constructivist models, which tend to evolve as the profession acquires new insights into the capacity of children to learn through play, new research on the brain, and greater evidence of the powerful effects of play on children's holistic development.

A good starting point is for ECE students to appreciate the roots of our profession. It is important for ECE students to become familiar with the philosophical and practical approaches of viable ECE models, question current practices and embrace those based on solid research evidence, and reflect on their own values and their experience. This foundation enables ECEs to evolve an approach and practices that best serve the children in their programs and their families. Canada is profoundly diverse in culture, geography, climate, and lifestyles. A one-size-fits-all model will not meet the varied needs and interests of Canadian families from coast to coast, even though some values and practices are likely to be common. Programs that respect and trust the integrity of children's freely chosen play may frame their philosophical approaches and take their planning cues and practices from the children and families they serve and still remain true to a philosophy based on the importance of play in childhood and developmentally appropriate outcomes.

The challenge in ECE is to create a setting and a climate for play and to plan programs that enhance children's play and guide their play in profitable directions. The well-planned early childhood education program is a catalyst for play, development, and learning; it fosters curiosity, self-expression, independence, interdependence, the self-confidence to have and pursue one's own ideas and to make wise choices, a desire to succeed, persistence with challenging tasks, mental health, and positive habits of mind that last a lifetime. ECEs need to know the learning processes that children engage in when they play as they gather meaning, uncover concepts, and understand what they see and do. All of these factors ensure that early childhood education in general and children's play in particular promote learning-to-learn; the achievement of outcomes in the physical, social, emotional, and cognitive domains; the ability to reflect, originate, and invent; and, most important of all, a sense of connection to other people and the natural world that provides hope, meaning, and fulfillment in children's lives.

A core belief represented in this text is that children in well-designed programs that adopt a developmental framework for curriculum and play-based principles for practice will make progress. Their progress depends on well-organized, strategic environments; a supportive emotional climate; meaningful play opportunities; freedom to choose what they will do and play from an array of interesting possibilities; and adults who know when and how to guide children's play in positive directions.

The Context for This Fifth Edition

The 21st century calls for an interdisciplinary approach within the early childhood education profession that is central to the development of our nation's human capital and the ongoing productivity and economic success of our nation. That is why this fifth edition draws on research and opinion from allied disciplines, including political and social sciences, economics, and philosophy. Although Canada made great strides in terms of its wealth, overall living standards, and global profile during the 20th century, our nation has surrendered elements of its economic strength, world leadership, and humanitarian reputation during the past decade. Expert analysts of Canada's status in the world, including the Organisation for Economic Co-operation and Development (OECD), have cautioned our nation about its failure to provide a national framework for early childhood education services and suggest that Canada's relatively poor showing on some status indicators, such as literacy rates, child poverty, and child health, may be related to the absence of a national strategy for our young children. It is time to affirm Canada's commitment to children and to the development of human capital by actively supporting access by all of Canada's children to early childhood education services that reflect national values, aspirations, and standards. In the global society and the new economy of this century, national prosperity depends on people's capacity to innovate, to find novel solutions to pressing problems, and to adapt to constant change and increasingly complex systems. The development of human capital begins when children are very young. The human foundation for healthy social and spiritual connection in a time of constant change, for success in learning, and for creative thinking and innovation for the future is laid during the early childhood period, from birth to age eight.

This fifth edition of *Empowering Children: Play-Based Curriculum for Lifelong Learning* continues to emphasize children's need for play not just as a pleasant pastime but because play is fundamental to children's development in all domains. This fifth edition also recognizes the profound demographic changes in our Canadian society and the urgent need to integrate children and their families who come from diverse cultures and who have their own values and beliefs about child-rearing priorities and early learning.

The importance of these early years to all later learning calls for a knowledgeable, systematic approach to planning and implementing sound, relevant ECE programs for Canada's young children. As in the earlier editions, the emphasis in this edition is on the links among play, the learning environment, child development, brain research, cultural priorities, and learning theory. All of these factors need to be examined so that children's play supports the achievement of developmental outcomes in the emotional, social, cognitive, and physical domains; promotes learning-to-learn; nurtures the ability to contemplate, originate, and invent; and fosters mental health and a positive approach to life.

The design of learning centres continues to be an organizing principle for this edition and forms the backbone of the text. Learning centres are concrete, visible, and tangible, and they help ECEs organize play so that all types of play are accessible and tempting to children. Learning centres help ECEs make efficient use of space and resources for play, foster constructive interactions, and facilitate learning that promotes discovery, elicits questions, encourages investigation, leads to concept formation, and supports communication. Developmental principles are linked to suggestions for designing learning centres and for choosing equipment, materials, and supplies. Play activities and learning experiences for children are included in the chapters on the learning centres in order to link theory and practice. A core belief represented in this text is that children in programs that adopt a clearly formulated set of planning principles, an explicit curriculum including clearly stated developmental outcomes, and strategic play-based learning practices will make developmental progress in all domains, regardless of their particular strengths, weaknesses, or disabilities.

This Textbook as a Learning Tool

Early childhood educators-in-training should gain from this textbook an enhanced sense of the importance of their professional roles in creating challenging play environments, in facilitating the optimum development of each child in all domains, and in helping children become eager learners and original thinkers. This fifth edition reinforces the values and the beliefs with which ECEs identify and explains how to put them into practice. The textbook uses the term *ECE* to refer to students preparing for professional practice and those who are already registered professionals. It is intended to be a how-to book that both students and practising ECEs may follow as they plan for play. It helps ECEs assess children's developmental progress; plan, implement, and evaluate play experiences and curriculum; and design play environments that promote children's ability to think for themselves, value things that matter, and achieve their goals. The chapters of this edition are organized to facilitate independent learning by students who may be enrolled in regular or distance education programs, full-time or part-time. The learning outcomes at the beginning of each chapter identify the knowledge and skills base that students should be able to demonstrate as a foundation for practice. Reflective practice is promoted by encouraging students to consider the points raised at the beginning of each chapter under the heading "Before reading this chapter, you should have..." The Learning Activities at the end of each chapter encourage students to apply the knowledge they have gained, review what they have read, and practise the skills they have learned. And they enable ECEs to add to their repertoire of resources for planning and implementing programs and activities by creating models, charts, and plans; designing tools that facilitate assessments of children's progress; and evaluating the curriculum, the environment, and planning strategies. Key words appear in bold type throughout the text. These words, and others, are defined in the Glossary at the end of the text, beginning on page 483. The end-of-chapter Summary explains the main thrust of the chapter without repeating the detail included in the chapter. The chapter should be read thoroughly before tackling the Learning Activities.

Changes to the Fifth Edition of *Empowering Children*

This edition incorporates many of the astute recommendations made by a team of reviewers from across Canada who have contributed their professional knowledge and insights related to changes and new developments that have occurred in the ECE profession. In so many ways, their insights and advice have made me reflect further on my approach for the fifth edition and have influenced my thinking about a viable approach for ECE in Canada. It was the reviewers' suggestions to add a chapter that discusses various curriculum models for ECE and to give more attention to the conclusions of recent research on the brain, project-based learning, and the urgent cultural diversity issues in programs. The fifth edition continues to emphasize the crucial role of play in early childhood; puts play at the centre of early childhood education philosophy; and shows how to employ play in ways that will ensure that children uncover concepts, acquire skills and knowledge, and make developmental progress while they are engaged with the play activities and experiences they choose.

Some reviewers asked that more attention be paid to the philosophy and practices of the schools of Reggio Emilia, which provide many examples of excellence and innovation in early childhood education from which our Canadian programs may learn and benefit. Our cultural and social contexts in Canada differ widely, however, from those of the Italian community in which their approach was first developed. This fifth edition makes a strong case for inventing a made-in-Canada approach—a model for early childhood education that fits our diverse Canadian contexts; represents distinct Canadian values; and equips our children with the knowledge, skills, awareness, and spiritual and moral fibre they will need to lead successful, fulfilling lives in our increasingly complex nation and the challenging world beyond. This edition continues, also, to recommend an advocacy role for ECEs as a professional obligation. Stable government funding and a legislated national framework for early childhood education would ensure that all children in Canada are able to access high-quality programs, through expanded early childhood education programs and full-day play-based kindergarten before they start formal schooling in grade one.

As always, reviewers, who represent a cross-section of program models across Canada, do not always agree in their perceptions of what should be emphasized and changed. Every attempt has been made to address the dichotomy of interests and opinion and to find a reasonable compromise. Nelson Education's ECE Resource Centre website, www.ece.nelson.com, continues to be a useful resource for readers. The website houses an expanded series of play activities and learning experiences for children that were formerly included in the text. Appendix A: Developmental Outcomes for Children Ages Two to Six of the textbook is also available on the website, as are links to other websites that are useful to ECE students and instructors.

Acknowledgments

I owe special thanks to my reviewers for this fifth edition of *Empowering Children.* I have found their reviews and recommendations to be perceptive, thoughtful, and balanced. Their expert opinions and generous advice have supported my belief in the value of play and its capacity to enhance development and learning in early childhood.

I thoroughly appreciate the supportive guidance and expertise of Nelson editors Alwynn Pinard, Theresa Fitzgerald, Claire Horsnell, and Strong Finish copy editor Heather Sangster.

Canada and the ECE profession recently lost Dr. J. Fraser Mustard, the internationally respected medical researcher and expert on the social, emotional, physical, and intellectual potential of young children. Dr. Mustard was instrumental in refocusing the Canadian child care debate to emphasise the role of early childhood education in the development of human potential. He was co-author, with the Hon. Margaret Norrie McCain, of *The Early Years Study: Reversing the Real Brain Drain* (1999); *The Early Years Study Three Years Later* (2002); and *The Early Years Study 2: Putting Science into Action*—studies that influenced provincial decisions to institute full-day kindergarten. *The Early Years Study 3: Making Decisions, Taking Action*, for which he was also a co-author, was published just days after Dr. Mustard's passing. His timely contribution will be missed and his wise leadership, energy and outspoken commitment to young children have inspired and guided the work of so many of us in the profession.

Pierre Giroux has patiently endured the writing of five editions of this book and he has encouraged and supported me every step of the way. I dedicate this edition to my son and daughter, Lyle and Dee, who both know intuitively what children need and crave and from whom I continue to learn. My grandchildren, Avi and Maya, remind me every day of the joyous, precious gift that is childhood.

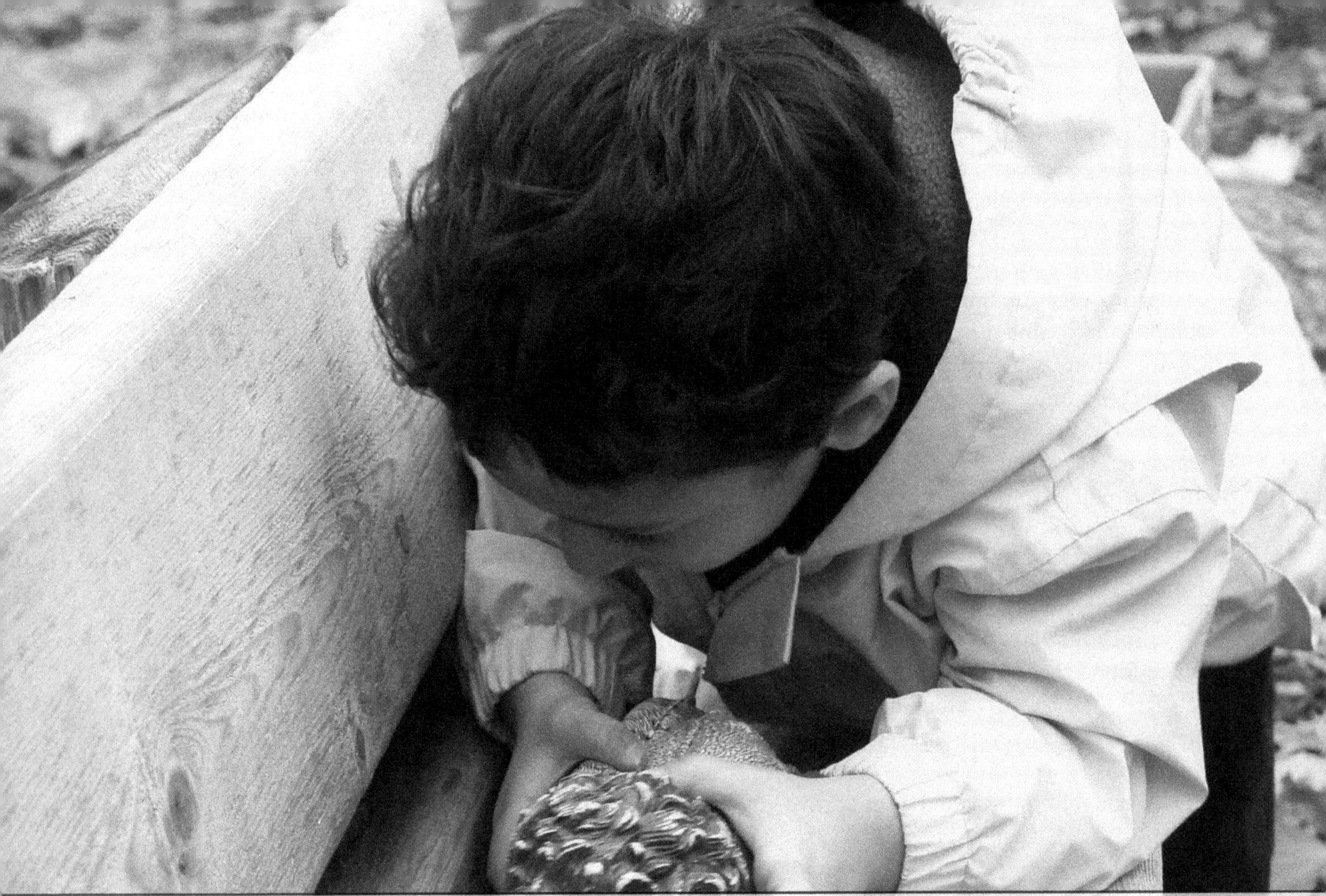

Section I

Setting the Scene: Perspectives and Contexts Related to Play

Section I introduces the following topics:

- key goals for early childhood education in the 21st century
- the political and social context for early childhood education in Canada today
- historical evolution of the meaning of play
- emergent curriculum and a new pedagogy of play and learning
- developmental stages of play, categories of play, and the social contexts of play
- current issues in early childhood education

“Play nourishes every aspect of children’s development. It forms the foundation of intellectual, social, physical, and emotional skills necessary for success in school and life” (Canadian Council on Learning, 2011). As an early childhood educator (ECE), you will play a central role, along with parents, in helping young children acquire, through play-based programs, the habits of mind, dispositions for learning, and developmental skills they need to optimize their human potential; to be happy, well-adjusted children; and to improve their chances for a successful life. You are entering a profession that originated in Canada about 70 years ago and has made progress in spite of the absence of public and political support. The postsecondary program you have entered will prepare you to work as an ECE professional, which includes becoming an advocate for young children in Canada. Your training should enable you to provide programs that support children’s physical and perceptual development, social competence, emotional stability, healthy attitudes, respect for themselves and others, ability to self-regulate, coping skills, persistence in overcoming challenges, and motivation and enthusiasm for learning—all key factors for successful living in the 21st century. To graduate, you should demonstrate the knowledge, skills, and dispositions you need to serve in a wide range of professional roles in early childhood education.

Chapter 1 explains the philosophical bias of this textbook and the political and social contexts for early childhood education in Canada. Early childhood education includes the years from birth to age eight; this textbook focuses on the years from ages two to six. Chapter 2 is about the history of play. Do not be discouraged by the density of historical facts; this chapter provides a brief outline that can be used as an ongoing resource, showing the origins of early childhood education as a discipline and tracing the pedagogical ideas and views of children and childhood to the present day. Over the past one hundred years, play has increased in status as new knowledge emerges about the key role of play in child development and learning. Some knowledge of the paradigm shifts and the historical evolution of theories of play is necessary so that ECEs can resist pressure from parents, the public, and policymakers to impose structure and academic learning on children much too early. The history tables in Chapter 2 may be used as a resource for later chapters, but they should be read and discussed early in the training program because the historical review provides a sense of both the origins and the integrity of the ECE profession.

Chapter 3 describes the role of play as the primary vehicle for development and learning for children ages two to six, and the nature and characteristics of types of play. Viable early childhood education depends on respect for children’s play and children’s right to choose their play and on knowing how various play styles contribute to each child’s development. Our ability to support the purity of children’s play depends on our knowing how play fuels the child’s imagination, enhances her sense of the world, and contributes to a “rich inner life” (Bettelheim, 1987b). Play is the essential medium for achieving developmental outcomes related to lifelong learning, good physical and mental health, positive attitudes, compassion, empathy, and a capacity for sustaining social relationships. It is increasingly the mission of ECEs to defend children’s right to be playful and to define play. The profession should not be coerced into forsaking the gift of childhood play to the interests of other disciplines and to pressures to raise test scores using outdated pedagogies. The ECE’s role is to observe children’s play; to plan, organize, and adapt the play environment to accommodate children’s choices; to provide the resources for play; and to offer opportunities for children to be full participants in a wide variety of categories, styles, and contexts for play.

Chapter 4 raises key issues related to children's development and opportunities to learn and adapt in a stressed society, where play has often been misunderstood and underestimated. Since the beginning of the 21st century, many health issues have become urgent; this chapter addresses issues related to children's mental and physical health and **spiritual development**. The urgency and impact of these issues make a strong case for protecting children's right to play outdoors as well as indoors, and underline their need for spontaneous, regular play in settings that allow children to be in close contact with nature and natural elements. A clear understanding of how play leads to learning is essential because the value of play is too often challenged by parents and school systems who believe, quite wrongly, that young children should be introduced to formal, academic learning at earlier ages. Even where full-day kindergarten is in place, the play-based mandate of these programs is at risk under several circumstances: where kindergarten classes split with grade one have a larger share of academic learning than the kindergarten children are ready for (Hammer, 2011); where kindergarten teachers are untrained in play-based pedagogy and resort to traditional teaching practices; and, where the kindergarten environments fail to provide organized learning centres that promote many categories and contexts for play-based learning and holistic development.

1 Early Childhood Education for a Creative Society

> "Tinkering at the margins will no longer do. We need a learning and development system that is in sync with the new creative economy....We need a system of learning and human development that mobilizes and harnesses human creative talent en masse."
>
> —Richard Florida, *The Great Reset* (2010)

Before Reading This Chapter, Have You

- discussed the assumptions and values upon which this textbook is based that are briefly outlined in the Preface and Introduction to Section I?
- explored this textbook to learn about its various components and what you should bring to the reading of each chapter?
- considered the role of play in your own childhood and how you learned while you were playing?
- examined your own views about school and learning and formulated a preliminary understanding of the relationship between play and learning?

Outcomes

After reading and understanding this chapter, you should be able to

- identify some global and national forces of the 21st century on the status and practice of early childhood education in Canada;
- communicate clearly why you have chosen to become an ECE; and
- explain why ECEs should be able to defend the role of play in early childhood education.

Political and Social Contexts for Early Childhood Education in Canada

The business sector, the education sector, and many of today's parents see the connection between early childhood education and a nation's economic prosperity. They want to ensure that children are prepared for success in learning and in life, but in Canada there is still no clear plan for achieving this vision. You are entering the profession at a time when the role and practice of ECE in most nations of the world are evolving to meet changing social, economic, and political demands. Globalization is already a central feature of the 21st century. This means that countries are in competition for the world's resources and are trying to either retain or acquire a standard of living that has been enjoyed for the past century primarily by countries of the Western world. Most Western nations know that their country's future prosperity and global competitiveness depend on the skills, knowledge, and dispositions of their children for getting along with one another, remaining healthy, and being engaged in learning and innovation. There is greater awareness of the impact of children's social conscience, empathy for others, and creative capacities on their own quality of life and on the quality of life of the societies they inhabit.

Canada has been slow to acknowledge the value of early childhood education. European nations funded public ECE programs for their children as early as the 1940s, right after the World War II. Canada remains the only Western nation that does not provide a national framework for early childhood education and the public funding to support it. Canada currently meets about 50 percent of the total demand for early learning and child care services for young children (*The Early Years Study 3* reports improvement). There is hope on the horizon as more provinces offer full-day kindergarten for all four- and five-year-olds, but early childhood education programs need to begin well before age four. Sadly, children under four have limited access to publicly funded programs, which leaves too many infants, toddlers, and young preschoolers in the care of untrained adults while their parents work. Informal arrangements offer no guarantee of quality or of developmental programming, much less of children's right to play and whether they will get adequate exercise or the freedom to safely explore and play outdoors, preferably in a natural setting. The federal government in 2006 implemented the Universal Child Care Benefit, which offers $1200 a year per child for families with dependent children under age six, instead of funding the actual cost of viable programs for young children. In its decision not to provide a national framework and federal funding for ECE programs, Canada stands in stark contrast to other nations of the world, which have invested significant portions of their gross domestic

Cooperative games

product in the care, nurture, play, development, and early learning of young children (McCain et al, 2011).

Canada's early childhood education programs depend largely on the integrity and competence of the people who manage and staff these programs. There are half-day programs and all-day private and nonprofit licensed child-care programs, some of which operate in dreary facilities that were not designed for children's play and daily living. There are also family resource centres and drop-in preschool programs, where parents and caregivers may bring children for a few hours each week to play with each other under parental supervision. At the provincial level, a growing array of full- and half-day junior and senior kindergarten programs is operated by the school systems. Most provinces and territories also offer a network of private-home, family-based child care. The administrative services that recruit and oversee them are licensed to monitor the quality of care provided in private homes, too often by minimally trained caregivers. There are also nursery school programs, some run by nonprofit agencies or cooperatives, for monthly fees, usually paid by families, that provide play-based programming for a few hours each week. These half-day programs primarily serve families with a stay-at-home parent or caregiver. Infant care for children under 12 months of age has declined as some parents who are eligible for maternity leave subsidies opt to remain at home with their infants for the first year. In recent years, families with means have increasingly hired nannies to provide in-home care for their children. Care of this kind is unregulated, and the value to young children depends on the training and commitment of the nanny, who is under parental supervision. This patchwork of paid services is usually amalgamated within municipal and provincial jurisdictions under "children's services" departments, each governed by its own regulations and policies, which do not conform to national standards for care, environments, professional training, or early development and learning curriculum. In 2009, Ontario inaugurated the first College of Early Childhood Educators in North America, which provides a legal framework for the work of all persons in Ontario who call themselves ECEs. Other Canadian jurisdictions may follow suit, and greater professional recognition may lead eventually to some harmonization of ECE standards nationally.

The effects of globalization in the first decade of the 21st century are altering the balance of power in the world. The **information age** has transformed societies and exposed the interdependence of nations. Global communications have been transformed by new technologies, and free trade has been accompanied by the rapid transport of natural resources, manufactured goods, and foods from and to all parts of the globe. Former Third World nations have made significant gains in their standard of living. The imperatives of survival and prosperity in a realigned world require developed nations to recognize new centres of power, acknowledge various threats to national security, and adapt to the changing flow of trade and money among nations. But the old order of life in the Western world is affected by climate change and environmental decay: global food production has decreased as a result of extreme climatic conditions, and vast populations living in lowlands migrate to seek safer places to live.

How do these dramatic changes relate to early childhood education in the 21st century? They motivate leaders, educators, and parents to re-evaluate the future for today's children, to speculate on what kind of adulthood they can anticipate, and to ask how children should be prepared so they can adapt to a world that their parents could not even have imagined when they themselves were children. It is important to equip them with the emotional, social, physical, and intellectual abilities they will need to adapt to change, to shape a viable future for themselves, and to contribute to a society that is socially just and life-sustaining. In the creative, knowledge-based society of the future, safety, security, and prosperity may depend much more on people's capacity to innovate, to find novel solutions to problems, and to deal effectively with increasingly complex systems and relationships.

Your Role in This Context

How do all these changes in the world affect you as an aspiring ECE? They emphasize the responsibilities attached to your professional role because you will be obliged not only to refer to the proven practices and values of past and current ECEs, but also to invent new approaches and to respond to changing needs without having clear precedents to follow. You are required to become a skilled practitioner and innovator in a field that cherishes childhood and play while preparing children for successful adaptation to a society that is changing dramatically. Your chosen profession will demand high levels of commitment in order to optimize children's potential; to help parents understand the forces their children face as they grow up; to prepare children for risks and opportunities that you have not likely encountered yourself; and to ground children emotionally, socially, spiritually, physically, and intellectually for a future that, at this time, we can only guess at.

How does all this change affect you personally? You may become an innovator who asks questions that invite new insights. You may become a role model for adults who find it hard to let go of deeply ingrained beliefs and practices and who cannot readily adapt to new challenges. You should consider the integrity of your own behaviour in a world where North America and Europe no longer claim dominion over the values, practices, and standards of other cultures and nations. You might consider what you value and whether they are the right values for the future. And you ought to question your past practices and evaluate whether they fit with new realities. When you have reflected on all of these questions and issues, you will probably be in a position to assess how your changing perceptions of the world and your sense of the future for today's children should influence what the children in your care experience, understand, and integrate into their daily routines, conversations, and aspirations. These expectations are daunting, but they also pose an exciting challenge as you learn and acquire a better sense of what may constitute a positive and healthy path into the future for yourself and the children you care for and guide. This reflection is the first step in developing your own philosophy of education, a task outlined in the last chapter of this book.

Canadian Challenges

The links between children's play, development, and early learning, and the later ability of human beings to perform at optimum levels in adulthood are clear and compelling. Most important is a stable emotional foundation that contributes to a healthy outlook, self-respect and empathy for others, and mental health. Children's futures also depend on their ability to cope with the complex natural and social forces that will have an impact on them throughout their lives. Technological advancement requires people who have the sophisticated abilities and knowledge to participate in the constant innovation that feeds the new economy. Transformation of the workplace from the industrial age to the information age has already occurred, and many people have been left out. The nature of work and everyday living in the information age has become more complex and demands higher levels of social and emotional competence, perceptual and physical skills, and thinking abilities. The development of human capital needed now and for the future should begin when children are very young. Early childhood education plays a significant role in the development of a nation's human capital (Mustard, 2004; Cleveland & Krashinsky, 2004; Florida, 2009).

On an individual level, there is growing evidence that the quality of children's experiences in the early years, even as early as the first six months of life, affects their ability as adults to handle stress, fight depression, and ward off physical and mental health problems. Children who develop optimally in early childhood are more successful in school, stay in school longer, and achieve success as adults in the workforce (Chetty, 2010; Human Resources Development Canada [HRDC], 2002; Mustard, 2010). The impact of early nutrition and exercise, especially the positive effects of physical play outdoors, preferably in environments where children have close, regular, and spontaneous contact with nature, is well documented (Louv, 2005; Pearlman-Hougie, 2010; Suzuki, 2010). The influence of early childhood experience on individual human development and on the success and sustainability of a whole society is profound (McCain et al, 2011).

A Renewed Vision for Early Childhood Education in Canada

The changing world calls upon us to reframe early childhood education in Canada so that it fits with the challenges we face as a nation, but also fully respects the rights of each child to a stable, healthy, safe childhood; to have regular, spontaneous contact with nature; and to experience a wide range of playful learning opportunities. The focus of the past several decades on nurturing, comfortable environments with warm, responsive caregivers, and enriched environments that value and promote play remains valid, but more expertise is needed. ECE goals acknowledge children's right to a happy, healthy, and stable childhood, one in which they feel confident in their environments, protected from harm, surrounded by people who love and nurture them, and where they are encouraged to explore and test their developing abilities through play that engages all developmental domains: physical, cognitive, social, and emotional. To achieve these goals, children need to engage in "playful learning" (Broadhead, Wood, & Howard, 2010, p. 181), purposeful activity, and timely challenges that move them steadily along a dynamic developmental continuum that makes the most of each child's individual potential. "Children develop only as the environment demands development" (Shenk, 2010, p. 35). Greater levels of accountability are required in the ECE profession to ensure that our programs for young children are delivering on their claims.

ECEs should be clear about the outcomes that children should have achieved by the time they start grade one and they should be able to explain how they are helping children achieve them through play. They should regularly assess and evaluate children's individual progress. These professional demands call for a balanced approach that protects and trusts children's play while ensuring that they make developmental progress. ECEs play a large role in the lives of young children, and the impact of their interactions and interventions is dynamic and lifelong. Children should enjoy and live their childhoods with freedom to explore, to play, and to "just be." To build a strong foundation for learning, children have to be well adapted at their present developmental stage; to be able to express themselves, learn, and grow at their own pace; and to be nurtured and protected according to their individual needs. Early childhood education programs help children adapt in healthy and constructive ways to the diverse contexts in which they are raised.

The world is wonderful.

A goal of early childhood education is to enable children to feel welcome in the environments they inhabit: their homes, schools, and communities. Programs help children feel included when they adapt their goals, strategies, and environments to the cultural, familial, and social particularities of the communities they serve. This is particularly important for First Nations children and also for the children of recent immigrant families. Effective programs blend the values and priorities of families with the challenges of the mainstream society in which their children are nurtured. Whatever culture children are reared in, we know that if they do not develop a strong foundation for learning in the early years, the benefits of formal public schooling later on are reduced. A strong foundation includes the acquisition of fundamental **cognitive skills** (e.g., perception, literacy, numeracy); constructive habits of mind (e.g., attending skills, eagerness to learn, curiosity, patience, persistence, and self-regulation); a disposition for learning, including acceptance of responsibility for their own learning; and wise use of time. It also ensures that children feel safe enough to play enthusiastically, to explore and take risks, and that they are valued for who they are and are healthy and strong enough to sustain challenges and competition from others. Equalizing the play opportunities for all children to achieve a full range of developmental outcomes is a key goal of early childhood education.

The Philosophical Bias of This Textbook

The philosophical bias of this fifth edition remains that play is of value in its own right, that spontaneous free play initiated by children needs to be protected, and that play is the primary vehicle for learning in early childhood. The devaluation of play creates human beings who are unable to deal with failure and unable to try again (Bettelheim, 1987b). Child development is a viable framework for observing and assessing children's individual developmental levels and needs and for determining, with children's input, which types of play activities and strategies will sustain children's interests, engage their energetic participation, and facilitate the child's successful learning. It is the role of the ECE to observe children in their play; to assess their individual needs and interests; and to plan and implement, in partnership with the interests and ideas expressed by the children and their parents, the environments for "playful learning" that will enable children to become all that they are capable of becoming. This role description captures the essence of **emergent curriculum**, in which program planning evolves from children's interests, but also factors in their unique developmental trajectories and their individual needs for challenge and stimulation in the untapped areas of their development and learning (Wien, 2008). It is important to connect children's developmental levels, abilities, needs, and interests in the curriculum (Essa, 2011). ECEs should also balance this requirement with a commitment to protect the quality and purity of children's play and to view "play as a bridge into a world of children's learning" (Broadhead et al., 2010, p. 178).

Canadian programs are obligated to support our culturally diverse population of children and their families in ways that respond directly to their cultural and family priorities. Families bring to Canada their own values about child-rearing priorities and early learning. We need to identify and respect their values, but we must also ensure that their children are able to adapt successfully to Canadian society. **Inclusive practice** extends to all children, irrespective of their physical or cognitive abilities, their economic conditions, or emotional challenges, and ECEs assume that children with special needs will make progress and achieve outcomes through individualized, play-based developmental programming. Research shows that play-based early childhood education improves all children's cognitive and academic performance, especially that of disadvantaged children. Evidence confirms that *early starters* in toddler and preschool programs have a significant academic advantage (Kamerman, 2001). These benefits are derived from programs that are nurturing and responsive to children's specific needs and actions, that value play, and that challenge them to make progress on all developmental outcomes, not just the ones easiest for them to achieve. Early childhood education programs are accountable when they observe, assess, and document children's play and their achievement of developmental outcomes.

Early childhood education should not be confused with formal academic instruction and pressures to accelerate children's performance in the traditional school subjects. ECE programs should foster children's curiosity and enthusiasm for discovery and learning, and cultivate disciplined learning-to-learn habits. Early childhood is not a time to emphasize learning achievement and competitiveness among children; it is a time to foster positive values about learning and to build a strong developmental foundation for a healthy, happy life. Greenspan (2007) identified 10 traits essential to achieving this goal: communication, creativity and vision, curiosity, empathy, engagement, emotional range, internal discipline, logical thinking, moral integrity, and self-awareness.

Navigating the Inevitable Pendulum Shifts in Education

The values and research of the 21st century have reinforced the theoretical beliefs and practices of constructivist philosophy and theory in early childhood education, but the journey has been full of bumps and detours. **Constructivist theory** originated in the 20th-century research and **epistemology** of Jean Piaget. Followers of Piaget (the so-called neo-Piagetians: Elkind, Kamii, DeVries, Kohlberg, Biber, and others) were the educational innovators of the 1970s through the 1990s who applied Piagetian **cognitive developmental theory** to educational models for young children. Within two decades, many of the central concepts of constructivism also penetrated mainstream educational theory. Constructivism holds that young children construct their own knowing and understanding through active interaction with concrete objects in their environment. By planning learning environments and activities for play that build on what children already know, we facilitate children's understanding and move them further in their development. Children understand a concept when they are able to transfer the learning acquired in one play context to another context. These principles hold true today, and their durability may be related to their reliance on children's play as the medium for development and learning.

The winding road of the past century, however, warns of the fragility of play as the centrepiece of early childhood education. The behaviourist tradition of the 1920s to the 1960s emphasized cultural transmission, programmed instruction based on right and wrong answers, external rewards, drill and repetition, and a prescriptive information-based curriculum. In the 1970s, the pendulum swung toward **open education** as a result of revelations coming out of the Summerhill experiment, the "freedom to learn" ideas of Carl Rogers, and the permissive strains in child-rearing philosophy. Classroom walls were taken down, children no longer "failed" a grade, and too many children were left to float aimlessly through the school system with insufficient attention paid to basic skills. The unfortunate coincidence in timing with the translation of Piaget's research during the late 1960s and the 1970s meant that many of the child-centred, discovery-oriented, and play-based educational ideas of the neo-Piagetians, as well as the progressive educational ideas that were contained in Ontario's Hall-Dennis Report (1968), were lumped with the open education movement as if they had all sprung from the same roots. Elementary education in particular suffered from the misrepresentation of the cognitive developmental movement and the misapplication of its practices. The subsequent failure of the elementary schools to interpret faithfully the Hall-Dennis Report and other progressive approaches in early primary education (junior kindergarten to grade three) undermined the play-based, constructivist approaches of the neo-Piagetian movement. Early in the 1990s, a "back to basics" approach emphasized standardized testing of children's performance on prescriptive academic competencies. During this period, the pendulum swung back to "teaching to the test," measuring knowledge gained, drill and practice, and other forms of passive rote teaching and learning characteristic of the cultural transmission approach. Early childhood education was negatively affected by this change, and some nursery schools in particular attracted parents who wanted their children to get an early jump on academic learning so that they could later compete successfully with their peers. Play-based learning was regarded by these parents as frivolous and unproductive. Even public child-care programs embraced increased structure and knowledge-based group learning time for "teaching." Early childhood educators should always resist this regrettable return to mechanistic learning approaches and disrespect for the value and role of play in early development and learning.

The following factors may have had the greatest impact on restoring the value of play in early childhood: the attention given to neuroscience and the dramatic discoveries in brain research of the first decade of this century, the seminal research of Howard Gardner on multiple intelligences in the 1980s and 1990s, and the persistent efforts of the neo-Piagetians. The pendulum is shifting back to play, but with many new insights on how to expand, enrich, and guide play toward deeper, more lasting results and with more articulate explanations of play-based methods, including projects. In the words of DeVries, Kwak, and Sales (2002, pp. 5–6), "We need to develop a way of thinking that helps us distinguish what is of educational benefit to children and what is not. A barrier to this goal is the tendency of early childhood educators to rely on abstract notions of play to justify and describe their play-oriented curriculum [which] . . . include vague, general statements to justify the play-oriented curriculum and vague characterizations to describe play in early childhood education." A primary learning outcome for ECE preparation programs (training and education) is to communicate clearly the pivotal role of various categories of play in early development and learning.

Future Trends in Early Childhood Education

In this young century, many new trends will have an impact on early childhood education. The funding being allocated to full-day kindergarten, for example, continues to be subject to public scrutiny and to demands for results that justify spending. "Canadians will need to be convinced that universal, full-day kindergarten is worth the expense. ... This country should be able to determine—with independent studies—whether it provided a bang for the billions" (Editorial, September 8, 2010, *The Globe and Mail*, p. A16). Along with skepticism about public funding for full-day kindergarten, there will be pressure to make kindergarten look more like primary-level (grades one to three) classrooms. Early childhood educators should resist pressure to introduce formal academic learning into their programs, and they should protect and defend children's right to play, demonstrating clearly how play-based programs facilitate children's optimal development in all domains: physical, affective, social, and cognitive. The onus is also on ECE and kindergarten teacher preparation programs to include skills that enable graduates to communicate clearly the outcomes of play-based learning. Graduates should not only achieve outcomes related to nurturing caregiving practices, developmental assessment, and play-based planning and curriculum implementation based on their assessments of children's individual progress; they should also be effective advocates for play-based programs for children from ages two to six.

Children's mental health is another emerging issue taking its place alongside children's physical health as a significant item in both research and public policy discussions. Credible research is showing the ill effects on children of poverty, poor diet and nutrition, lack of exercise, and too much time spent indoors. Children's alienation from nature and the growing alarm raised by Richard Louv about "nature-deficit disorder" (2008) has led to international debate over the need to create safe outdoor environments that encourage spontaneous and regular outdoor play in natural surroundings. We can expect more research that seeks to demonstrate that children's alienation from nature may contribute to the cause, or aggravate, a host of childhood illnesses and disabilities, including attention deficit disorder (ADD), hyperactivity, autism, and depression. Experts are also continuing to raise alarm bells about children's over-exposure to television and other technologies. Data on declining childhood health, the alarming increase in child obesity and mental illness, and children's lack of exercise are generating multidisciplinary discussion among professionals from health care, urban design and planning, psychology, architecture, environmental science, landscape design, and education. We are already seeing more attention being paid to outdoor programming for play-based learning; improved playground design with more "natural" playgrounds; more active efforts to bring children into closer contact with nature; and a push toward rigorous, planned physical fitness programming ("Breath of Fresh Air," Ioanna Roumeliotis, *The National*, CBC-TV, March 7, 2011). Recent studies have demonstrated the positive health benefits of contact with nature and greenery: improved mental acuity; reduced aggression and crime; reduced stress, depression, and anxiety; improved functioning of the body's immune system; lowered blood pressure; and an improved general sense of well-being and good health (Judge & Barish-Wreden, 2010). Issues related to children's mental health have also raised interest in the role of empathy in the formation of character, and considerably more attention is being given to children's social and emotional development and its impact on learning, adaptation, and success in life (Greenspan, 2007; Perry & Szalavitz, 2010; Rifkin, 2009).

One of the most exciting trends is the insight provided by neuroscience and the study of the brain into the plasticity of the brain throughout life—its ability to overcome early brain deficits and disabilities and to respond to thoughtful interventions to address the specific learning styles of children (Doidge, 2007; Mighton, 2007; Shenk, 2010).

With so many emerging trends that will have a significant impact on early childhood education in the future, it is refreshing to see other professions beginning to understand and appreciate the value of play, both indoors and outdoors, as a key function of childhood, one that is essential not only to building children's learning capacity but also to protecting and bolstering mental, emotional, and physical health.

Summary

Chapter 1 outlines the current political, social, and economic context for early childhood education programs in Canada and introduces some important professional concepts and terminology. It provides a brief introduction to the political and policy choices that need to be made in order to equip our nation's young children for the life and learning challenges that lie ahead in the 21st century. This chapter aims to establish a context for the study of early childhood education and to help readers understand the role of early childhood education in today's global society. Our Canadian multicultural context is another constant theme in this edition, which continues to emphasize the need for program approaches that integrate the cultural priorities of children and their families. The chapter highlights the importance of play as the foundation for healthy adaptation and learning throughout life. Students should become familiar with the bolded words in each chapter by referring to the glossary of definitions at the end of the textbook.

LEARNING ACTIVITIES

These learning activities require that students begin a journal of their growth to help them become reflective practitioners in ECE.

1. Build a collection of articles from the national and local press on various provincial initiatives to establish more accessible and higher quality early childhood education programs in Canada. Create a section in your journal where these articles will be preserved, annotated, and indexed.
2. In an 800-word (short) essay, explain why and how ECEs should defend the role of play in early childhood. Explain why Canadian governments should invest in universally accessible, play-based early childhood education programs for young children.
3. Children's acquisition of healthy "habits of mind"; positive attitudes toward learning; emotional stability and self-regulation; respect and empathy for others; and wonder about nature and the gift of life are important pillars in child development. Recall your own years spent in preschool and elementary school and describe your learning habits and your attitudes toward learning. If you could live those years again, how would you approach school and learning differently? What did school teach you about what to value and how to live your life? Record your answers to these questions in your journal.
4. An ECE is a "reflective practitioner" who regularly evaluates his or her choices, the quality of her or his work, and the impact of programs on the children. Discuss with your peers your memorable play experiences indoors and outdoors as a child and record yours in your journal. Explain how these remembered experiences might contribute to your emerging philosophy and approach to early childhood education.
5. Find an article in a local or national newspaper that addresses the topic of children's mental health. Write a short paragraph for your journal explaining the ways in which the article relates to early childhood education.

2 History of Play and Play Theory

> "Play is the lifeblood of childhood—it brings children joy, it nurtures and excites their creativity, it builds social skills, and it strengthens their bodies."
>
> —Silken Laumann, *Rediscovering the Joy of Play in Our Families and Our Communities* (2006)

Before Reading This Chapter, Have You

- considered the role of play in your own childhood?
- discussed with others the significance of play in development and learning?
- recalled what you learned as a child through play?

Outcomes

After reading and understanding this chapter, you should be able to

- describe the historical evolution of play in childhood;
- outline the evolution of classical and dynamic play theories; and,
- explain the importance of protecting children's free play and enhancing the impact of play.

The History of Play

Play has always been a significant part of human life at all ages. Play "lies at the core of creativity and innovation. Of all animal species, humans are the biggest players of all. We are built to play and built through play. When we play, we are engaged in the purest expression of our humanity, the truest expression of our individuality" (Brown, 2010, p. 5). Centuries ago, people directed their energy toward survival and the satisfaction of basic human needs. Even so, evidence suggests that people devised games, rituals, and dances to help them understand some of the unknown forces in the world that seemed to control them. Play has evolved from mystical rituals often associated with the supernatural, to the complex demonstrations of children's understanding of phenomena, events, concepts, and social environments as they engage in social play. The history of childhood records that the importance attached to play has ebbed and peaked through the generations and has been influenced by the prevailing attitudes toward children and the value of childhood. Although postmodern thinking challenged modernist notions that play is universal, the history of childhood shows that children have played through the centuries and in all cultures. Recognition of the importance of play through the centuries appears to be related to how much each era valued childhood as a distinct phase in the human life cycle, one that should be protected and nourished.

The contexts and characteristics of play—in other words, whether social, group-oriented, solitary, task-oriented, planned, spontaneous, or expressive—were not seen as particularly relevant to development until the 20th century. Appreciation of the instrumental uses of play to promote development and learning gathered momentum through the early work of Montessori and Dewey, the early nursery school movement, and, from the 1970s on, Piaget and the neo-Piagetians. In the 21st century, defending the value of play for its own sake and recognizing the positive impact of children's freely-chosen play on mental and physical health as well as intellectual growth have become important arguments against pressures for prescriptive curriculum content and academic learning in early childhood education (see Table 2–1).

TABLE 2–1

THE HISTORY AND EVOLUTION OF PLAY

Historical Period and Principal Philosophers	Meaning of Play in Childhood
Ancient Civilization (500 B.C.E.–500 C.E.) Plato c. 429–327 B.C.E. Aristotle c. 382–324 B.C.E. Cicero c. 106–43 B.C.E. Also Ancient Egyptians	• The Ancients understood the importance of children's play and its relevance to later development • Observing children playing in order to understand them better was emphasized • Children valued playthings such as balls, hoops, rattles, swings, skipping ropes
Middle Ages 900–1200 C.E.	• Distinctions between childhood and adulthood generally disappeared in the Middle Ages • Families were more concerned with the survival of their children than with their play

Table 2–1 continues on page 20

TABLE 2–1 ***(Continued)***

THE HISTORY AND EVOLUTION OF PLAY

Historical Period and Principal Philosophers	Meaning of Play in Childhood
Middle Ages (continued) 900–1200 C.E.	• Infant mortality was high, and surviving children were relied on for labour and service in adult society • Adult games and pleasures were available to children as well as to adults; children were hurried into the adult world as soon as possible and were frequently used as playthings for adults; sexual abuse was common
Renaissance and Reformation 1200–1700 C.E.	• Childhood was seen as a preparation for adulthood, and children's play was considered a serious activity and a vehicle for learning as long as it was pleasurable
Michel de Montaigne 1533–1592 Comenius 1592–1670	• Toys were used to encourage children's learning through play • Experience through play was valued
The Puritans 17th and 18th century North America	• The Puritans in North America during the 17th and 18th centuries were ambivalent about play, which varied according to location, ethnicity, and vocation; Puritans emphasized work-related play that went against children's basic natures • In England and the United States, play was suppressed longer than in Europe; in Britain in particular, play was viewed as the opposite of work and was considered to be irresponsible and in conflict with the Protestant work ethic
Modern Period 1700–1900 C.E.	• Children were encouraged to play according to their whims • Learning through play in the natural environment was encouraged
John Locke 1632–1704 Jean-Jacques Rousseau 1712–1778 Heinrich Pestalozzi 1746–1827 Friedrich Froebel 1782–1852 Robert Owen 1771–1858	• Experience and freedom in childhood were fundamental to development and the desire to learn • Children's well-being was an issue of public concern, and it was believed that children have their own way of seeing, thinking, and feeling that should be respected • Pestalozzi emphasized the importance of sensory experiences in learning and advocated freely chosen play to foster learning • Owen started the British Infant School in 1816, which combined elements of play in learning • European philosophers saw childhood as a distinct phase preceding adulthood, and they extolled the role of play in the formation of children's minds and souls—play is a "natural unfolding of the germinal leaves of childhood" (Froebel, 1887, pp. 54–55). • The first Froebelian kindergarten originated in Germany in 1837 and used specialized materials, games, and activities to promote specific kinds of learning • In Britain and the United States, children's play was severely restricted by their heavy labour in factories and on farms, with children working 12 hours a day, seven days a week • Play involved imitation of adults, who instilled responsibility and obligation to work, which stifled self-expression and opportunities for age-appropriate play

Table 2–1 continues on page 21

Historical Period and Principal Philosophers	Meaning of Play in Childhood
Early 20th century 1890–1950	• The importance of play to development and learning was revived in the 1920s
G. Stanley Hall 1844–1924 Sigmund Freud 1856–1939 and later neo-Freudians Susan Isaacs 1885–1948 Maria Montessori 1870–1952 John Dewey 1859–1952 Lev Vygotsky 1896–1934	• Play allowed children to channel primitive impulses and achieve self-control • Freudians saw play as a means of acting out painful experiences and dealing with emotional stress • Open-ended exploration, sensory awareness, and self-expression (unit blocks) were encouraged • Free exploration promoted emotional stability and maturity • Children's absorbent minds were ready to learn through play with structured, specific-purpose materials matched to their developmental stages • Play promoted all aspects of child development • A play-based, child-centred program was started at the University of Chicago that advocated the project method of learning through play • Social interaction and conversation between adults and children was regarded as the mechanism through which values, culture, customs, and beliefs are transmitted from generation to generation
Later 20th century 1950–1999	• Research found that children develop in predictable stages, that the environment and genetic inheritance are both instrumental, and that children construct knowledge and intellect by *doing*
Jean Piaget Erik Erikson Loris Malaguzzi Howard Gardner	• Children need play materials that respond to their actions on them and that challenge them to explore, test, create, manipulate, construct, and understand concepts • Children learn through active interaction with concrete things in the environment and need to play freely in order to find meaning and develop skills • Psychosocial theory emphasized the role of the environment in development and encouraged cooperative interactions, particularly through dramatic and sociodramatic play • A systems approach originated based on active learning through play (Reggio Emilia schools)
21st century Michael Meaney Steven Pinker Robert Sternberg Stephen Ceci Stanley Greenspan Martin L. Hoffman	• New research on the interaction of genes and the environment on human development will have an impact on play theory and early learning • New paradigms related to human development (Stanley Greenspan, Martin L. Hoffman) update our understanding of the influence of play at specific stages • New definitions of intelligence (Sternberg) and greater attention to the role of play throughout the lifespan will influence educational practice from early childhood onward

The Evolution of Theories of Play

Early theories about play and its role in childhood fall into two broad categories: classical and dynamic. J. Barnard Gilmore (1966) defined these two categories by concluding that the older **classical theories** tried to explain why people play and the **dynamic theories** focus on how people play.

Classical Theories

Classical theories, which prevailed from the 17th to the late 19th century, include the surplus energy theory, the relaxation theory, the pre-exercise theory, and the recapitulation theory (see Table 2–2).

Dynamic Theories

The more modern dynamic theories replaced classical theories in the 20th century. They are divided into two categories: psychoanalytic (see Table 2–3) and developmental theories (Gilmore, 1966).

PSYCHOANALYTIC THEORIES

Psychoanalytic theories originated with Sigmund Freud in the early 20th century and were elaborated by the neo-Freudians, Granville Stanley Hall, Arnold Gesell,

TABLE 2–2

CLASSICAL THEORIES

Surplus energy theory	When people have more energy than is needed for work, the excess is used in play.
Relaxation theory	Play is used to generate the energy needed for work. (This is less applicable to children's play.)
Pre-exercise theory	Children play to practise future roles in society; for example, little girls playing with dolls are rehearsing their roles as mothers; children are instinctively drawn to play that prepares them for adult behaviour. (This theory is influenced by Darwin's theory of evolution.)
Recapitulation theory	G. Stanley Hall's phrase "ontogeny recapitulates phylogeny" represented the belief that human development from infancy to adulthood parallels the evolution of humans as a species. Children's play resembles the behaviour of people in earlier times more than that of adults. In play, children re-enact the activities of each successive period in the evolution of the human race, such as playing with bows and arrows and making crude forts. (This theory is also influenced by Darwin's theory of evolution.)

TABLE 2–3

PSYCHOANALYTIC THEORIES

Freud	Sigmund Freud believed that play allows children to express themselves and to act out inner feelings they are unable to verbalize. Freudians believed that play helps children cope with reality, particularly when their reality is painful or confusing. The function of play is primarily emotional, as it reduces anxiety.
Erikson	Erik Erikson believed that play builds the ego by developing the physical and emotional skills that contribute to self-esteem. Erikson's psychosocial theory proposed three types of play: 1. autocosmic play with one's own body 2. microspheric play to acquire mastery over objects 3. macrospheric play with peers to cultivate a strong sense of self within culture and society

Erik Erikson, Evelyn Pitcher, and Katherine Read Baker. Psychoanalytic theorists, whose work was based on the theories of Sigmund Freud, believed that play served children's emotional well-being by fostering self-expression, role play, rehearsal of new experiences, and fantasy about unknown worlds.

The evolution of play theory has largely corresponded with our understanding of child development as a discipline. Early developmental theories evolved from the work of G. Stanley Hall and Arnold Gesell, who, in the 1940s, proposed that children develop according to a set sequence of developmental stages that roughly correspond to the ages of the children. These **maturationist theories** held that biological factors, rather than experience or learning, are primarily responsible for development, which is genetically predetermined and fixed throughout life. The **"nature versus nurture controversy"** captured the polar extremes of the early 20th century, occupied by the adherents of **behavioural science**, who believed that the environment was responsible for development and learning, and the developmentalists, who believed that development was intrinsically motivated and genetically programmed at birth. This debate, also known as the **heredity versus environment controversy** lasted well into the second half of the 20th century and has only been challenged significantly in the past decade or so by the findings of neuroscience and brain research.

DEVELOPMENTAL THEORIES

Developmental theorists of the latter years of the 20th century believed that genetic inheritance has significantly more influence than environmental factors in human development, although they acknowledged the influence of social, historical, and cultural factors and the impact of children's play on their development. Early childhood research has tended to focus in recent years on the influence of particular kinds of play on children's development. Most developmental theories attempted to describe characteristics of play, to show how positive play experiences facilitate intellectual growth, and to relate play to periods of change and developmental progress (Garvey, 1977). Two important developmental theories of play emerged from the work of Jean Piaget and Lev Vygotsky.

Jean Piaget's Cognitive Developmental Theory

Piagetian developmental theory focuses on the child's cognitive development. Children's play is seen as a tool for enhancing intellectual growth and for consolidating newly learned behaviours. Through play, children organize their experiences in the world, thereby better adapting to their environments. At the **sensorimotor stage** children need many opportunities to explore with their senses the physical characteristics of objects in the environment in order to understand concepts such as shape, size, and colour. Piaget believed that language labels help this conceptual understanding develop.

Piaget theorized that learning involves building **mental structures** acquired through the joint processes of assimilation and accommodation. **Assimilation** is the change that occurs when children try to fit the new learning experience into their existing mental structures. Typically, they respond to a new object or event in a way that is consistent with their existing **schema**. For example, a two-year-old may refer to a bee as a fly; a three-year-old refers to all men wearing overalls as builders. **Accommodation** occurs when children alter their existing mental structures to make a fit between what they already know and the new experience that unseats or challenges their current understanding. For example, when a child who has learned to grasp a large ball tossed to him by grabbing the ball with open arms and clasping it to his chest sees a smaller ball coming to him at a faster rate, he has to modify his open arm clasp by reaching toward the ball with his cupped hands. The new skill of catching a small ball thrown at higher speed requires that the child modify his existing ball-catching scheme to accommodate the smaller, faster ball. Piaget believed that development occurs as a result of the child's active interaction with things and experiences in the environment. Existing mental structures are adapted and built on by self-initiated, usually autonomous activity, within an environment that has been planned to address the child's developmental level, interests, and present capabilities.

Equilibration is the motivational factor for the learning that occurs as a result of the joint processes of assimilation and accommodation. When children achieve equilibration, they reach a new state of balance and a higher level of development. Through assimilation and accommodation, children gain intelligence. One aspect of becoming intelligent is the development of the thinking abilities children need to solve new problems and to originate new ideas (Piaget, 1972).

Piaget's Theory Related to Play

Piaget described three stages of cognitive development in childhood—the sensorimotor, **preoperational,** and **concrete operational** periods of development—that correspond to the four stages of children's play he described. The four stages of children's play are **practice** or **functional play** during the sensorimotor period (birth to 18 months); **symbolic play,** which includes **productive play** (2–4 years) and **reproductive play** (4–7 years) during the preoperational period (2–6 or 7 years); and **games-with-rules play** (6–11 or 12 years) during the concrete operational period.

PIAGET'S THEORY RELATED TO PLAY

Sensorimotor Play Stage: Practice or Functional Play (0–2 years)

Sensorimotor play involves the child's physical interaction with concrete objects in the environment in order to explore and to discover the physical properties of things. Children are busy gaining control over their movements, gathering information by way of the senses, learning to coordinate physical actions, and responding to the effects they have on things. Infants gain pleasure from mastering motor skills; therefore, much of their play involves repeated actions, called practice play, in which they appear to practise a newly acquired skill. Example: the infant who repeatedly drops objects from the high chair and watches the effect of these actions, or who enjoys playing pat-a-cake repeatedly, is engaging in sensorimotor play.

Preoperational Play Stage: Symbolic Play (Productive Play) (2–4 years)

In symbolic play, children learn to use symbols, or to make one object stand for another, as in using a wooden block to represent a car. At this stage, children generally use play materials to satisfy their own purposes, rather than to conform to any external standards imposed by adults. This productive play (two to four years) is usually characterized by focused activity in which children's play outcomes are increasingly recognizable to adults. For example, children may dress and undress a teddy bear, load and unload a dump truck, or fill a pail with sand and empty it repeatedly, and they seem happy to perform these actions for their own ends. As children begin to construct things, such as block houses, their play outcomes and products become more lifelike, more recognizable reproductions of objects in real life.

Preoperational Play Stage: Symbolic Play (Reproductive Play) (4–7 years)

A more advanced type of symbolic play, **reproductive play** occurs between the ages of four and seven, when children are able to represent remembered events, images, and actions using a variety of media. Reproductive play represents what children understand or want to understand about their environments and experiences. Initially, children often use artistic media to represent a remembered image; later, they might engage in pretend, **dramatic**, or **sociodramatic play**. Toward the end of the symbolic play stage, children become increasingly adept at using art, drama, music, and language to represent the real world and their experiences. **Representational thinking** is a key pillar in the child's development. It is fostered primarily through dramatic and sociodramatic play, as well as by play with many creative materials, such as blocks and artistic tools.

Concrete Operational Play Stage: Games-with-Rules Play (7–12 years)

Games-with-rules play appears during the school years as the child reaches the concrete operational period (around age seven), and begins to accept certain external limitations on his play, such as rules made by someone else. The increasing ability to think and behave objectively allows the child to participate more actively in groups, to become a team member, and to submit to the structure imposed by limits and rules. The child begins to make his own rules and to question existing ones; he collaborates in amending rules and accepts the binding nature of group-adopted rules for the duration of a game or a project.

Piaget's Definition of the Types of Knowledge Children Acquire

Piaget proposed that there are three principal types of knowledge that children acquire, through the various contexts in which they play; these types help us understand the many ways in which a healthy playroom climate supports many types and styles of learning. The three types of knowledge are physical knowledge, social-conventional knowledge, and logical-mathematical knowledge.

PHYSICAL KNOWLEDGE

Physical knowledge is largely sensory learning about the concrete, physical properties of objects, such as shape, size, colour, and texture. Infants begin to acquire physical knowledge right from birth. The entire sensorimotor period, up to 18 or 24 months of age, is primarily directed toward acquiring, through the senses, physical knowledge of the objects and people in the child's immediate surroundings. The learning climate that fosters the acquisition of physical knowledge is one in which children have ample opportunity for sensory exploration, to move freely, and to test and compare the physical properties of things based on their physical appearance. Children acquire physical knowledge from the moment of birth by manipulating things (touch), exploring with their eyes (vision), hearing, tasting, and smelling.

SOCIAL-CONVENTIONAL KNOWLEDGE

Families, communities, public institutions, and schools hand down **social-conventional knowledge** from one generation to another in the form of social rules, conventions, morals, values, facts, and information that are socially and culturally transmitted and that may be arbitrarily assigned. Street names, important

© Spencer Grant/PhotoEdit

Social-conventional knowledge

dates, safety rules, manners, social conventions, the functions of social institutions, and historical data are examples of social-conventional knowledge. During the preoperational period, children usually acquire social-conventional knowledge through verbal and cultural transmission from parents and from other adults. Later, school-age children, who are concrete operational, also acquire social-conventional knowledge in formal learning contexts from textbooks and other academic learning materials.

The inclusion of family members and guests representing the community in the program brings the outside world into the playroom. Children's social-conventional knowledge expands as they are introduced to a wide range of cultural and community customs, artifacts, occupations, and services. For example, inviting a mother to bring candles, cultural artifacts, and traditional clothing for the children to celebrate Divali, and to eat specially prepared Indian foods, recognizes the importance that South Asian cultures attach to their cultural festivals and helps all children in the program relate to the family traditions of their friends. The knowledge children gain of various societies and their important celebrations is an added bonus. It is important that the climate of the playroom reflects, on a daily basis, the culture of the children represented in the program and not just at special festival times of year. An inclusive environment ensures that all children see their culture represented in the playroom at all times of year and in many ways.

LOGICAL-MATHEMATICAL KNOWLEDGE

Logical-mathematical knowledge involves understanding relationships that are not directly observable. These are universal concepts and principles that are essential for numeracy, mathematics, and most logical thinking tasks. They include the ability to understand the largely abstract relationships that exist between concepts. For example, young children recognize the physical properties inherent in two red circles of equal size. They can perceive that each one is red and round. They may even identify the shape by its label, *circle*. Children recognize that the two circles are the same. What they may not understand is the quality of *twoness* created by putting the two red circles together, for that involves creating a relationship between the two objects that exists largely in the mind. The quality of twoness is inherent only in the relationship that one attaches to the two red circles. Take away one red circle and the quality of twoness vanishes from both circles, while the redness and the circular shape of each remain visible and the noun (circle) that describes them is unchanged (see Figure 2–1).

Red circle   Red circle

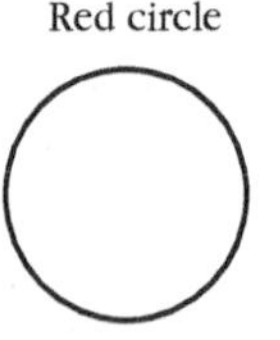

Figure 2–1

Arriving at an understanding of abstract concepts requires time and the opportunity to play with concrete materials that promote investigation, inquiry, testing, and trial and error. The old saying of Confucius, "What I hear I forget; what I see I remember; what I do I understand," captures what it means to acquire logical-mathematical knowledge in a climate that promotes inquiry through play.

Cognitive Developmental Theory and Developmentally Appropriate Practice (DAP)

Piaget's theories of **genetic epistemology** revolutionized thinking in early childhood education in North America in the 1960s and 1970s. The cognitive developmental theory that evolved from Piaget's work proposed that play is the child's vehicle for development and learning. Since the 1980s, largely as a result of Piaget's theory, there has been broad agreement that children need a wide range of developmentally appropriate play opportunities, in an organized environment which promotes hands-on, discovery oriented, self-directed, experiential learning with carefully selected play materials. These planned play experiences are important links among learning, the environment, and development in all domains: physical, social, emotional, and cognitive. In the 1980s and 1990s, **developmentally appropriate practice (DAP)** emphasized setting goals for ECE programs based on the tasks of development and assessing children's progress toward the achievement of developmental milestones (Bredekamp, 1987). Chapter 8 provides a more complete explanation of DAP.

Greater emphasis on purposefully planned environments with play experiences related to developmental outcomes appeared in the late 1990s. By about 2005, the instrumental uses of play were increasingly emphasized by research that reinforced the belief in the value of children's freely chosen play; the urgent need to protect children's play; and the importance of ensuring that children spend more time in physical play outdoors, preferably in close contact with natural surroundings. This progression in our understanding of play emphasized the need for flexible pedagogical approaches that accommodate children's interests and that focus on play that children choose.

Lev Vygotsky's Theory Related to Play

Vygotsky emphasized the role of the social environment in human development. He believed that cognitive development is dependent on social mediation that may be provided by ECEs, other adults, and peers, who provide "guided assistance" in helping children to achieve knowledge and new understanding. Like Piaget, Vygotsky believed in the value of play, but he attached greatest importance to the role of play in imposing certain rules and demands that cause children to gain control over their own behaviour. He saw play as social interaction that leads to knowledge and development. Vygotsky believed that, in play, children are active creators of the rules in the imaginary situation and are therefore able to go beyond their current level of development. Children become the active creators in pretend play or sociodramatic play of the very activity that produces opportunities for development and learning (Connery, John-Steiner, & Mayanovic-Shane, 2010).

Vygotsky's work was composed of ideas he gathered from his work with children with disabilities. His **zone of proximal development (ZPD)** (see Chapter 9, p. 160) was closely related to behavioural science and to remedial approaches for children with learning challenges, and not to approaches that promote active learning through play and guided discovery. Lambert & Clyde (2003, pp. 64–65) argued that Vygotsky did not regard children's exploratory play as valid, and viewed pre-rule play as transitory, providing a form of comfort only to children who were "deemed dependent and powerless due to their immaturity." Fraser (2000, p. 33), however, attributed to Vygotsky four key ideas that explain the relationship between play and learning that many educators believe are also relevant to constructivist practice in early childhood education.

1. Children actively construct knowledge.
2. Learning is related to experience and is enhanced by language.
3. Learning leads to development. Providing children with language labels helps children understand concepts more readily.
4. Language is central to cognitive development because it is through language that intellectual abilities such as symbolic thinking are transmitted.

Constructivist Theories of Play and Learning

The constructivist theories of Piaget, the neo-Piagetians, and Vygotsky emphasize children's construction of their intelligence through experience and active interaction with "things" in the environment (Piaget) and social interaction (Vygotsky). Constructivist theories describe learning as the result of experience, knowledge, and know-how, which are usually gained by hands-on interaction with things and phenomena in the environment. The anticipated outcome of constructivist education is the ability to integrate knowledge from various sources and apply what one knows to achieve a positive result. This **instrumental approach** to development and learning, as the acquisition of transferable skills and understanding, contrasts with traditional, industrial-age educational practices that relied on the memorization of quantities of information provided through **didactic teaching**.

EXAMPLE OF TWO DIFFERENT BELIEFS

A simple example explains the contrast in the beliefs underlying the two different theoretical positions. The memorization of numbers in a series, that is, being able to recite from 1 to 10 or 1 to 100 (behavioural approach), is less important than understanding the value attached to each number, the constancy of numbers (i.e., the number of objects does not change in spite of changes in the configuration of the objects), and notions of quantity and equality that enable one to compare, contrast, estimate, make inferences, and solve problems (constructivist approach).

Constructivist education is based on the premise that children gather meaning and understanding from their experience in the physical and social environment and construct their own knowledge, intelligence, and morality. This approach to curriculum using play-based approaches is based on the following principles of constructivist early childhood education:

1. Establish a cooperative sociomoral atmosphere for play.
2. Plan play activities based on children's interests.
3. Teach according to the type of knowledge children need to acquire, that is: physical knowledge, logical-mathematical knowledge, and social-conventional knowledge.
4. Evaluate curriculum in terms of its focus on inquiry, its relevance to the intellectual abilities of the children, its responsiveness to children's actions, and its ability to engage their attention and promote curiosity.

5. Ensure that the curriculum and the individual activities require children to think and to figure things out and promote children's reasoning.
6. Provide sufficient time for children's investigation and in-depth engagement.
7. Clarify the relationship between documentation and assessment of children's progress to the ongoing revision of curriculum and planning of play activities. (DeVries et al., 2002, pp. 36–51).

Courtesy of Dale Shipley

Absorbed in parallel play

The common meaning attributed to constructivist approaches to early learning is that children learn through their active engagement with things and people in the environment, thereby constructing their own meanings, making connections, and developing concepts. The constructivist theorists believe children can be guided to construct their intelligence and to achieve appropriate developmental milestones through play within carefully planned environments that build on the skills children have already achieved. As mentioned earlier, constructivist approaches provided the theoretical framework for developmentally appropriate practice (DAP), which put the child at the centre of the early childhood curriculum; DAP was first defined in the late 1980s by the National Association for the Education of Young Children (NAEYC) in the United States and continues to prevail well into the 21st century. (Refer to Chapter 8, p. 151 to learn more about DAP.)

Historical Interpretations of *Children Learn Through Play*

Children learn through play is a concept that has guided early childhood educators for decades. Exactly how children learn through play has been a subject of some controversy in the past and continues to generate debate in educational circles today. What we know is that children of all cultures play, and that culture influences the amount, type, and the content of play, although the underlying outcome is always developmental, making children's play across cultures quite similar. Children of all cultures "chase, roughhouse, explore, fantasize, practice, create play games with rules, and so forth" (Fromberg, 2004, p. 8).

For much of the 20th century, the role of play in children's lives dominated discussion of the optimal conditions under which children develop and learn. The concept of the individual as the cornerstone of Western societies contributed to the psychological and educational aspirations that characterized Western civilization in the 20th century: self-esteem, meeting basic needs, success, and self-actualization. Modernists believed that children's play is universal and independent of cultural influences no matter what conditions children encounter in their native environments (Johnson, Christie, & Wardle, 2005). Postmodern views (from the 1980s, 1990s, and beyond), however, challenged the imposition of universal truths on society and were more interested in diversity and inclusive practice, suggesting that

TABLE 2–4

HISTORICAL INTERPRETATIONS OF "CHILDREN LEARN THROUGH PLAY"

Time Period	Values	Practices
1920s–1950s Sigmund Freud	Early emotional experiences have a profound impact on adult personality. Play is seen as a necessary stage children go through.	Let children investigate freely and explore. Spontaneous play is best for the child.
G. Stanley Hall, Arnold Gesell	Children play to manage the primitive past practices of the human species and focus on acquiring social and mental skills. Genetic inheritance and maturation are prime motivators of development. Children go through stages in their play. Children's developmental stages may be understood by observing their play.	"Follow the child" and let him freely choose his own activity without adult interference or structure to guide him. Observations of their play should acknowledge the social settings in which play occurs.
Maria Montessori	Children's minds are absorbent, and there are sensitive periods when they are most ready to learn specific skills and concepts. Children act constructively in a free, well-planned environment.	Provide a rich learning environment with specific-purpose learning materials from which children may choose in order to promote purposeful and orderly activity.
John Dewey	Education is important to democratic society. Children should experience freedom in their play. School learning should be linked meaningfully to children's lives and build on their interests. Children are motivated by engaging actively with the environment. Play is distinct from work.	Projects comprise a significant portion of the curriculum and encourage children to engage in play activities linked to the longer-term investigation of a meaningful topic or question.
Margaret and Rachel McMillan, Lucy Sprague Mitchell, Caroline Pratt, Patty Smith Hill	Children should play unimpeded, in an open-ended environment. Free play facilitates children's healthy self-expression. The healthy functioning of the child at his age level is most important.	Children should engage in free play for most of the day. The teacher's role is to "follow the child" and avoid intervention in the children's free play. Teacher-directed strategies such as circle time are intended to socialize children and to impart knowledge.
William Blatz	Play is important for development to occur.	Founded the Institute of Child Study at the University of Toronto, which is based on principles of learning through play.
1940s–1970s		
The Behavioural Scientists J.B. Watson, E.L. Thorndike, B.F. Skinner, C. Bereiter, S. Engelmann	Play is less important than learning and work. Children's behaviour may be modified by controlling external stimuli. The environment is the most important function in development. Nurture is responsible for development. Programmed learning teaches correct knowledge and academic skills.	Behaviour modification is used to shape children's behaviour and learning. Learning activities are largely teacher-directed. Play is a reward for work and success. Head Start programs use programmed instruction to help children learn.

Table 2–4 continues on page 31

Time Period	Values	Practices
The Maturationist School neo-Freudians: Benjamin Spock, Harriet Johnson, Katherine Read Baker, Evelyn Pitcher, Virginia Axline	Nature is responsible for development for which there is a genetic predisposition. Children should play unimpeded, in an open-ended environment. Children benefit most from self-guided play with open-ended materials. Like the McMillan sisters, Mitchell, Pratt, and Hill, the neo-Freudians believe that free play facilitates children's healthy self-expression. Adult intervention impedes self-expression.	Free play and circle time dominate programs based on maturationist theories. It is important not to intervene in children's play but to provide an environment with many materials that children can explore freely.
1970s–1990s Cognitive Developmental School (Interactionists): Jean Piaget and the early neo-Piagetians, Jerome Bruner, Constance Kamii, David Weikart, Sara Smilansky, Lev Vygotsky (works were translated during this period)	Children's intelligence is constructed through assimilation and accommodation, leading to equilibration through active interaction with concrete objects in the environment. Language and social interaction are important means to convey society's values and expectations. Learning occurs through social interaction in group play situations. Vygotsky believes that play is the most important behaviour and educational activity in children's development and learning. Sociodramatic play, block play, and games-with-rules play are most useful for children ages four to six (Smilansky).	ECEs plan specific activities for children to explore concrete objects and build schema (mental structures). Children choose from a wide variety of play materials that respond to their actions on them. Key experiences are planned to ensure that children have opportunities to explore and develop skills and concepts. Adults should intervene in children's play to promote specific developmental skills. ECEs provide a "scaffold" to facilitate children's learning in progressively more complex tasks and play (Vygotsky and Bruner).
1970s–Present: David Elkind, Lawrence Kohlberg, Barbara Biber, Rheta DeVries, Eleanor Duckworth, Howard Gardner, Loris Malaguzzi, Dr. J. Fraser Mustard, and others	As the value of play was increasingly assaulted by the *back to basics* movement in the 1980s and 1990s, and with the pressures on young children to succeed in school (which led to more academics being pushed down into kindergartens and preschools), this group remains dedicated to the value of play as the primary source of children's development and learning. Purposeful, planned play experiences and activities lead to development and learning.	Programs should provide materials and rich environments for learning through play in order to promote children's development in all domains. Children develop their intelligences through play in carefully constructed environments that challenge them to explore and experience activities that lead to skills and conceptual development. It is important to encourage children to engage in various categories, styles, and contexts for play. The development of creative (divergent) thinking is encouraged.

there are really two approaches to raising and educating children: "a middle class, Eurocentric American approach and a minority approach" (Johnson et al., 2005, p. 6). The postmodern perspective believed that play serves the goals of Western society that foster independence, competitiveness, power, and domination in children. In the same period, play was seen by non-Western cultures as frivolous and incompatible with values of group loyalty, obedience, respect for elders, cooperation, and collectivism.

In the 21st century, we have already attributed greater importance to the role of play in development and learning, based on human development research that goes beyond the old dichotomy of ***nature versus nurture*** and sees development as the interaction between genes and the environment. Even notions that giftedness is ordained by genetic inheritance are no longer credible. Meaney (2001, pp. 50–61) claimed that "there are no genetic factors that function independently of the environment, and there are no environmental factors that function independently of the genome" (quoted in Shenk, 2010, p. 145). The claim that genetic inheritance is dependent on the environment, and vice versa, affirms that children's play in a strategic and challenging environment (not just repetitive or passive play, or "busy-ness") will inevitably have a significant impact on development.

The work of Stanley Greenspan introduced another dimension that is having an impact at a time of heightened concern about the mental and physical health of children. Greenspan (1997) proposed six levels in the development of human consciousness and stated that every individual is formed out of a relationship with others. Although the child's senses absorb information, it is the intimate relationships with the primary caregivers, and being cared for and loved, that have the deepest impact on the development of our essential humanity, including the ability to empathize with others. Human development research and theory in the 21st century emphasizes the development of empathy and "developed consciousness," which is the ability to experience basic emotions (Rifkin, 2009, p. 109). Martin L. Hoffman (2000) proposed five modes of empathic arousal in the developmental process as the child becomes increasingly adept at expressing empathy; these contribute to individual self-awareness and consciousness, all of which depend on role-taking, understanding the perspective of others, and "mediated associations," which allow the child to link another child's experience to his own experience. In this age of increasing social alienation, violence, and threats to civilization, many researchers are preoccupied with social consciousness, emotional self-expression, and the development of empathic sensibilities in children. Play theory will likely evolve to meet the challenges related to helping children become more socially engaged, emotionally stable, and connected to others, all crucial factors in mental health and well-being—as well as the survival of the human species.

Early childhood education in Canada today continues to put child development and learning through play at the centre of the learning process. Recent research suggests that it is the quality of children's play that matters. Children appear to play in order to understand the world around them, to express themselves, and to practise new skills. Their inner lives are enriched through daily interactions with events, people, and things, and play is pivotal in this process. While playing, children actively explore, manipulate, and respond to their environments and experiences. Through this interaction with the concrete environment, children develop intellectually and acquire social, emotional, and physical abilities. Unfettered play helps children become more sophisticated players whose imaginations, powers of invention, and positive sense of the world around them enrich their childhoods, nourish their spirits, and lay the foundation for independent thinking, creativity, and innovation.

Brown (2009, pp. 17–18) has confirmed the properties of play that apply for all ages: apparently purposeless (done for its own sake); voluntary; has inherent attraction; freedom from time, in the sense that we lose track of time; diminished consciousness of self, in that we stop worrying about how we appear to others; has improvisational potential, in that we are not locked into rigid patterns; and a wish to keep the play going ("continuation desire"). The importance of systematic planning for play based on key developmental goals for early childhood is paramount.

The overriding assumption of this textbook is that the simplest activities—those using basic, exploratory play materials—are always best for young children. However, ECEs should not equate the simplicity of play materials with an oversimplification of learning opportunities. The best play and learning experiences are those that permit children to have their own ideas (Duckworth, 1991). ECEs should plan environments and activities that encourage children to acquire new concepts through hands-on investigation of the complexities inherent in things, phenomena, and events. Play experiences that encourage self-directed and freely chosen action on concrete objects and events, especially objects that respond to children's actions on them, lead to sharper perceptions, increased knowledge, and enhanced understanding of progressively complex concepts. Children gain a sense of mastery over their environments and a stronger sense of self as they transform their world through play.

Summary

Chapter 2 provides an important historical foundation for students who are entering the early childhood education profession. The history and evolution of early childhood education as a discipline inform us about the origin of ideas and practices that we see today and explains why some beliefs and practices have been discarded or changed and new ones have been added. ECEs need to understand the historical evolution of the role of play in learning over several decades and even centuries. Throughout the 20th century, the value of play in learning has been challenged, but recent research confirms that play is children's natural way to learn during the early years, from birth to age six and beyond. Furthermore, play promotes conceptual understanding and transfer of learning from one context to another much better than rote learning. When environments and play are purposefully planned to challenge children, play fosters thinking and creativity. This chapter emphasizes that the usefulness of play as medium for development and learning should not infringe on children's right to choose what and how they play, and that it is crucial for children to have the time to pursue their play for their own ends. Even in cultures where children are pressed very early into adult responsibilities and work, when children have moments that are not organized and controlled and when they are not compelled to meet the requirements of the collective, they play. Children everywhere and throughout the ages demonstrate an inborn tendency to play, to discover and to engage freely in nonliteral, pleasurable activity that values process over product.

Learning Activities

1. Create a timeline chart that records in sequence the evolution of play theories.
2. In a couple of paragraphs, explain why it is important to protect children's free play.
3. Create a list of the key values associated with constructivist theories of play and learning.

3 Children Learn Through Play

"In the urge to categorize and define play, we may be in danger of overlooking the fact that children have their own definitions of play."

—ELIZABETH WOOD AND JANE ATTFIELD, *PLAY, LEARNING AND THE EARLY CHILDHOOD CURRICULUM* (2005)

BEFORE READING THIS CHAPTER, HAVE YOU

- understood the history and evolution of play and the historical interpretations of "children learn through play"? These sections help you to explain the ECE theories that influence ECE practices.
- linked Jean Piaget's theory of child development to children's play and learning?
- considered the role of play in your childhood and tried to define play according to your childhood experiences?
- reviewed the explanations of physical knowledge, social-conventional knowledge, and logical-mathematical knowledge in Chapter 2? These should be well understood before you proceed to Chapter 3.

OUTCOMES

After reading and understanding this chapter, you should be able to

- define play and outline the characteristics of play;
- provide examples, from your observations of children playing, that illustrate the categories of play;
- explain and give examples of the social stages of children's play;
- outline interpretations of "children learn through play" during the past 100 years; and
- state the principles that guide children's play and learning.

What Is Play?

Play is an absorbing, satisfying, and often joyful experience for children. Observing children at play often causes longing in adults, who recollect the times in their own childhood when they were able to abandon themselves totally to the interests of the moment. Any adult who has watched a young child hover over an insect or try to make intricate pathways with a stick in the sand has witnessed how all-consuming play can be. In play, the rest of the world is often shut out and the child's senses gravitate to the object of play. The child re-enters the real world when someone or something outside the playing commands his attention.

Play provides respite from daily demands and opens up the world to a child. No matter how eager ECEs are to provide purposeful play opportunities for children that enhance development and lead to learning, we must never forget that one of the greatest gifts of childhood is the ability to pursue seemingly insignificant interests and to endlessly explore tiny details. Play is a renewable resource in the life of a child that can be resumed at any moment. It may follow any path the child desires and will end when the child decides to move on to something else or when the demands of living in the world intrude on the child's agenda. Research shows that "play is a deeply intellectual and meaningful activity for children, closely linked to their self-regulated learning and **metacognition**, and vital to the development of appropriate self-knowledge and dispositions towards learning" (Moyles, 2010, p. xii).

Childhood is a time when "children are shielded so that they can play, and this play is quintessentially human" (Garbarino, 1989, p. 17). Children need opportunities for uninterrupted, spontaneous, freely chosen, absorbing play. These opportunities should be protected from interests that detract from extended play, such as non-essential "routines," pressures for direct instruction by adults, and frequent program changes that diminish the amount of time children may spend on a self-initiated play activity or project. The ability to release themselves to the pleasure, challenge, and fascination of the moment, to focus on details or tasks, however minor by adult standards, is a right of all children. Play is activity engaged in freely by the child in order to explore and interact with the environment and the people in the child's world. Children who are not given the opportunity to play may be forced too soon into the world of immediate demands, anxiety over things they cannot control, and experiences they are unable to comprehend. It is important to capitalize on children's natural tendency to play in order to guide their skill development, to help them adapt to their environments, and to facilitate their acquisition of knowledge and understanding of concepts.

CONNECT THE HISTORY AND THEORY IN CHAPTER 2 TO CHAPTER 3

As you learned in Chapter 2, knowledge about play has evolved over time. At one time, it was believed that play is what happens when energy is left over after work has been finished, or that play is a way of generating energy needed for work. Play was also seen as a largely therapeutic activity that helped children deal with complex emotions and difficult real-life situations. These dynamic theories gave way gradually to **developmental theories** of play. Piaget emphasized the self-regulating, autonomous nature of play, which has an important role in the construction of knowledge and understanding. Vygotsky emphasized the social processes involved in play, which he believed to be central to the construction of knowledge and the interaction of development and learning.

Characteristics of Play

An important characteristic of play is the player's active involvement, a factor that rules out passive behaviours, such as daydreaming or watching a video. One criterion of play is the ability of the player to pretend. Behaviour that is *non-literal*, or pretend, is immune from consequences, and the players understand that what is done is not what it appears to be. But even though play may be *non-literal*, ECEs should not treat children's play as if it were unreal (Bettelheim, 1987b). Play is very real to the child and is, in many ways, the child's true reality.

Play is *active*, undertaken voluntarily, and usually meaningful and enjoyable to the child. It may be means-oriented or process-oriented and purposeful, but the outcome of play does not have to be a product. Play is symbolic, in that it allows children to entertain possibilities beyond the here and now, and is characterized by a hypothetical disposition in which children ask "what if" questions. Given its voluntary nature, play may be *episodic*, for it may shift as children's goals and interests change spontaneously. Meaningful play is usually *absorbing* and appropriately challenging, stretching the child's abilities and imagination. To become successful players, children have to learn how to play—that is, to imagine, to negotiate their entry into play, to develop and sustain the roles they assume, and to defer gratification for the sake of the other players (Wood, 2010).

QUALITIES AND CHARACTERISTICS OF PLAY

- Personal attentiveness: watchfulness, observation, imitation, reciprocal engagement, curiosity, reflection, making conscious decisions and actions, developing flow and complexity in play.
- Personal involvement and motivation: taking risks, combining/offering ways of knowing and constructing the world, having the disposition to be playful and to act playfully (in "what if" and "as if" modes).
- Emotional engagement: playing in and with mood and feeling states (which also involves risk taking), spontaneity, resilience and responsiveness. Being a skilled player demands considerable resilience: as new friendships develop, children may be included or excluded according to an individual play leader, or the whims of the group.... Playing with emotions such as fear, anxiety and abandonment can lead to exuberant physical activity such as screaming, shouting, running, chasing/being chased, hiding/finding, being captured/released, being dead/coming alive.
- Imaginative potential: using everyday knowledge to inform and sustain play episodes, transforming ideas in the mind (making one thing stand for something else), dramatic exaggeration, evoking magical and superhero powers.
- Communicative potential and capability: attending, listening, co-constructing meanings, openness to multi-modal forms of representation, creating shared meanings and representations, using resources and materials—transforming their uses and meanings in imaginative ways, being multi-literate.
- Relational potential: trust, freedom to act differently in "what if" and "as if" modes, sense-making capacities—negotiating real-imaginary contexts, managing fluency, uncertainty and risk.
- Problem-creating and problem-solving potential: children have sufficient choice, freedom and control to develop strategic and flexible thinking skills.
- Evoking the spirit of play: going beyond boundaries, negotiating ideas, meanings and possibilities, experiencing transcendental and spiritual qualities. Playfulness, laughter, gleefulness, zaniness, wildness, dizzy play, clowning, fooling around, inventing rules and rituals are used to begin, maintain and end play.
- A sense of humour: wit, cognitive flexibility and spontaneity, telling and laughing at jokes and funny stories, teasing.

By considering the qualities of play and playfulness, practitioners can understand some of the complex cognitive processes and dispositions involved in becoming a skilled player, and the ways in which play activities impact on learning and development.

Source: Used with permission. E. Wood et al. (2010). Developing Integrated Pedagogical Approaches to Play and Learning, pp. 19–20. In *Play and Learning in the Early Years*. London, UK: Sage.

Play versus "Not Play"

Children's play is a rich source for learning and it is their natural way to learn. Because play takes many forms and ranges from simple to complex, with degrees of sophistication, play appears, therefore, to evolve in stages that correspond to the developmental stages of the child. Play also depends on the context in which it occurs. A child digging in the garden holding a pail and shovel, without reference to any task or product that must be achieved, is seen to be playing. A child who is compelled to undertake the same activity is not playing and may be deemed, by some, to be working. What distinguishes play from activity that is not play may be the intention behind it and the degree to which it is regulated externally and imposed upon the child.

Garvey (1977) claimed that play is often best understood by a consideration of what is *not play*. In determining what is play and what is *not play*, we should examine the behaviour in terms of its causes, motivations, and consequences. The key distinction between play and *not play* lies in the intentions behind the behaviour. Garvey believed that play has no external goals and is undertaken more for the process involved than for any particular purpose or end. It should be freely chosen by the player and should be spontaneous, enjoyable, and valued in and of itself.

Although Rubin, Fein, and Vandenberg's (1983) six factors that distinguish play from not play were written nearly three decades ago, they remain relevant today.

1. Play is intrinsically motivated; that is, it comes from inside the child and it is not motivated by competition or by social demands.
2. Play focuses on means, not ends; it is process-oriented rather than product-oriented.
3. Play occurs when objects are familiar; exploration occurs when objects are unfamiliar or not understood.
4. Play involves pretending, which means engaging in activities that have an "as if," representational, or non-literal quality.
5. Play is free of the externally imposed rules that distinguish play from games.
6. Play is characterized by the active involvement of the participant and, therefore, excludes daydreaming, flitting from one thing to another, and mindless exploration.

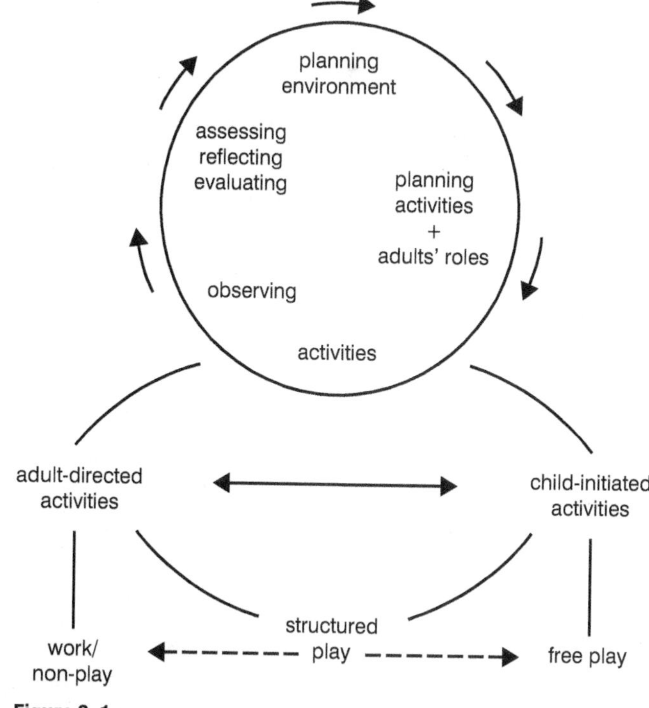

Figure 3–1
A model of integrated pedagogical approaches

Source: Used with permission. E. Wood et al. (2010). Developing Integrated Pedagogical Approaches to Play and Learning, p. 21. In *Play and Learning in the Early Years.* London, UK: Sage.*

Studies have shown that children differentiate play from *not play* by referring to "pretence" ("it's play because they are pretending"), distinguishing play from work (if it's not work, it's play), the use of "toys" (toys aren't work), the elements of choice involved, and the context in which it occurs (school) (Howard, 2010, p. 150). Wood et al. (2010, p. 20) advocate "integrated

*From *Play and Learning in the Early Years.* Edited by P. Broadhead, J. Howard, and E. Wood. 2010; p21. Reprinted by Permission of Sage Publications Inc.

pedagogical approaches" that combine adult-directed and child-initiated play, which are often complementary, and that both have elements of "playfulness" on a continuum of play from "work" to "pure play." DeVries (2002, p. 226) argued that it is important not to give work "a bad name" and recommended that we talk instead of *appropriate work* in early education, which helps children develop the capacity for work.

Many experts have attempted to differentiate play and work. Some claimed that play is activity done for its own sake, whereas work is done for some form of external reward. Montessori believed that play is the work of children. Dewey (1966 [1916]) introduced the notion that play may induce a desire for work that requires more thought and effort than does self-gratifying play. Within early childhood education today, play and work are not opposites, but they do have particular meanings. Elkind (1988) distinguished between work and play in Piagetian terms, calling work "accommodation" and play "assimilation." Work takes place when children have to alter their concepts or behaviour to better adapt to the demands of the world. For example, in learning how to tie their shoelaces, hold a fork, or hit a ball with a bat, children are accommodating, or working. When children use balls of clay or brushes and paint to represent thoughts or remembered images, or when they pretend that a swing is an airplane, they are *assimilating* or playing. When adults say that play is the child's work and equate work and play, they are doing the child and play a disservice (Elkind, 1987). Most ECEs believe that it is the nature of the activity in which children are engaged that determines whether they are working or playing. While it is acknowledged that each is viable as a means for development and learning, children should be allowed to play, as this is their natural means for cognitive and social development and emotional self-expression (Hughes, 1995). This is an important message for ECEs to convey to parents.

Research shows that young children are able to differentiate play and work activities. They make these distinctions largely according to the obligatory nature of the activity, the cognitive and physical effort required, the role of the teacher, and the amount of fun experienced while doing the activity (Wing, 1995). Marshall (1994) claimed that children are likely to perceive as work those activities that adults ask them to do or tasks that require thinking and figuring out. Yet, whatever differences exist between work and play in children's minds, they appear to appreciate opportunities for both. The child who spends an hour polishing the stones gathered at the beach and putting them carefully into a cabinet is highly engaged in worklike activity that is freely chosen, interesting to him, and full of potential for learning about similarities and differences, and a host of other knowledge. The child might even describe that he is "playing" with the stones, even while insisting that he is "working hard" to polish the stones for the display cabinet. Fromberg (2002, p. 20) claimed that "play is not the child's work in itself, nor is it a medium for learning in itself. We can think of play as an oscillating model that moves between process and product … an integration that transcends both the process and the product perspectives."

Wood (2010, p. 21) also recommends avoiding the work-play dichotomy by describing activities as "work" when they are controlled by adults, with prescribed teaching strategies, no choice or flexibility for the child, and defined outcomes; she sees "pure play" activities that are freely chosen and structured play activities that are more "worklike," such as doing a project or reading a story, as points along a continuum of play activities.

Issues arise when adults decide that play is something that children can do when they have finished their "work." Kindergartens used to provide limited play opportunities as a reward for work, which sent messages to children and parents alike that play is less important than work. This practice encouraged children to believe that work is whatever the ECE asked them to do, and, therefore, is less desirable and less interesting than play. This belief, if acquired by children, can undermine an attempt to instill in children a love of learning and the work that usually accompanies it. Although ECEs design the play environments that lead to development and learning, and often interact with children as "co-players" to extend and ramp up the complexity of their play, they should not dominate children's play so that it reflects adult plans and purposes (Wood, 2010).

The Value of Play

Children playing are at peace with themselves because they are engaged in activities they have chosen and that they have been directed to by their developmental needs (Brown, 2000). Most children play without prompting or direction from adults, and without a plan. For generations, children have developed and learned through spontaneous play. Why, then, do we spend time and energy finding ways to guide play in directions that are more purposeful?

By observing children at play, ECEs take note of the developmental skills that children have achieved. Part of the function of planning for play is to ensure that play activities showcase the child's developmental patterns as ECEs observe their play. Play is an important window to the child's level of understanding of the world around her. Play also integrates many aspects of development. When ECEs observe children playing, they are able to discern their command of language, their problem-solving skills, their ability to collaborate with others, their physical skills, and their emotional self-control (Fromberg, 2004). Elkind (2003) refers to *adult-functional* versus *child-experiential* perspectives on children's play. He reminds us that while there is value in play for the purpose of school readiness and lifelong learning, children play only for the pleasure of the activity and not to serve a purpose beyond what they are doing at the time. For children at play, the content is not important; they are focused on the moment and on the purposes that matter to them but perhaps not to the adults around them.

ECEs rely on children's natural inclination to play as they design environments, select resources, and plan activities and experiences that foster "absorbed" play, meaningful discovery and positive risk taking. Deep play steers young children toward new challenges, which have the power to transform their thinking and to actively engage their participation and motivations. In play, children integrate into their individual and group play experiences the cultural priorities and events that are important to them and their families. ECEs understand that play is instrumental in helping children overcome developmental gaps and delays, and that children's play is enhanced by a wise selection of materials and thoughtful environmental design. They believe that play is not "messing about" aimlessly, but that it should be meaningful, appealing, and engaging to the child. And it may be purposeful. Meaningful play offers regular and timely challenges and practice opportunities that lead ultimately to age-appropriate **developmental outcomes.**

Much has been written about the emergent curriculum, which requires that ECEs "trust in the power of play" to foster children's development and learning (Jones & Nimmo, 1998). A balanced approach to planning environments and curriculum for young children ensures that there is a mix of planned play activities in each learning centre and opportunities for children to freely explore the environment and to choose materials and play available to them, indoors and outdoors. Learning centres which are discussed in detail starting in Chapter 7 provide an organized physical framework for play activities that generally emphasize a particular developmental domain (e.g., physical, social), social context for play (e.g., solitary, parallel, cooperative), and category of play (e.g., sensory play, productive play, representational play). Balanced planning ensures that the *internal construction* of some of the play activities challenges children to develop specific skills or to discover phenomena and learn concepts that they may not have encountered before. The **internal construction of activities** refers to the teaching skill involved in selecting the resources needed to enhance children's play and in planning activities that allow children to *uncover* a concept for themselves as they play with the activity and to practise and develop new skills and understanding. The play equipment, materials, and supplies provided for children in each learning centre should challenge children to *uncover* and *discover* something new, and address the various **categories**, and **social contexts** of play that ECEs want to encourage.

EXAMPLE

An example of a play activity that encourages children to *uncover* a concept for themselves follows: The ECE sets out the water play table on a wheeled cart. She puts into the water table two sets of objects: one set of objects sinks because the objects are solid and heavy; the other set of objects are hollow and float. Only objects with these two distinguishing properties are put into this water table. What is the concept that children will *uncover* as they play at the water table?

Conditions Needed for Children to Learn Through Play

Play helps children find new ways to deal with reality. As children play, they explore the properties of things and extract information about their environments. They imitate, recreate, and rehearse roles that help them to understand and solve problems related to everyday life. They form relationships; share; cooperate; master their feelings; extend the range of their experience; test ideas; and form associations among things, events, and concepts.

Young children gain much of their knowledge about the world through the senses. The younger the children, the more dependent they are on sensory learning and on physical contact with their environment to learn and to know. Sensory-based play encourages children's active involvement and is meaningful to them because they find it easier to pay attention and to remain interested. When children's emotions are also involved in play situations, they are more open to the sensory information they receive. When children are able to be active as they play, they find learning easier.

Time also plays an important role in creating the right conditions for play and learning. Extended play periods are needed for children to explore and make discoveries, to elaborate on play themes, and to evolve a script in symbolic play. Allowing children the time they need to pursue their play and to achieve what they set out to do gives them the message that it is important to have goals, to achieve outcomes, and to use time well. It is essential that the daily program allow for extended and uninterrupted play times.

ECEs are required to consider many issues related to creating the right conditions for play. What is the proper balance between spontaneous and structured play, and between child-centred and adult-led play? Should the ECE plan specific play experiences that lead to predictable outcomes? To what extent should the individual developmental needs of each child determine the daily agenda of play and learning experiences? What is the role of developmental norms or milestones? These questions, and others, are considered in the following chapters. The following sections address what might be called the definitions and technicalities related to play; these are important details to understand.

Categories of Play

The multitude of ways in which children play alone and play together is difficult to capture in discrete classification systems. This textbook describes play in two ways: (1) the categories and styles of play in each category, which show the ways in which children interact with materials (see Table 3–1), and (2) the **social stages** and **social contexts** in which play occurs. It is important for ECEs to understand both in order to plan and to use environments and activities effectively to enhance children's play and to promote optimum development.

The categories of play include functional play, constructive play, symbolic play, and games-with-rules play. Several play styles comprise each category of play (see Table 3–1). The boundaries between categories and styles of play are often blurred, because children can engage in several play styles at the same time. Also, as their styles of play progress developmentally, children do not forsake earlier styles but, rather, continue with them throughout childhood. The categories of play are intertwined with the developmental stages (Fromberg, 2004; Mann, 1996).

Functional Play

Functional play consists mainly of simple, repetitive movements with or without concrete objects (Rubin, Fein, & Vandenberg, 1983). This play category dominates the sensorimotor stage of development, which occurs during the first two years of life. Functional play continues throughout childhood, but it largely characterizes the play of infants and toddlers, who explore objects physically, using their senses. Play becomes their way of understanding the properties of things in their world and of testing the reactions of objects to various forms of physical manipulation. Typical styles of play within this category include **repetitive** or practice play, **exploratory play**, and **testing play**.

Repetitive or practice play usually involves the repetition of physical behaviours that have already been mastered. Practice play is the earliest form of exploratory play and is characterized by the infant's sucking of objects, making sounds, listening, gazing, and following moving objects visually. Exploratory activities during the infant and toddler years include tasting, emptying, filling, inserting, pulling, stacking, pushing, rolling, and climbing.

From age two to age three, exploratory play involves arranging, heaping, combining, sorting, spreading, and transforming things in the environment. Later in this stage, children engage in verbal exploratory play by putting words and sounds together in new and often funny combinations. Interlocking materials, such as Lego; **modular materials**, such as small blocks; balls, rattles, keys, and drums; and stacking or nesting materials facilitate functional play. This style of play continues later with objects made to be manipulated in more than one way.

TABLE 3–1

CATEGORIES OF PLAY AND RELATED STYLES OF PLAY FOR EACH CATEGORY

Functional Play	**Symbolic Play**
Play styles: • exploratory play • repetitive or practice play • testing play	Play styles: • imitative play • pretend play • dramatic play • sociodramatic play • thematic play and sociodrama • fantasy play • representational play
Constructive Play	**Games-with-Rules Play**
Play styles: • productive play • creative play • reproductive play	Play styles: • rule-bound play • competitive play

Testing play appears early, when the child engages in motor testing by crawling into and out of small places. Later, children engage in testing play when they challenge their own ability to climb to the top of the climber and when they explore the capacity of the unit blocks to sustain a gigantic tower shape without falling over.

Constructive Play

Constructive play begins with productive play, which involves the child using materials to produce intended results. Productive play occurs from about two years of age, when children learn the uses of simple play materials and play with them to satisfy their own purposes. Constructive play includes creative play, such as building with blocks; constructing with Tinkertoy and other interlocking materials; sculpting with **malleable materials**, such as modelling clay or dough; and creating patterns or designs with modular materials, such as parquetry tiles and Lego. Children have to practise achieving their own goals in play before they are ready to adapt to externally imposed goals (Butler, Gotts, & Quisenberry, 1978). In constructive play, children interact with the play materials for their own purposes, often without any particular plan or strategy, to produce a specific outcome. Constructive play continues to be a common form of play in preschools and kindergartens when the right kinds of play materials are provided and children have the space and time to play with them for extended periods. At this later stage, children usually demonstrate reproductive play as they fashion a real-world object in their play, for example, with blocks. This style of play demonstrates more mature understanding of spatial relationships and the use of symbols so that the product of their play is often recognizable. As children's capacity for symbolic thought grows, they begin to construct objects that represent more imaginative or fantastical things (Johnson, Christie & Wardle, 2005, p. 64).

Symbolic Play

Symbolic play, and later **representational play**, involve the ability to use symbols in ways that are different from their usual purpose (Zigler, Singer, & Bishop-Josef, 2004). For example, the child may make one object stand for another, as in using puppets to represent the other children in the group, or in pretending that the table is a house. Being able to transform objects and events by imagining that they have different meanings lies at the heart of cognitive development and communication (Nourot & Van Hoorn, 1991). Planning activities for toddlers and preschoolers that encourage children to use objects symbolically—that is, making one object stand for another—is instrumental in promoting social-emotional and cognitive development, including literacy and numeracy skills.

Symbolic play occurs during the preoperational stage of development, which lasts from about age two to age six or seven years. At two years of age, the child's newly acquired ability to use objects as symbols begins to predominate over practice play. There are several styles of symbolic play often described as forms of **dramatic play**—imitative play, pretend play, sociodramatic play, and fantasy play—each of which involves "progressively symbolic distancing" from the object or event being represented (Nourot & Van Hoorn, 1991). These symbolic play styles are discussed in detail in Chapter 11, which describes symbolic thinking and representational thinking and the role of play in helping children progress from the use of concrete objects as symbols to the ability to use abstract symbols.

DRAMATIC PLAY

Imitative play is a symbolic play style that occurs during the first year of life and refers to the child's simple imitation of the actions of a parent or caregiver. The child enjoys games, such as playing pat-a-cake; making cooing or gurgling sounds along with a parent; or mimicking actions, such as hitting a cushion. Right from the early months of life, the infant can imitate other people and is particularly attentive to other children's actions. Early imitations closely resemble the actions of the adult or older child. Examples include a child who makes a clucking sound to mimic the sounds being made by an adult, rocking a doll in her arms and cooing softly, or a child hammering a saucepan with a wooden spoon like a drummer.

Pretend play is a universal characteristic of childhood, and studies show that children's pretend play is biologically based and occurs at similar times in child development in all cultures (Brooker, 2010, p. 29). Pretend play becomes increasingly more complex as children mature, and their pretend sequences develop along three transformational strands related to objects, roles, and action sequences: (1) pretend play with objects becomes increasingly independent of the features of the objects; (2) role play moves from personal and bodily related actions, such as pretending to brush hair, to imitation of others' activities, such as washing dishes; and (3) action sequences move from single pretend episodes, for example, bathing a baby, to multi-action sequences, such as dressing dolls and taking them for a walk to the store (Fein, 1975). Pretend play is a prerequisite for children to eventually master the elements of more complex dramatic play and of later pretend play with other children, which we call **sociodramatic play**.

Toward the end of the sensorimotor period, children begin to engage in pretend or dramatic play, in which they practise their own versions of adult behaviours rather than imitating only what they have seen. At this stage, children are beginning to think using symbols, meaning they can use an object to represent something else. For example, the child delights in pretending to be mommy or daddy by taking a doll for an outing in a carriage, or by pushing a stroller as if it were a shopping cart in the supermarket. The dramatic or pretend play of three-year-olds in the early stages of the preoperational period is usually predictable, and the representations are simple. Much of this early dramatic play tends to be solitary. Children at this stage generally prefer **props** that are familiar to them and that are similar physically to the objects and events being imitated. For example, they enjoy playing with child-sized replicas of household equipment, cars, trucks, telephones, and computers. Supporting this type of play is essential to children's development of their later ability to engage in sociodramatic play, which is an important milestone that all children should achieve (Zigler et al., 2004).

Thematic play is a more elaborate form of dramatic role play in which two or more children, usually younger than age four, play out a familiar theme. More repetitive than later versions of sociodramatic play, thematic play challenges children to listen and respond to the actions and language of the other player. Children often replay fragments of everyday living routines without integrating them into a longer role play sequence. This type of play appears to coincide with the child's rapid language development, which suggests that ECEs should encourage opportunities for thematic play as a rich resource for literacy learning (Segal, 2002).

Fantasy play is a variation of dramatic and sociodramatic play that usually begins to appear in the third year, as soon as children are able to use symbols. It is a "particular style of social pretend play that involves fantastic rather than realistic characters and situations, including story characters such as Goldilocks, Hansel and Gretel, and superheroes" (Saltz & Saltz, 1986, p. 159) such as Superman and Spiderman. Fantasy play that pursues a fantastical theme over an extended period is usually more mature than sociodramatic play, which represents more commonplace themes.

Successful experiences in make-believe or fantasy play depend on time playing alone and on an unstructured environment that permits flexible use of a wide range of materials and equipment in interesting ways. Fantasy play requires concentration and absorption in play, positive attitudes, healthy self-esteem, and a rich imagination that kindles the ability to dramatize with other children remembered themes from a favourite story or from a television program and assume the roles of the characters. Sometimes children assign roles and attempt to stay close to the plot that all players recognize or remember. The element of fantasy remains, as children see themselves as characters in the story and pour themselves wholeheartedly into becoming their fantastical characters.

SOCIODRAMATIC PLAY

Sociodramatic play is a more advanced and sophisticated form of dramatic play; it occurs as children mature, social play becomes predominant, and considerable social interaction and **cooperative play** are incorporated into pretend play. Smilansky (1993) called sociodramatic play the most important style of play for children, and Bredekamp (2004) believes that this type of play is most effective in developing school readiness abilities. Play becomes less predictable as more variables are involved. Sociodramatic play is most common during the **intuitive period**, which lasts from ages four to seven, a period characterized by the prelogical nature of children's thinking, when they gradually move away from reliance on what they perceive through the senses toward the eventual understanding of concepts. At this stage, children are becoming able to take the perspective of others, to connect similar objects and events, and to form classes or sets. It is during this intuitive period that children's role play evolves from dramatic play using realistic props and simple representations and becomes more complex and realistic. Sociodramatic play usually begins around age four; it is a more social and complex form of symbolic play that occurs when two or more children collaborate in dramatizing experiences from their physical and social environments. Sociodramatic play differs from fantasy play in that it involves dramatizing remembered experiences common to the children playing, such as going to the doctor or having lunch at a restaurant. Children older than four or five usually want their sociodramatic play to be as close to reality as possible.

EXAMPLE: AN EARLY FORM OF SOCIODRAMATIC PLAY

Lucy and Kai, age four, have been playing with the hollow blocks and appear to have constructed a house with a backyard and a surrounding fence. Lucy spies the dolls and stuffed animals sitting in the Daily Living centre and urges Kai to follow her to collect the dolls and animals, which they bring to their block structure. A simple dialogue follows. Lucy: "Let's pretend that this dolly is the mommy and the teddybear is the dog. You play the dog and I'll be the mommy. Now take the dog outside the fence. I'll call the dog to come home and you bring him back to the house." Kai: "I'll be the daddy and we can build a house for the dog in the yard." Lucy calls the dog: "Barney, come home." Kai brings the dog back to the backyard, then grabs some blocks; both children focus their attention on building the doghouse. At this stage, the children are unable to hold their dialogue for longer than a few simple exchanges and are easily distracted by the physical task, i.e., building the doghouse. As they develop their sociodramatic play skills, the plot lines of their dialogue become more complex and the play episode might be extended in time.

Along with the child's sharper perception of reality comes a desire to reproduce actions, events, and behaviours from the adult world. Children at this stage enjoy assuming adult roles, as if they are practising for the future or are trying to understand what it feels like to be someone else. As with dramatic play, sociodramatic play provides an opportunity for children to express feelings, solve problems related to their emotional lives, understand the conflicts of others, and experiment with new behaviours. At a more advanced stage, children prefer unstructured, abstract props that can become whatever they want. Cardboard boxes, hollow blocks, blankets, sticks, and furniture are examples of such abstract props. With time, children abandon the use of props in their sociodramatic play and rely more on verbalizing what they are doing, using, and thinking.

EXAMPLE

Lucy to Kai in the hollow block area, where they have built a large house and fenced backyard with a detached garage: "Let's pretend that this is our house and we are going to have a barbecue in the backyard. We'll invite friends and we'll cook hot dogs and roast marshmallows." Kai: "Can we invite Joey and Sri to come over with their sticks and make us a fire?" Lucy: "Let's pretend that we have a table and chairs here and we'll bring our drinks and have lunch. You can cook the hot dogs and I'll set the table and make us a cake."

Sociodramatic play helps children learn to take turns and understand that certain behaviours are important in specific social situations. The abilities to cooperate socially when assuming interdependent roles and to maintain a common *script* require considerable cognitive and social sophistication. Children need to be aware of typical roles in the social world and should be sensitive to the complexities of relationships. They also should be aware of social networks and be able to communicate, negotiate, and follow commonly understood sequences of social events. Symbolic play and later ability to assume complex roles are linked to language development, early literacy skills, and abstract thinking.

Sociodramatic play is vital to many aspects of cognitive development because several cognitive capabilities are required to maintain a sociodramatic script or pantomime. Singer and Lythcott (2002) maintain that sociodramatic play not only enhances children's readiness for school but also promotes social skills and creative development. In this particularly rich form of play, children have to be able to take a perspective other than their own, separate fantasy from reality, take turns, share, cooperate, negotiate, and pretend, without the presence of realistic props. They also have to remember the directions generally established by the group at the beginning of the play episode. Frequently, children embarking on a sociodramatic play situation will be heard negotiating roles, for example, by saying, "You can be the daddy, she'll be the mommy, and I'll be the baby." Another situation may see children setting the scene, as in, "Let's pretend that we've already done our shopping and have unpacked the groceries and now it's time to get dressed for the party."

Children also develop the capacity to remove themselves temporarily from the script or mime to renegotiate a role or alter the plot. Sometimes children will step out of their roles to prompt another child who has forgotten his part, whispering, for example, "Now go and answer the telephone and pretend you're talking to Spiderman." Sociodramatic and fantasy play significantly increase children's abilities to take a perspective other than their own and to understand the thoughts and feelings of others. Children whose social experiences are limited, who lack communication skills, and who have low self-esteem generally shun sociodramatic play completely or drop out very soon after the play has begun. *The sophistication and complexity of sociodramatic play as a stimulus for cognitive, social, and emotional skills makes it imperative that ECEs find ways to help all children become full participants in sociodramatic play episodes.* Opportunities for sociodramatic and fantasy play are vital to the development of representational abilities, which permit children to project themselves out of their immediate context into a pretend or fantasy world. Smilansky and Shefatya (1990) claimed that sociodramatic play expresses the child's need to model himself in thought, feeling, action, and reaction after the adults in his immediate surroundings, mainly parents, and that it arises from his intense desire to be like these adults. They concluded that since parents often overlook their roles in fostering sociodramatic play, early childhood programs should do all that they can to facilitate the acquisition of the basic tools of collective make-believe inherent in sociodramatic play.

Games-with-Rules Play

Play is characterized by freedom from all but self-imposed rules (which may be changed at will), by open-ended fantasy, and by the absence of any goals beyond the activity itself. Games, however, often involve **competitive play** styles, with agreed-on, often externally imposed, rules that require the use of materials in the manner in which they are intended for the game. They also have a goal or a purpose, such as winning the game. Whereas play is usually regarded as pure enjoyment, games are considered demanding and sometimes stressful.

Rule-bound play involves prearranged rules that children can accept and to which they are able to adapt. When two children play a board game or a game of tag, they must agree on the rules; this requires that children are able to control their behaviour within the limits established (Rogers & Sawyers, 1988; Segal, 2004). When children achieve the concrete operational stage of development, at about seven years of age, rule-bound play, or games with rules, predominate, and school-age children are usually able to understand the significance and stability of rules for the duration of the game or activity.

From age seven to age 12, the making and accepting of rules becomes an important part of children's play. Children in this concrete operational period are able to delay gratification, accept external limitations and authority, and challenge existing social expectations and rules in a reasonable manner. During the early stages of this period, children normally engage in board games, physical activities, and games with straightforward, externally imposed rules. These activities are favourites for children in after-school programs.

Competitive play allows children to develop and improve their abilities, to gain a clearer sense of their own levels of competence, to compare themselves to others, and to learn to be good sports by winning and losing graciously (Weininger, 1979). Children's increasing abilities to negotiate, form social contracts, question existing rules, collaborate in amending rules, and behave objectively prepare them for engaging in group projects and for becoming team members. Competitive play may describe two or more children playing in a group or two or more groups of children competing to win—for example, in team sports, relays, and other competitive challenges. Children aged six and up are generally ready for competitive play activities.

Social Play Stages

Parten (1933) was the first to classify children's play. In her classic study of the social interactions of two- to five-year-old children, she defined six increasingly complex levels of social play. She also found that children do not lose the ability to engage in earlier forms of social play as they get older and that children from ages four to six demonstrate all social contexts of play at different times.

Considerable learning in all **developmental domains** occurs because of social play (Parten, 1933; Smilansky & Shefatya, 1990). Language, physical, and cognitive abilities are fostered when children play together in either mixed-age or age-graded groupings. Social and emotional skills depend on children's play with each other in a variety of social groupings. Learning to listen, take turns, cooperate, share, empathize, show affection, be responsible, channel and communicate emotion acceptably, exercise restraint, delay gratification, and a host of other **affective development** abilities are addressed during social play.

The Contexts of Social Play

ONLOOKING PLAY

In **onlooking play**, a child observes children playing but does not physically participate. In this type of social play, sometimes called spectator play, the child remains on the periphery of the group and may later imitate the play behaviours he witnessed. Onlooking play is found in the play of children at all stages, which is one reason why we refer to these styles of social play as "contexts" instead of "stages."

SOLITARY PLAY

In **solitary play**, one child plays alone, although she is in a room where other children are playing. Solitary play may be egocentric, in that the child focuses on satisfying her own needs. Children at all stages engage in solitary play.

CONTEXTS OF SOCIAL PLAY
- Onlooking play
- Solitary play
- Parallel play
- Associative play
- Cooperative play/competitive play

PARALLEL PLAY

In **parallel play**, two children play side by side, each occupied by his activity and not interacting, though each may talk in monologue. The children usually do not exchange conversation or play materials. Parallel play is particularly prevalent among older toddlers and among three-year-olds.

ASSOCIATIVE PLAY

Associative play is loosely organized play in which children participate in a similar activity and may even exchange ideas or play materials but do not subordinate their individual interests to those of the group. For example, they may contribute to a mural without making particular reference to what the other children are adding. A child may imitate the play behaviours of another child but does not engage in interdependent play activity. Associative play is common among three- to four-year-olds.

COOPERATIVE PLAY

Cooperative play is paired or group social play that involves children with common goals who assume different roles or tasks under the leadership of usually one or two children. One example is two children cooperating in an art activity or in a science project. Another is intergroup play, in which two or more groups cooperate on a project toward a common end, such as making a mural or planning a puppet show. Play continues for a relatively long time and at a fairly high level of complexity. Cooperative play begins when children are about four and continues to the onset of the concrete operational period and beyond. Children become progressively more capable in their cooperative play between four and seven years of age, and ECEs should encourage their cooperative endeavours. Competitive play also occurs in the later preschool and kindergarten years when two or more children or two or more groups of children compete to win. Gentle competition may be introduced gradually when children are ready and relatively evenly matched.

Parallel play in the sand

Principles to Guide Play and Learning

Piaget's outline of the cognitive stages of development in childhood provided a framework for the emergence of developmental theories of play. As Piaget's developmental theory was elaborated upon by contemporary educators and by further research, a constructivist theory of play emerged (DeVries, 2004; Duckworth, 1991; Fromberg, 2004; Smilansky & Shefatya, 1993; Zigler, Singer, & Bishop-Josef, 2002). Vygotsky emphasized the impact of social interaction on play and learning and believed that development is facilitated by stimulating play environments in which children are encouraged to collaborate with their peers (Zigler et al., 2002). Some principles to explain and guide play and learning are described below.

Cooperative play

1. **Children construct their understanding of how the world works through active interaction with concrete objects, events, and people.** This principle comes from the knowledge that preoperational children, those approximately two to six years of age, are largely physical beings, for whom most learning occurs through the senses. Piaget believed that interaction with the environment through play is essential to children's ability to construct their own intelligence. Much of what children know and learn is perceptually bound, in that what they see is what they believe. Through active interaction with their environment—in other words, through hands-on play and social interactions—children acquire new knowledge and understanding. It is this **hands-on learning** within a planned environment that presents challenges in their play and helps children increase the complexity of their mental structures. As the concepts they understand and the knowledge they gain from active experience increase, children achieve higher levels of development.
2. **Children's understanding is facilitated by planning learning environments and activities for play that build on what children already know and that move them a step or two further.** ECEs help children build on existing knowledge and internalize and transform their learning to achieve new understanding. First, ECEs should know the children's developmental stages, interests, and present capabilities; then, they should plan environments, curriculum, and play and learning activities based on that knowledge. Children should be encouraged to explore, discover, think, and question. ECEs build learning activities around central concepts that emerge as children manipulate the play materials, alone and together, to find meaning. Vygotsky (1978) proposed that there is a "zone of proximal development," (ZPD) which is a space between what a child already knows and can do and the level of optimal development, which is usually achieved through play with more advanced peers or under an ECE's guidance. From this, the concept of scaffolding emerged, which is the process that occurs when older children or adults help a child move from his present level of understanding to a more advanced level. (See Chapter 9, p. 160, for a further explanation of scaffolding.) The scaffolding process is at work when ECEs use a hand-over-hand guidance strategy to help a child grasp a crayon and print a series of letters or when they ask children questions to help them probe more deeply into an activity in order to overcome an obstacle in their thinking.
3. **Young children learn best in informal settings.** Developmental educators have stressed the importance of **informal learning** for young children for four decades. David Elkind differentiated between **formal** and **informal education** when he described the "active classroom" (Elkind, 1976). Informal learning

occurs when children engage in play for its own sake, with materials or with others, or both, in activities planned to promote "structure formation"; **formal learning** is oriented toward "structure utilization," in activities usually initiated by the ECE, sometimes for a reward, and that make use of structures already formed (Elkind, 1976). For example, informal learning involves children's progress in understanding the concept of number through play that includes learning about sets, order, and number constancy, as opposed to formal learning, which includes performing operations with numbers, such as multiplication or division, at a later developmental stage.

4. **Informal, active learning practices are essential to children's healthy growth and development from ages two to six years.** Although informal learning is best for children under six, some educators and members of the public have continued to advocate a formal, back-to-basics, knowledge-based curriculum broken down into subject areas, along with rote learning, external reward systems, and standardized testing, and they believe it should begin as early as kindergarten. This approach is sometimes recommended as the answer to the need for educational reform. In the preoperational stage, children lay the foundation for later learning and build mental structures through active interaction with their environment, alone and with each other. Rushing young children prematurely into formal learning leads to the "miseducation" of children (Elkind, 1987). Issues related to children's readiness for formal learning are addressed in Chapter 4.
5. **Children understand a concept when they are able to transfer the learning acquired in one context to another context.** For example, a unit of several play activities that all address the fact that water can do many things leads children to a broader understanding of water and its many properties and related phenomena than does a single water play activity, such as sink and float at the water table. Units of activities guide children to make connections and to form concepts based on their active experience playing with concrete objects. Children take different amounts of time to achieve conceptual understanding through concrete experiences, especially when they are permitted to choose freely the activities they will pursue. Therefore, a unit of play activities should be left out long enough for children to make connections between the activities. When ECEs carefully observe children's play, they will be aware of which children have pursued play with the various activities in the unit and who has made the connections.
6. **The ECE's role is primarily to facilitate children's learning through play.** This means conducting regular and extended observations of children; assessing their participation and progress; and then planning rich play activities to sustain their involvement, capture their particular interest, and take the children to the next level of development. ECEs modify the environment as the children make developmental progress and are ready for new challenges in their play.
7. **Much has been written about the emergent curriculum, which relies on the ECE's understanding of children's current interests as well as their developmental stages and knowing what steps come next in a typical developmental sequence in each domain.** The ECE then weaves children's interests into the task of setting up resources and activities for all learning centres and outdoors, ensuring that they capture the children's current

preoccupations and engage them with the planned environment. Interesting activities, which children choose for themselves, invite attention to the activities for longer periods of time, allowing them to master skills, understand concepts, and integrate their new skills and understanding into their growing repertoire of abilities. When ECEs practise "playful pedagogies" that "create and sustain playful learning environments, enabling participation and engagement for all children, and considering diversity, equity and social justice" the intrinsic value of play is respected and programs promote rather than erode the status of play (Broadhead, Wood, & Howard, 2010, p. 181).

The Instrumental Uses of Play

Play is instrumental in stimulating and shaping child development and learning, which occur through constructive processes in which the previous knowledge the child brings to the play experience is modified by new experiences and discoveries initiated by the child. Understanding play includes having an appreciation of its instrumental function, meaning that play may be managed so as to foster children's development in specific domains. For example, if a child seldom plays in the Quiet-Thinking centre, where the literacy materials are located, the instrumental function of play may be achieved by moving the literacy-related materials into learning centres where the child does usually play. By selecting materials related to the play theme the child is pursuing, ECEs can expand and focus play activity. Why not ask a child to create road signs for the highway he is constructing out of hollow blocks, for example? Why not ask him to use rods, number symbols, or other markers to count and record the number of blocks he has used to build his bridge? Why not suggest that he recreate his block structure with modelling clay in the Creative centre?

EXAMPLE

Javier, a lively four-year-old, prefers to play outdoors or in the Active Role Play centre. His literacy skills are not well developed for his age. The ECE encourages him to play with materials that promote number, letter, and word recognition and perceptual and fine motor skills. To do so, she often moves a table with some puzzles, fine motor tasks, and a magnetic board with letters outdoors onto the patio and encourages Javier to play there with her for a while. At other times, she plays a story set to music (such as *Peter and the Wolf*) outdoors and encourages Javier and the other children to move according to the character and instrument in the story. In these ways and others, she actively exposes this child to early literacy tasks and perceptual skills in contexts that the child enjoys.

Play enables children to understand concepts and phenomena through hands-on interaction with objects. Through their sensory involvement with things, children manipulate and alter what is "out there" and try to fit new experiences with what they already know and understand. The ways in which play materials and props respond to children's actions on them lead children to better understand the things and the events in their own world, as well as the ways in which they interconnect. For example, as children play with blocks by stacking and aligning them, the blocks respond and take the shape the child intends. The new shape encourages the child's further actions. Responsive media, such as blocks, promote both physical knowledge and understanding of concepts.

The Emotional Impact of Play

Play serves children's emotional well-being by fostering self-expression, role play, rehearsal of new experiences, and fantasy about unknown worlds. **Open-ended materials**, such as blocks and paints or other artistic media, allow children to express themselves without being hindered by adult expectations or by pressures to produce a predefined outcome. Such play is accompanied by a sense of emotional release, as children use the materials to convey their deepest feelings and perceptions. When children explore materials freely and use them to fulfill their own purposes, they feel a sense of mastery over their world. Materials that the child controls and manipulates as he plays convey a sense that he has some influence over his world; this instills confidence, self-worth, and respect for others.

When children play with structured materials that present new challenges, they experience feelings of success when they finally master the tasks inherent in the materials. Feeling self-satisfaction and fulfillment in meeting challenges through play motivates children to set higher goals. **Self-esteem** is realized through successful experiences with appropriate materials in meaningful contexts. A child who plays and learns at his own speed knows when he has been successful, and this self-understanding, based on his own experience, makes it more difficult for external pressures and stress to shake his belief in himself. Children who play successfully and master challenging activities, in individual and social contexts, become less dependent on feedback from others. ECEs who allow children the time they need to finish their paintings and the block structures they are making recognize the importance of play to children as well as its instrumental value. The ECE who responds to a child's request to come and see what he has made, even though she must temporarily leave what she is doing, acknowledges the value of the child's play but also conveys a message that the child is most important.

Summary

Play is the catalyst for development and learning that fosters curiosity, independence and interdependence in learning, the self-confidence to have and pursue one's own ideas, a desire to succeed, persistence with challenging tasks, and habits of mind and dispositions for learning that last a lifetime. ECEs need to understand the learning processes that children bring to their play with responsive concrete objects, with each other, and individually so that they can gather meaning, uncover concepts, and understand what they see and do.

When play is under assault by pressures to introduce academic learning at earlier ages, it is incumbent upon ECEs to defend the value of play in children's development in all domains. ECEs should have a clear understanding of the categories, styles, and social contexts of play and how each contributes to development and learning. This professional knowledge is not possessed by everyone; it is unique to the ECE, who knows how to design curriculum, plan environments and activities, observe children's developmental needs and interests, record progress, and integrate what he learns about children's progress into the environment and the play activities. The more effectively ECEs can exploit the full potential of play environments, equipment, and materials to support all categories, styles, and contexts of play, the richer children's play and the program will be. The more successful the children are in their self-initiated play, the more likely that they will build a solid foundation for later success in learning. The more control they feel over their play environment and the more they persist and succeed with new play challenges, the more self-confidence they gain, the more deeply ingrained their self-esteem becomes, and the more self-reliant they become.

The ECE is an artist who possesses the unique ability to orchestrate environments, materials, and activities so as to optimize and enrich children's play and capitalize on the spontaneity of their freely chosen activities within a purposefully constructed setting. Chapter 3 is a cornerstone of this textbook because it explains the essential learning about play that ECEs should acquire in order to practise professionally.

LEARNING ACTIVITIES

1. Observe preschool children playing indoors and outdoors in a group setting. Report on three specific play activities by describing for each
   - the social stages and contexts of play observed and
   - the various categories and play styles you observe.
2. Use examples from their play to illustrate the categories of play and the social stages of play.
3. Create a table that relates the developmental stages of play to the categories of play and the social contexts of play.
4. Conduct a classroom debate on the resolution "Play is the child's work."
5. Explain the meaning of "instrumental function of play" and provide examples of instrumental play activities.

4 Issues Related to Play, Development, and Learning

"Education is inherently and inevitably an issue of human goals and human values."

—HOWARD GARDNER, *FIVE MINDS FOR THE FUTURE* (2006)

BEFORE READING THIS CHAPTER, HAVE YOU

- understood the historical development of early childhood education through the centuries?
- developed a good sense of the importance of children's play and play-based learning?
- recognized the theoretical foundations of constructivist early childhood education?
- learned the categories and social contexts of play and identified them in early childhood settings?

OUTCOMES

After reading and understanding this chapter, you should be able to

- explain the importance of spiritual development in early childhood;
- debate issues related to children's need for spontaneous, regular contact with nature;
- promote inclusive practice and value diversity in early learning programs;
- advocate for and persuade parents and the public of the value of play in early development and learning; and
- take a position on key issues and give reasons for your position.

What Are Issues?

An **issue** exists when a situation or conflict to be resolved contains at least two perspectives or opposing sets of conditions or ways to resolve the issue. Opposing values within the issue often generate the element of controversy. Most ECE professionals prefer to engage in constructive, collaborative pursuits in the interests of children, rather than to spend precious energy "taking sides" on issues that change with the times anyway. It is helpful, however, to understand the values and viewpoints behind issues that sometimes divide the profession. When the issues are clearly understood, more agreement than difference of opinion occurs among ECEs, administrators, and policymakers. This chapter addresses some issues particularly relevant in the lives of children today, such as how to build moral and spiritual fibre in children to gird them with skills and dispositions that will sustain them throughout life, and the importance of outdoor play and contact with nature to children's spiritual and physical development.

Wood and Attfield (2005) found that play is rich with meanings that children create for themselves and that, as they play, they inject their experience of the real world as if to add meaning to everyday events. To deprive children of the right to play is to prevent or stall their deeper insights into human interactions, their connectedness with nature, their thoughtful examination of nature's mysteries, and their reflection on meanings beyond what is immediately tangible and concrete. This chapter links children's play to the deeper issues of spirituality, connectedness with nature, respect for life in general, and the ultimate mandate of childhood, which is to help children become fully human.

Play and Children's Spiritual Development

This issue is on the minds of parents, school officials, governments, and the general public because of the apparently increasing incidence of mental illness and deviant behaviour in childhood and youth. In our pluralistic society, with its diverse values and cultures, we try to eliminate all forms of racial, religious, class, age, and gender prejudice. Programs frequently avoid topics that might be perceived by some groups as beliefs specific to the mainstream culture and, therefore, not valid within programs that serve children of many cultures and backgrounds. Perhaps because of the desire to be inclusive and "politically correct," spiritual development has been neglected. Neglect often stems from a fear of infringing upon the rights of individuals to adhere to their religious beliefs and because spirituality is often incorrectly equated with religious beliefs and practices. Religious beliefs, however, are more formal, often taught in or by an institution, and prescribe standards of behaviour.

Trousdale (2005) defined **spirituality** as the capacity for wonder; for interest in the nature and origin of things; and for reflection on how one relates to others, to oneself and to the world around us. Baumgartner and Buchanan (2010, p. 91) describe three common elements of spirituality: a sense of belonging, respect for self and others, and an awareness and appreciation of the unknown. These elements appear across religious and cultural boundaries. Goleman (2004) defined spiritual intelligence as the innate human need to connect with something larger than ourselves. Gardner (2004) proposed the existence of a ninth intelligence that he calls **existential intelligence**, which is the intelligence of concern with ultimate life issues, a concern closely related to spirituality. (See "Multiple Intelligences" in Chapter 8, pp. 143–145.) Spirituality is common to all cultures, no matter what their religious beliefs and irrespective of any religious affiliation. It is possible that when children are denied the right to explore their spiritual natures, they develop feelings of emptiness, futility, and alienation that may contribute to aberrant behaviour and mental illness. Children, as well as adults, need to believe they are a part of something larger than themselves.

Spirituality may be understood as a state of being concerned with the human soul or spirit that goes beyond the material world and external reality. It is often manifested by moments of reflection and wonder at the mysteries of life and consideration of the larger questions and fears that affect most human beings. In the broadest sense, spirituality is connectedness with the self and an understanding of what is greater than and beyond ourselves. In young children, we see hints of emerging spirituality when they ask such questions as "Where are the clouds going?" and "Where do babies come from?" and "What does dead mean?"

Bruno Bettelheim (1987b, p. 37) was interested in the spiritual development of the child. He believed that a "child, as well as an adult, needs plenty of what in German is called *Spielraum. Spielraum* means more than simply a "room to play in"; it implies space to grow spiritually and emotionally, as well as physically. Bettelheim (1987b, p. 177) believed that the development of "an inner life, including fantasies and daydreams, is one of the most constructive things a growing child can do." Play freely chosen encourages a child to become absorbed and to experience fully. Children who lose themselves in play—who escape to an inner world of imagination, dreams, and ideals—gain an enhanced sense of themselves as human beings. An important element of play is its capacity to provide an avenue to the soul, or to promote a deepening of the spirit and a fuller understanding of the self. Environments that provide *Spielraum* respect the importance of children's play at its deepest level.

The achievement of a rich inner life is often frustrated in our society and in families by packed schedules of routines, obligations, and immediate demands. Children's lives are often organized by the limitations of child care, the need to adapt to the group, and little time for quiet reflection and wonder. Too often, young children are coerced into adult-centred, direct instruction (Kirn & Cole, 2001) with little freedom to play. Some of us remember from our childhood the broad expanses of unplanned days at home and times when we listened alone to the sound of the wind in the trees, chased butterflies, waded in a muddy stream, and collected acorns and shiny stones, all without regard for time or obligation. It is in uninhibited contact with the natural world that play offers the greatest opportunities for developing the rich inner life of which Bettelheim spoke.

A happy, playful childhood is a reservoir of dreams, ideals, fond remembrances, moments of keen insight, and other treasures that are usually gathered when children are lost in doing something for its own sake. When children are robbed of opportunities for wonder and contemplation of the world and the mysteries around them, they are hurled too soon, and often without the inner resources they need, into a world of material values, preoccupation with the mundane, and fears related to uncertainty and the unknown. Far worse is the absence of opportunities for children to see themselves as part of a much larger whole that, initially, includes the family and community, and eventually broadens out to the rest of humanity. When children fail to see themselves as part of a larger picture, they do not ask the deeper questions in life. When their daily lives are a mundane round of short-term activities that have little meaning for them and do not inspire their imaginations and curiosity, they become restless and bored and sometimes afraid and empty. Emptiness, boredom, and fear coupled with a meagre sense of self-worth and meaning in life breed discontent, hyperactivity, and depression, which eventually may lead to acting out, mental illness, or even violence.

In studying the spiritual life of children, Robert Coles (1990) found it to be thoughtful and deep. He believed that children will try to understand the meaning of life and death in spite of the rigours present in their lives and that children should be allowed to question. Although children tend to glean what they need from their environments, their spiritual development depends on the wholesomeness, variety, and spontaneity of their everyday worlds. The overwhelming appeal of the Harry Potter books for school-aged children is a recent example of children's profound interest in moral issues; the relationship of good and evil; fear of death; and the obligations of friendship, courage, and loyalty. Although young children in the preoperational stage of their development have not yet mastered complex abstract concepts, they experience concrete evidence of the human condition in their interactions with family members, teachers, and other children; their loss of pets or loved ones; and their treatment of and by others. "We grow morally as a consequence of learning how to be with others, how to behave in this world, a learning promoted by taking to heart what we have seen and heard" (Coles, 1997, p. 5).

It may be easier to identify the effects of the absence of a rich spiritual life than to describe the benefits of its presence. Bettelheim (1987b) claimed that the absence of opportunities to spend energy on an inner life causes a child to turn to readily available stimuli such as television, computers, and video games. When children rely on modern media to fill the void caused by a lack of spontaneous play in the natural world and do not experience time for quiet contemplation, their perceptions of the world change dramatically. They learn to depend on fast-paced video images and sound, which raise their expectations of speed and heightened sensory stimulation and dull their sensitivity to the nuances of nature's visual, auditory, and other sensory pleasures. In our media-frenzied environment, large elements of childhood, including distinctions between adulthood and childhood, disappear and children are exposed too early to the interests and anxieties of adults (Postman, 1982). Children fail to gain a sense of control over their environments and their inner selves when they feel compelled by external stimuli instead of by their inner aspirations and a warm sense that their true spirit and identity resides within themselves. One of today's gravest issues may be children's lack of connection with life's larger meaning and with the human condition in its broadest sense. Early childhood programs should help children ask important questions; confront their human fears and anxieties; accept that much of life is a mystery; and see themselves as part of a continuum of humanity that instils humility, compassion, and empathy.

Respect for spiritual connections may be a key component of an inclusive environment, which recognizes that spirituality and the ceremony that often accompanies it are important in the lives and traditions of many cultural groups, especially First Nations peoples, who continue to remind us of our intimate connection to the earth. Programs that respect cultural diversity respect the cultural events and the ways in which they are celebrated by different cultures (Klein & Chen, 2001) while avoiding the temptation to make cultural festivals the centrepiece of their inclusive program. Recognizing the meanings of cultural events, rituals, and artifacts helps ECEs address children's questions of a spiritual nature and encourages them to see the similarities in cultural and spiritual traditions from one culture to another. It is important to achieve the right balance of attention to cultural festivals and to recognize the contribution of the cultures of all the children to the daily life of the program.

Children's Need for Spontaneous, Regular Contact with Nature and the Natural World

"A sense of wonder and joy in nature should be at the very center of ecological literacy" (Louv, 2008, p. 224). Children's relationship with nature is a fundamental touchstone for children's spiritual development and the development of "a rich inner life." The absence of regular, spontaneous contact with nature and the natural world in the lives of many children may be one of the most serious issues of our time. How can we expect children to grow up to value and protect nature, to feel connected to the natural world, and to appreciate the soothing, spiritual comforts that nature affords if they do not experience nature every day and revel in its changing beauty, variety, and mystery? Children who live in densely urban cities and towns, often in apartment developments, spend much of their childhood indoors. Contact with nature and natural play space is often limited to infrequent excursions to the local farm, or to the neighbourhood playground, which is frequently a concrete patch with a play structure. Parents often explain their children's indoor existence in terms of fear for their child's safety. Free play in the outdoors is often confined to "play dates," and supervised play in the unchanging environment of a playground. In recent years, urban planners have begun to connect children's needs for contact with nature to the importance of retaining natural spaces in new neighbourhoods. Ecologists and health care experts now recognize that children's infrequent contact with nature may be an impediment to mental health, physical health, and spiritual well-being and are increasingly linking children's inability to connect with nature to such childhood conditions as attention deficit disorder (ADD), depression, and some symptoms of autism (Kuo, 2009; Louv, 2008; Townsend, 2008).

When in contact with nature and its changing seasons, children feel connected to something much larger than themselves and develop a relationship with nature and natural surroundings that leaves a lifetime of precious memories. A fundamental issue is how to allocate a significant amount of time each day for outdoor play, including playful learning in natural surroundings, when access to such an environment is hard to find, and in a culture that does not fully comprehend the value of play. Just walking to the local park or playground every few days is not the answer, especially when designers replace elements of nature, such as trees, rocks, stumps, logs, stones, and loose materials, with pavement or sand-filled pits with manufactured climbing structures. It is children's right and need to play outdoors for significant segments of the day, and efforts should be made to ensure that children have regular and direct experience in nature. Some urban playgrounds include gardens where children can dig, plant, and tend "crops" as a nature-related activity—and this is a positive step forward. But children also need space where they can roam through bush and treed areas, hide in tall grasses, climb trees and rocks, and build with loose materials, such as rocks, timber, logs, branches, and stones. ECEs need to be advocates for natural playspaces in neighbourhoods and for playground design that retains the natural topography, plants and trees, and other natural elements.

The Importance of Outdoor Physical Exercise and Risk Taking

Play in natural spaces provides opportunities for being adventurous and taking risks. Risk taking is a part of life, and being able to assess and manage risk is an important life skill that allows children to push boundaries and extend limits (Tovey, 2010, pp. 81–82). Risk taking is positively related to emotional well-being, to becoming a good thinker, and to developing confidence in confronting physical challenges (Tishman & Perkins, 1993; Tovey, 2010).

As early as 1938, Susan Isaacs, an early ECE pioneer, addressed a meeting of the UK National Safety Congress: "If you are going to keep children safe … you must provide places in which they can get the thrills they need; there must be trees they can climb and ways in which they can safely get the experience of adventure and the sense of challenge that they crave" (Isaacs, 1938, p. 4). Empowering children is a matter of ensuring that children have the opportunities to take risks in safe environments (Tovey, 2010, p. 92). Yet government regulations and laws strive to eliminate all elements of risk from licensed environments and impose rigid standards on outdoor play environments. This practice makes it impossible for ECEs to plan for outdoor play in ways that recognize that children often seek, need, and benefit from risk taking. Clearly, this issue requires resolution.

Freedom versus Structure in Early Childhood Education

Freedom of choice for children in their play is an ideal that goes back to the writings of Rousseau and has been echoed as a guiding principle in early childhood education ever since. The Psychoanalytic School stressed the importance of freedom through its emphasis on self-expression, self-realization, and **autonomy** (Erikson, 1963; Rogers, 1969). The expression, *follow the child* became a mantra for the nursery school of the 1960s and 1970s, which was a product of the maturationist school of thought, when most forms of structure in programs for children were frowned upon (Weber, 1984). Piaget's work in the 1960s accelerated awareness of the extremely rapid brain development that occurs from birth to age six, which led neo-Piagetian educators to question the validity of a hands-off approach to early childhood education. In the 1970s and 1980s, Constance Kamii, Rheta DeVries, David Weikart, and others advocated greater intervention in early childhood environments in order to enhance the quality and benefits of play. They believed that facilitating children's interaction with responsive materials would challenge children, engage them in a process of uncovering concepts while playing with materials they choose, and enhance their understanding of concepts and phenomena. In 2007, David Elkind reinforced the belief that by structuring and enriching the environment we enhance the power of play.

To better understand this issue we must go back to the origins of the "free play" movement, which is a key factor in the **freedom-versus-structure debate**. The concept of freedom appeared early in the 20th century with the familiar term *free play,* which Patty Smith Hill (1868–1946) defined as follows: "In free play, the self makes its own choices, selections, and decisions, and thus absolute freedom is given to the play of the child's images and volition in expressing them" (Weber, 1984, p. 96). The idea of activity in learning expressed by Dewey (1859–1952) also supported the principle of freedom and advocated an emergent curriculum with the teacher as a facilitator of cooperative learning and inquiry through projects (Wolfe, 2000).

During the 1960s and early 1970s, Patty Smith Hill's concept of free play was interpreted by the maturationist proponents as non-interference in children's play, which led to a practice of setting up play materials and letting children go to it and an overemphasis on children's unguided exploration of open-ended materials as a means of promoting self-expression. This interpretation led to years of controversy with those who were advocating "active learning" through enhanced play environments and the obligation to plan for play. Later, Spodek and Saracho (2003) affirmed that even in free play there is considerable teacher influence. Others agreed that free play refers to the element of choice offered to children in the environment rich in opportunities for enhanced play that helps children become more effective players and achieve developmental outcomes.

In the 1970s, another complication arose. Freedom to express oneself became closely associated with the development of self-esteem, and during the 1980s and into the early 1990s, school systems began to include self-esteem as an explicit goal to be addressed by the curriculum (Leo, 1990). So tightly drawn was the link between schooling and children's self-esteem during those decades that children were almost never held back in school to complete learning challenges successfully and they were often praised for mediocre performances. "Child-centred education" became incorrectly associated with having few expectations of competence, and this, ultimately, gave child-centred education a bad name. Links between "freedom to be" and the development of self-esteem undermined the arguments for curriculum planning and strategic design of play-based learning environments. By 2000, however, the economic and social pressures of increased globalization contributed to a re-examination of educational values, and the former links between few expectations, constant praise, and self-esteem were largely replaced by the more appropriate link between self-esteem and personal achievement.

The debate about the worthiness of pure play and the imperatives related to helping children achieve foundational skills in ECE continued throughout the latter decades of the 20th century. Play advocates such as David Elkind (2007) kept insisting that it is play *and* foundational skills. The success and fame of the schools of Reggio Emilia during the latter half of the 1990s helped to reconcile both sides of the play versus structure issue, an influence that restored the credibility of developmental skills as viable outcomes and play-based intervention to help children achieve them. Reggio Emilia won converts to the integrity of planned activities that emerge from the interests of children and teachers, often taking the form of projects. Since then, the concept of freedom has reconciled children's freedom to choose within the structure of the planned play environment, and the term *curriculum* has gained renewed respectability. The schools of Reggio Emilia advocate an approach which builds on children's experiences and integrates their interests into meaningful, purposeful curriculum content that encourages collaboration; communication; and co-construction of themes, interests, and projects (Wood & Attfield, 2005). Of particular interest in the Reggio Emilia approach is that their environments are viewed as learning environments for teachers as well as for children. The "dichotomous distinctions between teacher-directed and child-initiated learning" (Katz & Chard,

2005, p. 328) tend to disappear when ECEs and children are engaged together in projects in which all are learning.

In the 1990s, however, another controversy was in full swing. The "back to basics" proponents blamed **child-centred learning** for the overall poor to mediocre academic performance of North American students relative to the children of other industrialized nations and criticized the *hands-off*, laissez-faire interpretation that was falsely attributed to child-centred education. They blamed children's less-than-stellar performances on standardized tests on the failure of child-centred education and included play-based early learning approaches in this broad category. More problems arose when these back to basics proponents inaccurately linked the achievement of outcomes and the traditional teaching approaches, including drill and practice, and teacher-directed activities. They failed to recognize that play-based approaches and developmental outcomes arise from a theoretical tradition that emphasizes children's understanding of concepts through active play and not rote learning achieved largely through memorization and the acquisition of factual knowledge. This misunderstanding led to regressive efforts in school systems to re-introduce programmed learning to replace the play-based approaches advocated by constructivist theorists and educators. The back to basics proponents failed to understand that for children who are preoperational, up to age five or six, outcomes should relate primarily to children's developing physical, cognitive, social, and emotional skills, which provide the foundation for reading, writing, math, and other subjects. They missed the point that these skills are developed in informal play settings that incorporate the acquisition of knowledge, skills, and dispositions to learn through play and that appeal to young children's natural curiosity and propensity to learn by doing. By 2000, children's achievement levels on some international tests had declined below the international norms, and this result led to a rethinking in Canada of educational accountability that by 2010 generated some improved results.

The 21st-century pressures of global competition have heightened the demands of some parents that their children prepare early for school success, sometimes starting as early as two. These demands have encouraged the rise of academically oriented preschool and kindergarten programs that regard play as ancillary to the instructional curriculum. ECEs should resist pressures to abandon or diminish learning through play or risk losing the progress that has been hard-won during the past 85 years. ECEs should be able to explain clearly the balance between freedom and structure, a balance that respects the value of play to young children's overall well-being and demonstrates that children are achieving, through play, the developmental outcomes that prepare them for success in school and lifelong learning. This professional obligation requires the ability to explain these points accurately and in some detail. Protecting and advocating for play affirms children's right to play and recognizes that what play means for children is just as important as what play does for children (Wood et al., 2010, p. 7).

Academic Subjects Are Not for Preschoolers

William Fowler, who taught at the University of Toronto for many years, wisely stated: "There is no effective knowledge which does not have structure, whether derived through spontaneous interaction with an environment or through a teacher ordering and explaining patterns to facilitate discovery and learning on the part of the child" (Fowler, 1971, p. 30). *Structure* refers to the extent to which teachers develop an instructional plan and organize the physical setting and the social environment for play that supports the achievement of learning goals (Kostelnik, 1992). Fromberg (2002, p. 20) saw play as a "form of disciplined freedom.... It continues throughout the lifespan and is valuable in itself as a vehicle for transporting and integrating development." *Freedom* is a factor of the control children have over the play situation. The freedom to decide whether or not to play, what to play, when to start and stop, and when to switch to another play activity generally motivates children to act. A developmental curriculum ensures that children's play occurs within a framework of explicit developmental outcomes.

An understanding of the importance of play is still not firmly established within the Canadian education system. Academic learning is not for children younger than six years. It may be introduced to children in small doses in grade one, and by grade four it predominates in the classroom. But the early years are a time to focus on building a developmental foundation for learning. Various forms of intelligence, including emotional and social intelligence, are often more effective determinants of success than mastery of academic skills (Bruno, 2011). Howard Gardner's research on intelligence since the 1980s changed the debate about intelligence by describing many intelligences in human beings, all of which should be cultivated during the early years. Cognitive scientists today believe that **intelligence** is both a generalized ability, which involves speed, perception, memory, and other generic cognitive tasks, as well as a set of several independent *intelligences* that may reflect the particular *talents* of each individual child. Howard Gardner (2004), Robert Sternberg (1988, 2005), and others have taken a broad view of intelligence as it relates to the ability to lead life successfully. Gardner's nine intelligences identify the characteristics and aptitudes of each intelligence. (For a description of Gardner's nine "multiple intelligences" see Chapter 8, pp. 144–145). Daniel Goleman (1995) proposed, for example, that **emotional intelligence** involves many aspects of the ability to self-regulate that are related to learning—abilities such as being able to motivate oneself, persist in the face of frustrations, control impulses and delay gratification, and regulate moods so as to focus on one task. In 1997, Goleman described **moral intelligence** as the mental capacity to determine how universal human principles, like the golden rule, should be applied to our personal values and goals. In 2008, Goleman described **social intelligence** which includes empathy and social cognition, and social facility, which is the ability to pick up on social cues and to influence others. More recently, Goleman (2009) defined **ecological intelligence** as an ability to understand one's relationship to the natural environment. None of these "intelligences" is currently measured by standard intelligence tests, yet they are vital to successful living.

The information age calls for high levels of performance in literacy; **numeracy**; **critical thinking** and problem solving; and perceptual, emotional, and interpersonal skills. Parents want to ensure that their children have what it takes to be successful learners and, later, to find a role in an increasingly competitive society. Building a strong physical, social, emotional, and cognitive foundation for later academic learning is a primary goal of constructivist, developmental, play-based early childhood education. DeVries et al. (2002) attributed the failure of jurisdictions to embrace the play-oriented curriculum for young children to the inability of critics and advocates to explain clearly the intentions, practices, and outcomes of play-based learning. Pushing academic, formal learning on children too soon, and for its own sake, may actually have the opposite effect of what parents want for their children, and it may even contribute to heightened test anxiety and to negative feelings about school (Eliot, 1999). Piaget described the problem as follows:

> In spite of the prophetic visions of the great educationists, play has always been considered, in traditional education, as a kind of mental waste matter, or at least a pseudo activity, without functional significance, and even harmful to children, keeping them from their homework." (Piaget, 1945, p. 151)

Piaget spent a lifetime proving that play is an important and necessary vehicle for helping children achieve the developmental outcomes that lead to success in learning. For the public to accept the role of play in helping young children develop the foundation they need for school success, ECEs should communicate clearly the values and practices of developmental, play-based programs, the standards by which programs can be evaluated, and the developmental outcomes that describe clearly the abilities that children will have achieved in order to be effective learners in the school years. Assessment of children's progress in all domains provides the cues for planning. It would not be wise, however, to establish outcomes that all preschool children must meet before they are allowed to start school. Developmental outcomes are useful guides for assessing children's progress and achievement and for planning the next steps in their development. Assessment of children's progress toward the achievement of outcomes helps ECEs decide where extra intervention through play may be needed.

Persuading Parents and Policymakers of the Value of Play in Early Learning

Convincing parents of the important role of play in learning during the early years is a significant issue that arises in the relationship between programs and families. Parents in the 21st century are sometimes preoccupied with how and whether their children will be prepared for productive roles in the workplace and this anxiety often translates into demands for schooling as they knew it. Some parents believe that returning to the content-based system they experienced is all that is needed to improve educational outcomes. Since parents were in school, however, much more has been learned about how young children learn. Learning success for the information age emphasizes the ability to perform complex tasks and roles. The acquisition of factual knowledge is only a stepping stone toward an integrated understanding of how to do something well. We have to remember that learning involves knowing, applying what one knows, and conceptual understanding of how one set of skills connects with other learning. Having the right dispositions for learning, which motivate us to progress further in our learning, and self-control or "willpower," are increasingly cited as essential for successful living (Baumeister & Tierney, 2011; Moffitt et al., 2010); their development begins through play in early childhood.

Janine Wiedel Photolibrary/Alamy

Grocery store

The complex interrelationship between play, the senses, hands-on interaction with concrete objects, conceptual understanding, and the acquisition of learning skills has to be articulated clearly and with conviction. When parents understand the rapid nature of children's brain development in the early years and the role of the senses in children's learning, it is easier to demonstrate the crucial role of play. When ECEs and parents work closely together to gather evidence of their children's progress on key developmental outcomes, parents soon discover the value of challenging play experiences that encourage children to explore, investigate, test, invent, and document. Talking in generalities about the value of play has little impact. Engaging parents in the process of documenting their child's progress at home is a more convincing approach to changing parents' minds about the role of play. Including parents more meaningfully in planning the program, observing their children, documenting their behaviours and performances at school and at home, and drawing conclusions based on what they see, often demonstrates to parents just how much they have underestimated the learning potential of play and the competence of their children when they have challenging play opportunities. Helping parents learn the value of ***playing with*** their children is another way to expose parents first-hand to the progress children make conceptually, physically, socially, and verbally when they are playing.

Through play, children learn skills for the 21st century. They

- use their knowledge and make choices in play that are increasingly complex and meaningful;
- play for extended periods with more elaborate challenges that encourage them to attend to the task at hand and finish what they start;
- invent sociodramatic play scripts that reflect their experiences, represent their understanding of these experiences, and assume greater complexity and sophistication;
- learn how to enter into and negotiate play and other social situations;
- approach problem solving using divergent thinking approaches that lead to alternative ways to address the problem, sometimes in collaboration with others; and
- risk asking increasingly complex questions.

Parental Involvement Facilitates Inclusive Practice

Similar characteristics of play are observed in children of all cultures, and parents are almost always interested in their children's success in school and in life. Sometimes, however, the priorities are different. Respect for diversity implies that a contemporary Canadian issue is the consideration we must give to understanding and addressing the educational goals and aspirations of different cultural groups, as well as the teaching and learning practices that parents of diverse cultures tend to favour. Bernhard, Hong, and Fish (2003) advised that ECEs should also be aware of other important adults in the homes of newcomers to Canada besides the parents, and that decision-making related to children may not rest solely with the parents.

Early childhood education serves children, parents, whole families, and their communities and society in general. An effective way to help parents understand the role of play is to involve parents and other caregivers directly in the program. Encouraging family involvement in programs is a key demonstration of **inclusive practice**. The reality is that involving families in programs in Canada's diverse urban communities poses significant challenges for ECEs and program supervisors and calls for a clear understanding of the specific ways in which families can participate, collaborate, and feel included. ECEs need to understand the cultures their children belong to in order to support their learning through play in culturally authentic ways. Wood (2010, p. 4) proposes "integrated pedagogies," which integrate the cultural values and child-rearing practices of families (see Figure 3-1, p. 37). Identifying and addressing the priorities of many families who have diverse values, whose experiences and backgrounds are different, and who have wide-ranging expectations of what the program will provide for them and their children is one of the more demanding requirements of Canadian programs, especially in the major cities. A question is how to balance responsibility to the children as a group, to the specific needs and interests of individual children, and to the families of the children. Describing viable types of family participation and engagement, including how to collaborate with families in planning curriculum for their children, is an important professional issue in Canada.

Courtesy of Charmaine Lee-Wah

Family participation

Many children from diverse cultures, in all socioeconomic categories, are living in families experiencing the stresses associated with long workdays, competing demands on time, the absence of a support system of extended family members, loneliness, financial pressures, and high societal expectations. The early childhood program sometimes replaces the extended family as the primary support system for new Canadian families. The more that programs involve families in their planning, decision making, consultation processes, and emotional support networks, the more included the children feel and the more empowered the family becomes. The creation of a social network of people committed to the well-being of children builds a community and a supportive infrastructure that sustains children and their families in countless ways. This notion of early childhood programs as "centres of exchange and relationship building among and between children, teachers, and families" (Katz & Chard, 2005, p. 317) is a cornerstone of the Reggio Emilia approach that engages parents directly in the organization and operation of the program. Parental involvement in their children's program helps parents to see for themselves the role of play in learning and to develop the skills they need to help their children learn through play at home.

Plan for Play So as To Be More Accountable

Another issue in ECE today is how to balance the pressures for accountability with the value of playful learning. Moyles (2010, p. xiii) claims that the early childhood education profession and children "have been put under great pressure to reach externally imposed goals; neither children nor adults perform well under pressure because it narrows thinking, rather than encouraging divergent, creative responses."

More work needs to be done to find an effective way to demonstrate accountability while protecting the purity of children's play.

> **EXAMPLE**
> A child will use eye-hand coordination, hand control, dexterity, perseverance, and self-control when he finally masters the tying of shoelaces. Or an adolescent will demonstrate **laterality,** coordination of upper and lower body movements, knowledge of the function of various car parts, and hand and foot control when they are able to drive a car with manual transmission. In early childhood, accountability for the development and learning achieved is likely to be based on children's demonstration that they can perform complex **developmental tasks,** such as tying shoelaces, riding a tricycle, and skipping in a cross-lateral pattern. It is also important, however, to observe children's progress in the execution of the discrete skills inherent in these developmental tasks, such as the perseverance, eye-hand coordination, and hand control involved in tying shoe laces. Both types of accountability and observation are essential for planning play activities.

The issues related to accountability are another example of the convergence of freedom and structure within ECE. Realistically, it may be children's demonstrations of the normal tasks of development, described as outcomes, that will convince parents, policymakers, and the general public of the value and function of play. Issues arise when governments choose to apply standardized tests of discrete skills and knowledge as suitable measures for the learning acquired, especially given the ways in which standardized tests often discriminate against children who are disadvantaged through circumstances that include poverty, other language learning, neglect, or disability.

Promoting accountability through children's achievement of developmental outcomes should not detract from the mission of ECE, which is to protect their play and to support, nurture, and guide children toward healthy habits of mind and body based on each child's developmental timetable and readiness to learn. Accountability requirements should not undermine playful learning. A question that might be debated is, "What are the reasonable expectations a school system should have of young children's development and readiness for school when they enter grade one?" How should these expectations be expressed? Answers include but are not limited to the significant developmental tasks described as outcomes for: emotional well-being; social interaction; ability to self-regulate; learning readiness; language and literacy; logical reasoning and numeracy; psychosocial development; and physical fitness, skills, and health. Appendix A provides a potential set of developmental outcomes for young children before they enter grade one. The Draft Version (2010–2011) of Ontario's Full Day Early Learning Kindergarten Program is another important resource.

Children learn through play that balances open-ended free play and more structured play opportunities. Wood's model of "integrated pedagogical approaches," which includes child-initiated and adult-directed activities, reflects sociocultural theories of learning, with practitioners playing important roles in leading and responding to children's choices, interests, and activities (Wood, 2010, p. 3). Integrated pedagogical approaches include flexible planning, observation, documentation, and reflective dialogue about children's learning. Educational goals are derived from children's interests and motivations and from the other activities they have chosen. Integrated pedagogical approaches connect children's emergent knowledge and understanding with the organized conceptual frameworks defined in the curriculum (Wood, 2010, p. 17).

ECEs should be engaged with children in their play to facilitate development in all domains and not just the developmental areas that children favour. We have seen that intervention in children's play has gained renewed respectability. Ideas that the development of the whole child just happens, and that self-expression is a simple matter of indiscriminately messing about with things, impede progress. The temptation to take the easier path and to replace play activities with formal academic learning and teaching practices at too early an age undermines children's right to play and to learn through play and misinterprets otherwise positive efforts toward greater accountability. As children's play becomes more sophisticated and as school-age children become capable of increasingly abstract thought, play remains valuable also throughout middle childhood, in many contexts, as a vehicle for learning.

EXAMPLE

Children should be able to perform simple arithmetic operations such as sums and subtraction using concrete objects; *classify* (or sort) a random set of objects based on two or more criteria they have selected and stated; skip in a cross-lateral pattern. Just as important, children should demonstrate the ability to perform such tasks as sustaining the story line in a sociodramatic play episode with other children. This relies on their integration of such discrete skills as focus on the task at hand; finish what one starts, collaborate with other children in maintaining the story line and one's own part in it, listen well, and follow directions. During the primary grades, many of the academic learning outcomes may be learned and evaluated though games-with-rules play and play-based projects in many subject areas, including art, music, physical education and health, social studies, and literacy learning. Examples include soccer tournaments, team-based hopscotch, chess or checkers tournaments, crossword puzzles, Scrabble games.

Summary

Understanding the issues that influence practice as well as the issues that sometimes divide a profession is an important aspect of becoming a professional. Some issues in the early childhood education field have been present for decades, while others have surfaced more recently as a result of the demands on families, the changing cultural composition of society, global, and local economic imperatives, and the mental and physical health of young children. This chapter has explored some professional issues related to play, including the ECE's role as an advocate for play as children's primary vehicle for learning. These issues include children's spiritual development in a world at a time when economic and social pressures tend to predominate and focus on narrow interests that offer immediate gratification. Some professional issues, such as the debate concerning the appropriate balance between freedom and structure and the imperatives related to inclusive practice, are specific to the diversity of our nation. Other issues are global and relate to the protection of human rights, including children's right to play and their freedom to choose and define their own play. Convincing parents of the importance of play to children's development and learning, and providing evidence of the learning that occurs through play, are priorities. Issues related to children's declining levels of physical fitness and health, regular contact with nature, and the influence of technologies on children's development and their daily lives are elaborated on in Chapters 18, 21, and 22.

LEARNING ACTIVITIES

1. Explain the points to be made on both sides of a debate on one of the following issues discussed in this chapter:
    a. A balance of freedom and structure protect the crucial role of play in early childhood education.
    b. The development of spirituality depends on children's exposure to the beauty and spontaneity of their everyday worlds, especially the outdoor natural world, and on their sense of wonder.
    c. Young children acquire through play the ability to demonstrate their achievement of the developmental tasks of early childhood.
    d. ECEs have to convince parents of the important role of play in children's development and learning.
2. A parent questions the value of play in your program and insists that you offer more academic, product-oriented activities to foster his child's readiness for school. What would you say to this parent? Explain the important function of play in parent-friendly language. This explanation may be made in the form of a pamphlet, a letter to parents to be displayed on the information board, or a detailed journal entry.
3. Consider the importance of spirituality in your life, what it looks like, how you acquired it, and how it enriches your life. Describe in writing an example of your spirituality. What types of activities would you favour in order to foster children's development of their spiritual nature?

Section II

Planning Play and Learning Environments

Section II addresses the following topics:

- features of the affective (social and emotional) climate in the environment that support children's play, development, and learning
- inclusive climate
- role of the schedule in facilitating play and development
- variety, complexity, and function of play equipment, materials, and supplies
- location and design of the learning centres
- organization of zones for play

The first step in planning play environments is to understand the interrelationship of the social and emotional characteristics (climate) of the playroom, the function of the play equipment, materials and supplies, and the design and organization of the learning centres. Section II examines these three components of play environments. Chapter 5 addresses the ingredients of a positive social and emotional (affective) climate for play and learning; Chapter 6 describes the variety, complexity, and function of equipment, materials, and supplies that are the child's tools for play. These are the "contents," or foreground, of the learning centres that children explore, manipulate, and use symbolically. Chapter 7 addresses the design of the physical space, including the organization of play zones, and the function, location, and design of the indoor learning centres.

5 Creating a Climate for Play, Development, and Learning

"Our abilities are not set in genetic stone. They are soft and sculptable, far into adulthood. With humility, with hope, and with extraordinary determination, greatness is something to which any kid—of any age—can aspire."

—David Shenk, *The Genius in All of Us* (2010)

Before Reading This Chapter, Have You

- completed the learning activities for the chapters in Section I and started your journal?
- visited a child-care centre and a kindergarten to observe the features of the environment, including the learning centres and the play materials, and to gauge the characteristics of the affective climate? (These visits will provide valuable reference points as you read the chapters in Section II.)

Outcomes

After reading and understanding this chapter, you should be able to

- describe the various affective (social-emotional) features in the environment that affect the climate for play and learning;
- explain the influence of the affective and sociomoral atmosphere in the playroom on children's behaviour;
- understand the relationship between the climate, play, and children's mental health;
- plan a daily schedule for half-day and full-day programs that support play, development, and learning; and
- explain how the affective climate influences children's play and learning styles and the developmental outcomes they achieve.

Features of a Healthy Affective Climate for Play

This chapter discusses the various elements that fit together in order to create a supportive, healthy, organized atmosphere and climate for children that nurtures brain development, facilitates play, fosters curiosity, allows risk taking, and whets children's appetite for learning. The ingredients of such a climate are wide-ranging and mutually interdependent, but the most important ingredient is the quality of the human interactions, especially the capacity of the environment to support children's stable emotional attachments with their primary adult caregivers and spontaneous interactions with other children (Perry, 2002). Studies suggest that we are losing "social capital" and that current lifestyles and environments are insufficient for children to form and maintain healthy relationships and to learn to "share, be empathic and understanding of others" (Perry, 2002, p. 97). Brain development is influenced most of all by the quality of children's relationships, and it is essential to invest as much in the social and emotional development of children as in their cognitive development. The relationships among the ECE staff and between the staff and the families of the children are also ingredients that influence the affective climate. Researchers are studying such ingredients as: Do parents have opportunities to talk to ECEs and children about the family's identity, traditions, home language, and priorities? Does the curriculum reflect the diversity of the children and families represented in the program and are their unique traditions and priorities visible in the environment? Do ECEs encourage children to speak their home language (Tobiassen & Gonzalez-Mena, 1999)? Ensuring that Canadian programs are truly respectful of the diversity of our population means that ECEs should foster children's pride in themselves, their families, and their culture (Bernhard, 2005). These aspects of climate are integral to inventing program models relevant to our Canadian cultural realities and family values.

Affective Climate

Climate refers to the mood and culture in an environment and is profoundly influenced by the qualities of emotional warmth, friendliness, a sense of physical and psychological safety, inclusion, and social acceptance. These qualities are key elements of climate that contribute to play that is rich and meaningful. The social and emotional climate in which children spend their daily lives determines the nature of children's mental health, which depends on a number of factors: the opportunity to play with other children; encouraging teachers and supportive caregivers; a safe and secure environment; and appropriate guidance and discipline (www.mentalhealthamerica.net/go/information/get-info/children-s-mental-health). The healthy climate ensures that children from diverse cultural backgrounds, and children with special needs, feel protected, secure, and connected to the physical and social environment of the classroom. They see familiar objects around them; their first language is respected, heard, and reflected wherever possible; play materials and books depict their cultural values; the foods of their culture are represented; and the environment has been adapted to children's special needs.

Climate also influences children's development and learning. When ECEs encourage children to explore with materials they can manipulate and allow them to pursue individual interests at their own pace, children make progress. Children need to be able to make mistakes and still be accepted and supported. When they forget rules, children should be able to trust that they will be reminded of them. A healthy affective climate accepts children's need to be secure before they will take risks; it is sensitive to their frailty and inexperience and accepts individual differences in their pace and style of learning. An inclusive climate recognizes that young children are instinctively accepting of each other and capitalizes on children's natural tendency toward inclusiveness (Richey & Wheeler, 2000).

"The first principle of constructivist education is that a sociomoral atmosphere must be cultivated in which respect for others is continually practised" (DeVries & Zan, 1995, p. 5). A **sociomoral** atmosphere emerges from the whole complex of interpersonal relationships and connections within an early childhood program. DeVries (1997) advocates the following five principles that foster a climate for development and learning:

1. Relate to children in cooperative ways.
2. Promote peer friendship and cooperation, including conflict resolution.
3. Cultivate a feeling of community and the construction of collective values.
4. Appeal to children's interests and engage their purposes.
5. Adapt to children's understanding.

The most important influence on affective climate is usually the ECE. When ECEs uphold children's rights to their own feelings, ideas, and opinions, and use their authority selectively, children gain confidence that nurtures their curiosity, motivation, initiative, and independence and encourages children to enter the play situation. The ECE supports the hesitant child's entry into play and builds her motivation to remain involved. ECEs set an example by showing children what the adults around them care about, what they find interesting and worthwhile, and what they spend time and energy on (DeVries & Zan, 1995; Katz, 1990). Children learn in environments that meet their developmental levels and interests and that tell them this is their place to roam, explore, and discover. Too many rules and boundaries tell children they have little influence on what happens in the classroom. A healthy climate assures children that who they are and what they do is important and that adults care deeply about their interests and motivations. When children are able to affect what happens in the environment, they feel that they share power with the adults. The affective climate engages children and ECEs together in making rules, choosing activities and projects, and rearranging the environment to accommodate spur-of-the-moment interests and pursuits. Children's sense of safety is enhanced in important ways when ECEs are clear about their expectations; convey their emotions and values honestly; express their values with sincerity and conviction; and, above all, show children in countless ways that they care profoundly about their well-being. The experienced ECE knows when and how to intervene in children's play to extend a play episode and encourage the full participation of each child.

Climate and Cleanliness

The cleanliness of the environment influences the affective climate. When environments are kept clean by washing tables and counters frequently and by sterilizing play materials, ECEs model attention to cleanliness that children learn to take for granted. By having children wipe or remove their shoes before entering the centre and wash their hands often, they encourage clean behaviours that become lifelong habits. ECEs' consistent attention to cleanliness reinforces the important role of custodian of the environment, which must be assumed by everyone. The floors should shine, stickiness should be removed from furniture and equipment, and play materials should be clean. Wise ECEs teach children early to assist with the cleaning tasks by providing cleaning materials, such as sponges, brushes, and dustpans. The clean environment gives messages to parents that the environment is cared for, that children's health and safety matter, and that high standards of care prevail within the program.

Messy play

Maintaining a clean environment, however, does not preclude messy play and untidy play space. There is a difference between dirty and untidy. Children naturally gravitate toward messy play activities such as dough, finger paint, and blocks. A climate that permits children to make a mess but also encourages them to tidy up fosters a sense of comfort that facilitates children's creative use of materials. A healthy respect for the environment does not mean that it should be tidy at all times, but children should participate in leaving the centre tidy after their play there has ended.

Affective Climate Contributes to Child Guidance

The goals of child guidance are self-control, self-regulation, and respect and consideration for others. The child's ability to empathize with others is a key factor that determines his readiness to control aggressive impulses and channel emotions. Children learn to self-regulate by making their own choices, by learning the consequences of those choices, and accepting responsibility for their actions and choices. Opportunities in their play for children to choose among real alternatives, to follow through with their decisions, and to take responsibility for them contribute to children's ability to self-regulate. Interesting environments and activities encourage children to play more purposefully, manage their own behaviours and, sometimes, the behaviours of other children, and they reduce the need for adult intervention. When children have plenty of interesting things to do, they seldom become restless or out-of-bounds. We know that a delicate balance must be struck between adults and children that allows both to have power, yet respects the rights of all members of the classroom. Children need to feel they are able to affect what happens in their environments. Katz (1974) claimed that children feel psychologically safe when they perceive that what they do really matters to others. Children are quick to learn who has the power in a relationship, and they become resentful and act out when they discover the adult has all the power. The reverse is also true; that is, children feel insecure when they encounter adults who give them too much power and provide too few boundaries. We should not underestimate the impact of an equitable climate in which adults and children share power, a play environment in which children know their limits and feel secure enough to explore and express themselves,

Purposeful play

and a social context that provides built-in cues to children about expected behaviours and limits and that conveys respect for others.

A healthy affective climate empowers children to become fully engaged in their play. When children have real choices and are encouraged to exercise choice safely and with consideration for the rights of others, they learn respect. Children's appreciation of fairness makes them more willing to comply in situations that demand it. Children want adults to assume their authority appropriately, to establish clear boundaries, and to guide their behaviour with kindness, warmth, sensitivity, and concern for the developing ego and spirit of each child. Clear limits, interesting things to do, opportunities for meaningful self-expression, and a climate in which children are supported when they make mistakes guide and inform children without manipulating them or inducing guilt.

Influence of Climate on Children's Learning

Children's inner lives develop in a playroom climate where they are encouraged to reflect on events, ask questions when they occur to them, and receive answers or promises to respond later. A healthy climate provides time, space, and emotional support for dreaming and contemplation; is unhurried and flexible; offers varied sensory experiences that facilitate self-expression and experimentation; and engages the imagination. The climate influences children's play styles and affects the process and outcomes of play. Children need opportunities for physical exploration of the environment; they like to interact with each other; and they require time to uncover the mysteries of natural phenomena and the complexities of concepts, at their own speed and in their own ways. The affective climate of the playroom determines the extent to which children feel safe and free to let themselves go in their play, knowing that they can count on the adults in the room to protect their safety and support them when they blunder. This factor is especially important for the child from a disadvantaged home, where circumstances may not inspire the child's confidence or their freedom to become absorbed in play.

Creating a Constructivist Learning Climate

Children acquire physical, social-conventional, and logical-mathematical knowledge in informal settings that promote freely chosen activity within carefully designed environments that promote hands-on experience with things, events, and people (Elkind, 1977). Constructivist theory describes the learning process whereby children create and extend their mental structures, frameworks, and understanding through their own experiences. (Review the explanation of constructivist theory in Chapter 2.) Learning tends to follow development and children's ability to understand a concept depends first on their sensory experience of an object or event during solitary play and then on their ability to connect objects and experiences and understand relationships in various contexts. Piaget believed that conceptual understanding can be achieved without language, although language helps to clarify and shape that understanding. Lev Vygotsky (1896–1934) also influenced our understanding of how children construct their knowledge and understanding. Unlike Piaget, Vygotsky maintained that language leads thought and that labelling objects helps children understand concepts, and he stressed the importance of the social climate in learning. Vygotsky believed that children develop concepts and thinking abilities in much the same way as they acquire cultural and social knowledge, that is, in a social context, with the help of adults and peers. Both philosophers believed in the importance of play to development and learning, but Vygotsky emphasized the importance of social mediation, especially for very young children whose learning is facilitated with the guided assistance of adults.

Social mediation occurs largely through language and speech, which connects the child socially and culturally to others, allowing children to absorb and share their thoughts and feelings as well as their ideas (Miller, 2010, p. 342). A constructivist learning climate promotes and supports children's ability to understand and use language to communicate with others, think, act, and express themselves. The constructivist climate also recognizes that children develop at different rates and that they have unique learning styles. To accommodate different rates and styles of learning, children should be encouraged to select activities themselves, pursue them in their own ways, set their own goals, decide when they have finished, and document and communicate what they have done. To individualize activities and programs for children means that ECEs plan and set up activities that meet the developmental needs and interests of each child in the group.

The Need for Active and Quiet Play

Children have physical needs for both active and quiet play. ECE programs, which some children attend for as many as 10 hours a day, five days a week, and sometimes 50 weeks a year, occupy a major chunk of time in young children's lives. Being expected to maintain a consistent and often rigorous daily routine, most of it spent in groups, is tiring enough for adults but can be stifling for children. When children remain in groups for most of these long periods, it is no wonder that they sometimes become competitive, manipulative, anxious, aggressive, or resentful.

A healthy affective climate allows a child to be alone for a while during the day, and to enjoy some privacy and relief from the group at times; this is essential for mental health, especially for children who crave moments of solitude. Scandinavian programs ensure that small nooks with covered foam mattresses or beanbag chairs are built in to the environment to provide cozy spaces for children to curl up alone when they need a break from the group. A healthy affective climate in group care respects children's need for moments of privacy and provides for some down time during the day when not much is expected of them. Children, like adults, differ widely in their requirements for social contact with others; some enjoy time by themselves, thrive on moments of quiet reflection, and may even find the pressures of the group oppressive and threatening, especially if there are no moments for escape. *Creating an affective climate that respects individual needs for space and freedom to choose, instead of making children feel unusual or antisocial if they prefer to be alone, is an essential support for mental health.*

Children learn at different rates and employ unique learning styles for each task. Therefore, small-group or individual play activities are usually more effective than large-group, adult-centred activities in helping children to acquire physical knowledge and abstract concepts (logical-mathematical understanding). Individual and small-group activities also allow for greater hands-on involvement with things in the environment. Large-group activities are useful for learning social skills, language, some musical skills, and for practising physical skills. An appropriate balance of small-group, large-group, and individual play activities is an important element of a positive climate for learning.

The Influence of Physical Characteristics

Child-sized furniture and shelves and cupboards placed at children's levels make the environment accessible to children and contribute to feelings of belonging, independence, and self-worth. Placing natural flowers and leaves for children to touch and smell on low tables stirs their appreciation of nature's beauty. Accessories such as placemats, curtains, and cushions that are pretty and soft create a homelike atmosphere and reduce the institutional feel of an environment composed mostly of hard surfaces and geometric shapes. Pictures and paintings hung at a child's eye level reinforce the message that children are important. A playroom arranged so that children can touch and explore the beautiful things placed within their reach conveys the message "This is your place to discover and to enjoy."

Successful play environments are aesthetically pleasing and provide abundant sensory stimulation and appeal. By including both soft and hard surfaces, rough and smooth textures, muted and bright colours, curved and sharp contours, and natural and artificial materials, the designer creates an environment of contrast and variation. A cushioned rocking chair or a comfortable sofa in a quiet corner are often children's favourite places because they provide sensory relief from hard surfaces and offer comforting reminders of home. Round instead of square tables and soft washable area carpets contribute to a positive affective climate. Smooth, hard surfaces such as plastic, vinyl, and laminate add to the durability and practicality of equipment and materials more than wood, textiles, cork, and rubber building products; therefore, practical and utilitarian features often replace the comfortable, homey, and aesthetically pleasing amenities that most of us need and enjoy. Building products and materials that are easy to maintain and durable have obvious advantages, yet the aesthetic and sensory characteristics of an environment may be just as important, for they help form habits, values, and choices that affect the quality of life. Playroom environments planned with aesthetics in mind invite cuddling up in a chair with a stuffed animal; learning to wipe the paint off our hands before touching the flowered cushion; or feeling the soft texture of the quilted placemats when helping to set the table for lunch.

Climate also affects spiritual development. Children need authentic environments that include properties of the natural world. Comfortable surroundings and private spaces to retreat to contribute to intellectual and physical meanderings that nourish the spirit. Natural objects and materials, such as wood, cork, plants, earth, water, wool, and stones, add authenticity and natural content to playrooms. Beautiful surroundings instill hope, inspire a sense of organization and meaning, and provide a standard that children can aspire to achieve. The dreary, cluttered, make-do environments we see in some underresourced Canadian programs are a powerful reminder of our advocacy role and of how much there is left for us to do. Our play and learning environments should reflect the rich abundance of beautiful, natural building products that Canada offers.

Importance of Lighting and Colour to the Climate

LIGHTING

"Research indicates that light has measurable effects on psychological and physical wellbeing" (Schreiber, 1996, p. 11). In children's play and learning environments, natural and artificial light affects children's learning experiences and their sense of comfort and security. Plenty of daylight sources are especially important in full-day programs because sunlight not only destroys mould and bacteria and provides vitamin D, but also affects the mood and climate of the environment (Caples, 1996). Because ECEs find it useful to be able to control light sources, classroom design should consider using window shades, plenty of light switches, and variable lighting appropriate to specific areas of the environment. As much natural light as possible should be captured in the play environment for aesthetic as well as health reasons, especially for centres located in northern regions where winter daylight hours are limited.

Crowther (2003) cites several sources (Hathaway, 1994; Liberman, 1991; Ott, 1976) that have linked poor or fluorescent lighting to increased hyperactivity, decreased productivity, and poorer health in children. Other studies have shown that the use of full-spectrum fluorescent lighting, which is the closest match to solar light, may result in decreased cavities and absenteeism and improved growth and productivity. Standard fluorescent (cool white) lighting has long been suspect in terms of how it affects mood, health, behaviour, and eyesight. Full-spectrum light supplements have positive effects on learning, energy levels, resistance to common illnesses, and dental and overall physical health. Incandescent and full-spectrum lighting also add warmth to the mood and climate of the environment and ensure more flexibility in lighting specific play and learning activities (Schreiber, 1996).

Two factors related to lighting have recently captured attention. One is the decline in the intake of vitamin D by children (and adults) who have become regular users of sunscreens and who avoid the sunshine based on warnings about skin cancer and other forms of skin damage. Because vitamin D is a vital ingredient for good health, and given that sunshine is a key element in the production of vitamin D, it is important for programs to balance the amount of light and sunshine to which children are exposed. Another factor is Seasonal Affective Disorder (SAD), which afflicts children in northern countries during long winters. Crowther (2003) cites a study by Giedd (1998) that claimed to have found a high incidence of SAD among children in the United States. She recommends the following lighting suggestions for early childhood settings: ensure that children play outdoors in all weather for at least an hour a day (extreme cold or heat would be exceptions); place indoor units of play near open windows or where natural light can penetrate; use full-spectrum fluorescent lighting; and use mirrors to reflect natural light indoors.

COLOUR

Colour influences the climate and the aesthetic quality of the environment in addition to affecting the behaviour of children and adults. Colours should be chosen for their known psychological impact; for example, reds are exciting, purples and greens are said to be stabilizing and soothing, and yellows are restful. The widespread use of primary colours and pastels in early childhood programs encourages experimentation with colour and greater sensitivity to the typical colour palettes of other cultures, which make the environment more inclusive (Caples, 1996). Suitable blends of colour and varied textures, particularly in natural products, enhance the physical and sensory quality of the play environment. Also, studies have shown that colour may be used instrumentally to elicit various kinds of behaviour, mood (Liberman, 1991), and physical responses such as raising blood pressure. Generally, it is thought that pastel and warm colours are calming and relaxing, while bright, primary colours tend to stimulate and excite. An approach might be to use the pastel and warm colours as background and use the primary colours, which attract children's attention, in the foreground.

The Inclusive Climate

Inclusion is a generic concept that embraces children and families of all cultures, religions, socioeconomic status, physical and intellectual abilities, and sexual orientations. Children's understanding of family as a concept is enhanced by their interaction with children from all types of families. "Inclusion refers to theoretical, social, and curricular means for ensuring that all children are fully accepted members of the learning communities in which they participate" (Mallory, 1994). In a general sense, inclusion refers to practices that invite full participation and *membership* for all individuals irrespective of differences and special needs. Mallory and New (1994) suggest that for early childhood education to become more inclusive, the traditional theoretical and empirical knowledge base of child development should be broadened. Assessment, teaching, and program-planning approaches that respond to the different cultural realities of young children are essential components. Above all, authentic inclusiveness is demonstrated by ECEs who consistently model acceptant behaviours, understanding, and sensitivity toward others (Elswood, 1999).

EXAMPLE

Wilson (2001, p. 3) quotes Kate, age five, who defines family as "people who love each other." This definition provides a beautifully expanded understanding of family that also extends to the family relationships of same-sex parents and their children. Trust a child to help us all sharpen our concept of family! Early childhood education programs are the vanguard in promoting inclusive attitudes, values, understanding, and appreciation of various family constructs, including the common bonds of love, respect, nurturing, and protection on which they depend.

Inclusion, therefore, is a term that applies to issues related to the inclusion of people from diverse races, ethnic backgrounds, sexual orientations, and religious groups. Being "inclusive" implies the obligation to actively encourage the expression of interests, views, perceptions, and suggestions made by all families and to pursue bias-free practices that respect different perspectives and priorities. Children respond to pictures, **artifacts**, clothing, implements, and foods that represent the cultural heritage of their families and provide reminders of home. Stimulating environments that respect diversity are those to which all children in the group can relate all the time. Multicultural elements should not be singled out for special attention only at times when traditional celebrations occur. An inclusive environment is one that represents consistently the cultures of the children in the program. Children will appreciate various cultures when, for example, a child's mother plays the sitar during the morning group time, a traditional Chinese fan decorates the wall, and soft leather moccasins are available to wear. Using woven rugs to enhance the Daily Living centre and displaying on the walls artwork from regions representing the cultural backgrounds of the children and staff create an inclusive environment all year and not just at holiday times.

Often the term *inclusion* is used in the context of issues related to children with special needs. All children, whether or not they have disabilities, learn through play. The integration of the child who experiences physical, cognitive, or affective challenges or a multitude of issues that cross developmental domains, is based on the assumption that children with disabilities are more similar to all children than they are different. ECEs have to ensure that the child with disabilities makes progress in spite of the disability. This goal is met by providing materials, a play environment, and interpersonal support that minimize the effect of the child's disability while maximizing the child's strengths. In well-planned, play-based programs in which children with disabilities are integrated with children without disabilities, opportunities exist for all the children to make developmental progress.

Sometimes the challenges for ECEs in inclusive environments are considerable. A broader range of developmental activities is frequently needed to address the individual capabilities and interests of children with disabilities. Special materials and media, such as computers or symbol boards, minimize the effects of the disability and allow the child to achieve the objectives of play. Whatever accommodations have to be made, the ECE should ensure that the child learns through play with things that she can manage successfully. Providing children with disabilities with materials suitable for a much younger child is not reasonable accommodation. Placing children with disabilities in structured, prescriptive educational settings robs them of their right to learn through play. Programs that depend solely on direct teaching, or that try to compensate for children's disabilities by manipulating their behaviour, are inconsistent with the philosophy of early childhood education advocated here. Inclusive environments ensure that ECEs regularly monitor the progress of all children and make relevant accommodations and modifications to play and learning environments and experiences to ensure all children's optimal development.

An inclusive climate also ensures that children with special needs can function as independently as they are able to within the environment. Wide pathways in the classroom and spacious entry points into the learning centres make it possible for the child with physical challenges to move from one part of the classroom to another. Modifying the outdoor environment by raising garden beds to children's waist levels enables all children to tend and harvest the vegetables and flowers they have helped to plant. Providing equipment for upper body strength for the child without the use of her legs allows for fitness and strength activities that are within the child's grasp. Children who are deaf need visual signs and signals from the environment to help them understand the cycle of the day. Children with visual impairment rely on the stability of the environment in order to find their way and access materials for play.

Climate and Technology

The presence of technology in the early childhood playroom reflects North American reality and mainstream culture. Issues related to technology will be addressed further in Chapter 18. Computers, CD players, and videos add features of today's world that are almost as familiar as the child-sized stove and refrigerator. When integrated into the program at a child's level of development and understanding, technology may add to the climate's authenticity. Today's children often master children's technology by age three and frequently use digital cameras by age four.

By age five, they are often able to read on the computer screen and they frequently learn to type words on the keyboard before they can print and write. To deprive a child of all technologies in the 21st century may be as futile as depriving a child of all exposure to television was in the second half of the 20th century. Some experts claim that the effects of technology may be robbing children of necessary human contact and deep relationships that are the essential foundation for empathy (Perry & Szalavitz, 2010). The NAEYC Position Statement on Technology in Early Childhood Education (2011) is an important resource for ECEs on the judicious use of technologies with young children. Recent research on the health effects of new technologies, especially cellphones and other wireless devices, including cordless phones, raises concerns about children's use of wireless devices. Until more is known about their potential ill effects, wireless technologies should be excluded from preschools and kindergartens. *ECEs should remember that children's development and learning primarily occur in the three-dimensional world as they manipulate concrete objects in the environment.*

The Role of a Schedule

The daily schedule of routines and playtime can either undermine or promote the effectiveness of children's play opportunities. In some environments, children regularly meander, engage in repetitive activity, or otherwise while away the time. In others, they are tightly organized into an endless round of adult-led activities. The schedule should support a positive climate for play that ensures that there is sufficient choice for them to be meaningfully engaged in play for much of the day. A wise ECE will also permit a child to opt out of the scheduled activities for the day when the child feels a need to do so.

Playtimes are often undermined by scheduled routines that keep interrupting children's play. This negative effect is brought about by those who believe that the pace, daily agenda, and routines should provide frequent changes of activity. Sometimes small blocks of time are scheduled for specific kinds of play, such as free play, group time, outdoor play, organized games, and quiet playtime. Interspersed in these allocations of playtime are washroom routines, snacktimes, naptimes, mealtimes, and the inevitable transition periods intended to form smooth bridges from one type of activity to another. With packed schedules like these, children barely manage to have one full hour of uninterrupted playtime in a whole day. They are bombarded with reminders that it is time to tidy up, to get dressed, or to move to another area of the school or centre.

Program schedules that assume children have short **attention spans** foster play that is product-oriented. Short intervals of play interspersed with frequent routines encourage children to choose activities that can be completed in one short sitting. Projects and two- or three-stage activities are often unfinished or interrupted by the time children have to move on to something else. In such programs, the schedule becomes the master of the day—it is invested with the power to interrupt and to disengage the attention and involvement of children in their play. Consequently, play loses its meaning and much of the potential it might have had to motivate and to provide feelings of success and mastery. One Canadian study showed that schedules that provided short intervals of play actually decreased children's attention spans from the time they entered the program until they left it (Nash, 1989).

Scheduling Time for ECEs

ECEs, who have so many responsibilities, need time to sit down or to have something to drink and eat, as well as time to plan and set up activities. Early childhood programs are unlike retail stores or factories, where staff check in and out for 10-minute breaks and for lunch. Ratios of children to adults are affected every time an ECE leaves the room, and children's play is sacrificed when the break schedule dominates the lives of the ECEs and the children. ECEs are never off duty when they are in the school or centre (see Table 5–1). But being professional does not mean always assuming a teaching role. ECEs need down time—allotments of time when they may do some thinking for the next day, have a cup of tea, and relax for a few minutes. Schedules should recognize and acknowledge the ECEs' needs by moving away from conventional "break" times, and by building time into the schedule for a quiet time with a small group of children. This practice helps to establish a more homelike climate. Sometimes, ECEs need to stand back and examine the demands they place on themselves and on children to always be busy.

Scheduling Routines

The approach to scheduling recommended in Tables 5–1 to 5–4 assumes that most children are able to use the washroom largely on their own. This approach means that the toilets and sinks are located just off the playroom and can be supervised by ECEs through glass enclosures or over half-walls. Two-year-old children naturally require more direct attention and assistance, and the regularity and consistency of the routine become part of the learning agenda for each day.

TABLE 5–1

EXAMPLE OF A DAILY SCHEDULE FOR A FULL-DAY PROGRAM

7:30 a.m.	Arrival; greeting; warm drink or snack; early arrivals play in the learning centres
8:30 a.m.	Group planning time with the ECE to talk about the day ahead
8:45 a.m.	Playtime in learning centres with planned activities that are set up
10:00 a.m.	Snack brought to snack table for children to help themselves; four chairs at the table to accommodate four children at a time; children wash their hands with soap at a sink before they sit at the table
10:30 a.m.	Reminder regarding washroom; planned physical program in the gymnasium, psychomotor room, or outdoors; some group physical activities may be led by the ECE
11:45 a.m.	Tidy up and preparation for lunch; washroom; lunchtime
12:45 p.m.	Naptime; quiet play in learning centres for children who require no more than an hour of rest
2:15 p.m.	Story time with the ECE in small groups
2:45 p.m.	Playtime outdoors or indoors in learning centres, depending on the weather
4:00 p.m.	Playtime continues; snack offered at the snack table indoors or outdoors, depending on the weather and on the presence of insects and hot sun or severe cold outdoors
4:30 p.m.	Group time with the ECE to discuss the day, to share plans for the next day, to work on a group project, or perhaps to make some play materials for the next day or perhaps some "down-time"
5:00 p.m.	Preparation for home, while some children continue to play in learning centres

TABLE 5–2

SCHEDULE FOR THE ECES

7:30 a.m.	Set up learning centres for play according to weekly plan
8:00 a.m.	Greet children and parents and guide children to quiet play area and breakfast snack as appropriate
8:45 a.m.	Planning time with small group to introduce activities in the learning centres
9:00 a.m.	Facilitate children's play with activities and observe/record
10:00 a.m.	Snack, washroom break (while playtime continues)
10:20 a.m.	Lead routines as needed and prepare children for outdoors
10:30 a.m.	Lead planned group physical activity indoors (gymnasium) or outdoors
11:45 a.m.	Prepare children for lunch and serve lunch
12:45 p.m.	Prepare children for naptime. Prepare learning centres for afternoon play period indoors or outdoors (During this period, ECEs often take their lunch breaks.)
2:45 p.m.	Facilitate children's play with planned activities, indoors or outdoors, depending on season/weather and observe/record
4:00 p.m.	Snack and playtime continues indoors with planned activities in learning centres. Then lead group time to plan, work on a group project, or make play materials for next day or schedule some "down-time"
5:15 p.m.	Light snack, quiet play time, and preparation for going home

The schedule in Table 5–1 omits many events that will inevitably occur during the course of the day. Time for dressing and undressing before and after outdoor play, for example, is not listed. Children are assumed to be capable of using the washroom independently, although ECEs may remind certain children to use the washroom. An informal approach to managing children's frequent need to use the washroom is less disruptive to their play and less institutional.

Schedule Planning to Meet Children's Needs

The daily schedule should coincide with the natural rhythms of children's days and contribute to their physical and emotional well-being. It also should reflect the goals of the program. Programs that state, for example, that the goals for children are independence, freedom to choose, decision-making abilities, and attending skills should not implement schedules that rigidly insist children remain in bed for the whole naptime even though they cannot sleep, or schedules that prevent a child from finishing an activity that requires just a few more minutes.

That ECEs and children require timeframes and limitations to accomplish necessary tasks in a day is a given. One question, however, remains: What needs to be done in a day? Children must arrive, settle in, have frequent snacks and a meal, rest, and prepare for going home. They also need to use the washroom frequently. For the rest of the day, children should be able to engage in child-initiated play, with time set aside for organized group play activities such as physical or music programs.

Longer play periods encourage deeper involvement in play and more complex play activities, including group play, individual play, constructive play, and role play. Shorter play periods encourage unoccupied behaviour and functional productive play (Christie & Wardle, 1992). The daily schedule should be adjusted to ensure that longer play periods occur every day.

TABLE 5–3

SCHEDULE FOR A HALF-DAY PROGRAM

8:45 a.m.	Arrival and greeting
9:00 a.m.	Planning time in small group
9:10 a.m.	Playtime in the learning centres, where activities have been planned and set up for children to choose their preferred activity
10:30 a.m.	Snack is available for children.
10:45 a.m.	Small-group activities with ECEs—e.g., reading a book, cooking activity, musical activity; planning for next day and sharing experiences they have had—this timeframe may be used for small-group activities and adult-led larger activities
11:15 a.m.	Physical play indoors or outdoors depending on weather, with some planned activities in groups and independent play
11:45 a.m.	Preparation for going home

TABLE 5–4

INTEGRATED DAY—KINDERGARTEN TO CHILD CARE

7:30 a.m.	Arrival at the school; breakfast snack and quiet time with books and puzzles
8:45 a.m.	Move into the kindergarten room
9:00 a.m.	Kindergarten program play at learning centres with planned activities
10:00 a.m.	Snack and group time to review the day with the ECE; group sharing
10:20 a.m.	Planned small-group activities in the learning centres continues
11:10 a.m.	Outdoor play with planned physical program or a physical program indoors in a gym or active play room
12:00 noon	Move to early learning and care program and preparation for lunch; lunch followed by quiet time
1:10 p.m.	Project time: cardboard carpentry project, unit block or hollow block play, planning for concert or parade
2:00 p.m.	Music program—music and movement, singing, listening, dancing, marching—indoors
2:40 p.m.	Story time—continuing story in small groups with ECEs—also finger puppets, puppets, feltboard stories, and stories told by children
3:15 p.m.	Snacktime and prop boxes at super units to promote sociodramatic play episodes in small groups
4:15 p.m.	Preparation for outdoor play (depends on seasonal light factors)
5:15 p.m.	Drink and light vegetable snack and quiet time with books and puzzles or to work on projects begun earlier before going home

The daily schedule is the skeleton of the day; it determines the quality and complexity of play and whether a day is good or bad. The quality of the affective climate and the effectiveness of the environment often rely on the emphases and flexibility within the schedule and the amount of time children are allowed to become deeply involved in their play.

Principles of Schedule Planning

1. The schedule should be open and loose enough to allow for unexpected occurrences, changes in the plan, and children's spontaneous needs and interests.

2. The schedule should be regular but not inflexible. The order in which events occur during the day will remain fairly constant most days, but the times may vary, depending on a range of factors, including weather conditions, special plans, and the needs of other groups to use facilities or equipment.
3. The schedule should provide for alternating periods of quiet and active experiences. Moving from active to quieter activities will reduce the likelihood that excitement will escalate and cause children to tire more quickly.
4. The schedule should provide a variety of activities and outlets for children at any given time, whether indoors or outdoors. Children have different activity level requirements; some are able to play actively for long periods without becoming overexcited or fatigued, whereas others can engage in seated or quiet activity for long periods without becoming restless or bored. Each play period should permit children to choose either more active or quieter pursuits. Quiet corners allow for privacy and individual play; active role play areas encourage social interaction and motor activity.
5. The schedule should provide a balance of indoor and outdoor play. Most children love the outdoors, but on extremely cold days no one enjoys being outside. In the summer, the heat and the sunshine can become oppressive in the afternoons. Common sense should prevail on days when it is too cold or damp or hot for children to play comfortably outdoors, and the schedule must be adjusted accordingly. In climates where both indoor and outdoor playtimes are possible and the number of staff is sufficient to meet ratios both inside and outside, schedules should permit freedom of movement between the playground and the indoor playroom. This type of arrangement is often referred to as an indoor/outdoor program.
6. Schedules should account for seasonal changes in children's needs. The schedule planned for September may not suit the needs of children in December or May. Knowledge of the needs and the rhythms of children will lead to changes in the schedule to accommodate changing weather conditions and children's energy levels.
7. Children should have enough time to become deeply involved in what they are doing. Schedules requiring that children be continually herded from one place to another or from one activity to another reduce children's powers of concentration and delay the development of attending abilities. Asking a child to leave an activity before he is finished exacts a cost in terms of the message the ECE sends the child. On the one hand, he may hear the ECE say that it is important to "finish what you start," and on the other, he may experience discomfort and frustration at being urged by the same ECE to leave what he is doing to join a small group, when a few more minutes would have allowed him to experience the satisfaction of completion and success.
8. Schedules should allow sufficient time for transitions from one activity to another or from an activity to a routine. Children are notoriously poor at hurrying, especially when they know someone wants them to. Transition times are not wasted times; when used well, they allow valuable time for ECEs to relate to children individually.

9. Schedules should provide for a suitable balance between playtimes when children can choose to play alone or in small groups, and time for group learning and projects. Unstructured playtimes help children learn to make responsible choices, develop autonomy and initiative, and pursue their own interests and goals. Group learning times teach children to function as members of a group and allow ECEs to relate to the group as a whole and to instil in children a sense of group identity and belonging. Group times also promote a sense of common mission, especially when the ECE and the children together use the time to plan and carry out meaningful projects that arise from children's interests and choices (Katz & Chard, 1989). The periods of unstructured playtime, when children may play alone or with others at activities of their own choosing, should take a larger portion of the day than the group learning times. This approach to scheduling recognizes the importance of child-initiated play and active, hands-on sensory involvement with concrete objects and the physical environment.
10. Schedules also should account for the needs of the adults who work with young children. Although these needs should not supersede those of the children, the ECE's role is demanding. ECEs also need variety in their tasks and some opportunity for choice. The schedule should make the best possible use of human resources by encouraging ECEs to do what they most enjoy doing. ECEs also need help with some of the tedious, time-consuming tasks involved in caring for children. They should be able to share simple chores with children during down-times, such as tidying the cupboard, cutting **collage materials,** setting the table, and planning for the next day's activities. In these ways, children learn to use time well (Nash, 1989).
11. Schedules should reflect the interests and the needs of children and their families and should allow time for ECEs to involve parents as much as possible in the lives of their children and in the program. Schedules should ensure that ECEs have comfortable periods of contact with parents at arrival and departure times.

Summary

A healthy affective climate fosters positive relationships between adults and children that promote mutual respect and affection. Children have to know that what they believe and how they feel are important to the adults who care for them. The aesthetic appeal of the environment, including colours, textures, contours, cleanliness, and tidiness, contributes to an atmosphere of safety, beauty, and harmony. Group times foster a sense of belonging and identity and allow for self-expression. Children are encouraged to choose from a wide range of play and learning opportunities and are permitted to pursue activities at their own pace. ECEs' needs are addressed so that they may administer more effectively to the needs of children. Schedules are based on children's natural rhythms and are flexible enough to allow for change. Schedules provide for large blocks of playtime and minimize the importance of rigid, institutional routines. Together, these ingredients of a healthy affective climate will positively influence the effectiveness of the physical setting and the developmental challenges children encounter in their play.

LEARNING ACTIVITIES

1. Observe three play and learning environments for young children. Using the guidelines outlined in this chapter, develop a set of criteria for such categories as social and emotional characteristics, physical features, schedules, and small-group and large-group play times that will help you determine whether the climate contributes to development and learning through play.
2. Analyze three sample daily schedules for three separate programs for young children. From the schedules, determine the length of the uninterrupted play periods. Evaluate whether the program's daily schedule appears to promote engaged play and learning. Suggest ways to alter the schedule to make it more compatible with the principles described in this chapter.
3. Visit an early childhood education program that has a diverse population of children. Describe the cultural features of the classroom environment. Do the classroom climate and environment reflect the diverse family backgrounds of the children in the program?

6 Play Materials, Equipment, and Supplies

> "Children's play is influenced as much by the form of materials as by the child's purposes in play."
>
> —WILLIAM FOWLER, *INFANT AND CHILD CARE* (1980)

BEFORE READING THIS CHAPTER, HAVE YOU

- observed children playing with equipment, materials, and supplies in a preschool or kindergarten program?
- visited a store to familiarize yourself with the play materials parents are encouraged to buy for their children?
- observed how children in preschools and kindergartens use the play materials?
- noted the types of play equipment, materials, and supplies in each learning centre?

OUTCOMES

After reading and understanding this chapter, you should be able to

- differentiate equipment, materials, and supplies;
- describe the features of the various types of play materials;
- explain the selection criteria and appropriate uses of open-ended, specific-purpose, and two- and three-dimensional materials to promote development and learning;
- calculate the **complexity** of the play environment using simple formulas;
- determine the **variety** of play environments;
- optimize storage space in playrooms; and
- choose equipment, materials, and supplies that support inclusive practice.

The Tools of the Profession

Play **equipment**, **materials**, and **supplies** are the tools for early childhood education. Therefore, understanding the intrinsic purposes, variability, and extendibility of the many materials children play with is an essential teaching skill. Knowing how to design the environment for play and use the space effectively depends on understanding the potential of play equipment and materials. Just as an artist should be well acquainted with the tools for creating a range of artistic products, so should an ECE be knowledgeable about the intrinsic play value and optimal uses of the "things" in the environment to promote play, development, and learning. Strangely enough, this is a skill often overlooked. Because a key function of early childhood education is to enhance the quality of children's play and to promote "pure play," and because children's development depends largely on their interactions with things in the environment, knowledge of the play potential of equipment, materials, and supplies is essential. Knowing how equipment and materials are used optimally and how to modify and adapt them for various play purposes so as to encourage specific categories and social contexts of play, and to support children with special needs, is the hallmark of the competent ECE. Constructivist educators adapt equipment, materials, and supplies to meet diverse needs and know how to exploit their potential by using and reusing materials in a variety of play contexts and for a multitude of purposes.

EXAMPLES

Tabletop blocks can double as materials for sorting, seriating, and counting; **Cuisenaire rods** may be used as materials for fine motor tabletop construction; fabric and felt pieces may be used for sorting and also for forming patterns; buttons and shells are interesting materials to classify; pine cones and acorns double as art supplies as well as materials to explore in the Science Discovery centre; puzzle pieces may be used for tracing in the art area.

Toys

In ECE, the language of *play equipment, materials*, and *supplies* is preferable to the word *toys*, which refers to a wide range of playthings, including commercial products designed to amuse children and encourage passive observation. Examples include battery-operated hamsters that squeak, giggle, and zoom around on wheels and dolls made of plush nylon that sing in harmony. *Toys* that often require minimal effort by the child do not necessarily enrich play and are only marginally responsive to children's actions on them, whereas play materials generally respond to children's actions on them and involve significant play potential.

In the rich play environment one does not typically find many toys. Try to make an electric train, for example, respond to a child's actions on it, or try to modify its purpose or structure in any way. The most that can be achieved is for the child to manipulate controls to speed up or slow down the train and to change the surrounding scenery. Well-planned play environments contain play materials that respond to children's actions on them, to become what the child wants them to become and to adapt to the child's maturing skills. Responsive play materials enhance the richness of children's play, are valuable tools for early development and learning, and represent value for cost.

CHALLENGE YOUR LEARNING ABOUT RESPONSIVE PLAY MATERIALS

Compare, for example, the responsiveness of unit blocks versus a spinning top; of paint, paint brushes, and blank newsprint versus a colouring book; of a Lego set versus a replica of Disney's fairy castle; of a ball versus a hand-held windmill. Make a list of the responsive materials you used to play with as a child. Then, list the toys you have seen in the stores and comment on their degree of responsiveness to children's actions on them. Develop a rating scale to rate each toy in terms of its responsive qualities, play value, and value for cost.

The best play materials invite exploration, manipulation, and adaptation; provide sensory stimulation; and promote challenging, independent, and creative pursuits. Art materials and blocks foster **creative-constructive play**; realistic artifacts of cars, animals, and dolls, for example, support early pretend play; **convergent materials** promote **task orientation** and problem solving; and hollow blocks support creative-constructive play and dramatic play. ECEs select play materials, supplies, and equipment that are rich in their capacity to promote development.

Equipment

Equipment forms the infrastructure of the play environment and refers to the furniture, storage containers, and large items of play equipment that are often used to define the boundaries of a learning centre and to denote the type of play encouraged there. Equipment makes a stable footprint on the floor; that is, it covers floor space more or less permanently. Tables, children's chairs, water tables, climbers, and playhouses are examples of equipment. The choice of equipment and its location influence the quality and type of learning through play that occurs. Important criteria for choosing equipment are appearance, practicality, durability, portability, adaptability, versatility, texture, contour, size, shape, and overall aesthetic quality.

Because most children's furniture comes in standard sizes, the criteria for choice are often limited to quality of construction, building materials used, and whether or not accessories are included. All equipment should be joined with screws, rather than simply with nails and glue. Solid wood or plywood is stronger than particleboard and resists splintering. Some sturdy equipment is now available in safe products made of recycled materials. Surfaces should be easy to clean and covered with nontoxic paints or stain.

Equipment

Materials

"Irrespective of whether objects employed in play are natural or social in origin, or whether the play involves social behaviour, much of any play consists of manipulations of materials" (Fowler, 1980, p. 166). Materials are the smaller objects that children can play with and transform. Whereas equipment provides the infrastructure for the environment, materials are part of the foreground; they support the developmental outcomes of the curriculum. Children develop and learn through their play with materials as well as through their social play.

ECEs should consider criteria such as durability, variety, safety, cleanliness, attractiveness, responsiveness, and versatility in selecting materials and should choose materials that represent the cultural diversity of the children and their families. The most cost-effective and valuable materials in a learning environment are those that are extendable and grow with the child, that may be used for more than one purpose, that address a wide range of objectives, and that invite open-ended play. Materials such as unit blocks, Lego, and other modular materials fit this description. Art materials—such as clay; weaving and sewing devices; and various implements for carving, painting, and drawing—add challenge and encourage experimentation by children. Books and music that reflect the children's cultural origins enhance the inclusiveness of the environment.

Supplies

Supplies are the consumable items that should be replenished periodically. Examples include paper of various kinds, crayons, paints, paste, wood, chalk, modelling clay, brushes, sand, markers, and cardboard boxes—anything that gets used up over time or becomes ragged and needs to be replaced. In our product-rich society, the choice of supplies and materials is seemingly limitless. ECEs generally choose supplies that are easy to manipulate and store, and that are durable, colourful, attractive, and clean. Plastic bins, paper containers reinforced with adhesive covering, and fitted shelves for storage should be purchased along with supplies to ensure that they can be labelled, properly cared for, used effectively, and replenished when supplies diminish. When choosing equipment for storage, ECEs should take into account the specifications necessary for all supplies to be accommodated neatly, accessibly, and attractively. Children are interested in the variety and the appearance of supplies. Such factors as whether the paper is shiny; the crayons, paints, and stamp pads have unusual colours or erasers have different shapes, often determine whether a child will choose one activity over others.

Types of Play Materials

Play materials are of two main types: open-ended materials and structured, specific-purpose materials. Within these two broad categories are subclasses of materials. Generally, the number and the nature of the tasks for which children use them define the two types.

Open-Ended Materials

Open-ended materials have an indefinite number of outcomes and an indefinite amount of flexibility in the ways children can use them (Fowler, 1980). The outcomes may be planned or spontaneous, and there are usually no rules—or only simple ones, outlining the steps to follow. Open-ended materials may be modular or free-form. Modular materials usually lead to construction play. Materials such as Lego, unit blocks, Tinkertoy, parquetry tiles, and tabletop blocks are modular. They have many pieces, or multiple units, usually of uniform shapes and sizes, which are made to fit together in specific ways. These materials consist of discrete, rigid forms, or modules, that have been designed with fixed units of measurement, such as inches or centimetres, to allow them to be arranged into a variety of structures. Sets of unit blocks include units in various shapes and sizes, but the units are usually exact multiples of one basic unit (see Chapter 20, p. 377, Figure 20–1). Structures that children build using modular materials are often formed using add-on processes, since the units cannot be altered in either shape or form. Modular materials are sometimes referred to as **non-continuous materials**.

Free-form materials are more concerned with how things flow (rather than fit) together to make the whole (Fowler, 1980, p. 171). These materials, which Fowler called "surface diffusible, free-form materials," are generally used for painting and drawing. They include paint; markers; brushes; sponges; chalk; crayons; and various kinds of paper, wood, and clay. These media allow free-form shaping only within the limitations of the surface area being used (i.e., the size and shape of the paper or slate). Free-form natural substances, such as earth, sand, and water, which are sometimes called **continuous materials**, are often used for construction purposes, as in building sandcastles, and making canals and mud huts. These substances are much harder to control and to manipulate toward specified outcomes than are rigid, modular materials, as it is difficult to maintain the consistency and shape of free-form substances. Various types of malleable materials such as clay and dough are continuous materials that have more predictable properties and children can use them to build lifelike representations.

Specific-Purpose Materials

Specific-purpose materials have an internal structure that guides the outcome of play and provides the steps to follow in reaching the outcome. Sometimes called **means-ends materials** (Fowler, 1980, p. 151), they include pegboards, formboard and jigsaw puzzles, and dominoes, all of which have somewhat predictable results. Although these materials are used for specific-purposes, they can be used for other purposes. For example, dominoes can double as building blocks; pick-up sticks as colour sorting materials; and beads and Lego blocks as objects for classification. For the most part, however, specific-purpose materials are kept together as sets to be used in standard ways toward a precise, predictable product and outcome.

Specific-purpose materials promote design concepts and content concepts (Fowler, 1980). Formboard puzzles use the design concepts of shapes, configurations of shapes, and interlocking and inlaid shapes to form patterns and abstract representations. Some structured materials are designed to help children practise and learn the concepts of seriation, classification, number, size, part–whole, and functional relationships. Many educational materials fall into this category, including sets of objects for children to classify, rods for seriation, interlocking blocks for identifying part–whole relationships, and stacking cups for ordering by size. When children play with specific-purpose materials they experience feelings of success when they master the tasks inherent in the materials. Feeling pride in meeting challenges through play motivates children to set higher goals. Self-esteem is enhanced through successful experiences with appropriate materials in meaningful contexts. ECEs who allow children the time they need to finish their puzzles and other tabletop activities with specific-purpose materials recognize the function and instrumental value of play. The ECE who responds to a child's request to come and see what he has made, even though she must temporarily leave what she is doing, is acknowledging the importance of the child's play.

Two-Dimensional and Three-Dimensional Materials

Materials may also be differentiated according to whether they are two- or three-dimensional. **Two-dimensional materials** are those with flat surface areas, such as drawings on paper, collages on paper or cardboard, and formboard puzzles. Such materials often carry representations that have length and width but little depth. **Three-dimensional materials** have length, width, and depth. A two-dimensional material might be a wooden puzzle piece the colour and shape of an apple, or a picture of an apple flashed on a computer monitor. A three-dimensional material would be a real apple or a lifelike representation, which has length, width, and depth. The prevalence of screen-based technologies has vastly increased children's exposure to the two-dimensional world. This makes it all the more important to balance children's experience with two-dimensional and three-dimensional materials that provide opportunities to transfer learning they have achieved first in the concrete, three-dimensional environment to the two-dimensional computer screen.

Many play materials, especially open-ended ones, are increasingly found in both three-dimensions and two-dimensions on the screen, such as block puzzles. The ease with which children learn to perform various computer functions—that is, to reposition, roll, transform, change shape, and reconstruct *objects* on the computer screen—demonstrates children's ability to transfer learning acquired in one context to a different context. Children more fully understand transformations when they have experience with both three- and two-dimensional versions of them. (See Figure 6–1 for a summary of the types of play and learning materials.)

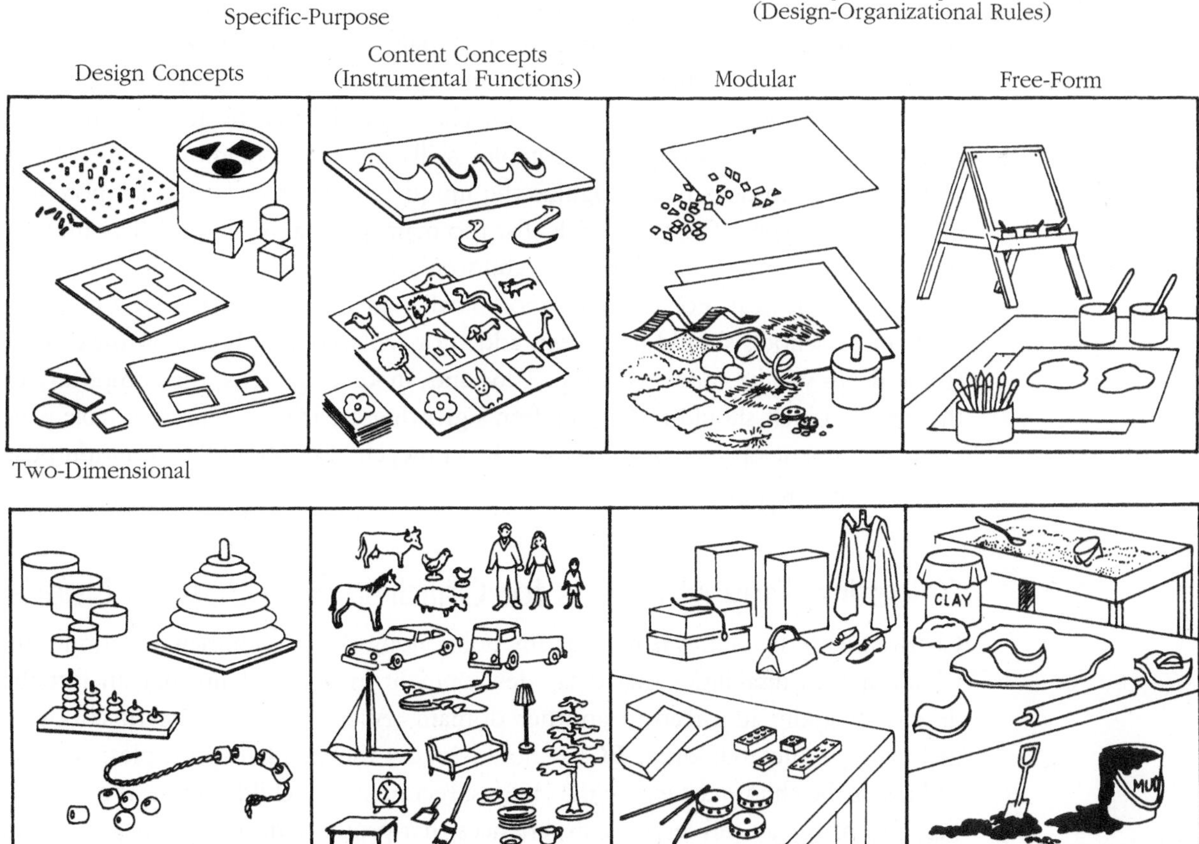

Figure 6–1
Major types of play and learning materials

Source: W. Fowler, *Infant and Child Care: A Guide to Education in Group Settings* (Toronto: Allyn & Bacon, 1980). Used with permission.

Play Materials to Promote Development and Learning

When children are actively involved with concrete materials in the environment, they first learn about the physical properties of objects and later form concepts based on the relationships among objects they see and experience. They relate textures they have touched and sounds they have heard to direction, specific persons, and messages. They feel the shape of a letter or number by tracing these symbols in sand or salt trays, or by shaping their own bodies in the same configuration as the number or letter on the magnetic board. The value children gain from any play material depends on the match the ECE is able to make between the material and the developmental level of the child who will be playing with it.

Materials should accommodate the wide range of developmental levels and abilities represented in the program. For example, specific-purpose materials like puzzles are used to stimulate more complex and conceptual learning, instead of simple sensory exploration of materials like stuffed animals.

Play materials should move children from sensorimotor, physical exploration of the materials to an understanding of the many relationships that exist among materials and the environment. The presentation of play materials should also change as the children make developmental progress. The playroom should not look the same in June as it did in September. The continued presence in the playroom in June of the same puzzles, manipulative materials, tabletop construction materials, and creative materials that were present in September indicates a program that is not developmentally based and does not challenge children to achieve outcomes that represent progressively more complex skills and understanding. It also shows that the program does not recognize the unique characteristics and play potential of the various types of play materials. Far too many programs fall into this category. Play environments should build on children's ongoing developmental progress throughout the year. For example, more challenging creative materials and **super units** in preschools should have been added or replaced **simple** or **complex** units, (these terms will be addressed on p. 106) and, in kindergartens, the complexity of the play materials should reflect children's growing capacity to represent, role play, perform numeric operations, and read. Over time, children should use multipurpose materials in new ways.

Selecting Play Materials for Children with Special Needs

Children with disabilities may be at any point along the developmental continuum. Children with disabilities that delay development in one domain may, in fact, be developmentally advanced in another domain (Allen et al., 2006). In choosing materials for these children, ECEs should follow the standard principles: observe and assess the child; start where the child is; recognize the child's interests and abilities; and plan play and learning experiences that promote developmental progress. The arrangement of materials should provide clear messages to the children about how they are to be used and for what purpose; mixed messages should be avoided (Allen et al., 2006). Often, children with disabilities need a greater amount of adult intervention in their play to guide them over difficult hurdles, but the fundamental approaches to early childhood education apply; that is, children learn through self-directed, hands-on interaction with things and experiences—and the curriculum and activities should meet the special needs and interests of all children and encourage as much autonomy and freedom of choice as possible.

A key principle for choosing materials for children with disabilities is to ensure that the materials can be adapted to each child's needs to help them experience success. Choosing materials suitable for a much younger child is not an appropriate solution for the child with disabilities. Manipulative materials are especially adaptable and can be used successfully by children with special needs. Materials should be placed at various levels to allow children to access them independently from a seated position on the floor, from a wheelchair, or standing with a brace (Allen et al., 2006). The obligation to adapt materials to increase a child's likelihood of success often requires us to think through the various ways in which play with a material may be modified to account for the child's particular challenges. For example, ECEs may tape down more intricate puzzle pieces, leaving those pieces free that are easier to manipulate; limit the number of modular pieces in a set, such as nesting cups, for a child with a short attention span; or provide a lace of leather or plastic, rather than a string, for stringing beads (Allen et al., 2006). Visual cues on posters or plaques on the wall may also be used to guide children to the appropriate use of materials.

Play Materials as Responsive Media for Learning

The most effective materials for development are those that children can manipulate and change. Creative materials fall into this category, along with blocks; other construction materials such as Lego, Tinkertoy, cardboard, or boxes; and materials used in woodworking and in sewing. Paints, paste, papers, collage, and clay also respond to the child's actions. Initially, they are used in sensory ways; at later stages, children play with them in more purposeful ways and use greater skill in shaping them with tools and hands.

The responsive play environment includes a wide range of flexible, open-ended materials. Effective learning in early childhood is a two-way street. The child's manipulation of things in the environment and the ways in which the materials respond create a dynamic interaction between the child and the play environment as the child moves from physical exploration and experimentation to an understanding of interrelationships in the physical world. Play materials vary greatly in the potential they offer for meaningful learning and understanding.

EXAMPLES OF THE VARIABLE COMPLEXITY OF PLAY MATERIALS

Play materials vary in complexity in many ways: (1) irregularity of shape and colour; (2) number of parts; (3) size of parts; (4) the intricacy of the interrelations among parts, including the types of connecting mechanisms, e.g., snaps, hooks, Velcro; (5) toughness of the parts and interconnecting mechanisms (Fowler, 1980, p. 173). Compare the differences in complexity among the following: a set of Lego for making a robot; a Fisher-Price farm; a chunky animal jigsaw puzzle in plywood; a doll and doll clothing with snap fasteners; a drum; a feltboard with felt animals; nesting cups; a dollhouse and furniture. Consider the difference in play and learning potential, for instance, between a windup mechanical car set and a set of tabletop blocks. Once children wind up the cars and observe their movements a few times, their interest wanes. The cars respond to the child's winding of the mechanical key by moving along the track or floor and, perhaps, by making car sounds. They do not change their shape, alter their play potential, or provide variety and flexibility in the ways they can be used. The play potential of the windup car set is more passive than active, and the child's role is largely that of observer.

Tabletop blocks, on the other hand, take the shape that the child creates during play. They respond to the child's actions, and the new configuration invites the child to continue to shape the blocks into a planned or purely exploratory structure. The flexibility and the inherent potential of the blocks to inspire a child's creativity depend on the child's action on them. A variety of responses by both the child and by the blocks themselves are possible. The play that occurs is a two-way interaction between the child and the play materials. As the child explores the blocks and uses them for his purposes, he learns about their properties and eventually uses them to represent a plan. The blocks respond more flexibly and creatively as the child's ability to manipulate and use them expands. Experiencing the physical properties of the blocks leads the child to understand the various ways in which the blocks may interrelate to create a variety of structures. In this way, blocks are truly constructivist play materials. Children's growing understanding of blocks as play materials leads to more sophisticated building and creating and to the acquisition of **spatial intelligence**.

Specific-purpose play materials also respond to children's actions, although they bring about specialized kinds of learning, usually the development of a discrete skill or the understanding of a concept. For example, dominoes promote visual discrimination of the similar configurations of dots on a tile. They also promote understanding of quantity when the child recognizes that the tile with five dots should be placed next to another tile with five dots. The child should understand the concept of matching likenesses, which, in this case, usually involves recognizing similar patterns of dots. Sometimes colour, shape, and tactile clues provide additional sensory information for making appropriate juxtapositions. Of course, dominoes may also become, at any given time, materials that demonstrate cause and effect by tipping one tile in a series of tiles placed at regular intervals and watching the wave of motion that occurs.

When play environments provide diverse materials to promote a comprehensive range of developmentally appropriate sensory, conceptual, and social learning, children are less likely to use materials for unintended purposes. Nonetheless, one of the beneficial characteristics of many specific-purpose materials is that they contain possibilities for more flexible use. A good example is the multiple uses of Cuisenaire rods that can transform from instruments of measurement, to tabletop blocks, to seriation materials, to matching, to sorting sets, and to demonstrating mathematical operations.

Criteria for Selecting Play Materials

In selecting play materials for the learning environment, ECEs should consider practical, economic, aesthetic, and developmental/educational criteria (see Table 6–1).

Practical Criteria

Practical criteria for selecting play materials include safety, adaptability, inclusive qualities, cleanliness, ease of storage, functional quality, and multipurpose use.

TABLE 6–1

CRITERIA FOR SELECTING PLAY MATERIALS

Practical Criteria	Economic Criteria	Aesthetic Criteria	Developmental/ Educational Criteria
safety	cost	form/line	interest
adaptability	quantity needed	colour	relevance to real life
inclusive qualities	sturdiness/ durability	proportion	responsive
cleanliness		composition	representational
storage/size	reusability	design/structure	familiarity
functionality		properties	
multipurpose			

SAFETY

ECEs should not rely exclusively on either government standards or systematic testing of a limited range of play materials on the market by the Canadian Toy Testing Council. Non-commercially produced materials made by private manufacturing companies and by local craftspeople should be carefully screened to ensure their compliance with safety standards. Parents and ECEs should remain vigilant and check for the presence of toxic substances in all commercial and hand-made play materials, especially those available at craft fairs and those that are imported.

Safety features that should be examined include the durability of the material, the size of detachable parts, the presence of sharp edges, and the ease of cleaning and disinfecting. Play materials that break easily may leave rough edges that can cut the skin and sharp pieces that can be swallowed. Wood preservatives containing insecticidal agents can be absorbed through contact with uncovered skin. Materials with joints or ridges may harbour bacteria, which can lead to infections. Safety is also influenced by the developmental appropriateness of materials or equipment for each child, for example, a wooden rocking horse may be safe for one two-year-old but not for a child who cannot yet balance and hold on.

ADAPTABILITY

Adaptability is a practical consideration that recognizes that programs generally have to stretch budgets. The selection of play materials that are adaptable and expandable to a variety of purposes also stretches children's imaginations as they will invent ways to integrate a piece of equipment or a play material into their play. Open-ended materials are generally more adaptable than specific-purpose materials. The adaptability of materials in the environment also depends on the ECE's ability to see their inherent potential for play. Materials should be placed in learning centres in ways that will lead to more flexible use.

INCLUSIVE QUALITIES

Materials that are truly inclusive permit children with developmental challenges to play independently and to take risks; they invite independent play instead of posing barriers that require adult intervention. The play environment should contain an adequate supply of similar materials for children to choose that would allow the child who takes longer to complete a task to finish what she is attempting to achieve. An insufficient number of sets of materials in a classroom, for example, may intimidate children with special needs who watch others playing with the materials efficiently and independently. Inclusive practice also implies the selection of materials that encourage boys to play with dolls and girls to play with construction sets, as they choose. Materials present in learning centres either reinforce masculine and feminine stereotypes or reduce the dominance of gender stereotypes. Play materials should also represent the cultural backgrounds of the children, including the mainstream culture; for example, cultural clothing, hats and shoes in the dramatic play areas, cooking implements from many cultures, and puzzles from around the world.

CLEANLINESS

Play materials made of artificial products, such as plastics, are often easier to clean than those made of wood, sponge, or cloth. Yet ECEs should balance the need to keep play materials clean with consideration for the aesthetic quality of the learning environment. Natural materials, such as wood and fabric, add interest, tactile variation, and beauty and can often be washed easily and frequently. The frequency of cleaning and disinfecting play materials also depends on the ages and the vulnerability of the children. In programs where children still explore by putting most materials into their mouths, or at times when the incidence of illness is high, ECEs need to choose materials that are easily washed and disinfected.

EASE OF STORAGE

The amount of storage needed in a play environment is often underestimated; so is the ease of access to ensure that ECEs and children can put things away. Natural wood or brightly painted storage pieces that are easily cleaned, with wide cupboard door openings and strong hinges, enhance the storage potential of the classroom and contribute to the quality of play. The issue of where and how to store play materials not in use is especially important in programs where space is limited. Materials such as balance beams, skipping ropes, skateboards, and tumbling mats, which are easily stored and address many of the same physical skills, may be more practical than a large climbing apparatus.

FUNCTIONALITY

Materials and equipment that do not perform the function for which they appear to have been designed easily discourage children. Play equipment and materials for groups of children should function well and with a minimum of adult intervention. The equipment or material should be built to sustain a range of exploration and testing by children, who may handle and manipulate the unit in a variety of ways. Generally, the simpler the structure of the equipment or material and the greater its freedom from unnecessary detail, the more functional it will be.

MULTIPURPOSE USE

The extent to which the playroom provides materials that have many uses and functions is usually a measure of the flexibility and play potential of the learning environment. Play materials that children can move to other learning centres and use to meet a variety of their own purposes in play hold particular interest for children and provide added versatility for children and flexibility for ECEs in their planning. Multipurpose materials are essentially creative, since children decide how to use them in their play. The more abstract the materials, such as unit blocks, hollow blocks, large blankets, planks and poles, the more complex and challenging the play may become. Materials such as tentlike structures, tunnels, Lego, and other modular sets are inherently multipurpose. The environment should contain some materials that have no intrinsic play purpose but may be used for many purposes (for example, blankets, spare chairs, sheets, flags, string and rope, pieces of hose, tires, and large and small boxes). As a general rule, the lifelike materials, such as the Fisher-Price garage and airport, are more suitable for the younger child, who is still in the "seeing is believing" stage of development. Older preschoolers who are symbolic thinkers benefit immeasurably from more abstract play materials that challenge them to make one thing represent a purpose that the child intends, instead of something dictated by the design and obvious intention of the more concrete **artifact**. Because our role as ECEs is to encourage children's ability to engage in representational thinking, it is vitally important to include in the play environment materials of an abstract nature that challenge children to use the material for their own purposes.

CHALLENGE YOUR LEARNING ABOUT PLAY MATERIALS

Visit a preschool or kindergarten and observe the play materials. List the materials that challenge children to use the play materials for their own purposes. What are the "abstract" characteristics of the materials in your list?

Economic Criteria

COST

The actual cost of equipment or a material is based on the number of times it will be used in a day or week and the length of time it will serve without repair or replacement. Higher cost does not necessarily mean higher quality or greater usefulness and effectiveness. It is usually more economical in the end, however, to pay more for play equipment and materials that will endure manipulation by many children in many different ways over many years.

The higher purchase cost of unit blocks and sturdy tricycles is usually compensated for by their greater longevity and aesthetic appeal for their entire lifetime. It may be wise to economize, instead, on supplies such as paper, paste, paint, and sand, as long as the supplies meet safety and health standards.

QUANTITY NEEDED

Quantity is another economic factor that may help ECEs decide whether to introduce a play material. Sometimes more is better. For example, the presence of one or two tricycles in a playground only causes problems; half a set of unit blocks is virtually useless for a group of children and limits play opportunities rather than expanding them. When budgets are not flexible enough to purchase a sufficient number of an item, it is often best to delay the purchase and to fundraise in order to purchase valuable play equipment and materials in sufficient quantities.

STURDINESS AND DURABILITY

Equipment and materials need to be sturdy enough to allow children to play freely without fear of breaking the item. Sometimes broken equipment or materials leave splinters or sharp edges that pose a safety hazard. When materials do break down through extensive use, they need to be repairable by an ECE or parent, to avoid an unanticipated expense for repair. Materials that are sturdy and that can be repaired easily show children how to look after and mend things when they break.

It is important to teach children the benefits of reusing materials that can be repaired and refurbished rather than to replace them. Passing equipment and materials on from one group of children to the next group teaches children to respect their playthings so that they will be preserved for continued use by others.

Aesthetic Criteria

Beautiful materials are more interesting and attractive to children. Colour, shape, size, proportion, design, and the quality of construction affect the appeal of materials and contribute to the aesthetic quality of the environment. Form, colour, and proportion influence children's choice of materials and the development of aesthetic values. One of the great lessons of the Reggio Emilia schools relates to the beauty of the environments and the materials found in them, many of which are hand-made by parents and children. The Scandinavian countries also consider beautiful materials to be an essential feature of the early learning environment. Dolls and stuffed animals with stylized or exaggerated features are often not as appealing, even to children, as more lifelike representations. Cartoon creatures hung on the walls have less aesthetic appeal and represent a distorted view of the world that ECEs should not reinforce. The presence of beautiful objects in the environment, including photos and paintings that represent reality, helps children see beauty and harmony in the everyday world around them. Through well-designed materials, children learn to appreciate how line, form, composition, and structure are relevant to the function and context in which the material will be used. Learning to respect and care for beautiful things in a meaningful context helps children become sensitive to aesthetic values and principles.

Developmental/Educational Criteria

ECEs should set up concrete play materials in a physical context that provides messages to children about what they are to learn and how they are to learn it. This is one way to ensure that the environment becomes the third teacher. For example, placing beakers, jugs, and measuring cups of different shapes on the water table provides cues to children that pouring and comparing are intended for play at the water table that day. Children may, however, simply fill and empty each container without comparing just for the pleasure of watching the water swoosh from one container to the other. They may pour water from a tall, thin beaker into a stubby measuring cup without determining that the same amount of water will fill each container. Eventually, even without adult intervention, carefully selected play materials such as these do promote the learning of concepts—in this case, the concepts of equality and volume.

Two criteria that determine the developmental and play value of materials in programs are the interest they provide for young children and their relevance to the child's everyday experience. **Interest** is a criterion that determines the extent to which children are motivated to play with materials. Usually, the most interesting materials are simple ones that can be used in various ways by children of different developmental levels. Materials should be fun and should provide children with hours of pleasure during months, or even years, of use. The most interesting materials are those that respond to the child's actions and that require the child to use his own energy, ideas, and capabilities in order to make them "work" or use them in novel ways. A pretend telephone encourages a child to speak and to manipulate the buttons or dial numbers; a sturdy wooden box can be used as a platform, for storage or as a prop.

Relevance is a measure of the extent to which a material relates to a child's cultural context and life experiences. For example, a tractor usually means less to a city child than a fire engine. Playrooms should be a microcosm of the child's world—they should include equipment and materials that are familiar and that represent everyday reality. For instance, learning about family and the child's neighbourhood is more meaningful than learning about times, places, people, and things that lie beyond the child's experience and comprehension. That is why play with realistic-looking models of dinosaurs is sometimes less meaningful for children than representations of animals, people, or things that are familiar to them in their own environments.

Relevant materials form a bridge between the world of play and the real world. They help children to understand everyday living concepts, such as family relationships, community roles, culture, festivals, and traditions and they foster role play of the adult behaviours that children associate with these props. Materials that encourage children to rehearse real-life events, such as a hospital visit, an airplane trip, a visit to the dentist, or a trip to the zoo, also help children adapt more readily to unfamiliar and potentially frightening experiences.

Play materials promote development in specific domains. For example, large and small muscles of the body, as well as manipulative and perceptual abilities, are developed when children play with hoops, beanbags, racquets, ropes, balls, and climbing apparatus. Children develop physical abilities, such as **cardiovascular stamina**, muscular endurance, **agility**, **flexibility**, and speed, as well as body awareness and **kinaesthetic discrimination**, when playing games with targets, balls, flags, and bats and cognitive development occurs, for example, when children play with specific-purpose materials that address concepts of colour, time, space, number, and size.

Reusability of Materials

Children demonstrate earnest attempts to protect and respect nature and natural resources when adults model environmentally conscious practices such as reusing materials in the classroom. Many resource books explain in detail the steps to follow in making specific-purpose play and learning materials from recycled products, e.g., Workjobs manuals. Items frequently discarded such as packaging, cardboard boxes, wood pieces, jars, magazines and fabrics may become resources for making play materials. Care should be taken, however, to avoid using materials that may contain toxic substances. Programs that reuse materials in learning centres and for storage purposes should provide bins for the collection of recyclable materials. Joint efforts by parents and ECEs provide powerful messages to children about the importance of working together to use resources sustainably.

Storing Play Materials

Storage units have an impact on the quality of the play environment. The strategic placement of storage racks, shelves, and compartments for bins containing supplies and materials makes it easier for children to think for themselves without relying on adults to choose and provide what they believe children need. Storage units should be located close to the materials and supplies they store. Specially designed shelving for materials and supplies in the Creative Arts centre, for example, will maximize the use of storage space and provide ready visibility and accessibility for children. The neat display materials in custom-crafted shelving enhances the aesthetic quality of the space. Materials should be labelled using both words and pictures on containers and shelves to make it easier for children to return them to their proper place. Many types of customized storage units for art materials, modular materials, graphic and construction supplies, and specific-purpose materials that are accessible to children, influence the flow of the program, and raise the morale and effectiveness of the ECEs.

Flexible storage units ensure that the environment has plenty of space to store materials not in use. Storage units should allow for the shelves or cupboards to become a table or counter surface; a divider between learning centres; a place to hang children's art work or posters, indicating the type of play anticipated in a learning centre; or as a prop to encourage and enhance sociodramatic play. Storage units should enhance the aesthetic quality of the classroom.

When children have access to materials and supplies within each learning centre, the ECE has more time to observe children, to facilitate their play and learning, to observe their skills in the use of the materials, and to assist them when they need help.

The Contents of Play Space

One of the most important teaching skills is to organize the contents of the play space to optimize the play and learning potential of each play unit. In a well-organized play environment all units of play have a purpose, each unit is located so as to complement the others located close by, and each unit is set up so as to give messages to children about what they might explore or do there. The programs of Reggio Emilia provide helpful examples, especially when designing a play environment from scratch instead of retro-fitting rooms that have been designed for another purpose. The Reggio Emilia schools are designed especially to reflect the values and goals of the larger community, with a central space in the school, usually with plenty of natural light, that resembles the central square so typical of Italian towns and cities. This central space serves as a crossroads among various groups of children and as a place to display children's creations and messages for parents. Natural light is an important feature of Reggio Emilia schools, and this feature is enhanced by the use of mirrors, illuminated light tables, and many large windows that can be opened to let in the light and sounds of the outside environment (New, 2005).

It is a fact of life in many Canadian schools and centres, however, that the space allocated for programs is often a church basement, recreation centre, or other facility not specifically designed for young children. Kritchevsky, Prescott, and Walling's classic book, *Planning Environments for Young Children: Physical Space* (1977), has solved many practical problems. The formulas they provided have been widely employed to optimize the use of space and to ensure that the contents of space are interesting to children, well positioned, and challenge children to engage with the play units for longer periods of time. Play space has two parts: the **contents**, which are the play units themselves, and **potential units**, which are empty spaces in a room or a yard to which a play material of one kind or another can be added. *Space planning should provide sufficient space around equipment and play materials for children to play with them effectively and this surrounding space is considered part of the play unit.*

The Variety and Complexity of the Play Environment

Knowing how to ensure sufficient variety and complexity in the environment are essential teaching skills. Play units may be classified according to their variety and complexity.

Variety

Variety is the potential of the play unit to accommodate different kinds of play activity, such as digging, pouring, building, stacking, and twirling. Variety permits children to try a number of different kinds of activity, with the result that these activities hold their interest longer and expose them to learning a wider range of skills. Measurements of the degrees of complexity and variety in an environment indicate the extent to which children will find the environment interesting and involving. *Variety relates to the number of different kinds of play units in the playroom or playground that invite diverse types of activity.* When ECEs expect children to play for long periods in an area and to make their own choices about what to play with, variety becomes an important factor in planning. Insufficient variety limits children's choices and reduces interest and participation. ECEs can evaluate the variety of the environment by assessing the kinds of play possible for each play unit; this provides an overall sense of the variety offered by the play activities available throughout the playroom. The following analysis offers a range of variety in play for 12 children depending on how long the children will be using the playground. Greater variety is required when children are expected to play in an area for a long period.

EXAMPLE

A playground for preschoolers has 12 riding vehicles, a rocking boat, a tumble tub, a climbing apparatus with boxes and boards, a dirt area with scooper trucks, and a sand table with shovels. The ECE's task is to link the variety, the time allocated for play, and the number of children present and determine if there is sufficient variety.

Analysis of variety:

- vehicles—riding, balancing, pedalling
- rocking boat—rocking, climbing, pretending
- climber with boxes and boards—climbing, stacking, hauling, building
- dirt area with scooper trucks—digging, pushing, loading, scooping, emptying, pretending
- sand table with shovels—digging, scooping, pouring, comparing, mixing

Complexity

Complexity measures the capacity of the indoor and outdoor play environment to keep children interested for a reasonable time. Complexity is calculated by determining the potential of each play unit for active manipulation by children. The addition of accessories or sub-parts to play units produces greater complexity.

When preschool children are expected to play for more than 20 minutes in a playroom, a high degree of complexity adds to the amount of choice available to children and makes the environment more interesting. The degree of complexity will normally decrease for older children and increase for younger children. Older children usually have more mature attending skills such as longer attention spans. If an area is insufficiently complex, ECEs often have to compensate through their own active participation or intervention, a factor that may compromise the quality of the play. Groups of toddlers (up to 30 months of age) in an environment for 20 minutes or longer may require five or six play places per child. Three- and four-year-olds require approximately three to four play places each, while five- and six-year-olds may require two to three play places per child for a play period of about one hour.

RECOMMENDED NUMBER OF PLAY PLACES

18–30 months of age	5–6 play places
3- and 4-year-olds	3–4 play places
5- and 6-year-olds	2–3 play places

Units of Play: Simple, Complex, and Super Units

Kritchevsky et al. (1977) identify three types of play units: simple units, complex units, and super units. Each type varies in its capacity to keep children interested and in the number of children it can accommodate for play at one time. The ECE's ability to identify and create simple, complex, and super units in the environment, and to locate them strategically to promote purposeful play are important teaching skills. It is in knowing what type of play unit is needed, where to place it, and how to furnish it to engage children's attention that the ECE becomes the expert professional who can treat materials and equipment flexibly, optimize the value of the contents of the playroom, and ultimately provide the most stimulating environment for play and learning. ECEs should know how many play places they have created in each centre and the ratio of play places to the number of children who will be playing in the environment.

Knowing the importance of the organization of the environment for play and learning and of optimizing the environment's potential as the third teacher, it is practical for ECEs to become familiar with the descriptions of each play unit and its potential for play in order to be fully in command of the environment at all times; to be able to modify the environment at a moment's notice; and to explain clearly to parents and others how the environment is contributing to the quality of children's play and, thereby, to their development and learning.

SIMPLE UNITS

A simple unit has one primary purpose in play and is generally used by one child at a time for the intended purpose (Kritchevsky et al., 1977). Usually, it does not have sub-parts. A child's drum, telephone, spinning top, and tricycle are examples of materials used in relatively fixed ways. Some simple units, such as a tape player, a cash register with coins, and a Rock-A-Stack, have component parts but still exist for one main play purpose. As play with a simple unit will usually accommodate only one child at a time, a simple unit is allocated one play place in calculating the complexity of the play environment. Simple unit = one play place.

COMPLEX UNITS

A complex unit is "a play unit with sub-parts or a juxtaposition of two essentially different play materials which enable the child to manipulate or improvise" (Kritchevsky et al., 1977, p. 11). Complex units are allocated four play places in the calculation of complexity. A dollhouse with furniture, a doctor's kit and dolls, a water table with containers for pouring and measuring, and a puppet theatre with hand puppets are examples of complex units with built-in flexibility for various styles and types of play. Complex units require sufficient space for a small group of children to use the same material, either cooperatively or independently. Complex units of play can be created by combining two or more simple units or by adding simple units to one that is complex. When two or more simple units, such as a telephone and note pads, or a tape recorder and a few sets of earphones, are placed together, a complex unit has been created. Complex unit = 4 play places.

SUPER UNITS

A super unit is "a complex unit which has one or more additional play materials, i.e., three or more play materials juxtaposed" (Kritchevsky et al., 1977, p. 11). For example, ECEs and children may create super units by adding boxes, ramps, and boards to a climber in the Active Role Play centre, or by combining a cash register, a telephone, a counter, and shelves stocked with grocery boxes and tins to make a supermarket. Super units are usually the play stations that have been set up by either the ECE or the children for sociodramatic play. These would include a hospital or doctor's office super unit, an office super unit, or a hairdresser's super unit. Super units may be set up in potential space in the classroom and are often close to the role play zone or the office area in the Project centre. A super unit is usually allocated six to eight play places in calculating complexity if the space in which the super unit is set up can reasonably accommodate six to eight children. Super unit = six to eight play places.

Adding blankets and tables to the playhouse area outdoors or creating a post office in the Project centre by setting up a counter and a desk with stamps, envelopes, and a mail slot are examples of super units that ECEs or children may create. Often, the best ideas for creating super units come from the children themselves. A super unit accommodates the most children at once and usually holds their interest the longest, as it provides the potential for sociodramatic play. Six or up to eight children can usually play together in super units. The role of super units in promoting sociodramatic play cannot be over-emphasized; there are few better ways to promote the development of literacy and thinking abilities and for children to use imagery, invent scripts, collaborate, solve problems, and revise strategies as they develop their sociodramatic play episodes. Super units provide exceptionally rich settings for play that helps children understand a wide range of social skills—such as how to enter group play; how to cooperate; how to take turns, listen, and respond; how to go with the flow and give and take—skills that are especially important for children from homes where there is stress, poverty, or other factors that inhibit social learning. All environments for preschool and kindergarten children should contain at least one super unit at all times, and these should change with children's interests and individual developmental needs.

CALCULATING COMPLEXITY

The first step in calculating the complexity of a learning environment is to identify the play units in the playroom or playground as simple, complex, or super units. Each unit is then assigned either one, four, or six to eight play places, depending on whether it is a simple, complex, or super unit. The number of children accommodated in the super unit will usually depend on the amount of space available for the unit. The number of play places is added up, and the total is then divided by the number of children in the play environment. The **quotient** indicates the number of available play places per child, which is the measure of complexity of the playroom or play zone.

EXAMPLE

The number of play places in the environment when all simple, complex, and super units have been counted is 34. There are 16 preschoolers playing in the environment at any given time. When you divide 34 play places by 16 children you have 2.1 play places for each preschooler. When you refer to the table on page 106 that indicates the optimum number of play places that an environment should provide for each preschooler in order to ensure sufficient complexity, you will see that the environment described in this example is not sufficiently complex as three to four play places per child are required. The ECE's task is then to add approximately 14 to 18 more play places to the environment in order to ensure that it is sufficiently complex. In reality, how many play places the ECE will add depends on the space available in the playroom and the learning centre. He may decide to add two more super units if there is sufficient space, or he may add four more complex units to the space to increase the number of play places. If your program is located in cramped quarters, the potential of the program to accommodate sufficient complexity is limited. This makes decisions related to the location of the preschool or kindergarten play and learning environment highly dependent on the total amount of space needed to accommodate sufficient variety and complexity in order to optimize the environment's play and learning potential.

CALCULATING COMPLEXITY

simple unit = 1 play place
complex unit = 4 play places
super unit = 6 to 8 play places

1. Identify play units as simple, complex, or super.
2. Assign the number of play places to each play unit.
3. Calculate the total number of play places set up in the play and learning environment.
4. Divide the total number of play places by the number of children in the environment. The answer you get is the quotient. For example, 34 ÷ 16 = 2.1 (the quotient).
5. The quotient is the indicator of complexity, that is, 2.1 play places per child.
6. Check the indicator of complexity against the recommended number of play places per child (see p. 106)

It is important that ECEs overcome any math anxiety they may have in order to master the technicalities involved in planning play and learning environments. Here is an example of the calculation of complexity in the environment.

EXAMPLE

A learning environment for 16 three-year-olds playing for one hour contains the following play units arranged in five learning centres:

- a one-metre-square water table with jugs and plastic bottles (1 complex unit = 4 play places)
- string painting at a round table for four (4 simple units = 4 play places)
- four single-sided easels (4 simple units = 4 play places)
- a small listening centre with two headsets (1 simple unit = 2 play places)
- a climber with slide, firefighter's pole, and helmets (1 super unit = 6 or 8 play places)
- a table and four chairs with a tea set (1 complex unit = 4 play places)
- two sets of unit blocks with wooden accessories (1 complex unit = 4 play places)
- four hoops (4 simple units = 4 play places)
- a beanbag target toss with four beanbags (1 complex unit = 4 play places)

The number of play places in the example above is calculated by adding the amounts in parentheses together: 4 + 4 + 4 + 2 + 8 + 4 + 4 + 4 + 4 = 38 play places (or 36 play places if the super unit accommodates six children).

To determine the complexity of the learning environment, the total number of play places (38) is divided by the number of children who will be playing in the area at one time (16). The quotient provides the number of play places available per child, which is 2.4. This is the measure of complexity.

Do 2.4 play places per three-year-old child in this play environment represent sufficient complexity? The guidelines suggest that three-year-olds require between three and four play places per child. Therefore, we conclude that this learning environment has insufficient complexity and that additional play units need to be added. The ECE's task is to decide how many more complex units to add to the space and whether or not there is sufficient space and interest on the part of children to add another super unit. When an environment cannot accommodate sufficient complexity, either the number of children playing in the environment should be reduced or more space should be added. Too often, the solution that is adopted, sometimes out of necessity, is to restrict children's choices of play activities or to introduce longer periods in adult-directed large-group activities. These solutions tend to contradict the purpose and goals of early childhood programs.

The scenario in the preceding example is often seen in real learning environments. Frequently, the causes of aggressive or restless behaviour and mindless flitting about can be traced to insufficient complexity in a learning environment. When they have discovered the cause, ECEs have to determine which other units of play to add and where to locate them, keeping in mind the need to adhere to guidelines with respect to pathways and amount of covered versus uncovered space, and so on (Chapter 7). It is important to remember that the variety and complexity of the play and learning environment have a direct influence on children's play behaviours. *When the balance of variety and complexity is optimal, the need for ECEs to intervene to guide children's behaviour is minimized.*

The guidelines with respect to the number of play places for the units of play should not always be taken literally. For example, a climber with ramps and hollow blocks (super unit) may be located in a space that accommodates only four or six children. A table with a dollhouse, furniture, and small dolls (complex unit) may have only enough space to accommodate three children. Using good judgment and the guidelines, ECEs can determine an approximate indication of the degree of complexity in the environment. When too much or too little complexity exists, they will be able to make appropriate amendments by following the Kritchevsky, Prescott, and Walling formulas.

Summary

Equipment, materials, and supplies are the tools of the trade in early childhood education. Effective early childhood education depends on the ECE's ability to match materials and supplies to the categories and social stages of play intended and to the developmental levels and needs of each child. Well-designed learning environments ensure there is a balance of specific-purpose and open-ended materials to promote a wide range of developmental abilities. ECEs need to select materials according to specific practical, economic, developmental, and aesthetic criteria. Storing play materials close to the centres where they are used most frequently encourages children's independence in learning and frees ECEs to observe and facilitate children's play. *Ensuring that the equipment, materials, and supplies represent the diverse cultures of the children and families in the program promotes inclusive practice.* Calculating the complexity of the play environment enhances the quality and duration of children's play. Ensuring sufficient variety in the environment motivates interest and children's active participation. These are important skills for ECEs to master.

LEARNING ACTIVITIES

1. In a preschool or kindergarten, which may be your field placement, make an inventory of the play materials and equipment. Augment your inventory by consulting equipment and materials catalogues. Create a detailed inventory of play materials and equipment suitable for children ages two to six. Choose categories from those used in this textbook to classify the various types of play materials—for example, open-ended, specific-purpose, and two-dimensional/three-dimensional materials. Consult the chapters related to the various learning centres for ideas for play materials. Leave plenty of blank space in your inventory to make additions and to jot down ideas for adapting materials and for using them for several purposes. Ensure that your inventory includes a selection of equipment and materials that may be adapted easily for children with special needs and check that the range of play materials is culturally diverse and inclusive. Repeat this activity for the outdoor play environment.
2. Create an inventory of various types of storage units that encourage multiple uses and provide aesthetically appealing additions to the environment. Use current equipment catalogues to augment your inventory. Evaluate the materials in your inventory (from Learning Activity 1) to ensure that the majority of the materials would respond to children's actions on them. Revise your inventory to ensure there is a mix of convergent and divergent materials, three-dimensional and two-dimensional materials, as well as plenty of continuous and free-form materials.

3. Visit a preschool or kindergarten classroom. Identify the units of play in the room as simple, complex, or super units. Calculate the number of play places. Determine the complexity of the play and learning environment by dividing the number of play places by the number of children using the space at the time of your visit. For how long were the children expected to play in the environment? Was there sufficient complexity? Explain your answer. What changes would you make to ensure that the complexity of the environment is sufficient to interest and engage the children?
4. Determine the variety of the learning environment you have visited. List the activities and materials you would add to augment the variety. Indicate how the variety of the play has been enhanced by the materials and activities you have added.

7 Planning Space and Learning Centres

"Children develop only as the environment demands development."

—Mandel Sherman and Cora B. Key,
"The Intelligence of Isolated Mountain Children" (1932)

Before Reading This Chapter, Have You

- understood the play potential of various types of play materials?
- differentiated simple, complex, and super units of play?
- determined the variety and complexity of play environments?

Outcomes

After reading and understanding this chapter, you should be able to

- provide a rationale for the organization of space, the placement of storage units, and the creation of pathways to facilitate play and learning;
- apply principles for the location and design of learning centres;
- explain the role of play zones in the design of the play and learning environment; and
- conduct a Learning Environment Audit (Appendix B).

Many models exist for planning play space that reflects the culture and values in which they operate. Reggio Emilia schools, for example, provide environments that reflect an emphasis on relationships; collaboration in order to achieve collective aims; and respect for a wide range of ideas, divergent thinking, and creative expression. These values are also reflected in the attention the Reggio Emilia schools pay to problem-based curriculum and project learning. North American values, in contrast, often emphasize preparing children for academic success in school, the development of social skills, and communication with others. These values are visible in the attention paid to individual performance, language and literacy, and getting along well with others. The design of space should be closely linked to the values and priorities of the program.

The Function of Learning Centres

A **learning centre** is a clearly defined area that houses equipment, materials, and supplies that promote similar categories of play and social contexts of play and where the materials complement one another. Learning centres have visible boundaries, a predictable climate for play, and emphasize play related to developmental outcomes. For example, the Active Role Play centre emphasizes cooperative role play in groups with enough space for children to be active and move about freely. The Quiet Thinking centre encourages children to play individually at activities that require concentration, individual effort, and the development of learning-to-learn skills. Exceptions occur frequently and no hard and fast rules should be imposed. Children decide the nature of their play and choose the materials that support their play, and choice requires flexibility in how the learning centres are used. There are many approaches to organizing space and planning learning centres. A developmental rationale provides a framework for combining child development theory, play theory, principles of learning, and diversity considerations. Space constraints, however, sometimes challenge the implementation of an "ideal" plan, and common sense must prevail.

The learning centre approach "provides an intentional strategy for the active involvement of children, experience-based learning and individualization in relation to children's developmental abilities, interests, and learning styles" (Myers & Maurer, 1987, p. 21). Well-organized and well-defined learning centres provide messages to children about the behaviours, the kinds of activities, and the level of involvement expected of them (Houle, 1987; Ministry of Education, Ontario, 2010; NAEYC, 2009). Frost, Wortham, and Reifel (2005) advocate a logical arrangement of learning centres, which increases the frequency and quality of play and promotes learning. Early childhood education in the United Kingdom and Australia has, for over a decade, linked learning centres to the outcomes explicit within the curriculum (MacNaughton, 2003). A logical arrangement is one in which compatible materials are close together and set apart from incompatible materials and equipment. A well-designed classroom frees the ECE to observe children and to facilitate their play and learning, rather than resort to direct teaching or a supervisory role. A variety of activities are set up daily in each learning centre. Children are motivated to choose from these activities when ECEs include them in planning and encourage them to express their interests and to suggest what they would like to play and do.

Learning Centres Support Specific Categories of Play

The learning centre is the basic unit of classroom organization. Its main purpose is to organize space, equipment, materials, and supplies so that children know what tools are available for them and what kinds of play are possible in the learning centre. Promoting specific kinds of play in each learning centre makes it easier for ECEs to observe and interpret children's play and to assess the developmental progress they are making. Learning and development, however, are not always so neatly organized. What children learn and how they develop are rarely determined by boundaries or by divisions of space and resources. Yet, clearly defined learning centres do help ECEs and children to optimize the space available and ensure that the environment provides a wide spectrum of play opportunities. A key challenge is to ensure that the developmental outcomes identified in the curriculum (see Chapter 9) are linked directly to the design of learning centres and to the categories, stages, and social contexts of play encouraged in each centre (see Table 7–1).

TABLE 7–1

LINKS AMONG OUTCOMES, LEARNING CENTRES, AND PLAY

Developmental Outcomes	Learning Centres	Major Categories of Play	Stages/Social Contexts of Play	Play Materials (examples):
Social-Emotional:				
pro-social skills social relations social perceptions expressing self early moral understanding self-regulation empathy with others	Daily Living Active Role Play Outdoor active areas	imitative practice productive pretend/dramatic sociodramatic fantasy	onlooking solitary parallel associative cooperative	housekeeping equipment doll beds table and chairs dressup clothing/props musical instruments hollow blocks ramps, etc.
Physical:				
basic movements physical abilities perceptual skills body awareness skilled movements	Active Role Play Creative Arts outdoor active areas large muscle vehicle trails open areas	symbolic dramatic sociodramatic creative-constructive games-with-rules	solitary parallel cooperative competitive	hollow blocks ramps boards climber playhouse props musical instruments balance beam trampoline
Cognitive:				
memory basic concepts attending skills learning-to-learn skills sensory-perceptual skills problem solving language/logical thinking creative thinking symbolic thinking representation	Quiet Thinking Creative Arts Project Centre Science Discovery Unit Blocks	practice productive symbolic creative-constructive reproductive sociodramatic fantasy	solitary parallel associative cooperative competitive	books water/sand table discovery table exploring table theme table Workjobs puzzles/board games modular materials other specific purpose materials unit blocks and accessories computer props arts materials/paints, clay, wood/fabric

ECEs influence the styles of play that will occur in a learning centre by setting up materials and activities and by organizing storage units to provide messages about what children are likely to play and do in that centre. Children should choose the learning centre where they want to play. Some ECEs conduct a planning circle soon after children arrive in the morning, let the children know what is available in the learning centres that day, and then let them select where they want to play. Others prefer to put up planning boards with depictions of the various centres on cards, which children can carry with them and deposit in a rack near the **play station**.

Children may also opt to return to a project begun earlier or to begin one with an ECE, who helps them assemble the materials they need.

Each learning centre may accommodate two or three activities with the materials and supplies needed; children decide which activities they will play with and how they will play. Children also have the option of choosing their own play activity by accessing materials from storage shelves and setting them up. Their choices determine, to a great extent, what the outcomes of their play will be, even when they choose activities that have already been set up by the ECE. *The learning centres are an organized and complex juxtaposition of complementary and integrated resources for play designed to enrich play and to move children further in their development.* Although the outcomes are not predictable in any precise way, the careful selection and arrangement of materials for activities enhance the probability that certain outcomes will be achieved.

Learning Centres Support Child Development

Learning centres address a comprehensive range of developmental outcomes based on the normal tasks of development in the social, emotional, physical, and cognitive domains to help children make progress across all domains. Developmental outcomes provide input to the organization of space and curriculum design. The location and organization of learning centres should reflect the individual needs of children in the group, as determined by the ECE's observations and assessments and, of course, the space available to the program. Therefore, early childhood playrooms will not all have the same learning centres, nor will the same proportion of total space be allocated to specific learning centres from program to program. The configuration, the space that is allocated, and the contents of the learning centres will vary from program to program, depending on children's identified needs and on the specific developmental outcomes stated in the program curriculum.

The identification of developmental objectives through the systematic observation and assessment of each child's progress is essential knowledge for planning and setting up learning centres. The distinction between developmental outcomes and developmental objectives is addressed in Chapter 9. Table 7–1 shows the potential links between developmental outcomes and learning centres, as well as between categories of play, social stages and contexts of play, and units of play. The criteria for selecting appropriate learning materials for each centre were addressed in Chapter 6. Grouping equipment, materials, and activities developmentally promotes the learning potential of each unit of play by locating it near others with related developmental objectives. A rational arrangement helps children see the relationships between their interests and ideas and the activities, and between materials and play opportunities.

EMOTIONAL DEVELOPMENT

Play experiences that promote emotional development encourage children to express themselves using a variety of media and methods and to interact, communicate, cooperate, care, wonder, and reflect. When learning centres offer opportunities for children to be successful in the play that they pursue, children gain emotional control and feel a sense of self-worth based on their achievements. This means that materials and activities should be matched to the developing abilities and the emotional needs of each child in the program. Not all activities are planned and intended for all children; ECEs may encourage a child to become involved in the activities best suited to her needs. When she chooses an activity beyond her developing capacity, the ECE offers support and encouragement or simplifies the activity sufficiently to allow the child to feel a sense of progress, if not ultimate success. Care must be taken, however, not to remove all elements of challenge, as children also need to persist in their efforts when confronted with obstacles. Emotional self-regulation and self-esteem are largely fostered by children's successful involvements socially, physically, and cognitively. Emotional and mental health needs are met, to a large extent, by children's individual sense that they have some control over their environment, that they are able to succeed in the environment, and that their caregivers care passionately about them and their progress (Katz, 1974).

SOCIAL DEVELOPMENT

Between the ages of two and six, children have to master certain developmental tasks to build a strong foundation for later development and learning, and their social development is a key to successful learning. Children are developing a sense of self through many forms of self-expression, are learning to communicate, and are acquiring socially desirable ways of interacting and cooperating. Play is essential to the social well-being of the developing child. Children need opportunities to interact with each other and to conform to group requirements established by persons or events outside of themselves. Often children require support as they cope with the harsh realities of the group, where the needs and interests are varied and adult attention must be shared. Children differ widely in their ability to adapt to the group and to learn the complex skills associated with successful social interactions, and not all children are eager group players. This is particularly true of children whose contact with other children has been limited. Children need opportunities to practise their social skills in many types of environments, indoors and outdoors, and these play opportunities, like all others, should be planned according to the needs of the individual child and not on the assumption that everyone enjoys groups. Play and social development outdoors will be addressed in Chapter 22.

PHYSICAL DEVELOPMENT

Physical development includes sensory and perceptual experience, motor skills, fitness, body awareness and health, and physical abilities. All learning centres contribute to a range of physical skills. The Creative Arts centre primarily promotes sensory-perceptual and **fine motor skills**; the Active Role Play centre primarily encourages motor development, coordination, and physical abilities; and the Daily Living centre usually facilitates body awareness, spatial awareness, and motor skills. The Quiet Thinking and Project centres mainly foster development of sensory-perceptual, fine motor skills, and coordination. Unit blocks challenge children's perceptual, fine, and gross motor skills; coordination; and balance. Outdoor play provides opportunities for freer bodily expression and for mastery in all areas—sensory skills, muscular development, coordination, perceptual awareness, and fitness. Playgrounds should promote children's contact with nature while offering freedom for children to run, jump, and climb and develop their physical abilities and motor and coordination skills (see Chapter 22). Playgrounds in Canada need attention to ensure that they compensate for the confined lifestyles, especially of inner-city children who do not have regular opportunities for spontaneous play outdoors unless they are supervised by adults. These children are sometimes at risk of impaired physical development and health problems later in life.

COGNITIVE DEVELOPMENT

Cognitive development includes acquiring skills related to perceptual processing, memory, attending abilities, logical reasoning, language and communication, conceptual understanding, knowledge related to everyday living (**conventional knowledge**), and problem solving. All learning centres provide opportunities for cognitive development. Ginsburg, Inoiue, and Seo (1999) found that young children acquire complex mathematical concepts and conduct mathematical operations when play activities incorporate the underlying skills and concepts related to numbers and math, such as building with blocks or construction sets. Play promotes a wide range of academic skills needed for children to succeed in school, such as emotional self-regulation, delayed gratification, taking another's perspective, taking turns, flexible thinking, sequencing the order of events, and recognizing one's independence from others (Singer, Plaskon, & Schweder, 2003). Smilansky and Shefatya (1990) believed that symbolic play, including dramatic and sociodramatic role play, are especially rich in their ability to promote cognitive development. Cognitive skills are also addressed during outdoor play, where children use language and interact more readily, exercise their bodies with abandon, receive an abundance of sensory messages, grapple with the cognitive challenges of games and team activities, learn to assess risk, and plan grandiose construction projects with naturally occurring objects.

The Seven Indoor Learning Centres

This textbook describes seven indoor learning centres. Programs may choose to have more or fewer learning centres, and much of the decision will rest on the amount of space available to the program, as well as the developmental outcomes of the curriculum and the priorities of the parents and the program. There are also several outdoor learning centres; these will be described in Chapter 22.

Daily Living Centre

This centre supports and encourages dramatic play and children's active representation of the life around them. Sometimes referred to as the "household play" or housekeeping area, this centre facilitates role play and dramatization, which means that social interaction, collaboration, and cooperation are encouraged. The Daily Living centre comprises several play areas or play stations: household play; dolls area; a dressup corner; sometimes a puppet theatre; and, ideally, space for a potential unit, all of which support interaction and communication in small groups. Kritchevsky, Prescott, and Walling (1977, p. 9) define potential units as "empty space which is surrounded in large part by visible and/or tangible boundaries."

Active Role Play Centre

This centre also features dramatic and sociodramatic play; it encourages active role play in a larger space that allows for active movement, social interaction, and larger-scale activities such as musical shows, parades, construction with hollow blocks, and large muscle play. Where space allows, an indoor climber or playhouse may be a centrepiece that supports expansive role play, including **superhero play**.

Musical instruments are often stored in this area to encourage children to add music to their play. This learning centre might also include space for a potential unit or super unit such as a stage and musical props, a spaceship, or a construction site.

Quiet Thinking Centre

This centre encourages individual play with materials designed to promote language, literacy, numeracy, learning-to-learn skills, and thinking. Although children may also play together at a game or a puzzle, or read a book to another child, this centre is generally intended for play that requires the mastery of attending skills such as task orientation (focusing on the task at hand), avoiding distraction, and completing what a child starts. Therefore, this centre usually includes a book nook; a puzzle table; a display table; a number and math play station; tabletop blocks and interlocking materials such as parquetry or Lego; and, possibly, a corner for Workjobs (Chapter 17).

Project Centre

This centre is the technology "hub" of the environment, which may house one or two computers and a printer; a listening table with audio equipment; a viewing centre with a projector for slides and possibly an old View-Master; an office area; storage for various books, CDs, DVDs; and a project corner with a table. The project area emphasis of this centre implies social interaction, collaboration on projects, and busy dynamics. The equipment, materials, and supplies in this learning centre teach children about organizing and storing materials for easy access and use in projects, the importance of research, and the various tools and supplies that make project work easier and the products more satisfying.

Creative Arts Centre

This centre is one of the busiest, as it provides space, materials, and supplies for children to create their representations and productions, using a wide range of visual arts media and plastic materials, such as clay and papier mâché. Ideally, space should allow for setting up an art area for drawing and painting with at least two easels, tables for wet and dry art, a workbench, a sewing table, a marble slab for clay, and an area for cardboard construction and perhaps mural-making, which requires more space. Play in this centre calls for storage units for supplies and counter space and hangers for drying and displaying children's works of art.

Unit Blocks Centre

This centre should not be omitted from any preschool or kindergarten environment, as it is a key space for encouraging representational thinking, which is especially important for the four- to-six-year-old. All that is required is a square space, bounded on three sides by shelves or low walls to contain the unit blocks; a soft but flat, tightly woven carpet; and two sets of unit blocks. Unfortunately, too many programs sacrifice this space in favour of adding to other learning centres, and they do not recognize what they are losing in terms of its unique potential for play, development, and learning. Primarily an area for social interaction and collaboration on construction projects that involve divergent thinking, creativity, spatial intelligence, logical thinking, problem solving, communication, and a host of other developmental skills, this centre is noisy and busy and needs to be thoughtfully located. If space in the main playroom does not allow, this centre may be located in a separate but nearby room, perhaps alongside the Active Role Play centre. Chapter 20 outlines the function and layout of the Unit Blocks centre.

Science Discovery Centre

This centre encourages curiosity, investigation, and inquiry using a wide range of natural and manufactured materials and allows for individual pursuits as well as collaborative play and projects. It houses the wet and dry sand tables; the water play table; an exploring table; a resource and discovery display table; a potential unit that may allow for setting up a seasonal display; possibly an aquarium, pet corner, and terrarium; and space for storing supplies and materials. Ideally, this centre will include a water source and may be located next to the Creative Arts centre in order to share the sink and taps. Expanded space in this centre allows for projects and experiments with larger items of equipment, such as ramps and pulleys.

In summary, learning centres are intended to enhance the quality of play and put the child at the centre of the environment. They expose play and learning opportunities, rather than closing options for children. Effective planning of learning centres frees the ECE to observe and facilitate children's play and learning. A beautiful, comfortable setting with a place for everything and space to move freely is more likely to be maintained and to promote learning, whereas a crowded, haphazard environment offers little incentive and no precedent for children in their daily activities. Learning centres also foster behaviours that promote participation in play activities. The ECE has to decide how to schedule routines, what rules to establish for appropriate behaviour in learning centres, how to convey clearly the limits on behaviour, and how many learning centres to introduce or change at one time. ECEs should keep a list of the limits that have been explained to children and of those which need reminders. The learning centre that provides clear messages to children about the kind of behaviour that is anticipated is the most effective guidance strategy that ECEs employ. *When the activities available in each learning centre are at the children's level, are interesting to them, change at appropriate times, and are relevant to their daily lives, the frequency with which ECEs have to intervene in children's play in order to guide children's behaviour diminishes.*

Locating the Play and Learning Environment

The location of the playroom and the arrangement of physical space should foster a strong relationship between play and the developmental outcomes of the program. The environment should provide space for five main types of play experiences: (1) quiet, calm play; (2) play with structured materials; (3) discovery play with constructive, expressive, creative materials; (4) dramatic and sociodramatic play; (5) play involving gross motor activities. Each area should accommodate children with disabilities. One school of thought suggests that smaller, partially partitioned areas within learning centres for specific kinds of play activities may support higher quality play (Christie & Johnsen, 1987).

Indoor learning centres often represent some aspects of the adult world. For example, a well-designed household play area for three-year-olds will likely have miniature versions of household appliances, cupboards, tables, and chairs. Familiar miniature models of things found at home, such as an ironing board and iron, a telephone, clothes racks, dolls' beds, a mirror, and a rocking chair, contribute to the homelike setting and support dramatic play. Four- and five-year-olds need a flexible area that allows for relational role play and representation with the help of props that replicate aspects of the adult world. The office area in the Project centre contains computers and other devices that replicate a real office, such as printers, projectors, cameras, and audio equipment.

Decisions regarding the location of the play environment within a school or centre are usually the first and the most important ones to be made in planning a program. Sometimes the options are few, especially if a program is borrowing space from a school, apartment block, church, or community centre. Many questions should be asked when deciding where to locate the play environment. Where are the access points (entrances and exits, gates, walkways, and parking spaces) of the building located? Are direct entry and exit possible from the street, parking lot, and playground? Where are the emergency exits? On what floor of the building is the program located, and how easily can children manage stairs if there are some? Where are the washrooms, the gymnasium or active play area, and the cloakroom? Where does natural light enter the play space? Most important of all, how many children will be using the space at any given time and what is the ratio of space to the number of play units needed in order to ensure sufficient complexity and variety in the play and learning environment?

Ideally, an indoor learning environment for young children will have one room large enough to accommodate all the children at one time, and include space for all or most learning centres that may be partially partitioned by storage units or other equipment or furniture. When space is at a premium, a gross motor play area for active, physical play may have to be located outside the main playroom. Program planners who have to cope with several small rooms that will accommodate only two or three learning centres at a time should be particularly careful to ensure that the centres located in one small room are compatible. When active play areas are placed close to quiet, solitary-play areas, noise and high levels of physical activity may disturb the quiet play of children who are engaged in activities that require concentration. Imposing rules in environmentally-induced situations such as these lessens the freedom and the independence of the children in the program and diminishes the quality of play.

Organizing Space: The Play Zones

Before locating the learning centres, ECEs should consider the various **play zones** in the overall space occupied by the program. Defining the play zones is an important first step in planning the physical layout of the playroom. Play zones locate similar categories, styles, stages, and contexts of play adjacent to or close to each other as much as possible. Organizing the environment according to zones that accommodate complementary learning centres minimizes the distractions for children while they are playing and promotes the transfer of learning from one centre to another.

When children are able to transfer the learning gained in one context to another context, ECEs can be reasonably sure that real learning has occurred (Piaget, 1969).

For example, children who explore concepts of measurement at the water table may decide to test similar concepts at the sand table. Activities related to comparisons of size and measurement, for example, may be set up at a table in the Quiet Thinking centre; in the Project centre, using a software package or a children's website related to size and measurement; or in the Unit Blocks centre. This transfer of the learning gained in one centre to another centre reinforces learning and teaches children that there are usually many different ways to find answers, to understand a concept, and to solve similar problems.

Zones provide cues to children about the kind of play expected in each area of the classroom. Zones also help ECEs organize equipment, storage units, and play materials close to where they will be used, for maximum efficiency. Zones are designed to accommodate a type or category of play that is encouraged, more than the domain of development and the specific developmental outcomes they address. Three potential play zones are the **role play zone**, the **concept learning zone**, and the **creative discovery zone** (see Figure 7–1).

Role Play Zone

The role play zone may also be called the *social* or *interactive* zone, since this is where children are encouraged to play together while they engage in pretend play, acting out roles familiar to them in their daily lives. This zone is pivotal in the development of cognitive capabilities, especially the ability to use symbols; to engage in symbolic thinking; and to represent with the help of props for pretend, dramatic, and sociodramatic play. This zone is also the most physically active area in the playroom because the emphasis is on "doing," constructing, and active movement where space allows. The two learning centres that make up this zone, where social interaction predominates, are the Daily Living centre and the Active Role Play centre. Preschool and kindergarten children are encouraged to be interdependent in their play as they pretend and recreate roles observed in their everyday lives, as they represent their imaginings with actions (as in fantasy play), and as they evolve a script familiar to

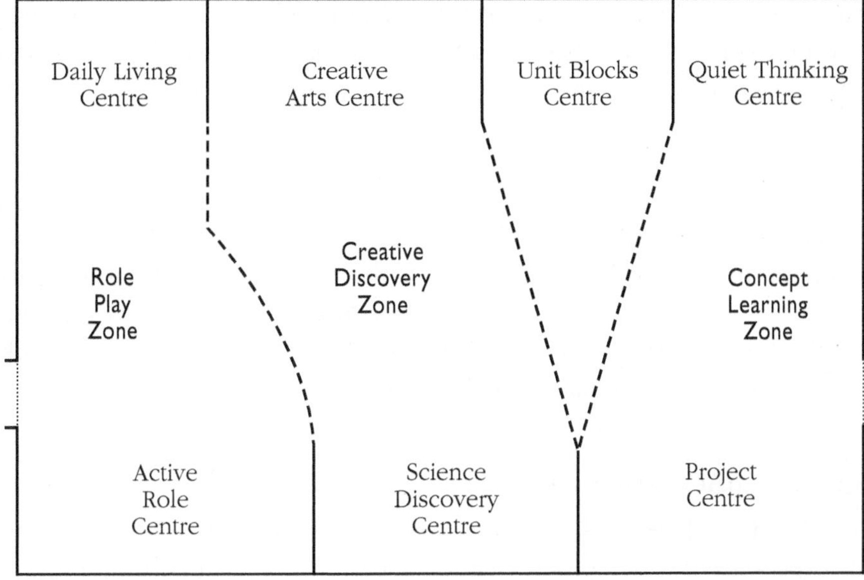

Figure 7–1
Play zones

them during their sociodramatic play episodes. Dramatic or sociodramatic play may occur elsewhere and need not be confined to the role play zone, but ensuring that there is a zone that encourages role play is a key organizational principle. Perhaps, most important of all, is the role of this zone in fostering self-expression, children's ability to interpret the world close to them; as such, it is a key zone for observing children's emotional and mental health and their interactive skills.

Concept Learning Zone

Young children also like to play alone sometimes, and reasons have been stated earlier in this book for encouraging them to do so for part of each day. Although most programs place a high value on children's social play, children also need to play individually and to engage in worthwhile solitary pursuits, especially if they spend a large part of each day in group programs. Children need to experience the satisfaction of single-handed achievement, which can be fully realized only when they tackle activities and persist with challenges on their own. Individual pursuit of goals and perseverance with challenging activities are the primary builders of the **learning-to-learn skills**. The play environment should dedicate space where children can play individually with specific-purpose materials that help them to learn concepts and symbols and to practise fine motor, manipulative, and perceptual skills. When a child experiments alone with modular materials, she is challenged to develop her own ideas and to figure out how to realize her own plans. When children are involved in solitary, self-directed, and small-group play, adults' time with individual children is often maximized.

This zone encourages quiet, individual play with specific-purpose activities, which address cognitive, perceptual, and fine motor skills, and modular construction materials. In the Quiet Thinking centre, children learn by manipulating two- and three-dimensional concrete materials. The concepts or skills to be learned are embedded in the materials themselves. Formboard puzzles; classification and seriation kits; pre-math and pre-reading activities; and a host of modular construction materials, such as Lego, are meant for individual tabletop play. A Project centre may be located near the Quiet Thinking centre in the concept learning zone to promote the transference of skills and concepts practised with the concrete materials. In the Project centre, children are able to transfer the conceptual and perceptual learning gained with concrete materials to the computer screen using programs and websites that provide similar challenges.

Although children may go to the concept learning zone to play alone or with others and to master objectives individually or together, it is understood that play in this zone is not boisterous and that greater attention to the task (task orientation) is required. Projects that require children to use office materials and equipment and the computer usually involve collaboration with others, but the play is quieter than in other zones. Children practise and master concepts in all learning centres, but the concept learning zone promotes the development of learning-to-learn, thinking, problem-solving, and attending skills that will last a lifetime.

Creative Discovery Zone

Children need ample opportunity to express themselves and to represent the world as they experience it with a variety of open-ended media, such as paint; paper; clay; wood; cardboard boxes; and fabric, needles and thread for sewing. The Creative Discovery zone provides these media, as well as materials for artistic experimentation and exploration of naturally occurring objects that may be incorporated into art, such as shells, stones, and pieces of wood. This zone promotes the discovery of concepts related to the natural transformations of materials, such as water and sand. In this zone, children seek a number of ways to solve a problem or try a new strategy when the first one does not work.

The play materials and supplies associated with the Creative Arts centre, which is located in this zone, are largely open-ended and abstract. Children are encouraged to originate their own plan with the media provided, to devise a strategy for achieving their plan or idea, to follow through and try alternatives when necessary, to represent their own ideas, and to report on what they have achieved. Play may be individual or collaborative, and children are encouraged to talk with each other about their works of art or their projects.

The Science Discovery centre, also located in this zone, is an area where children observe, manipulate, and explore an array of naturally occurring objects that are part of their everyday world. This area reinforces the importance of the natural world and its phenomena. Young children engage in scientific discovery indoors, outdoors, and in all learning centres, but the dedication of one centre to science exploration ensures that both planned and spontaneous opportunities to develop a science orientation are available to children every day.

The Unit Blocks centre may be located in the Creative Discovery zone because unit blocks are open-ended, creative materials that promote symbolic thinking and representational skills. Placing the Unit Blocks centre with the Creative Arts and Science Discovery centres allows children to transfer the creative ideas and problem-solving skills used with visual arts media and science discovery to their play with three-dimensional blocks. ECEs sometimes prefer to locate the Unit Blocks close to the Active Role Play centre and the Daily Living centre to facilitate the extension of children's role play episodes using structures made of blocks. Others see play with unit blocks as a way to reinforce language and concepts discovered in the Quiet Thinking centre. Whatever strategy ECEs pursue, they should always be able to explain their reasons for locating a learning centre in a specific zone and for the juxtaposition of the various zones.

The Design and Setup of Learning Centres in the Play Zones

The design of learning centres should reflect features that are recognizable to children in their daily lives, such as various technologies and household implements. These features facilitate planning, provide direction, shape the number of options available, and guide ECEs toward philosophically consistent and socially relevant choices. Children need practical learning challenges in their play that allow them to explore and understand concepts in a variety of ways. "In real situations, children develop multiple access routes to their knowledge" (Duckworth, 1987, p. 49). Learning centres, with activities set up from which children choose what they want to play, provide children with authentic challenges and with concrete objects to explore and manipulate, and they build meaning. Learning centres are designed to facilitate children's independence in learning, alone or with others, so that children can explore; experiment; test; and experience phenomena in a physical, sensory way in order to understand them (Prascow, 2002).

A rational approach to designing a learning environment is based on the developmental outcomes each learning centre intends to address. The use of the term *learning centre* underlines the importance of facilitating children's achievement of developmental outcomes in their play. ECEs also allow for *possible learning outcomes,* which, in children's play, are not always the same as the intended outcomes. Flexible planning of environments for play should allow for both child-initiated and adult-initiated activities that combine free play and directed play and allow for the achievement of learning outcomes that have not been anticipated.

FACTORS TO CONSIDER WHEN SETTING UP A PLAY AND LEARNING ENVIRONMENT

- How many learning centres are needed and how much space is available for each centre?
- Should each learning centre be a permanent fixture in the learning environment?
- What is the primary rationale to be followed in creating the learning centres?
- Is there evidence that the learning centres address all developmental domains (e.g., cognitive, physical-sensory, social-emotional, and creative-expressive goals)?
- How many children can each learning centre accommodate at any given time?
- Do learning centres allow for flexible use of space and are there enough potential play spaces in the classroom?
- Are visual partitions such as shelves and bulletin boards used effectively to define and separate one centre from another so as to make a good use of space?
- Are there quiet places for children to retreat to in order to find respite from the normal activity levels of the classroom? Are these quiet places made inviting and comfortable for the children?
- Is there an optimal mix of open-ended (divergent) and closed (convergent) materials available to children?
- Is there evidence of space that may be used for projects of some duration so that children can leave out their materials and their achievements for the day?

When Programs Occupy Two or More Playrooms

Many programs experience space constraints because they operate in restricted and multipurpose environments not specifically designed for play-based programs for young children. *Programs that rely on two or more smaller rooms for setting up learning centres, as opposed to one large room for all learning centres, usually have difficult decisions to make about how to locate zones and learning centres.* In this situation, it is particularly important to locate complementary centres together. It is more complicated to manage each centre and to plan complementary activities in environments made up of a number of small rooms. When programs have to use more than one room, the active play and socially interactive centres are sometimes put in one room (i.e., the Active Role Play and Daily Living centres are arranged together, and the Quiet Thinking, Project Learning, Science Discovery, and Creative Arts centres are located in another room). This challenge has no easy solution; compromises are always necessary and the outcomes are not always what the ECE would prefer.

Densely Organized Space

The organization of space also affects the quality and ease of social interaction in a program. In densely organized space, where there is the least possible amount of space between play units, children are guided toward interactive play; thus, the development of social skills becomes paramount. Programs with goals that emphasize social learning facilitate interactive and group play through densely organized space.

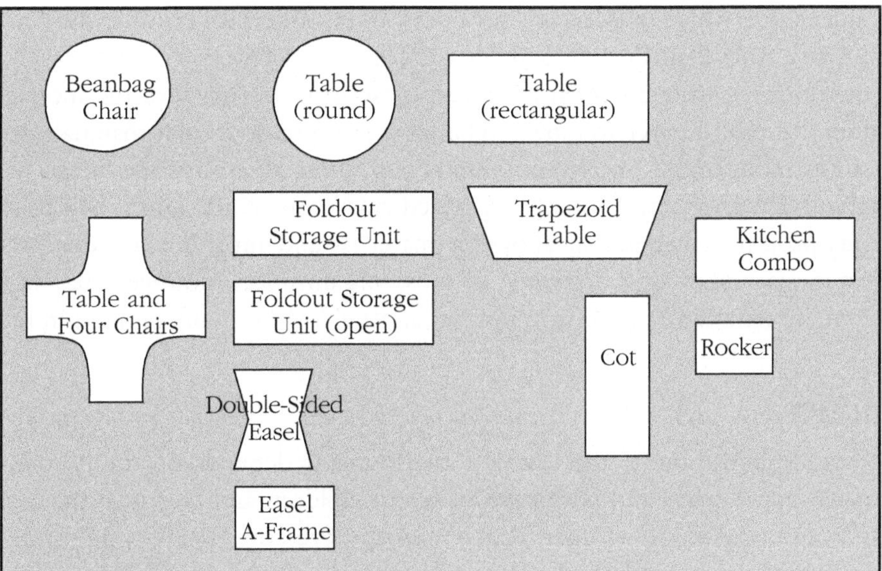

Figure 7–2
Paper templates representing the footprints of major items of furniture and equipment in learning centres

TIPS FOR DESIGNING A LEARNING CENTRE

Several useful aids make the tasks involved in designing learning centres easier for ECEs.

1. **Make templates of equipment and furniture.** Most equipment, furniture, and storage units for the early learning environment come in relatively standard sizes. To design a classroom, it is useful to make metric-sized cut-outs to use as templates that represent the footprint for each major item of equipment, furniture, and storage in the classroom (see Figure 7–2). The items should be drawn at the same scale as the drawing of the floor plan of the playroom. The playroom drawing (see Figure 7–3) indicates doorways; built-in units; windows; electrical outlets; water sources; and other unchangeable elements, such as telephone cables, intercoms, or computer cables. Simple cardboard or bristol board templates can be made and used to experiment with the locating of learning centres and the play units within them. The templates can be used to trace the location of units and centres on the playroom drawing once final decisions have been made.
2. **Draw a plan to determine layout and pathways.** When decisions have been made about where to locate learning centres, plans are ready to be committed to paper. Once a suitable arrangement for the equipment and furniture has been determined, it is important to check whether there are clear pathways that lead children into and out of learning centres (see Figure 7–4) and whether there is sufficient play space around each play unit, including enough space to accommodate children with disabilities. Adjustments can be made easily on paper before physically shifting heavy furniture and equipment.

Loosely Organized Space

Loosely organized space provides more empty space per child and conveys a sense of openness. Open, spacious environments often contain more potential units of play and broader pathways. Potential units (i.e., potential play spaces) are useful for setting up props for a super unit to facilitate sociodramatic play that replicates situations that take place, for example, in a hospital, a restaurant, an office, or a beauty salon. A potential unit may also be a small corner, an empty table, or space under an awning. A program that provides time and space for significant projects of some duration requires access to potential units of play large enough to accommodate children working together, and an adult. Potential units are usually located in learning centres where projects are most likely to be undertaken such as the Creative Arts, Active Role Play, Project, and Science Discovery centres.

Environments with potential units and loose organization give the message to children that they are free to move, to be active, to spread out play materials, and to play alone more often. Therefore, loose organization often suits the longer period of the full-day program. A loosely organized environment also lends itself to spontaneous project activities that allow for materials and furniture to be assembled wherever space allows. A downside of loose organization, however, may be that children are tempted to roam and interact aimlessly without any purpose in mind.

Pathways

Effective organization of the learning environment depends on the presence of adequate empty space and **pathways** visible to children and that help them move easily from one place to another. Kritchevsky and Prescott (1969, p. 17) state that "a clear path is broad, elongated and easily visible.... Paths are difficult to describe in words, but when they are well-defined they are easily seen." Learning centre environments ensure that pathways are visible from a child's eye level and easy to find (see Figures 7–3 and 7–4).

Clear pathways in the learning environment lead children from one area of the classroom into another, without distracting them along the way with equipment or materials that encroach on the path. For example, in outdoor play, a child who is setting out from the garden area and heading toward the sandbox may be enticed into climbing instead, if the climbing equipment and its surrounding play space intrude on the pathway. Sometimes a pathway is clear but it does not lead to all learning centres. Some areas in learning centres may be hidden and, therefore, seldom used. In planning physical space, it is important to ensure that pathways are clearly defined, that boundaries of learning centres and play spaces surrounding equipment are clearly visible, and that major pathways lead to and from all learning centres (Nash, 1989). When children with physical disabilities who are in wheelchairs need access to the learning environment, pathways have to be wide enough to allow the wheelchair to pass through easily. Sometimes, this may mean sacrificing a barrier that encloses the learning centre or reducing the number of play stations in the learning centre to accommodate the wheelchair at the play stations.

According to Kritchevsky et al. (1977), when there are clear pathways through space

- children playing at one unit will not interfere with children at another unit,
- adults and children do not need to pass through play units and their surrounding space to get from one place to another,
- no play units are permanently hidden, and
- there is no dead space.

Dead Space

Dead space is a large amount of empty space roughly square or circular in shape and without any visible or tangible boundaries (Kritchevsky et al., 1977). Dead space is sometimes found in the centre of a classroom or a playground, where the pathways and the boundaries of play areas are not clearly defined. Often out-of-bounds running or play develops, and ECEs have to intervene. Dead space can usually be

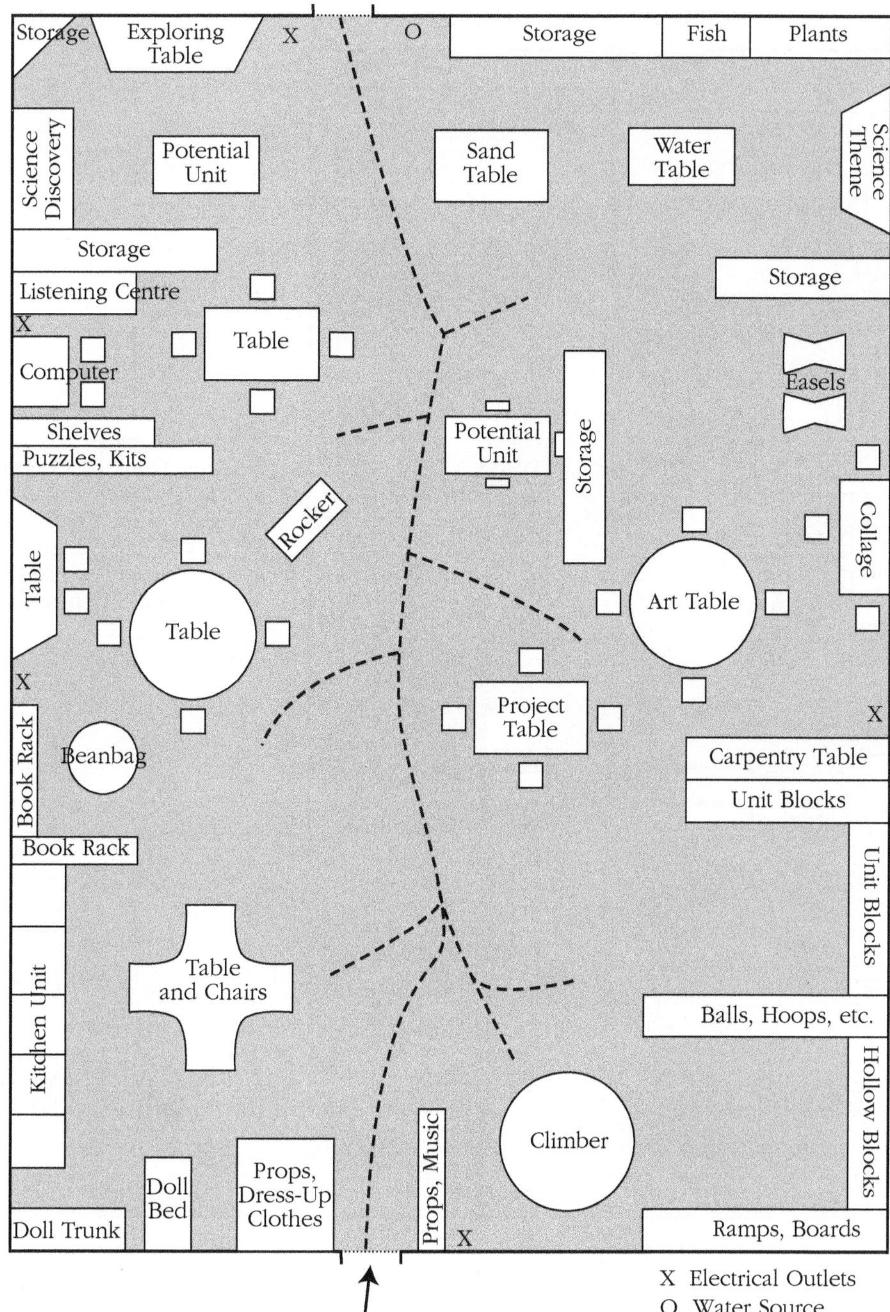

Figure 7–3
A playroom diagram

eliminated by adding a play unit or by moving some equipment or furniture. Setting up the materials and equipment for children to work on a project can also be an effective way to eliminate the dead space.

Amount of Empty Space

An important criterion of good physical organization of space is the amount of empty versus covered space in the classroom. Kritchevsky et al. (1977) propose that, as a general rule of thumb, one-third to one-half of the surface in a room or a yard should be uncovered to facilitate good organization of space. Larger groups

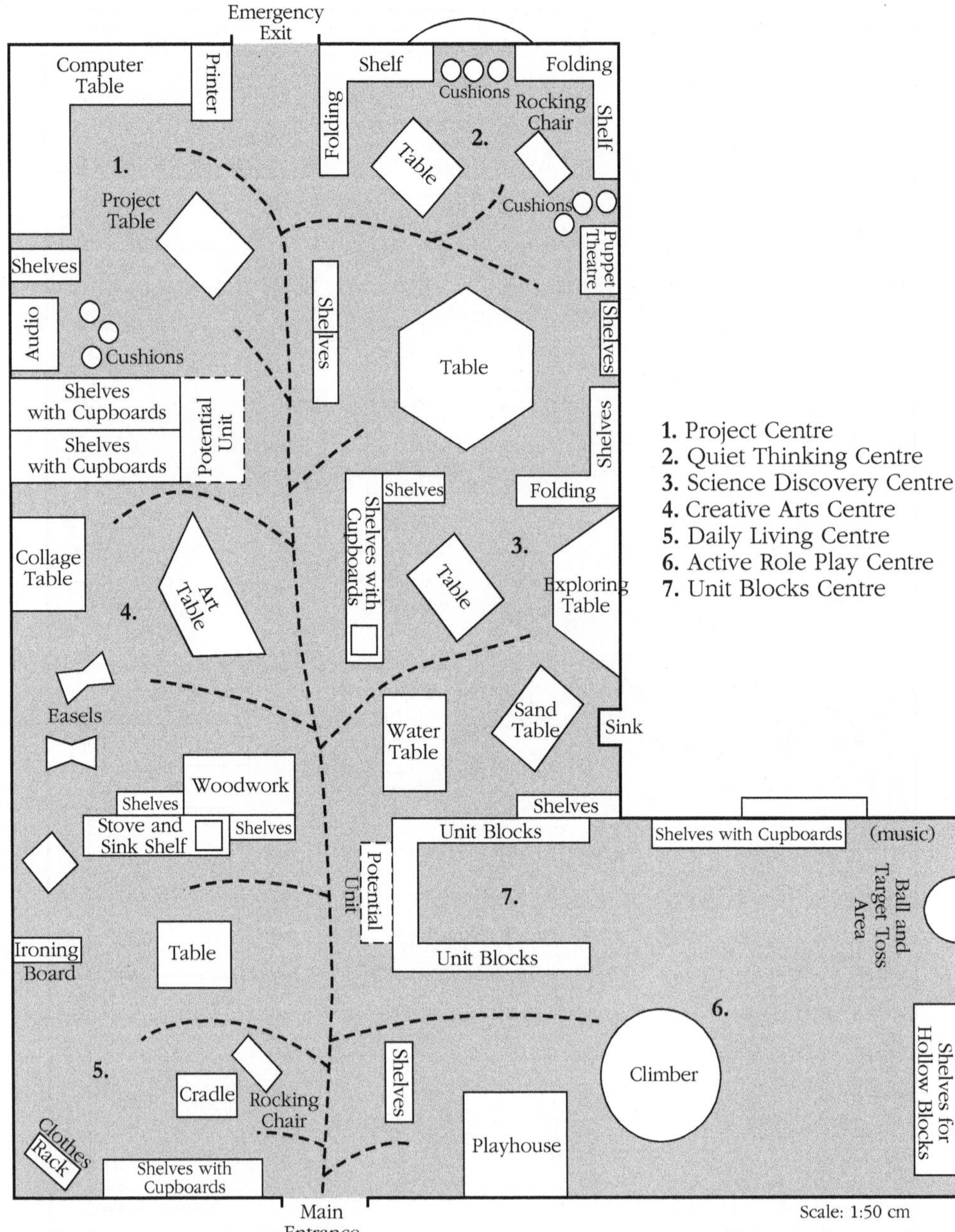

Figure 7–4
Learning centres and pathways

of children need a larger proportion of empty space (i.e., about one-half of the surface should be uncovered). The total amount of space in a classroom is related to the number of children who will use the room at one time. The ratios of total space available per child are regulated by provincial legislation in Canada and differ slightly among the provinces.

The layout diagrams in Figures 7–3 and 7–4 represent a variety of constraints and configurations that ECEs often meet in the real world. Committing the environmental design decisions to paper allows teaching teams to make suggestions and to see the developmental rationale behind the plan. ECEs are able to ensure that the clarity of pathways and the amount of empty space comply with accepted principles.

Organizing Space to Facilitate Play and Learning

Spatial cues in the arrangement of play stations and learning centres stimulate specific kinds of behaviour, play, and learning. The organization of space teaches children about respecting the play and learning environment. Clean, tidy, well-organized areas for play and storage; shiny, smooth surfaces; and furniture in good repair, are environmental characteristics that encourage children to look after the equipment and the materials and to tidy up when they have finished playing. Poorly organized space may lead to conflict between the goals of the program and the behaviours caused by the setting. When space is used carelessly, rules and other forms of constraint, such as locked cupboards and frequent adult intervention, are often needed to provide the cues for behaviour that the environment has failed to communicate. The presence of many rules and constraints reduces the freedom children have to explore, experiment, and choose, and conflicts with the main aims of programs.

Storage Units

Effective organization of space requires ease of supervision and the efficient placement of storage units discussed in Chapter 6. The shape of the space and the distribution of things within that space should allow adults to see and to be seen easily. Movable equipment and furniture allow for more control over the physical setting and portable storage is usually better than built-in or permanent storage, as it allows for flexibility. The placement of permanent, larger equipment, such as swings and climbers, and non-movable counters and storage units, requires careful consideration. Many types of customized storage units have the added benefit of ensuring that materials and supplies are accessible to children to optimize their choices.

Inaccessible storage areas for materials that adults should control—for example, costly supplies, personal belongings, and cleaning agents—are also needed (Caples, 1996). A balance between stationary storage areas, such as built-in cupboards, and mobile units on wheels in each learning centre adds to the stability of the environment and allows ECEs to adapt learning centres to the evolving curriculum as children make developmental progress.

Label containers with words and pictures

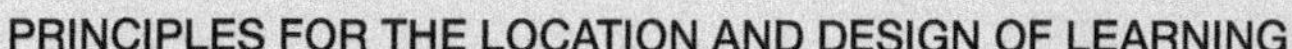

PRINCIPLES FOR THE LOCATION AND DESIGN OF LEARNING

1. **Juxtapose centres in a zone of the playroom that addresses similar categories, stages, and contexts of play.** This increases the likelihood that children will rely on the environment to provide messages about what is expected of them in each learning centre, and it usually prolongs the time that children stay with an activity. Place active, noisier centres close together. The identification of play zones—for example, zones that promote social interaction and dramatic play (role play zone), those that promote exploration of things and discovery of concepts (creative discovery zone), and those that promote greater attention to the learning of concepts (concept learning)—provides a sound rationale for locating the learning centres.
2. **Separate clean and messy learning centres.** Wet, messy play materials are best confined to tiled areas near a water source. The Creative Arts centre and the Science Discovery centre will likely be close to each other for this practical purpose, as well as to facilitate transfer of learning. Carpeted areas in other centres provide warmth, soft surfaces to sit on, as well as sound absorption. They give messages to children that quieter, cleaner, individual play will occur in these areas.

3. **Dedicate more space to learning centres addressing developmental outcomes and objectives that have priority, as determined by the individual assessments of children's developmental needs** (see Chapter 9). The sizes of the learning centres vary depending on the priority of the developmental outcomes to be achieved by the children. Physical limitations, such as amount of space available, size and amount of equipment and materials needed in the learning centre, location of pathways, and space for storage, also influence the size and configuration of learning centres. Portable storage units allow flexibility in room arrangement, alteration of the boundaries of learning centres, and changes in curriculum priorities.
4. **Locate portable storage units close to the learning centres.** Enabling children to access their own materials frees ECEs to facilitate learning and to observe children's play. Ample space tailor-made for supplies and materials draws attention to their aesthetic features and usefulness in the environment (New, 1993). When children choose materials for themselves, they learn to make basic decisions in matching the media and materials to be used and in planning what they want to pursue in their play. ECEs also show children how to take proper care of each learning centre and its materials and the location of easily accessible storage units in each centre facilitates children's active participation in tidy up, a learning activity that promotes cooperation, memory recall, motor capabilities, and attending skills.
5. **Ensure that learning centres are clearly visible from major pathways.** It should be possible for adults to see into the learning centres from most points in the room. Dividers between the centres should be high enough for children to feel enclosed in a centre but low enough for ECEs to monitor play effectively without interfering or being overly intrusive. Houle (1987) recommended that the freestanding backdrop of a learning centre be one metre high or less so as to allow ECEs to see into all areas at all times. Freestanding dividers also provide maximum flexibility to adjust the size or shape of a learning centre to incorporate new categories of play, or to accommodate more, or fewer, children. Flexible boundaries ensure that the centres and activities change as children make progress.
6. **Let the arrangement of equipment, materials, and supplies in the learning centre communicate the limits and boundaries for play.** Certain ground rules are necessary for each learning centre and should vary according to the nature of the play anticipated there. These rules can be kept to a minimum when the physical arrangement of the learning centres is consistent with the provision of materials, use of space, and presence of boundaries and other physical cues. There should be sufficient space for children to move freely from one learning centre to another and to play without obstructing the play of other children. Children will participate eagerly in setting reasonable ground rules and will help to maintain them when the physical environment, materials, and activities provide consistent messages. Children usually respect the limits and the physical boundaries around play stations that promote specific kinds of play.
7. **Account for practical details.** Unchangeable features such as electrical outlets, walkways, doors, windows, noise levels, built-in units, water sources, and cable outlets all influence classroom design. To conserve space, which is usually at a premium in learning environments, furniture may be arranged to provide clearer pathways or to divide learning centres. Multipurpose furniture such as tables and chests of drawers, can be used as play surfaces for children or for storage. An empty table or corner can be designated as potential space, as long as it is bounded by dividers, furniture, or storage units. Walls with bulletin boards at children's eye level may display posters or photographs that offer further clues about the style of play encouraged in the centre. A range of materials and supplies is accessible and may be used in flexible ways. When they come from the learning environment itself, messages about the care and maintenance of the learning environment's aesthetic quality are most effective.
8. **Vary textures and colours.** Textures and colours may extend the messages of the centre. A mixture of hard, soft, upholstered, painted, and natural textures in a playroom creates a homier atmosphere and also adds variety, which allows children to become familiar with the properties of various materials. Variations in texture stimulate the senses, which play an important role in learning. Hard, smooth surfaces can be easily cleaned and returned to their original state after use. Soft, nubby textures promote relaxation and require greater care in use. The shine and sleekness of materials of today can be combined with the warmth and character of worn products, such as weathered wood, sand-blasted brick, and cork.

9. **The selective use of colour can have a direct effect on moods and feelings.** Red, yellow, orange, and brown are generally considered warm colours and make a room appear smaller and cozier. Blues are cool and detached, create feelings of space and may contribute to slow, deliberate behaviours. Greens are believed to be calming and easier to tolerate for longer periods. Balancing colours skillfully can create a harmonious setting that will suit any time of year and many variations in behaviour and activity.
10. **Consider exposure to natural and artificial light.** The combination of colour and light from both natural and artificial sources is also part of playroom design. Maximizing the amount of natural light a room will receive, especially during the dark winter months, is essential in designing rooms in northern climates. Playrooms with an eastern exposure are bright in the morning but darker later in the day; a western exposure has the opposite effect. Rooms with a southern exposure usually receive the largest amount of natural light.
11. **In playrooms where fewer winter daylight hours necessitate the use of artificial light, choices about the kinds of artificial lighting to use can offset the disadvantages of the absence of natural light.** Pot lighting recessed in the ceiling, or reflected light in a cove ceiling using incandescent light sources, is the most natural kind of artificial light and the easiest to tolerate for long hours. Standard fluorescent lighting should be avoided, although full-spectrum fluorescent lighting may substitute.
12. **Create a diverse learning environment in all learning centres.** Including cultural artifacts, ornaments, and other accessories as permanent fixtures in the classroom should be standard practice. Ensuring a diverse learning environment all of the time addresses multicultural goals more effectively than special activities honouring specific festival times although these also have a place. The languages of the families the program serves, including print, songs, and gestures, should be represented in the playroom. Objects from various cultures, such as artwork, tools and fabric add texture and colour that brighten and add interest to the classroom throughout the year. To be truly inclusive, Gonzalez-Mena (2005) recommends that programs also recognize the dominant culture as a **culture** and not as a universal reality. This approach means that the artifacts and accessories of the mainstream culture will coexist along with those of other cultures to create an inclusive playroom culture that is distinct from that of the environment outside the classroom. Living in this inclusive culture on a daily basis has a significant impact on the child, who absorbs the messages delivered by the environment in which she plays and interacts with others that lead to lifelong habits of mind and attitudes and that are firmly rooted in her childhood memories.

Analyze the Learning Environment

Designing the learning environment calls for systematic analysis of children's interests; their developmental levels, style, and pace of learning; and their participation levels in various types of activities. Data collected while observing children at play provide the basis on which environments may be altered and redesigned. ECEs should frequently evaluate the play space to ensure that the close relationship between developmental outcomes and environmental design remains stable. Factors to analyze include:

- Are children able to choose and initiate their own learning?
- Does the environment provide a variety of developmentally appropriate play opportunities indoors and outdoors?
- Does the environment change according to the needs, developing abilities, and interests of the children?
- Do ECEs function as facilitators of children's learning, or do they have to intervene frequently and lead most activities?

The Learning Environment Audit, which appears as Appendix B, pages 479–482, addresses several evaluation factors relating to the design of the physical environment. Activities checklists, which are discussed in Chapter 10, focus on evaluating children's levels of participation and their mastery of the objectives of self-directed learning experiences.

Summary

Well-planned indoor learning environments provide young children with a window to the world beyond and an invitation to discovery that will help them stretch, imagine, and grow. When children encounter an interesting setting at their eye level, they are challenged to explore, test, and manipulate. Effective learning environments support many zones for compatible categories and social contexts of play and are comfortable, warm, attractive, bright, and full of promise. Children have freedom to move, to choose from a wide range of alternatives, to meet and play with others, and to be alone. When key principles for the location and design of learning centres are followed, children transfer the learning they acquire in one centre to another centre, they find their way easily from one learning centre to another, and they understand the limits and the behaviours expected in each area of the playrooms. Children of all cultures are able to see relevant objects from their home lives reflected in the learning centres at all times.

LEARNING ACTIVITIES

1. Using the Learning Environment Audit in Appendix B as a guide, create a chart you will use to evaluate the design and location of learning centres. Include the design features and principles described in this chapter. Be sure to include the features related to location, aesthetics, lighting, organization, and contents.
2. Redesign an existing preschool learning environment using graph paper and a set of templates you made to represent the major items of equipment and furniture. Create a scale drawing of the dimensions and unchangeable features of the room or rooms where learning centres have been set up. Provide a written rationale for your redesign based on the principles for the location and design of learning centres (see pp. 129–131).
3. Using graph paper and your templates, draw a learning environment and the learning centres that represent the design features and principles that you have learned in this chapter. Provide a written rationale for your diagram. Discuss the ways in which your learning environment and the learning centres might be adapted to various physical constraints you might encounter, such as doorways, natural light sources, water sources, and electrical outlets.

Section III
Curriculum for Young Children

Section III introduces the following topics:

- the foundations of curriculum, including the values, practices, and standards on which curriculum is based
- principles of learning in early childhood
- familiar curriculum models and approaches
- a generic curriculum framework, based on child development, that emerges from children's interests and is grounded in play
- observing and assessing children's developmental progress and capturing their interests in order to plan the next steps in a play-based curriculum
- planning play activities, learning experiences, and projects that address developmental objectives
- direct and indirect methods to facilitate children's learning through play
- evaluating the curriculum's effectiveness

Section III emphasizes that there is not one curriculum model that meets all needs. ECEs need to understand the values, practices, and standards upon which curriculum is based so that its intentions and strategies are clear and consistent. Examining various curriculum models provides examples of how to blend curriculum with the cultural, environmental, and philosophical worldviews of the people and interests the program serves. Curriculum usually starts with the children's needs, and accounts for the priorities of their parents and the community they live in. This approach emulates the curriculum foundations for the schools of Reggio Emilia, which respond to local interests; it also recognizes that children's development drives the curriculum. Fostering play that is freely chosen, hands-on, open to children's decisions about how they will use the play materials, and flexible enough to respond to their ideas about how they will play with the materials provided is a central strategy.

Chapter 8 addresses the foundations of curriculum and some familiar curriculum models and approaches; Chapter 9 describes the components of a generic curriculum framework and their interrelationships; and Chapter 10 describes tools and systems for planning play activities, learning experiences, and projects that address developmental outcomes and objectives.

8 Curriculum Foundations and Models for Early Childhood Education

"Curriculum for young children has structure and purpose; it is not just 'what happens.'"

—Elizabeth Jones and James Nimmo, *Emergent Curriculum* (1994)

Before Reading This Chapter, Have You

- reviewed the essential features of a healthy climate for play and learning?
- differentiated equipment, materials, and supplies and simple, complex, and super units for play?
- become familiar with the learning centres and their location in the playroom?
- understood the factors related to planning play space?

Outcomes

After reading and understanding this chapter, you should be able to

- describe the influences on curriculum for young children today;
- identify the values, practices, and standards that you would choose as inputs to ECE curriculum;
- describe key features of familiar curriculum models for ECE;
- outline Gardner's theory of multiple intelligences and its influence on our understanding of intelligence; and
- link your knowledge of emergent curriculum and developmentally appropriate practice (DAP) to the task of constructing a curriculum for young children.

Curriculum Foundations

A **curriculum** is a system of intentions and plans to promote development and learning based on an educational philosophy and a consistent theoretical approach. Mallory and New (1994, p. 4) cite "a concern regarding the degree of congruence between the values, beliefs, and goals embedded in typical early childhood programs that ultimately affects inclusiveness and effectiveness." As logical as it seems, ECEs know that congruence is difficult to achieve when one is faced with many competing philosophies. A priority for staff in an early childhood education program is to establish a coherent philosophy that works within their context and for the children and families they serve. The curriculum should make explicit the values, practices, and standards that the program represents. Chapter 8 addresses the philosophical and theoretical values and principles that drive play-based, developmental curriculum and briefly describes some models within the constructivist philosophical tradition. Chapter 9 focuses on the complex task of designing a curriculum, which is best achieved using a written framework that articulates clearly the relationships among the various elements of the curriculum.

Values

Values are beliefs that motivate behaviour. Early childhood education is based on the belief that children are motivated largely from within. This belief also assumes that children usually pass through stages in a predictable sequence, although not necessarily at the same ages. Each stage is characterized by cognitive styles and physical abilities very different from those of an adult. Cultural differences also exist. These are mediated by the values and priorities of families and the opportunities for development provided to the children. Since cognitive development in early childhood is largely sensory and physical, children's knowledge of the world around them and the maturation of their thought processes depend on their freedom to explore, manipulate, and be physically active.

Developmental theory values individualized curriculum because no two children learn at the same rate, to the same level, or in the same way. Children need freedom to engage in learning that is interesting and matches their needs and abilities. Real learning occurs when children integrate new understandings from their concrete experiences, a process that takes time and patience. Children build developmental foundations for learning that accommodate more and more complex challenges that lead eventually to higher levels of functioning as adults. This belief is central to the concept of lifelong learning. In the absence of a strong developmental foundation that covers all domains—physical, social, emotional, and cognitive—children's opportunities for rich life experiences are diminished and their life choices are narrower.

Values are also linked to specific theories of development, learning, and play that have evolved over hundreds of years (Chapter 2). Various models for early childhood programs profess to follow one set of values more than others; these value differences are evident in the models described in this chapter. For example, the Montessori schools typically place a high value on children's development of *learning to learn skills* that will help them become effective learners; the HighScope model values children's cognitive development as a preparation for school; the Bank Street model emphasizes children's development through social experiences; the schools of Reggio Emilia place a high value on creativity and problem solving as well as promoting the social values and conventions of the communities in which they reside.

Practices

Professional ECE practices related to curriculum are derived from an understanding of the value of play, knowledge of child development, and knowledge of how children learn. This professional knowledge base, along with the knowledge of how to design and set up the environment, guides curriculum design, program planning, and the methods and behaviours ECEs choose to facilitate children's play and learning. Play-based practices are the strategies for implementing developmental curriculum for young children.

PLAY-BASED CURRICULUM PRACTICES

1. The playroom offers an array of challenging play alternatives that are meaningful and accessible to children to choose for themselves.
2. Equipment, materials, and supplies are organized into well-defined learning centres that provide clear messages to children about what they are likely to be doing, practising, and learning in each centre (Chapter 7).
3. Play activities are based on observations of the children playing, together and individually, to ensure that the activities capture children's interests, motivate their participation, and facilitate developmental progress from their present level to a higher level. Unplanned, randomly selected activities that fail to account for assessments of the individual development and the interests of the children often amount to little more than busy work.
4. Planned play activities move from simple to complex, beginning with concrete learning challenges in which the concepts or skills to be mastered are clear and observable to the child. For example, simple, concrete, sensory sorting activities based on the visual or tactile differences children detect gradually lead to more abstract challenges that move the child from sensory exploration and dependence on what they see, to sorting according to criteria that exist only in the mind of the child.
5. A balance of **convergent** (structured) and **divergent** (open-ended) **activities** should be provided in the learning centres. Structured experiences with specific-purpose materials such as puzzles and stacking sets provide built-in cues regarding what is to be done and learned with the materials. For example, stacking cups and jigsaw puzzles have clear tasks to be accomplished that are visible to the child as she plays. Open-ended activities, such as easel painting, sociodramatic play, and block play, offer opportunities for children to explore materials; invent plans, procedures, and scripts; try several approaches; make decisions; and achieve their own goals.
6. Activities and experiences that promote all categories of play and many social contexts for play are essential in the well-planned curriculum.
7. A balance of individual and group activities and experiences that address children's unique learning styles and preferences is provided. This practice makes it more likely that children will learn to play alone on some activities; this provides an opportunity for the ECE to focus on the progress of one child in a play activity and to intervene as necessary. Balance ensures that children experience opportunities to play in small groups in sociodramatic play episodes with super units such as a grocery store, and to play in group games outdoors and in the playroom. Group play experiences provide ECEs with the opportunity to assess children's social progress, their communication skills, their ability to navigate group dynamics, and a host of other social abilities.
8. Projects comprised of a sequence of activities encourage children to collaborate over an extended time period in order to achieve the desired result. Projects should be interesting to the children, facilitate inclusion of all children who want to participate, and motivate children to explore multiple avenues (Katz & Chard, 2005). The challenge is to encourage children's interest in projects that link school, home, and community; to foster collaborative thinking and problem solving; to promote learning-to-learn skills; and to stretch children's interests and abilities beyond what is familiar to them. Projects are addressed in Chapter 18.
9. Ongoing assessment of children's progress is based on their achievement of the developmental objectives related to the play activities and experiences. ECEs note the categories and the social contexts of their play, and the sequence of steps children pursue in order to succeed with the activity. These assessments inform curriculum, including the next steps in activity planning.

EXAMPLE

An example of simple to complex might include sorting two sets of objects according to one prescribed visible criterion (such as green buttons and red buttons), followed by sorting according to two or three prescribed, visible criteria (such as "all the brown bears go into one pile and all the yellow cats go into a different pile"), followed by sorting according to visible criteria chosen by the child herself from an array of objects (such as large coloured tabletop blocks and small coloured pegs from a pegboard), and, eventually, followed by sorting a random selection of objects according to non-visible criteria identified by the child—which is a much more abstract task, as in sorting "things to eat with," "things to cook with," "things that make sounds."

Standards

The **standards** in an ECE curriculum refer to the developmental outcomes linked to the developmental tasks of early childhood. The standards cover all major developmental domains—physical, social, emotional and cognitive. Progress toward the standards may be assessed by observing children's achievement of **benchmarks** that describe the bite-sized chunks of learning that lead to the achievement of the outcomes. In developmental programs, the standards are stated as developmental outcomes that describe the performance observed by the ECE that indicates that the development has occurred. The benchmarks are usually reflected in the developmental objectives, which are handy descriptors that help ECEs recognize when children are making progress. Children's developmental progress is assessed by observing their participation and success in planned and spontaneous play activities that require progressively higher levels of skill, knowledge, and conceptual understanding. These levels may be adjusted through repeated observations of several children in order to determine realistic expectations for individual children and the group.

ECEs observe children's behaviours as they begin a series of activities, assess their developmental levels, monitor the developmental skills they demonstrate in various activities, and assess their progress from the point at which the learning process began. Assessment is a sophisticated skill that requires knowledge of child development and well-developed observation and recording skills (see Chapter 9). The value of observation and assessment depends on the ECE's ability to choose play materials and plan activities that move children beyond their current developmental levels (see Chapter 10).

EXAMPLE

Let's say that learning to skip in a cross-lateral pattern (right foot and left arm forward followed by left foot and right arm forward, with a hop and a step), by age five, is the developmental outcome. The benchmarks in learning to skip in a cross-lateral pattern, which is a complex coordination task, may be defined as: balance on one foot, upper body coordination with lower body; right-side body coordination with left side, walking, then marching in a cross-lateral pattern, followed by skipping. ECEs may encourage children to begin the learning process by walking through the right-left, upper- and lower-body coordination, marching, then introducing the hop and step. Breaking down this complex task into bite-sized chunks (i.e., planning activities that encourage practice of each discrete skill) facilitates learning, allows children to succeed at each stage in the learning process, and allows the ECE to observe clearly where the child may be having difficulty and when he has achieved each discrete skill. The discrete skills involved in the complex task are usually expressed as developmental objectives. Some children may achieve the complex developmental outcome on one or two tries; other children will take it one step at a time and need assistance and coaching along the way. What is important is that all children learn to skip in a cross-lateral pattern, as this skill is fundamental to team sports, many individual athletic pursuits, dancing, swimming, and a host of later physical endeavours. It is alarming to note in a group of middle school or adolescent children, not to mention adults, how many have never learned to skip. Can you skip?

But let's not forget: Setting standards and promoting and monitoring developmental progress should not be confused with attempting to accelerate children's development. Effective curriculum promotes children's progress at their own rate and according to their unique learning styles and interests. Evidence that each child is progressing developmentally from the point at which assessment began is most important. Articulating the values, practices, and standards of the curriculum is essential to planning effective programs, and they are usually the starting point for building a sound curriculum.

How Social and Political Factors Influence Curriculum for Young Children

Traditional educational approaches based on simply exposing children to "developmentally appropriate experiences and materials are *not* effective enough to promote children's achievement of developmental and learning outcomes for a more complex world" (Andrews & Lupart, 1993, p. 637). *Purposeful early childhood education supports and intervenes to help children achieve developmental outcomes that prepare them for lifelong learning, thinking, and problem solving; encourage community participation; provide outlets for stress; promote mental health; and foster spiritual fulfillment.* A curriculum for the 21st century should emphasize the development of habits of mind that prepare children for later participation in a global society (Andrews & Lupart, 1993). Although research shows that early experiences do not necessarily determine development, Bruer (1999) emphasized that they are predispositional, influencing the likelihood that development will occur and that certain skills and understandings will be achieved. These beliefs provide a rationale for creating *an intentional curriculum framework* within which children's interests and ideas, and parents' priorities, may be integrated.

The new agenda for education from birth to retirement and beyond emphasizes the importance of achievement in learning, however it is attained and manifested. Research has revealed that, while brain development occurs rapidly during the early years, it continues throughout life, including during old age (Doidge, 2007). We need to ensure that children have the physical, intellectual, and emotional foundation they will need to meet increasingly complex learning challenges in school, work, and everyday living. The technology revolution has fundamentally altered the ways in which human beings communicate and learn and has had a significant impact on learning during childhood. Children are using complex software, cellphones, videos, cameras, and other technologies to investigate, inquire, communicate, experiment, and learn some skills at much earlier ages and in ways never imagined 40 years ago. These technologies are also having some perverse effects, in that children are increasingly sedentary; stay indoors more; and lack the stimulation, spontaneity, and physical exercise associated with active play with three-dimensional objects, indoors and outdoors. The rates of obesity; physical ailments; and such diseases as diabetes and cardiac and circulatory problems, formerly absent in childhood, are increasing. While it is true that safety and lifestyle issues also contribute to children's lack of fitness, poor diet, and obesity, the prevalence of technologies in society has contributed in major ways to children's inactivity and lethargy.

Curriculum for young children should recognize and address these influences, which are counterproductive to cognitive, social, physical, and emotional development. Children learn social skills by interacting with other children and adults; they learn emotional coping skills by experiencing frustration, disappointment, and hurt; and they experience the joy and exhilaration of success when they achieve physical and social goals while playing outdoors with friends.

The political influences on curriculum for young children are numerous. They include parents' beliefs about the importance of individual success versus group collaboration and the importance of the individual versus the public good; a community's preoccupation with conformity to accepted norms and beliefs versus commitment to freedom of expression without boundaries; beliefs about the value of group participation versus individual pursuits; and values attached to spiritual well-being versus the achievement of marketable skills. Curriculum decisions are always subject to political considerations of one kind or another and should be recognized and made explicit as values that drive curriculum design and planning.

How Culture Influences Curriculum for Young Children

We live in a multicultural society with pluralistic values and a mind-numbing range of individual needs, priorities, pressures, and challenges. The diversity of Canadian society provides a fertile proving ground for a generic approach to curriculum that respects the priorities of various cultures and families, while helping children identify with, and relate to, their day-to-day environments. Cultural priorities and family values vary widely; some families consider collective, shared goals to be far more important than individual achievement and success. Other families want, above all, for their children to compete successfully in a world that values personal wealth, influence, and independence. A curriculum framework for young children in Canada is obligated to respect diverse cultural priorities and other differences while focusing on goals that support children within their families and also reflect values of the larger society. And those societal values are also significant because children need to be able to adapt to and cope with mainstream conventions and expectations. Research reported by Ali (2005) found that newcomer parents often struggle to provide for the most basic needs of their children, needs compounded by the cultural barriers parents face when they immigrate. Canada is challenged to break new ground in finding more ways to support new Canadians. The path toward a curriculum framework that embraces diverse cultural realities and expectations is not obvious—but one must be carved.

How Neuroscience and the Study of the Brain Influence ECE Curriculum

In recent years, the discipline of neuroscience and the study of the brain have provided a wealth of understanding about the brain and learning. The plasticity of the brain in early childhood remains a cornerstone in early childhood education theory and practice, and Doidge (2007, p. 60) argues that it is important to "get it right early," before children drift into bad habits they have to unlearn. Advances in neuroscience and brain research have had a significant impact on beliefs about the role of early childhood education, on what it can claim to mean and do in the lives of children, and on how curriculum can take full advantage of the special cognitive strengths and conditions present in the young child. Recent discoveries have demonstrated that the number of connections among neurons or synapses in the childhood brain is 50 percent greater

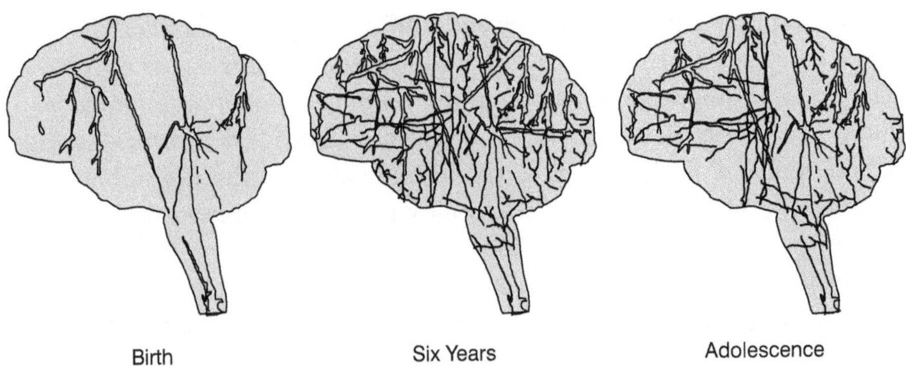

Figure 8–1
The development of synapses in early childhood

Source: Palaiologou, I. "Physical Development." In I. Palaiologou. Ed. (2010). *The Early Years Foundation Stage: Theory and Practice*, pp. 178–189.*

than in the adult brain, and that a massive "pruning back" begins in the brain during adolescence (Doidge, 2007, p. 42). Research has shown that notions of the brain as a muscle that improves with exercise are well founded. New learning about "critical periods," which were first proposed by Freud in the early 20th century, have demonstrated that these periods, when a child is best able to learn a certain set of skills, such as a second language, are usually short-lived. We now know, for example, that children should be introduced to new languages at an early age and that second language learning involves complex interactions between the home language, the new language, and the child's developing brain (Chumak-Horbatsch, 2010). Neuroscience is making an enormous contribution to early childhood education by reinforcing the importance of early exercise of the brain, learning good intellectual habits while very young, and taking full advantage of the plasticity and malleability of the young brain.

The recent advances by neuroscientists resonate with the work of many experts in early childhood learning over the past several decades. Howard Gardner (1991, p. 5) stated that by the age of five, children have developed a well-defined "unschooled mind," consisting of simple and often misguided theories about mind and matter based on their immature perspective of the world. The formidable task of the school years is to refashion the immature preschooler into a more sophisticated thinker and conceptualizer, a task at which schools often fail. Gardner (1991, p. 111) maintained that:

> The mind of the five-year-old persists in most of us, in most of our daily activities, with only the disciplinary expert escaping fully from its powerful clutches in certain areas of expertise. In some sense, the purpose of education should be to revise the misconceptions and stereotypes that reliably arise all around the world in the first half-decade of life. But, at the same time, education should try to preserve the most remarkable features of the young mind—its adventurousness, its generativity, its resourcefulness, and its flashes of flexibility and creativity.

Neuroscience provides a sound empirical foundation for constructivist curriculum that fosters children's acquisition of a broad range and a deeper level of developmental skills and greater efficiency in the application of these skills. Constructivist environments encourage children to adopt a healthy and realistic world view and offer clear choices for play that facilitate development and learning in all domains. As well as allowing for spontaneous free play and emergent curriculum, the learning centres and planned activities encourage purposeful play that intentionally leads children to make viable connections, discover valid concepts, and explore real phenomena as they interact with an array of things, experiences, and events. The more interesting this array of experiences, the more motivated children are to probe more deeply, to ask more questions, to persist beyond obstacles in their path, and to discover. For many neuroscientists and education experts, **motivation** is the key to intelligence (Sternberg, 2005).

New Definitions of Intelligence

Old notions that intelligence is a generalized, measurable ability largely fixed at birth were dispelled in the 20th century and replaced by new knowledge related to the plasticity of the brain, which implies that no ability is fixed and that the brain is "always learning how to learn" (Merzenich, 2001, p. 68). Sternberg claimed that "intelligence represents a set of competencies in development and is neither fixed, nor generalized, but rather a dynamic, diffuse and ongoing process that results in different types of intelligence rather than a single entity" (Sternberg, 2005, p. 18). His new definition of intelligence proposed that skills develop as results of gene-environment interaction; he referred to intelligence as a process driven by metacognition, learning and thinking skills, knowledge, and motivation, of which the driving force is motivation. (Sternberg, quoted in Shenk, 2010, p. 190). These elements are discussed in Chapter 15 on "learning to learn" and in other chapters in Section IV.

This revised definition of intelligence resonated with Gardner's paradigm of "multiple intelligences," or talents. Although misrepresentations of human intelligence were dispelled by scientists during the 20th century, old mythologies die hard, and outdated views persist even today and in places where they shouldn't, including in our schools. John Mighton (2003, p. 19), in *The Myth of Ability,* explained this phenomenon: "I believe the answer lies in the profound inertia of human thought: when an entire society believes something is impossible, it suppresses, by its very way of life, the evidence that would contradict that belief." Mighton's development of the Junior Undiscovered Math Prodigies (JUMP) program forced a rethinking of the old notion of "giftedness," casting doubt on the exclusive role of genetics in human intelligence. Mighton's astute observations supported the conclusions of other Canadian researchers such as Meaney (2001), who claimed that abilities emerge from the interaction of genes and the environment, and that if one changes the genes or the environment, the result in terms of development and learning may be different. ECE curriculum is obligated to build on new research evidence related to intelligence and learning. Our task as educators is to understand how nature and the environment interact and how our temperament, intelligence, and talent are subject to the developmental process (Shenk, 2010, pp. 26–28).

Curriculum and the Theory of Multiple Intelligences

Revised definitions of intelligence provided an illuminating new context for the earlier work of Howard Gardner on multiple intelligences (1983, 1996, 2004). Gardner described nine "intelligences" as a series of distinct abilities or "talents" rather than a general capacity and proposed that the key question is "How are you smart?" rather than "How smart are you?" (Gardner, 2000). Gardner advocated a view of curriculum that mobilizes the development of "multiple intelligences." His theory supported the view that not every child needs to acquire the same body of knowledge at the same time. The explosion of information makes it impossible for any individual to acquire more than a fraction of the available knowledge. Understanding basic concepts and practising learning-to-learn skills are more important during the early years than acquiring prescribed facts and subject-based knowledge. Gardner (1999) believed that to be equipped for future productive roles and to be "intelligent," children need to learn to think mathematically, historically, ethically, humanely, locally, and creatively. In 2006, Gardner proposed "Five Minds for the Future": the disciplined mind; the synthesizing mind; the creating mind; the respectful mind; and the ethical mind.

Gardner's *Frames of Mind* (1983), as well as his later publications, build on Piaget's theoretical foundation. Gardner's nine independent intelligences have their own set of specific devices, and each responds to different challenges and tasks. Gardner proposed that people have different blends of intelligences and different levels of intelligence in each area. These wide differences should be accounted for in play environments, since the central task of early childhood education is to find out what "crystallizes" each child's learning (Gardner, 1999). We can find out where children's aptitudes, interests, and talents lie by exposing them to a wide range of learning opportunities that address all the intelligences and various styles of learning. Gardner (2004) proposed three distinct uses of the term *intelligence*:

1. Intelligence is a property of all human beings. (All of us possess these nine intelligences in varying degrees.)
2. Intelligence is a dimension on which human beings differ. No two people—not even identical twins—possess exactly the same profile of intelligences.
3. Intelligences should not be confused with learning styles, nor should multiple intelligences become an educational goal in itself (Gardner, 2004, p. xvii).

MULTIPLE INTELLIGENCES

Linguistic: This intelligence involves sensitivity to the different functions of language, including its ability to convince, stimulate, excite, convey information, and entertain. It is common among people who read and write well; who like to tell stories; and who have a talent for memorizing names, dates, and trivia.

Logical-mathematical: This intelligence involves the ability to sustain long chains of reasoning, to use analogies skilfully, to recognize and solve problems, and to discriminate patterns before being able to articulate what one is thinking. It is common among people who like mathematics, reasoning and logical tasks, problem solving, and doing experiments.

Visual-spatial: This intelligence involves the ability to transform and modify initial perceptions; to mentally take a position other than one's own physical position; to recreate aspects of one's visual experience even in the absence of the physical stimuli; to orient oneself in a physical context; and to work with graphic depictions of space, such as maps, diagrams, and geometrical forms. This talent is demonstrated in people who are good at solving puzzles, reading charts and maps, and navigating mazes.

Musical: This intelligence appears very early and involves pitch, rhythm, timbre, and tonal memory, all of which originate in the auditory-oral sphere. People strong in musical intelligence like singing, listening to music, playing an instrument, and responding to music by keeping time or dancing, and they are good at remembering melodies.

Bodily-kinesthetic: This intelligence is seen in people who are able to use their bodies in highly differentiated and skilled ways for expressive and goal-directed purposes. It includes the ability to work skilfully with objects in fine motor and gross motor ways and to master the movements of one's body in such sports as hockey, basketball, and diving.

Interpersonal: This intelligence is abundant in people who like to be with others and who are able to perceive their moods, motivations, and intentions. These people are good at leading, organizing, communicating, and manipulating others. High levels of interpersonal intelligence are often seen in those who become politicians, religious leaders, therapists, and counsellors.

Intrapersonal: The person with good knowledge of the self, who is able to understand and pursue inner feelings and instincts, is one with intrapersonal intelligence. These people often prefer to work alone and at their own pace on individual projects within their own space and pursuing their own ends.

Naturalistic: This intelligence is typical of the botanist who is able to notice small differences and make tiny discriminations among phenomena in the natural environment. People with high levels of naturalistic intelligence are often employed in roles that have to do with the environment, natural science, horticulture, and climate predictions.

Existential: This refers to the intelligence of concern with ultimate life issues, or "the intelligence of big questions" (Gardner, 2004, p. xvii). People with existential intelligence ponder the mysteries and questions of life and death and are preoccupied with humankind's relationship to the universe and nature. Theologians, poets and other writers, astronomers and other scientists are frequently among those with high levels of existential intelligence. (Gardner, 2004)

Curriculum for a Disciplined Mind

Gardner's theory of multiple intelligences, as well as developmentally appropriate practice (DAP) and emergent curriculum have influenced the ECE approach to curriculum design and planning. The level of organization present in the planned environment, according to Howard Gardner (1996), helps children master the early symbol systems of the culture, while it also fosters innovation and creativity. In planning the learning environment, ECEs are guided by the constructivist principle that children learn as much from their mistakes as from their successes. Teachers in Reggio Emilia schools recognize this principle by purposefully planning for mistakes to happen and by encouraging children to begin a project with no clear sense of what it might turn out to be (New, 1993).

Purposeful planning of the learning environment should lead to children's progress and achievement and not to adult control of what children do, the tasks they undertake, and the products they accomplish. Well-organized learning centres, and the direction provided by the play activities and experiences, comprise a rich play environment in which children's bodies and minds are challenged, their imaginations are sparked, and their motivations are kindled.

ECE Curriculum Models

Before building a curriculum framework, however, we should be familiar with various curriculum models out there, each of which addresses constructivist principles. Programs often claim that they follow a specific curriculum model, for example, the "Reggio model," "emergent curriculum," or HighScope. As we examine various models, it is important to distinguish between curriculum models and curriculum approaches. "Multiple intelligences," "developmentally appropriate practice" (DAP), and "emergent curriculum" explain approaches to implementing curriculum for young children that may be employed in either recognized "models" or a generic curriculum. None of these *approaches* prescribes a specific model, but they do emphasize certain generally accepted developmental principles that explain and influence children's development and learning. A curriculum *model* is more prescriptive in that it tends to emphasize specific developmental goals, values, practices, and standards.

Educational models are often developed for a specific context or a particular set of priorities that are important and meaningful at the time. For example, the *écoles maternelles* model evolved after the World War II to encourage French families to have more children and to provide physical and emotional support for orphaned and fatherless children. The HighScope model (Perry Project) was developed to raise the performance levels of disadvantaged children in a Head Start program in the Detroit area in the hope that early intervention would improve their success in school, and it did. Some models have broad applicability to many contexts, and all models inform early childhood education practice. Contexts and priorities are constantly changing, however, and circumstances frequently arise that create needs and interests that one model alone cannot address. For example, the mental health and physical needs of children and issues related to children living in poverty are among today's pre-occupations. It is fair to say that some existing models can be adapted to fit unique contexts and needs, but more often than not, the values and practices of the original model are so diluted that it becomes barely recognizable. Perhaps a viable Canadian approach is to evolve a model that addresses our multicultural priorities, social justice imperatives, and competitiveness rather than to retrofit models that addressed a period in time, a culture, and philosophical values that worked in a different context. When ECEs know the generic components and principles of curriculum and can design curriculum frameworks that are flexible, respond to changing needs, and are based on assessment of individual children's developmental progress, it is easier to identify the elements of other curriculum models that would be compatible within our own contexts. Canadian ECE curriculum might address issues, for example, related to children who experience English-as-a second-language challenges and respond to cultural priorities such as those related to First Nations peoples. *A purposeful, strategic, and responsive curriculum framework reflects the priorities of families and communities served by the program; the ideas and interests that emerge from the children,; and applies values, practices, and standards relevant to best practice in play-based, developmental early childhood education.* A made-in-Canada curriculum framework would ensure optimum flexibility for interpretation by the diverse populations living in Canada, including First Nations. Select elements of familiar models may be incorporated into the values, practices, and standards of Canada's curriculum framework. A few relevant models are outlined briefly in the sections that follow.

The Montessori Model

The Montessori schools, which are privately owned and operated, remain popular worldwide and in Canada. In 1907, Dr. Maria Montessori opened the first school for slum children in Rome, Italy, called the Casa dei Bambini, or Children's House, which became the prototype for the Montessori model. Many of the values and practices in the Montessori schools have influenced mainstream early childhood education practice today. These include

- an emphasis on observing the play activities of children to guide preparation of the learning environment;
- reliance on a carefully prepared environment to optimize children's choices of play activity;
- an emphasis on spontaneous, independent, and purposeful activity;
- value placed on helping children become independent and self-regulating;
- the use of specific-purpose materials to train the senses, develop skills, and prepare the intellect; and
- the importance of developing the habits of mind that contribute to self-discipline and later academic learning.

Although Montessori referred to the development of independent learning skills as "work," much of the medium for learning involved children's freely chosen play with specially designed materials. Montessori's concepts of "sensitive periods" and "the absorbent mind" often over-shadowed a primary Montessori value, which was, and still is, to promote children's adaptation over time as a "consequence of a child's active interaction with the environment." The Montessori model encourages educators to "focus on what children can do at each stage of development and to appreciate the special intellectual power, social affinity and creative potential of each stage" (Feez, 2010, p. 26).

Over the past century, the Montessori model has been misinterpreted, distorted, and also embraced and appreciated for its contribution to early childhood education. Although it has not been considered a "mainstream" ECE model in Canada, its endurance for a century is a testament to the success of the model. Although Montessori schools have sometimes been criticized for limiting creativity and reducing play to preparation for academic learning, the model has evolved to meet many social, emotional, and physical needs of children while continuing to employ sensory and conceptual materials and emphasizing the development of self-regulation and practical life skills. It is important to note that Maria Montessori was a contemporary of Jean Piaget and John Dewey, both of whom learned from her work and informed hers. Similarities also exist between Montessori's work and that of Lev Vygotsky, who described her approach as "organized development rather than learning," and who, like Montessori, saw the environment as the source of development and not just the setting in which it occurred (Feez, 2010, p. 167).

The Schools of Reggio Emilia

The schools of Reggio Emilia in the Italian city by the same name were established after World War II by a group of women who needed to work in order to help rebuild their war-torn region. These women were motivated by a determination to make fundamental changes for women in the workforce but also to protect the rights of their children to high-quality learning experiences (Fraser, 2000). Loris Malaguzzi, on hearing of these efforts, joined this group as a young teacher and over the years provided much of their inspiration and leadership. The Reggio Emilia schools, which are embedded in the tradition of Rousseau, Pestalozzi, Froebel, and Dewey, are excellent examples of a program model that emphasizes the importance of establishing the right climate for learning. Canadian ECE programs have emulated values and practices of the Reggio schools programs, and some claim to be "Reggio models." Although the Reggio Emilia schools are designed to fit the cultural context, social values, and economic conditions of the northern Italian community they serve, many of the practices fit our multi-ethnic culture and the value that people living in Canada, especially First Nations, place on our natural environments. Perhaps the foremost lesson Reggio schools teach to other nations is that the first obligation of early childhood education is to respond effectively to the children and families in their own communities rather than to transplant a model designed for another context. Listen to the wise words of Sergio Spaggiari of Reggio Emilia: "If you want to be like us, don't copy us. We have never copied anyone. If you want to be like us, be original" (New, 2005, p. 332). Bruner (1996) also reminded us of the importance of ensuring there is an authentic match between the culture and the educational approach for children. The lesson for Canadian early childhood education is that our program models for young children should reflect the cultural mosaic of our communities, and that, while we can borrow ideas and practices from Reggio Emilia and other models that may be relevant to our values and contexts, ultimately, we are obligated to apply approaches and design curriculum that serve our own needs and interests. This lesson frames the Canadian challenge, especially at a time when the mix of cultures in Canada is rapidly outgrowing the predominance of the English- or French-speaking Caucasian population.

Several aspects of the Reggio Emilia model might be considered generic to programs for young children, and other aspects are compatible with the Canadian milieu. Generic aspects include the promotion of the environment as the "third teacher"—organized to convey messages to children about the categories and styles of play anticipated in each area or zone. The Reggio Emilia schools also ensure that materials, design features, and functional pieces—such as message boards and the groupings of furniture and work spaces—facilitate adult and child partnerships in projects and planning sessions. We might also borrow climatic features that facilitate more frequent communication and connection between individuals and among groups of children and that offer regular opportunities for children from other playrooms or programs to interact, develop relationships, and collaborate in projects that move into common areas of the school (New, 2005).

The schools of Reggio Emilia believe that the curriculum emerges from the interests and ideas of the children, but that the curriculum should be "negotiated" by children and teachers jointly (Fraser, 2000). These schools see the curriculum proceeding through three phases: design, documentation, and discourse. Children are involved in the design phase and represent symbolically their ideas about the content so that their teachers can assess their level of knowledge and understanding of the topic; then, the children record their plans and the paths they intend to pursue. The documentation phase describes the process teachers and children followed as they pursued a project, and this documentation serves as a basis for planning future steps. During the discourse phase, teachers pay close attention to the language being heard and spoken and ask questions to uncover the meanings behind the words children use, as well as the reasons for them (Fraser, 2010, p. 128). These practices and others are relevant to Canadian curriculum and are frequently adopted by our programs.

Écoles Maternelles

Less attention has been given in Canada to the *école maternelle* model, which has been a central feature of French public policy since the 1940s; yet it remains one of the most developed models for early childhood education. French families have access to publicly funded, "free" early childhood education for their children from age two on, for eight hours a day, Monday to Friday, with optional after-school programs operated by many municipalities from 4:30 to 6:30 p.m. Approximately 99 percent of French children are enrolled in the *écoles maternelles.*

Most distinctive about these programs is the degree of elaboration of their curriculum and the philosophy and intentions that drive the programs. Three central principles are at the heart of the *écoles maternelles*, which are governed by the French Ministry of Education: to "school," which means to prepare children for learning in the elementary schools at the age of six; to socialize the child for life in French culture, which is multicultural; and to learn and to exercise physical, creative, and cognitive skills, including the ability to reflect and imagine, to explore widely, and to become knowledgeable. Learning to be an effective learner is a priority in these beautiful schools, which are designed specifically for young children. French citizens place a high value on emotional self-control; propriety in social interactions and behaviours; and respect for the public good, including for immigrants, who form a large segment of the French population—and the *écoles maternelles* reflect these values. Teachers in the *écoles maternelles* have a minimum of three years of university training and are respected professionals who provide significant support to parents.

The curriculum of the *écoles maternelles* rests on intensive observations of children at play with a wide range of materials selected to promote specific developmental skills. Documentation of children's progress is achieved through planned, regular observations and a portfolio for each child that contains all of the child's "productions," or photographs of what they have completed, for the teachers to assess and use in their program planning. Technologies play a significant role, and children use them to extend their play in the three-dimensional world and to solve problems that they have encountered in their play. A rigorous physical program is governed by a curriculum laid out by the Ministry and followed daily by teachers, who lead children through a series of planned physical activities, indoors and outdoors. Although the curriculum is more structured than we would see in Canada today, the results are promising, especially for children with disabilities, who make excellent progress and often start regular public schooling on a par with their classmates who are not disabled. Even given the structure in the child's day in the *école maternelle*, there is plenty of evidence of freely chosen play, including convergent and divergent activities with specific-purpose and open-ended materials, examples of children's original and creative use of art supplies, and props for sociodramatic play and sociodrama. The extent to which teachers are able to respond to queries about any child, on a moment's notice, indicates how diligent teachers are in their observations, assessments, and ability to infer the next developmental outcomes they should pursue (Shipley, 1989).

The Bank Street Model

This model originated from the pioneering work of Harriet Johnson, Lucy Sprague Mitchell, and Caroline Pratt, who together founded the Bureau of Educational Experiments in New York City in 1916, which later became the Bank Street College of Education. This influential model is based on the contributions of Jean Piaget and his followers, who believed that young children learn primarily through their interaction with concrete objects in the environment; this model became known in the 1970s as the "developmental-interaction" approach (Kohlberg & Mayer, 1972). Many of the principles practised by Bank Street have become standard early childhood education practice worldwide and form the backbone of developmentally appropriate practice and constructivist approaches. Hallmarks of the Bank Street model are its focus on development of "the whole child," the belief that motivation is intrinsic and that children's cognitive and affective development are intertwined. Children's ego identity and competence are believed to evolve from their interactions with other people and with things and events.

A unique feature of the Bank Street model is the belief that all aspects of child development are interconnected, which is manifest in the "integrated curriculum" that extends from the classroom into the community. Teachers play a key role in this model as observers of children's play and development, as facilitators of their learning through play, and as designers of a well-defined environment that gives clear messages to children about what they are to do with the materials. Handmade materials are considered useful as they can be tailored to meet the needs of individual children who may help to make them. Teachers assume that children are capable of choosing and learning from their play with activities without much intervention or planning of the environment by adults. Bank Street models emphasize helping children develop a strong sense of self; become independent in their play and learning; master the skills inherent in the activities; and, through their successes, feel confident and become eager learners able to take risks, pursue their own goals, and solve problems.

The HighScope Cognitively Oriented Curriculum

This model was developed by David Weikart of the HighScope Foundation of Ypsilanti, Michigan, as a response to the need for a head-start program for disadvantaged children. The curriculum approach was a main feature of the Perry Preschool Project, a longitudinal research project that followed children from early childhood to adulthood, and was widely recognized in the 1970s and 1980s for its claim to have raised the intelligence levels and overall competence of the disadvantaged children it served. Influenced directly by the work of Jean Piaget, the model focused on children's acquisition of the cognitive skills associated with school success. The structured curriculum approach highlighted "key experiences" for children and a "plan, do, review" delivery of activities that was frequently teacher-centred. Children choose activities freely from a variety of materials laid out in clearly defined areas for play; these play periods are interspersed with small-group and large-group activities that are largely teacher-led.

The comprehensive and well-defined curriculum covers 10 areas of development, including creative representation, language and literacy, initiative and social relations, movement, music, classification, seriation, number, space, and time. Large elements of the curriculum plans are derived from Piaget's theories related to how children develop "schema" that lead to an understanding of concepts, especially those related to number, order, classification, time, and space. Language development is reinforced by encouraging children to talk through their experiences and to describe what they are doing and feeling. The HighScope Foundation provides specialized training in the delivery of the cognitively oriented curriculum to ECEs all over North America and beyond, and the HighScope Press publishes detailed curriculum documents.

Three Approaches that Influence ECE Curriculum Design and Implementation

Multiple Intelligences

The distinction between *models* and *approaches* was made on page 145. Multiple intelligences has also been addressed on page 144. This paradigm holds that nine "intelligences" are present in all human beings but at widely variant levels. Although Howard

Gardner has always maintained that these intelligences should not be seen as goals to frame curriculum and outcomes to be achieved, the theory behind this approach has influenced curriculum models for the past three decades. It is evident that the concept of multiple intelligences is compatible with neuroscience and recent brain research discoveries, which underline the "plasticity" of the brain throughout life and undermine the old notion of a generalized intelligence factor as measured by the IQ (intelligence quotient) test. Most current curriculum models recognize Gardner's contribution to curriculum for young children. The educational practices that have evolved from *multiple intelligences* have significantly influenced how we perceive the overall mission of early childhood education and how we use this approach to help us design environments and curriculum to address all nine aspects of intelligence.

Developmentally Appropriate Practice (DAP)

The DAP movement began officially in 1987 with the publication of the position paper by Sue Bredekamp entitled "Developmentally Appropriate Practice in Early Childhood Programs: Serving Children from Birth through Age 8." This seminal paper, published by the National Association for the Education of Young Children (NAEYC), has had an impact on professional practice in Canada, the United States, and worldwide.

DAP is "informed by what we know from theory and literature about how children develop and learn" and became a mainstream approach in ECE in North America in the late 1980s (Copple & Bredekamp, 2009). Three position statements on DAP have been published by the NAEYC from 1987 to today. They elaborate on the definition and implementation of DAP as theoretical knowledge expands about child development, the impact of culture on children, and the nature of early learning. A generic curriculum framework should account for the "DAP approach" and its principles and recommended practices, which have evolved over three decades. DAP includes five interrelated dimensions: assessing children's development and learning; designing appropriate curriculum; teaching and facilitating play to enhance development and learning; supporting a caring community of learners; and establishing reciprocal relationships with families. DAP "is not a curriculum; it is not a rigid set of standards that dictate practice. Rather, it is a framework, a philosophy, or an approach to working with young children" (Bredekamp & Rosegrant, 1992, p. 4). DAP reminds us about the following three important bases for decision-making about curriculum:

- what we know about child development and the nature of learning in early childhood, along with an understanding of the order in which development often occurs and what types of experiences facilitate learning and development;
- what we have learned about each child based on observations of the child in a number of settings and play experiences, so that we can respond to individual differences and interests, including different family backgrounds, and choose developmental outcomes, teaching styles, play categories, and social contexts for play that are supportive of the child's individual development, including children with disabilities and children who are disadvantaged; and
- what we understand about the family, community, social contexts, and other priorities, so that we can ensure that our programs and activities for individual children are relevant to and respect real needs and individual interests.

Emergent Curriculum

A discussion of a curriculum framework for early childhood should include an understanding of the assumptions, values, principles, and strategies of the approach known as emergent curriculum. The word *emergent* emphasizes that planning needs to emerge from the daily life of the children and adults in the program, especially from the children's interests (Jones & Nimmo, 1994). The word *curriculum* implies advance planning by ECEs, or schools, who determine the agenda to be pursued.

Emergent curriculum has many healthy roots, all of which reflect the importance of children's input into the play opportunities they will have in their environments, which is a key principle of the schools of Reggio Emilia. Jones and Nimmo (1994) identify several origins of emergent curriculum: children's play, comments, and questions; adult interests, that is, the interests of parents as well as ECEs; things, people, and events occurring in the environment; and the developmental tasks of early childhood. Curriculum that emerges from these origins is called "emergent" because it evolves, changes direction as connections are made, and is open to new possibilities and opportunities as children play (Jones & Reynolds, 1992). Emergent curriculum is not just a matter of going with the flow and observing what children do; it is guided by observing children as they play and by using that information to create activities and projects that capitalize on their interests and on knowing what they need to experience and learn next. In this sense, emergent curriculum has a structure, but not the kind of structure that presupposes specific activities for all children. Emergent curriculum is also guided by the direction in which children are headed, that is, the normal tasks of development and their natural progression through play toward the achievement of the developmental outcomes that have been identified for each child. Curriculum also emerges by observing children's responses to activities and experiences and by becoming knowledgeable about what motivates each child; what captures their interest; what kinds of supports they may need in their play; and how they respond to new challenges, taking risks, and overcoming obstacles. In this sense too, emergent curriculum is not a curriculum model but, rather, an approach to curriculum that emphasizes planning and setting up activities based on each child's developmental and motivational trajectory.

Emergent curriculum adds *processes* for curriculum development. It focuses attention on curriculum *content* personally meaningful to children because the child's construction of meaning is a key to learning and motivation (Goulet, 2001). Emergent curriculum also affirms that spontaneous choices by children should be respected and pursued and, where possible, linked to the curriculum framework. When ECEs "trust in the power of play" (Jones & Nimmo, 1999), the teaching emphasis turns to ensuring that play opportunities are rich, varied, and absorbing in order to spawn ideas and impulses that arise from the children themselves.

Emergent curriculum does not imply an absence of planning or the absence of a framework to guide activities and teaching in the early learning environment. Neither does emergent curriculum mean that children should meander within the environment while ECEs wait for an idea or interest to reveal itself. Jones and Nimmo (1999) state that children need to become "competent players," and therein lies the challenge for ECEs. Building the curriculum framework challenges ECEs to create a rich blend of environmental design and program and unit planning within a developmental backdrop that facilitates all categories of play and challenges children's thinking, stimulates ideas, elicits curiosity and lasting interest, and prompts questions and inquiry.

Recent studies support linking emergent curriculum with intention and purposeful planning for play. These links are particularly evident, for example, in the *play-literacy interface,* which implies that well-planned play can serve **literacy** by "a) providing settings that promote literacy activity, skill and strategies; b) serving as a language experience that can build connections between oral and written modes of expression; and, c) providing opportunities to teach and learn literacy" (Roskos & Christie, 2001, p. 59–89). These findings do not imply that ECEs should limit play in order to emphasize literacy. Rather, they underline that play should be seen as the catalyst through which children are exposed to and use language in a variety of forms—expressive (speaking), receptive (hearing), reading, writing, drawing, and role playing. Instead of reducing opportunities for sociodramatic play in favour of instruction in letters and sounds, the links between play and literacy are firmly grounded in creating more opportunities for children to interact and assume roles in increasingly elaborate and extended sociodramatic play episodes. Much of the responsibility for ensuring the prevalence of sociodramatic play opportunities falls to the ECE, who provides the environments and the props that stimulate this particularly rich form of play. Here, again, is an example of the importance of the curriculum backdrop that fosters the emergence of freely chosen, child-initiated play that assumes the significance and meaning the child intends. For example, providing writing tools in dramatic play areas increases children's writing tendencies (Bredekamp, 2004). Setting up an office in the Project centre gives children the props they need to assume roles and collaborate in a sociodramatic play episode in which they also read, print, listen, speak, and exchange information and ideas.

Emergent curriculum is compatible with developmental curriculum. A developmental curriculum framework includes statements of purpose and a range of teaching and learning methods that may be chosen by ECEs to facilitate children's achievement of outcomes, and it describes the resources and tools for assessing children's achievement. A generic framework does not dictate specific activities, themes, or interests that should be addressed; these are part of the monthly and weekly program plans. The activities and **learning experiences** that emerge from the interests and ideas of children and ECEs, along with events that emerge spontaneously from children's play and their daily lives, are inserted within the developmental framework.

When children's interests are factored into the curriculum framework, the relationships among developmental outcomes, developmental objectives, resources, activities, and assessment strategies remain the same. Jones and Nimmo (1994, p. 5) explain the approach this way:

> In an emergent curriculum we take the children as our models and our co-players. We are the stage directors; curriculum is teacher's responsibility, not the children's. People who hear the words *emergent curriculum* may wrongly assume that everything simply emerges from the children. The children's ideas are an important source of curriculum but only one of many possible sources that reflect the complex ecology of their lives. Teachers need to have both the ideas and a vision of where the players might adventure together. The teacher, the responsible adult, is the organizer who sets the stage, times the acts, and keeps the basic drama together. On those days when all the parts come together, the result is truly magic.

THEMES WITHIN A PLAY-BASED DEVELOPMENTAL CURRICULUM FRAMEWORK

The play-based developmental curriculum framework provides a generic model that accommodates a variety of theoretical approaches; a wide range of values, practices, and standards; an eclectic mix of environmental design strategies and program plans; and many teaching methods. A curriculum framework also accommodates planning that is knowledge-based and subject-based, usually through themes that interest the children. A child will not say, for example, "This week I want to work on my fine motor skills." She may, however, express an interest in making a cloth collage with the colourful fabric patches that one parent brought to the sewing table on Monday. The idea may spread among the children that it would be fun to make a quilt as a group project instead of an individual collage, and this discussion may lead to an investigation of what a quilt looks like and how to make one. At this point, the quilt project idea has been adopted. The idea emerged from the children and the gesture of one parent sharing scraps of cloth. From there, the ECE encourages the children to discuss the project and elaborate it further; then he links it to the developmental outcomes and objectives contained in the curriculum. It becomes important to the children to make the quilt together, and it is what matters to them most at the time. It is the ECE's role to define the project, find and organize the resources children may need, identify potential steps in the project, and monitor the children's progress as they proceed.

Identifying a Canadian Approach to Curriculum Design

A major purpose of ECE curriculum is to help children develop a strong foundation for lifelong learning while living their childhoods to their fullest possible potential. This value implies that children are protected, nurtured, challenged, and respected; that they play freely; and that they experience a *good day*. A strong foundation includes positive dispositions for learning, that is, habits of mind built on a strong sense of self, a respect for learning, a curious nature, a regard for truth, a facility for self-regulation, and an ability to delay gratification. Early childhood education fosters a range of thinking styles and encourages children to use them judiciously (i.e., thoughtfully, in the appropriate context, and with sound judgment). It also instills positive health habits that include physical exercise and fitness, a healthy diet, and respect for the body. Spiritual growth, the appreciation of beauty, and artistic expression are also goals for early learning. Effective curriculum fosters sociomoral dispositions, including empathy, compassion, and respect for people of all cultures. These dispositions rely on the ability to communicate effectively, to interact positively, and to maintain constructive relationships. Goleman's (2006) concept of *social intelligence,* added to his earlier definition of *emotional intelligence,* claims that children inherit the potential for healthy adaptation, socially and emotionally, but he emphasized that the neural circuitry for both is constructed through learning experiences designed to help children build social and emotional skills. ECE programs generally assign a high priority to emotional intelligence and social intelligence outcomes.

A Canadian curriculum model should be clear and easy to explain to parents and other stakeholders. Effective curriculum design requires that ECEs collaborate in the creation of a model and plans that are well understood and supported by the teaching team. Why plan a curriculum? The answer is simple and unequivocal. Without planning, the hard work of nurturing and helping children develop may be hit-and-miss, arbitrary, and fragmented. ECEs' time and program resources would be expended for no useful purpose. It is true that children develop and learn in the absence of a planned curriculum; children are curious, resourceful, and usually motivated to explore their environments. Children, like adults, however, benefit from some structure and sense of direction in their daily lives, and planning injects purpose and potential into the child's play. It helps children choose meaningful play activities and pursue worthwhile interests instead of drifting aimlessly, even though there may be times when children should be allowed to drift aimlessly—and these should be recognized. Given the precious resources dedicated to programs and the aim of capitalizing on this exceptionally vibrant stage in development and learning, a curriculum and planning are needed to justify funding, to use scarce resources effectively, and to ensure that results are available and convincing to stakeholders. A well-articulated curriculum respects children's right to make progress and to feel, from an early age, a sense of personal achievement.

Summary

An ECE philosophy that identifies values, practices, and standards and that capitalizes on the findings of neuroscience, brain research, child development, and educational theory all contribute to the foundations for curriculum. Choices of educational outcomes, the design of environments, activity and program planning, and observation and assessment strategies are influenced by three recognized "approaches" to curriculum: multiple intelligences, developmentally appropriate practice (DAP), and emergent curriculum. ECEs benefit from knowledge about familiar models for early childhood education, such as Montessori schools, *écoles maternelles*, Reggio Emilia, HighScope, and Bank Street schools. Equipped with knowledge related to the key elements that constitute curriculum, ECEs are prepared to design a curriculum framework that best fits the needs and interests of their children and families, the context in which the program operates, and the sociopolitical and economic challenges of the broader environment.

Learning Activities

1. Visit two programs, each of which represents a different curriculum model. Describe the characteristics of the model which you observed and provide short examples for each characteristic. Identify the role of the ECE during your visit. Collect brochures that advertise and explain the purpose and goals of the program. Was there consistency between the program literature and what you observed? Retain your comments in your journal.
2. Assume that you are asked to list a set of values for the program in which you are teaching that will be used to draft a curriculum framework. Explain the values that you would choose for your draft. Link the three approaches—multiple intelligences, DAP, and emergent curriculum—to your list.
3. Read a book or an article by Howard Gardner in which he addresses the topic of multiple intelligences. Which of these intelligences do you believe you were encouraged to develop when you were in elementary school? How did you do so? Were there any that you did not develop fully? Explain why. Record your answers in your journal.

9 Developmental Curriculum Framework

> "Curriculum is a framework for developing a coherent set of learning experiences that enables children to reach the identified goals."
>
> —Carol Copple and Sue Bredekamp, NAEYE Position Statement (2009)

Before Reading This Chapter, Have You

- observed various models for early childhood curriculum and compared and contrasted their environmental and program features?
- appreciated the cultural, social, and political influences on ECE curriculum?
- understood the role of values, practices, and standards in the task of building a curriculum framework?
- understood the influence of the three approaches to curriculum discussed in Chapter 8?

Outcomes

After reading and understanding this chapter, you should be able to

- create and use tools to observe children and assess their developmental progress;
- build a framework for curriculum planning based on assessments of children's development and interests, developmental outcomes, and developmental objectives;
- apply practices related to authentic assessment; and
- apply principles of early learning to planning curriculum based on developmental outcomes.

Inputs to the Curriculum Framework

Curriculum is a complex instrument for facilitating learning that includes various components. These components are identified and defined in the "Curriculum Components" box below. A **curriculum framework** influences the curriculum design and typically starts with intentions, which may be stated as **goals.** Goals are **inputs** to the curriculum. The inputs are based on ECEs' and parents' understanding of the broad aims for their children; they include the input to curriculum planning derived from the assessment reports. In Chapter 8, we saw that inputs are also influenced by values sometimes expressed as the philosophy, goals, or a vision for the program.

CURRICULUM COMPONENTS

- **Curriculum** "is intentions or plans ..., not activities, but a blueprint for activities ... that articulates the relationships among its different elements" (Pratt, 1980, p. 4).
- **Program** refers to activities and experiences that are planned and implemented that organize and describe the content of the program.
- **Curriculum design** refers to the deliberate choice of intentions (which include developmental outcomes and objectives), strategies to address the intentions, and ways to determine whether the intentions have been fulfilled.
- A **curriculum framework** lays out the elements of curriculum design and includes the elements listed below.
    - **Developmental goals** or intentions are inputs to curriculum and are derived from assessment reports and the interests and priorities of ECEs, children, parents, and communities
    - **Developmental outcomes** are "results" that describe complex, reliable and verifiable demonstrations by children in their play that they have achieved the tasks of development relevant to their age.
    - **Developmental objectives** describe sequential and incremental steps toward the achievement of developmental outcomes; developmental objectives are attached to play activities and experiences that are planned, based on the interests shown by children, to encourage and enhance play and help children make developmental progress.
    - **Implementation strategies** refer to the design of environments (Chapter 7); the choice of equipment, materials, and supplies for play (Chapter 6); and the planning of play activities, learning experiences, and projects to address the developmental objectives (see Chapters 10 and 18).
    - **Methods** are implementation strategies that describe *direct* and *indirect* ways to enhance children's play and to facilitate development and learning through play.
    - **Observation strategies** involve tools and practices for observing children at play in order to learn more about the whole child, to gauge their developmental progress, and to determine their interests.
    - **Assessment** is a systematic procedure for gathering and examining evidence of children's developmental progress that relies on observation records, parental input, ECE's perceptions, and other input; the results of assessment form the basis of reports that become inputs that guide the next steps in program and activity planning and individual development plans.

Inputs to the curriculum emerge from the cultural composition of the families served by the program and their priorities for their children. Inputs are usually reflected in the developmental outcomes, which are based on the developmental tasks. Research on human development has, for over a century, added to our understanding of the developmental tasks of early childhood. These inputs influence the design of the environment, the curriculum emphasis and special interests, the approach to observation and assessment, and also the criteria for program evaluation. Appendix A presents a comprehensive set of developmental outcomes based on the developmental tasks of early childhood. When these developmental outcomes are understood, it is easier to follow the steps in curriculum planning. The sensory, hands-on nature of children's learning in early childhood, which has been established over decades of research, also informs curriculum. Neuroscience and psychology influence what we believe about the nature of intelligence and the plasticity of the brain, and are increasingly relevant to ECE curriculum. Educational theory related to the unique ways in which young children learn has considerable impact on curriculum content and methods for teaching and learning. This discussion will begin with the principles of learning in early childhood.

STEPS IN CURRICULUM DESIGN

A. Know the *principles of learning* in early childhood.
B. Identify the *intentions* or *goals* of the curriculum for children in a program.
C. Observe children and assess their progress in all developmental domains.
D. State the *developmental outcomes* of the curriculum framework for each developmental domain based on the goals (intentions) and assessments of children's developmental progress.
E. Identify developmental objectives related to the developmental outcomes (in ascending order of complexity).
F. Ensure that the layout design, organization, and provisioning of the learning centres in the playroom and outdoor play areas reflect the developmental outcomes of the program. (Resources were addressed in Chapter 6 and use of space in indoor environments in Chapter 7.)
G. Plan *activities* for play and learning related to the developmental objectives, i.e., program planning (see Chapter 10).
H. Describe the play-based *teaching and learning methods* that will be used to facilitate children's achievement of the developmental objectives.
I. Plan curriculum content and design *curriculum webs* that link the curriculum content (i.e., activities and projects) to developmental outcomes and objectives.
J. *Evaluate* the curriculum.

A. Know the Principles of Learning in Early Childhood

The following 13 principles link an understanding of how young children learn to the curriculum framework. Applying these principles requires a unique blend of expertise and professionalism on the part of the ECE that is not possessed by untrained staff. These principles are derived from a century or more of input from the philosophers and educational theorists referred to in Chapter 2.

1. Children learn largely through the senses; therefore, they require plenty of opportunities for sensory involvement with their environment.
2. Children learn when they can explore and experiment in an environment that allows them freedom to move, to choose among real alternatives, and to pursue activities at their own pace, at their own developmental levels, and according to their unique learning styles.
3. Children learn by doing—by interacting with concrete objects in the environment. Studies show that learning by doing involves "playful learning," which means that "playfulness is linked to learning via all aspects of children's development—cognitive, social, physical, and emotional, and via their home and curriculum experiences, all of which contribute to their wellbeing" (Broadhead et al., 2010, p. 182).

4. Learning is most effective when children are interested in what they are learning and are able to choose and pursue play activities in their own way. (This is a fundamental principle of emergent curriculum.) When children learn in a context meaningful to them and that they have discovered for themselves, their learning will generally be remembered.
5. Children learn in an environment where they feel psychologically safe, where they are able to take risks and make mistakes, and where they receive encouragement and well-timed, guided support in learning.
6. Preoperational children learn best in informal settings where they engage in active, hands-on play, leading to learning that is experiential and process-oriented. Learning occurs through interaction with concrete objects that respond to their actions on them. Formal learning is appropriate for concrete-operational children, starting at age six or seven, when they begin to use the tools that aid formal learning, such as textbooks and tests. In informal settings, children with disabilities often need direct intervention in their playful learning to help them overcome physical, cognitive, or emotional disabilities and make developmental progress.
7. When the concept or the skill to be learned is inherent in a play activity, children may uncover or discover the concept on their own. Example: concept of "sink and float" with objects that either sink or float at the water table. Children also uncover concepts when their play is open-ended and exploratory, whereby the concept reveals itself as children explore the properties of the materials. Examples: thick versus runny paint on newsprint; the packing qualities of wet versus dry sand.
8. Early learning experiences are most effective when they take children from simple to more complex levels of knowledge, skill, and understanding; from concrete to abstract concepts; and from general to specific. Examples: number recognition before constancy of number; bead stringing with laces and large beads of three colours to thread and needle with small multicoloured beads in self-repeating patterns.
9. Revisiting knowledge, skills, and concepts in a variety of contexts different from that in which the learning first took place reinforces and transfers the learning from one context to another. Examples: making patterns with parquetry; forming patterns with blocks and making patterns on the computer screen.
10. Learning is most effective when play experiences build on what children already know and take them one step further. The new learning task should be just far enough from what the child already knows to be challenging, but not so far as to discourage and frustrate. This education principle is known as **optimal discrepancy** (Piaget, 1969). Vygotsky's (1978) zone of proximal development (ZPD) is also relevant here. This means that children learn efficiently when the learning of new knowledge, skills, or concepts is supported by ECEs or peers in a context just above what they have already achieved. These supports for learning are also built into the staging of specific-purpose materials used in Montessori programs.
11. Recognize the child's **learning style**, which refers to each child's preference for a style of learning consistent with his developmental level

and interests as well as his reliance on tactile, auditory, or visual stimuli in the environment. Each child may employ a range of learning styles depending on the play situation, and learning styles vary widely among children (Gardner, 1989). Some children learn best through listening to, interpreting, and acting on auditory messages. Tactile learners have to touch and feel things to form concepts that endure. These children like to test, experiment, and manipulate materials. Some children are observers and are relatively passive in their learning. Other children prefer learning in social contexts by imitating and collaborating with their peers. Still others are solitary learners who prefer to play alone, to pursue their own objectives and interests, and to reach conclusions at their own pace. Some children learn best in a quiet, orderly environment, where activity and noise levels are kept to a minimum and where they are able to remain at the task for long periods. Other children need plenty of activity, room to move, frequent breaks, and many opportunities to change from one activity to another. *Activity planning for each learning centre should account for the wide variety of learning styles and children's preferred contexts for learning. Early childhood is a time for children to experience many different ways to learn.*

12. Children are deemed to have learned when they are able to transfer the learning gained in one context to another context. Piaget (1969) claimed that there are two kinds of learning. One kind refers to the acquisition of new responses within specific contexts; that is, the child has learned the skills appropriate to the context but has not generalized the concept to another context. The second kind of learning occurs when the child has acquired new mental structures that transfer the learning gained in one setting to a learning challenge in another setting. Piaget believed that the latter type of learning endures.

13. Activities should begin at the child's developmental level, and significant learning challenges should be sequenced, step by step, in an order and at a pace relevant to the child. It is helpful to provide models or demonstrations of successful task completion. When a child encounters an obstacle to her success in an activity, the ECE may decide to intervene to help the child overcome a temporary stumbling block, or make a suggestion that will reveal an alternative approach. This is an example of **scaffolding**.

SCAFFOLDING

A **scaffold** is anything an ECE provides that enables a child to perform a skill or understand a concept (Vinson, 2001). It is the process of helping a child to overcome obstacles to learning within a unit of activities in order to move to the next level. As children learn at their own rates, the speed with which they progress developmentally varies from child to child, and within each child, depending on the nature of the learning experience. Learning occurs most readily when the new learning to be acquired contains elements of something already familiar to the child. Piaget describes the *optimal discrepancy* that should be present in any new learning experience; this means the distance between what the child knows already and what the child has to learn within a specific activity should be optimal, or *just right*. Too little discrepancy between what is known already and what needs to be learned will fail to challenge or motivate the child. Too much discrepancy may frustrate the child and discourage learning. Scaffolding is related to Vygotsky's sociohistoric theory (1978), which suggests that young children actually co-construct knowledge with the assistance of others and in association with others. He described the scaffolding process in terms of guided assistance to a child as she reaches a **Zone of**

Proximal Development, the point at which learning may slow down or stop unless she is helped to overcome the difficulty she has encountered. Without well-timed intervention, the child may pursue the wrong direction or switch to another activity. The adult who is helping the child needs to simplify the steps leading to the concept, ask questions to discern what the child understands, supply the right amount of suggestion, and coach or provide physical assistance at the right time in the child's learning cycle. Jerome Bruner (1976) was one of the first to recognize scaffolding, which attempts to facilitate learning by breaking down what is to be learned into building blocks and adapting each block to the learning styles, interests, and developmental needs of each child. This simplification of the learning process makes it more likely that the child will perform all tasks associated with learning something significant, thereby maintaining her interest and motivation. ECEs also help children adjust their performance so as to successfully complete the learning goal. Scaffolding techniques are important for children with disabilities, who often need more support and intervention in the learning process, adjustments in activities, alterations in resources, feedback on performance, and direct assistance from teachers.

B. Identify Intentions and State Goals for the Curriculum

Goals describe, in broad terms, the long-term aims or intentions of programs and reflect a vision over time for children's play, development, and learning. Goals are influenced by cultural, social, and political conditions and priorities, as we saw in Chapter 8. Inputs include, for example, an emphasis on an arts or literacy program, or on ESL programming, or perhaps a religious focus for private denominational programs. Planning the curriculum accounts for priorities most highly valued by interested and concerned persons, who include ECEs, parents, governments, the school system, and the community. For curriculum goals to reflect the priorities of the families implies that ECEs understand parents' hopes for their children and are persistent in helping parents communicate their interests. This often means finding ways to overcome language barriers so that parents can communicate and understand clearly the aims and rationale for the program and ask questions to reveal any concerns or doubts they may have.

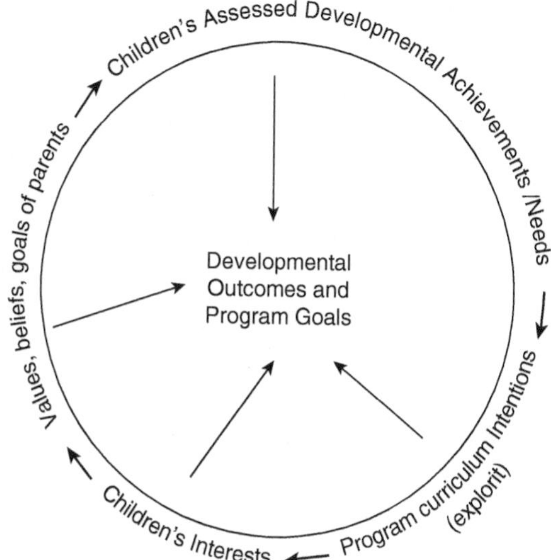

Figure 9–1
Curriculum intentions or goals as inputs to curriculum

C. Observe Children and Assess Their Progress in All Developmental Domains

This step usually begins any new planning cycle. It is important to observe and record accurately children at play in a variety of learning centres and social contexts, including outdoor play. Observation reports support the assessment of children's developmental progress in all domains and their interests and strengths. **Assessment reports** usually lead to the creation of an individual development plan (IDP) for each child.

Broadhead et al. (2010, p. 183) suggest that "observation sits at the heart of understanding the links between play and learning, and the significance of playful meanings and intentions for young children." This perspective enhances the role of observation and recommends sustained observations of children at play—which includes listening to their conversations, querying them about their intentions, and engaging them in conversations about what they are doing or planning. Supporting children's playful learning requires reflection by the ECE, whose purpose is to "locate children's play choices and activities within a wider theoretical framework of the nature of playful learning" (Broadhead et al., 2010, p. 183).

There are many tools and strategies for observing children as they play and interact throughout the program day; these are outlined in numerous publications that describe observation and assessment approaches. Recommended strategies for observation that emphasize playful learning do not consist primarily of brief observations using checklists, but rather recommend using children's interests and ideas as starting points for conversations with children about their play, a practice that contributes to an "emergent" approach to curriculum. Learning through play takes many forms and can be documented using a range of observation tools, photographs, samples of work, videos, and audio recordings (Glazzard & Percival, 2010, p. 19). ECEs describe children's participation in play, group, and individual activities and their behaviours or responses to situations and events. Observations, which are intended to enhance play, record the ECE's response to conversations with children about their intentions, what they imagine, and what they are thinking. Palaiologou & Bangs (2010, p. 59) note that

> the systematic collection of information about children's development and learning helps professionals to: collect and gather evidence that can offer an accurate picture of children, their learning and development; understand the reasons behind children's behaviour; recognize stages in development; inform planning and assessment; provide opportunities for collaboration with parents and other professionals; find out about children as individuals; monitor progress; inform curriculum planning; enable staff to evaluate their practice; and, provide a focus for discussion and improvement.

AUTHENTIC ASSESSMENT

In recent years, attention has focused on **authentic assessment** in early childhood education programs. Gober (2002, p. 3) explains that assessment is really "taking stock" of children's growth and development, and that authentic assessment documents and evaluates growth and development, over time, using real-life situations. Scientific observation and assessment involve rigorous, scientific procedures, designed and implemented by experts, but, for the purposes of early childhood education, observation and assessments should be practical, efficient, and integrated into the daily planning cycle. Assessment is used to identify where support is needed (Glazzard & Percival, 2010, p. 3). The key is to ensure that observations are recorded in some fashion and to not rely on memory or good intentions to capture at the end of the day what has been observed earlier in the day.

Authentic assessment uses a wide range of tools to simplify the process of gathering information for the assessment report. Several resource books describe methods (time samples, event samples, interval samples, anecdotal records) and tools that may be used for record-keeping, including self-adhesive notes, checklists, notebooks and clipboards, and digital cameras to photograph the child at play (Wright, 2010). Many programs set up a **portfolio** for each child, a large file with subdivided sections for the developmental domains that store samples of children's productions; the observation records, checklists, and tapes; photographs of children's interactions with people; materials and equipment; and anecdotal notes recording play and social behaviours, preferences, and habits. Computer files have become standard tools for collecting and storing information about children's progress; they allow greater flexibility in record-keeping and tabulating input, and they facilitate the preparation of assessment reports. A summary of common strategies is provided below, but students are advised to consult resource books on observation strategies.

OBSERVATION STRATEGIES

Time sampling: uses an observation checklist and a time counter set for a specific interval of time—e.g., 60 seconds—to record on the checklist at prescribed intervals, usually at different times during the day.

Interval sampling: to target simple behaviours during specified timeframes, the actual amount of time spent on an activity is recorded and tabulated. Frequency sampling counts how many unique incidences of a behaviour occur over a timeframe.

Event sampling: periodic observations during a limited timeframe to determine in which activities the child participates, often using video cameras to record the episode.

Anecdotal records: to capture a significant event or a story that provides insight into a characteristic of a child and to describe it, one occurrence at a time, usually during playtime and when children are interacting with peers. Anecdotal records are best undertaken as the day begins or as the child moves to a new activity and should be recorded on the spot. This approach is often used to gain insight into concerns about behaviour.

Adapted from R. Wright (2010). *Multifaceted Assessment for Early Childhood Education* (pp. 87–89). Thousand Oaks, CA: Sage.

OBSERVATION AND ASSESSMENT

Assessing children's development is both the starting point and the end point of the program planning cycle, a circular process that is ongoing, constantly evolving and sometimes changing direction. Observing and assessing tasks function in tandem. They start with observations, which are made easier and clearer when the environment for play is well organized and when learning centres are clearly defined and materials are readily accessible to children so that they can initiate their own activities. The schedule has to allow sufficient time for children to become fully engaged. As time is often a stumbling block to observation, the well-planned environment, which gives cues to children about what they can play with and uncluttered space to pursue their chosen play activity, frees up time during play periods for ECEs to grab a notepad and take notes while the children play. Thoughtful planning of the environment is a key strategy for ensuring the integrity of the curriculum, which depends on accurate input from observations and careful assessments of children's developmental progress. Planning also requires scheduling practices that protect long play periods free of unnecessary routines and allow children to remain with activities long enough for ECEs to really see what children can do and understand. Given the challenges of finding staff time to observe children, Palaiologou and Bangs (2010) recommend involving parents in collecting information about children by contributing anecdotes from home and completing answers to questions in booklets, which shed more light on, for example, children's play interests and visits that they enjoy.

Simpler, efficient means of observing and recording children's developmental progress seem to work best when there isn't time for the more sustained observations of children's play recommended by Wood et al. (2010). Tools that assist in gathering data related to individual children should record the child's participation in the play activities; the child's achievement of the developmental objectives; and, whenever possible, examples to prove that the child has transferred the learning achieved in one unit of play activities to new activities and contexts. Checklists are among the simplest assessment tools available. Gober (2002) maintains that the checklists used should always be objective, include the dates of observations, and add evidence and anecdotes to support the checklist information. Practicality suggests that observation tools should be easy for ECEs to use while they are busy with other tasks or while they are working with children. Accurate assessment of each child often leads to the individualizing of curriculum according to the child's needs and interests with specific developmental objectives becoming part of his individual development plan (IDP) (see pp. 165–166).

More detailed and lengthy observations are also essential for assessment reports, and time should be taken to write a detailed account of a child's behaviour and performance during a sustained period of time. For example, resource teachers expect more detailed observations of children with special needs. The object of assessment is to understand the whole child, to become familiar with their play and learning styles, and not only to document the child's achievement of the developmental objectives and outcomes. Detailed records describe children's play, what interests them, how they communicate and interact, where they stumble, how they respond to obstacles to successful completion of activities, and examples of their social and emotional development and well-being. ECEs should always be alert to behavioural signs that may suggest a budding mental health or learning to learn issue.

The success of a play activity may be partly revealed by the child's participation, whether the child completed what she intended to do, and her level of achievement of the activity's objectives. The curriculum framework includes assessment methods and the tools used to determine the children's level of participation in the activities linked to each developmental objective, and children's achievement of the objectives. Activities checklists are addressed in Chapter 10, p. 193. For greater efficiency, ECEs may identify certain "benchmark activities" that reveal the child's progress on key indicators, such as the level of readiness with which the child is approaching the activity, ability to sustain play and problem solve to overcome obstacles, degree of success with the objectives, persistence in the presence of distractions and other challenges, and the extent to which children are "good players." **Benchmark activities** are addressed on pages 139 and 171. The relationship of the activity to the child's skill and understanding of the task inherent in the activity should be noted. It is important to also record perceptions gained through conversations with children about their play, their aspirations, and their intentions in addition to children's achievement of developmental objectives. The importance of play and "learning through play" calls for much more than a record of directly observable behaviours, and more intensive investigation reaps dividends.

ASSESSMENT REPORTS

Assessment means synthesizing information about the "whole child," usually gathered through systematic observation methods, in order to ascertain a child's progress in all developmental domains: social, emotional, physical, and cognitive. Assessment examines all documentation compiled during observations, including examples and photographs of children's "productions." Assessment demands that ECEs learn to listen, examine, hypothesize, intervene, evaluate, and then reflect and design (Meisels, 2000). In addition to careful review of observation records and samples of children's productions, ECEs discuss with their colleagues the inferences they are making from the observation records and samples in order to test their individual perceptions and analysis and invite alternative viewpoints. The ECE responsible for each child will usually compile the assessment report, which is a succinct summary of the review process, and this summary is also shared with colleagues whose input is invited. The assessment report is linked to the developmental outcomes of the curriculum and to the individual development plan for the child. Recommendations are made in the report to promote the child's continued developmental progress.

Assessment reports provide information for meetings with parents to discuss their child's progress and the ECE's recommendations. The first priority in meeting parents is to put them at ease, to encourage them to ask questions and discuss what they have observed about their child, and to invite them to provide information about how the child spends her time at home (Wright, 2010). This approach is often followed by a positive description by the ECE of the child's progress and a review of the assessment report, which may raise issues and questions about how best to help the child make further developmental progress. Once a consensus with the parents is reached, the recommendations may be framed as objectives for the child's individual development plan, and the cycle continues. The recommendations also include the child's perceived interests and ideas, as this information helps ECEs motivate his participation in activities. The assessment process and reports involve considerable reflection, collaboration, and consultation among ECEs and with parents.

INDIVIDUAL DEVELOPMENT PLANS (IDP)

Individual development plans have already been mentioned. An **individual development plan (IDP)** is a variation of the individual education plan (IEP), which is a recognized instrument used by resource teachers and other specialists for children with disabilities. An IDP may take many forms but in its simplest form usually includes a written summary of the child's development and interests, along with a series of objectives for the child to pursue as next steps in the curriculum. Often, program staff determine together the formats they wish to use for the IDPs, which may be simple or more complex depending on the skills and confidence of the ECEs using them.

The purpose of observation and assessment is to ensure that each child is understood holistically—and that includes developmental progress in all domains: the child's interests, what motivates the child, how the child behaves in a range of situations, how the child interacts with other children, and the level of sophistication of her play (Percival, 2010). Observations help ECEs gain a composite sketch of the child as a whole; this information may then be transferred to a plan that provides direction for the individual child. The IDPs for all children provide input to the overall curriculum for the group.

TABLE 9–1

ELEMENTS OF AN INDIVIDUAL DEVELOPMENT PLAN (IDP)

ECEs often have their own formats for IDPs, but there are several common elements that appear in whatever format is used.

- child's current developmental level for all domains
- developmental objectives for the child to focus on over a few weeks or months
- child's interests and the play activities she appears to enjoy most
- recommendation of play activities to be encouraged in all learning centres
- descriptions of child's preferred play styles and learning styles: e.g., solitary, associative, collaborative, in role play, active physical play, projects, etc.; recommendations to encourage the child to try other play styles outside of his comfort zone
- descriptions of typical play behaviours and objectives for play
- descriptions of typical social behaviours and objectives for play
- language and communication skills and recommended objectives
- physical skills and recommended objectives for further practice and development: e.g., body awareness, basic fundamental movements, sensory-perceptual abilities, physical abilities, skilled movements, and healthy attitudes

CURRICULUM AND THE CHILD WITH DISABILITIES

McCollum and Bair (1994, p. 86) state that "early childhood special education is, first and foremost, intervention: the underlying purpose and hope is to change the trajectory of development from what it would have been without intervention." Dogmatic views that all learning should be active, that direct teaching always negates active learning, and that tasks should be introduced in a specific sequence are not helpful for children who need teachers to intervene in their learning and to address their unique developmental sequences and needs. Children of all developmental levels, from the most delayed to the most gifted, need sensory play and learning experiences, and environments that help them explore, question, and build concepts. They also need ECEs who encourage and guide them to use their strengths to the best possible advantage (Allen, Paasche, Cornell, & Engel, 1998). Edmiaston, Dolezal, Doolittle, Erickson, and Merrit (2000) suggested that, historically, special education was grounded in behavioural science and direct instruction, which does not fit with the constructivist framework. The narrow definition of the goals of individual education plans (IEPs) may be broadened, however, to reflect a constructivist orientation and a focus on the whole child (Allen et al., 2006). Understanding involves internal change; such change occurs more readily when children are able to experience their world for themselves through hands-on interaction with concrete objects in the environment. ECEs have to use teaching methods that accommodate children's interests and their learning styles, aptitudes, and developmental patterns and levels, and they must design and adapt the environment accordingly. Once a learning environment has been set up, the ECE can then encourage and support play and learning ideas that emerge from the children's interests, promote their self-directed learning, and plan appropriate intervention.

SUMMARY OF THE DEVELOPMENTAL ASSESSMENT AND PLANNING PROCESS

1. Analyze the notes recorded by considering children's use of the materials, supplies, and equipment and achievement of the objectives of the activities and the learning that has occurred.
2. Formulate developmental objectives to take children from objectives they have already achieved to the next steps in development and learning.
3. Create a profile for each child that describes the child's preferred play styles and learning styles, behaviour, and progress made toward each developmental outcome. Curriculum outcomes are an amalgamation of the identified developmental outcomes for each child; they are an integrated set of outcomes for the whole group.
4. Plan activities that address the developmental objectives identified for each child in the group. In age-graded groups of children, the developmental stages and abilities of the children may be somewhat similar; this simplifies the planning task for ECEs.
5. Plan activities for children with special needs directly related to their development and adapt activities used for the typical child so that the child with special needs can engage in play with other children in the group.

D. State the Developmental Outcomes of the Curriculum

Children vary widely in their developmental patterns and the rate at which they make progress, and their progress across the developmental domains is uneven. The term *developmental outcomes* describes children's reliable and verifiable demonstrations of developmental progress related to the tasks of development. Developmental outcomes are usually demonstrated by children before they are deemed to be ready for the next program level, such as toddler to preschool, preschooler to kindergarten, and kindergarten to grade one. Outcomes rely on a "*design back*" approach to ensure that the internal composition of the outcome is well understood. This approach supports children's learning by defining the incremental steps toward the achievement of each outcome. These incremental steps are described as *developmental objectives,* and they generally occur in a rational flow from simple to complex, general to specific, and concrete to abstract.

In ECE, we may also apply the "distance-from-self criterion" (Holt, 1989), meaning that the curriculum starts close to the child's own life experience and context and expands outwards, moving the child gradually into less familiar territory. (See Figure 21-2 on p. 408.) This is why, for example, it is often best to introduce children to stories about domestic pets and local animals before stories and activities on dinosaurs or elephants and tigers. The outcome statements that guide the curriculum and individual development plans and frame the assessment reports describe, over the long term, the integrated learning that children should be able to demonstrate and apply at the end of a defined timeframe.

In addition to describing the developmental tasks of early childhood, outcome statements in curriculum may also reflect the social usefulness and cultural importance of specific skills, knowledge, and dispositions, and they are relevant to the larger physical and social environment. For example, in areas with an abundance of lakes, rivers, and streams, knowledge- and skill-based outcomes related to safety near water are viable outcomes. Appreciating similarities and differences among families is important, especially in diverse societies such as ours. First Nations families value teaching their children about their spiritual beliefs and respect for natural environments. Religious programs emphasize knowledge related to the beliefs and practices of their religious group. Knowledge-based outcomes are valid for ECE programs, provided they are relevant to the child's experience and social context.

Developmental outcomes do not rigidly define standards of performance that must be achieved by all children under specific conditions, nor do they set up prescribed expectations to be achieved within a specific timeframe, such as "the child will use scissors to cut out patterns stamped on construction paper by December" or "the child will tie her shoelaces without assistance or coaching before the first day of school." Outcomes do, however, describe significant developmental milestones (e.g., ties shoelaces successfully; rides a tricycle independently), which are complex performances that include many discrete skills or incremental steps. The thoughtful statement of developmental outcomes is an essential backbone of the play-based developmental curriculum framework.

When developmental outcomes are clearly understood, the objectives leading to their attainment can be sequenced from simple to complex. An important teaching skill is to break down, into bite-sized chunks, the components of practice and learning related to a complex task in order to achieve the outcome. Experienced ECEs know how concepts are formed, how knowledge is acquired, and how skills are mastered. *The ability to arrange learning steps in a rational sequence that leads to the attainment of higher levels of learning is a professional skill that differentiates well-trained educators from untrained staff.*

Developmental outcomes are observable, written descriptions of what the child should do to demonstrate achievement of the outcome (Appendix A). Usually, the demonstration depends on integrating knowledge and skills and applying them, that is, "knowing that" and "knowing how." Outcomes describe applications that are complex because they represent the integration of skills, knowledge, and dispositions in an authentic context and not a singular skill, such as "hop forward three steps" or "string beads with laces" (which would be objectives). For example, an outcome statement might be, "The child has fully participated in sociodramatic play from the start to the finish of a play episode"; this involves incremental skills such as sustaining a "script," taking and providing cues, listening actively, and collaborating with the other children. The developmental outcome should be challenging enough to require the child to combine what she knows with what she is able to do. To achieve an effective result, the child should reliably demonstrate the outcome more than once and perform it well and happily. Developmental outcomes require that ECEs observe and assess children's development at regular intervals rather than assume that the essential development has occurred just because the child has been exposed to a particular set of play and learning experiences (Shipley, 1997).

EXAMPLE

Developmental outcome: Represent, using unit blocks, a multilayered structure or building that is recognizable and that the child can name.

"What would be the incremental steps leading to a child's being able to accomplish this complex and somewhat abstract task?" The answer to this question would provide the "design back" steps to be stated as developmental objectives, in ascending order of difficulty, as in: stack unit blocks; build vertical, three-dimensional structures with the unit blocks; make patterns with the various unit blocks; use all block sizes and shapes to form a structure; recognize the symbolic nature of unit blocks and name the structure (e.g., "see my condominium"); announce (a plan for) what the child will build with the unit blocks today; execute a recognizable facsimile using the blocks; use decorative unit blocks to elaborate upon the basic structure according to the child's plan. ECEs might shorten or lengthen this ordered list of developmental objectives, or change the order somewhat, depending on children's familiarity with unit blocks, but the "design back" approach features the incremental steps children typically take in order to achieve this outcome.

E. Identify the Developmental Objectives Related to Developmental Outcomes

TABLE 9–2

EXAMPLES OF THE RELATIONSHIP BETWEEN GOALS, DEVELOPMENTAL OUTCOMES, AND DEVELOPMENTAL OBJECTIVES

Goals	Examples of Developmental Outcomes	Examples of Developmental Objectives Leading to Developmental Outcomes
develop pro-social skills (affective domain)	the child participates successfully in a sustained sociodramatic play episode	the child assumes a role assigned by another child; pursues an agreed-on "script" for the play episode; negotiates changes to roles and scripts; responds to cues; provides cues; listens actively
develop visual-perceptual skills (physical domain)	the child controls the movement of his eyes	the child discriminates embedded forms from other forms; differentiates figure from ground; scans a page from left to right; tracks a moving object on a screen or in the air
develop logical concepts	the child understands the concept of number	the child demonstrates one-to-one correspondence; counts objects in a set; understands that the number of objects does not change according to the properties of the objects counted (and the configuration of the set)

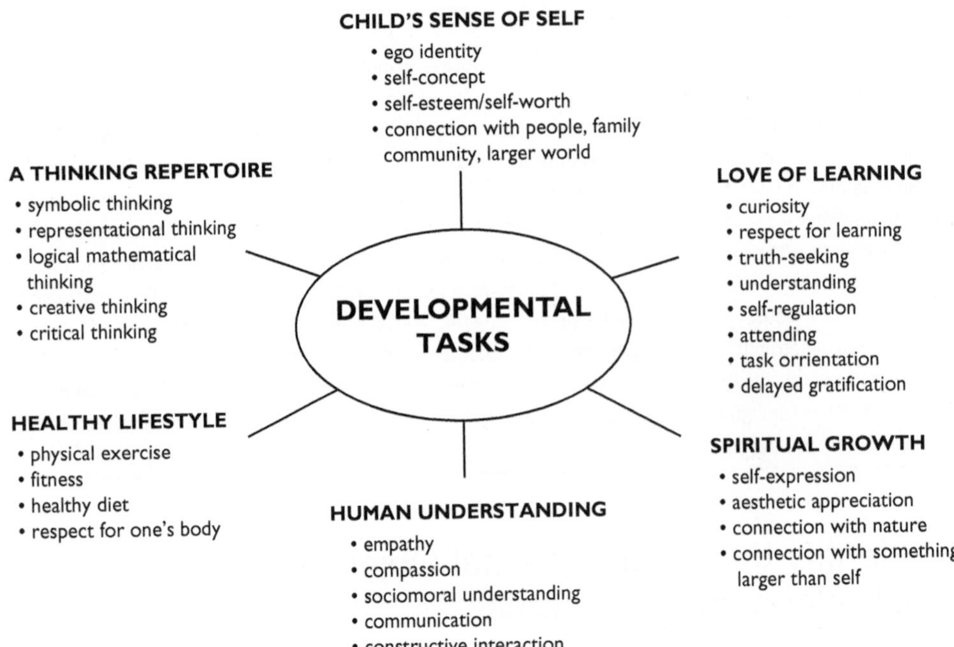

Figure 9–2
Developmental tasks for lifelong learning

DEVELOPMENTAL OBJECTIVES

Developmental objectives are short descriptions of observable skills, knowledge, concepts, or behaviours. They describe the stepping stones that lead children incrementally toward the achievement of developmental outcomes. Objectives serve as markers and guides for planning and help ECEs sequence activities from simple to complex (developmental sequencing), keeping in mind that the pace and order in which children acquire skills, knowledge, and concepts may vary from child to child. The developmental objectives are linked directly to activity planning; play-based activities are planned to address the objectives. (Activity planning using the activity card system (A-cards) is the subject of Chapter 10.) Developmental objectives are aligned with single activities or a unit of activities or learning experiences.

EXAMPLE

A few entry-level developmental objectives related to the following developmental outcome: "*demonstrate classification skills*"

- Match blocks of three colours and three shapes.
- Sort blocks by colour categories.
- Sort blocks by shape categories.
- Sort blocks by putting the same colour and shape in each category (e.g., all the red square blocks, all the yellow round blocks).

F. Plan Design and Layout of the Playroom Environment

Ensure that the layout and design of the playroom environment reflect the developmental outcomes of the program, i.e., the location and organization of the learning centres and the selection of play equipment, materials, and supplies accessible to children in each learning centre, indoors and outdoors. (This step was addressed in detail in Chapters 6 and 7 and should be reviewed.)

G. Plan Activities for Play and Learning

The curriculum may identify specific activities and learning experiences that serve as benchmark activities; these activities make it easier for ECEs to observe children's participation and assess their developmental progress. Benchmark activities are the play activities within the curriculum that may be described on an *activity card* cross-referenced to the *activity card system* (A-cards) (see Chapter 10). The A-cards include an evaluation component for each planned activity. For each developmental outcome, a series of benchmark activities that clearly mark a child's incremental progress with respect to the developmental outcome is identified in the curriculum to facilitate observation and assessment. The benchmark activities should be consistent with the children's interests, play and learning styles, and inputs to curriculum, which include goals and priorities. For example, these may be units of activities, such as the provision of various bead-stringing activities, which promote hand control, fine motor skills, eye-hand coordination, visual acuity, and ability to detect patterns. This range of physical and perceptual skills in ascending order of difficulty may lead to more mature bead stringing activities, such as stringing beads in self-selected repeating patterns. The benchmark activities noted in the curriculum should be revised as children make progress, so that they accurately reflect the developmental levels of the majority of the children in the group. Observations allow ECEs to spot quickly any disconnect between the children's development and interests and the activities provided for them.

WHY IS PURPOSEFUL PLANNING OF BENCHMARK ACTIVITIES AN IMPORTANT PART OF CURRICULUM?

Children cannot be depended upon to carve out an educational agenda that will take them down roads formerly untravelled or that will require them to struggle now and then with alternatives and obstacles to solve a new problem or to learn a new skill. For children to make developmental progress in all domains, using some benchmark activities ensures that a comprehensive range of physical, social, emotional, and cognitive objectives are planned and that children's progress with these activities is observed and assessed. This strategy removes some of the guesswork from assessment and purposefully matches a standard set of activities and objectives to the developmental tasks of childhood in each domain. There are always, in the developmentally appropriate play environment, many opportunities for children to initiate their own play activities with materials and supplies accessible to them in the learning centres.

EXAMPLES OF BENCHMARK ACTIVITIES

Social skills—activities that address ability to initiate play with others, give and take, ability to take and provide cues, helpfulness to others; e.g., projects in the Creative Arts centre, exploration activities, listening games, games involving taking turns; dramatic play activities—activities addressing language, role-playing, social skills, and self-expression, e.g., super units which encourage sociodramatic play and sociodrama, that involve children in acting out remembered stories

Emotional skills—activities that encourage self expression, empathy, respect for others, self-regulation, e.g., play with dolls, super units such as hospitals or veterinary clinics; group games

Physical abilities—activities that specifically address flexibility, agility, balance, endurance, and stamina, e.g., running races, balancing on logs, throwing and catching a ball, negotiating an obstacle course

Perceptual abilities—activities addressing various levels of perceptual, eye-hand coordination, and manipulative skills, e.g., stringing beads, doing puzzles, cutting collage pieces, tossing beanbags

Cognitive activities—activities addressing logical concepts such as classification and visual-perceptual and knowledge-based skills, e.g., sorting sets of objects with one similarity and with two or three similarities; seriating sets of objects

H. Describe the Play-based Methods for Teaching and Learning

Methods include the skills ECEs employ to facilitate children's play and developmental progress. Methods are closely related to the **play styles** and learning styles of children. The choice of a method for an activity depends much more on how children play and learn than on how ECEs teach. In early childhood education, we know that children learn largely through their senses and through their interaction with concrete objects in the environment. Therefore, the methods used to facilitate children's progress are largely child-centred; that is, they rely on setting the stage within the environment for children to explore, test, discover, and manipulate in the context of their play. The ECE needs to know when and how to intervene in children's play to help them make the most of their environment. Child-centred methods mean that children choose their activities from a strategic array of equipment, materials, and supplies in the learning centres that are planned to help children *uncover* knowledge and concepts and practise skills as they play. For child-centred methods to result in optimal developmental progress and learning, the environment must truly be the *third teacher*, after the parents and the ECEs. Progress in learning does not occur willy-nilly simply by letting children loose in any environment stocked with a random selection of play materials. The interaction of the child with the environment is carefully orchestrated by the skilled ECE who understands how to design and organize the environment, plan and set up activities, and use resources effectively, to facilitate and enhance play.

Developmental, play-based methods favour learning opportunities in which children are active and self-directed. Methods are active when children initiate their play and choose from a set of alternative activities. *Teacher-directed* methods are needed when ECEs read a story, teach a song or finger play, or lead a physical exercise in the gymnasium. Both **direct** and **indirect methods** are compatible with the developmental approach. The challenge for ECEs is to choose a method to facilitate children's achievement of the developmental objectives for the activity, to enhance the quality of play, and to ensure that the learning process is satisfying enough to motivate further developmental progress.

INDIRECT METHODS

Indirect methods are used when ECEs rely mostly on skilful and selective planning of the environment and materials to promote play and development. This method implies a willingness to relinquish to children much of the responsibility for their own learning as they play within the planned environment. *Indirect methods* encourage children to be investigators, explorers, and originators, rather than followers of someone else's ideas and solutions. In indirect teaching, the ECE often becomes an observer of children's play in the learning centre, as well as a **guide** who helps children manipulate a tool or solve a puzzle. As a **resource person**, the ECE responds to children's questions about phenomena or objects, helps them find supplies and materials they need for a project, or joins in their search for new ways of building or making something. The ECE as **facilitator** is always looking for opportunities to enrich and extend children's play and learning in an activity, such as to find new or alternative solutions to problems, to encourage children to ask questions that will lead to the discovery of new concepts, and to help children find new words with which to communicate effectively.

Exploratory and **discovery-oriented methods** are the most common examples of indirect teaching approaches. When using these methods, ECEs prearrange specific materials and supplies to stimulate exploratory play and discovery through sensory play and manipulation of the materials provided. Sometimes materials are simply accessible to children for their own exploration, rather than set up as activities. A ready supply of loose materials, such as wood, old bricks, sticks, and rocks found outdoors, and crayons, paper, blocks, markers, scissors, glue, and fabric pieces indoors, can be useful in a variety of projects and smaller tasks that children choose.

Materials may also be carefully selected and set up in learning centres with specific play purposes in mind; they may be included in science table exhibits and discovery activities, for example, to examine various kinds of bark with magnifying glasses; pour, measure, and compare with beakers at the water table; and create collages in the Creative Arts centre.

Child-initiated methods are fostered in the unit block and hollow block areas; at art tables; at tables with construction materials, such as Lego, tabletop blocks, and modular building materials; and in natural settings outdoors. Environments with an abundance of natural, modular, and open-ended materials arouse children's imagination, encourage them to use what is around them in new and different ways each day, and allow them to set their own goals. In this context, children decide which activities they will be involved in, what materials they will use, and how they will use them. Self-correcting activities, such as puzzles and Workjobs, are child-initiated when children are free to choose when they will pursue them. As well, ECEs encourage children to pursue the activities at their own pace and according to their individual learning styles. Child-initiated methods may also apply in small group settings when children choose or suggest an activity they want to pursue. ECEs are particularly useful as resource persons when the children are involved in "writing" their own stories, planning a field trip, tackling a long-term project, or making an "invention" when they need an adult to encourage and support their efforts.

The developmental, play-based approach supports initiative and self-motivation in learning, which are important lifelong learning skills. One of the more difficult professional skills for ECEs to acquire is the ability to know when to step back and let children be active, self-directed learners. Experience provides ample evidence to ECEs that children are capable of learning through their freely chosen, independent play with concrete objects in their environment and that the freedom to pursue their own interests motivates children toward further learning.

TEACHER-DIRECTED METHODS

Direct teaching assumes that the ECE not only decides, in advance of the learning experience, which objectives are to be addressed and how they will be addressed, but also leads, models or demonstrates, and guides the activity to its anticipated learning outcome. The ECE assumes a central role in a directed activity, both in a physical and an intellectual sense. He may be at the head of the circle or at the front of a line to call out instructions and give commands. **Teacher-directed methods** are sometimes referred to as *teacher-centred* or *teacher-as-leader* techniques.

One teacher-directed method is **teacher demonstration**, which is often appropriate for gymnasium or playground activities in which the ECE physically demonstrates, with or without the help of the children, how to perform a specific movement or skill. ECEs often demonstrate the use of implements, such as a hammer, screwdriver, or spatula. The **teacher-as-model method** suits such activities as follow the leader, hokey pokey, and finger plays. When ECEs lead an activity such as an obstacle course, a cooking experience, or a musical game, they support children's eagerness to be involved and ensure that the experience is successful and fun.

Activity-centred methods, such as popping corn, cooking, breaking the piñata, making a jack-o'-lantern, and cleaning pet cages, require direct methods such as teacher demonstration to ensure children's safety and the success of the activity. These methods raise the likelihood that certain kinds of learning experiences occur, because the materials provided suggest the activity to be pursued; the objectives to be addressed; and, usually, the steps to be followed to reach the anticipated outcomes. Although these kinds of activities are closely supervised and have clearly stated limits, they also contain elements of discovery and active interaction.

Dependence on the planned environment for children's self-initiated play does not rule out some teacher-directed or teacher-led activities. Purposeful curriculum for young children depends on teacher-led small-group or large-group activities for a part of every day. Small-group cooking activities, or large-group games and activities within a physical program, for example, are usually teacher-led and involve demonstration, direction, modelling, and instruction. At some times in the day, ECEs may choose to work with children in groups in order to provide a chance for children to identify with their group, to share information, to learn cooperatively, and to practise communicating effectively. As in all educational settings, it is important to avoid the dogmatism that says that only one type of methodology is acceptable. A skilled ECE possesses a wide repertoire of *indirect* and *direct* teaching methods and the knowledge of how and when to use each method to promote optimum play, development, and learning.

I. Plan Curriculum Content

The curriculum planning task includes identifying the central subjects, themes, or topics in which to integrate the many parts of the curriculum framework that comprise the developmental, play-based curriculum. These subjects or topics, which we typically refer to as "content," emerge from the children's interests that have been identified through observation, assessment, and just listening to children as they express what they like to do and experience. Subjects and topics frame activities, experiences, and projects; they often include a set of related knowledge or concepts (e.g., ice-water-rivers-lakes); or classification concepts in a developmental sequence; or large themes, such as the ecology of a forest or maintaining a garden over four seasons. Linking topics or themes to activities promotes meaningful learning connected to what children know already and can do, and to the next steps in their development.

Activities are linked to the list of developmental objectives that has been compiled based on assessments of children, and the developmental objectives are linked to the developmental outcomes. This integration of interesting themes and activities into the larger curriculum framework is where emergent curriculum and developmentally appropriate practice (DAP) intersect and are fully realized. Building the curriculum framework is open to children's input as they ask questions, suggest things they'd like to know and do, and talk about their special interests, which are factors at the heart of emergent curriculum. The project method, discussed in Chapter 10, pages 190–192, and Chapter 18, Project Learning, pages 337–338, is another example of curriculum planning that emerges from the interests and needs of children and is linked to the developmental outcomes identified in the curriculum.

What mechanisms help ECEs create these links? There are two common approaches; one is a "development-based webbing approach" and the other may be called a "theme-based webbing approach" because it groups activities related to a major interest area such as "learning about the properties of water" or a topic that emerges as a result of children's field trip to a garden nursery, which led to their wanting to plan and grow a garden. Activity planning is facilitated by the use of **curriculum webs** that map subject areas or topics that interest children the most (based on children's input) and that also map the developmental outcomes.

USING THEMES AS A VEHICLE FOR DEVELOPMENT AND LEARNING

The subject and content areas or topics that typically interest young children may be referred to as **themes** although they are not themes that have been preplanned by ECEs because "children need to know about them" or because they interest the ECEs. Themes serve as an overlay on the curriculum framework; they knit together units of activities with developmental outcomes and objectives that reflect children's interests as they arise from excursions, films, or programs they may have seen, books they have read, and the questions they ask. Themes allow for exploration of seasons and exploration of phenomena and remarkable events that children may have experienced such as flooding, construction projects, and moving to a new house.

In earlier decades, themes had a "bad name" because they were largely knowledge-based and provided the framework—the background and foreground—for all program planning. Theme-based approaches in the past often reflected adult interests. They tended to be "one-off" constructs, often for one week at a time, that revolved around the festival times of the year and special days such as Valentine's Day and Halloween. Sometimes, they failed to connect all elements of the curriculum, and opportunities for learning were lost in the preoccupation over the theme as the "destination" rather than the "vehicle" for learning. The "theme of the week" idea sometimes assumed that children were interested in cute and contrived definitions of what is important and it failed to connect themes to children's deeper questions and actual experiences. The fact that "themes of the week" were often planned in advance also meant that children were left out of the discussion in favour of the "new ideas" of the moment that often appeared at workshops or in craft-based resource books. This approach did not explicitly link the themes to children's development, nor did it encourage the transfer of learning from one unit of activities to another. When used to promote development, themes can serve as the link between related units of activities and learning experiences that build on earlier learning and the children's experience, and encourage children to transfer learning from one unit to another.

Palaiologou, Walsh, Dunphy, Lyle, and Thomas-Williams (2010, p. 25) suggest seven key principles for the design of effective curriculum: challenge and enjoyment; breadth (a range of experiences in a variety of contexts); progression (each stage building on the previous stage); depth (helps children develop their capacity for thinking and learning); personalization and choice (content to meet interests of each child and allowing personal choice); coherence (clear links between the various topics and extended activities to integrate various strands of learning); and relevance (related to their lives). Webbing or mapping techniques and theme-based strands are useful tools to help ECEs integrate these principles into their curriculum planning.

Developmental outcomes and themes may be combined so that both the developmental outcomes and the themes form the structure that binds the curriculum. Themes do not dominate the curriculum and they are usually appropriate for the season of the year. They may emerge from a recent event that has captured the

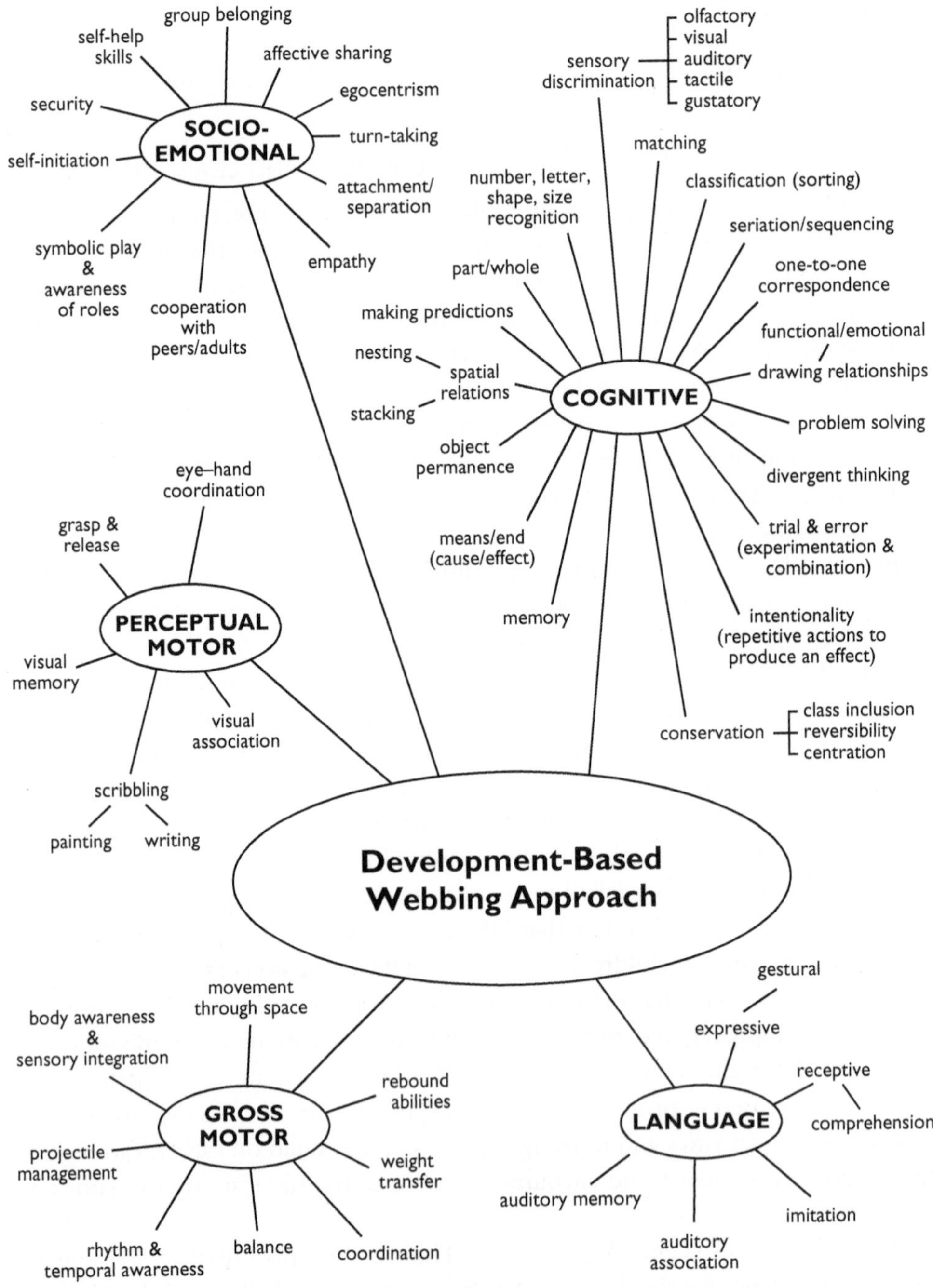

Figure 9–3

A development-based webbing approach*

Source: Nadia Saderman Hall and Valerie Rhomberg (1995), *The Affective Curriculum: Teaching the Anti-Bias Approach to Young Children*. Toronto, ON: ITP Nelson (p. 63).

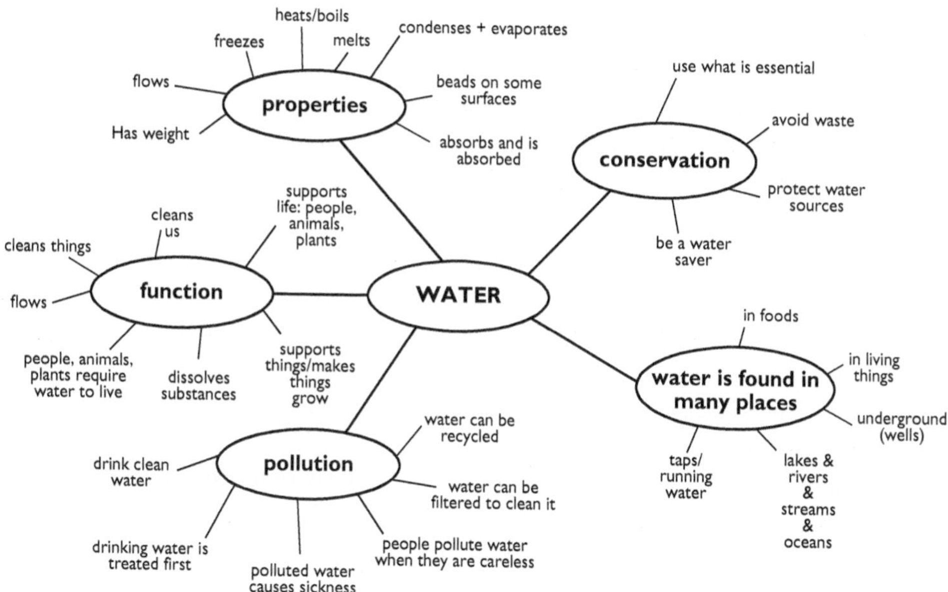

Figure 9–4
A theme-based webbing approach*

imaginations of the children and may vary in the amount of time they take to unfold because it is difficult to connect with the developmental outcomes within in a short timeframe if opportunities to explore related concepts do always arise at the same time. The knowledge gained from themes of short duration is sometimes disconnected and remains in limbo. Some themes take a season to develop fully; still others occur over the space of an entire school year. A series of connected activities sometimes turn into extended **projects** that unfold over time, such as studies of gardens-seeds-plants-flowers-vegetables-preparing soil-working soil-fertilizing soil-tilling soil-harvesting-cleanup.

EXAMPLE

Many ideas for curriculum come from things and events happening in the environment. One college lab school spent a year on a curriculum that emerged as the construction of the huge campus athletic centre beside the ECE lab school evolved over four seasons. The ECEs found ways to link the indoor and outdoor activities to the exciting events happening beside their school, which they spent time each day observing and discussing with the children as the construction proceeded. It became evident that this construction project, which fascinated the children, could be a major theme for the curriculum that would bind together the developmental outcomes and objectives and provide a wealth of related topics for activities and projects. The ECEs first arranged the playroom environment to ensure that it would accommodate activities and projects related to the central construction theme. The dry and wet sand tables in the Science Discovery centre assumed greater prominence, and a larger sand table was constructed, while other play stations in that centre were removed to make space. Children began to anticipate the activities they would play next as they observed the construction taking shape next door. The Active Role Play centre became a resource for construction hats, tools, large trucks, shovels, hollow blocks, wooden planks, pulleys, and pipes and rods for building. Outdoors, the sand and loose materials areas were transformed into sites for digging a foundation and building a replica of the athletic centre. The book nook displayed books about buildings and construction, and the office area contained photos of beautiful buildings and blueprints.

*From HALL/RHOMBERG. *The Affective Curriculum*, 1E. © 1995 Nelson Education Ltd. Reproduced by permission. www.cengage.com/permissions

J. Evaluate the Curriculum

Greater accountability creates new demands for ECEs and programs. Added professional standards support the demand for increased salaries (Canadian Council on Learning, 2011) that adequately reflect the responsibility of ECEs to ensure that children achieve developmental outcomes appropriate to their age levels. Greater recognition of the ECE profession also creates obligations. *The continuing challenge is for the early childhood profession to deliver on the claims that high-quality early childhood education has a powerful impact on children's later learning, on their lives as a whole, and on the ultimate success and credibility of a society dependent on the human capital of its citizens.*

Evaluation that is ongoing and dedicated to improving the quality of programs and performance is called **formative evaluation**; it is an important component of the developmental approach to early childhood education and a component upon which effective curriculum depends. Evaluation practices enable ECEs to review and revise outcomes, activities, methods, and other curriculum components. Assessment reports are important because they reveal the developmental progress of each child. Evaluation is an ongoing process in which the ECE uses a variety of instruments to acquire information related to the coherence of the curriculum, which includes environmental design and organization, developmental outcomes, objectives, activities, and methods. Program evaluation casts judgment on the success of the program and prescribes changes that should be made to the curriculum to enhance children's play and their achievement of the outcomes. Evaluation strategies ask questions, once children have played with the activities included in the curriculum, that provide information about the success of the curriculum; this evaluation procedure may use Activities Checklists, which are addressed in Chapter 10, along with the Activity Card (A-cards) system. The information from activity evaluation helps ECEs determine whether or not to amend the activities to make them more interesting and challenging or whether to leave them out longer for children who still need to achieve the objectives, and shows them how to extend and elaborate the activities to take children's learning a step further.

Curriculum evaluation involves constant monitoring of the relevance and quality of the developmental outcomes and the coherence of all the curriculum components. The integrity of the curriculum as a reflection of the program goals is also a focus of curriculum evaluation. The integration of assessments of children's development at the beginning, the ongoing monitoring of children's developmental progress, and the evaluation strategies at the end of a curriculum cycle support a continuing round of observing, assessing, planning, implementing, and evaluating, followed by appropriate revisions to curriculum for the next cycle.

Program evaluation takes a broad view of the program, going beyond the curriculum, and includes the climate and social interactions within the program; the roles of ECEs and parents; the timing, quality, and viability of adult interventions; the influence of routines, transitions, and schedules on the program; food; safety; and a host of other factors. Systematic evaluation permits ECEs to make decisions based on precise methods rather than on guesswork or intuition. As ECEs become more comfortable using simple evaluation techniques and learn to evaluate regularly and systematically, they may adopt more comprehensive, standardized tools designed by evaluation experts.

Worthwhile evaluation requires an efficient, workable system. When evaluation is carried out regularly and reveals information that is practical and relevant, the savings of time, energy, and resources can be significant. Effective evaluation instruments need not be complicated or sophisticated; often the most effective are those designed by the ECEs themselves for use in their own contexts to reveal the data and information they need in order to plan effectively. Many types can be employed regularly and efficiently.

Summary

This chapter provides a framework for a generic curriculum. Programming related to each of the learning centres is addressed in the following chapters. Definitions and examples should be read carefully to understand the concepts contained in the terminology used. A generic *framework* for ECE curriculum is open enough to accommodate features of various models that fit with the program inputs and developmental outcomes. A curriculum framework links the various components of curriculum to form a coherent whole. It will be easier for ECEs to use this generic framework once they have understood the terminology and applied the concepts in specific programs.

Learning Activities

1. Write a developmental outcome statement for each developmental domain—physical, cognitive, social, and emotional. For each outcome statement, provide a series of sequenced developmental objectives that outlines the incremental steps toward achievement of the outcome in ascending order (easiest to most difficult).
2. Link two benchmark activities to one of the developmental objectives for each developmental outcome you identified in Learning Activity 1. Indicate the learning centre or outdoor play area where the benchmark activities would most likely be set up for play.
3. Design a chart that includes all components of the curriculum framework including: developmental outcomes, developmental objectives, benchmark activities, methods, and observation tools and assessment. On your chart, identify a developmental outcome (using Appendix A), and complete all other sections of the chart. This chart may be the beginning of your set of curriculum charts covering all developmental domains.

10 Activity Planning

> "Play opportunities which are meaningful to children provide rich learning environments to support children's development. The interconnectedness of play and learning means that in any play situation, a learning opportunity is also evident."
>
> —Natalie Canning, *Reflective Practice in the Early Years* (2010)

Before Reading This Chapter, Have You

- created a curriculum chart that includes the components and terminology related to a generic curriculum framework? (Chapter 9)
- applied principles of learning in early childhood to the identification of benchmark activities for curriculum?
- stated developmental outcomes and identified developmental objectives from simple to complex related to each outcome?
- practised the various methods for facilitating play and learning?
- applied various observation strategies in observing children?

Outcomes

After reading and understanding this chapter, you should be able to

- plan and implement activities using the activity card template to address developmental objectives;
- use activity cards to plan units of activities that lead progressively toward developmental outcomes;
- plan projects composed of units of activities that emerge from children's interests;
- create and use evaluation tools that provide an efficient way to evaluate the curriculum; and
- demonstrate accountability by evaluating the success of activities, learning experiences, and projects in addressing the developmental objectives and outcomes.

Activity Planning Is Important

In activity planning, ECEs carefully select equipment, materials, and supplies that they set up at a play station for a purpose. Generally, they are aware of how children will play with and learn from the intended activity because they have planned the activity in advance. ECEs have to know that the children are ready to use these materials and that they have the skills they need to engage meaningfully with the materials and to practise the inherent tasks. Purposeful activities that guide children toward objectives facilitate systematic observation of children's developmental progress. ECEs anticipate what children are likely to do with the materials, and they know what to look for as children play.

When play is always left up to children alone and they are permitted to use materials randomly, their play is often physical and exploratory, and its purpose is known only to the child. Although we know that open-ended, exploratory play is as important and beneficial as the purposeful play being discussed in this chapter, it is a rare child who will choose to play outside of his comfort zone and also persist in trying to solve a difficult problem he encounters in his play, without encouragement and support. A key role of the ECE is to encourage children to try activities that call for skills, exploration, and risks they may not have ventured into before. Many children are reluctant to explore or experiment in areas that are unfamiliar, or uncertain, without assurances that they will be supported if they run into difficulties. The influence of home life is so dynamic that when activities are not purposefully planned, children are often content with play that repeats their play at home and that does not stretch and challenge their capabilities. The early years lay the foundation for the development of skills, knowledge, and concepts that will be used later in formal learning settings. Days filled with open-ended play that may become repetitive and redundant, with materials that never change, in an environment that remains the same from fall through spring, waste children's precious time. Children are challenged to grow when ECEs systematically plan a wide range of interesting, novel activities to address all developmental domains.

Effective planning of activities and learning experiences is based on the following assumptions about the role of play in learning, to which you were introduced earlier in this textbook:

- Children should choose from a range of planned play activities set up at learning centres and play stations.
- Children should be able to select materials from shelves or bins and use them for their own purposes in their play.
- Children's learning through play depends largely on the quality, variety, and accessibility of materials in the environment that respond to children's actions on them.
- Flexible use of play materials and the accessibility of resources promote children's self-expression and decision making.
- Children's play is important; therefore, schedules and routines should support and extend play and learning times and not interrupt their play with unnecessary routines and transitions.
- The development of a rich inner life occurs during play in unstructured, natural environments, often outdoors, where the child has the privacy and the freedom to explore physically and intellectually.

- ECEs should plan some activities every day that address, systematically, a wide range of developmental abilities in all domains and in all learning centres, including the outdoor playground.
- ECEs should encourage and interest children in engaging in planned activities and learning experiences, as well as open, exploratory, free play.
- Purposeful activities that guide children toward specific objectives, whether they emerge from children's ideas or from adults', facilitate systematic observation of children's developmental progress.

Activities to Enhance Play and Learning

The early years pass by quickly, and children have much to experience and to learn. Purposeful planning acknowledges the value of children's time and the importance of ensuring that they will make progress in all developmental domains. The planned environment shapes children's choice of play activities and introduces them to a wide range of play styles and learning opportunities. Within the curriculum framework, the central unit of planning for learning through play is the activity. *An activity is an event circumscribed by a time frame, a context, or a specific setting that includes materials that may be used flexibly or whose use is prescribed. ECEs may plan activities or children may initiate them. The term* activity *also applies to play that is spontaneous, with materials selected by children from shelves and used for their own purposes.* Projects, for example, may contain several discrete activities that emerge from the interests children pursue as the project unfolds.

Planned activities should be systematic, be available every day, and contribute to children's developmental progress. Activity plans describe the ways in which children will most likely interact with materials and supplies and how they will practise developmental skills. Planned activities include those that have specific developmental objectives that clearly describe the purpose of the activity and how materials should be used, such as solving puzzles and matching shapes. Planned activities also include creative, open-ended play, as in painting, building roadways in the sand, and working with cardboard as a building material, where there is not a defined product or end point, but where the choice of materials and supplies suggests that certain kinds of play and learning will result.

All planning begins with an understanding of children's developmental stages and the skills and learning they have demonstrated based on what the observations and assessments have revealed. Each planned activity should contain elements of skill and knowledge familiar to the child, as well as new challenges intended to help the child grow. Some activities address objectives that can be mastered in one sitting. Most allow for periods of practice, followed by eventual learning of the skills, acquisition of new knowledge, or understanding of new concepts inherent in the activity. When ECEs plan activities that build on children's present strengths and take them one step further, their programs are dynamic and change as the children do. For example, programs that move with children's development are very different in the spring than they were the previous fall. Planned activities that involve challenge and new experiences reduce the likelihood that children will be bored or restless. The stimulation they find day after day absorbs much of their energy and motivates them to learn and to grow. As a result, ECEs spend less time intervening and guiding children's behaviour and more time facilitating their learning and assessing their progress.

The key to successful planning lies in carefully observing and assessing children to determine their present capabilities, future needs, and interests. ECEs take the information gathered and identify the next steps that children should be encouraged to take; they solicit children's input by discussing with them what they like to do, by listening to their responses and comments during play, and by keeping records of the kinds of activities in which children show interest and participate most often.

Activity planning includes those activities to be undertaken by children who play individually and activities that call for large- or small-group participation. Activities designed for children to play alone are usually located in learning centres where play is quiet, requires concentration, and is unlikely to be interrupted by boisterous play close by. Usually, the learning to be derived from the individual activity is inherent in the nature of the materials and the way in which the ECE arranges them on a table or in a quiet corner. Group activities are often planned for outdoors and for indoor learning centres where children cooperate, collaborate, and need to move about actively; they encourage interaction and cooperation, and emphasize social skills and emotional control. Adult-led group activities are especially suited to psychomotor play and physical development. In unplanned activities, children select materials from learning centres to accomplish their own loosely defined purposes, which evolve as they proceed. Learning environments should allow for both planned and unplanned activities because considerable development and learning, as well as fun, are derived from both.

Learning Experiences

Learning experiences are harder to define because they are composed of planned and unplanned episodes of play for which the outcomes are not as clear-cut. They are largely open-ended, and the outcome of the learning experience is not predictable for each child, nor is it necessarily the same from child to child. The developmental objectives may be understood in general terms, but the learning to be achieved is not as intentional as it is for an activity. Although some of the conclusions reached by children participating in a learning experience may be similar, the nature of the experience is such that each child will glean something unique and may participate in the experience with different intentions and levels of engagement. Examples of learning experiences would be a field trip to the local fire department, planning with the children a picnic lunch to be taken to the local park, or attending a concert. Children enter into learning experiences with their personal goals and their own interests and motivations. The learning they achieve from experiences like these is unique to them and more difficult to interpret through observation. It is generally by talking with children about the experience that ECEs gain a more complete understanding of the nature of the learning achieved by each child and the perspective from which he has approached the experience and taken in all of the stimuli.

Planning learning experiences for children within the context of the curriculum framework is an important teaching skill. Frequent opportunities for children to participate in these larger experiences allow them to glean from the experience whatever it is they are inclined to appreciate and figure out. Learning experiences require careful planning and an understanding of the learning inherent in various types of experiences. Fieldtrips, like walking to the garden centre, and excursions, like going to a petting zoo, are usually planned ahead; other learning experiences include inviting a visitor to demonstrate how to make a quilt, or watching a children's film. Some learning experiences, such as playing a musical instrument in a band, lend themselves quite readily to the development of a project, such as putting on a concert for parents. Learning experiences should be exciting, rich events in the child's week that open doors to children by expanding their imaginations and wonder about the world, exposing them to the environment beyond the playroom, and providing reference points for them in their daily lives. These will be the remembered events of childhood; they enrich the child's repertoire of interactions and understanding of the contexts in which they live.

Children do not always have to be involved in activities that have a clear purpose or an intended outcome. They also need time for passive play and opportunities to find and follow their own pursuits. Developmental programs are flexible and allow children to be uninvolved when they want to be. Planning activities and learning experiences does not mean that every minute of the day is planned or that the developmental objectives are always clearly articulated or that the learning experience will be standardized for all. Gazing at the clouds in the sky while lying on the grass in the playground is not a planned activity or learning experience if it occurs spontaneously and has no clear purpose. Passing time in this way does, however, provide important opportunities for relaxation, wonder, and just *being*. Resourceful ECEs capitalize on spontaneous events to promote incidental learning and to arouse curiosity and imagination in children. These are the teachable moments when ECEs may ask children to follow the movement of the clouds with their eyes or to find the duck or the elephant shape among the cloud formations, to focus on an airplane moving in and out of the clouds, or to imagine what it would be like to be a bird flying through the clouds. Experiences like these may also provide practice in using ocular motor skills (pursuit and tracking), in recognizing shapes, in discriminating embedded shapes, in finding new words, and in imagining. ECEs also need to respect and support children's wishes to drift a little, at times. Sensory experiences, such as running a stick through a stream to watch the currents and ripples it makes, contribute to the joy of childhood and provide precious moments of surrender to the senses and relationship with nature. Times such as these provide a wealth of opportunity for developing respect for the environment and reflection; they feed the soul, calm the nervous system, and induce contentment and serenity. Moments like these make important contributions to mental health.

The Activity Card (A-Card) System

The *activity card* (or *A-card*) *system* is useful in a number of ways. Inexperienced ECEs sometimes resort to direct teaching methods initially, until they have mastered the methods for implementing activities. The aim of the A-card system is to teach planning skills, to practise various methods for implementing activities, and to become proficient at planning activities in order to respond immediately to a child who makes a suggestion for an activity or who expresses an interest in pursuing something that captures his attention. The degree of responsiveness needed by the ECE to act quickly on an idea (think on her feet), or to suggest how an interest might be extended, depends on an understanding of the components of activity planning and knowing how to implement them somewhat effortlessly.

The A-card system helps ECEs develop a diverse repertoire of activities related to developmental objectives, apply a repertoire of teaching methods, sequence activities in order of their complexity, account for children's learning styles, and evaluate the success of the activities in encouraging children's participation and success. Once ECEs master the skills inherent in the A-card system, they are more adept at thinking on their feet. The A-card system then becomes a repository for activity ideas filed under various headings. The A-card system may, therefore, be regarded as a prop to support practice and learning of many aspects of activity planning and implementation. The key to successful planning lies in carefully observing and assessing children to determine their present capabilities, future needs, and interests. ECEs take the information gathered and identify the next steps that children should be encouraged to take.

The activity card system, clarifies the links among developmental outcomes; developmental objectives; resources (equipment, materials, and supplies); teaching and learning methods; assessment methods and tools; and evaluation. The system outlines the progression of developmental objectives that lead to the achievement of the explicit developmental outcomes. Activity planning is the basis of program planning and of curriculum implementation. A system for planning activities ensures that a degree of objectivity and structure guides this essential component of the ECEs role. The A-card system facilitates planning within a short period and enables ECEs to change activities if they do not appear to be working. Activity card systems accomplish four main goals:

- provide an inventory of activity ideas and resources for all learning centres by building a system of activity cards described according to the usual order in which learning occurs
- may be filed for easy retrieval of activities and learning experiences, which promote specific developmental objectives and developmental outcomes
- reinforce the importance of play-based, developmental activity planning by making it easier to find, plan, and articulate activities and learning experiences that address a wide range of developmental objectives, themes, and interests, in all learning centres
- identify key activities called *benchmark activities* that may be cited on the curriculum framework; these become the criteria for determining the child's developmental progress, the success of the curriculum in helping children achieve the developmental outcomes, and the readiness of the child for the next steps in the learning process.

EXAMPLE: FRAMEWORK FOR A SYSTEM OF ACTIVITY

When planning an activity, an ECE should

- name the activity;
- list the developmental objectives;
- state the previous experience children need to participate successfully in the activity (sequence experience needed in a developmental progression where possible);
- select the equipment, materials, and supplies (the resources used in the activity);
- describe the play-based teaching and learning methods that allow children to be self-directed in their play with the activities or the adult-led teaching methods to be used; and
- evaluate the success of the activity in helping children achieve the developmental objectives.

The Purpose of the System

The A-card system streamlines program planning. It is best to use index cards that are 10 centimetres by 15 centimetres (approximately 4 inches by 6 inches), although smaller cards may be preferred. Activity cards outline the information referred to in Figure 10–1 in a clear and abbreviated format. Figure 10–2 shows a format to be followed. The A-card system provides a permanent record, on cards, of activities that have been carefully planned, implemented, and evaluated. Any activity may be related to two or more developmental outcomes, likely from two or more domains, or it may be related to only one developmental outcome. The related outcomes may be summarized on the A-cards using a coding system. Activity cards are helpful tools for emergent curriculum, as they allow ideas for projects and activities that come from the children to be documented and saved. Documenting activity ideas carefully, even after the fact, helps ECEs make the link between children's freely chosen play that emerges spontaneously and the developmental outcomes of the curriculum.

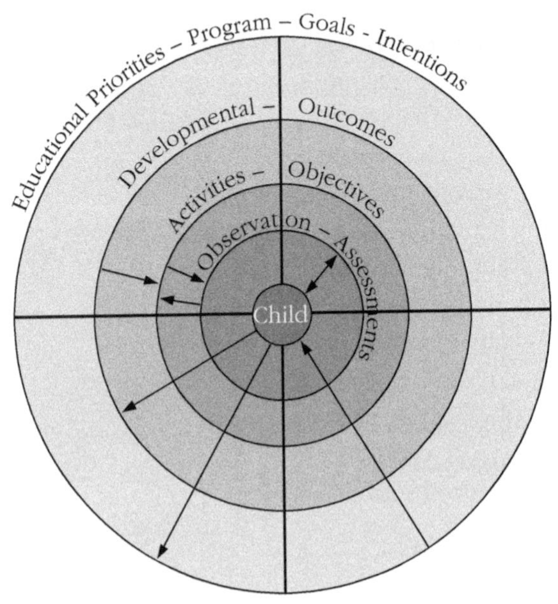

Figure 10–1
Framework showing how activities link to the curriculum

The Filing System

Activity cards may be filed according to the learning centre in which they will most frequently be used. For example, the file box for storing A-cards might be divided into seven sections, one for each of the main learning centres in the indoor learning environment: Active Role Play, Daily Living, Quiet Thinking, Project, Unit Blocks, Science Discovery, and Creative Arts. Each section should contain A-cards describing activities most likely to be set up in that learning centre, although activities may be presented anywhere in the indoor or outdoor learning environment. A separate section or a separate A-card file

NAME OF ACTIVITY:

DEVELOPMENTAL OBJECTIVES:

PREVIOUS EXPERIENCE NEEDED:

RESOURCES/MATERIALS:

TEACHING/LEARNING METHODS:

EVALUATION [on flip side of card]

Figure 10–2
Activity card

should be added for outdoor play activities in the playground; this file should also be divided according to the outdoor learning centres. Outdoor play is addressed in Chapter 22.

An alternative would be to file A-cards according to the developmental domain that the activities primarily address. In this example, the file for storing the A-cards might be divided into four sections, which roughly correspond to the four main developmental domains: physical, social, emotional, and cognitive. The developmental domain sections might also be sub-divided into categories that are more discrete, for example: physical, social, emotional, cognitive, creative, language and literacy, and perceptual (combines cognitive and physical perceptual skills).

Once a basic filing system has been chosen—that is, either according to sections that designate learning centres or to sections that designate developmental domains—a coding system may be developed that cross-references the activities from the learning centre to the developmental outcome, or vice versa. For example, a colour coding system may be used for the A-cards with developmental objectives that relate primarily to one developmental domain—with a different colour assigned to each domain. The coloured cards are then filed according to the sections that designate learning centres. ECEs tend to be very creative in building their cross-referencing systems.

EXAMPLE: SERIATION STAGES

The skills involved in ordering objects by size and length, known as **seriation**, can be ranked in order of difficulty by using specific-purpose materials designed to take children progressively through the steps involved in learning to seriate, which is an important logical concept. Simple stacking and nesting materials are usually the first seriation materials introduced to children, whose play with them is initially sensory and exploratory. After a while, children grasp the notion of the vertical sequential stacking or nesting of the various components of the set of materials, often through trial and error. Eventually, they are able to approximate the correct order in the sequence determined by the equal **gradations** between each set of items in the series. An intermediate step in the learning sequence would be the child's ability to order objects horizontally, leaving one gradation in size between each item. At this stage, the child may not have grasped the concept of a common baseline but may have ordered the objects correctly. Metric-sized rods (called Cuisenaire rods) in 10 lengths, with a one-centimetre gradation between each size in the series, are a helpful seriation material. Being able to order the rods in ascending or descending order, following a straight line that goes in one direction only, with one gradation in size separating each item in the series; using a common baseline for all items; and seeing the relationship of the parts to the whole series are clear signs that the child is well on the way to understanding the concept of seriation (Figure 10–3).

TYPES OF SERIATION MATERIALS

- Stacking materials that assume a common baseline, such as stacking bears, stacking Russian dolls, stacking cups that nest one inside the other or on top of one another, for vertical seriation.
- Sets of several items that are alike in all aspects but size, where each item is one gradation larger than the earlier one in the series for horizontal seriation. Children learn to seriate the items in each set according to size, eventually observing the one gradation of difference between each item in the series.
- Two sets of objects for which each item in one series might differ in size from the item related to the same order in the other series, in which children use double seriation—also horizontal—to seriate the objects.
- Cuisenaire rods or other tall blocks or rods that are seriated horizontally, respecting a common baseline, so that the finished product represents a set of stairs moving in one direction only, with the same gradation between each item in the series.
- USING A-CARDS, PLAN A UNIT OF SERIATION ACTIVITIES.

Intermediate step in learning concept of seriation

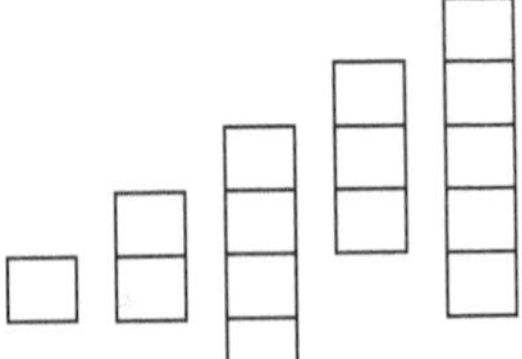

Mature concept of seriation

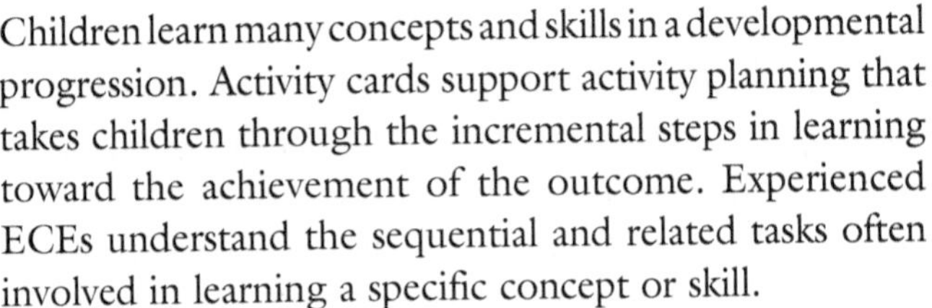

Figure 10–3
Stages in seriation

Developmental Sequencing

Children learn many concepts and skills in a developmental progression. Activity cards support activity planning that takes children through the incremental steps in learning toward the achievement of the outcome. Experienced ECEs understand the sequential and related tasks often involved in learning a specific concept or skill.

Previous Experience Needed

In the A-card system, "*Previous experience needed*" indicates the order in which activities should be sequenced developmentally. This section of the A-card lists the skills, tasks, or concepts children should have mastered before tackling the present activity. Take the example of bead stringing. Initially, children explore large beads and strings in a sensory way, examining their size, shape, and the holes for the laces to pass through. Children may experiment for a long time, trying to insert the shoelace into the large hole in a large wooden bead that is easy to grasp (sensorimotor play). To succeed with simple bead stringing, children need to have sufficient hand control and eye–hand coordination. Therefore, activities such as large jigsaw puzzles, matching shapes to a pattern, and pouring activities could be identified under "Previous experience needed." As they gain experience with these materials, they begin to string beads at random, with no particular end in mind other than to practise inserting the string through the hole and stacking several beads on a knotted string (practice play). Eventually, children graduate to stringing small, multicoloured sets of beads with shoelaces or thread and needle, perhaps using self-repeating patterns ordered by colour, size, shape, and property (wood, plastic, metal). The A-cards will state the level of bead-stringing the child should have attained prior to working with a more advanced activity and materials. This item on the A-card ensures that ECEs respect the concept of developmental sequencing of activities from simple to more complex (refer to Tables 10–1 and 10–2 on pp. 190–191).

TABLE 10–1

ACTIVITY CARD FOR A FIRST-LEVEL BEAD-STRINGING ACTIVITY

NAME OF ACTIVITY: bead stringing (simple)

DEVELOPMENTAL OBJECTIVES: coordinate eye–hand movements, develop pincer movements (thumb–forefinger), control hand movements, track beads on the string (ocular-motor skill)

PREVIOUS EXPERIENCE NEEDED: brush painting, moulding clay, formboard puzzles, pouring

MATERIALS: large wooden beads of many colours and shapes, shoelaces

METHOD: place beads with laces on a table; partially string one lace with beads of any colour or shape; leave model on table; let children play (child-initiated, self-directed play). When a child experiences difficulty threading the bead onto the lace, use a hand-over-hand approach to guide the child's hand. Recognize effort, time spent on the task, and any progress made.

EVALUATION: [on reverse side of card]

Did most children participate and string a few beads? Did they understand the task?

Did some children achieve the developmental objectives (i.e., was the activity appropriate to the developmental levels of the children for whom the activity was planned)?

Did children figure out more complex ways of stringing the beads?

Next time, I would …

TABLE 10–2

ACTIVITY CARD FOR A MORE ADVANCED BEAD-STRINGING ACTIVITY

NAME OF ACTIVITY: bead-stringing according to size and colour
DEVELOPMENTAL OBJECTIVES: recognize same/different; match similar beads according to size or colour; classification
PREVIOUS EXPERIENCE NEEDED: simple bead-stringing activities; simple matching and sorting activities according to colour and size; pouring; moulding
MATERIALS: small and large wooden beads of three primary colours, laces
METHOD: place beads with laces in a basket on a table; partly string one lace with large red beads, another lace with small red beads, another lace with large yellow beads, another with small yellow beads, and so on. Leave on the table for children to play; observe (child-initiated, self-directed play).
EVALUATION: [on reverse side of card]

Resources and Materials

Equipment, materials for play and learning, and supplies are the resources and media that facilitate children's development. Chapter 6 addressed the equipment, materials, supplies, and media needed in programs, as well as the adaptation of materials and equipment for children with special needs. ECEs have to understand the play and learning potential of a wide range of materials and supplies in order to match the right play materials to developmental objectives. A list of the materials and supplies that the activity requires for children to achieve the developmental objectives should be stated on the A-card. In some cases, items of *equipment* need to be stated also: some examples would be a balance beam for an obstacle course, a net or goal posts for a beanbag toss, or a climbing apparatus for an activity with props that will be used to promote sociodramatic play.

Describe the Teaching and Learning Methods for the Activity

Chapter 9 (pp. 172–174, Section H), describes the methods that will be used by ECEs to introduce and facilitate children's learning through play for each developmental outcome. The methods may indicate the type and style (context of play) in which the developmental outcome is likely to be addressed and the learning centre where the activity will be set up and played. The types of interactions that ECEs may have with children to facilitate their play, including questions they will ask to promote understanding or help they may offer to improve their skills, are included on the activity card. Remember that the curriculum framework should guide ECEs in setting up the environment and facilitating play so as to optimize the value of children's play and to promote their development of specific skills and understanding. The activity card provides a space to indicate which methods would be preferred in order to address the developmental objectives of the activity. A brief description of how the activity would be introduced to the children and in which centre, and how to facilitate children's learning while they are playing with the activity, is essential. The A-card includes in the methods section key questions that ECEs may ask in order to stretch children's thinking and extend their play; it should also include ways to adapt the activity for children with special needs.

The stages in the child's development of bead-stringing skills, for example, may be identified on the A-card beside "Method" to clarify the usual order in which children progress in their play with these materials. Of course, many skills are practised at the same time in any activity. For example, in bead stringing, children are practising the hand control and eye–hand coordination also needed for pouring. They are also developing physical perception through the ocular motor skills of **fixation** and accommodation, the ability to discriminate **figure from ground**, and **depth perception**. ECEs should always be aware of the complementary functions of a variety of activities and materials in promoting development. Children have their own learning styles, which include learning at their own pace and at times when they are ready.

Children need to explore, ask questions, and find out for themselves. When ECEs have time to sit with children playing and to observe their strategies and choices, they are in a better position to facilitate learning by making a suggestion or by asking a pertinent question. Adult intervention is needed when children meet challenges within an activity, need redirection, or require assistance with tasks and skills inherent in the activity. Here we see in action both Vygotsky's (1978) theory of the zone of proximal development and Bruner's (1986) concept of how skilled teachers build a scaffold in order to help children over the challenging steps in learning.

Planning Projects—The Project Method

Projects can be undertaken almost anywhere in the playroom, as well as outdoors. The Project centre (Chapter 18) is especially well equipped for projects because it supports research and production related to projects in all learning centres. The **project method** is introduced in this chapter because projects usually involve a related series of activities implemented over time as the children progress with the project. The project method is particularly effective in fostering the development of attending and learning-to-learn skills. As projects are often undertaken by children working in pairs or in small groups, the project approach works best in learning centres that encourage small-group play and cooperative learning.

John Dewey was the first North American to recommend projects to promote learning, and they became an extension of his two philosophical themes—democracy and experience—which were elaborated upon in his writings and in the University of Chicago laboratory school he founded in the early 1900s. He believed that children should be encouraged to cooperate in the reproduction of events and experiences of interest to them, and to construct knowledge through their investigation and experimentation with authentic materials found in everyday living experiences (Dewey, 1900). In this way, Dewey believed that children learn to collaborate within a democratic context and develop a capacity for sustained exploration of subjects and themes, both current and historical.

William H. Kilpatrick, in the first decade of the 20th century, built upon the ideas of John Dewey by formulating the "Project Method" around children's "wholehearted purposeful activity proceeding in a social environment" (quoted in Weber, 1969, p. 111). Kilpatrick believed that useful projects for young children should involve manual and motor activities as well as cognitive and aesthetic experiences. His version of the project method was predicated on the construction of a significant plan in some external form, such as putting on a play or building a raft. He believed that projects enhance aesthetic enjoyment, promote problem solving, help children resolve an intellectual challenge (such as whether, or when, or under what conditions snow melts or evaporates), and help them acquire some new knowledge or skill (Weber, 1969). Since Dewey's time, the project approach to learning in early childhood has been elaborated the world over. The Danish programs and the *écoles maternelles* in France reinforce the importance of extended projects over a long duration. The schools of Reggio Emilia value long-term projects that replicate daily living and social life. Projects provide excellent examples of collaboration among ECEs and children in capturing children's interests and evolving ideas for projects and a plan for achieving their common goals (Helm & Beneke, 2003).

Katz and Chard (1989, p. 3) described the aim of projects to "cultivate the life of the young child's mind … not only knowledge and skills, but also emotional, moral and aesthetic sensibilities." A project was defined as an in-depth study of a topic, engaged in by one or more children, which would extend over several days or weeks, depending on the children's interests and developmental levels, their experience with projects, and the complexity of the topic addressed. A later book by Helm and Katz (2011), *Young Investigators: The Project Approach in the Early Years*, second edition, provides an expanded framework for projects, which is addressed in Chapter 18. As a teaching method, projects focus not only on the content to be learned, but also on the process of learning. Projects challenge children's interactions with their peers as they work on their project, and ECEs have to develop skills to facilitate children's interactions with the people, objects, and the environment in which the project evolves. Projects may occur in the playground or in the community close to the program (e.g., planning, designing, making, harvesting, and maintaining a garden). The most successful projects revolve around the experiences and events that interest children most and are familiar to them in their own surroundings.

Projects are important for children with special needs, for those who are learning a second language, and for children living in poverty because they provide a rich vehicle for promoting literacy, for facilitating children's task orientation and attending skills, and for engaging in collaborative learning with their peer group. Meaningful longer-term projects are worked on over time, and are comprised of several activities in several stages. They help children integrate components of knowledge, skills, and dispositions as the projects challenge them to stretch and to persevere. The planning of units of activities united by a common theme or purpose usually leads to the planning of projects.

The project approach is an essential method that contributes to a balanced approach to helping children learn. Shorter episodes of play are balanced by projects that demand persistence, the ability to return to an activity after an interruption and to overcome obstacles in following a plan, and the realization of a long-term goal that the children helped determine. Projects are essential components of curriculum and activity planning to develop learning-to-learn skills, to engage children's interest, and to teach research skills. They require space, because they usually involve several sittings and therefore need to be left out for children and ECEs to return to after an interruption. The planning of specific projects will be addressed in later chapters on learning centres, and especially in Chapter 18.

Katz and Chard (1989) recommended the project approach for preschool and kindergarten children, which, they claim, serves five major purposes:

1. Projects engage children's minds in ways that deepen their understanding of their own experiences and their environments.

2. Projects provide a balance of types of play and learning activities and are emergent and less structured than many discrete activities.
3. Projects encourage children and ECEs to see school and learning as relevant to real life, especially when projects are authentic and relate to real things and events.
4. Projects foster cooperation among children and build a community ethos.
5. Projects serve as stimuli for ECEs, who have to be actively involved in learning and research themselves when projects relate to authentic events. Longer-term projects ask children to define the project, know the steps involved, formulate and implement plans, and communicate what they have accomplished.

Chard (2001) provides some criteria that help children and ECEs choose projects that optimize children's learning. Does the project

- build on what children know?
- foster social relationships and collaboration?
- allow children to apply literacy and numeracy skills?
- add meaning to their lives; encourage children to research a topic of interest to them using various tools?

Accountability and Evaluating Activities

The need for greater **accountability** creates new demands for early childhood programs. Professional standards support the demand for increased salaries that adequately reflect the responsibility of ECEs to ensure that children achieve developmental outcomes appropriate to their age levels. Greater recognition of the value of early childhood education also creates obligations. *The continuing challenge is for the early childhood profession to deliver on the claims that high-quality early childhood education has a powerful impact on children's later learning, on their lives as a whole, and on the ultimate success and credibility of a society dependent on the human capital of its citizens.*

Worthwhile evaluation of activities requires an efficient, workable system. When evaluation is carried out regularly and reveals information that is practical and relevant, the savings of time, energy, and resources can be significant. Systems need not be complicated or sophisticated. Effective activity evaluation is part of a workable system. Many types of evaluation, including the evaluation of activities, can be employed regularly in a minimum of time. As with curriculum evaluation, the efficient and effective evaluation of activities may be facilitated by using tools created by the ECE. For activity evaluation, checklists provide a quick way to ensure that the activity planning process has accounted for the key planning elements, and they allow for checking the effectiveness of the activity after it has been implemented with children. One activity checklist may be created to ensure that all elements of activity planning have been addressed. Another checklist may be devised to evaluate activities following implementation. Some ECEs prefer to write this evaluation on the back of the activity cards using a simple question and answer format.

- Did the activity address the stated outcomes?
- Did the children participate?
- Did all or most of the children achieve the objectives?
- In what ways might the activity be presented or conducted differently next time?

ECEs may select a set of evaluation criteria for an activity from a comprehensive list of questions. Not all questions will apply to all activities.

TABLE 10–3

ACTIVITY PLANNING CHECKLIST (BEFORE IMPLEMENTING THE ACTIVITY)

Questions	Yes	No	Notes
Does the activity address the developmental objectives stated on the A-card?			
Are the materials developmentally appropriate?			
Is the sequencing of the activity appropriate (e.g., simple to complex)?			
Does the activity offer choice in the way the activity is to be pursued?			
Is the activity closed or open-ended?			
Does the activity focus on the process or the product?			
Does the activity have a clear ending? Who decides when the activity is finished?			
Does the activity provide the child with a clear message that the child has succeeded?			
Does the activity promote positive social behaviour?			

TABLE 10–4

ACTIVITY EVALUATION CHECKLIST (DURING AND AFTER IMPLEMENTING THE ACTIVITY)

Questions	Yes	No	Notes
Do children choose this activity? Do they follow through and finish the activity?			
Do children use the materials for the purposes intended?			
Is the purpose of the activity clear to children when they see the activity set up? Does the set-up provide messages or cues to children about how to play with the activity?			
Is there some choice in the way the activity is to be pursued?			
Is the activity closed or open-ended? Does the activity focus on process or product?			
What comments do children make about the activity?			
Does the activity encourage children to use new words?			
Do children return willingly to the activity after an interruption?			

Table 10–4 continues on page 196

TABLE 10–4 ***(Continued)***

ACTIVITY EVALUATION CHECKLIST (DURING AND AFTER IMPLEMENTING THE ACTIVITY)

Do the children appear to relax during the activity?			
Are the methods used appropriate to the activity?			
Does the activity encourage children to focus and to develop learning-to-learn skills (e.g., task orientation, blocking out distractions)?			
Comments			

Summary

This chapter focuses on activity planning and includes a systematic planning approach for activities. Units of activities, related by theme or purpose, often lead to projects that occupy children over an extended period of time. Projects will be addressed more fully in Chapter 18. The skills involved in activity planning are fundamental to the teaching role and should be fully mastered by ECEs in order for them to be effective professionals. A systematic approach to activity planning is advocated because of the need to ensure that many developmental skills are covered. The use of a system also facilitates planning and ensures that the sequencing of activities and the planning tasks become second nature. The activity card system is recommended as a way to become familiar with the elements of activity planning; once the activity card system has been mastered, the actual writing of activity cards becomes less important as a planning tool and more relevant as a way of retaining and storing a repertoire of retrievable resources and records for future reference. It is recommended that ECEs create and maintain a file for all of their activity cards. The indexing of the cards may be achieved using either the developmental domains (e.g., physical, cognitive, social, emotional, creative) or the learning centres as the main categories. Once the activity file has been established, perhaps by also cross-referencing developmental domains and developmental objectives with the learning centres, the file becomes an excellent resource for students and beginning teachers and to help ECEs explain to parents the purpose of each activity and how it contributes to development and learning.

LEARNING ACTIVITIES

1. State one developmental outcome for four- to five-year-olds. Identify four developmental objectives that relate to the outcome you have stated.
2. Using the activity card format in Figures 10–1 and 10–2, and following the description of the components of an activity card, plan four activities that address the developmental outcome and developmental objectives you identified in Learning Activity 1.

3. Use the Activity Planning Checklist in Table 10–3 to evaluate your planning of the activities.
4. Use the Activity Evaluation Checklist in Table 10–4 to evaluate the four activities in Learning Activity 3 that you implemented with the children.
5. Develop your own activity card system by writing a series of 20 activity cards with developmental objectives that address at least one developmental outcome for each developmental domain. One series of activities should represent activities linked by a common purpose, for a unit or a project, and include sequenced activities that lead children toward the achievement of the outcome.
6. Design a *filing system* and a *cross-referencing system* that will allow you to use activities you have planned for a variety of outcomes and in various learning centres.
7. Write activity cards for two activities or learning experiences that were suggested by children and that emerged from their interests and ideas. File these cards in your activity card system and code them for cross-referencing.
8. Begin to build your curriculum chart by adding to your chart the benchmark activities you have planned, next to the developmental objectives they address, and in the context of the developmental outcome to which the activity cards and the objectives relate.
9. Select a child to observe in a program during an extended play period. Ensure that you understand the developmental objectives of the activities that have been planned for the child in each learning centre. Use a checklist to record the child's participation in one or more activities and her apparent levels of achievement of the objectives of the activities.

Section IV
Facilitating Symbolic Play

Section IV addresses the following topics:

- definition and types of symbolic thinking and symbolic play
- facilitating fantasy play: pretend play, including dramatic and sociodramatic role play
- planning the Daily Living centre and the Active Role Play centre to encourage and enhance dramatic and sociodramatic role play
- planning play stations within the Daily Living and Active Role Play centres
- music as an accompaniment to daily living, and to enhance the imagination and all experience
- using music to promote movement, self-expression, and mental health
- representational thinking using props
- adapting the environment for children with disabilities to enhance their role play and musical self-expression

Section IV emphasizes the role of symbolic thinking and symbolic play in children's development and learning and the particular importance of two learning centres in fostering children's ability to engage in symbolic and representational thinking through various stages of pretend play. Chapter 11 describes how children develop the ability to think symbolically and to represent using symbols as they engage in symbolic play; it identifies the reasons why the various stages of symbolic play from pretend through to dramatic and sociodramatic role play, often known as fantasy play (Paley, 2004), are essential to children's holistic development, especially to their abstract thinking ability; and also describes how to facilitate pretend, dramatic, and sociodramatic role play. Chapter 12 describes the Daily Living centre and the props and activities needed to enhance role play in the context of familiar household artifacts. Chapter 13 shows how the Active Role Play centre promotes symbolic thinking and representation through play that uses props, construction materials, musical instruments, and costumes. Chapter 14 focuses on the importance of music to enhance children's lives and to stimulate the imagination and support their fantasies, to promote movement, representation, and self-expression through music, and to foster physical well-being and mental health.

11 Symbolic Play

> "Fantasy play is the essential, irreplaceable curriculum of the first years of life."
>
> —Howard Gardner, "Introduction," *Multiple Intelligences* (2004)

Before Reading This Chapter, Have You

- recalled your own play during childhood that involved engaging in pretend play alone, with another child, and in small groups, and identified your favourite play themes?
- observed children's pretend play in the housekeeping area and with dolls and stuffed animals?
- observed children's pretend play in small groups in which they assume roles in a play episode with a sustained "script"?

Outcomes

After reading and understanding this chapter, you should be able to:

- describe the various stages and characteristics of symbolic play;
- explain the function of symbolic play in promoting children's development and learning;
- facilitate sociodramatic play;
- explain the relationship between children's sociodramatic play and representational thinking; and
- describe the relationship between sociodramatic play and emotional development, self-regulation, and mental health.

The Development of Symbolic Thinking

Between the ages of two and four, children develop the ability to form mental symbols, which is to represent things or events that are absent, using concrete or abstract symbols. Symbols enable human beings to "venture mentally beyond the here and now, in time and space" (Bruce, 2010, p. 106). As they engage in symbolic thinking, children begin to make meaning from everyday experiences, as well as the more profound experiences in their lives related to taking risks, separation, death, parting, loss, and fear.

The capacity to form a substitute in his mind for something he cannot see or touch frees the child from earlier dependence on the presence of the concrete object in order to think. Piaget claimed that children form mental symbols through imitation, that is, by making one object stand for another, and that this ability to signify bridges the distance between sensorimotor thought (dependence on what one perceives) and later intelligence using a range of symbols such as language and number. In the early stages of symbolic thought, the symbol is always related to the child's direct experience and the meaning that the individual child attaches to the symbol. As children progress through the various stages of play, they move from simple imitation and pretend play, for example, using a stuffed animal to represent a baby, using words to describe present wants and actions (e.g., "doos [juice], now"), and then to describing absent things and events (e.g., "Mommy gone"). Piaget believed that language plays a limited role in the development of symbolic thought because the young child thinks non-verbally, whereas the development of language depends very much on the nature of children's thinking. He believed that children always have the language they need to express what they are thinking. Vygotsky, on the other hand, believed that the use of language is a major contributor to the child's development of thought.

In the preschool period, while children are at a peak of creativity, they need to be encouraged to be something other than what they are and to *act out* and to dramatize what they imagine (Cobb, 1977). Vygotsky (1978) found that young children perceive the meaning of objects, and the objects themselves, as the same, and he saw this dependency on the concrete realism of objects as preventing children from thinking abstractly. For example, a young child who finds a large plastic spoon and then pretends to eat or to feed a doll with the spoon is using the spoon in its usual context. As their play matures, children begin to use objects representationally, as pivots that help them mentally represent the meanings of words. **Pivots** are objects that children use to represent something other than the object itself, such as when they use a unit block to represent a car. When this happens, the child is separating the meaning of the object from the object itself. Similarly, the child who uses the plastic spoon pivotally as a wand in a dramatization is viewing the spoon abstractly, out of its normal context, as representing something else. As children's representational abilities develop and they are able to assign meaning mentally using imaginary objects, they become less dependent on pivots. Vygotsky saw children's use of pivots in their play as a significant stage in the development of symbolic thinking. Recognizing the contributions of both Piaget and Vygotsky to our understanding of the development of thought—and language—one challenge is to understand the role of play in helping children use symbols to represent what they are thinking, because the ability to represent is a critical aspect of both the ability to think and of intelligence.

Symbolic Play

Symbolic play involves the child's growing ability to move from pretend play to representation using role play and drama. Piaget described four categories of play: exercise play, which is the sensorimotor play of infancy; symbolic play, which is related to the development of representational thinking; constructive play, which represents a mature form of symbolic play involving "adaptations" (mechanical constructions, etc.) or solutions to problems and "intelligent creations"; and games-with-rules play, which depends on children's cognitive and sociomoral abilities (Piaget & Inhelder, 1969, p. 59). Representation becomes the "*shorthand* by which the human mind can transcend space and time, reconstruct the past, anticipate and plan for the future" (Sigel & Cocking, 1977, p. 168).

Symbolic play leading to representational thinking is a key developmental task of the early childhood years from age two to seven, which suggests that symbolic thinking and pretend are critical to the development of mature thought (DeVries & Kohlberg, 1990). It is important, therefore, to understand the child's progression in the use of symbols through imitation, language, pretend play, and representation and to provide rich opportunities for play that exercises these developing abilities (DeVries & Kohlberg, 1990, p. 26). Representational thinking plays a critical role in thought because "it … evokes what lies outside the immediate perceptual and active field" (Piaget, 1962, p. 273).

Children's symbolic play in the early stages involves making one thing stand for another (as in, making a block represent a car being steered along a track). At later stages, children begin to play "as if" they were a mommy or a daddy caring for a baby, for example, or a daddy going to work with his tool kit. More mature symbolic play involves assuming roles that call for children to practise the social skills related to give and take, sharing, communicating, waiting and taking turns, listening, collaborating, and including others in their play. Symbolic play helps children "coordinate and bring together their learning. It orchestrates their feelings, ideas and relationships with their families, friends, and culture. It also develops their physical and embodied self. It develops their abstract thinking" (Bruce, 2010, p. 114). Vygotsky claimed that play is crucial to children's development of symbolic representation in its many forms, from language symbols, number symbols, and musical scores to dance and dramatic representations, as well as all forms of visual art and products of visual imagination. Symbolic play facilitates representation using a number of media in which an object or event is portrayed or depicted in some medium or by some mode: for example, imitation through bodily actions; making one thing stand for or represent another; using word symbols (signs) or number symbols to represent a thought or an idea; drawing a picture to represent a thing or an event; pretend, dramatization, or role play to represent an event or a series of events; or construction to represent an object or an idea. Today, researchers also believe that "play is recognized as the first medium through which children explore the use of symbol systems, most obviously through pretence. Play becomes a transition from the purely situational constraints of early childhood to the adult capability for abstract thought" (Whitehead, 2010, p. 164).

Symbolic play is a critical building block in lifelong learning because it helps children develop their abstract thinking, reasoning, and problem solving abilities and helps build a foundation for literacy and numeracy skills. Gradually, children relinquish their dependence on *seeing is believing* and understand the realities that lie beyond the concrete physical world. Children's engagement in symbolic play is fed by the imagination, which conjures up images of what might be—"if I were a daddy," or "if I were a nurse who could make people feel better." Symbolic play stimulates imaginative thinking. The power to imagine is a human quality that affects all corners of our lives. Maxine Green (2002, pp. 35–36) stated that "it may be the recovery of imagination that lessens the social paralysis we see around us and restores the sense that something can be done in the name of what is decent and humane." Children who cannot imagine a different world or a different life are inhibited in their ability to rise above their circumstances, to dream and to strive. Green goes on to say that "imagination is as important in the lives of ECEs as it is in the lives of their (children), in part because teachers who are incapable of thinking imaginatively ... are probably unable to communicate to the young what the use of imagination signifies."

Pretend Play

Pretend play is a term used to describe the very early stages of symbolic play. It is also used as a generic term to refer to play in which children pretend, as in dramatic and sociodramatic play. Segal (2002) cites the work of McCune (1986) to describe five levels of pretend play between 10 months and two years. Children's ability to make an object represent another is not visible in the earliest stage of symbolic play, which begins during the sensorimotor period, when children are able to use actions to convey meanings, usually at the end of their first year. This early type of symbolic play, referred to as pretend play, involves a child's momentary, short-lived imitation of remembered actions. A child closing her eyes and pretending to sleep while lying on the doll crib, for example, is engaging in early pretend play that becomes more elaborate and representational as the child matures. During the second year, a child is able to use words and objects to stand in for other objects or to represent meaning; for example, a child may raise a cup and say, "Doos [juice]," or pick up her blanket and put her thumb in her mouth as it gets close to naptime.

The development of symbolic thought is a major developmental task of the two- to four-year-old child. Children's abilities to use symbols generally move, as with other skills, from the simple to the more complex. That is, they need more realistic props initially, such as a telephone or truck, then more abstract props that they may use as pivots, such as a block for a car or a rolled blanket for a baby. Finally, children use verbal representation, rather than a concrete prop, to assign imaginary meaning (e.g., "Pretend I'm holding a sign that says 'Stop'"). From about two to four years of age, children often engage in dramatic play alone (solitary play) or beside another child (parallel play). They may play together or with an adult, or they may involve the other player in a passive, objective role and retain control of the pretend roles. For example, a child may say to the stuffed animals or to a child nearby, "Watch out, here comes Mr. Moon," as she runs by, but she will not necessarily rely on other children to participate in her fantasy. Children are at a critical stage in their cognitive development during this period, when they are making the transition from using concrete objects in their usual

Assuming social roles

remembered context to using objects as symbols to represent something else. This stage is a transitional period between symbolic and representational thinking when the child is engaged in **decentred pretend**, either alone or with another child, in an activity usually performed by someone else, for example, feeding the doll in a high chair or rocking a teddy bear.

Dramatic Play

Later pretend play involves enacting two or more different schemes in a realistic sequence, as in undressing the doll, putting the doll in the bath water, drying the doll, and then dressing the doll. These activities are often seen in the Daily Living centre. This is the stage of sustained pretend play referred to as dramatic play, in which children identify with events they remember, imitating each action as closely as possible. This type of play is common in children under age three or four. The next stage of dramatic play shows more planning on the child's part as he relates what he intends to do and then re-enacts a familiar event, such as packing up the cart with the packsacks, food, and blankets to go on a camping trip, symbolically playing out an event that he has witnessed at home. Dramatic play sows the seeds of imagination for more elaborate forms of symbolic play, in which children dramatize real or imagined events, such as going to the supermarket or the hospital, which they do in super units set up in the Active Role Play or Daily Living centres. As dramatic play enhances school readiness, the development of social skills, and various forms of creative achievement (Singer & Lythcott, 2002), the environment, the props provided, and adults need to encourage it.

Sociodramatic Play

Role play becomes more sophisticated as children develop the ability to collaborate with other children and to sustain a script for their role play of events both real and imagined. As children develop their capacities for representing ideas, they are able to recreate roles, situations, and sequences of events, first with the use of props and later without props. Children's ability to use symbols and to pretend in their play are significant indicators of their cognitive maturity.

To pretend in a reciprocal dramatic play situation with others, the child must have acquired knowledge of social roles and relationships and must be able to communicate and negotiate effectively with other players (Garvey, 1977). The development of dramatic play tends to parallel language development, so that by the time children are communicating freely with others, they are ready to engage in social role play. The focus on social roles and interaction, rather than on objects, distinguishes dramatic and sociodramatic play from other types of play (Smilansky & Shefatya, 1990).

Sociodramatic play is dramatic play involving two or more children who assume related roles and follow one another's cues in acting out an event or a social context from the adult world. This is usually a world that has emerged from the child's own experience, but it might also emerge from their imagination (fantasy) of what is probable in the adult world based on what they have seen on television or video. Examples include play that replicates mommy and daddy going to work, play that imitates going on a safari, or play that recreates the experience of visiting the local fire station, for example, climbing on the truck and using the hoses to put out the fire. Because the motivation and the script for representing remembered experiences come from within the child, sociodramatic play provides a window to the child's inner world. Anxieties, fears, and dreams become visible as children reveal their innermost thoughts and attempt to unravel the subtleties in their own relationships, those they observe, and those they imagine. Observing sociodramatic play offers a peek into the children's emotional and mental health.

Language, perception, and memory play important roles in sociodramatic play. Pelligrini (1980) demonstrates that sociodramatic play is important to young children's development of many intellectual and social capacities. For example, children's abilities to **decentre** (to become less egocentric) and to become more **sociocentric** (to focus more on the group than on the self) seem to be determined by the ease and frequency with which children engage in sociodramatic play (Rubin, 1980). To sustain a play episode with their peers, children must be able and willing to take a perspective other than their own. Children who are able to decentre also develop the ability to easily explain information in words because they cannot assume their peers understand what they are trying to do or say simply through their actions (Pelligrini, 1984). Their play is punctuated with brief explanations, such as, "Okay, I'll pretend now to be afraid and run away, and you can coax me back." This ability to use explicit language is essential for children to evolve more complex and abstract themes and roles and to sustain a sociodramatic play episode. Therefore, children who engage successfully in dramatic and sociodramatic play appear to be better readers and writers than children who engage primarily in functional and constructive play (Pelligrini, 1984).

In sociodramatic play, concrete objects and play materials are less important than what children do and say and the ways in which they interact with one another as they work out a pretend episode and collaborate in developing the script that accompanies their theme. Divergent and **convergent thinking** skills, problem-solving abilities, and the ability to take a perspective other than their own are more important to successful sociodramatic play experiences than the materials they use. Although prop boxes are useful tools to extend children's play themes, they play a supporting role at this stage. Social skills, such as the ability to initiate interaction, to accept other children's ideas, and to observe and follow the interpretations of others, are also involved. Memory skills used in remembering many past experiences and behavioural subtleties are important to the child's desire to represent real life.

Children often have to rely on other children to participate in re-creating an event or a social exchange. To engage in sociodramatic play successfully, children have to cooperate with other children in negotiating and assigning roles, carry them out over time, and agree on a *script* related to the event or relationship they are representing. Sometimes, a whole play episode can be spent negotiating roles. As their symbolic play becomes more abstract, children engage in deeper levels of negotiation and begin to plot out story lines and scripts that evolve according to a time line. Vygotsky's theory proposed that children function above their normal levels of ability when challenged by peers in their play to maintain social interaction and to entertain perspectives other than their own. The common problems peers have to resolve in their social play provide rich experiences for daily living.

Sociodramatic play is more mature when children begin to observe that social communication is more than a series of isolated behaviours and is, instead, composed of a complex network of interdependent behaviours and responses. For example, children playing in a super unit such as a supermarket will generally assume the recognizable roles of the cashier, the shopper or customer, or the grocery packer or shelf stocker. From three-and-a-half to five years of age, they exhibit growing awareness of the interdependence of the roles; the conventions or customs that govern the roles; and the kind of verbal banter that often accompanies, for example, shopping and checking out groceries at the counter. Their dialogue is often familiar: "Yes, Jessica, the prices are getting higher every week." "Nice day today." "Would you like to have a cart to carry these bags to your car?"

Children's aims in sociodramatic play are much more than simply to imitate observed behaviours. They try to act out as closely as possible the actions and reactions they have observed, as a way of understanding the meanings of those actions and reactions. Making meaning is a significant goal for children who enter sociodramatic play. Children learn through witnessing, experiencing, remembering, and portraying real-life interactions and adults' actions. Their desire to represent reality in sociodramatic play is consistent with their increasing interest in depicting real life in all creative endeavours—an interest that continues into the **early primary years**. Sociodramatic play opportunities are powerful agents in the development of all aspects of **social cognition** as well as language development, literacy (cultural literacy and numeracy), emotional expression and self-awareness, perspective-taking, the development and application of imagination, social interaction, memory, sensory perception, mental health, and physical development. When children build and then create their own play episodes around, for example, such imagined experiences as fire rescue, Olympic challenges, and fort construction, the limbs and muscles enter into the construction process and eventual implementation of their play episode, and some of their enactments require highly coordinated physical movements and agility. The learning outcomes to be achieved when children engage in sociodramatic play are so profound that this category of play should be an intentional component of the preschool and kindergarten curriculum. Zealous attempts by school boards to reduce or remove scheduled time for play and to substitute academic learning and seat work are alarmingly counterproductive and fly in the face of all that we know about the developmental skills that children achieve through sociodramatic play.

Facilitating Sociodramatic Play

The well-planned play environment allocates sufficient space and also the tools for pretend, dramatic, and sociodramatic play to flourish and mature in the Daily Living, Active Role Play, Unit Blocks, and Creative Arts centres, and outdoors in the playground, to ensure that children achieve outcomes related to symbolic and representational thinking. A major component of ECEs' roles in facilitating sociodramatic play is establishing a play and learning environment to support and encourage this play category. This includes planning the schedule to allow for long, unhurried play periods and arranging space to maximize children's freedom to play without interference or interruption. The creative play in which children engage whereby two or more children take cues from one another and jointly create a script that is familiar and meaningful to all the children requires time and freedom from interruption. ECEs have to provide a supportive environment and learning centres with realistic and abstract props, with sufficient space for movement, and with some protection from the heavy traffic areas and noise from other centres. Once children have learned how to use realistic props in their sociodramatic play, such as the familiar firefighters' hats or nurses' or doctors' kits, they can be helped to assign meaning and function to abstract materials as they play out an imagined episode such as travelling to a space station, using unit blocks or hollow blocks, to represent something they have never seen or experienced. A key to helping children become sophisticated "players" lies in moving them along the continuum of pretend play from their reliance on "realistic" props to being able to ascribe value and function to abstract objects that become something else in the mind of the child. This is another reason why play with unit blocks and hollow blocks is so important; these abstract materials, especially in the absence of realistic props, facilitate children's ability to create and sustain an imaginary episode that relies on abstract props and language to enact in some detail an event that appears real but only exists in their minds, such as making a trip to the moon. This is a point at which children have engaged in sophisticated representational thinking.

The community and the various roles people play are important facilitators of sociodramatic play, especially if children have firsthand opportunities to explore many aspects of their own community and second-hand opportunities to explore the communities of others in faraway places. Excursions into the community are a major resource that fuels children's symbolic play, making it richer and more varied. The impact of field trips becomes obvious as ECEs observe and listen to children the day after they have visited a farm or a police station. Adults facilitate symbolic play by building into the schedule many opportunities for children to go out into the community to experience how it operates, who does what, and the resources available. Sometimes, these field trips may be planned spontaneously, or they may be more deliberate, as in planning to visit the local radio station and encouraging children to work on a project that will prepare them for the visit. Following the field trip, the resourceful ECE provides the resources needed for children to build their own super unit to replicate the venue they had visited the previous day.

ECE Role in Facilitating Sociodramatic Play

Because dramatic play focuses mainly on social roles and interaction, ECEs can facilitate sociodramatic play by helping children become more aware of their social surroundings and by encouraging their interest in the interactions and activities of real life. For example, when children imitate the gestures of a police officer directing traffic, the ECE may acknowledge the action and perhaps enter the play briefly by asking to be helped to cross the street safely. ECEs encourage sociodramatic play episodes and validate children's pretend play and imitative behaviour when they enter the pretend episode and challenge children to elaborate and sustain their play.

Smilansky and Shefatya (1990) noted that the learning potential of pretend play is vastly underestimated in most programs for young children. Smilansky (1968) advocated that teacher education should emphasize the instrumental value of all levels of pretend play so as to facilitate age-appropriate development and learning, especially during the symbolic play stage. Jones and Reynolds (1992, p. 1) supported this view, stating that to become a "master player" is the height of developmental achievement for children ages three to five because master players are skilled at representing their experiences symbolically in self-initiated improvisa-

Negotiating roles

tional drama. Sometimes alone, sometimes in collaboration with others, children play out their fantasies and the events of their daily lives. Vygotsky believed that children's tendency to talk to themselves while playing is important to children's learning to represent ideas in language and to use language to self-regulate their activities (Berk, Mann, & Ogan, 2006). Through pretend play, young children consolidate their understanding of the world, their language, and their social skills. Karpov (2005) claimed that sociodramatic play is the leading activity during early childhood. *There is broad consensus that learning to facilitate pretend play in its various forms and stages, especially ensuring that children become effective players in sociodramatic play contexts, is a challenge that ECEs should master.*

Vygotsky's symbolic play theory also emphasized the role of the ECE, parent, or older child in developing symbolic play skills in young children. The physical learning environment, adults, peers, and older children serve as agents that buttress children's immature attempts to make meaning within the play environment (Gowen, 1995). The more sophisticated play partner has to understand the developmental sequence of symbolic play, and know where the less experienced child is in the sequence, in order to be able to cue in to the child's play behaviour without taking over.

Sometimes ECEs feel uncomfortable and unable to find a role for themselves when children are engaged in dramatic play. Dramatic and sociodramatic play offer children the chance to reconstruct their own experiences and to pursue their own agendas. ECEs should be able to help children extend their symbolic play without imposing their own vision of how children should play or what they should pretend, symbolize, or dramatize. ECEs also have to trust that children are usually able to create their own interpretations of experiences. There are often times, however, when ECEs should assume a role in the sociodramatic play episode in order to rescue a script that is faltering and inject new language and a sub-plot that will sustain children's sociodramatic play. ECEs contribute positively to children's sociodramatic play when they take children to interesting places and read them stories that relate to real-life events. From the well of their own experience, children draw the ideas and the motivation for dramatizing and trying to understand the world around them. Enriching experiences in the outside world, in the neighbourhood, and in the broader community are all the more crucial for children whose everyday experiences at home are limited by economic pressures and burdened parents.

Once sociodramatic play has become well established in a program, ECEs more often observe rather than feel they have to intervene. Unless children's play poses some risk to themselves or to others, ECEs may permit children to play out even negative episodes (Sawyers & Rogers, 1988). Pretend violence, for example, is common in preoperational children (Bettelheim, 1987a). It is better for ECEs to observe carefully and to try to determine the purpose and the meaning behind the negative feelings demonstrated, than to risk stopping the play prematurely. The same thinking applies to permitting children to use props in different and unusual ways that often stretch the imagination, as well as to letting them act out bizarre roles that seem to have no bearing on real life (Sawyers & Rogers, 1988). When children need help in holding onto an idea or a script, or in choosing a new direction for their role play, the ECE may intervene with a question or a comment, or even briefly assume a role without interrupting or changing the nature of the episode being dramatized. For example, the ECE may say, "I'll be the grandfather and take the baby for a walk so that the mommy can take the bus to see her friend in the hospital." The Reggio Emilia schools emphasize the value of children's co-construction of their knowledge as they interact and develop their symbolic play episode. Children are not only practising roles themselves; they are also learning to depend on each other and the adult as they explore the world of relationships and roles and create a sense of belonging that are the fundamental aims of their programs. Just as the development of concepts through interaction with objects builds a foundation for later learning of academic skills, so do children's early relationship experiences provide a foundation for their future relationships.

Learning centres that promote dramatic and sociodramatic play foster an emergent curriculum that children build for themselves as they interact. Gowen (1995) summarizes some teaching techniques for promoting symbolic play, which are based on Vygotsky's theory:

- Comment on what the child is doing by following up on cues.
- Imitate the child's action.
- Reinforce the child's symbolic play by saying, for example, "Your table looks so pretty."
- Make indirect suggestions, such as, "Maybe it's time for your baby to go to bed now."
- Make direct suggestions, such as, "Pretend that the climber is your space station."
- Model symbolic play behaviours for children (Gowen, 1995, pp. 75–84).

Sociodramatic Play and Mental Health

The value of sociodramatic play to mental health and the emotional development of children is often underestimated. "Secure emotional attachments in young children have been found to be associated with a range of positive emotional, social and cognitive outcomes, and ... are closely linked to the amount and sophistication of children's play" Whitebread (2010, p. 171). Palaiologou (2010, pp. 132–133) contends that

> during make-believe play, preschool children act out and respond to one another's pretend feelings. Their play is rich in references to emotional states ... [and] they explore and gain control of fear-arousing experiences when, for example, they play the role of a doctor or a dentist, or pretend to be searching for monsters. As a result, they are better able to understand the feelings of others and also to regulate their own.

By role playing the experience of their beloved pet dying and being buried, children gingerly approach their fear of the loss of a parent or grandparent and anticipate how it will make them feel. Through their role play using the dollhouse or puppets, they rehearse and try to unravel their feelings of being excluded from the group or being bullied by others.

Dramatic and sociodramatic play also contribute significantly to children's ability to make friends (Segal 2002). As children pretend in their play, they gradually communicate their wishes to another child or to the group and begin to involve others using words or gestures, or by using them as props, as in, "You stand there and pretend you are a robot." When children reverse the roles of parent and child in their dramatic play, they gain a sense of power; when children act out fears and anxieties, they gain coping skills and feel less vulnerable. The richness and results to be gained from dramatic play demand that ECEs ensure that the play environment is set up for this style of play and that the playroom climate and the available resources (equipment, materials, and supplies) support and extend pretend play at every stage and in many contexts.

Perhaps, above all other benefits, dramatic and sociodramatic play help children come to terms with their feelings and, possibly, those of others, as they replay a memorable event. The unfortunate irony is that, too often, the children who most need the reassurance and meaning-making of sociodramatic play are the same children who have not been supported to achieve the level of symbolic and representational thinking essential for sociodramatic play to have its full beneficial impact on their emotional development. It is not a given that all children will become adept "players," with all the cognitive and social skills they need to engage in the level of sociodramatic play essential to all other aspects of their healthy development. The onus is on ECEs and other adults in children's lives to ensure that children are provided with opportunities and encouragement to progress from simple imitation and pretend play to sociodramatic play that is sufficiently complex to contribute to their meaning-making, social cognition, and emotional and mental health. Many excellent resources are available to ECEs so that they may help children become expert sociodramatic "players."

SUMMARY OF THE VALUE OF SOCIODRAMATIC PLAY

Sociodramatic play facilitates the following developmental abilities and is, in turn, enhanced by children's progress in these areas:

- dreaming and engaging the imagination
- taking a perspective other than their own
- decentring and being more sociocentric
- thinking abstractly—that is, assigning imaginary meanings to objects—and representationally
- using explicit language or explaining clearly
- managing and expressing fear and anxiety by dramatizing events and things that frighten and trouble children
- engaging in symbolic play that calls on children to use progressively more abstract objects to represent things, people, and events
- evolving more complex and abstract roles and scripts for their dramatizations
- conversing, reading, and writing to improve literacy skills
- learning about the social environment;
- making friends more easily
- expressing feelings and lending meanings to events, especially those that are troubling

The Value of Sociodramatic Play to Self-Regulation

The role of play in self-regulation and children's control over their learning will be revisited in Chapter 15. Vygotsky (1978) linked play to children's growing ability to control and regulate their own learning, and he suggested that play may contribute to intentional learning and problem solving, especially that which requires effort and attention (Whitebread, 2010, p. 164). Vygotsky linked children's ability to regulate their learning to their understanding of their own "zone of proximal development" (ZPD), which tends to determine the level of challenge they can handle. Like more recent play researchers, Vygotsky believed that sociodramatic play offers the richest form of learning, partly because it provides practice in self-regulation as children play collaboratively with others and maintain a group-determined "script." Children also have to actively control their own emotional investment in the play episode as they wait for their cue to speak and act, respond to the cues of others, listen attentively to the evolving script, and help steer the action forward in order to sustain the play. Vygotsky believed that children's tendency to talk to themselves while playing is important to children's learning to represent ideas in language and to use language to self-regulate their activities (Berk et al., 2006).

Superhero Play

Superhero play, a particularly explicit form of fantasy play, appears in the simple pretend dramatizations of children in the Daily Living centre, especially if a potential unit of play has been set up using a prop box containing costumes, hats, and other props related to a popular TV or book character, but it is more likely that **superheroes** will be enacted by children in the Active Role Play centre. Children's superheroes are as fickle as the latest fashion trend, but they are important to the children who admire them, sleep with their artifacts under their pillows, and carry them in their packsacks wherever they go. Superhero characters may appear as puppets that help children dramatize a TV episode they have seen. As long as puppets or dolls representing the current superheroes of the day are nonviolent and conducive to constructive thoughts and behaviours, they can be useful props to help children engage in pretend and sociodramatic play. It is helpful for children to imagine their hero involved in some fantastic adventure that challenges children's ability to fantasize, dream, conjure up possibilities for risk and adventure, and to play out a script for his hero. Fantasy play that often involves children's superheroes will be addressed again in Chapter 13.

Sociodramatic Play to Support Inclusive Practice

Sociodramatic play seems to occur at more complex levels in children from advantaged homes, whereas children who are disadvantaged seem less inclined to engage in sociodramatic play, and when they do, it is often of short duration and is not as complex (Smilansky & Shefatya, 1990). Children who are newcomers are similarly less inclined to risk using a new language in order to enter into a sociodramatic play episode. Children need encouragement to include newcomers in their play as "good play is taught by children to one another" (Smilansky, 1992). ECEs have to know when and how to facilitate sociodramatic play so that all children may benefit from its rich possibilities.

The power of sociodramatic play is enhanced when ECEs promote and support play episodes that replicate the experiences lived by minority group children in a context and an environment with which they cannot fully identify. Imagine the impact on children from other cultures who are encouraged to participate in a sociodramatic play episode that underscores their feelings of exclusion from the group, that attempts to portray their feelings about being excluded, and that dramatizes these experiences for children of the mainstream culture. The children's play *Elijah's Kite* provides an example of the impact of the dramatization of societal scourges such as bullying, on both the victim and the perpetrators. In diverse classrooms, adults' imaginations and creativity are challenged to foster the invention of sociodramatic play episodes that uncover children's deep sense of being ostracized from the group, of being different, and, even more important, of being similar to all other children.

Sociodrama

Sociodrama is the enactment of a story or of some other dramatic form. Sometimes called creative drama, sociodrama is externally motivated, and its roles and behaviours are limited by the events, actions, and script of a story (Smilansky & Shefatya, 1990). For example, children may recreate a favourite television program by assuming the roles of the characters and by sticking as closely as possible to the television script. ECEs enhance children's creative thinking and appreciation of literature when they provide props and encourage children to act out the stories they have enjoyed together.

The ECEs role in facilitating sociodrama is different from that involved in sociodramatic play; she reads a story to the children until they are familiar with the plot and with the characters, and she encourages them to assign or negotiate roles. The ECE then helps children remember the dialogue and the actions, perhaps by prompting them with repetitions of the story line. Because children's dramatization of a favourite story evolves over time, props, costumes, and the storybook should be left out for several weeks to allow children to become more familiar with the story; to look carefully at the visual depiction of the characters; to hone their roles and dialogue; and even to make adaptations to the story, such as changing the ending. To increase the likelihood that children's literature will influence play, Carlsson-Paige and Levin (1990, pp. 167–170) suggest that ECEs follow these steps:

- Set up a routine for choosing new books to read.
- Select books that relate to themes present in the children's dramatic play.
- Choose books that have dramatic events, powerful characters, appealing illustrations, and special features that can be easily dramatized or that will add new concepts to children's play.
- Read favourite books repeatedly and return to them at regular intervals.
- Read books that have sequels or that have the same characters.
- Choose a favourite author for children to become familiar with.
- Try books that allow children to make up their own endings.
- Help children bring characters, dramatic events, and salient aspects of books into their play.
- Use books that are inclusive, in that they represent boys and girls of various cultural backgrounds, and are free of gender, racial, economic, and ethnic stereotypes.

Choosing Stories for Children's Sociodrama Projects

Think of sociodrama as a project that occurs over time rather than as a simple re-enactment without any advance planning. It is wise to ease into sociodrama as a project by starting with children's re-enactments of rhymes and simple stories involving one or two scenes. ECEs should pause frequently in their reading of a story to ask children to act out the actions of familiar animals in a story, or to repeat with them the dialogue spoken by a character in the story she is reading. These early steps with younger children prepare them gradually for the enactment of stories with two or three scenes connected by a narrative or by dialogue invented by the children. When choosing stories for re-enactment, ECEs usually select those with familiar, repetitive sounds and dialogue that can be easily remembered and sequenced by children. The number of characters in the story selected for sociodrama should expand gradually as children take turns dramatizing the simple actions of two or three central characters and become ready for more complex storylines. It is always best to choose a story well loved by children; this is usually one in which children can relate to the characters, who exhibit behaviours and feelings that are familiar to them, as well as to challenges they experience in their own families. Studies have shown a positive link between children's ability to retell a story and their play with representational objects such as flannel characters and paper cutouts (Karpov, 2005).

Choosing stories with explicit cultural themes adds a significant dimension to the story re-enactment, as it raises the profile of a specific cultural group and provides a context in which children can more closely identify with the culture represented in the story. Finding costumes and sets may be challenging, but it is also more interesting for the children and may involve families who assist with the ***production*** by providing clothing for costumes, supplying simple words in another language for the dialogue, providing props related to the culture represented in the story, and designing sets that depict a cultural context familiar to some children but not to all. Sociodrama projects related to diverse cultures represent more elaborate projects that unfold over time.

Negotiating roles for children to play within a story re-enactment sometimes demands that the ECE preselect the role most appropriate for each child to increase the likelihood of challenge and success. The ECE has to devise a plan for convincing each child to assume a role most closely related to the child's developmental levels. Sometimes, children have different ideas of who they want to play, and the coaching demands on ECEs increase as they help children prepare for roles that stretch each child's abilities. In cases where a child may choose a difficult role, ECEs may need to prompt and intervene to help the child remember a line, an action, or the cue for his part. There are benefits to children to be gained by both preselecting roles and letting children negotiate their own roles, always bearing in mind that these sociodramas are not subject to scrutiny by demanding critics. Sociodrama projects are definitely examples of learning activities where the developmental and learning outcomes to be achieved by the children, not to mention the fun and laughter involved in planning and executing the activity, are much more important than the actual production. These activities are truly times when "getting there is half the fun." The process is more important than the product.

EXAMPLE OF AN ADVANCED STORY RE-ENACTMENT BY FOUR- AND FIVE-YEAR-OLD CHILDREN

Read to the children *Make Way for Ducklings* by Robert McCloskey (1969). Leave the illustrated book out on a table in the book nook for children to examine the illustrations and review the various characters in the book. Let the children know that you will be asking them to act out the story. Talk to them about the setting for the actual story (i.e., Boston, Massachusetts, in the United States) and explain to them that this is a large coastal city in the United States of America. Locate Boston on a map. After researching the neighbourhood to assess its potential, ask the children if they would like to set the story in their own neighbourhoods instead.

With the children, determine where in their neighbourhoods they might find a place where ducks might live in families and where the ducks might have to cross busy streets in order to find a safe place to live. Consider making a field expedition to the spots in the neighbourhood suggested in order to learn the street names and some local landmarks.

Re-read the story to the children to identify the characters in the story: Mr. and Mrs. Mallard; Michael the policeman; Clancy (an old lady); and ducklings Jack, Kack, Lack, Mack, Nack, Ouack, Pack, and Quack. The children playing these parts might practise walking like ducklings. Find the props and costumes needed for Michael, the old lady, and Mr. and Mrs. Mallard. Ask the children playing the parts of the ducklings to order themselves according to the order suggested by the story. How might the children costume themselves to look like sibling ducklings? Note the connection between the ducklings' names and the letters in the alphabet. Discuss with the children how they would make the traffic sounds and depict the cars and trucks on the busy streets where the ducklings need to cross. Where would they enact their dramatization of the story (e.g., in the playground, in the Active Role Play centre)?

Identify the dialogue for each character in the story. Sequence the order of actions and events in the story with the children. Draw a map with the children that identifies the key places in the story—either the Boston sites actually referred to in the story, or the sites in the local community that they have chosen to be the setting for the action. At this point in planning the dramatization, the ECE might identify some learning outcomes for this project. What would be the likely developmental and learning outcomes for the children, given the many planning steps involved in preparing for the dramatization? The learning outcomes will be substantial because of the challenges represented by the story and the planning stages involved in helping children locate the setting and sites for the story. For stories with several scenes, as in *Make Way for Ducklings*, the ECE is usually the narrator of the story; she has the children perform the actions of the various characters, with simple dialogue added by the children, as she reads the story. Rehearsal of the dramatization of the story with the children is essential. This usually involves talking about the feelings of the ducklings and their "parents," and how the children might portray these feelings. Because there are many steps in the story and many different scenes, tackle each scene individually with the children before connecting all scenes into one dramatization. Determine with the children when they are ready to dramatize the story for other groups of children in the school or centre.

Summary

Children's fantasy play, referred to in this chapter as pretend, dramatic, and sociodramatic play, and sociodrama deserves high priority in all preschools and kindergartens. Role play is often the focus of the Daily Living centre and of the Active Role Play centre, where realistic props are widely accessible. Role play may also occur in the Unit Block centre, where children engage in imagining, fantasizing, creating, representational thinking, social collaboration, and emotional expression, using a range of abstract props.

Symbolic thinking is an essential milestone in cognitive development fostered by children's all types of symbolic play. All children should be encouraged to engage in pretend play from toddlerhood to kindergarten and the early grades and beyond because of the immense capacity of role play to contribute to representational thinking, to social and emotional development and mental health. Because the ability to think symbolically is also an essential foundation for academic skills, sociodramatic play should be accessible every day to all children in the preschool and kindergarten program.

LEARNING ACTIVITIES

1. Observe the pretend play of young preschoolers in a group setting and describe episodes that imitate the remembered actions of others.
2. Describe examples from observations of symbolic play in which children used objects as pivots.

3. Observe a sustained sociodramatic play episode in which children negotiate roles and develop a script. Describe the role of the ECE, or another adult or an older child, in supporting and extending the children's play.
4. Select a children's story that would be an appropriate vehicle for facilitating sociodrama with a group of four- to five-year-olds. For this activity refer to the example in the box on page 212.
5. List some examples of children's stories/books that would be useful candidates for children's dramatizations.
6. With your peers, debate the advantages of sociodrama derived from children's literature versus sociodrama based on television shows.
7. Create a prop box containing relatively abstract and readily available items that children could use to engage in a sustained play episode. The prop box might relate to the Olympic Games, the dramatization of a recent movie for children and families, the dramatization of a children's story or book, or a field trip.

12 The Daily Living Centre

"It is in the development of their themes and characters and plots that children explain their thinking.... If fantasy play provides the nourishing habitat for the growth of cognitive, narrative, and social connectivity in young children, then it is surely the staging area for our common enterprise: an early school experience that best represents the natural development of young children."

—Vivian Gussin Paley, *A Child's Work: The Importance of Fantasy Play* (2004)

Before Reading This Chapter, Have You

- made connections between symbolic thinking and children's dramatic and sociodramatic play?
- observed pretend and dramatic play episodes in several social contexts?
- linked children's ability to use symbols to their growing ability to represent (engage in representational thinking)?
- linked children's use of symbols (symbolic thinking) and the development of literacy, numeracy, and creative expression?

Outcomes

After reading and understanding this chapter, you should be able to

- organize and set up the Daily Living centre to ensure that the play stations and activities reflect the children's developmental needs and interests and various social contexts and categories of play;
- provide the Daily Living centre with equipment, materials, and supplies to support and enhance fantasy play, from early pretend to sociodramatic play; and
- create prop boxes to encourage and enhance dramatic and sociodramatic play.

Purpose of the Daily Living Centre

Often referred to as the **dramatic play area** or the *household play* area, the Daily Living centre helps children to express their feelings and emotional needs, engage in fantasy, act on their tender impulses to care for others, demonstrate **empathy**, and play together collaboratively and cooperatively. The Daily Living centre should support play that progresses from simple imitation and pretend to more complex role play involving sociodramatic play episodes and sociodrama.

The Daily Living centre sets the cultural tone for the program because it attempts to replicate the child's home environment and to provide a place where home life and school life are bridged by the familiar artifacts of daily living in the family. It is because children relate easily to environments that contain items they recognize from home that this learning centre should represent the cultures of the children's families by including furniture, implements, clothing, and other stable features of the domestic environment with which each child may identify. In Canada, the creation of Daily Living centres that reflect the diversity of our population is no longer optional. One exception might be First Nations communities with their homogeneous populations, where environments largely reflect the artifacts, implements, and furnishings particular to the culture of their community.

One of the primary obligations of early childhood education is to build the **social capital** of the nation. Effective early childhood educators exploit the classroom environment and its contents to support this goal. The words of Dr. Robert Glossop of the Vanier Institute of the Family (2002) in an interview for *Link* (Roots of Empathy newsletter) are relevant in this context:

> There are two kinds of social capital. There is the bonding type, which is to feel closely affiliated with those who are like you, and there is the bridging type of social capital, which is to feel closely affiliated with people who are different from you. In our society, when there is increasing diversity by virtue of heritage, race, culture, religion, language and so on, whatever we can do to give people an opportunity to experience not only how we differ from one another but what we hold in common is a vital contribution.

In the 21st century, daily living has been altered profoundly by changing employment and workday demands; the presence everywhere of technologies; the increasing diversity in our culture; new economic realities for families, business, and governments; unfamiliar global threats; and changing family configurations and pressures. The environment and play materials should not limit the ways that families can be defined. The Daily Living centre should also reflect the lifestyles of families by attracting boys and girls to the kitchen and doll play stations, by supporting play that is not gender-biased, and by affirming a range of family constellations. It should support children's attempts to find consolation and refuge in an environment dedicated to fostering empathy with others, promoting emotional self-expression, encouraging sharing and cooperation, and reinforcing kindness and consideration. The Daily Living centre environment is sometimes a context in which issues related to bullying, violence, fear, and disrespect may be played out by children who are trying to understand what they experience. The vigilant ECE will respond to signals from children whose pretend, dramatic, and sociodramatic play episodes reveal needs that should be attended to and meanings that should be explored in order to support children and their families through some of the complex issues of our times.

Symbolic Play in the Daily Living Centre

This learning centre supports symbolic play, from simple imitation and pretend to more sophisticated dramatic and sociodramatic play and sociodrama. The dramatic play area with its many props and dress-up clothes encourages children to act out behaviours and roles they see at home and in the community. Standard items in the Daily Living centre include the kitchen and laundry furniture and equipment, the dolls, and a doll bed area. Familiar clothing and accessories should be placed on racks that are easy to for children to reach. Children begin by imitating simple actions, such as pretending to be mommy rocking the baby in his arms and folding the sheets on the doll beds. In Daily Living centres that include enough space for a super unit, children may be challenged to extend their play as they set up the furniture and props for a tea party or restaurant, or for operating a beauty salon. The space used to set up potential units or super units should not disturb the kitchen and doll play areas, which should remain as stable features of the Daily Living centre.

Given today's food culture and the diversity of foods we can access easily, the tools and space for cooking allow children to experiment with "pretend" cooking, using dough, but also to do some "real" cooking, perhaps using foods with which they are unfamiliar but which relate to the home experiences of some children in the group. This centre is one that may introduce children to a wide range of foods to touch, smell, and taste, in addition to their lunchtime and snack food experiences. Cooking implements are an important feature of this centre, where ECEs may set up small-group or individual cooking activities to do with the children. Parents may be invited to the centre to demonstrate to children the preparation of foods from their culture and include the children in a cooking activity and a sampling. Broadening children's food horizons and encouraging them to sample foods with which they are unfamiliar enhances their experience and appreciation of the cultural differences and the similarities that exist—for example, the various types of bread typically consumed by other cultures. This learning centre contributes to children's attitudes toward food and informs them about healthy eating for appropriate nutrition, body building, energy, and prevention of illness. A resource table in this or another centre may encourage children to look at books and pictures of healthy foods and the full range of food groups.

In the Daily Living centre, props represent household items and lifestyle gear typically found in children's homes, including miniature appliances and furniture; ironing boards; storage closets for hats, shoes, and clothing; a table and chairs; household linens; and supplies for housekeeping. Children practise roles from the family and the community that are familiar and meaningful to them. They borrow props from this centre, such as dolls and dress-up clothing, to use in their play in other learning centres. A flexible arrangement of equipment and materials in this centre ensures that children are able to evolve many types of symbolic play, not just play related to home and domesticity. Shopping bags, strollers, and baskets enhance role play related to going out into the community to meet friends, to shop, to go to work, and to attend functions. Props should be flexible enough to symbolize whatever the child has in mind. Dolls and puppets encourage children to role play various expressions of emotion. Dress-up clothing such as scarves, capes, shawls, and other multipurpose items becomes what the child intends. Costumes are better placed in the Active Role Play centre.

As children become increasingly capable of using symbols and assuming roles and are able to represent real and imagined experiences and events, their play in groups more accurately reproduces the world as they experience it. Sociodramatic play encourages a level of intimacy among children who implicitly agree to pursue common aims in their pretend play. This style of play teaches children that families are both similar and different, that people behave in predictable and unpredictable ways, that there are happy feelings and sad feelings, and that events and contexts are continually changing. As children act out a play episode related to family life, for example, they generally acknowledge their own feelings and those of others, and they learn to empathize with others.

The physical setting, materials, and the climate of the Daily Living centre provide messages to children that they may assume the roles of the adult world and they may allow their imaginations to dictate the flow of their play, alone or together.

Facilitating Development in the Daily Living Centre

Significant everyday living concepts are explored and learned in the Daily Living centre, which is a particularly rich area for fostering all categories of play and addressing many developmental tasks. Play with dough and kitchen implements promotes fine motor development and eye–hand coordination; pretend play with dolls and household props promotes symbolic thinking, imagination, problem solving, and language and communication skills. Sociodramatic play in super units such as supermarkets, restaurants, or offices promotes language development, literacy, symbolic and representational thinking, logical reasoning, communication skills, memory, attending skills, and perception—the list goes on. Children learn to take a perspective other than their own and to negotiate role-taking when they collaborate to recreate routine events from daily life. Social-conventional learning occurs as children contribute concepts they have observed while participating in family events, such as, "This is my brother's bar mitzvah," and "Let's pack the basket to go camping." Cooperative play with props also promotes manipulative abilities (e.g., doing up zippers, tying bows, rolling dough, and stacking dishes) and teaches factual information, such as, "This is a garlic press," "My daddy wears coveralls to fix cars," and "Angie's family eats with chopsticks like these."

Nash (1989) discussed two related types of learning that occur in this centre: that of factual concepts and of feelings concepts. Factual concepts relate to everyday life. They are the answers to such questions as, What is a restaurant, a briefcase, a condominium? Can boys be nurses? What is it like where my mommy works? Children assume roles they see in their neighbourhoods, such as the grocer, dentist, barber, or librarian. Feelings are explored through play that allows children to act out highly emotional situations that are often more complex than they can describe in words. What is it like to have a baby sister? Can I look after a baby too? What does it mean to be unemployed? Why are my daddy and mommy angry? Such questions arouse intense feelings in children which they are often at a loss to understand without 'trying on' the roles involved. Role play allows adults to observe the situations that children are trying to cope with and understand, and which they often must learn to accept or challenge. Children find some answers to calm their fears and begin to cast some light on the complexities of everyday living as they assume grown-up roles for themselves.

The child who pretends to care for a baby sister, or who pretends to be mommy leaving for work in the morning with a briefcase, comes closer to understanding what life will be like with a new baby in the house and what her mother's life is like when she is away from her. Children express feelings about their own life experiences: for example, they may express anger that mommy is always too tired to play and fear that they may be displaced by the new baby. One child was overheard to express his fear of being a "trade-in" before his new sibling was born. When the child replayed a scene in which he had accompanied his parents to trade in the old car for a new, larger one in recent weeks, an observant ECE concluded that he was afraid that his father and expectant mother would trade him in for the new baby brother or sister.

Gender Issues and Stereotypic Play

Anyone who has observed children closely knows that boys and girls play differently; these and other gender differences seem sometimes to be hard-wired at birth. Research has demonstrated that boys also learn differently (Brizendine, 2009). A function of the early learning environment is to provide opportunities for boys and girls to choose and pursue their own play preferences within an available mix of play opportunities that foster, for example, doll play, rough-and-tumble play, and construction play that invites both sexes to play together and learn from one another. Play and learning differences between boys and girls should be addressed in the preschool period and certainly during kindergarten and the early primary years (Abraham, 2010). The importance of ensuring that boys have ample opportunities to choose their own play preferences and learning styles is explored further in Chapter 13. We know that gender roles in North American culture have changed significantly with many more women in the workforce. Eliot (2010) claims that, in spite of significant societal changes, parents still tend, often unconsciously, to socialize their children to traditional gender roles at very young ages and to have different expectations of their child's school performance and preferred learning styles. She contends that there should be a much greater balance in the play and learning activities offered to boys and girls—for example, girls should be encouraged to engage in construction play and physically active play, and boys should be reinforced for participating in nurturing play. Eliot (2010) argues that most gender differences are relatively small and that there is considerable overlap in the learning interests and styles of boys and girls. Not all little girls dream of being princesses, and not all little boys are interested in war play and the stereotypic superheroes. The stark facts, however, that the academic performance of boys has slipped dramatically relative to that of girls, that many more boys than girls drop out of high school before graduation, and that females outnumber males in many postsecondary programs, suggest that the ways in which we socialize young boys and girls, the early learning opportunities we offer them, the context of those opportunities, and the play and learning expectations we have of them are overdue for revision (Cappon, 2010; Drolet, 2007).

The research landscape related to gender differences, however, remains murky in spite of political pressures to resolve issues related to the relatively poorer performance of boys in school from the early grades on. Brizendine (2006, 2010) has studied the male brain and the female brain; she found that the behaviour and play patterns of boys versus girls remain relatively constant during the early years and beyond, despite attempts to socialize both genders to the play styles and traditional roles of the opposite gender. She claims that scientists have learned that, no matter how much influence we may wish to have,

> girls will play house and dress up their dollies, and boys will race around fighting imaginary foes, building and destroying, and seeking new thrills. Regardless of how we think children should play, boys are more interested in competitive games, and girls are more interested in cooperative games. This innate brain wiring is apparently different enough that behavioural studies show that boys spend 65% of their free time in competitive games, while girls spend only 35%. And when girls are playing, they take turns more often than boys (Brizendine, 2009, p. 18).

Whether or not we agree that males' and females' brains are different by nature (Brizendine, 2006, pp. 13–27), "experience, practice, and interaction with others can modify neurons and brain wiring.... Gender education and biology collaborate to make us who we are." For ECEs, the challenge may be to ensure that boys and girls have access to the mind-shaping, bodily exercise, and social and emotional experiences of the other gender, encouraging boys to invest time and energy in verbal, quieter, nurturing play with one or two other players, and girls to engage in rough and tumble, competitive play and construction activities with larger groups. It is beneficial to encourage boys to assume the role of nurse, and girls to that of veterinarian; to ask girls to repair the broken dollhouse chair, and boys to fold and put away the bedding for the doll cribs; to encourage the boys to be the cooks, and the girls to "mow the lawn" in the playhouse. We need to find ways for boys to engage in nurturing, cooperative play by introducing resources that boys typically choose, so that they can, for example, "put the baby in the car and take him for a drive" or use a car or truck to paint on newsprint. The Daily Living centre should also provide play materials that reflect gender differences and have posters and pictures on walls of men and women in non-stereotypic roles that reflect the lifestyles of parents who are lesbian, gay, bisexual, or transgendered.

When ECEs address the gender differences they observe in children's play and when they try to balance their play by encouraging, but not coercing, children to engage in play typical of the opposite gender, they are also addressing cultural differences and helping children of other cultures to adapt to the society outside their home. We see many cultural differences in the ways that boys are treated and the expectations of them versus those for girls in the same family. Brooker (2010, p. 30) claims that "cultural variations in children's play may be the result of adult constraints imposed on children's play induced by cultural values more than inherent choices and motivations." The ECE who is trying to help the young boy from a family in which gender roles are very much divided along traditional lines, for example, understand that he, too, should shoulder some responsibility for tidying up the housekeeping area where he has been playing, is addressing not only the child's understanding of gender roles, but also his obligation to share the burden for what in his family may be viewed as "female work." The challenge for the ECE is to help children of other cultures "bridge the distance" between the child's family environment and his adopted culture, where he will go to school and work, and live out much of his life. The ECE has to undertake this challenge without alienating the parents for whom such role-sharing may be threatening and unwelcome. A challenge like this is one example of the complexity of contemporary life in a multicultural, pluralistic society such as our own.

Variations in children's play by gender are also relevant to children in single-parent homes and to the influence of socioeconomic differences between children living in poverty and those from more affluent families. Children from single-parent homes may have only the mother as a role model. Children from poor homes often have fewer home-based examples to reference in their dramatic play because there may be less food, fewer resources, less contact with the world beyond their immediate neighbourhood. Neuroscientists in Canada and the United States are studying how low socioeconomic status is affecting academic performance, mental and physical health, and the wiring of the brain, in order to shed light on new early childhood interventions that may reduce the impact of poverty on academic outcomes and quality of life in general. Some Ottawa-based research is also focusing on cognitive strengths that may result from poverty in childhood, such as brain features that may be associated with greater resilience (McIlroy, 2010).

The very nature of children's dramatic play in the housekeeping area of the playroom is changing as the contexts of children's lives and experiences change.

> In Western societies, the traditional housekeeping and family games played in home corners are also being changed, by children themselves, as they introduce new themes and artefacts and construct new meanings from their own experiences of life outside the classroom. Through their play, children frequently reveal how life is lived in re-constituted families or in homes where no one works (Brooker, 2010, p. 31).

Increasingly, we see role play whereby children try to replicate the actions of their hard-pressed parents and the influences of the media culture and ever-present technologies in their homes. Encouraging children to import from other learning centres the materials they need to represent what they imagine and to make meaning of what they live each day supports their attempts to understand their home experience through role play. Children have a profound need to make meaning through pretend, to allow full rein to their imaginations, and to work through the complex mix of contradictions and emotions that they experience in their daily lives.

Organization and Design of the Daily Living Centre

Equipment, Materials, and Supplies

A Daily Living centre will typically include the following elements (see Figure 12–1).

EQUIPMENT

- **Household Play:** refrigerator; stove; microwave oven; dish cupboard; sink; kitchen implements (including specialized food preparation implements used by a variety of cultures); small table with chairs; chest of drawers for storage; sheets, blankets, pillows, towels; full-length shatter-proof mirror; rugs or mats
- **Role Play:** storage shelves for equipment and rack for dress-up clothing, hats, shoes, purses, shopping carts, wagons, baskets, shopping bags, including items in all categories that address various cultural groups represented by the children
- **Doll Play:** cradle, highchair, child-sized bed, rocking chair, and dresser for doll clothes

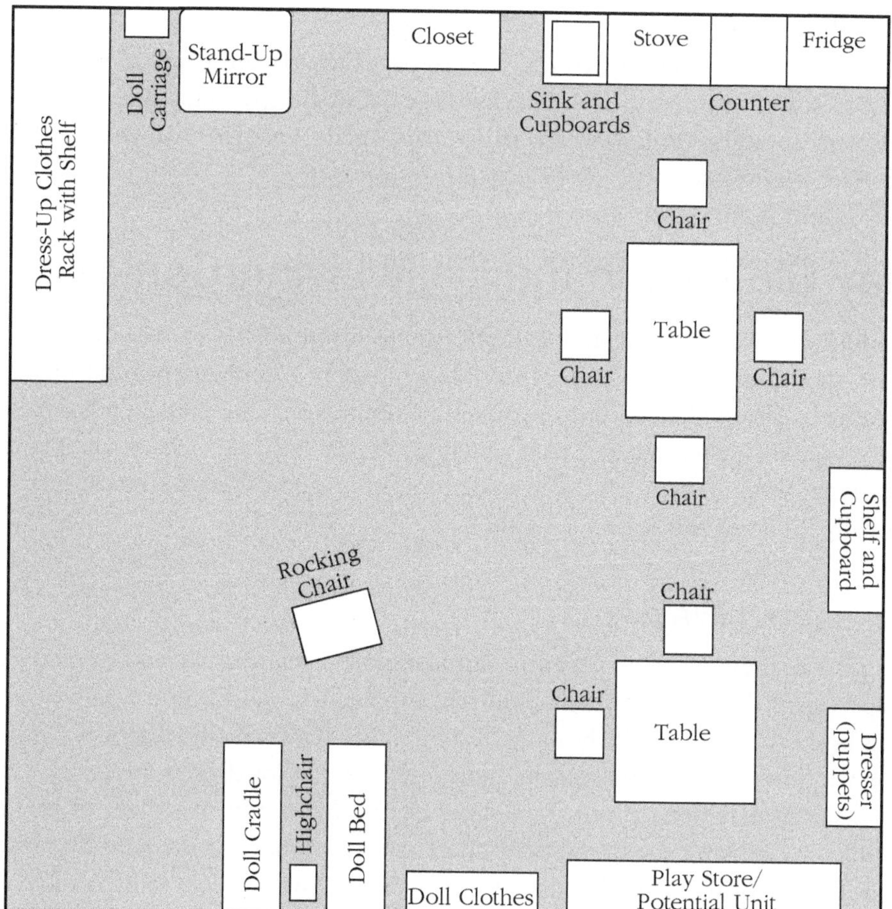

Figure 12–1
The Daily Living centre

MATERIALS

- **Household Play:** baking utensils, dishes, cutlery, baking pans, pots, measuring cups and spoons; various types of culturally relevant serving dishes for eating; cooking implements and dishes relevant to different cultures; kitchen organizers and hooks; laundry and cleaning equipment; iron and ironing board; tea towels, sponges, dish rack; mirror; laundry basket; hand vacuum, broom, mop, and dustpan; tablecloths, cloth placemats, cushions
- **Role Play:** male and female small-sized adult clothing from various cultures, including capes, robes, nightwear, scarves, shawls, gloves, shoes, and slippers; familiar occupational clothing, including safety helmets, hats, shoes, lunch bucket, briefcase, masks, and wigs; mirror; prop boxes containing props for a store, hospital, restaurant, library, or barber shop play; and items for specific cultural, historical, and mythical themes. Prop boxes should be set up one or two at a time, as setting up too many leads to confusion and to over-stimulation. Both the clothes closet and prop boxes should be readily accessible for children playing in the Active Role Play centre, where play related to various "occupational" groups often occurs and where helmets, policemen's hats, farmers' implements, uniforms, and parade clothes are often needed
- **Doll Play:** assorted dolls, ethnic doll accessories, beds and bedding, baby bottles, doll clothing, doll stroller, doll bathtub, doll highchair, and miscellaneous items, such as telephone or cell phone, stuffed toys, doll house and furniture, and small cars and trucks

SUPPLIES

- Dough or modelling clay, cloths, towels, paper towels and napkins, tissues, mild liquid soap, tissues, cotton swabs, bandages, dish cloths, wrappings, paper bags, dusters, sponges, tin foil, waxed paper, paper plates, napkins and cups, plastic cutlery, and glasses

Play Stations in the Daily Living Centre

In addition to equipment and materials for a household area, the Daily Living centre should include specialized play areas, such as a kitchen and doll play area, that may be clearly defined or have no visible boundaries. Including a potential unit where special or theme-based play activities may be set up, such as role play in a school, pet shop, or doctor's office, adds complexity and variety to the play activities normally found in this learning centre.

Household Play Area

At a glance, the household play area in most playrooms resembles a basic house or an apartment. It should contain child-sized appliances and furniture, as well as the items listed above under the heading "Equipment, Materials, and Supplies." A miniature window with curtains may be built onto the wall or divider, pretty placemats and cushions may decorate the tables and chairs, and a nontoxic plant or two may be added to enhance the domesticity and cozy atmosphere. Posters on the walls or small, framed prints should add to the diversity of the environment. A table with four chairs is usually located in the household area. Here, children can use dough or modelling clay as props for moulding and cutting cookies or for rolling out dough. In this context, dough is properly used as a prop that enhances symbolic play, rather than as a creative substance. The texture and consistency of the dough and the use of specialized implements, such as rolling pins, cookie cutters, and cutlery, also allow children to practise fine motor skills, eye–hand coordination, hand control, and a wide range of other manipulative and perceptual abilities.

A miniature house or apartment setting provides clear messages to children that play re-creating family and household events and roles is encouraged. Through playing with props, children explore the complex relationships and responsibilities in a typical household and become aware of the similarities between their lives at home and those of their peers. For example, children recognize that chopsticks are eating implements like knives and forks, and that the wok is another kind of cooking pan. All families have both particular and universal rituals associated with mealtimes. All cultural groups spend time in food preparation and rely on specific tools to facilitate meal planning and cooking. The household play area is a powerful learning environment for reinforcing the similarities and appreciating the differences that exist across cultures.

Household area

Where space permits, the household play area provides a setting in which ECEs, visiting parents, or other guests may conduct individual cooking activities with small groups of children. These activities can also be used to demonstrate the ethnic mix of children in the group. Individual-portion cookery is most appropriate for young children and reduces possible hazards associated with infection. ECEs should observe guidelines for conducting cooking activities that local health authorities in some jurisdictions have established. In addition, individual-portion cooking activities allow children to compare their results, to make adjustments to their own cooking techniques, and to form relationships between the way things look before they go into the microwave or oven and how they turn out (DeVries, Zan, Hildebrandt, Edmiaston, & Sales, 2002).

Dressing up for role play

ACTIVITIES IN THE HOUSEHOLD PLAY AREA FOR CHILDREN AGES TWO TO FOUR

1. Provide supplies so that children can wash the dishes (perhaps those used for snack) using real water and suds in the sink. Encourage cooperative play by suggesting that another child help by drying the dishes.
2. Children typically find solace in playing with water and suds, and some will play at this station for long periods of time, which makes play at this play station an opportunity to introduce bathing the "babies" which appeals to their instincts for nurturing and caregiving.
3. Encourage the children to practise using chopsticks to pick up small pieces of pea-sized play dough they have made.
4. Have the children polish the shoes from the dress-up area. This cooperative task also involves waiting for the polish to dry and shining the shoes with cloths and brushes.
5. Provide tweezers to put cotton balls in small cups to use as symbols to represent various foods.
6. Have the children sift and measure, using sifters and measuring cups, to create a cornmeal or flour mixture. Provide rolling pins with dough.
7. Provide dusters for children to dust tables, counters, and shelves, which provide practice in caring for the environment.

ACTIVITIES IN THE HOUSEHOLD PLAY AREA FOR CHILDREN AGES FOUR TO SIX

1. Have the children stack measuring cups, measuring spoons, and scoops in seriated order. Include cultural implements as items to be stacked and seriated.
2. Have the children make their own snacks by peeling and sectioning tangerines or mandarin oranges and placing wafers at the side of their napkins or plate.
3. Assemble a collection of dirty golf balls that the children can clean with a toothbrush and liquid soap at the sink or in a bowl of sudsy water.
4. Provide miscellaneous materials for the children to sort according to texture (e.g., pieces of plastic, sticks, sandpaper, rocks, foam rubber, Styrofoam, textured fabrics) and to define their own criteria for sorting.

Dolls and Doll Furniture Area

The main items of equipment in this area are doll cribs, a trunk or drawers for doll clothes, a doll highchair, and a doll stroller or carriage. The explicit purpose of this area is to promote children's role play of family and caregiving roles, such as mother, father, teacher, babysitter, doctor, and nurse. The ability to care for and nurture others is an important emotional objective for early childhood, which sows the seeds

Doll play area

of empathy upon which all positive human relationships are founded and provides the basis for morally responsible behaviour. Gordon (2006, p. 117) speaks of "emotional literacy that is frequently described as the ability to recognize, understand, cope with and express our emotions in appropriate ways." The doll play area allows children to express their tender responses to those they perceive as more vulnerable than themselves and to hold others to account for behaviours that they consider to be inappropriate.

Children's mental health is affected by how they feel about and treat other people and by whether they are able to extend themselves in caring for others (Yardley, 1988). Practising the gestures, behaviours, and language associated with caregiving helps children internalize and understand feelings associated with close, dependent relationships. The ability to care for and look after others is a powerful emotional capacity that promotes self-expression, empathy, and compassion, and it is a learning priority for children in most cultures. These affective characteristics are also closely related to developing a spiritual life in which children learn respect and reverence for life, express feelings of wonder, and act out attitudes of consideration and concern for others.

Play with dolls may take many forms. A young child who cradles a doll tenderly and coos softly while curled up on a cushion in a corner begins to sense what it is like to extend himself in the care of another human being. Besides imitating the actions of a mother or father rocking the baby, the child is rehearsing a familiar caregiving role and imagining what it is like to be a parent. The doll play area provides opportunities for many categories and social contexts of play, including associative play, in which children play with dolls individually, but alongside other children, rehearsing their own mental scripts without interacting. Social interaction occurs when children cooperate and combine their dramatic play scripts to take specific roles and to follow a jointly conceived plan that unfolds as play continues. One child may appoint himself the daddy, another child the mommy, and another the baby, and then may announce to his playmates the script to be followed, and the other two children happily comply with the plan. Sometimes considerable negotiation occurs, with all children participating in the allocation of roles. Some families continue to build rituals and regular family-centred experiences into their children's lives, but the reality these days is that the family sometimes delegates this responsibility to child-care programs, schools, and teachers (Smilansky, 1990). In the doll play and household play areas, ECEs provide the environment and materials with which children may help one another dramatize and practise familiar rituals from their own families, which often include extended family members. Children learn much from each other as they observe other children playing out their family rituals, including the diverse practices that accompany mealtimes, bedtimes, and especially family gatherings and celebrations that have many cultural variations.

The doll play area provides a place to encourage nonstereotypic play and tolerance for others. Dolls representing many cultural and racial groups help to break down stereotyped views and to develop enlightened attitudes and positive relationships among ethnic groups. Most important of all, ECEs should encourage and support role play by boys and girls in the doll play area, which should be arranged to provide cues to boys that they are welcome and that this is an area in which they can express themselves emotionally, develop nurturing skills, and practise caregiving roles with babies. Children are encouraged to take the dolls to other learning centres (for example, to the Active Role Play or Quiet Thinking centres) for use as props in their play and for the emotional sustenance they provide. In setting up the dolls at play stations outside the Daily Living centre, ECEs encourage children who would not normally choose the dolls area to incorporate dolls into their play in other learning centres. This practice is especially important for boys who need to be encouraged to bring dolls as props into their play in the Active Role Play centre and outdoors.

ACTIVITIES IN THE DOLLS AREA FOR CHILDREN AGES TWO TO FOUR

1. Invite the children to dress dolls in a variety of clothes with different types of fasteners, such as snaps, buttons, Velcro, ties, buckles, and hooks and eyes.
2. Ask the children to tidy and sort the doll clothes in drawers or in the trunk.
3. Have the children fold towels, blankets, and sheets for cribs; have them make up doll cribs with bedding and tuck the dolls in.
4. Play lullabies on the tape or record player and encourage children to sing along to their "babies."
5. Promote pretend play episodes that involve daily living in their families with parents, pet dogs and cats, looking after babies, tidying up the kitchen area, washing dishes.
6. Rotate family photos and albums on a table.

ACTIVITIES IN THE DOLLS AREA FOR CHILDREN AGES FOUR TO SIX

1. Promote sociodramatic play episodes in the Daily Living centre by creating a potential unit that may feature a tea room, a doctor's or dentist's office, or a hairdressing salon, using dolls, tables and chairs, telephones, and personal care items such as brushes, combs, as props.
2. Challenge the children to engage in sociodramatic play by setting up a hospital with typical hospital artifacts to promote doctor or nurse role play using the dolls as patients.
3. Have the children read stories in which various cultures are represented, and provide dolls dressed like characters in the story.
4. Provide a frame for a dollhouse, along with balsa wood or cardboard and glue for children to add room partitions and other household features including miniature furniture.
5. Encourage children to demonstrate to their friends the ways in which they celebrate special holidays and family celebrations.

Potential Play Units

The Daily Living centre is an ideal location for a potential play space large enough to set up the props for a super unit involving a restaurant, supermarket, or other role play that replicates ordinary events in children's daily lives. Potential play space is important because it allows room and the materials needed for children to extend

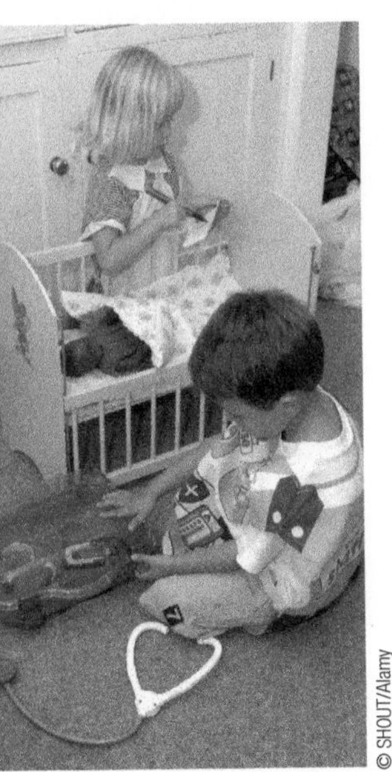
© SHOUT/Alamy

Props for the Daily Living centre

their pretend play into more imaginative play in which they jointly create their scripts and interact in the fulfillment of roles that they prescribe for themselves and for others. It is important that this type of play be accommodated in a part of the Daily Living centre where it will not interfere with the play of children who want to use the household play or doll play areas. When a classroom is not large enough to accommodate a potential unit in the Daily Living centre, the potential play space should be located in or adjacent to the Active Role Play centre.

Dress-up Clothing and Props

Dress-up clothing and props should be stored in mobile wooden cabinets that open to define a boundary for play space and are closed when not in use. Hooks may be used to hang clothing. Sometimes shelves for storing hats, belts, shoes, purses, and the like are built into the cabinet. A typical dress-up and props area contains a wide selection of adult clothing for both genders that is in good repair, preferably washable, and in small sizes. Clothing may include dresses, overalls, pants, uniforms, gowns, aprons, blazers, coats, skirts, shirts, and a variety of shoes, including low-heeled and slightly higher-heeled, for both day and evening wear, and some for sports. Multicultural clothing for everyday and ceremonial occasions enriches play and children's experience of other lifestyles and customs within North America and in other countries. Shawls, hats, scarves, capes, and jewellery add to the dramatic value of the dress-up area and encourage children to try out the accessories of other cultural groups. All clothing must be easy for children to put on and take off. Sometimes difficult zippers or fasteners need to be replaced with Velcro strips, especially in integrated programs where children with special needs may have difficulty pulling clothing over limbs or moving freely. Dramatic and sociodramatic play are facilitated by the real-life quality that adult-style props add to children's pretend play. Capes, briefcases, canes, hats representing occupational groups, lunch bags, shopping bags, and numerous other everyday objects add to the duration, depth, and realism of symbolic play.

When children assume roles familiar to them in their lives, they gain a better understanding of what it must be like to be an adult in that role. By simply putting on clothing that represents a role that is strange yet interesting to them, children achieve a clearer sense of self and may wonder, "Should I become a police officer? A farmer? A television personality? Maybe a nurse?" Roles never before imagined for themselves or for others come into clearer focus by virtue of dressing up in the concrete symbols of the role. Similarly, when children try on the clothing of other cultures, they sometimes find they move and carry their bodies differently than in their own clothing, and they may experience greater physical freedom or restriction. Ensuring that the dress-up clothing and props may be easily accessed by children playing in the Active Role play centre will ensure that sociodramatic play episodes will evolve and continue elsewhere in the environment.

Adding clothing and props in the Daily Living centre enhances and extends sociodramatic play by providing cues to the group that enable children to add a new role to their play or pursue a new story line. Clothing and props are visual cues that ECEs may add to alter the roles and life experiences being dramatized if they see children are running out of ideas. ECEs may gain further insight into the aspirations, motivations, and interests of children by tuning in to their conversations and assumptions as the children follow a plan or evolve their script.

Prop Boxes

Prop boxes are essential for the Daily Living centre, where the emphasis is on fostering children's imaginations and on encouraging them to express themselves, including their deepest emotions, through play. Each prop box should be aesthetically pleasing, decorated, and filled with items that relate to a specific theme in daily life for which the items in the prop box would trigger ideas and scripts related to their everyday world. As much as possible, the prop boxes should contain the real items taken from the adult world and not child-sized replicas. To ensure their portability to all areas of the learning environment, prop boxes should be light enough for children to transport either by carrying them or in a cart they can wheel to the potential space. Examples of prop boxes appropriate for preschool children include themes related to the pet store, fishing expeditions, a bakery, a supermarket, or other places in the community that children frequent with their families. Prop boxes related to play involving an office, bank, post office, or library are more likely placed in the Project centre or near the book corner. Prop boxes related to active play, such as underwater diving stations, fire station, or police station, are better located near the Active Role Play centre or in the playground. As always, when children are encouraged to provide ideas for prop boxes, the range of interests and subjects they represent expands enormously. Prop boxes should also represent diverse cultures and lifestyles. To ensure the dramatic potential of prop boxes, items contained within them should include abstract as well as lifelike props that support and do not limit the potential for pretending and imagining (Crowther, 2003).

Prop boxes for the Daily Living centre containing items related to the theme intended should be made from sturdy cardboard or wood and be decorated and labelled. Because sociodramatic play episodes usually attract several children at a time, the potential unit that is set up would normally be considered a super unit that would account for approximately six to eight play places. There should be a sufficient number of items in each prop box to ensure that all children have access to at least one prop at a time, and that they challenge children to integrate the prop into the dramatic script they evolve together. Prop boxes enhance children's social-conventional knowledge, particularly when they introduce real items from the adult world that they see at home or in the community but that they neither understood nor used before. Creative ECEs keep adding items to prop boxes to ensure that the play episodes are different, and of longer duration, each time children play with the props. Prop boxes can often double as resource tools for science activities, telling stories, doing projects, and enhancing literacy and language.

The variety and range of the prop boxes introduce children to hobbies, recreational pastimes, or work-related pursuits that they may not have imagined on their own. As these new interests are awakened in children, they prompt ECEs to develop curriculum and activities that build on children's new interests as well as on their greater knowledge and conceptual understanding. This, in turn, ensures that their sociodramatic play is more realistic, better informed, more challenging, and creative. Interesting, creative, and relevant prop boxes, and the potential play spaces to set them up as super units, are essential contributors to the learning environment and ensure that the activities address children's preoccupations, passions, and aspirations.

ACTIVITIES IN THE DRESS-UP AND PROPS AREA FOR CHILDREN AGES TWO TO FOUR

1. Set up adult clothing in small sizes that is easy to put on and fasten and that represents the kind of clothing their family members would wear. Include small-size shoes with low heels.
2. Add accessories such as purses, shopping bags, and sporting gear to enhance children's play themes, including accessories familiar to the cultures of the children in the program, and props that represent aspects of daily life that may be unfamiliar to some children. (This facilitates children teaching each other, as Smilansky suggested (see Chapter 11)).
3. Provide clothing that enhances certain body parts, such as chaps for the legs, tall riding boots, belts for the waist, gloves, knee supports, and hats.

ACTIVITIES IN THE DRESS-UP AND PROPS AREA FOR CHILDREN AGES FOUR TO SIX

1. Add working clothes, uniforms, briefcases, computer carrying cases, overalls, back packs, and lunch bags to the dress-up/prop area to facilitate children's dramatic or sociodramatic play involving the roles of mothers and fathers going to work.
2. Suggest a familiar role to a group of children who are already dressed up in clothing reminiscent of an event or an experience that you know they have recently had.
3. Set up a pet hospital using medical kits, an ironing board as an examination table, hospital gowns, masks, gloves, and stuffed animals.
4. Distribute clothing and jewellery with unusual fasteners for children to practise fastening and unfastening on one another, as well as on themselves (include clips, snaps, buckles, small and large buttons, laces, clasps, and spring fasteners).
5. Set up prop boxes that encourage children to role play an event that has had an emotional impact on a child or children in the program. Perhaps there has been a flood or a storm that has blown over trees and requires cleanup. Observe the play to ensure that the children affected are helped to express their feelings and others learn how to empathize with them.

Puppets and Dollhouse Area

Puppets are props that children use to help them evolve an imagined episode using the puppets to symbolize various characters. Most early childhood playrooms provide a puppet theatre, puppets of various kinds, and a dollhouse with miniature furniture. The puppet theatre should be mobile so that it can be taken to another learning centre where play with puppets is a priority for the children. A simple puppet theatre, which can be constructed of plywood, sturdy pressboard, or heavy cardboard, is an essential item of equipment in every playroom. The curtained window in the puppet theatre gives children the confidence to express feelings and perceptions and to enact situations that they would be unlikely to communicate without having the puppets as props. These play materials may also be located in the Quiet Thinking centre, but in or near the Daily Living centre they are primarily intended to encourage dramatic play with the puppets or with the miniature dolls in the dollhouse. Children's identification with a puppet or with a miniature doll in a dollhouse is not as complete or active as when they assume the role themselves. They may, however, feel less inhibited about expressing anger, sadness, hurt, confusion, or aggressive feelings through an arm's-length drama using puppets or miniature dolls as props. In the Quiet Thinking centre, ECEs frequently use puppets during group time to talk to the children or to enhance the telling or reading of a story. When ECEs engage in dialogue with a puppet, they model conversation that facilitates language development, as well as children's understanding of the rules for engaging in polite conversation.

As props, puppets are particularly useful for young children whose pretend play episodes depend on props to help them follow a theme, create a storyline, communicate, and imitate remembered actions. Puppets come in many shapes and sizes, from finger puppets to hand puppets, to large, lifelike personifications of real people or familiar storybook or video characters. Children who are more prop-dependent in their dramatic play will usually choose puppets that are more realistic depictions of the characters in their theatrical episode. The ECE's role is to observe children's play with puppets, to determine when they should be challenged to use more generic puppets (that is, those that do not resemble any particular character), which demand more of children's imaginations and their ability to represent using abstract objects. When purchasing puppets, it is wise, therefore, to choose puppets that can be used for more than one dramatic purpose and that are abstract enough to become what the child intends (Crowther, 2003). It is best to avoid Disney or other cartoon characters, which limit both the characters these puppets can assume and the play episode and the script evolved by the children in their puppet dramatizations.

ACTIVITIES IN THE PUPPETS AND DOLLHOUSE AREA FOR CHILDREN AGES TWO TO FOUR

1. Provide dolls and hand puppets representing many cultures.
2. Consider locating the puppet theatre in the Quiet Thinking centre, as children often use the puppets while looking at books and reading stories.
3. Provide a doll or a puppet for a child who appears troubled and is unable to tell the ECE what is troubling him. Ask him to let the doll or puppet explain how he feels.
4. Use finger puppets to tell a story about how the child felt when he had no one to play with.

ACTIVITIES IN THE PUPPETS AND DOLLHOUSE AREA FOR CHILDREN AGES FOUR TO SIX

1. Read a story and suggest that children act out a scene from the story using the clothing and props.
2. Encourage children to use dolls and puppets to tell a story to the other children.
3. Ask a child who is sad or out of sorts to use a puppet to describe how she is feeling that day.
4. To ease tensions that may exist between children, encourage the children to use the puppets and puppet theatre to "act out" or express the feelings they have.

Summary

The Daily Living centre is an essential feature of the play environment, which fosters children's symbolic thinking through pretend, dramatic, and sociodramatic play. The play stations emphasize children's ability to care for others, to cooperate and collaborate in their play with other children, and to try on pretend roles as a way to understand the adult world. Several play stations make up the Daily Living centre; these include the household play area; the dolls and doll beds area and, possibly, the dollhouse, which should be portable to other learning centres as the need arises; the dress-up corner; the puppets and puppet theatre, and the potential play areas for setting up super units to encourage sociodramatic play using prop boxes.

LEARNING ACTIVITIES

1. Visit a kindergarten or preschool classroom to observe children's symbolic play with dolls and doll furniture and with household play equipment and materials. Describe the symbolic play observed in this learning centre.
2. For the same setting as in Learning Activity 1, record the incidence of play materials that promote bias-free values and attitudes, such as ethnic cooking utensils, specific articles of clothing from other cultures, and so on. Make recommendations for additions to the learning centre to enhance its inclusive qualities.
3. Choose two activities from three of the play stations in the Daily Living centre or a potential unit. Create six activity cards following the activity card format presented in Chapter 10. Ensure that at least three activities encourage sociodramatic play for kindergarten children (four to six years).
4. Create a prop box for a specific sociodramatic play episode. Include accessories and attachments to enhance and extend the play as children become more accustomed to the theme represented by the prop box.
5. Observe children's dramatic and sociodramatic play and note the gender roles assumed by the children. Describe examples of children assuming non-stereotypic gender roles.

13 The Active Role Play Centre

"Childhood is not something we leave behind. The achievements and experiences of childhood are *constituents* of our later selves."

—KIERAN EGAN, *PRIMARY UNDERSTANDING: EDUCATION IN EARLY CHILDHOOD* (1988)

BEFORE READING THIS CHAPTER, HAVE YOU

- linked the equipment, materials, and supplies present in the symbolic play areas of the Daily Living centre, the Active Role Play centre, and outdoors to the categories of play and children's typical play themes?
- observed children's active play with hollow blocks, in a playhouse, and making music with instruments?

OUTCOMES

After reading and understanding this chapter, you should be able to

- plan and set up the Active Role Play centre to promote movement and active role play, including sociodramatic play;
- include children with disabilities in active role play activities;
- ensure that the Active Role Play centre provides space and opportunities for boys to choose and sustain their preferred play and learning styles;
- design the Active Role Play centre with the hollow blocks, ramps, and other props to sustain role play for significant periods of time;
- set up props, including musical instruments and costumes, within children's reach to facilitate the spontaneous integration of music into play;
- promote creative-constructive play with props, hollow blocks, and other building materials such as tracks, bridges and tunnels;
- encourage positive superhero play and risk taking; and introduce cooperative games in small groups.

The Purpose of the Active Role Play Centre

The Active Role Play centre is the area of the playroom where play is active, children use larger materials and equipment for play, and noise levels may be elevated. This centre compensates for longer days indoors when the weather is inclement and darkness descends earlier. Although children should play outdoors for significant parts of every day, Canadians know that there are days in winter and summer that are not conducive to lengthy outdoor play periods given our extreme climate patterns. The Active Role Play centre is, therefore, an essential area where children may let off steam, engage in physically challenging activities, practise using their bodies in many forms of movement to music and in sport, engage in rough-and-tumble and superhero play, and construct super-sized representations of the ideas and the structures they imagine or those they wish to replicate from their experience, books, or favourite programs.

The Active Role Play centre promotes role play with themes that include reasonable freedom of movement and some physical risk taking and adventure with large equipment, construction materials, and props. Children develop physically while engaging in symbolic play with active play equipment and materials; they assume roles that call for action, space, and freedom to move. When children assume roles, they practise expressing themselves verbally and physically, use divergent thinking skills, increase their language competence, develop their bodies, and enhance their **self-concept**. This is a learning centre where children play cooperatively to co-construct their understanding of the social world and collaborate in their sociodramatic play to re-create events, sequences, and roles that they observe in the community. In doing so, they rely on one another, consider the perspectives of others, learn to support one another, and listen to and observe another child's representation of a reality she understands. The added space for large-muscle activity, and the large props and equipment, allow children to plan larger-than-life, expansive roles, especially if fieldtrips are planned so as to add ideas and themes that foster and enrich sustained sociodramatic play.

The climber; hollow blocks; planks and ramps; props such as blankets, firefighters' hats, and hoses; big cardboard boxes; and a playhouse or climbing structure encourage active, social play, and risk taking. The open space encourages more vigorous role play than the closer quarters of the Daily Living centre. Children should have room to build large structures with hollow blocks onto which they can climb or to make intricate road networks for cars and trucks. Ramps and planks allow children to cordon off a large play structure or a playhouse made of blocks. ECEs may encourage children to develop their own super units in the Active Role Play centre, such as a space station, an undersea exploration site, or a fire station. For this reason, children should have ready access to the prop boxes and dress-up clothes, which may be stored either in the Daily Living centre or in the Active Role Play centre. Ideally, the space in this centre will allow for periods when children can leave their structures standing over several days to return to their play and continue the themes they may have begun in the super unit they have built.

Props in the Active Role Play Centre

To support active role play, children often need props to extend and enhance role play. These props may be abstract or realistic depending on the sophistication of the players. Prop boxes related to adventure and superhero themes belong in the Active

Role Play centre or outdoors. As storage space allows, they should be routinely accessible to children. Musical instruments should be freely available to children to support their dramatic play themes and movement to music, and to incorporate their own music into role play of concerts, parades, marches, dance theatre, and drama.

Facilitating Development and Learning in the Active Role Play Centre

Developmental goals in this learning centre include fostering teamwork; building social relationships; communication and language; self-expression using props for role play; symbolic thinking; physical development, including physical abilities, gross and fine motor skills, fitness, coordination, and body awareness; active problem solving; spatial concepts; and a wide range of social skills. Children's sense of self is closely related to their perceptions of the competence of their own bodies in physical activities. The muscles, skeleton, and proportions of the body are, for the most part, genetically determined and should be well developed by the later stages of early childhood. Practice and plenty of opportunities for movement promote coordination and the development of physical abilities such as strength, **endurance**, agility, **balance**, and the ability to make physical adjustments to space by crouching, stretching, and bending.

We know that the young child has an intimate and compelling relationship with the concrete world. The responsive environment gives back messages as the child acts on it. Environments indoors and outdoors that are physically challenging have much in common with environments that are cognitively stimulating; both are rich in concrete objects, in media to explore, in sensory experiences, in problems to solve, and in opportunities for risk taking. ECEs provide new play and learning opportunities when children have mastered former challenges.

Physical development is linked to cognitive, emotional, and social development. In the cognitive domain, ECEs may foster the understanding of such concepts as space, direction, time–space orientation, position, distance, and body awareness through physical activity. Think of the learning that takes place when children run an obstacle course. They bend, climb, stretch, jump, hop, and roll while passing through the obstacle course, and they build muscles and motor skills in the process. They are also learning directional prepositions, such as *around, over, through,* and *between*. To negotiate the obstacles correctly, children have to attend to the ECE's verbal instructions or to pictorial signs at each station; then, they must be able to execute those instructions successfully. When trying to squeeze through a tunnel, they have to figure out how small to make their bodies, and, thus, they develop spatial awareness, which is a cognitive skill, along with muscular and motor competence.

Although children also learn through spontaneous play in unplanned environments, their physical development is enhanced through play in an environment that promotes regular, active involvement addressing a comprehensive range of physical skills such as tumbling, marching, teacher-directed physical exercises, and group games. Sociodramatic play themes often require space to move in a coordinated fashion, balance, bend, stretch, climb, sway, and perform a host of other physical abilities and motor movements. **Cooperative games** may incorporate physical development as well as the learning of colours, time, size, numbers, social behaviour, language, cultural awareness, and other everyday living concepts.

Children find it easier to communicate and to use language fluently while performing physical tasks. Words learned in the context of a physical experience are usually understood and are seldom forgotten. For example, an ECE may respond to hollow block play in the Active Role Play centre by saying, "It looks a little like a condominium to me," to a child who does not know what to call the multilevel structure she has constructed with hollow blocks. The ECE's suggestion of a word at that moment is likely to make a more lasting impression than would a group activity on words that describe types of homes.

Children are particularly vulnerable to criticism or mockery of their physical abilities or appearance. A positive self-concept is, in the early years, linked to children's abilities to use their bodies effectively and to be admired and accepted by their peers (Pica, 2004). Physical activity, whether competently executed or not, also has the side effect of releasing and channelling emotion and pent-up energy. Therefore, creative physical programming, combined with the props needed to support sociodramatic play themes, facilitates children's social adaptation, emotional well-being, spiritual growth, creativity, and intellectual growth.

Creativity, language, representation, and self-expression are fostered when children assume roles, such as those of a firefighter, a police officer, a deep-sea diver, or an astronaut. In this centre, children also solve problems, such as "How many hollow blocks do I need to stand on to be as high as the top of the climber?" Children practise communication and representation, and they form relationships and develop social skills as they collaborate in building a space station with blocks, blankets, and the climber. As well, children use logical thinking skills to estimate how many giant steps will bring them to the end of the room. The Active Role Play centre is a rich environment for the development of the whole child.

Protecting the Rights and Interests of Boys in the Active Role Play Centre

Creative-constructive play is important in this centre, and boys and girls both benefit from this play style, although, possibly, in different ways. Making this centre accessible and attractive to both genders is a subtle skill, especially when the large climbing equipment or hollow block structure built by the boys tends to dominate the space. Recent research tells us that there are learning benefits to encouraging girls and boys to play together in the Active Role Play centre, as each gender may be pursuing its own "script" while interacting in boisterous play that often involves running, chasing, capturing, hiding, and play fighting, all of which create positive emotional engagement among the players (Jarvis, 2010).

In the past decade, a dramatic shift has occurred globally in the performance of boys in school, along with higher failure and dropout rates for boys, to the point that in Canada, men now account for only 40 percent of university undergraduates. "We don't pay nearly enough attention to [boys'] needs and aspirations, take seriously their interests, and what motivates them, whether it's reading comics or science fiction" (Cappon, 2010). There is a sense that we make many assumptions about male children without the research to confirm our assumptions. And the result is that boys are underperforming academically when they reach school. This phenomenon is occurring in spite of the shift in the economy to work that requires sophisticated intellectual and social skills rather than manual labour. Alarm in Canada over the declining academic performance of boys is finally attracting the attention of parents and educators, who see the need to defeminize the schools while ensuring that supports are not removed from girls. There are lessons to be learned at the preschool and kindergarten levels to ensure that boys' preferred play styles, which have an impact on their learning, are protected and nurtured by following a few key principles:

- The different play and learning styles of boys and girls should be factored into playroom and playground design.
- Boys' preferences for boisterous action and rough-and-tumble play should be supported by the play environment and the climate for play.
- Boys should be encouraged to move actively, build, lift, climb, challenge one another, take risks, and compete.

Supporting boisterous play in the Active Role Play centre does not mean excluding girls or making the centre less appealing to them. Girls also enjoy boisterous play often characterized by running, chasing, racing, climbing, sliding, and competing, albeit sometimes with different "ends" in mind and propelled by agendas that are different from the boys'. Girls are often attracted by the props built by the boys (e.g., forts, houses, bridges, and roads), which they employ as props for their own fantasy, social, and sociodramatic play themes. The alert ECE will observe times when girls are likely more welcome to enter the play of boys in the Active Role Play centre to contribute to and possibly sustain the boys' active play. There are also times when girls may be encouraged to use the structures built by the boys when the boys have moved on to another centre. The ways in which the different play styles of boys and girls influence each other and their gender roles and identities—and contribute to their social, emotional, physical, and intellectual development—need more attention and further research.

Rough-and-Tumble Play

Rough-and-tumble play is often mistaken for aggression, although it is an important play style that holds considerable benefits for young children of both genders. This form of play is characterized by chasing, climbing, playful wrestling, and tackling, all of which include energetic physical exercise. Just as there has been a decline in children's exposure to regular, spontaneous contact with nature for safety reasons, today's children are often "protected" from vigorous rough-and-tumble play for safety reasons, but also because we have succumbed, perhaps too much, to values that overly promote the virtues of cooperation and collaboration and disparage competition. We often miss the point of children's rough-and-tumble play by forgetting the fun and excitement generated when children challenge one another's prowess, out-run or out-climb each other, engage in pretend play of "scary" roles, and enjoy the energy and emotional release that comes from rough-and-tumble activity (Tannock, 2008). ECEs need to ensure that children are playing with a smile on their faces, rather than with intentions to harm others, even though there might be some element of "settling scores" contained within rough-and-tumble play. Some observers of the changes in gender roles in our society claim that our attitudes toward rough-and-tumble play, and toward built-in gender differences, may have feminized boys and subjugated their natural impulses to values that seek to neutralize gender differences, all in a quest for equality that distorts essential human nature. Jarvis (2010, p. 63) suggests that "male fascination with physical competition has been present for many generations, represented in the discourse of both historical and contemporary cultures" and provides research evidence of continued gender differences in play. Similar studies suggest that natural instincts for rough-and-tumble play should not be stifled because children, like other mammals, are creating important neural connections in the areas of the brain that govern emotion and sociability (Jarvis, 2010, p. 62).

Superhero Play

Discussion of children's superhero play, which usually begins in the preschool period, is also relevant to the Active Role Play centre because this is often the venue for this type of role play. Children have had superheroes for as long as children's play has been observed and documented. In the Middle Ages, children played at being knights and infidels, just as today's children play Spider-Man and Batman. The popularity of superheroes escalates and declines with the times, like fashions and fads that come and go. The various media introduce children from a very young age to contemporary childhood heroes and heroines, and their influence on young children is pervasive and powerful. Their superheroes live on their sheets and pillowcases, T-shirts, pyjamas, and even their socks. It would be futile to rule out superhero play; instead, it might be practical for programs to capture the appeal of these characters to help children understand the fickle attraction of power, to juxtapose power with empathy and compassion for others, and to challenge children to take risks that build confidence and character. Engaging young children in discussion about their superheroes, particularly to explore their sense of adventure and their understanding of achievement, helps them relate to the values of courage, strength, striving, and persistence. Observant ECEs will use children's superheroes to build interesting prop boxes, plan challenging activities that capitalize on their attraction to superheroes, and reinforce the importance of effort leading to success that some of the more noble characters represent to children.

Superhero play has many benefits for children (Sluss, 2005). Issues related to superhero play sometimes focus on the level of aggression and violence that often accompanies children's role playing of various heroes. There is no denying the negative impact of violent television and video, from which children should be protected. The fear is that engaging in rough-and-tumble play behaviour will somehow increase the chances that children will become aggressive and violent adults. That fear, as well as moral indignation at the prevalence of violence in society today, sometimes leads ECEs to ban superhero play in the learning environment. Adults tend to project their own feelings about aggression and violence onto children's superhero play, instead of trying to understand and use this role play constructively. ECEs who recognize the presence of superhero play throughout history will instead search for stories and poems that introduce children to admirable superhero characters to emulate, with a view to replacing, or at least reducing, the appeal of mindless, violent television and video characters. Creating a unit of activities around such favourite characters such as Winnie the Pooh and Christopher Robin and Harry Potter reinforces for children many traditional values, such as courage, honesty, loyalty, and kindness, that are too often forgotten in contemporary adventure films and stories.

Superhero play is closely associated with rough-and-tumble play, which often includes play-fighting (Pelligrini, 1991). Vigorous kinds of superhero play are, for many children, a useful outlet for the basic human urges that contain violence and aggression (Kostelnik, Whiren, & Stein, 1986). Used positively, superhero play, and even pretend violence, can help children gain some control over their aggressive feelings (Bettelheim, 1987a). Assuming the superhero role allows children to feel physically, and to understand more vividly, the confusing forces of good and evil that superheroes or antiheroes often represent. Passive watching of superheroes on television does not permit children to experience the mysterious forces the hero represents as readily as they would by trying on the role for themselves. In children's minds, superheroes take on the superhuman characteristics they are meant to depict. Positive heroes are usually good in an absolute sense, with extraordinary qualities of wisdom, bravery, strength, and power. They demonstrate skills and mystical powers that children often wish they had. In addition, they usually overcome or defeat any counterforce that attempts to thwart them; they seem to have all the answers, they seem to be in control, and they are usually popular and admired members of their own social group (Kostelnik et al., 1986).

Sometimes children want to assume the roles of the antiheroes whose characteristics are all bad. This moving back and forth between superhero and antihero roles puts children in touch with the opposing forces of good and evil and helps them feel these forces physically and emotionally. Their play heroes avoid the ambiguities and the conflicting behaviours and values that children so often see in the adults around them, and that are often confusing and disturbing to them. Just as assuming the roles of caregiver, parent, or ECE allows children to experience the feelings of nurturing and power associated with these roles, so superhero play allows children to unravel some of the mysteries surrounding good and evil. Superhero play that is well supervised, understood, and appreciated by adults for its humanizing potential, as well as for its universal appeal to the animal instincts deep within every person, can become a powerful agent in the young child's moral and spiritual development.

EXAMPLE

Kostelnik et al. (1986, p. 7) provided some useful suggestions to help ECEs capitalize on the positive and growth-enhancing characteristics of superhero play in planning curriculum and activities.

- Help children recognize the humane characteristics of superheroes.
- Discuss real-life heroes and heroines.
- Talk about the pretend world of acting.
- Limit the time and place for superhero play.
- Explore related concepts, especially those related to courage, compassion, and standing up for good against evil.
- Help children develop goals for superheroes that go beyond the normal storyline.
- Help children de-escalate rough-and-tumble play that gets out of hand.
- Make it clear that harmful aggression, such as hitting, is unacceptable.
- Give children some control over their choices and allow them to role play what matters to them.
- Praise children's attempts at mastery, particularly the kind of mastery that takes time and persistence.

Once ECEs have decided that the benefits of superhero play outweigh the potential hazards, the next step is to ensure this play style is well managed and guided. Limits help children differentiate between fantasy and reality (Austin, 1986). Effective supervision of superhero play includes recognizing the danger signs and anticipating when play is likely to turn to harmful aggression and violence. When children's voices and faces show anger, when they utter threats and playful interaction stops, ECEs need to redirect the play and offer suggestions for more constructive activity.

Locating the Active Role Play Centre

When the Active Role Play centre is situated close to the Daily Living centre, the range of potential role play activities is maximized. The preferred juxtaposition of these centres allows props to be shared, role play to be extended from one centre to the other, and larger groups of children to be accommodated. This juxtaposition may also link the preferred role play themes of girls in the Daily Living centre to those of the boys playing in the adjacent Active Role Play centre. This accommodation promotes collaborative sociodramatic play between the girls, who may have one set of objectives in their play, and the boys, who may have a different set of objectives. Jarvis (2010, p. 69) observed mixed-gender play in which boys and girls were playing together with different purposes in mind and found that "children involved in mixed-gender chasing were practising complex social skills, simultaneously competing and colluding within a highly gendered, independently directed activity."

Chapter 7, on planning space, referred to the necessity at times for the Active Role Play centre to be located apart from the regular playroom that houses most or all other learning centres. It is not an ideal arrangement, but sometimes alternative space has to be found for active play. Isolating this learning centre from the others has disadvantages in that it is more difficult to transfer play and learning between centres; another is that there are fewer opportunities to combine props, materials, and accessories from another role play area. However, separation from the other learning centres may mean that a greater amount of space is available to the Active Role Play centre, especially if it is located in a basement or in a specially-designed psychomotor room or gymnasium. Larger space allows staff to permanently install large, stationary equipment, such as tunnels, ramps, spheres, climbing apparatus, and even vehicles and vehicle pathways, and to leave open space for sociodramatic play.

Role play is so important for children that ways should be found to extend play begun in the Active Role Play centre into the psychomotor room and the playground where children have more room to move and to continue their sociodramatic themes and active play. Schaffer, Wood, and Willougby (2002) note that preschool children who are encouraged, trained, and have enough space to engage in role play and pretend perform better on tests of cognition, language, and creativity than children who pretend less often. It is also possible in a large room to set up sports and field equipment for children to have regular, physical play and an exercise program. This accommodation should also address the need for children to experience active play with hollow blocks and other large materials for construction, to engage in creative-constructive and sociodramatic play, and to access the props and dress-up equipment from the Daily Living centre to support active role play. When alternative space must be found for the Active Role Play centre, adjoining space or space close to the main playroom, well lit with natural light, and with shelves, storage areas for props, and furniture or storage units that may be used to cordon off an area for sustained construction play, is a reasonable solution. A potential play space to accommodate a super unit is also an essential component of the Active Role Play centre, and ways should be found to create such a self-contained area even in a large, open room.

Active Role Play

When the Active Role Play centre has space for a potential unit of play, children may be encouraged to build a frame for their sociodramatic play theme and to leave the structure intact for as long as the children's play theme endures. An empty corner with boundaries may become a place for children to create a super unit, such as a courier depot for trucks and cars; an auto repair shop; or a fire department with hoses, ramps, trucks, helmets, and rubber boots. As this learning centre usually becomes the venue for active play indoors, it becomes a substitute for the playground on days when it is too cold, wet, or hot for children to play outdoors. On such days, the Active Role Play centre becomes the principal area where children can stretch their limbs, be active and noisy, and release energy. ECEs have to put away some props, accessories, and play materials temporarily to provide more room for large-muscle play, for organized physical activities, and for cooperative games.

Organization and Design of the Active Role Play Centre

The Active Role Play centre should include a large-muscle play area (physical activities), a playhouse area (role play), a hollow blocks area with various props (physical and role play), a music and movement area (physical, role play, creative), and space for a potential unit (see Figure 13–1).

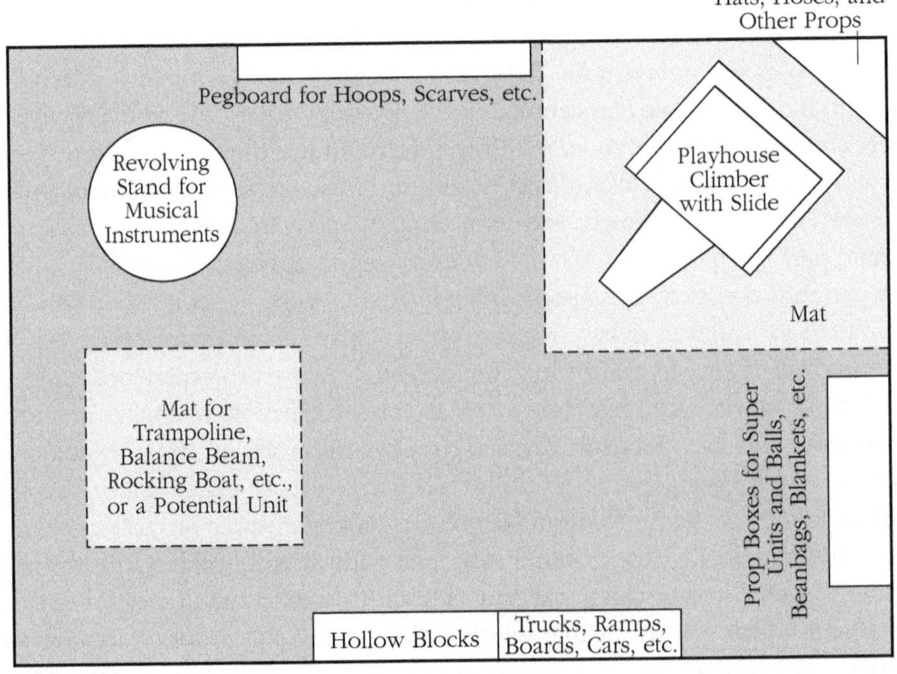

Figure 13–1
The Active Role Play centre

Equipment, Materials, and Supplies

- **Equipment:** climbing apparatus, shelves for materials, shelves for hollow blocks, boards, planks, ramps; props rack; and pegboard wall for hanging props and materials
- **Materials:** prop boxes to promote a variety of themes; authentic musical instruments (not toys); dress-up hats and helmets, including head coverings representing various cultural groups; hoses; blankets; hollow blocks; artifact sets (such as a Fisher-Price village, airport, farm, school, hospital, garage, castle, and zoo for younger children); large trucks, wagons, and cars; large boxes and tunnels; skipping ropes; hoops; balls; cylinders; punching bag; balance beam; large ropes; beanbags; rocking boat, springboard, and box horse; parachutes (small for indoors); trampoline (with tumbling mats for soft landings); props for role play, such as wooden chairs and blankets (to make a space station); and a firefighter's pole and ladder
- **Supplies:** fabric to make flags and banners; construction paper; newsprint; large markers and cardboard for signs and posters; cardboard boxes; ropes; duct tape

Sociodramatic Play in the Active Role Play Centre

The Active Role Play centre integrates active play with role play involving groups of children playing cooperatively in order to plan, implement the plan, and evolve a script around an event or the play station they have created using the materials available to them. The provision of creative-constructive materials such as hollow blocks, boards and planks, blankets, ropes, tunnels, rubber mats, and other large-muscle equipment, contributes to children's ability to represent using abstract materials to construct a frame or a *set* for their sociodramatic play episode.

As stated throughout this textbook, sociodramatic play is an essential ingredient in children's development and learning, especially during the preschool and kindergarten period, from ages four to six. Programs should reserve space for children to build sets that frame the theme of their play episode and add props to support the evolution of their ideas and their script. The dynamic interaction among children who are collaborating to evolve a storyline, to maintain the story, and to achieve their goals involves cognitive skills such as representational thinking, imagination and communication, as well as social interdependence, social adaptation, the ability to form social relationships, and cooperation. Emotional skills such as self-regulation, trusting others, and forming attachments also arise from active play contexts in which children feel pride in something they have achieved together. Sociodramatic play allows preschool and kindergarten children to learn while doing, to execute a plan, and to make adjustments. When physically active sociodramatic play is encouraged in larger spaces, its benefits are optimized.

Cooperative Games in the Active Role Play Centre

Cooperative learning activities provide opportunities for children to work actively together to achieve a common outcome. As early as 1929, John Dewey was advocating cooperative learning on projects, an approach referred to as the project method. Cooperative games for young children were advocated by Orlick (1981), who suggested that children as young as four were capable of collaborating in group games under the leadership of a teacher. Chambers, Patten, Schaeff, & Mau (1996) proposed that the egocentricity of young children may be offset by their curiosity and their need to be active and to socialize as long as the groups remain, at least in the early stages, no larger than three children so that children do not have to accommodate multiple perspectives. Because cooperative learning is challenging for some children, opportunities to practise cooperating in play need to be built in to the curriculum. When introducing cooperative activities and games to young children, it is important to provide frequent feedback and to keep the activities short, active, simple, and noncompetitive. The interactivity of simple cooperative games challenges children to play together and try something new.

Cooperative games involve children in pairs or small groups and may be played indoors in the Active Role Play centre when they cannot be played outdoors. They are characterized by asking children to play as a team toward achieving a common outcome, by the inclusion of all children in the game without any elimination of participants as the game is played, and by the absence of competition, in that there are no losers and no winners. The attraction for children, and what keeps them interested in the game, is their focus on the achievement of a common goal, which is accompanied by helping each other and empathizing with each other's failed attempts when a movement or action does not go as planned. To be successful, cooperative games rely on the social competence of children who have to agree on a strategy, collaborate to execute the strategy, and ensure that their individual efforts contribute to the realization of the common goal. Cooperative games should be introduced gradually to children, starting with games that have a simple and achievable goal for preschoolers. In kindergarten and beyond, children are ready for more complicated negotiation and the assignment of individual tasks to master as they each perform a different skill to achieve the desired end result. Cooperative games require that children take a perspective other than their own. When ECEs observe that children have developed some ability to do so, they know the children are ready for cooperative games.

As the name suggests, cooperative games require children to plan and help one another in teams, and doing so fosters mutual interdependence, reliability, and trust—qualities that help children build positive interpersonal relationships. Cooperative games also promote cognitive skills, such as language and communication, the ability to represent physically what is said, and understanding of concepts such as shape, size, direction, and speed. Problem solving and negotiation of strategies are so much a part of cooperative games that children also develop the ability to build on each other's ideas and contributions, and to use trial and error in order to uncover the most efficient path to achievement of the outcome. When a strategy does not immediately achieve the desired result, children's ability to try another strategy, to openly share their discouragement, to encourage each other, and to respect each child's contribution are significantly challenged. Cooperative games are a rich medium for helping children develop the task-orientation skills and self-regulation that are needed for any team endeavour in which they rely on, and learn from, each other. In addition to promoting social and cognitive skills, cooperative games provide practice in many fundamental movement patterns, help children develop their large muscles, acquire physical and motor fitness skills, develop body awareness, and prepare themselves for later participation in team sports.

ECEs ensure that the Active Role Play centre is equipped with the materials and equipment needed for cooperative play indoors. The props stored in this centre, such as large blocks, hoops, and ropes, as well as signs, posts, and barriers, support cooperative play, such as building and navigating obstacle courses, staging a parade using the musical instruments and costumes, or having each child pretend to be a different animal in an animal parade. Another challenge for ECEs in facilitating children's participation in cooperative play is to lead without taking over the planning and the negotiating of strategy as well as its implementation. ECEs have to reconcile themselves to seeing children plan inefficiently, making some errors of judgement, and failing several times in their attempts to achieve the goal, all the while encouraging the children to try again.

Play Stations in the Active Role Play Centre

Large-Muscle Play Area

Large-muscle play in the Active Role Play centre requires materials and equipment that allow children to move freely; to use their muscles for short periods of time, as in climbing, pushing, and pulling; and to coordinate large-muscle movements in performing specific tasks, such as running, jumping, hopping, leaping, galloping, marching, and skipping. In spacious Active Role Play centres, tunnels, spheres, and climbers may be left out for children to play freely and to explore. Large building equipment, hollow blocks, planks, tumble boards, trampolines, rocking boats, and mats encourage children to lift, press, push, bounce, sway, tumble, and perform other movements designed to develop muscles of the legs, arms, and torso. Balance beams, balance boards, punching bags, skipping ropes, parachutes, hula-hoops, and vehicles promote gross motor movements, which require greater precision in controlling the muscles. All of these materials may be useful for children to create the sets for their sociodramatic play episodes.

ACTIVITIES IN THE LARGE-MUSCLE PLAY AREA FOR CHILDREN AGES TWO TO FOUR

1. Children walk or march in a band, each playing a musical instrument.
2. Children dramatize a parade with costumes and possibly a float pulled on a wagon. (Prop box for a parade is located nearby. Costumes should be stored on hooks or in cupboards accessible to the children.)
3. Dramatic jumping: Children pretend to be rabbits, kangaroos, grasshoppers, frogs, popcorn, and so on. Children may engage in this activity to music.
4. Dramatic hopping: Children imitate bouncing ball movements to musical accompaniment.

ACTIVITIES IN THE LARGE-MUSCLE PLAY AREA FOR CHILDREN AGES FOUR TO SIX

1. Children dramatize walking as if they are in a tornado, walking on leaves, walking in deep snow, walking in mud, or on ice, using music to guide their steps.
2. Pretend parade in which children wear costumes to define their roles and gallop, march, skip, and change direction using a musical cue.

3. Children create a sporting goods store in the playhouse using a prop box to extend their roles and the script they evolve. The prop box contains such items as sleeping gear, walking sticks, hats and clothing for rugged sports, backpacks, and boots.
4. Children play a cooperative version of kick-the-ball by holding hands and forming a circle to keep the ball moving within their circle, while holding hands and kicking the ball back and forth across the circle. If the ball stops or goes outside the circle, the game is over and they try again.
5. Getting from here to there. The ECE sets up squares of construction paper fastened to the floor in the Active Role Play centre. Children have to figure out how to jump or hop from one square to another, ensuring that they touch all squares without touching the same square twice.

Hollow Blocks Play Area

Hollow blocks belong in the Active Role Play centre because their size and weight promote large-muscle development and because they are highly adaptable props that promote symbolic play. Although it may be tempting to put the hollow blocks and the unit blocks together, this should be steadfastly avoided. Unit blocks are abstract and designed to foster logical-mathematical concepts, spatial intelligence, creative thinking, problem solving, and symbolic thinking. Hollow blocks have some of the same characteristics but they are largely creative-constructive play materials, which challenge children to construct representations of real structures. Hollow blocks also serve as props that become whatever children want them to be, and they may be used to extend children's sociodramatic play beyond the constraints of the climber and ramps by making a super unit, such as a concert stage or an airport. Sometimes hollow blocks are stored with the large dump trucks, with machinery such as steam shovels and tractors, and with accessories such as wooden tree stands, large wooden houses and buildings, and a wooden train set. Hollow blocks enable children to build walls, to create a set for a sociodramatic play episode, to partition an area of the Active Role Play centre, or to build a path or runway. The space allocated to the hollow blocks area may also make it an appropriate setting for sociodrama, which calls for freedom of movement and large props that can be positioned easily to create a set for a play. Flexible space even allows for building a small stage with necessary props, where children may act out the roles and actions of a story or a favourite program.

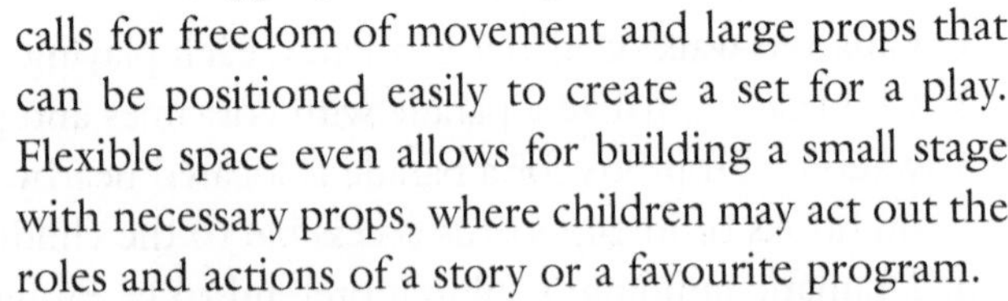

Use hollow blocks as props.

Children may interact with hollow blocks in purely sensorimotor ways. Two-year-olds, especially, enjoy lifting, pulling, pushing, and tugging large objects, all of which develop the large muscles and gross motor skills. Older children may stack hollow blocks to support a blanket being used for a tent or fort. Laid out in a grid along the floor, the blocks become clear boundaries for a village or become roads for a network of highways. As crude, abstract symbols that can easily assume any role that children assign to them, hollow blocks stimulate the representational thinking and imagination that support sociodramatic play in the

Active Role Play centre. The inherent safety of hollow blocks as a play material makes it unnecessary for ECEs to impose undue limits on play, such as restricting the height of structures to the point that building loses its challenge and fun.

The hollow blocks play area also may become the site for physical science discovery activities. This area can be converted into a place for building ramps to investigate planes and inclines; relationships between motion, speed, and distance; the motion and use of pulleys; the balance of weights and counterweights; the swinging of a pendulum hung from the ceiling to a table holding a fulcrum; the use of levers and wedges for lifting; and many other physical science experiences that require space for children to use large materials. The typical Science Discovery centre may be too small for experiments requiring large equipment and materials for testing and exploring the many mechanical and physical phenomena that interest children.

ACTIVITIES IN THE HOLLOW BLOCKS AREA FOR CHILDREN AGES TWO TO FOUR

1. Visit a construction site and watch the bricklayers form a regular pattern with the bricks. Encourage children to practise bricklaying by building a wall or foundation using the blocks.
2. Have children use wagons to load, stack, and unload the hollow blocks as they deliver them from the Active Role Play centre to the playground, where they are needed to create a larger structure that cannot be built indoors.
3. Build a parking garage for the large trucks and cars. Encourage the children to role play the parking lot attendant and the drivers finding places to park. Use a prop box containing traffic signals, stop signs, steering wheel, a bus, and trees on stands.
4. Build stairs using the planks and boards that allow children to climb up onto and down from a platform.

ACTIVITIES IN THE HOLLOW BLOCKS AREA FOR CHILDREN AGES FOUR TO SIX

1. Visit a local construction site. Later, suggest that children set up a construction site using the hollow blocks, ramps, trucks, backhoes, cranes, and whatever else they find to enhance their site.
2. Create a steeplechase track, using hollow blocks for children to step over as part of the daily exercise program. Show children pictures of the fences, hedges, and water traps that make up a typical steeplechase track.
3. Build a podium for presenting Olympic medals to participants for jumping, hopping, and marching. Use a prop box for hats, coats, gold medals, and sports paraphernalia. Adapt this activity so that children with special needs have opportunities to win a medal.

Accessories and Props Area

Storage Space

An area for storing the accessories and props that children may use in a multitude of ways in their sociodramatic play should be designated. Hanging larger props and play materials from pegboards with hooks, stacking them on open shelves, or storing them in large wooden boxes with lift-up lids make these materials easily accessible to children at a moment's notice. Ideally, children should be able to reach play materials themselves when the mood strikes or when they have a sudden flash of an idea that requires a prop. Keep in mind that a wide range of creative props, including authentic items from the adult world, such as an old telephone, a large basket, a cupboard on wheels, helps children with the "wonderful ideas" that Duckworth (1987) spoke of many years ago. The richness and variety of the props enhance children's abilities to think symbolically, to imagine, to plan, and to use props to represent something that they have in mind. When the props are visible to the eye, it is more likely they will be used in the Active Role Play centre to support sociodramatic play episodes. To provide ideas, posters may be displayed that depict interesting places and events that are familiar to the children, such as the Winter Olympics, a skating show, or a trip to a water park.

Setting Up the Accessories and Props Area

The accessories and props area should be located close to the hollow blocks and out of the way of the climber, tricycles, tunnels, large cylinders, and spheres. An uncluttered pathway to the accessories and props allows children to easily and safely pull hoops or hats off wall hooks or to lift the drums and other musical instruments out of the storage shelves or box. Space used to house a table or to create a boundary that partly seals off the accessories and props area from the rest of the centre may become useful potential space to set up as a super unit, such as a sports shop, a car or truck repair station, a construction site, or a music store. Prop boxes, each containing items addressing a specific theme, should be available in the accessories and props area to facilitate children's creation of super units for sociodramatic play so that there is at least one super unit available in the playroom at all times. Review the section on prop boxes in Chapter 12.

Music in the Active Role Play Centre

The role of music in children's play and development is addressed in Chapter 14. Because the Active Role Play centre encourages role play as well as movement activities, music is often a natural accompaniment and enhancement to the activities in this learning centre. For example, children may stage impromptu parades using musical instruments and costumes in this centre. Storing the more fragile musical instruments in a cupboard with doors that are easy to open in the accessories and props area ensures that they remain out of the line of fire when not being used, while remaining accessible to the children. Musical instruments that are more durable and safe for children to choose and use independently should be placed on shelves within easy reach for children to integrate music into their role play. Although children should be encouraged to make their own music with authentic instruments representing diverse cultures, it is useful to include a CD or tape player in the Active Role Play centre to use as a musical accompaniment for the active role play that occurs in this centre.

When children are exposed to appropriate music during the day, they are more likely to integrate music spontaneously into their active play. A predisposition toward music as an accompaniment to various tasks, to alter mood, and to ease the burden of challenging tasks is developed early in life. Children should be encouraged to choose when and how to add music to their role play and to engage in large-muscle play, such as marching, skipping, and dancing, in time to music. Storing instruments such as drums, tambourines, rhythm sticks, and triangles on shelves within easy reach facilitates spontaneous movement to music the children make themselves and instils a lifelong reliance on music to add richness, depth, and meaning to many activities.

The Playhouse Structure Area

Ideally, the Active Role Play centre would be large enough to hold a stand-alone playhouse or a combination playhouse and climber that children can enter and use as the focal point for their sociodramatic play. It is helpful if the structure comes equipped with simple climbing apparatuses, such as a slide, a ramp, and steps, especially if the Active Role Play centre is too small to house a full-sized climber. Basic, solid, and unadorned structures are best. The absence of accessories enhances the abstract nature of the structure, which makes it easier for children to imagine that the structure is anything they want it to be in their play. Structures that are rough-hewn—with four walls, a roof, a window, a door, and some built-in climbing potential—encourage children to decorate the structure themselves, by adding cushions and curtains to create a domestic atmosphere or by adding a sign and a counter with a telephone and a cash register to represent a business. A roof allows the structure to become a private place, when necessary, where children may find some refuge and quiet. Houses with removable roofs provide added flexibility for the ECE, who may, at times, want to monitor or to observe children's play in this area. Situating the play structure in an area where there is some space around it to add wagons, blocks, and ramps permits children to use the structure as the centrepiece for any super unit they may want to create. A plain A-frame wooden structure, for example, can become a house or chalet, a school or store, a cabin for a camping expedition, or a station. The addition of themed items from prop boxes may support role play in the playhouse, or the children may invent an original story line without the addition of lifelike accessories that may inhibit the child's imagination.

Readers are encouraged to review the section on gender issues in Chapter 12, pages 220–222. Derman-Sparks and Ramsey (2005) claim that gender role stereotyping remains prevalent in our society largely because of the widespread use of gender to divide, differentiate, and condition people according to stereotypic roles for commercial purposes. Television programs and commercials, consumer advertising, and other media are widely used to reinforce the images and stereotypes that businesses want to imbed in our society. Parents and schools are hard-pressed to combat

© Frank Siteman / PhotoEdit

Accessories and props in Active Role Play centre

these pressures, and ECEs are faced with the difficult task of trying to instil more balanced values. The playhouse area is where children assume roles related to domestic life, which provides an opportunity to encourage boys and girls to share household tasks that they are role playing. This is another area, however, where cultural values and expectations tend to differ widely, both within cultures and cross-culturally, and ECEs need to consult parents with respect to encouraging nonstereotypic play and explain to them the rationale behind the approach they plan to take. In cultures where gender roles are clearly differentiated, it may confuse children to encourage them to assume a role normally assigned to the opposite gender in their families. Ormrod (2006) cautions that programs should try to avoid the *cultural mismatch* that can undermine attempts to help children adjust to their school settings. Here is another area where Canadian preschools and kindergartens need to find a balanced and sensitive approach to fostering the role-sharing so necessary in families, given the typical pressures facing two-parent households where both parents work outside the home.

Gentle approaches to addressing gender role issues, such as encouraging boys and girls to assume household tasks in the playhouse area, include ensuring that the dress-up clothing, costumes, and accessories contain nonstereotypic items that can be worn with ease by both boys and girls (Crowther, 2005). ECEs should encourage boys to contribute items to the playhouse area that are typically found in the hollow blocks and props area, and to recognize girls who assume nonstereotypic tasks with the woodworking tools to fix something that has broken in the playhouse. A subtle approach to fostering nonstereotypic gender play seems to work best, as we know that children pick up on these subtleties no matter what their cultural background and soon begin conveying to their parents their sense of the legitimacy of roles that are not gender-biased. The cultural sensitivities involved in this type of role play make this a classic example of issues that need to be discussed honestly and openly with parents with a view to acknowledging their cultural biases, and to suggesting alternative approaches that demonstrate compromise.

ECEs often observe sexual play in the playhouse area that calls for sensitive management by adults, who use these occasions as *teachable moments*, when they can guide children's play in the right direction by acknowledging sexual differences and by reinforcing the importance of respect for one's own body and that of others. The sad reality is that many young children are exposed much too early to adult sexual activity on television and film and then develop a precocious curiosity that is sometimes acted out in the program. When this happens, ECEs have to intervene to redirect children while, at the same time, acknowledging the curiosity that each gender has about the other as matter-of-factly as possible. Reinforcing values of respectfulness, personal privacy, and healthy attitudes toward the body is essential. Occasions such as these potentially offer opportunities to link sexuality to personal responsibility and a sense of wonder about life and humanity. There is no denying the challenge these moments create for ECEs, who often have to come up with right responses, maintain positive attitudes, and offer constructive redirection on the spur of the moment, usually when they have several other things to do at the same time. The wise ECE will create scenarios ahead of time so as to be able to draw upon positive approaches when the occasion demands and avoid being caught off-guard without a suitable response to the situation.

Integrating Children with Disabilities in the Active Role Play Centre

Integrated programs should intervene in the physical development of the child to minimize the delaying effects of inactivity and of motor disabilities on the development of the body as a whole. Therefore, the Active Role Play centre, as well as the outdoor play areas, must be adapted (1) to challenge children with physical disabilities and developmental delays to practise motor play and (2) to accommodate activities that capitalize on their capabilities. In planning the environment and play activities, ECEs should provide physical activities that take children with disabilities or delayed development through the normal progressions in development as much as possible. An important obligation of the ECE is to ensure that the child with physical disabilities remains active and is able to play in the Active Role Play centre (Allen et al., 2006). Integrating children with disabilities involves creating an affective climate in which they feel psychologically safe and are willing to take risks; they may also need more adult support in order to learn how to play physically.

The popularity of the Special Olympics and the excellent athletes with disabilities who compete with courage, competence, and determination have drawn attention in recent years to the importance and viability of active play for children with disabilities. The development of a healthy personality is closely associated with children's confidence and trust in their own bodies (Erikson, 1963). Therefore, ECEs should help the child with a physical disability to minimize its impact and to maximize her sense of achievement in overcoming physical obstacles to the limits her body will allow. Before age six, all children are developing their motor skills, and children with physical disabilities are no exception; they require physical programs that are adapted to their individual needs and abilities. Full integration of children with physical disabilities and delayed development will occur when all children in the group share responsibility for helping the child with a disability deal with the challenges of the large-muscle play area. ECEs should encourage children without disabilities to appreciate their shared responsibility in helping others participate in their role play, games and other activities. These opportunities help children become aware of the needs of others and more sensitive to the appropriate times to offer help. Role play often provides the inspiration for active play in this centre. Children can often agree on a suitable role for the child with disabilities to play in which the effects of the disability will be minimized, while enabling some physical involvement in the play.

Adapting the Environment for the Child with Disabilities

ECEs have to adapt the learning environment to provide equipment and materials suited to the capabilities of children with disabilities. As well, ECEs often have to intervene to help children with disabilities accomplish physical goals. For example, the ECE may adapt an obstacle course so that the child with cerebral palsy may surmount an obstacle close to the ground by crawling and pulling herself using the upper part of her body. Programs should take into account the nature of the child's disabilities and then should adapt the learning environment accordingly. ECEs who have made careful observations can remove many of the obstacles to a child's freedom of movement and interaction with other children.

GUIDELINES FOR ADAPTING THE ENVIRONMENT FOR CHILDREN WITH PHYSICAL DISABILITIES

- How does the setting appear at a child's level? Are there interesting things to see and touch, such as windows, mirrors, mobiles, aquariums, and other materials?
- Is there room for a wheelchair user or a child with minimal mobility to negotiate in and out of spaces and turn around?
- Are shelves and tables at a comfortable level for a child's height? Is there a place (preferably more than one) that can accommodate a child in each activity area?
- Are shelves, tables, sinks, and other fixtures sturdy enough to hold the weight of a child with minimal mobility who may need support?
- Are **prosthetic devices** (such as a standing cuff) easily accessible in the areas where children might practise standing or sitting without an adult's assistance while engaged in an activity?
- Are some of the play materials accessible to a child without assistance, even if he is minimally mobile?
- Is the sound level of the room satisfactory for a child with a hearing impairment? Are there some special quiet areas for children to work with minimal noise distraction?
- Does the environment contain sufficient contrasts to attract the notice of a visually impaired child? Do contrasts of colour and light complement contrasts of texture and height?
- Are the cues (colour, change of levels, or dividers) that designate different areas clear and consistent?
- How much of the environment is designed for self-management or self-engagement? How frequently do children use these opportunities? Does a child need training to use these opportunities?
- Does the arrangement of the room allow for quiet and social places to meet children's changing needs?

Source: From A.K. Rogers-Warren (1982), Behavioral ecology in classrooms for young handicapped children. ***Topics in Early Childhood Special Education***, 2(1), 21–32. Adapted with permission of PRO-ED, Inc., Publishers.*

Summary

The Active Role Play centre is a focal point for children's role play, physical development, and symbolic and representational thinking Ideally, the Active Role Play centre will be located close to the Daily Living centre, but when space does not allow this, it is wise to find a location where children have freedom to move and to leave out play structures or super units they have built and want to return to, and to encourage children to incorporate music into their role play episodes. The close connection between active role play; sociodramatic play; and children's physical, cognitive, and social development requires that this centre be given a place of prominence in the preschool and kindergarten setting.

Issues related to gender play often arise in the Active Role Play centre, especially the play house. It is wise for ECEs to involve parents in discussion of issues related to gender play to assess their priorities for their children. But at the same time they must advocate the program's philosophy, which is to minimize stereotypic gender role play and to foster nonstereotypic role play and role sharing while ensuring that the innate differences between boys' and girls' play preferences and learning styles are respected and recognized in the curriculum.

Many challenges arise for ECEs in planning and implementing activities in this centre. ECEs have to know in advance where they stand and how they will respond

---

to superhero play, issues related to gender roles, and sexual play incidents, so as to avoid being caught off-guard during busy play periods. This is an area of the playroom where teachable moments arise on a regular basis. These moments call for active intervention and responsible guidance by ECEs who have thought through where they stand on a wide range of cultural, societal, spiritual, and human issues.

Learning Activities

1. Describe the creation of a stage in the Active Role Play centre for children to engage in creative drama (sociodrama) related to a favourite story. Include tasks that children can undertake to help you build the stage and the ways in which they can help gather and create the props and costumes for their creative drama.
2. Create a prop box to support a sociodramatic play theme in the Active Role Play centre. Write three activity cards that outline how you would introduce activities to the children using the props in the prop box, the questions you would ask to stimulate their imaginations, and the role you would play in trying to extend their play episode.
3. Describe how you would adapt one play area in the Active Role Play centre to encourage active role play by the child with disabilities.
4. Discuss in class play-related issues that arise in the preschool and kindergarten classroom on such topics as attitudes toward superheroes and superhero play; rough-and-tumble play; gender play; and sexual play. Each discussion group should produce a short document outlining the values and attitudes to convey to children, some guidelines for responding to each type of play, and desirable learning outcomes for young children in the context of these various examples of play.

14 Music and Movement in the Active Role Play Centre

"Music is a moral law. It gives a soul to the universe, wings to the mind, flight to the imagination, a charm to sadness, gaiety and life to everything."

—Plato

Before Reading This Chapter, Have You

- considered the role of music in your own life?
- observed young children singing, playing musical instruments, and making music?
- turned to music as a source of solace in times of distress, to ease pain, to express joy, for quiet contemplation and reflection?
- tried to play a musical instrument before any training?
- listened to and assessed the quality, variety, and developmental potential of music produced for children?

Outcomes

After reading and understanding this chapter, you should be able to

- use music to facilitate children's development in all domains;
- use music to alter the mood and climate for play and learning;
- explain the role of music and movement to children's symbolic thinking and representation in the Active Role Play centre;
- build music and singing into all aspects of curriculum; and
- introduce dance into the music and movement program.

Music Is Important to Children

The best reason for a vital music program in early childhood education is that music is important to children. Simply observing the look on children's faces when they sing a familiar song in unison, or when someone plays a tune they all recognize on the autoharp, convinces even the lay observer of music's power to focus children's attention, transport them to a different mood, and move them to express themselves. Music influences child development and provides an avenue for creative expression. Early exposure to music provides children with a valuable tool to help them regulate their emotions; to gain insight into their feelings; and to mediate periods of stress, pain, loneliness, and exuberance. Of great importance in today's world, and to contemporary research on human development, is the development of empathy. Empathy is closely related to children's developing spirituality, and music contributes to children's ability to empathize with others (Shenk, 2010). When associated with special events and times of the year, music becomes a significant reference point in people's lives, from childhood on. The ability to appreciate and to be moved by music can be a coping mechanism to relieve stress and deal with loneliness and despair. Music has the power to alter mood, to enhance pleasure, to strengthen memory by association with an event, and to add beauty and depth to children's lives and to our own. Recent studies show that when children ages four to six participate in a music program involving rhythm, pitch, and melody, they performed significantly better on verbal intelligence tests (McIlroy, 2011).

"Perhaps the most important thing about music is the child's ability to enjoy both making and listening to it, and this ability needs to be 'caught'" (Cass-Beggs, 1974, p. 5). Too often, educators neglect music, which means that this crucial medium for self-expression, emotional development, creativity, social experience, and physical and perceptual development is unavailable to children. By allocating space in the Active Role Play centre for music-making and active movement, and an accessible place for storing musical instruments, ECEs ensure that music is a priority and that music and movement become part of the daily routine.

Music helps children grasp the symbolism in language associated with song and chants. *Peter and the Wolf,* the classic story and music by Prokoviev, where the defining sound of each musical instrument stands for one of the characters, is often used to help children connect musical sound and symbol. Music adds coherence to the activities in which children typically engage; it helps children associate a musical piece with a specific feeling, a certain type of movement pattern or activity, or a memory of an event or a story, or thoughts about other people.

Children enjoy making and listening to music, and music experiences support learning in a number of domains (Kim & Robinson, 2010). Howard Gardner (1983, p. 99) found that musical intelligence is a "distinct way of knowing" and that "of all the gifts with which individuals may be endowed, none emerges earlier than musical talent." Yet we see far too little music in preschool and kindergarten programs, especially considering that music is a powerful accompaniment to learning through play. Although this chapter emphasizes the role of music in the Active Role Play centre, music should be heard and played and moved to throughout the curriculum, indoors and outdoors. Listening, singing, playing, moving to, and inventing music should be part of every child's experience, so much so that it becomes integral to all aspects of their lives.

Music helps children develop cognitive skills.

Music Education for Young Children

"Except among children with unusual musical talent or exceptional opportunities, there is little further musical development after the school years begin" (Gardner, 1983, p. 109).

Gardner advocates the provision of a music program for young children, whose keen sensory capacities and fluent use of symbols and metaphors make the early years a period of heightened "creative orientation" (Gardner 1989, p. 298). Planned music programs allow ECEs to recognize exceptional talent and to intervene accordingly. Gardner (1996) sees musical intelligence as one of several intelligences that involve heightened perceptual discrimination, body awareness, a sense of **rhythm**, and sensitivity to **pitch** and **melody**. He links music concepts and appreciation to an understanding of concepts found in physics and mathematics, such as sensitivity to timing, counting, pausing, intervals, patterns, and repetitions. ECEs may detect children with unusual talents or musical intelligence by providing musical experiences and opportunities for children to make their own music (Gardner, 1989).

For generations, music educators have demonstrated their interest in advancing musical literacy in young children. Both Carl Orff and Zoltan Kodaly (Andress, 1998) used methods whereby children begin to read simple notations of two syllables and gradually incorporate more pitches and syllabic variations. Their approaches involve the initial practice of certain patterns before teaching children songs. Kodaly created a music program based on folk songs for children in Hungary in the 1940s; his program focused on singing and on playing simple percussion instruments. The Kodaly method emphasizes children's developing vocal and reading skills and introduces in-tune singing with *solfège,* beginning with *sol-mi* and *sol-la* until the five pitches, *do, re, mi, sol, la*, are included. He stressed the importance of sight-reading and believed that musical training would develop the whole personality of the child.

The Orff process is a comprehensive program based on song, speech, body rhythms, movement, and specially designed instruments leading to imitation, exploration, and creation (Andress, 1998). Children are encouraged to stamp, clap, and tap to accompany speech used in chants, rhymes, and poetry before they play instruments. In Germany, in the late 19th and early 20th centuries, Orff saw movement as the heart of music education and developed a teaching approach that enabled children to integrate language, music, and movement. Children were encouraged to move according to the beat and rhythm before they used the movement patterns for creative and expressive purposes (Andress, 2003). Dalcroze (1865–1950), who taught in Switzerland during the 20th century, also believed the body was the vehicle for music expression and focused on teaching eurhythmics to integrate body, sound, and interpretation of music. All three music educators believed in the power of music to affect the cognitive, physical, social, and emotional development and growth of young children.

The Ontario Ministry of Education's draft music standards for full-day early learning in kindergartens (2010–2011, pp. 97–102) identify five outcomes that children should have demonstrated by the end of senior kindergarten:

1. demonstrate an awareness of themselves as musicians through engaging in music activities;
2. demonstrate basic knowledge and skills gained through exposure to music and music activities;
3. use problem-solving strategies when experimenting with the skills, materials, processes, and techniques used in music, individually and with others;
4. express responses to a variety of forms of music, including those from other cultures; and
5. communicate ideas through music.

These outcomes view music as a vehicle for learning, problem solving, intercultural knowledge, and communication. Music also contributes to children's self-knowledge, their relationship to others, their emotional responses, and their ability to manage and interpret their emotions. The National Standards for Music at the pre-K level in the United States (1994) emphasize creating, responding to, and understanding music as a part of daily life and for self-expression. The connection between music and intellectual development is generally well established in the education sector, while the relationship between music and children's emotional well-being and mental health has often been underestimated. It is a mandate of early childhood education to foster music appreciation and musical expression in young children so that music becomes, and continues to be, a critical element in a life well lived.

Music and Brain Development

Penn (2005) found that theories related to brain development revolve around several key questions related to how the brain develops, whether brain functions are segmented or modularized, and the significance of neural connections in brain function. Conventional theory suggests that singing and experiencing music in a variety of ways exercises the brain and strengthens the synapses between brain cells; this has an impact on the sensory and perceptual systems, cognition and metacognition, movement and coordination, and the memory systems. It is the simultaneous engagement of all the senses, muscles, and the intellect in making music that appears to involve the entire cerebral cortex and to strengthen the connections among neurons. Similar claims are made that movement experiences from birth to age five are essential to neural stimulation, the development of basic motor skills, and cognitive development, and that these should be a daily factor in children's lives (Pica, 2004). These theories require further investigation, but the role of music in encouraging children's participation in activities and in evoking powerful emotional responses to living and learning in many contexts cannot be denied.

Music Supports Symbolic Play

Music facilitates symbolic play and the imagination, which influence children's spirituality, creativity, and the richness of their play. Music has a significant place in all learning centres, but its connection to the Active Role Play centre gives music a "home base" in the classroom; music is also an energizing accompaniment to role play and symbolic thinking. Music requires space, which is available in the Active Role Play centre, where there should be room for children to march, play instruments, "drum up" a spur-of-the-moment parade, dance, listen to music as an accompaniment to play, and use music as a stimulus for a sociodramatic play episode, such as putting on a concert, imitating a rock band, or running a dance competition.

Music has the added function of stimulating the imagination as children conjure up ideas based on the music they hear and they begin to role play characters in their imagined story, or walk like animals that resemble the musical sounds they hear. As children become accomplished listeners to various types of music, they fabricate connections in their own minds between the music they hear and familiar characters in stories, and these connections extend to interpreting their imagined or real stories in the form of dance or pantomime. A particular style or familiar piece of music may become a symbol in their minds for a favourite character, or a remembered event, or a routine or task that they have associated with the musical piece. Think of the vision evoked in your mind by the "Wedding March" or the "Skaters' Waltz" or the theme music from *Gone with the Wind.* Music is a key trigger for the imagination and symbolic thinking when music listening is closely associated with various categories of play in all centres of the playroom. These connections between music and play are particularly acute in the Daily Living and Active Role Play centres, although music also adds richness to outdoor play, the Creative Arts centre, the Unit Blocks, and the Science centre.

Music as a Way of Life

Early childhood is the best time to introduce children to music and to the relaxation, internal harmony, and a sense of well-being and connection with others that music can contribute to living. A large part of the influence of music in our lives is the way it makes us feel. People who possess extraordinary musical intelligence are more aesthetically sensitive to the particular qualities of music and are able to hear tones, rhythms, and musical patterns in their heads; usually they are able to listen more consciously to music, recognizing and describing its melody, rhythm, and tonal qualities. All children, however, who are exposed to music in a variety of forms, will develop an appreciation for musical representations that enhances their lives in some way. ECEs do not have to be musicians or have a good singing voice in order to provide essential musical programming for young children. All that is needed is an appreciation of music as a way of life, as a powerful vehicle for child development, and the willingness to make music happen in the program (Pica, 2004). A repertoire of music does not have to be large; children crave repetition and familiar tempos easy for them to replicate. As children master the music in a song or instrumental piece, it is time to add movement to the music.

Using musical instruments to represent and interpret what words or actions alone cannot convey, supports creative self-expression, which develops in the early years. When musical instruments are accessible, children are able to explore the construction and sounds of the instruments themselves. Encouraging children to make their own music, with instruments and with singing, rather than resorting to technology, is consistent with the principle that children learn best when they are involved actively, which includes moving to the music. Children learn about sound by creating it, as well as by listening to it, and they respond to rhythm and harmony. Live music from instruments has a calming effect on children, even when the beat is lively and they move in time with the rhythm of the musical instruments.

Instruments are the tools of music, and children should learn to care for and respect them (Houle, 1987). When children are able to select and use musical instruments spontaneously, they develop an ear for the kinds of sounds specific instruments make. Making instruments available prompts children to add music to their sociodramatic play. Compact discs or tapes should not replace children's experience of making music by playing the instruments themselves, but if musical instruments are scarce, recorded music is a worthy substitute. There is an abundance of good music on compact discs performed by musicians who understand what children enjoy and who reach them intellectually, emotionally, and aesthetically through their recordings. The musical recordings of British Columbia's Graham Walker, for example, have enchanted children and adults for years. Children learn to recognize and sing along with favourite songs they hear while they work at puzzles or construction, and they often link particular kinds of play to the music they hear. Music may also be used in programs to provide cues to children about transitions during the day or to change the level of activity and responsiveness in the room.

Music for Spiritual Development and Self-Expression

Most people respond emotionally to music that reaches into their deepest feelings and sensibilities. Music is a powerful vehicle for self-expression and an antidote to anxiety and anger. Emotional well-being, which is influenced by self-esteem and by the ability to use acceptable emotional outlets, may be enhanced through musical self-expression. For those most open to its magic, choosing music to accompany both life's darker moments and its joyous moments enhances the meaning of life and one's connection with the human condition. For disturbed or anxious children, music provides the means for releasing pent-up feelings, for calming a troubled spirit, and for relieving emotional anxieties. The effect of music on a group of children is obvious to ECEs who regularly pick up an autoharp and play to children while they await the arrival of their parents after a long day, or who organize an impromptu singsong to calm a restless group. Live music with instruments, whether played by the adult, by children, or by both, has positive mood-altering capacities that may be relied on daily.

As mentioned earlier, music is closely connected to children's empathy and developing spirituality. When it is associated in children's minds with experiences of awe and wonder, music becomes a significant trigger for the child's developing spirituality and sense of connection with elements of life larger than the self. Rifkin (2009, p. 170) claims that "empathic consciousness starts with awe.... that inspires all human imagination.... Imagination ... is impossible without wonder, and wonder is impossible without awe. Empathy represents the deepest expression of awe, and understandably is regarded as the most spiritual of human qualities." Traditionally, children have associated music with various experiences of "religiosity," such as church services; with death or sadness; with cultural festival times; and with holiday celebrations. When music is enlisted to accompany experiences of everyday living, playing outdoors on a beautiful day, shared experiences in school and in families, and moments of deep communication with others, it is invested with the added power to feel what the other is feeling, to take a broader perspective, and to care about preserving the connection one shares with others. In this sense, music has the capacity to foster empathy, which is the "soul of democracy" (Rifkin, 2009, p. 161) and the truest form of connection with others. We all know that great music by the famous composers can inspire and instill awe and wonder in the minds of adults who have been exposed to the power of music from an early age. Those few people who are not moved by music lack access to an important vehicle for achieving solace and strength, and they do not have access to music as a source of mental health and emotional stability. Music both supports a mood and has the power to distract from a prevailing mood. It can conjure up visual images and stimulate physical reactions. And in the Active Role Play centre, music may induce shy, introverted children to move to rhythm and sound, an action they would not risk without the prompting that music provides.

Music Supports All Development

Music is a key accompaniment to development in all domains because it has the power to release inhibitions, to motivate action and risk taking, to induce joy into play and movement, and to support children's attempts to move their bodies in harmony with sound and rhythm. Music in the physical curriculum ensures that children make connections between the body, mind, emotions, and social challenges. Before exploring the role of music in a physical curriculum, readers are advised to consult Appendix A, which identifies physical outcomes and developmental objectives. Children's language abilities are stretched when confronted with the challenge of demonstrating cognitive concepts in physical ways. Children find it easier to communicate and use language fluently while they are performing physical tasks, and words learned in the context of physical activities, particularly when accompanied by music and singing, are seldom forgotten.

Perhaps most important of all, music helps children express and interpret their feelings, instilling in a young mind that may be troubled and confused, some sense of order and connection between the music they hear and the emotions of sadness, happiness, fear, doubt, and even shame. For this reason, children should be exposed to many types of music—music that conveys joy, sadness, apprehension, silliness, and hope. There is within music the power to connect with the innermost feelings and to induce a sense of being a part of something larger than the self, and a part of human life experience that has been experienced by others. For the young soul whose mind has been opened to its power and sensibility, music can reduce loneliness, convey hope, allay fear, and induce order into a confusing environment. Music has been, and always will be, a fundamental element of meaning-making in life for those who believe in its persuasive qualities. Music has the power to develop sensitivity for feelings, impressions and images, to alter moods, restore and maintain health, and to enrich children's aesthetic sense (Pica 2010, pp. 30–31).

DEVELOPMENTAL STAGES OF MUSICAL EXPERIENCES

"As with motor development, every child progresses through the stages of musical development at his or her own pace. Although the sequence of developmental stages remains the same for all children, the ages at which they reach and pass through each stage can vary from child to child."

Infants

Birth to 8 months Display receptiveness to music with their eyes, eventually turning their heads toward its source; **3 to 6 months** Respond to sounds by vocalizing; **10 to 18 months** Indicate the types of music they like and dislike; **10 months to 18 months** Rock, bounce, or clap hands to music, though not necessarily rhythmically; **13 to 16 months** Attempt to sing sounds to music; **18 months** Attempt to sing songs with words; **All ages** Enjoy having their names sung in songs.

2-year-olds

Continue to use their bodies in response to music; can learn short simple songs; show an increasing ability to follow directions in songs; respond enthusiastically to favourite songs, often asking to hear them repeatedly; may sing parts of songs (often not on pitch) but seldom sing with a group; enjoy experimenting with sounds, using everything from household objects to musical instruments; discriminate among songs

3-year-olds

Have greater rhythmic ability; can recognize and sing parts of familiar tunes, though usually not on pitch; make up their own songs; walk, run, and jump to music; enjoy dramatizing songs

4-year-olds

Can grasp basic musical concepts, such as tempo, volume, and pitch; show a dramatic increase in vocal range and rhythmic ability; create new lyrics for songs; enjoy more complex songs; love silly songs; prefer "active" listening (singing, moving, doing finger plays, accompanying music with instruments)

5- to 6-year-olds

Can reproduce a melody; begin to synchronize movements with the music's rhythm; enjoy singing and moving with a group; enjoy call-and-response songs; have fairly established musical preferences; can perform two movements simultaneously (e.g., marching and playing a rhythm instrument)

7- to 8-year-olds

Are learning to read lyrics; can learn simple folk dances; enjoy musical duets; may display a desire to study dance or play an instrument; can synchronize movements to the beat of the music; can compare three or more sounds

Source: Rae Pica (2010). *Experiences in Movement & Music: Birth to Age 8* (4th ed.). Belmont, CA: Wadsworth/Cengage Learning. Cengage distributed through Thomson Learning, Toronto. pp. 35–37.*

Music and Movement Help Children Develop Physical and Cognitive Skills

The development of the child's body and mind are closely intertwined; that is, physical development affects cognitive development, and vice versa. Young children are primarily physical beings. Their image of themselves and of the world beyond arises largely from their physical experience in the concrete world. The child's concept of self contributes to her self-confidence and overall sense of well-being. How the child views her own body, how well she is able to use it to achieve her own goals and to feel her effect on the world around her, and how she believes others regard her physically, have a crucial and lasting impact on the child's sense of self-worth, and on her social, emotional, and cognitive development during the early years. From birth to age three, children learn about themselves primarily through their sensory experiences, which are said to be largely *sensorimotor*; that is, their awareness and actions are built

*From PICA. *Experiences in Movement*, 3E. © 2004 Wadsworth, a part of Cengage Learning, Inc. Reproduced by permission. www.cengage.com/permissions

largely on messages received from the senses. About age three, children's reliance on sensory perception in knowing themselves and their world is modified by their growing ability to use symbols, to remember, to see themselves as separate from the concrete world, and to form mental associations. Although they are still dependent on the concrete world and their senses, they now possess cognitive skills that augment the purely sensory ways of knowing that are typical of the younger child.

Davies (2003, p. 3) sees the body as the "instrument of action … for which there are three important and interrelated categories: *dynamics* which relates to how the instrument (body) moves; *space* which refers to the ways in which the body inhabits and uses space; *relationships* which identifies ways in which the body acts and interacts with people and objects." Children gain physical competence and a repertoire of movement patterns as they develop **action schemas** that involve the integration of **dynamics** (weight, time, flow) and **space** (size, extension, zone, direction, level, pathways, and patterns). Introducing music into the movement curriculum facilitates this integration. Music education is much more than just listening and singing and should involve children in making their own music and in moving to music. Pica (2004, p. 35) states that "if children are to fully experience music, they should explore it as a whole, being given opportunities to listen, sing, play, create and *move*." When set to music, active movement always seems smoother and more enjoyable. Music, drama, movement, and dance have always been compatible, and musical instruments and planned physical activities are also compatible with other materials and activities in the Active Role Play centre.

Where space allows, ECEs are wise to create a music and movement area within the Active Role Play centre that is dedicated to playing instruments, listening to music, and experimenting with sound and movement, including dance, with and without adult supervision (Pica, 2004). This centre should be provisioned with percussion instruments (maracas, tambourines, castanets, rhythm sticks, and cymbals), melodic instruments (keyboard, xylophone, and bells), a prop box with props to enhance movement to rhythm and beat, and clothing and accessories to promote dance and various forms of drama set to music. When this area is updated frequently with new props and instruments and new articles of clothing and accessories, children are motivated to be active and to attempt new forms of movement set to music. A music area "should function as a support to the singing, listening and playing that goes on among children and adults" (Watts, 1991, p. 75).

When the Active Role Play centre is not large enough for group physical activities set to music, the playground, a gymnasium, or a psychomotor room provides the space for movement to music where the compatibility of music, physical exercise, motor skill development, and perceptual abilities may be fully exploited. Group activities set to music, especially music that includes verbal directions or musical cues to children about how they are to move, engage the whole body and mind of the child who is engaged in listening, comprehending, managing her physical movements, and expressing herself or interpreting the music.

PHYSICAL SKILLS FACILITATED BY MUSIC AND MOVEMENT AND DANCE

Locomotion: walk, run, jump, hop, gallop, march, skip, and climb

Nonlocomotor movements: bend, curl, stretch, sway, turn, twist, swing, reach, lift, push, pull, and twirl

Physical abilities: fitness, including muscular strength, muscular endurance, flexibility, cardiovascular endurance, circulatory-respiratory endurance; motor fitness, such as balance, speed, agility, power, and coordination

Body awareness and body image, along with spatial awareness, laterality and directionality, and temporal awareness are also factors in children's physical ability and motivation to dance (see Appendix A).

Children's physical growth affects their progress in all domains. When children move efficiently and feel their bodies respond to physical demands, progress is concrete and observable to them, and the satisfactions they feel provide a general sense of well-being, pride in accomplishment, joy at meeting challenges, and a heightened sense of self-worth. Efficient movement becomes another source of self-expression, an outlet for feelings and desires, and a means to greater appreciation of the aesthetic quality of well-executed movement.

Physical curriculum enhances cognitive abilities. In the cognitive domain, concept learning, such as understanding of space, direction, time–space orientation, position, and distance, is achieved through physical activity. When an ECE plays compatible music and says, "Walk like a duck," "Hop forward four times," or "Clap to the rhythm beat," she is asking children to connect concepts, music, and movement; to solve problems involving representational thinking; and to process and interpret sensory messages. Perceptual processing skills are linked to the accurate reception (acuity) of sensory messages that develop through practice and repetition.

Children also gain knowledge and understanding through physical and cooperative games that teach colour, time, size, numerical order, social protocol, language, cultural awareness, and other everyday living concepts. When music and song are added to the mix of physical programming to promote physical skills and cognitive understanding, the senses, body, mind, emotions, and creative impulses are fully engaged in the learning process. Without music in their daily lives, children do not have access to its lifelong benefits. Music helps children practise and achieve almost any developmental outcome, and musical accompaniment to movement activities and exercises enhances the physical experience and motivates children to try harder and to become more invested in the experience. Children will often be inclined to risk and to abandon themselves more completely in movement activities accompanied by music. As well, music promotes sensory-perceptual skills, such as listening, using **auditory discrimination** (recognizing various tones, rhythms, and sounds), and applying **auditory-motor integration** (coordinating one's body movements to the command of musical sounds). By actively listening and by imitating a musical beat, children heighten their perceptual skills and learn to distinguish among different sounds.

Children feel a sense of harmony when they integrate their bodies, souls, minds, and emotions in the execution of a march, a dance, or an interpretive movement activity. They discover rhythm and melody by moving to music, and their bodies move more responsively when music guides the tempo and the direction of the movement. Music may be used to teach math, to facilitate language and literacy, and to enable symbolic and representational thinking. Because music is abstract, children practise abstract thinking when listening to music. Children also develop cognitive skills, such as memory, and classification skills, including the abilities to recognize groups of sounds and rhythms and to replicate patterns of musical sounds. As well, music enhances language skills; by singing songs, children learn language appreciation, vocabulary, **syntax**, and rhyme.

Props to Enhance Music and Movement

When children hear music, their natural inclination is to move in ways that correspond to their own experiences with music—that is, to march, sway, dance, clap, skip, or pretend to be part of a band. Props to accompany movement and music in the Active Role Play centre or outdoors add to the variety of movement. Scarves and hats from the Daily Living centre may be used as children dance; a baton, a cape, or coattails help an aspiring conductor lead his orchestra. A small platform or strong boxes to simulate a stage may be part of the Active Role Play centre, and a microphone and music stand may be kept near the musical instruments. ECEs should make use of whatever props they can find to foster children's love of a range of music.

Hildebrandt and Zan (2003) encourage ECEs to let children make their own instruments as a way of helping children understand the various aspects of musical sound: pitch, **loudness**, **timbre**, and **duration**. By making their own instruments, children become aware of the differences in sounds, experiment with actions and materials that produce different sounds, experience the regularities and understand cause-and-effect relationships between actions and materials and various sounds. Various reusable materials make interesting sounds, starting with drink cans, bottles, aluminum plates, paper or polystyrene cups, elastic bands, and containers of rice.

Children need opportunities to develop and grow through music in self-directed play, as well as in planned group activities. ECEs should introduce children to musical instruments through demonstration and practice in group learning periods before they make them accessible to children throughout the day. Plenty of practise using musical instruments in group activities teaches children to care for the instrument, use it optimally to enhance sound, and appreciate the challenge of learning to make music. Listening to an experienced musician play an instrument provides a rich example of the range and intricacy of the music to be made by persevering in learning to play an instrument well.

Storing Musical Instruments

Musical instruments should be stored close to the space where music and movement activities will take place, and away from the construction activities, so as to avoid adding to the noise level that is usually high in these play areas. Making musical instruments available to children in a separate hallway or an alcove may be necessary, but doing so limits the integration of instruments into active and sociodramatic play. Having musical instruments available for a wide range of play activities "makes them a more natural, accessible and integrated part of the curriculum, much like books and pencils for language arts" (Watts, 1991, p. 78). Instruments should be located away from the listening area, where children listen to CDs, maybe old records, MP3 players, and the radio. The music-making area is more active and noisy than the listening area and accommodates musical instruments and accessories for movement to music. The listening area may be located in the Project centre or in the Quiet Thinking centre.

Because some musical instruments should be available to children at all times, the centre should provide accessible storage for simple, sturdy instruments that children may select themselves and play spontaneously. It is best to group instruments together on wide shelves or in cupboards for safe and optimal access according to their primary purpose; for example, for movement activities, for listening activities, and for making music. Cupboards with doors make a good storage space for precious and fragile instruments, which the ECE can access to use with the children, whereas open shelves can store the simpler, more durable instruments. Rhythm sticks, drums, maracas, and triangles, for example, may be simple musical accompaniments for an impromptu parade or for a concert that the children present. Watts (1991, p. 79) recommends that instruments available in the music making area be changed at least once a week and that the changes be "from hand drums to tambourines or tambourines to cymbals, rather than from one kind of stick to another." There should always be a plentiful supply of musical instruments that reflect cultural preferences, such as maracas, and drums from many countries.

Music for Inclusive Practice

Music is a vehicle used to disseminate the "culture" of nations, to represent a period in time that has passed, and to protect, over the generations, the culture of childhood. More than 40 years ago, Edith Fowke (1969, p. 6) wrote in her book for Canadian children called *Sally Go Round the Sun* that "the most traditional folklore is fast dying out because the people who used to sing songs and tell stories for their own amusement are now listening to records or watching television." Although today's reality is that children are preoccupied by iPods and Leapsters as well as apps and videos, her message is as timely today as it was then. It is a tribute, in part, to grandmothers and to the ability of children to communicate within their own childhood culture and to have their own priorities, that some of the traditional **rhymes**, chants, clapping games, songs, and nonsense verses remain alive in playgrounds in spite of contemporary technological distractions. ECEs today generally monitor the words and meanings used in the traditional rhymes, lullabies, and chants to ensure that their messages and meanings convey values and ideals that we want our children to emulate in our multicultural society. The politically incorrect "Peter Peter Pumpkin Eater," for example, is a candidate for removal from the culture of childhood, or at least for revision to reflect more enlightened preoccupations!

Music can "break down barriers of race and language, for in a variety of forms, music is common to all races and is enjoyed by all races, and the enjoyment can transcend the cultural differences of race and language" (Cass-Beggs, 1974, p. 3). Music is a universal language, and a part of every culture's identity and festivals (Lazdauskas, 1996). Singing, for example, is a natural vehicle for the enhancement of cultural awareness and appreciation of cultural differences, and a powerful force for transmitting and transforming culture (Sluss, 2005). Children should be encouraged to listen to and sing the songs of many cultures, even to sing them in the language of the culture. All cultures create their own music, and each culture tends to emphasize a different quality of the music. Some focus more on pitch and rhythm; others are identified by a unique timbre. Providing opportunities for children to learn the songs of other cultures heightens their responsiveness to the unique cultural qualities of music and develops their auditory discrimination abilities.

Crowther (2003, p. 98) referred to music as "a great gift to give to all children," which, as already mentioned, has the capacity to soothe and relax, to help solve problems, and to express emotions, for children of all cultures. In diverse societies like ours, the music of various cultures provides a window to the values and priorities of the culture, but also provides an avenue for communication that is unmatched by language and other symbol systems. Children who recognize the musical sounds of their culture in an environment otherwise unfamiliar relax visibly to the familiar beat and rhythm patterns, or to the soft melody of a lullaby, or to the staccato of First Nations dance music. Recognizing that music is an important vehicle for inclusive practice also means that music is an effective ingredient for communication and interaction with children with special needs. Music makes it easier to expand the movement repertoire of children with disabilities.

Learning Through Music

Music provides a unique medium for symbolic learning, as music has its own symbol system and serves as an important language for communicating with others. Because much of music is repetition, children's attention is captured by hearing the same rhythm and tones over and over and associating these repetitions with words and movements in song, dance, and other forms of movement to music. Pica (2010, p. 197) describes five aspects of musical experiences that children should encounter every day: listening attentively and focusing to perceive differences in tones, rhythm, and other elements; singing; playing instruments and doing something such as marching or movements while playing; creating music using instruments, bells, or rhythm sticks; and musical elements. The musical elements include: tempo (speed and timing of the piece); volume (dynamics such as loudness or softness); articulation (the punctuation of notes as in staccato, or legato, the smooth flowing of music without pauses); pitch (high or low musical tone and accuracy of the note); timbre (tonal quality); phrases (divisions in a composition like phrases in a sentence); form (the overall design or organization of the phrases with repeating or contrasting phrases); mood (feelings evoked by the music); and rhythm or melody (patterns of sounds and silences into groupings) (Pica, 2010, pp. 199–205). Children practise and develop these elements and concepts through singing, chanting, moving, playing instruments, listening to music, and making up tunes and songs. Children learn the musical elements and musical skills through direct instruction in planned group experiences and through spontaneous, child-initiated and self-directed experiences with musical instruments, songs, and movement. Playing music of various styles, periods, cultures, and textures exposes children to most musical elements. Encouraging children to move to various musical styles enables the integration of music with physical development and coordination.

Singing

The way in which singing opens up an avenue to the human spirit is rivalled only by physical exertion and the exploration of nature. To the accompaniment of musical instruments or without, song has a way of transporting us beyond the here and now and of releasing energy, enlarging the emotions, and sharpening the perceptions, inducing awe, and stimulating the imagination—all elements of the child's developing spirituality. Children should be encouraged to sing in all areas of the learning environment, whenever the mood strikes them, not only to experience the voice as a wonderfully flexible musical instrument, but also as food for the soul, as a way to safely release emotions, to have fun with sounds and language, and to communicate what may not be expressed as well in words.

© Gabe Palmer / Alamy

Singing and physical activity are compatible. partners.

Singing and physical activity are compatible partners, and movement activities that call for singing, with or without instruments, should occur daily in the Active Role Play centre and outdoors. The uplifting elements of song are integrated by children when they hear others singing and when they learn to sing throughout the day and in all kinds of places. Allowing themselves to be moved by music is an act of trust cultivated when children are encouraged to sing to make the sadness go away, to express the joy they feel on a sunny day, to celebrate their appreciation of one another, to play with language and sound, and to make the work easier and the physical exertion seem lighter. In active role play, singing is a natural accompaniment that reinforces the link between cognition and psychomotor development and often makes difficult physical tasks easier to accomplish.

Children are ready for singing as soon as they begin to talk. Prior to that stage, infants and toddlers have usually responded to familiar lullabies and nursery rhymes whose tunes they recognize and want repeated. Because songs tend to emphasize syllables and segments of words, singing helps children develop word recognition and reading skills. Some adults introduce children to singing by encouraging them to chant familiar verses in unison; this approach is sometimes easier for ECEs who may feel uncomfortable about their own singing and musicality. Playing a CD softly in the background of the songs to be sung with the children allows timid adults to rely on the melody from the tape and encourage the children to follow along. ECEs have to work hard, however, at overcoming any self-consciousness they may have about singing, so that children will sing. Self-consciousness about singing usually evaporates quickly when the joy of making sounds and music and singing together take over and all participate happily without regard for staying in tune. A love of singing in early childhood often turns into a lifelong love of music and song that many children pursue through choir and music lessons during their school years.

Music and Dance

Dance is a form of expressive movement that may begin by learning to handle flags, ribbons, scarves, and other expressive materials while moving in rhythm to the music. Dance is a complex form of movement that "arises out of the connections and coordination between movement and the senses" (Bruce & Ockelford, 2010, p. 109). Dancing rests on the ability to coordinate the sounds one hears with the execution of rhythmic movements, usually following a set pattern. Children's ability to create and perform dance rests on their earlier development of a movement repertoire that includes physical abilities, locomotor and nonlocomotor skills, and coordinated movements. Because dance is a form of communication and creative interpretation, there is also a symbolic connection between dance and the story that dance is trying to convey, or the meaning it is attempting to portray. Children's natural inclination toward dance as a form of self-expression may be seen early in the toddler period, as children move their upper bodies to the sounds of music coming from the CD player or car radio. To facilitate dance and the integrated movements that arise from it, a variety of resources are needed in the Active Role Play centre, and a movement program that takes children, systematically, through various stages in the development of basic fundamental movements.

Davies (2003) notes that certain movement patterns are used frequently by young children who are learning to dance: running and leaping, turning and twisting, landing and rolling, moving and stopping suddenly, making straight and curved patterns, reaching high and crouching low. Movement combinations are facilitated when ECEs select music and rhythm matched to the movement combinations and encourage children to string together several movement combinations as the rhythm changes.

MUSIC AND MOVEMENT ACTIVITIES FOR CHILDREN AGES TWO AND THREE

1. Sing simple songs such as "Twinkle, Twinkle, Little Star," "Rock-a-bye Baby," "I'm a Little Teapot," and "Mary Had a Little Lamb" with the children. Demonstrate movements to accompany the song and have the children imitate your actions.

2. Play classical ballet music and have the children bend and stretch and sway to the sound of the music. Demonstrate actions and then let the children think of movements for themselves that relate to the rhythm and melody of the music.
3. Clap to the beat of music with a familiar beat. Then remove the music and have children try to replicate the same beat and pattern of clapping.
4. *Find the bell.* Children in the group close their eyes and one child is asked by the ECE to take the bell, and to run and hide. Once in position, the child rings the bell and the children have to find the child by linking sound, direction, and distance.
5. *Tambourine game.* Use a code of signals on the tambourine, with each code signalling a basic movement, such as walk, jump, hop, crawl, slide, and gallop. Start with one movement to a code at first, and gradually increase the code of signals to three or four at a time and have the children perform the movement.

MUSIC AND MOVEMENT ACTIVITIES FOR CHILDREN AGES FOUR TO SIX

1. Have the children sing action songs involving movements, including bend and stretch, reach for the sky, sway like a tree, and sway like a sailboat in the wind.
2. Invite the children to listen and then repeat the teacher's rhythmical patterns of clapping. Vary the patterns and rhythm so that children have to listen carefully for changes in the clapping pattern. Play or sing a song and clap the rhythm of the song simultaneously.
3. Play *Peter and the Wolf*, and have the children imitate the movements of the characters in the story by trying to keep time with the rhythm and beat of the instruments.
4. Sing songs that have actions and movements associated with the songs—"I'm a Little Teapot," "Hokey Pokey," and "Row, Row, Row Your Boat"—and have the children do the movements as they sing.
5. *Guess who said it.* Children stand in a circle and close their eyes. The ECE or a child secretly taps one child in the group on the shoulder and the designated child sings a song or chants some lines from a verse. Children guess whose voice they are hearing.
6. *Carpet dance.* Each child stands on a small carpet sample. To move, the child has to twist and turn by rotating his hips and making the carpet move. Once the basic movement is mastered and the child makes the carpet move, play music to have children dance on their carpet to music.

MUSICAL ACTIVITIES WITH INSTRUMENTS

1. Play musical instruments in the rocking boat and try to coordinate the rhythm of the instruments with the rocking motion of the boat.
2. Count the beats of the drum, or listen to the beats in a song with a catchy rhythm, to sensitize children to the importance of timing in music.
3. Make musical instruments with the children using familiar reusable materials. Limit the number of materials children have available to them so they can understand the cause-and-effect relationship between the material and the sound. Have children demonstrate their instruments.
4. Plan a parade using musical instruments from the cupboards or with instruments that children have made. Use costumes and other accessories to add to the atmosphere.

Summary

Music is an important accompaniment to everyday living for adults and children, and appreciation of music, as well as the development of musical talent, develops very early. Music contributes significantly to development in all domains, but music has the greatest influence over physical, cognitive, emotional, and spiritual development when combined with movement. Children's natural tendency to respond to music is evident from infancy as they rock and turn to rhythmic sounds and try to imitate simple rhymes and songs sung to them. Too often the power of music to influence development is under-estimated. Children should be exposed to music and movement programs and activities on a daily basis, and ECEs should overcome any reticence they may have about singing and dance by observing the immense power of music and movement to alter mood; to influence behaviour; and to awaken interest, imagination, and action in children. Although it is desirable for children to make their own music through the frequent use of musical instruments readily accessible to them in their play, CDs and other media may be used to ensure that music becomes a significant part of each day. Music is a particularly effective accompaniment to movement through dance and many other forms of physical activity.

LEARNING ACTIVITIES

1. Outline in two paragraphs the role of music and musical instruments in the Active Role Play centre as a stimulus for sociodramatic play and active play.
2. Create a scale drawing of the Active Role Play centre. On your drawing, show clearly where the storage areas for musical instruments will be located. Ensure that children have easy access to the musical instruments for their spontaneous play. Include a space dedicated to music and movement.
3. List the guidelines you will provide for children in their play with musical instruments.
4. Choose four musical activities from the lists provided. Write activity cards for these activities following the format outlined in Chapter 10.
5. If you are not a musician, draw up a plan for your professional development, which will include familiarizing yourself with simple musical instruments and the particular characteristics of the music of various cultures, so that you can incorporate music into your work with young children from diverse backgrounds.
6. Observe a kindergarten or preschool program, noting particularly the various ways in which music is integrated into the program. Suggest additional ways to integrate musical instruments into the environment and to expose children to a wide range of music, including music meant especially for children.
7. Plan a field trip to a musical event suitable for children (concert, choir rehearsal). Outline the ways in which you will introduce the event to the children and how you will further their appreciation of the event when they return to the centre.

Section V

Play and Learning-to-Learn

Section V addresses the following topics:

- contributions of neuroscience to aspects of play, development, and learning
- play to foster motivation, attending, and learning-to-learn
- playing alone; individual play
- cultural interpretations of cognitive development and learning success
- constructivist early childhood education strategies for language and literacy
- language learning, literacy, and early reading in the Quiet Thinking centre
- logical concepts: number, order, classification, and early mathematical understanding through play in the Quiet Thinking centre
- the Project centre and issues related to the use of technologies, including computers, as play and learning tools for children and for projects

Section V explains that play is the essential medium for learning in early childhood and that play should be enhanced to exploit its rich potential for the development of skills, knowledge, and dispositions for later formal learning and a lifelong motivation to learn. Learning-to-learn includes attending skills and task orientation, as well as the all-important ability to motivate oneself (intrinsic motivation) and to be self-directed, and not to depend on external motivators, such as rewards. Attending skills are facilitated by play that is challenging, interesting, and thoughtful. Attending skills include knowing how to use time well, to search for and use resources, to block out distractions, to return to a task after an interruption, to ask questions, and to attend to a task until it is finished. These skills are commonly referred to as the ability "to focus." Galinsky (2010) cites focus and self-control as the first of "seven essential life skills."

Chapter 15 discusses the role of play in learning-to-learn and in preparing for later formal academic learning. Attending, task orientation, motivation, and other dispositions to learn are related to success in school and in life. Being able to play individually and becoming an effective *player* during early childhood are important first steps toward success in formal learning. Play that emphasizes language and literacy in the Quiet Thinking centre is addressed in Chapter 16. Chapter 17 describes how play with concrete objects contributes to the development of logical thinking and abstract concepts that lead to number sense and numeration, measurement, classification, seriation, spatial sense, relationships and patterns, and probability. Chapter 18 explores the role of technologies to complement children's play in the three-dimensional environment, and the role of projects that may be started, implemented, or finished in the Project centre.

15 The Quiet Thinking Centre: Learning-to-Learn

"It's not that I'm so smart. It's just that I stay with problems longer."

—ALBERT EINSTEIN

BEFORE READING THIS CHAPTER, HAVE YOU

- identified your own favoured learning style?
- considered the habits of mind you possess that facilitate your learning?
- recognized where your own approach to attending and task orientation needs improvement?

OUTCOMES

After reading and understanding this chapter, you should be able to

- explain some links between brain development, cognition, and early learning;
- facilitate children's development through play of the habits of mind, dispositions for learning, attending, and task orientation skills that equip children for school success and lifelong learning; and
- be a role model for the motivation and excitement of learning, persistence, and overcoming obstacles needed to achieve success.

Learning-to-Learn Fosters Lifelong Learning

Educators have discovered through decades of experience that achievement in school is influenced as much by children's **learning-to-learn** and attending skills as by their native intelligence. Research has confirmed that the brain remains plastic and capable of change and increasing complexity throughout the lifespan when the environment challenges and encourages ongoing progress. We have also learned that intelligence is a lifelong process, not an entity present at birth and that remains relatively fixed throughout life (Sternberg, 2005; Doidge, 2007; Shenk, 2010). Every child can grow smarter if the environment demands it, and a primary mandate of early childhood education programs is to ensure that it does. We all know of exceptionally talented individuals who have failed to achieve their potential because of poorly developed learning habits, an absence of intrinsic motivation to do what it takes to succeed, and an inability to delay gratification. These skills are closely identified with the "executive functions of the brain," all of which involve the prefrontal cortex, which "manages" our attention, emotions, and behaviour and helps us achieve our goals (Galinsky, 2010, p. 4). That is why business and government leaders since the early 1990s, and more recently neuroscientists, have emphasized that an individual's acquisition of learning-to-learn skills, including **self-control**, is the key to adaptation and a predictor of success in the knowledge economy (Moffitt, 2011).

Dispositions for learning include task orientation skills, such as being able to choose an activity, begin the activity, plan, resist distractions, persevere in the face of obstacles, overcome the obstacles, and complete a task. The ability to return to a task after an interruption, to use time wisely, to block out distractions, and to delay gratification are the key attending skills. A learning-to-learn curriculum is framed by an understanding of children's readiness for further exploration and challenge. A valid curriculum should ensure that children experience success by tackling worthwhile tasks and completing them, alone and with others, by learning the meaning of effort, by persevering, and by achieving outcomes. Learning-to-learn may be the greatest overall determinant of success in school for most children. The ability to attend, self-control, conscientiousness, and perseverance are essential goals of early childhood education and for life in general (Moffitt, 2011).

The development of lifelong learning abilities originates well before children have begun to tackle academic skills in the early primary grades. The ability to be motivated and purposeful in an activity, to be task oriented, to plan systematically, and to practise efficient strategies for learning are skills that many adults wrongly assume are either innate or are learned by children on their own. Most children develop these skills while they are young only when the environment offers opportunities and incentives to do so, and when it challenges children to practise and achieve these outcomes. Whatever their inherited genetic abilities, and however talented children may be, without the ability to be self-regulating, to organize and plan, to persevere, and to delay gratification, their cognitive potential may be wasted. The earlier children learn these skills, the better (Shute, 2011). The ability to plan systematically, as with so many other aptitudes for learning and organization skills, is learned in an environment that encourages and enables children to derive more value from their play (Casey & Lippmann, 1991).

Brain Development and Learning-to-Learn

Knowing the rudiments of brain development helps us understand how children learn. The brain develops faster than any other part of the body during the early years; it has attained approximately 75 percent of its adult weight by age three, 90 percent of adult weight by age five, and has reached full size by age seven (Eliot, 1999). The brain's physical growth is outstripped, however, by the enormous changes in its internal structure. Although the infant at birth has most of the **neurons** it will need, the connections, or **synapses**, are just beginning their rapid production in the prenatal period and during the first two years of life. This process of **synaptogenesis** is a factor of genetic programming, but we now know that intelligence, like other traits, is a process—a result of a complex interplay within a dynamic system (Bruer, 1999). "One moves along the [intelligence] continuum as one acquires a broader range of skills, a deeper level of the skills one already has, and increased efficiency in the use of these skills" (Sternberg, 2005, quoted in Shenk, 2009, p. 42). The well-organized, challenging play environment motivates, challenges, and stimulates the developing mind in positive directions.

As children encounter new learning experiences, they use and reuse many of the early synapses in the brain, while others tend to disappear in a process referred to as **synaptic pruning**, which many theorists believe continues well into adulthood. The adding of new synapses, along with the pruning of those that are no longer useful, are simultaneous processes that add to the brain's efficiency (see Chapter 8, p. 142, Figure 8–1). A process called **myelination,** in which the **axons** of the neuron gradually become coated with myelin, allows the neurons to fire more rapidly. This process produces more effective learning. Research suggests that myelination continues from early childhood into early adulthood, especially in the **cortex** (Merzenich, 2001). Infants achieve a major cognitive landmark at eight to nine months of age when they are able, for the first time, to integrate their understanding of the world into a simple but meaningful plan of action. The next cognitive leap occurs around 18 months of age, when children's sensory and motor control systems in the brain are nearly complete and the left hemisphere of the brain has matured considerably. This is the time when language begins to appear and children are ready to focus on acquiring cognitive concepts, symbolic thinking, and self-awareness. At this stage, children also develop the ability to regulate their actions, to control automatic reflexes, and to resist some temptations. The emergence of self-control, even at this young age, is a significant milestone because it is the key to disciplined learning (Eliot, 1999). At this stage, children can be offered simple play materials with built-in limitations, such as shape puzzles and interlocking blocks, and some amount of sustained activity with these materials should be anticipated.

Between the ages of three and four, another cognitive transition occurs, one that coincides with improved communication between the right side of the brain (perception) and the left side of the brain (analytic reasoning). At this stage, children begin to realize that appearance and reality are not necessarily the same. For example, children are able to retain their knowledge that snow is white even when they examine snow through red plastic glasses (Ormrod, 2006). Closer to the age of five, children's ability to distinguish appearance from reality matures; we observe this in their growing ability to sort sets of objects according to several criteria at a time based on their physical characteristics initially (e.g., colour, shape), then their utility (e.g., kitchen versus workshop utensils), and then abstract concepts (e.g., objects that are dangerous and those that are safe). Constructivists believe that children come to understand simple concepts like these largely through their ongoing interaction with concrete objects in the environment. Vygotsky would also say that the use of language to describe the objects contributes to children's **perceptual acuity** and conceptual understanding.

From about age three, children begin to understand that the perceptions and thoughts of others may be different from their own. This represents a leap that moves them beyond the **egocentricity** and **sensorimotor** abilities of their toddler years and into preoperational thought, and the ability to relate to others with greater restraint, empathy, and sociability. The period from three to five years is, therefore, a precious one for sociodramatic play and creative-constructive play, which call for children to collaborate with others, assume roles, and represent ideas. By age six, children whose playful learning is well developed are usually ready for some early academic challenges owing to the maturation of their perceptual, analytic, language, and other cognitive processes. They have often achieved the necessary self-regulation and self-awareness for the attending and task-orientation challenges of formal schooling.

We now know that brain development occurs throughout the lifespan and that cognitive development is, therefore, a lifelong enterprise (Brown & Bjorklund, 1998; Doidge, 2007). This knowledge puts pressure on the entire educational continuum to ensure that children, adolescents, and adults continue to exercise their brains, entertain new intellectual challenges, and overcome deficits that they may have experienced in an earlier developmental phase (Ormrod, 2006). Whatever future research will teach us about brain development and the lifespan, we know that early exercise of the brain contributes to the formation of synapses between neurons and that these connections and synaptic pruning promote increasingly efficient thought processes that allow young children to learn faster and to participate more readily in thinking challenges. Increasingly, research on the role of play in learning, imagining, creating, symbolizing, problem solving, metacognition, and self-regulation is expanding our understanding of play as a prerequisite for development and learning, including social connectedness, emotional well-being, and physical health (Whitebread, 2010).

Piaget's Beliefs about How Children Learn

Constructivist principles of learning state that children are active learners who, when exposed to well-organized play materials and challenging learning opportunities, are more able to uncover concepts as they manipulate materials and interact with things in the environment. Piaget explained how concept formation and new learning occur; he described *schemes*, which are organized systems of thoughts or actions. Schemes develop through the joint processes of assimilation and accommodation leading to equilibration. Children in stimulating environments are continuously confronted with learning challenges that create an imbalance between what the child knows now and can do, and what the new learning task is demanding of him. In order to achieve a new state of equilibrium, the child tries to understand the new concept or skill in terms of what he knows already (assimilation), and when the new learning does not fit his existing mental structures or *schemes*, he tries to modify his existing scheme to accommodate the new learning challenge (accommodation).

The imbalance between assimilation and accommodation creates a temporary period of ***disequilibrium*** for the child, who is driven to correct the imbalance and regain equilibrium by developing new schemes or revising existing schemes. This process eventually leads to equilibration, which is a temporary state before some new learning challenge confronts the child. Equilibration and children's drive to return to equilibrium is the intrinsic force that leads children to develop increasingly complex skills and thought processes (Ginsberg & Opper, 1969).

UNDERSTANDING THESE CONCEPTS IN TERMS OF YOUR OWN LEARNING

Think of your own experience learning to drive a car, especially a car with a manual gear shift. Recall the disequilibrium you felt as you tried to coordinate your perspective of the road, the steering wheel, the pressure of your foot on the accelerator, watching in the rear-view mirror for traffic behind you, and observing the roadside traffic signs, not to mention the oncoming traffic and the centre line of the road. Add to this complexity the need to also shift gears by coordinating the action of your hands and your left foot as you speed up, slow down, or stop according to the traffic signals and the traffic around you. This example illustrates the nature of the disequilibrium that we all feel when the mental structures (schemes) and knowledge we have already acquired are no match for the new learning challenge that confronts us. As we practise and persist with the challenge, the coordination of hand, eye, and foot become more instinctive and automatic and we learn to focus our attention on the road and the traffic, rather than on which foot to use for the brake and which foot for the clutch, and how to work the turn signals. As our actions become more coordinated, a sense of equilibrium returns and we are ready for the next learning challenge, which is usually to apply what we have read about the rules of the road. Children experience similar disequilibrium when they are learning to ride a bicycle, hit a baseball thrown to them from a distance, or string a set of multicoloured beads with different properties (wood, plastic, glass) and shapes according to self-repeating patterns.

Piaget's Three Types of Knowledge as They Apply to Learning-to-Learn

Piaget (1969) identified three types of knowledge: ***physical, social-conventional,*** and ***logical-mathematical,*** as noted in Chapter 2, pages 25–26. Physical knowledge includes knowledge of the physical properties of things in the environment that the child discovers as he explores. Social-conventional knowledge involves factual information derived culturally and agreed upon by society. Children acquire social-conventional knowledge largely through their social relationships at home, in school, and in their neighbourhood from peers, older children, and adults who pass on to them everyday living concepts, cultural conventions, expectations, and factual data. They learn from children's books and other print material, television programs, videos, CD-ROMs, and educational software. Thus, the sources of physical and social-conventional knowledge lie largely outside the child.

The source of logical-mathematical knowledge, however, lies within the child; in other words, it is intrinsic. Logical-mathematical knowledge is mainly about acquiring concepts, which includes an understanding of what is true, even in the face of apparent or physical contradictions. This type of knowledge is created when children form relationships between and among objects. As they manipulate objects in order to see the relationships, they begin to form relationships that exist only in the mind and that are, therefore, abstract. Logical-mathematical knowledge involves physical learning in terms of perceiving the physical characteristics of objects, such as, ***round*** and ***silver***, and social-conventional learning such as ***coin*** and ***dime***, but it also requires conceptual understanding of the abstract characteristics, such as, ***worth the same as 10 pennies.***

Children are acquiring logical-mathematical knowledge from the time they become capable of rudimentary thought, but logical-mathematical concepts and *abstract* understanding depend on the child's discovery of relationships among things and phenomena. Logical-mathematical thinking progresses from a relatively simple understanding of the concepts of same-versus-different and part-versus-whole, to a more complex understanding of the concepts of cause and effect and ordering. Children's active manipulation of play materials helps them uncover, discover, construct, and eventually understand relationships. When children play with modular materials, such as beads and strings, pegs and pegboards, bingo chips, Cuisenaire rods, Lego, and tabletop blocks, they compare, contrast, arrange, sort, measure, count, quantify, and relate things in many different ways, eventually discovering relationships for themselves.

Structure building occurs when each component of the concept to be learned is visible, understandable, and meaningful to the child. (For example, it is inappropriate to expect that when they reach kindergarten or grade one, children will accept on faith alone that 2 + 2 = 4; they need to understand concepts of quantity, equality, and number constancy before they can grasp the meaning of even simple mathematical equations like this one).

Vygotsky's Sociocultural Learning Theory

Vygotsky's research, predominantly on children with developmental disabilities, produced a perspective on children's learning based on the role of adults and other children in fostering children's cognitive abilities. His social learning theories emphasized the following points:

- Adults convey to children, through formal and informal means, an approach to interpreting and responding to the world.
- Thought and language are intertwined during the early years from about the age of two, when children begin to organize and express their thoughts using words.
- Children's social interactions and activities promote the development of complex cognitive processes that they gradually transfer to independent learning situations.
- Children learn more efficiently when they are assisted with challenging tasks through a process called scaffolding. The key to effective scaffolding is in matching the assistance offered to the child, exactly to the child's learning needs (Kail & Zolner, 2005).
- Well-organized play that includes new tasks and experiences stretches children cognitively (Ormrod, 2006, pp. 34–37).

Information Processing Theory

Information processing theory, which emerged in the late 1950s, initially proposed that the functions of the human brain were similar to the operations performed by computers, but, as research has revealed the enormous complexities and plasticity of the brain, this theory has assumed a more constructivist bias, similar to the beliefs of Piaget and Vygotsky.

Ormrod (2006, p. 43) states that "information processing theory is actually a collection of theories that emphasize the development of cognitive processes—processes through which children acquire, interpret, remember, manipulate, and make use of information." These theorists believe that children's cognitive processes and abilities develop through more steady and gradual *trends* rather than discrete stages. They propose that children learn faster, remember more, and can think about increasingly complex tasks as they grow (Ormrod, 2006).

Kail and Zolner (2005) propose that:

> For both Piaget and information-processing theorists, children's thinking becomes more sophisticated as children develop.... Whereas Piaget emphasized the "whole" of cognitive development, information processing emphasizes the "parts." ... Piaget emphasized qualitative change in cognition ... [whereas] changes in information-processing ability typically produce a steady increase in cognitive skill. Information-processing approaches focus on cognitive change as continual and gradual, implying a focus on quantitative changes rather than qualitative change. Qualitative change refers to change in type or essence (quality), whereas quantitative change refers to change in amount or value (quantity). Since both types of change play a role in development, here, too, Piaget's theory and information processing theory complement each other. (Kail & Zolner, 2005, p. 20)

Summarizing Theories of Cognitive Development

All three theories of cognitive development are increasingly seen as complementary; the qualitative emphasis of Piaget's work, Vygotsky's sociocultural theory, and the quantitative emphasis of information processing combine to produce a more holistic understanding of cognitive development. Whatever theory one prefers, they all seem to subscribe to some fundamental understandings:

- children's thinking is qualitatively different at various ages;
- children construct their knowledge and understanding through play and active exploration of things in the environment;
- learning and development are built on a foundation of earlier learning;
- challenging play opportunities promote development and learning; and,
- social interactions enhance cognitive development and language acquisition.

Metacognition, Self-Regulation, and Structuring Play to Promote Concept Learning

Section IV addressed the value of play to children's development of the higher order thinking skills, including symbolic thinking and representation. Children's ability to attend in the face of learning that is complex also requires motivation, intention, and a commitment to meet the challenges presented by their play. Brown (1987, pp. 65–116) identified metacognition as a key learning skill that involves "experience" (self-awareness of mental processing and the ability to reflect upon it);

"knowledge" (knowledge that arises from metacognition about one's own mental processing and preferred cognitive strategies for dealing with tasks); and "control" (the ability to choose and use strategies appropriately in relevant contexts so as to achieve mastery). Metacognition, the knowledge and ability to think about cognition, is often linked to **"theory of mind,"** which is the ability to think about thought. There is some agreement among researchers that an early theory of mind occurs between ages three and five and develops gradually between ages two and six (Bergen, 2002).

Rifkin (2009) describes theory of mind as "I know, you know, and I know that you know," which he claims proves that "the development of thought itself... necessitates relationship to others. We can only know ourselves in relationship to others, and.... Language itself, the ability to form thoughts with words, only emerges in relationships with others" (Rifkin, 2009, p. 148). Whitebread (2010, p. 162) links metacognition to the concept of self-regulation described by Vygotsky, who saw learning in early childhood as "a process of moving from other-regulation (performing a task while supported by an adult or peer) to self-regulation (performing tasks independently)." An understanding of metacognitive processes in early learning is important because we know that learning-to-learn skills and habits of mind develop in early childhood and may be fostered and supported by play activities (Bruner, 1972). Sternberg (1985) described three cognitive processes: knowledge acquisition components; performance components (implementing learned cognitive procedures and strategies); and metacomponents (higher-order processes used to select and coordinate the activities of the other two components in relation to the task at hand and to plan, monitor, and evaluate task performance). He claimed that it is the metacomponents that distinguish able learners from those who struggle when confronted with something new and unfamiliar. Recent research has even linked self-regulation and cognitive control mechanisms to emotional and social development and to motivational drives to learn and overcome hurdles. Self-regulatory abilities have an impact especially on deliberate, intentional learning that requires effort, planning, the choice of which organizational strategies to use, and the ability to evaluate what one has learned (Whitebread, 2010, p. 163).

What does this body of research mean to ECEs who are mandated to challenge, support, and guide children's play during the early years? It means that ECEs are not only required to provide play opportunities that match children's developmental levels so that they can practise and repeat familiar actions. They must also think through the next steps in the learning process for children who need to develop new strategies and a theory of mind that enables them to engage with unfamiliar tasks and cognitive challenges, to go beyond what they know already, to actively choose how they will tackle new problems, to persevere as they implement their selected plan, and to adjust their plan as they proceed. Allowing children to simply walk away from an appropriate new challenge they have not previously encountered may mean that we are failing to capitalize on an important teachable moment. The ECE has to constantly evaluate how to adjust an activity and its inherent challenges (scaffold the learning required by the activity), support the child's effort, encourage her perseverance even in the face of some inevitable missteps, and keep her interested and focused on examining what she has tried and failed and what other options might work instead. "Persistence is the difference between mediocrity and enormous success" (Shenk, 2009, p. 113).

Motivation Is the Key to Successful Achievement

Today's changing economic order and emphasis on creativity and innovation demand that children become effective learners, able to adapt and to solve novel problems. We should support children's intrinsic motivation, self-improvement, and independent learning and provide the time it takes for children to practise skills related to delaying gratification, persistence and planning. The challenge for ECEs is to help children internalize their motivation to complete a task successfully, that is, to become self-motivated. Motivation is a mix of many ingredients that include faith in oneself; self-knowledge or knowing what one is capable of; the ability to visualize what success would look like; the ability to ignore impulsive actions and delay gratification (drop the activity in order to do something easier and more fun); and sufficient time to persist, try different strategies, revise plans, and try again. Time is a key factor in helping children become self-motivated and successful learners. Brain research tells us that the brain circuits that control a person's persistence are plastic and alterable (Doidge, 2007; Shenk, 2010, p. 113). Adults help children shape these circuits by modelling self-control, setting up challenging play activities that encourage practice and persistence, supporting and believing in their ultimate success, praising their persistence and progress, and seeing failure at any step along the way as an opportunity to try a different approach. When ECEs and parents believe that intelligence is malleable and incremental, they are more likely to motivate the children they care for to adopt significant goals and achieve them.

Cultural Interpretations of Cognitive Development and Learning Success

The brain is dominated by the language of its culture, and culture changes the brain's architecture from a very early age (Doidge, 2007, p. 300). For the past 50 years, considerable attention has been paid to the differences in the rates at which children learn certain types of skills. The cultural environment has a direct bearing on whether and how people challenge themselves and others to compete and to achieve (Shenk, 2010, p. 121) Culture also affects the emergence of concrete operational thinking in young children, broad differences in aptitudes, the time it takes to learn certain types of skills, and our awareness of the considerable variation in the *multiple intelligences* that children demonstrate (Gardner, 1999; Ormrod, 2006). The distinctive characteristics of intelligence in divergent populations are also culturally related: those whose life experiences are embedded in different forms of social organization; those who require survival skills that are unique to their culture and environments; those who adhere to unusual customs and beliefs; and those who solve problems using techniques that match their environments (Sternberg, 2005). Attention has also been paid to the wide range of aptitudes we see in children with special needs.

Perhaps one of Vygotsky's most important contributions to early childhood education is found in the perspectives he offered on the impact of culture on cognitive development (Kail & Zolner, 2005, p. 20). Ormrod (2006) provides the following comment on Vygotsky's belief in the role of culture on cognition:

> A society's culture ...guides children in certain directions by encouraging them to pay attention to particular stimuli (and not to others) and to engage in particular activities (and not in others). And it provides a lens through which children come to construct culturally appropriate interpretations of their experiences. We see obvious effects of culture in many of children's everyday activities—in the books they read, the jokes they tell, the roles they enact in pretend play, the extracurricular activities they pursue—but we must remember that culture permeates children's unobservable thinking processes as well. (Ormrod, 2006, p. 37)

In Canada, the cultural diversity issues challenge ECEs to work with parents to ensure that the cognitive skills parents value most are recognized and supported in their programs. The emergence and timing of certain cognitive abilities depend on the value attached to that particular form of learning by the culture of the family and community. Another diversity challenge is to identify the developmental skills that are learned earlier, and more capably, by children of one culture, and those areas of development in which children of another culture will exhibit superior skills and knowledge. Then, the challenge is to develop programs that broaden the developmental and learning opportunities for all children.

While independence and self-help skills may be valued by mainstream North American culture, dependence on adults for children's physical care and support is the goal for families of certain European and Asian traditions (Kotsopoulos, 2005). The rates at which children achieve developmental milestones in any domain—cognitive, physical, and affective—depend very much on what is valued and supported by the culture. The challenge is to accept culturally relevant assessments of children's developmental progress and to design curricula and programs that support a wide range of cultural priorities, including those of the mainstream culture.

Attending and Learning-to-Learn

Like so many other dispositions, positive work-study habits begin early (Stipek, 1982). According to Gardner (1991, p. 136), "the successful student is one who learns how to use research materials, libraries, note cards and computer files, as well as knowledgeable parents, teachers, older students, and classmates, in order to master those tasks of schools that are not transparently clear." Children are ready to practise attending, organizing, planning, and problem-solving skills in preschool and when they are encouraged to practise these skills, they exhibit the improved thinking abilities of successful learners. Most cultural groups in Canada support the view that more attention should be paid to children's development of learning-to-learn skills.

The current popularity of Montessori programs is partly due to the importance these programs place on the development of attending and learning-to-learn skills largely through play with specific purpose materials. Montessori programs emphasize children's ability to choose, start, and finish activities; avoid distractions; and return to an activity after an interruption. Just as the profession promotes the development of the divergent thinking abilities fostered by the creative arts, dramatic play, physical activity, and social play, so the profession also respects the importance of convergent thinking skills that are practised and acquired through play with specific-purpose materials, in settings that encourage some individual play and that motivate children to overcome obstacles they meet until they finally succeed.

Before Montessori, Froebel's 19th-century kindergarten relied heavily on play materials consisting of solid geometrical shapes, tablets, lines, and points, which were an integral part of a programmed curriculum. Specific-purpose play materials for focused skill development, coexisting with continuous, creative materials for open-ended playful learning and self-expression, have been present in programs for the past two hundred years. The Quiet Thinking centre accommodates a wide range of specific-purpose materials and play activities that address learning-to-learn and attending, and early literacy and numeracy concepts.

Task orientation involves choosing and beginning an activity, overcoming obstacles, following through, completing the task, and being able to report that the task is finished—skills that are related to intrinsic motivation. Being able to consider options and to choose personal goals, whether learning-related or more playful, for self-improvement or for leisure, originate in early childhood play, especially the ability to enter into play; to become and remain engaged in play; and to avoid boredom, messing about, and wasting time. These influence children's readiness for later academic learning and are dispositions for learning that contribute to a life of fulfillment.

Brown and Fenske (2010, pp. 5–8) studied the strategies of highly successful individuals and found that they all … are good at tuning out distractions and choosing the best way to focus on a task and get the best outcome; they are energetic and sustain their energy; and they appear to adapt in exceptional ways over time to the demands of the tasks before them, harnessing the plasticity of their brains to help them succeed. Successful people appear to exhibit self-awareness, focus, motivation, memory (so as to predict and improve), emotional balance (to recognize and anticipate emotional responses in self and others and adjust), resilience (to be able to reframe failures and start over), and adaptability to changing circumstances (Brown & Fenske, 2010, p. 90). These characteristics are fostered by providing a curriculum with play opportunities that challenge young children to practise these vital skills.

LEARNING-TO-LEARN SKILLS

Attending

- able to focus and concentrate
- able to use resources effectively (e.g., teachers, peers, older children)
- able to block out distractions
- able to return to an activity after an interruption
- able to reframe failures and start over

Task Orientation Skills

- choose an activity from alternatives and adapt to its demands
- start the activity (this is harder for some children than it may appear)
- persist with the activity and adapt to circumstances
- overcome obstacles and seek help as needed
- finish and report on the activity

Attention Span: This is the amount of time a child spends at a task that is appropriate and interesting (the length of time spent is less important than the quality of the time children devote to the activity, that is, their task orientation).

Motivation: Sternberg (2005) claimed that motivation drives all key elements involved in building intelligence, including learning skills, thinking skills, metacognitive skills, and knowledge.

Concept Formation

Forming a **concept** involves understanding the relationships that exist among objects, people, and events. Hiebert and Lefevre (1986) described conceptual knowledge as a web of knowledge, or a network in which the linking relationships are as important as the discrete pieces of information. **Concept formation** is achieved by constructing relationships between separate pieces of information, an ability that Bruner (1960) described as the essence of discovery learning. In Piagetian terms, concept formation occurs through the equilibration process, when new or previously unrelated pieces of information are assimilated into existing mental structures that alter to accommodate the new level of understanding. In this way, new information becomes part of an existing network or concept (Hiebert & Lefevre, 1986). Concept formation is fundamental to the development of both reasoning and logical thinking skills. As children gain an understanding of concepts, their abilities to organize their experiences and to perceive a natural order in the world contribute to rational thinking.

The source of understanding, or of concept formation, lies within children, since they comprehend the concepts in their own ways. To become self-directed learners children must play, experiment, cooperate, and be interested in learning. The role of the play environment is to respond to the child's level of interest, action, experience, and development. The modular and specific-purpose materials in the Quiet Thinking centre, such as the beads, tabletop blocks and tiles, and puzzles with various purposes, are examples of play materials that respond to children's actions on them. Play materials such as Lego allow children to construct relationships and to understand spatial concepts. Play with modular materials, such as seriated sets, sorting kits, and small building blocks, helps children to understand the logical relationships of seriation, **classification**, **number**, and **conservation**. Children need time and space to discover many relationships as they play with responsive materials. Children should be developmentally ready in order to engage with specific-purpose materials that pose a challenge. The child's maturity should be considered before a child is left to tackle the challenges typically inherent in such materials as stacking cups, jigsaw puzzles, parquetry, and Lego blocks. When adults impose concept learning on children before they are ready, or when they try to teach concepts as if they were the same as physical or social-conventional knowledge, children become confused and discouraged. When asked to tackle activities that require them to ignore what they perceive, and rely instead on a concept they know in order to solve a problem or finish a task, children who have not grasped the relevant abstract concept become frustrated. For example, when a child has not grasped the concept of number, he may memorize the sum $1 + 1 = 2$, although it has little meaning for him. When older children learn to perform arithmetical operations by memorizing rules and tables, and by following formulas without understanding the concepts behind them, the operation becomes mainly mechanical and verbal, rather than logical, and children cannot progress in math (Mighton, 2003). When the rules and verbal explanations that have been memorized fail them and they have to rely, instead, on logic and understanding, children are unable to solve abstract mathematical problems.

EXAMPLE

Children begin to form concepts by playing with a variety of objects similar to one another in one or more ways. The ways in which the objects are similar represent the concept, or the criterion, that integrates the objects. Children have achieved concept formation when they are able to classify other objects correctly as either members or non-members of the set. For example, a red bingo chip and a yellow bingo chip are different, at least according to the criterion of colour. When children recognize that the chips are different, they create a relationship between the two chips that pertains to the criterion of colour. In placing the two objects in relationship to each other and comparing them based on the criterion of colour, the concept of *same-different* becomes apparent.

Develop a Culture of Thinking in the Early Childhood Program

Like so many other aspects of development and learning, thinking is not something that one falls into or that happens without active engagement and effort; thinking is an intensely active pursuit, and the fact is, people differ widely in their ability to think purposefully and effectively. The usual products or results of thinking are an idea; a plan; an insight; some new understanding; and, sometimes, a decision. Not everyone achieves any of these outcomes, however, by following a set of prescribed steps. They generally employ many of the skills that comprise "thinking," such as: comparing, contrasting, deducing, inferring, describing, predicting, analyzing, synthesizing, evaluating, or judging. A goal of early childhood education is that children develop an early ability to think effectively, which means that they are able to employ early versions of thinking skills as they organize their thoughts, plan how to tackle an activity, consider their results, and determine whether or not they meet their own expectations. An essential skill related to effective thinking is the ability to recognize situations and challenges that call for thinking. When the need for thinking is built in to the play activities provided, children acquire the ability to know when to stop and think. When the playroom becomes a "culture of thinking," children are immersed in play challenges that require them to "stop and think" before they engage with the activity (Salmon, 2010).

The Importance of Individual Play in Learning-to-Learn

The value of individual play in order to learn concepts has endured for two centuries (Nourot, 2005). Young children need time and opportunities to play alone with concrete materials in order to understand basic concepts in their own ways. The Quiet Thinking centre is dedicated to this purpose. Hands-on learning through play is a learning style that reflects young children's strong sensory orientation. Until the concrete operational stage, which begins about age seven, children generally manipulate and explore concrete objects through the senses to form concepts. Children learn about their position in space in relation to other things in their environment through real experiences, such as feeling the distance between themselves and others at a table. Later, when they are school age, children understand concepts in the absence of the sensory stimulus, but in the early years, offering children opportunities to explore concrete objects individually is fundamental to their development.

The Quiet Thinking centre is dedicated to "thinking," and, as such, it is an area reserved for relatively quiet play; individual pursuit of play activities; opportunities to engage with unfamiliar materials, problems to unravel and solve; and, sometimes, a requirement to report what has been learned. Children's reports may be as diverse and unintended as they wish. What is important is the requirement that children develop the ability to reflect on what they have done and what they have learned (that is important to them), and communicate their understanding of what the activity called upon them to do and achieve. *The protocol that surrounds quiet play, with individual activities that require children to form and use thinking skills in the execution of an activity, is the intended purpose of the Quiet Thinking centre.*

The Quiet Thinking centre and the specific-purpose materials provided there encourage children to sit down, usually alone, to tackle an activity and to finish it before they move on to something else. The agenda is to provide opportunities to practise attending and task orientation, to experience what it means to play alone with a challenging activity, to avoid distractions, and to organize and plan an approach to solving the challenges posed by the activities. "Getting there is half the fun" is relevant to the Quiet Thinking centre, where the emphasis is on organizing one's thoughts, choosing an activity, planning ahead, starting and finishing, overcoming obstacles, reframing the "problem" that should be solved, persisting in spite of challenges, and knowing when one has succeeded. Although these thinking skills are also practised daily in all other learning centres and outdoors, the Quiet Thinking centre ensures that children are exposed to particular challenges in their play that they might not choose to experience unless they are encouraged to do so. A learning centre dedicated to "quiet thinking" and individual play makes it easier for ECEs to observe and record a child's approach to a new challenge, her attending and task orientation skills, and her command of the ability to think and reflect on what she plans or is doing, which involves metacognitive abilities. Therefore, an ECE should always be present in this centre, asking questions, recording actions and responses, noting progress or lack of it, and offering assistance and encouragement to help a child overcome a setback.

The Quiet Thinking Centre Promotes Learning-to-Learn

The Quiet Thinking centre emphasizes individual, hands-on, self-directed learning at planned activities with specific-purpose materials as described in Chapter 6. ECEs set up the activities; children choose an activity, decide initially how they will use the materials, and eventually use the materials for the purpose intended. The specific-purpose activities encourage children to play with the materials and to learn from them. These materials help children form concepts and master the generic skills involved in being purposeful, organized, enthusiastic learners. Solitary play and individual pursuits allow for thinking, reflection, and working at one's own speed. The environment in this learning centre gives messages to children that this is an area where they are encouraged to play alone, finish what they start, and tidy up the activity when they have finished. Structure in this centre refers to the ECE's careful planning of play materials and activities with implicit developmental objectives, at play stations that address the developmental levels and interests of individual children. Photographs and posters of children playing individually with materials support a climate for quiet play. Providing many simple units of play in this centre also conveys messages to children about play behaviours expected in this learning centre.

Children develop good attending skills and task orientation when ECEs acknowledge children's interest and involvement in the process of learning, as well as their completion of challenging tasks. When children are able to choose activities suited to their own abilities, they gradually sense the amount of time needed to begin and finish an activity. Some children need help understanding the nature of the task involved in a chosen activity. The ECE's timely guidance helps children realize that they should try to understand a task before beginning, and then plan how they will proceed.

There are times each day that should be devoted to physically active play and social learning opportunities for children to practise, for example, cooperation, sharing, turn-taking, helping others, and compromise. We know that cognitive concepts and attending skills are also gained through social and cooperative learning experiences. Collaboration with other children on activities and projects helps children experience the vast potential of human relationships in achieving goals—and acquire the knowledge that several heads are often better than one when trying to meet a challenge. The profession typically emphasizes the importance of social interaction and cooperation in learning. Young children also need to learn, however, that there is a time and place for independent play and solitary endeavours, as well as for group projects and playing with others, and some children are much more attuned than others to playing alone. The increased incidence of attention deficit hyperactivity disorder (ADHD) in young children supports the provision of quiet, individualized play environments where the child is able to practise playing alone and relying on his own resources in an environment where he is encouraged to focus on a single task for a short time and, eventually, for an extended period of time. The organized environment of the Quiet Thinking centre simplifies the choices for children, limits distractions, and supports concentrated effort on a task that allows the child to witness his own progress. Social and cooperative play experiences in other learning centres reinforce the understanding children have acquired through solitary play in this centre. Conversely, playing alone with materials prompts children to try out for themselves ideas they have observed or evolved in groups.

It is essential that the schedule encourages children to play alone for parts of the day, at activities that capture their imagination and interest; challenge them to find and depend on their own resources; learn to choose, start, follow through, and finish something; work independently for the most part; and know when to ask for help. The development of attending skills depends on a schedule that provides sufficient time for children to pursue meaningful activities: some that can be completed in one sitting and some that take longer because they are more complex. Choosing activities from alternatives offered is an important skill in itself. Children might select activities from a planning board that presents pictures or symbols of activities available in each learning centre on a given day (Casey & Lippmann, 1991; Nash, 1989). Programs should provide a balance of short, one-step activities and longer, two- and three-step or multi-step activities, some of which require children to return to them after an interruption. Between the ages of three and four, after experience with sociodramatic and organized group activities and individually with solitary activities for which there is a recognizable beginning and end, children are ready for projects that are a particularly effective way for children to practise attending and task-orientation skills in groups. Projects are featured in Chapter 18.

Outcomes Guide ECEs in Helping Children Become Effective Learners

For decades, accountability and purposeful planning were resisted. In today's political and economic climate, however, it is difficult to persuade the public and politicians of the urgency of investing public funds in programs for young children if there is no form of accountability attached to the investment. Programs that simply preach that *children learn through play*, and that focus only on social skills that prepare them for school, are unconvincing unless they provide evidence to show that children have also achieved effective learning-to-learn skills. Too many children reach grade one unable to cope with the school curriculum. A systematic approach that defines the developmental outcomes to be achieved by young children should include a clear explanation of the learning-to-learn and attending skills that children should demonstrate by the time they start grade one and how the program will help them achieve the outcomes. Outcomes clarify what young children can and should be learning; bridge preschool and primary school curriculum; and hold programs accountable for what they are teaching and for what young children are learning (Seefeldt, 2005).

The environment and the curriculum for learning are inseparable ingredients in terms of meeting explicit outcomes. ECEs need to be purposeful in their planning and in the ways they choose to intervene in children's play to ensure that developmental progress is achieved in culturally appropriate ways. Today, it is more accepted that planned opportunities for children to learn specific skills will occur, that they will be presented to children in a clear and organized fashion, that these activities will have explicit developmental objectives, and that children's achievement of the objectives while they play will be facilitated by the skilful and timely intervention of the ECEs.

Hands-on learning

Solitary play fosters persistence.

Learning-to-learn

ACTIVITIES TO PROMOTE LEARNING-TO-LEARN SKILLS FOR CHILDREN AGES THREE AND FOUR

1. Suggest that children play with formboard and jigsaw puzzles, which have clear beginnings and endings and an internal structure that dictates the steps to follow to successfully complete the activity. Have children play with specific-purpose materials, such as attribute blocks, classification kits of various kinds, seriation materials, Lotto games, and one-to-one correspondence kits; these materials provide practice in defining the task, beginning, following through, and finishing.
2. Provide a table for children to play exclusively with the simpler Workjobs kits and encourage them to "read" the labels (codes, text, and picture labels) and return the Workjobs to the

shelves after completing them. Suggest that children ask for help when they encounter challenges they cannot address alone (see Workjobs box).

WORKJOBS

Mary Baratta-Lorton's series of books called *Workjobs* and *Workjobs* II (1972 and 1979) became popular in the 1970s and 1980s because of concern for the environment and attention to recycling and protecting natural resources. Play materials made from recycled materials are popular once again because of their value in promoting learning to learn and attending skills. Workjobs are another example of specific-purpose materials, similar to those originated by Froebel and Montessori, which promote hands-on play. Each Workjob fosters specific skills and concepts. Since the early 1970s, several approaches to creating play and learning materials from recycled products, or from *beautiful junk*, have emerged. That the materials are usually homemade enhances their affordability for programs when resources are scarce. The building of a complete inventory of Workjobs is a practical way to involve parents and family members in the life of the program and to help them understand the learning that is gained by children through play.

Workjobs should occupy a special place on low shelves that are accessible to children and should be stored in individual kits with word and picture labels. Children can then see which Workjob is contained in each box or sack before removing it form the shelf. The shelves for Workjobs may be located close to an open carpeted area in the Quiet Thinking centre, where children may play with their kits on the floor and then replace them on the shelves. Some ECEs specify a time of day for all children to play with the Workjobs kits. This regularity frees ECEs to observe and to assess children's mastery of the developmental skills addressed by each kit, as well as to work individually with children on difficult or unfamiliar tasks. The designation of a time of day for Workjobs depends on whether a sufficiently large inventory of kits is available to permit plenty of choice for children.

Workjobs challenge children to develop a wide range of learning-to-learn skills necessary for effective learning through the following tasks:

- find alternative solutions to the problem presented by the Workjob;
- practise and repeat an action, persevere;
- plan, anticipate a result, and form a hypothesis;
- test the solution;
- communicate what has been done or completed;
- transfer to other activities, the learning gained by doing the Workjob;
- find the Workjob's proper place on the shelf; and
- put away the Workjob in the box as it was found.

ACTIVITIES TO PROMOTE LEARNING-TO-LEARN SKILLS FOR CHILDREN AGES FOUR TO SIX

1. Set up the Cuisenaire rods arranged in seriated order from smallest to largest, following a common baseline. Provide a second set of rods for children to try to replicate the model. Encourage children to use the rods freely to explore their properties and potential to illustrate such concepts as addition, subtraction, and fractions (part/whole relationships).
2. Challenge children to match words and pictures in photos or on cards. (See Activities in Chapters 16 and 17 for three- to six-year-olds.)
3. Set out challenging puzzles, etc., which capitalize on children's previous experience.

Summary

Chapter 15 emphasizes the role of the Quiet Thinking centre in helping children acquire the learning-to-learn skills and dispositions for learning that have a significant impact on success in school and in life. A viable curriculum for young children should address outcomes that relate to task orientation and attending, including the ability to delay gratification, use time well, block out distractions, and return to a task after an interruption. The achievement of these skills helps children become self-regulating so that they learn to think and to persist with difficult thinking challenges. To help children achieve these developmental outcomes, ECEs have to understand the rudiments of brain development and the nature of learning in the early years. The Quiet Thinking centre is specifically dedicated to encouraging children to play alone, to practise learning skills related to task orientation, attending, perseverance, and self-control, and to experience what it means to overcome obstacles in learning and use resources effectively.

Children develop conceptual understanding through their play with concrete objects, and this chapter emphasizes how specific-purpose, responsive play materials facilitate concept formation. The role of the ECE includes the provision of play activities that challenge children to develop task orientation skills, to seek help, to block out distractions, and to use time wisely. Children have individual learning styles, unique aptitudes for certain types of learning tasks, and different approaches to learning; this is especially true for children with special needs. We also know that Canadian early childhood curriculum should account for the diverse priorities of parents for the education of their children.

Learning Activities

1. Create a personal inventory of the learning-to-learn skills that you acquired during your years of schooling. Describe how you acquired these skills. Are there any learning-to-learn skills that you have not yet mastered? What factors contributed to your success and to the difficulties you experienced as a learner? Build a list of teaching practices essential to facilitating children's acquisition of learning-to-learn skills. From this list, create a checklist so you can review the play and learning environment and your curriculum plan to ensure that the activities address attending and task orientation skills, including self-control and perseverance.
2. Explain the relationship between thinking and learning-to-learn. Describe the thinking strategies that you turn to when you are confronted with an unfamiliar problem or task. Do you have a plan to develop thinking strategies that will improve your ability to solve problems and deal with complex learning challenges? Describe your plan and include it in your journal.

16 The Quiet Thinking Centre: Language, Early Literacy, and Reading

"Literacy is learning to read the world and not just the words on a page."

—Paulo Freire and Donald Macedo,
Literacy: Reading the Word and the World (1987)

Before Reading This Chapter, Have You

- considered your own literacy level and reading interests?
- explored the world of children's books?
- read stories to children and observed their questions and interests?
- evaluated the language you use when you speak with children?

Outcomes

After reading and understanding this chapter, you should be able to

- explain literacy in the context of early childhood education;
- relate symbolic play to language and literacy development;
- describe the influence of culture on literacy;
- outline the environmental factors and developmental skills that lead children to reading;
- set up play stations to promote language, literacy, and reading in the Quiet Thinking centre; and
- plan activities and units of learning to support literacy, reading, and writing in the Quiet Thinking centre.

The Nature of Language Development, Literacy, and Reading

Language development is largely a social process facilitated by interaction with others (Bruner, 1983; Doidge, 2007; Palaiologou, 2010). Language is also born in the context of caring relationships (Perry, 2010). Perceptual skills also play a large role in children's ability to read and write. Palaiologou (2010, p. 144) defines **emergent literacy** as "a set of skills, knowledge, and attitudinal precursors to formal reading and writing and the environment that supports these precursors." She identifies the following competencies linked to emergent literacy: awareness of language; conventions of print; emergent writing; phonological awareness; phoneme correspondence; attitudes that promote reading and writing, such as interacting with books; and an environment that encourages shared book reading, symbol recognition, and alphabet play. One might question, Why emphasize language, literacy, and learning to read and write in the Quiet Thinking centre when these abilities are also acquired during social interactions, warm connections with others, active outdoor play, role play, and creative exploration? One answer might be that the Quiet Thinking centre emphasizes children's development of perceptual skills (visual and auditory, in particular), their ability to use symbols, and the learning-to-learn skills crucial to literacy and reading. Perceptual skills are fostered and are more readily assessed in the relatively quiet environment of this centre.

Language Learning

Experts remain divided on whether children develop language or whether it is acquired as "grammar grows in the mind" (Chomsky, 1980, p. 134). For Noam Chomsky, whose work has had a great impact on the understanding of language, language is not something we learn (Saxton, 2010). His "language acquisition device" was viewed by some experts as an explanation that language is innate and unfolds over time. Development, however, implies learning and genetic factors. Piaget believed that it is the child's experience with things and the knowledge that the child constructs from that experience that leads to the development of language (Saxton, 2010, p. 21). There is still no definitive answer to the question of how children come to understand and use language proficiently within a few short years. Neuroscience may potentially shed more light on an evolutionary explanation of the origin of human language (Rifkin, 2009). Some research suggests that language might have evolved from primates through the exercise of hand movements in play (gesturing) and grooming (Dunbar, 1996; McNeill, 1992). The development of language may have been driven, not by an innate, universal grammar, but by bodily gestures, grooming, and play that led to "gossip" and ultimately to language. McNeill (1992) found that gestures and language develop together and that speech is usually accompanied by hand movements, facial expressions, and bodily gestures.

Whitehead (2010, pp. 46–50) outlines four conventional views of children's language learning:

1. Behaviourist: All behaviours, including language, are learned through imitation of parents and caregivers, who provide positive reinforcement.
2. Cognitive: Language development and acquisition are part of the general intellectual abilities associated with cognitive development (Piaget and Vygotsky).

Language is the product of general human cognitive abilities and interaction between children and their surrounding environments; the storage and retrieval of linguistic information is similar to the storage and retrieval of other knowledge. Language comprehension, usage, and creativity rely on cognitive abilities similar to those used in non-linguistic tasks. The more we understand the development of language, the more we understand the human mind (Lesman, 2011).

3. Nativist: Humans are programmed to learn language due to innate and universal language-specific abilities hard-wired into the brain. Noam Chomsky (1972) proposed a "language acquisition device" (LAD) and a "universal grammar," whereby children deduce the structure of language from exposure to it.
4. Social interactionist: This view emphasizes the social purposes for language, which gives incentive to children to learn language so that they can participate in a social group (Bruner, 1983).

Language Development

Children construct their understanding of language in the first few months of life, long before they actually use formal language. At about 15 to 18 months of age, children begin to combine two actions in their play and to use two-word sentences, for example, "Mommy go" (Palaiologou, 2010, p. 142). The most concentrated period of language development occurs between ages two and five, when children master the sounds of their own language and those of others in their communities. An understanding of the syntax of language usually occurs by age five; by age six, language development slows and focuses on learning new words and their meanings, until age 12, when vocabulary development also slows.

Early language development is linked to the child's understanding of symbols, demonstrated by her ability to use one object to stand for another, a skill that develops very early. Symbolic thinking is linked to the child's developing ability to understand that letters stand for sounds and that words and names represent things, people, and feelings. Language development depends on social interaction and active play in an environment rich in opportunities to interact with things. As soon as children understand that objects have an existence independent of their own capacity to see and touch them, they begin to acquire the ability to use objects as symbols. Using blocks to create a tower, running a block along the carpet as if it were a vehicle, and drawing a square with a triangle on top to represent a house are early examples of the ability to use symbols. Through play with concrete materials, children are challenged to find the words they need to communicate what they are doing with things. The role of play in language learning cannot be overestimated. The earliest type of symbolic play begins when children imitate remembered events, about the same time as they begin to acquire language, during the second year. Dramatic play becomes increasingly complex throughout the preoperational period, and language and dramatic play develop simultaneously, since they both involve symbolic thinking. As children progress from simple imitations of single events to complex dramatizations of familiar episodes from everyday life, often involving several roles, they develop the ability to use language that is more elaborate and to communicate effectively. Pretend play and language involve symbolic representation as children use words as well as objects and actions to represent other things or events. Johnson, Christie, and Wardle (2005, pp. 138–139) state that sociodramatic play requires children to use the "lexical" and "syntactical" features of language to evolve a play episode. The script that accompanies it strengthens their representational competence and helps children acquire the skills they need to understand and use **decontextualized language**, which conveys meaning independently of context.

Humans pass through similar stages in their language development but ultimately develop their own language styles. Language learning has four main parts: **phonology**, which pertains to the production of sound; syntax, which involves the rules by which words are put together into sentences; **semantics**, which relates words to reality and intended meanings; and **pragmatics**, which refers to the rules of effective communication in a given context (Hughes, 1995). Children are influenced by the rhythm, accent, and pace of the language models close to them, and they pick up sloppy language habits related to syntax, use of the vernacular, imprecise use of words, and poor enunciation when that is what they hear in the environment. We know that when adults model the correct syntax and pronunciation of words so that children hear language correctly, children make progress; if they hear unclear or distorted models of speech, their language learning is impeded. Children do not learn language by being corrected by adults. Their ability to understand the construction and rules of language develops over time and through a series of stages. Even though they hear and understand the language used by adults, they continue to use their own constructions. We all recall times when we have tried to correct children's language by repeating a sentence using proper syntax:

Child: I don't gots my mittens.
ECE: You don't have your mittens?
Child: Yes, Jamie have gots my mittens.

Children acquire the grammatical structure of their language in a predictable developmental order, which some theorists believe is closely related to the child's level of cognitive development (Berko Gleason, 1989). Piaget (1955 [1926]) believed that children always have the language they need to express what they are capable of thinking at any stage. Kamii (1972) emphasized the importance of stimulating thinking and general cognitive growth to promote language development. Vygotsky (1978) stressed the importance of language as a vehicle of social interaction and, unlike Piaget, believed that language is central to thinking and cognitive development in general. Bruner (1983) stressed that language development depends on rich social learning environments and on plenty of opportunities for cognitive growth. Pinker (2007) refers to language as "the stuff of thought" that enables the child to be a full participant in active, **experiential learning** in a well-planned environment that facilitates language and literacy. ECEs witness every day the powerful influence of social play in large and small groups on children's use of syntax, learning of new words, and the ease with which they pick up the language of pop culture.

Language and the Use of Symbols

Learning to use language depends on the child's ability to use symbols and engage in symbolic thinking. As children become verbal, around age two, they are interested in language and learn to use letters for sounds and words to represent things and, eventually, intentions and meanings. Young children usually learn language more easily than they acquire abstract logical concepts. The language learning process involves the symbolic task of associating letters with sounds and words with meanings. An environment rich in materials for symbolic play is therefore important to language development. This process is different from learning abstract concepts, which involves understanding relationships that often cannot be seen. Both types of learning require times when children are encouraged to focus on an activity and interact individually with materials. The Quiet Thinking centre provides play opportunities whereby children can work independently with literacy materials such puzzles; magnetic letter boards; feltboards; books; and a host of other materials that support language and early reading. Although language learning is addressed in all learning centres, the Quiet Thinking centre helps children acquire the perceptual abilities associated with language, especially visual and listening abilities; the learning of language symbols; and an appreciation of books and the power of words.

The Meaning of Literacy

The development of literacy begins in infancy and is intensified long before children go to school, especially when parents read to their children from infancy. Literacy is not acquired through skill and practice; it is more deeply ingrained and comprehensive (Jalongo, Fennimore, & Stamp, 2004, p. 62). Literacy is a manifestation of one's experience in society and one's perception of the environment and the self in the environment. Many kinds of literacies influence an individual's relationship with the society in which he lives, for example, musical, computer, cultural, media, environmental, and global literacy all define our interactions with our world.

ECEs should not only be knowledgeable about many types of literacy, but also sensitized to the cultural priorities of families from diverse backgrounds whose goals for their children are culturally biased and whose experiences of the world differ widely. To support literacy, ECEs have to find and construct a *common language* among children that accounts for the experiences that have influenced children's lives and identities, which may have alienated children from the broader community in which they now live, and which reflect the ways in which children live their lives outside of the school or program (Jalongo et al., 2004).

Language and Literacy in a Culturally Diverse Society

Language and literacy learning in Canadian ECE programs are more complex than in homogeneous societies where one language predominates. In our diverse nation, literacy means different things to people of diverse cultures, and literacy is closely related to **home language**. The first language of a growing majority of children in many Canadian urban centres is neither English nor French. The term **transitional literacy** describes the characteristics of the learning process children go through in adding another first language to the language they learn and use in the home (Barone, Mallette, & Hong Xu, 2005).

Newcomers to Canada believe that when children retain their home language, they retain their "membership in the ethnic culture" and are able to communicate with immediate and extended family members (Chumak-Horbatsch, 2010, p. 19). Cultures that emphasize extended family connections and celebrations expose children to emotionally based relationships with a wider range of individuals, each with their own stories and perspectives to share with the children. In cultures that value extracurricular participation in sports activities, music lessons, gymnastics, or ballet, for example, children experience literacy challenges in more structured and prescriptive contexts. Some First Nations value environmental knowledge and the ability to meet physical and resource-based challenges. Some cultures promote a literacy related to spiritual fulfillment, the attainment of inner serenity, and peaceful and respectful coexistence. Literacy goals are culturally bound, and literacy levels in children should be measured according to the priorities of each child's culture of origin as well as by the standards relevant to the broader culture in which they live. Challenges arise when children are transported from one set of cultural priorities to an unfamiliar culture that makes new demands on their skills and perspectives but does little to bridge the distance between the literacy valued by their culture of origin and the new culture into which they have been thrust. ECEs work with families to build cultural bridges for children and ensure that assessments of children's literacy factor in the cultural contexts in which they live. Developing a common culture within the program that is supported by the bridges built between the home and the school—by communication with children about the values and contributions made by each child to the group and by inventing, collaboratively, a set of common values, assumptions, and understandings—creates a richly textured playroom culture. From this common culture, literacies emerge that embrace the input of each child and each cultural group represented.

Home Language

Experts in language learning now advocate that children should be encouraged to retain their home language while learning another first language (English or French) within their programs and schools. Young children tend to acquire language skills in their home language and then transfer what they have learned in their home language to learning the **other first language (OFL)**. Encouraging children to continue to use their home language, at home and at school, allows them to capitalize on their level of language learning in their home language. Because language and thought are so closely intertwined, any interruption in the use of home language while the child is learning a new language not only results in a child's inability to communicate effectively but also inhibits the development of the cognitive thinking processes ripe for development in early childhood.

Bilingual children who actively use more than one language experience cognitive and social advantages (Chumak-Horbatsch, 2010). Communication and language include body language, gestures, facial expression, and movement, as well as verbal language, and children bring their own experience of language in their homes and communities to the preschool and kindergarten setting (Scottish Consultative Council on Curriculum, 1999, p. 15). So another reason to value and encourage home language is to ensure that children are able to respond confidently to others, to state their needs and thoughts, and to express their feelings in their home language. Practices like this expose all children in the program to other languages, while also emphasizing their development of competence in English or French. Planning a curriculum for language and literacy development that includes the home languages of the children, as well as English or French, calls for close collaboration with parents and the careful monitoring of the language of learning in the program. Curriculum outcomes and objectives for activities should readily accommodate children's reliance on home language by importing songs, music, stories, rhymes, and finger plays of their own culture and by providing opportunities for them to converse with adults who speak their language. Allen et al. (2006) suggested that ECEs who speak the home languages of children in the program should introduce new concepts in the child's home language and encourage parents to reinforce these concepts at home.

Learning a Second Language in Early Childhood

The critical period for learning language is between infancy and age eight and puberty, when both first and second languages are processed in the same part of the brain. Because the brain map is dominated by the language of the child's culture, and because culture changes our cognitive architecture, second languages are processed more easily in the same part of the brain as the first language. After this critical period, second languages are not processed in the same part of the brain as the native language (Doidge, 2007). Recent research supports the advantages of learning more than one language during early childhood, and suggests that bilingual children demonstrate more "cognitive flexibility" (Lesman, 2011, p. 26). Doidge (2007) claimed that children who learn two or more languages during the critical period and subsequently become bilingual store all the sounds of the languages they have learned in one single large centre of the brain. The ability to learn a second language without an accent after puberty is also limited.

Cummins (2003) stated that there are three types of language proficiency that children should achieve in order to master the language of the dominant culture. These are conversational fluency, which allows children to communicate; discrete language skills, such as alphabet, decoding skills, spelling patterns, and grammatical rules; and academic language, which includes the finer points of tense, style, and reading comprehension. Although some claim that young children do not learn languages any more effortlessly than do adults (Soto, 1991), it appears that the earlier children start to learn another language, the more proficient they will eventually become. A second language should be learned naturally, in an authentic context. And what children learn in one language transfers to the other language they are learning.

Literacy Depends on Experience

Empowering children includes giving a voice and an identity to children whose experience outside the home and the school is limited and enabling them to find ways to lead, influence others, display their unique talents, and have their own "moments in the sunshine." Recent movements away from the deficit model no longer see children as cognitively deficient if they are not reading by grade one; we recognize that the development of reading and literacy originates long before children are involved in formal schooling. (Sulzby & Teale, 2003). This understanding underlines the importance of creating a playroom culture that embraces the language abilities and literacy of all children and involves them in projects that reflect their daily life and their collective exploration of the neighbourhood and beyond.

In addition to ensuring that the playroom is a microcosm of the larger world outside, children whose experience of the world is relatively narrow have a greater need to get out into the community and to gain experience beyond the preschool or kindergarten. Technologies offer an opportunity for virtual experience of the outside world in addition to actual excursions to the local library, museums and other destinations on a regular basis. Concerted efforts should be made to recognize the contributions of the child whose experiences and reach within the community have been limited and to integrate them fully into the playroom culture, where they are able to assume significant roles and leadership opportunities and are encouraged to talk about experiences that occur in class each day. Jalongo et al. (2004) cautioned that

> Every single skill or approach that can enhance literacy abilities in children can be interrupted or rendered ineffective by low expectations and negative attitudes toward children.... [ECEs] must work with diligence to create and enhance positive conceptualizations of all young children that lead to what is always possible—recognition of the current strengths and abilities of the child, and the opening of opportunity for future growth and development. (Jalongo et al., 2004, p. 68)

The Role of Perceptual Skills in Language and Reading

Most developmental skills related to language learning and reading involve sensory perception. Visual and auditory perception are especially vital to fluency in both verbal and written language and, later, reading. Language learning is influenced by hearing the language of others, and by imitating and practising it, but it is also a visual learning task, in which printed words and spoken words are accessible visually as children look at text and watch the movement of the lips and mouth as words are spoken. Language is usually received through the eyes and ears, but it also may be tactilely received, as in the case of Braille for persons who are blind or visually impaired. The later ability to read also depends on a complex network of physical and cognitive perceptual skills (see Appendix A) that children practise as they acquire basic language abilities. The value of singing and rhyme in language acquisition should not be underestimated. Songs sung and rhymes chanted by children enhance the resonance of syllables and words, stimulate the memory of sounds and phrases, sharpen the meaning of language as it is affected by tone and register, and provide a wonderful opportunity for fun with words.

Helping Children Acquire Perceptual Skills for Language and Reading

The Quiet Thinking centre relies, for the most part, on play with a rich mix of specific-purpose and open-ended materials that children explore individually and collaboratively. Children's acquisition of the perceptual skills related to language, literacy, and reading is facilitated by play with materials and activities that address specific abilities. ECEs are active observers in the Quiet Thinking centre, monitoring children's perceptual progress and ensuring that there are no gaps in children's play experiences with the perceptual materials. As always, the ECE assumes a non-intrusive but active role in modifying activities to make them more interesting to children who may have avoided an earlier version of an activity, or by finding new ways to interest a child in an activity that involves eye–hand coordination at the cutting table, or identifying sounds at the listening table. Small-group activities may be planned that involve guessing the direction from which sounds are coming or identifying the sources of sounds; playing I Spy; following the text or pictures from left to right in a book, on a poster, or screen; responding to auditory cues related to directional positioning; perceiving differences and similarities in sounds and tones; and moving the eyes from one target to another. All children should experience opportunities to practise the full range of auditory and visual perceptual skills, and instances where a child may need more intervention and encouragement should be noted. When a child experiences ongoing difficulty with perceptual activities, the child should be referred for additional support and intervention.

Technology can be a useful tool to help ECEs determine where children may be experiencing gaps in their perceptual abilities and to provide practice that is play-based and fun for children, even if it is of the two-dimensional kind. Well-designed software is available for children aged three and up that engages their perceptual abilities while they have fun with games that improve a wide range of perceptual skills related to reading and writing. Play with software-based activities on a computer or Leapster may provide practice and foster learning, although it should not replace or predominate over play with concrete objects in the three-dimensional world.

Learning to Read

Understanding exactly how a child learns to read, that is, the steps and the order of learning and the integration of many factors, is a little like trying to unravel the mysteries of language learning. It is difficult and unwise, therefore, to assume that all children learn to read in a set order and following specific techniques because the particular combination of life circumstances, enrichment opportunities, direct teaching, perceptual abilities, language development, life experience, and a host of other factors influence children's early reading capabilities.

Interest in reading starts as soon as children are read to and introduced to the world of print, literature, and graphics. When all forms of language and communication are valued and supported by the environment, children will be interested in trying to read long before they are exposed to formal reading instruction. The learning environment should promote a culture of respect and enjoyment of reading in many contexts. Children of other cultures should see their home language reflected in the language arts area using posters, books, and signs that include words familiar to them. Children's early efforts to read should be encouraged and valued on their own merit; these early attempts do not have to match adult expectations of "good reading."

Learning to read is not a linear process, and one approach does not fit all children. Many elements and influences are incorporated in any instance of learning to read (Jalongo et al., 2004). The act of reading includes fluent processing and coordination of word recognition, understanding of the text, contextualizing of the content, identifying the nature of the composition—whether it is rhyme, poetry, narrative, or direct speech—and the rhythm of the words as they appear on the page. Reading, as in decoding any system of symbols, involves the **semiotic function**, which is the ability to obtain meaning from words, pictures, musical tones, or gestures. The act of reading is more art than science, and the teaching of reading challenges ECEs to be alert and sensitive to the myriad ingredients that contribute to effective reading in children.

Children's ability to read emerges in a natural way when they hear language often, are encouraged to use language to express themselves, and are exposed to a supportive and literate environment—one rich in print, stories, and song—at home and in the preschool and kindergarten programs. A key ingredient for learning to read is literacy learning, which must be built into the playroom culture. Early readers—children who read fluently at four and five years of age—have usually integrated many types of life experiences; have mastered learning-to-learn skills and specific perceptual, physical, social, and cognitive skills; and are motivated by a desire to be part of the reading culture. Early reading is influenced by development in all domains, not just cognitive. Factors that lead to reading include adults' reading to children from the first year of life; casual and frequent conversation with children about meaningful events and things that matter in their lives; exposing children to a wide range of cultural, family, and community events; broadening children's reach within the neighbourhood and society in which they live; and modelling to children a love of literature and the joys of being able to access information and ideas from books, rhymes, and songs.

Play with language through verse and poetry, and with language learning materials such as puzzles, lotto games, magnetic letters, flannelboards, and books of all kinds, expose children to the world of letters, words, sounds, symbols, and meaning. A program that emphasizes literacy learning that is culturally based and emphasizes learning to "read the world," is more likely to produce eager readers (Freire & Macedo, 1987). Neuman and Roskos (1994) proposed three rules for helping children learn to read: (1) understand how literacy can be useful to children; (2) use literacy creatively to help children construct new understanding; and (3) use literacy to facilitate interactions with others. An important ingredient in learning to read is having regular, meaningful, rich conversations with children about things that matter to them and in which they are fully engaged—instead of *telling* children, giving instructions, asking short-answer questions, and using pat phrases. Early readers have nearly always been exposed to literate adults who have, themselves, a strong command of language, and who raise questions that require more than short answers, who provide full answers to children's questions, and who speak in a way that challenges children to reach for understanding.

© Jim West / Alamy

Link language symbols to pictures.

Learning to read, like learning a new language, depends, to a great extent, on total immersion in the culture of the language and a literacy culture; it is also influenced by their relationships with others and the emotional climate in which children are read to. The contribution of visual and auditory perceptual development is fundamental to learning the mechanics and techniques of reading as children detect figure from ground, scan sentences for meaning as they also decipher words, move eyes smoothly from left to right across the page, and sound out combinations of syllables as they strive for word recognition. Symbolic thinking plays a role as children integrate the notion of storyline and script in evolving their sociodramatic play episodes and transfer this skill to reading a story for themselves.

Reading depends on the richness of a child's vocabulary and is usually a factor of exposure to words through conversation and in the context of physical activity of some kind. Reading also depends on language learning that emphasizes syntax, which involves the ability to combine words correctly to form sentences and paragraphs that are meaningful and clear. Learning the pragmatics of conversation, such as when to speak, when to refrain from speaking to allow someone else to speak, and how to tailor what we say and how we say it to the target audience, also contributes to a child's growing ability to read, especially when reading dialogue. Physical activity and challenges not only support the mastery of perceptual skills but also provide balance in the day for children who find it difficult to sit still long enough to read. Emotional stability, and the sense that one is cherished and protected, give the child the courage to release himself to the adventures and surprises found in reading books and poems. Undoubtedly, learning to read is much more than drill and practice of the language arts; reading engages all developmental domains (as well as the imagination and the spirit) and brings about a sense of wonder about the mysteries of the world and the courage to explore, risk, and understand more. If children are taught the principles related to the reading process, they will discern much of the rest and rely on their own cognitive resources to unpack the text (Resnick & Hall, 1998). There are, however, specific, identifiable skills to be taught, which include the ability to infer the meanings as well as all the visual and auditory physical perceptual and cognitive processing skills that enable children to decode the text (Table 16–1).

The key to teaching reading appears to be *balance*, that is, the blending of several program elements and the inclusion of phonics and literature in the reading program. The ECE needs to understand the contributions of language and linguistics, including phonology, semantics, syntax, and pragmatics. They have to understand motivations to read and how to establish the right emotional climate for reading, as well as, how to stretch them to try reading beyond their comfort levels. They should facilitate discussion among children about the reading they have engaged in and listen actively to the children's discussion in order to know what they understand (Calfee & Hendrick, 2004). An important element is the ECE's knowledge of each child's literacy and language levels, and her ability to adapt reading instruction to individual needs for emotional support, motivation, and assistance with language development.

Learning to Write

Children who read early are usually inclined to write early. As with reading, their ability to write emerges when they are immersed in a world of print, books, signs, posters, and materials that foster symbolic play. The environment encourages children to write, just as it does to read, and it helps when ECEs treat children as writers who have important things to say. When children see models of writing and understand that writing is another form of communication, they are usually eager to

TABLE 16–1

SENSORY-PERCEPTUAL SKILLS RELATED TO LANGUAGE AND READING

Visual Skills—Physical

Form discrimination

Recognize basic form and shape.
Recognize similarities and differences in simple one- and two-dimensional forms and shapes.
Recognize shape symbols in the environment.
Understand shape constancy.

Depth perception

Accurately judge distance and height.

Figure–ground perception

Select a figure from a detailed picture or poster.
Find small objects or creatures in illustrated books.
Look at only one part of a picture at a time and ignore other areas.
Shift attention from one part of a picture to another or from one detail to another.

Ocular Motor Skills

Adjust near-far focusing (accommodation).
Move eyes from one target to another (fixation).
Follow a moving target without moving the head (pursuit).
Track or use the eyes to make a series of long sweeps (saccades) smoothly across a page, board, or screen (tracking).

Visual Skills—Cognitive

Identify and label objects seen.
Identify similarities and differences.
Match similar objects.
Identify an object when only part is revealed.
Identify familiar objects from pictures.
Pick out small details in a visual field.

Auditory Skills—Physical

Recognize sound sources.
Listen to auditory clues.
Hear differences and similarities in sounds and tones.
Detect one tonal quality from an auditory field.
Detect auditory figure-from-ground sounds (i.e., background from foreground sounds).
Hear repeated patterns of sound and silence.
Execute well-timed responses to auditory cues.

Auditory Skills—Cognitive

Identify and label sounds.
Focus on a sound and attend to it.
Link what is heard to its source.
Interpret sounds.
Match sounds according to similarities.
Differentiate musical notes: high/low; harsh/soft.
Identify where a sound is coming from (direction).
Follow the sound.
Follow verbal instructions.

try their own version of writing. Talking to children about their writing encourages their interest, as does talking to them about their drawing (Hughes & Ellis, 1998). Children's interest is enhanced when they can form letters and symbols and when they understand that writing allows them to capture a thought or an idea forever and pass it on to others. Cultures that value the written word and fluency in writing have a long tradition of encouraging children to write at an early age and believe it enhances reading, symbolic thinking, and representation.

Writing using computers will be addressed in Chapter 18. There is no denying the fascination children have for computers as tools for their "productions," and to experiment with creative design, writing, and problem solving. High quality software provides practice with number and letter symbol recognition, responds to auditory and visual prompts, and provides practice of many perceptual abilities. While it may be difficult to attract boys to the cutting activities that help them develop the hand control, ocular-motor skills, and depth perception needed for writing, many boys will line up for a chance to use a software program that focuses on these skills but that happens to take the form of an exciting computer game.

Organization and Design of the Quiet Thinking Centre

The Quiet Thinking centre contains a reading area, including book shelves and a cozy place to curl up with a book; a tabletop play area; a sensory exploration or display table; and an area for play with specific-purpose materials (see Figure 16–1). A writing station (perhaps a desk) equipped with various types of paper, cards, envelopes, pads, staplers, paperclips, and hole punchers, along with implements for writing, such as pencils, pens, markers, chalk, and chalkboards may also be included in this centre (and may be replicated in the Project centre). Resources such as picture files and photo albums may be placed on shelves or on the display table. Where space allows, this centre also includes a listening table, or a potential play space where the audio equipment borrowed from the Project centre can be set up along with the earphones. All play stations in this learning centre encourage individual involvement and quiet behaviours, but it is important to be flexible, as there may be times when ECEs want, for example, to encourage a collaborative activity with word games or books, or to encourage children to talk about the things they find in the picture file. Sometimes children simply enjoy collaborating in using the flannelboard and felts while telling or reading a story. Materials in the Quiet Thinking centre should be labelled with pictures and words to reinforce the use of letters and word symbols, and to model the functional value of written language, drawings, and other symbols of everyday living. In keeping with the intention to reinforce home language in the classroom, the centre should feature signs and word symbols in the home languages of the children represented in the group.

Equipment, Materials, and Supplies

- **Equipment:** bookshelves consisting of a regular bookshelf and a display rack for books; carpet; large cushions/beanbag chair, a desk, adult rocking chair or armchair, and child-sized rocking chair; storage shelves and rack for puzzles; chairs and two tables; magnetic board; chalkboard; table for listening equipment (recording devices, CD player, and headphones)

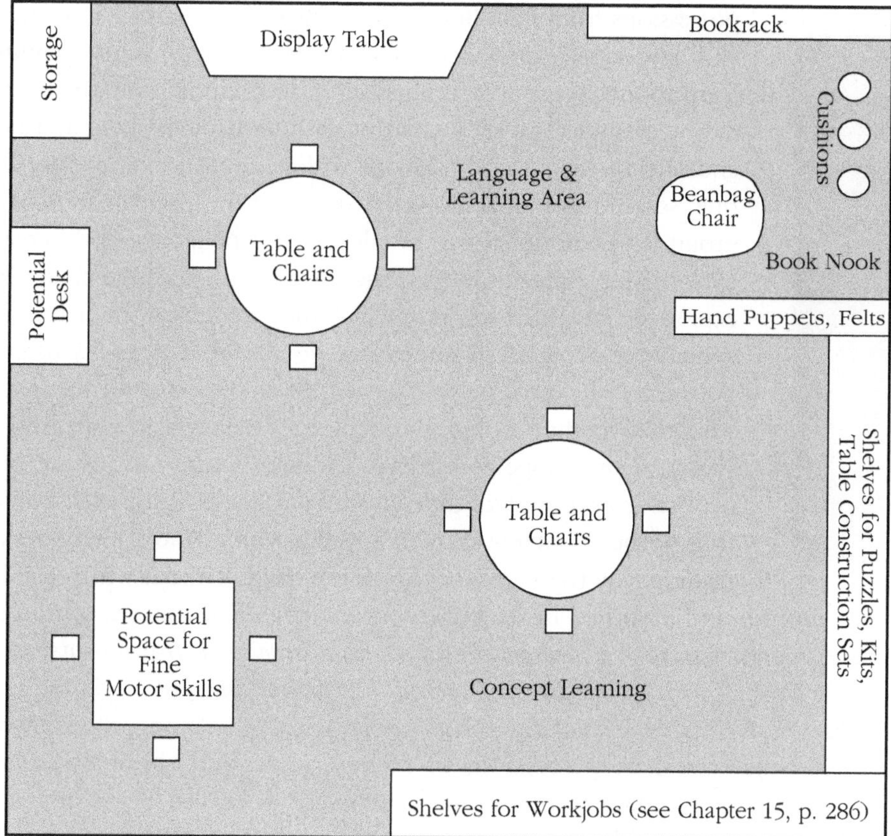

Figure 16-1 The Quiet Thinking centre

- **Literacy materials:** early reading materials, including picture books, storybooks in languages representing the cultural composition of the group, child-made books, activity books, and visual-discrimination books with detailed illustrations; picture files; photo albums; felt books; clipboards, flannelboard, and felt pieces; posters; letter and number sets; magnetic board and magnetic letters; small flip chart stand; formboard and jigsaw puzzles; textured fabric kits; lotto, card, and board games; picture blocks; language-based Workjobs; audio cassettes and CDs
- **Thinking materials:** sets of modular materials for classification, seriation, number, and conservation; part–whole kits; dominoes; pegboards and pegs; beads and strings; sequence sets; parquetry tiles; people pieces; pattern, attribute, tabletop, and nesting blocks; centimetre and colour cubes; counting chips; Cuisenaire rods; Tinkertoy and Lego sets; abacus; beakers and cups; dolls; rings; and sorting sets
- **Supplies:** crayons, pencils, pens, pencil crayons, felt-tipped markers (water-based and non-toxic), paper, chalk, string or cord, brads, (for making books), cardboard, and Bristol board; notepads, invitation cards, order forms, bills

Play Stations in the Quiet Thinking Centre

Book Nook

Beautiful books transport children to another world, even when they are simply looking at pictures, feeling the shiny pages, tracing around shapes, and softly caressing a book's beautiful cover. For many people, well-worn books are the most treasured

Maya "reading" to her "children."

possessions from childhood. Books provide a sensory, intellectual, and emotional experience for children. Through books, children learn about experiences, events, and places remote from themselves. Sitting snuggled up on a chair or cushion while looking at a book and letting their minds drift provides relief from the daily routine, solace from an anxious day, respite from the demands of the group, and emotional and intellectual escape into a world created by someone else. Books feed the imagination and free children to explore an imagined world in which they are the centre of attention and able to accomplish something wonderful. The ability to enjoy books, and to read, helps children develop *vision* and to imagine what they might become, the challenges they will attempt, and the successes they hope to achieve. Children's early visions are often derived from the ideas they glean from books and the marvellous feats of the characters in the books they enjoy. Above all, books and reading feed the *rich inner life* of the child, without which children become anxious and absorbed in temporary issues, mundane concerns, and petty details. *Children who learn to love books and the freedom of spirit they provide, receive a precious boost for a rich inner life and mental health that may last a lifetime.*

Literacy is facilitated by talking about books with and among children; this encourages them to share perceptions of themes, plots, and characters, and to expand their understanding of the meanings inherent in books. These interactive experiences that focus on books are essential to literacy development because they provide common topics for conversation and the pragmatics of discourse. Books introduce ideas for sociodramatic play episodes and for projects, expand children's repertoire of second-hand experience obtained through books, and inform and instruct. The book nook should be a place where a child may read, look at a book, or talk to another child about a book, with or without an adult present. As children discover that another child has extracted a meaning, theme, or message from a book that had escaped them, they become aware that people have various perspectives and that they notice and value different things. These collaborative experiences contribute to theory of mind (which involves understanding one's own and other people's thoughts and feelings) and help children learn that people differ in their perspectives on values, knowledge, events, and issues (Ormrod, 2006).

LOCATION OF THE BOOK NOOK

The book nook is best located in a comfortable corner created by two adjoining dividers to provide some privacy and seclusion from the tabletop play areas of the Quiet Thinking centre. If the area is large enough, it can include an upholstered chair, a rocking chair with cushions, or a beanbag chair to allow children to curl up with the books. Pretty, bright cushion covers and a washable quilt or knitted blanket add colour and warmth to this corner. This is prime space in which to introduce the fabric patterns and textures of other cultures. Framed prints, posters, or paintings on the wall in the book nook stretch the mind and spirit and are visual reminders that this is also a place for dreaming, imagining, and thinking. Works of art from many cultures broaden children's understanding of what is beautiful and rich in potential for discovery and learning.

The bookshelves house two kinds of books: one may house the program's collection of books, with spines facing outward on a bookrack that may display up to

30 attractive books at children's eye level; these may change weekly. ECEs should replace torn, dirty books and those with pages missing because books that have been well cared for encourage respect for the books and their careful handling. Books should be shelved by category. The variety and type of books will depend on the ages of the children. Younger children mainly enjoy picture books with large print and illustrations that feature human and animal families; colours; shapes; pop-up pictures; number and letter symbols; familiar nursery rhymes; popular characters; and familiar landscapes, such as farms, the countryside, and cities. Older children's favourite storybooks should always be on the shelves, as well as a weekly selection of new or theme-oriented books to spark children's interest. Stories written in the home languages of the children should be placed prominently.

ECEs should clarify and model certain behaviours when they introduce children to the Book Nook. These behaviours include washing sticky or paint-covered hands before looking at a book, turning the pages carefully, replacing the book on the rack when finished, and holding the books properly so as not to bend the cover or break the binding. Children need to be shown how books should be held by pointing out the often fragile binding that holds the pages together, and by encouraging children to feel the pages so they understand that they may tear easily unless handled gently. Modelling respect for books reinforces the relationship between books and new learning, and between books and the world of ideas and imagination. Hopefully, books for children will never be replaced by e-readers.

The careful selection of books to support special themes or occasions helps to integrate the Book Nook into the learning environment. For example, when children are learning about road safety, it is useful to have books on that topic available in the book nook. Flannelboards and felt cutouts representing familiar characters from children's favourite books encourage children to tell stories based on those they have heard, and those they have *read*. Children should always have access to the flannelboard and felts in this area once they have been introduced to their proper care and handling, so as to dramatize, using the felts, a favourite story.

SELECTING CHILDREN'S LITERATURE FOR THE BOOK NOOK

The role of children's literature in promoting symbolic play, particularly sociodrama, was addressed in Chapter 11. The benefits of children's literature in fostering an appreciation of reading; a love of literature; an aesthetic appreciation of language, including other languages; and stimulation of the imagination are inestimable. Children should be involved with books from infancy. An important factor in stimulating a love of literature is choosing good books for children that capture their imagination and provide fascination, a taste of discovery and adventure, fodder for dreaming, and precious insights. Books of rhymes and poetry should be prominently featured as another example of a form of literature and language, and to enhance children's appreciation of the cadence and rhythm of words, their rhyming characteristics, and the use of **onomatopoeia** (words formed from a sound associated with the item being named, e.g., *crack, boom, sizzle*) in rhymes and poetry.

Fromberg (1995) suggests the following criteria for choosing books for young children:

- the characters should have integrity, should be believable, and should be real enough for children to identify with them;
- the characters should have wholesome, human relationships in a wide range of cultural contexts;

- the book should address egalitarian values related to gender roles, culture, race, sexual orientation, and ethnicity;
- there should be a satisfying ending;
- the content should be significant and may be playful;
- the book should use language beautifully and correctly in whatever language it is written;
- each book should have just one story; and
- illustrations should be integrated with the text and should be aesthetically appealing.

The book nook contributes to children's literacy as well as language learning and early reading. This play station in the Quiet Thinking centre should include many resources, such as photo albums, picture files, children's magazines, and posters, that bring the outside world into the centre and motivate children to explore, ask questions, and talk to each other. These resources should be updated frequently and address the changing seasons and celebratory events that appeal to children, respond to program themes, and provide ideas for projects that arise from stories and poems. The picture file is a particularly rich resource for stimulating language development; promoting conversation among children; and introducing them to creatures, places, events, and phenomena that lie outside their individual experience. It is also an ideal vehicle for promoting cultural awareness and affirming the cultural affiliations of all children in the group by providing photos of places or countries where some of the children were born, and maps showing the locations of places important to the children.

Gross and Ortiz (1994, p. 32) promote the practice of using children's literature to "develop positive attitudes toward people with disabilities and to encourage positive peer relationships among children of differing abilities." ECEs should review books carefully before reading them to children to ensure that the messages are accurate and reflect positive attitudes, which include portraying people with disabilities as competent and independent, emphasizing their commonalities with all children, describing them respectfully, and evoking children's empathy.

ACTIVITIES IN THE BOOK NOOK FOR CHILDREN AGES TWO TO FOUR

1. Provide props, such as teddy bears, stuffed animals, dolls, crowns, and scarves, that relate to a new book on the shelves. Children may use or wear the props while reading the new book.
2. Include a flannelboard with felt characters representing the characters of favourite books, or of a new book. Encourage children to tell the story using the felt characters after the story has been read or while looking at the storybook.
3. Talk with children about the characters in the book and what they like or dislike about them.

ACTIVITIES IN THE BOOK NOOK FOR CHILDREN AGES FOUR TO SIX

1. Set up a book-repair shop in the Creative Arts centre or in the Project centre (Chapter 18). Remove all damaged books from the shelves and racks. Show children how to wipe finger marks off pages with a damp cloth or how to repair torn pages and binding with glue. Reinforce the importance of caring for books and of repairing those that still have potential. Support the idea that books are precious possessions.

2. Provide an informal story time every day. Later in the year, choose a story that is serialized (i.e., read over three or four story-reading sessions) to promote attending skills and enjoyment of more complex literature, to build anticipation, and to develop memory.
3. Include children's magazines, such as *Owl, Chickadee, Turtle,* and *Children's Digest,* on the bookracks. Introduce children to the concept of magazine subscriptions and address new topics with each new edition.
4. Encourage children to bring photographs, maps, or pictures from magazines, or books from home, to add to the picture file. Laminate the pictures or engage the children in inserting the pictures in an album to place on the book rack.
5. Talk with children about a book they have just read, or read recently, and imagine another ending for the book. Ask them to change a key event in the story, which leads to a different conclusion.

Language Learning Area

The language play station should provide two tables with chairs, specific-purpose materials, modular materials, small construction materials, storage shelves for puzzles, a theme table, possibly a chalkboard and chalk, a magnetic board on a stand, and a puppet theatre. The resources and activities should address a wide range of emergent reading skills and visual-perceptual abilities fundamental to speaking, listening, reading, and writing. Where space allows, provide a desk with two chairs, with graphic tools, such as felt-tipped markers, crayons, pencils, and chalk and a chalkboard; various sizes and types of paper, index cards, and file boxes; writing folders for each child; and materials for making books.

Sometimes referred to as the tabletop area, the language arts area provides materials that introduce children to letters and words, and promote visual-perceptual abilities. Tabletop construction toys, such as Lego, Tinkertoy, pegboards, and table blocks, foster development of spatial concepts, figure–ground perception, depth perception, left-to-right progression, scanning, visual tracking, and other visual skills. The many kits, baskets, and bins containing modular, specific-purpose, and construction materials in this area require efficient, easily accessed storage space. Storage units with compartments are useful, as are movable storage shelves and cupboards, which may serve as boundaries for the language learning area.

Children benefit from play that promotes access to concrete symbols, such as letters, shapes, pictures, and three-dimensional objects. Children should be encouraged to construct their own symbols of objects using tabletop blocks and interlocking materials. They need time to explore letter and word symbols through their senses, for example, by copying or tracing felt letters in books, or by printing letter symbols on salt or sand trays. The language learning play station teaches children to recognize and interpret sounds and letter symbols, to link language symbols to pictures, and to enjoy printing and creating books. To absorb the full impact of books and other literacy materials, children need to concentrate in a relatively quiet environment where they may individually explore the play and learning materials.

ACTIVITIES IN THE LANGUAGE LEARNING AREA FOR CHILDREN AGES TWO TO FOUR

1. Set up magnetic letters and numbers and magnet boards to promote directional positioning of letter and number symbols.

2. Provide salt trays and sand trays to encourage children to shape and form letter symbols and to practise directional positioning.
3. Set up picture and letter blocks to encourage children to form pictures and words.
4. Provide alphabet sets with wooden or plastic letters to promote children's sensorimotor and physical-perceptual exploration of the shapes of letters.

ACTIVITIES IN THE LANGUAGE LEARNING AREA FOR CHILDREN AGES FOUR TO SIX

1. Encourage children to use the Lego sets to create symbols or models of structures they see in the community.
2. Provide an old View-Master and slides, kaleidoscopes, and a slide projector to promote visual-perceptual abilities and bring the outside world into the playroom.
3. Set up Ready to Read sets with a letter, and a picture of an object that begins with the letter, together on each card.
4. Ensure that a well-stocked, beautiful picture file is available for children to inspect on their own or with others and encourage them to talk about the pictures.

The Listening Table

A table may be set up in the language learning area or it might be a permanent fixture to accommodate the listening equipment from the Project centre, such as the tape recorder, headphones, and a CD player. CDs provide practice in auditory learning as children are required to listen, to use their imaginations, and to understand without seeing a visual accompaniment—a skill often underdeveloped in children who spend considerable time watching videos or television. Some CDs give children verbal instructions to carry out, along with accompanying print materials; these provide practice in following verbal directions by carrying out the directions with the symbols, letters, or word pictures without benefit of a visual stimulus. Children may also spend a quiet time listening to a story on tape, telling their own story, or reciting a rhyme on the tape recorder.

Display Table

A display table is often a potential space in the Quiet Thinking centre that may be set up to address a special theme or to introduce a new topic for exploration. The display table may be used to promote new books and to address emergent reading, problem solving, and perceptual and fine-motor skills. If space is at a premium, the display table can double as a listening table periodically. A picture file is sometimes placed at the display table along with photo albums and resource files that relate to a topic or project the children are currently exploring. Small picture files on cards stored in 10 centimetre by 15 centimetre file-card boxes provide as much enjoyment as larger pictures mounted on construction paper, and they are just as effective in stimulating language.

ECEs should change the display table every couple of weeks so that children become accustomed to checking to see what is there for them to explore. Interesting display tables stimulate language by adding new vocabulary and by encouraging conversation. Some popular items for the display table are pictures of people; travel photographs; special occasion displays of winter carnival time, festivals, and holidays; cultural displays; calendars; books; famous paintings and portraits; photography books; albums; and catalogues.

A cutting activity may be set up at this table if it cannot be accommodated in the Creative Arts centre. Cutting activities often involve tracing, drawing, and cutting with the purpose of staying within the boundaries or lines. Through cutting activities, children acquire skills in lateral movement, left-to-right progression, figure–ground perception, manipulation, fine-motor movements, eye–hand coordination, and many other perceptual-motor and physical abilities related to reading and writing.

Summary

Chapter 16 takes a broad view of literacy as *reading the world*—and not just the word—in the sense that literacy is deeply ingrained and is a manifestation of one's experience in society and one's perception of the environment and the self in the environment. Therefore, literacy development in early childhood requires that children are offered many types of experiences and are exposed to varied environments that influence the children's relationship with the society in which they live. Cultural factors have an enormous influence on literacy development, which is also highly dependent on the child's exposure to the language of their culture, their home language. Literacy goals are both bound by the home culture and influenced by the standards of the adoptive culture. ECEs need to work with families to build cultural bridges for children who have to adapt to the literacy valued by their culture of origin and to the literacy required by the new culture in which they live and are schooled.

The child's ability to understand, to use many symbol systems, and to think symbolically have an impact on language and literacy. The learning process involves the symbolic task of associating letters with sounds and words with meanings, which is quite different from learning abstract concepts that involve understanding relationships that cannot be seen. Although theories diverge on how children acquire language and the relationship between thought and language, the importance of excellent language models for young children, the role of play with meaningful materials, and exposure to the wealth of experience that pictures and stories open up to children cannot be overestimated. When children have acquired the ability to see words as symbols and are able to contextualize the content, when they have acquired the cognitive-perceptual and physical-perceptual skills they need for reading, and when they have been immersed in a culture that values books and reading, they will learn to read.

Learning Activities

1. Work with a group to create a literacy album for the display table.
2. Create your own guide for the selection of children's literature following the criteria outlined in this chapter. In your guide, start a list of favourite books and stories for preschool and kindergarten children. For each book, include

the author, date of publication, title, publisher, and place of publishing. After each entry, record why you like the book, its main themes or storyline, and the messages it conveys to children. Comment on the aesthetic quality of the publication.

3. Make a tape of activities with verbal instructions for children to implement with concrete materials, books, or picture files to promote listening abilities.
4. Create a picture file of interesting places in the world, animals (domestic, wild, from all regions), sea creatures, and various geographical features. Laminate the photos and file them in an attractive box, or seal them in a photo album with plastic cover pages.
5. Compile a list of literacy materials—kits, sets, puzzles, games, software—along with the distributors' names, for use at the language learning table.

17 The Quiet Thinking Centre: Logical Concepts

> "Play is the very best medium for the young child to develop and learn and is 'the curriculum children have for themselves.'"
>
> —VIVIAN GUSSIN PALEY
>
> *A CHILD'S WORK: THE IMPORTANCE OF FANTASY PLAY* (2004)

BEFORE READING THIS CHAPTER, HAVE YOU

- considered your own attitude toward mathematics?
- observed young children sorting materials, counting, and putting objects in order?

OUTCOMES

After reading and understanding this chapter, you should be able to

- describe how logical concepts are formed by young children;
- explain the influence of social, symbolic, and individual play on young children's concept formation;
- outline the ways in which children learn concepts related to number, quantity, equality, and order; and
- equip the Quiet Thinking centre with materials that promote concept formation: number, class, seriation, and conservation.

Early Mathematical Understanding

Mathematics is another language for making meaning and making sense of the world. Young children develop an early mathematical understanding in environments that encourage them to explore, think, and play with ideas (Carruthers & Worthington, 2010). Early mathematical understanding includes

- ability to count, understand quantity and equality, and to perform simple arithmetic operations (calculate);
- understanding of space, shape, and measures;
- seeing and forming patterns; and
- organizing information, estimating, and deducing probability.

The breadth of knowing associated with all four strands of early mathematical understanding is acquired in all kinds of environments, indoors and outdoors, and in all play contexts, including symbolic play. Just as children begin to understand that letters and words signify meaning, so they develop an early understanding of numbers as symbols to represent something, in the same way that role play provides a context for reading and writing. Perspectives of *multimodal play,* in which children explore meanings with a wide range of things, help children understand that marks made on paper can stand for something else (Carruthers & Worthington, 2006). An environment rich in symbols that helps children learn to use letters and words also enables children to understand the context for using numbers and mathematical symbols.

Children's play with concrete objects, including specific-purpose play materials, helps them uncover for themselves concepts related to mathematical understanding while playing individually or with another child. In this learning centre, ECEs are able to observe the changes in each child's thinking that accompany their growing awareness of number and math symbols as a mathematical language for knowing their world. Understanding these concepts does not normally proceed in a linear fashion, although the concepts do build on one another. *The role of the ECE in the Quiet Thinking centre is to facilitate play with carefully selected materials, to encourage children to reflect, and to help children make the crucial connections that lead to concept formation.*

Concept Development in Early Childhood

Research on the development of the brain has influenced our understanding of how children acquire abstract thinking abilities, which include logical concepts such as number concept, classification, seriation, and conservation. We know that brain development is influenced by both genetic and environmental factors (Doidge, 2007). The development of brain circuits, which are required for cognitive processes, is a product of strategic interactions between specific biological characteristics and certain kinds of environmental stimulation (Segalowitz, 1995). Chapter 15 emphasized that children need to be able to form and reinforce connections and relationships largely through the senses. The more they repeat the same actions on different materials (e.g., objects that sink and objects that float) and see the same result in terms of effect, the more likely they are to deduce a concept such as the relationship between weight and buoyancy. What children uncover through discovery is more lasting and easier for them to recall (Gallenstein, 2003).

Early in life, children "need to make sense of numeracy and mathematics which are evolving life skills, almost like a language, that enable them to face both certain and uncertain situations with greater confidence" (Needham, 2010, p. 155). Mathematical learning and language and literacy learning, although different, are mutually interdependent as children come to terms with words and concepts that are linked, such as more and less, longer and shorter, and nearer and farther. And like language development and literacy are of a social nature, so too are the early stages of concept formation. Children also acquire, through social play, the social conventional meaning of number and social uses of number, and they learn to recite number words during play while singing, chanting, and doing simple finger plays. Play is essential to concept formation, and "mathematics is an inherently social activity" (Schoenfeld, 1992, p. 3) because mathematical knowledge and skills relate to so much of daily living and social interactions.

Understanding logical concepts, however, involves an internal construction that something is true in spite of its obvious physical and perceptual contradictions. Children grapple individually and on their own timetable with the challenges of accepting what they know over the perception of what they see, and they benefit, therefore, from individual play time with concrete objects that allow them to eventually "uncover" a concept on their own. Concepts are the building blocks of the mind and knowledge that help us organize and categorize information (Charlesworth & Lind, 2010). Concept development begins with the exploration typical of the infant and toddler during the sensorimotor period (approximately birth to 18 months), as children are tied to sensory understanding of their world. During the preoperational period, from about age two and a half to age six or seven, children develop concepts, including an understanding of number, as they manipulate concrete materials, use number symbols, and move away from "seeing is believing" to become more independent in their understanding of abstract concepts, which they cannot see, touch, or feel. Concrete operational thinking usually develops between the ages of five and seven, once children have acquired the logical concepts of seriation, classification, number, and conservation, and are able to apply these concepts to mathematical operations and problem solving. While they are still dependent on the concrete objects to reinforce understanding and to test solutions, they are increasingly guided by principles and concepts in their thinking and deductions (Charlesworth, 2005).

The theories of Piaget (1969) and Vygotsky (1978) represent somewhat different interpretations of the relationship between cognitive development and concept learning. Piaget believed that cognitive learning occurs when a child interacts with concrete objects and events in the environment that build on what she knows and challenge her to move beyond her current cognitive level. The child's constant need to maintain equilibrium impels her progress from one cognitive stage and concept to more elaborate concepts. Piaget rejected any notion that children's learning is the result of exposure to specific content in teacher-directed learning situations, and therefore, emphasized children's acquisition of conceptual understanding at their own pace, during individual or parallel play experiences relevant to their individual interests and abilities. He believed that the child should control the time he needs to discover, uncover, and understand concepts. Constructivists who followed Piaget assumed that "mathematical knowledge—like all knowledge—is not directly absorbed but is constructed by each individual (Resnick, 1989, p. 162).

Therefore, the practice of having children in groups recite the numbers from one to 10 and back again while introducing children to the sight and sound of numbers has little impact on children's understanding of the meaning and logic of numbers, which depends on each child's ability to construct logical relationships based on play experiences.

Like Piaget, Vygotsky believed that children actively construct their own system for understanding phenomena through their individual cognitive structures. Vygotsky, however, emphasized the role of social interaction with other children and adults in the development of concepts. His view of the role of symbolic play in learning precipitated a more culturally oriented view that "regards development as a collective process in which children help to shape and share in their own developmental experiences through their participation in everyday cultural routines" (Mallory & New, 1994, pp. 73–74). Following Vygotsky's theory, ECEs would encourage children to talk with each other about their challenges with (logical-mathematical) play materials, a collaborative approach that contributes to the child's developing theory of mind. In this context, ECEs provide activities that children can achieve only with the help of others, offer sufficient support with difficult challenges (scaffold children's learning), and gradually withdraw the support and encourage children to work in pairs or small groups (Ormrod, 2006).

Bruner (1966, 1986), like Piaget, believed in **discovery learning**, but he took a different approach to children's learning by proposing three modes of intellectual development that all children go through and that are not limited to age and stage of development. He referred to the **enactive mode**, which emphasizes actions on concrete objects; the **iconic mode**, which includes visual representation and images; and the **symbolic mode**, in which the learner has to represent using numbers, letters, or words in increasingly abstract contexts. Using this paradigm, Bruner sought to understand how children think, how they learn, and how best to help them learn (Howe & Jones, 1993). Bruner emphasized the importance of providing the right kinds of materials for children to manipulate, of observing children as they play with the materials, and of encouraging children to work together in order to solve the problem or complete the task. He believed that discovery learning helps children learn how to learn and develop problem-solving skills that allow them to transfer learning from one context to a new context.

The Importance of Understanding Logical Concepts

When children do not have opportunities to uncover and understand the logical-mathematical concepts in early childhood, they are unprepared for the demands of mathematics when they begin formal schooling. When children are able to see the relationship between concrete objects through hands-on play with carefully structured sets of materials they gradually understand the concept that lies behind the number symbols. As they begin to understand number abstractly, they are less dependent on the presence of the concrete objects.

For too many children, however, mathematics becomes a subject learned by rote, by memorizing times tables, formulas, and equations without any real understanding of their logical basis. Unlike other types of learning, mathematics has its own signs and symbols and involves "progression in preparation for absorbing other concepts" (Needham, 2010, p. 156). If one step in the learning process is omitted or not fully understood, all later learning related to the concept in question is inhibited or ruled out (Mighton, 2003). If children have not understood the abstract concepts related to number and mathematics, when they are required to solve problems using logical concepts, they become lost and sometimes give up. Many of these children fall into the trap of believing that they *cannot do math and science.* Some teachers, parents, and school systems have, in the past, quite wrongly perpetuated the myth that there is something mysterious about learning math that does not pertain to other subjects, and that some people can do math and others cannot. This myth is a particularly dangerous one to perpetuate in a world that depends increasingly on higher-level, abstract thinking skills to address social, economic, and political challenges. *Because the information age relies on the logical-conceptual abilities of workers who can handle abstract thinking and complex problem solving tasks, a learning deficit in numeracy and logical understanding may have a lifelong negative effect, not the least of which may be fewer opportunities in life and work.* This problem is compounded when we consider the impact on a society's ability to innovate and compete.

ECEs are obligated to overcome any math anxiety they may harbour from their own schooling. Unless children are exposed to well-planned learning experiences in number concepts, logical-mathematical learning deficits accumulate throughout the school years and the child becomes increasingly frustrated by mathematics and science, and possibly by school and learning as well. If ECEs intervene appropriately with children who take longer than others to progress through the stages in concept formation, and guide their assumptions, children will make progress. The key role of the environment in concept development is particularly evident in studies showing that disadvantaged children derive significant long-term benefit from positive environmental stimulation and early cognitive intervention begun in infancy (Eliot, 1999).

Smith (2001) found little evidence to support any cultural or gender differences in the ways children understand and apply math and science concepts in early childhood. All children have the capacity to understand concept of number and basic science provided that they have play experiences that help them perceive differences, effects, and changes; manipulate the materials; and eventually understand abstract relationships in the absence of the concrete materials. To achieve concept of number before starting grade one, girls and boys must be encouraged to play with kits of materials *to explore, manipulate, match, sort, classify, order, seriate, sequence, count, equate, measure,* and *quantify.* Although logical concepts are also explored and developed in social and collaborative contexts such as the Science Discovery, Project, and Unit Blocks centres, children need opportunities and time to play individually with kits, sets, and structured materials designed to help them uncover the concept as they explore the materials and perceive their various relationships. Consider, for example, the learning that a child achieves when, after many attempts to randomly put a series of wooden ducks of graduated sizes in a row, he suddenly discovers, when he stands them up instead of lying them down, that they form steps that move in one direction only (up or down) and that the difference in the sizes of each duck in the ordered series is exactly the same.

Logical-Mathematical Understanding

Achieving an understanding of an underlying, unifying concept among objects or events involves making a mental leap from the external, physical, observable reality of things or objects and the knowledge of their social-conventional meaning, to the realm of concept formation. Logical-mathematical knowledge originates within the individual and involves constructing relationships among objects that have no existence in external reality (Kamii & DeClark, 1985). Learning logical concepts—number, seriation, classification, and conservation—is a function of children's gradual understanding of the concrete and abstract relationships that exist among items in a **set**. This kind of learning takes time and patience and depends on the individual learning style and experience of the learner.

Logical-mathematical learning consists of understanding relationships, such as same-different, more-less, part-whole, and cause-effect, as well as number operations, such as 2 + 2 = 4. This kind of conceptual understanding defines a relationship not directly observable because the source of logical-mathematical understanding is inherent in the relationship itself, which exists in the mind. For example, a red button and a blue button placed side by side constitute two buttons. This understanding is different from knowing their observable characteristics and properties, such as their colour, their shape, and the substance of which they are made (e.g., plastic or wood). Logical-mathematical concepts are universal, in that they are the same in all cultures. This fact implies that all children need to learn logical-mathematical concepts no matter what their cultural backgrounds. Because acquiring an understanding of these relationships is an internal process that relies on children's individual perceptual skills, it also implies that playing alone with concrete objects helps all children discover relationships through their manipulation of objects. This approach does not deny the contribution of social play in all other learning centres to supporting children's understanding of concepts and to affirming that the concepts they understand are shared by others.

Facilitating Children's Understanding of Logical Concepts in the Quiet Thinking Centre

Greenberg (1994, p. 16) explained the futility of trying to introduce and teach children logical concepts, including numbers, through group activities:

> A fundamental principle of teaching is that we first have to engage the mind of the learner. As everyone who works with groups of young children knows, it's next to impossible to get the undivided attention of a large group—to ensure that each child is grappling intellectually with the problem; therefore, we can see that trying to present a 'math lesson' to a group is almost always developmentally inappropriate.

Knowing that children have to construct their understanding of concepts does not imply that we should abandon children to their own devices. Children have individual needs for assistance, clarification, and encouragement when they approach challenging learning tasks. ECEs create an environment that promotes self-directed learning, but they should remain close by to answer questions, to guide children in ways that will help motivate them, and to respond to their needs. The rate and efficiency with which children's conceptual understanding develops depends a lot on our sensitivity to children's individual needs. When children experience success in meeting challenges and in learning abstract concepts, they approach advanced learning tasks with greater enthusiasm and with confidence. The mastery of logical concepts and the ability to reason, to reflect on their learning, and to think abstractly, are essential skills for success in school and in life.

The Quiet Thinking centre emphasizes children's individual play or play with another child, with two- and three-dimensional materials. Preschool children who enjoy matching and sorting activities, board games involving counting and classifying, and nonsense rhymes, are more likely to do well in math and to enjoy learning activities that involve reasoning and logic. Children affirm their conceptual understanding in social and cultural contexts as they compare what they understand to what their peers understand; or their conceptual understanding receives a reality check when confronted with the fact that their understanding differs from that of another child and they are compelled to revisit what they understand.

CONCEPT LEARNING RELATED TO MATHEMATICS AND PROBLEM SOLVING

- Connect mathematical concepts to evidence of mathematics in daily living.
- Learn to classify, or how to sort and group objects according to some similar characteristic or characteristics, e.g., the square objects, the round red objects, the blue wooden triangles.
- Learn to seriate, which helps children focus on the relationships among objects as they place them in a logical order or sequence.
- Learn to count, which involves rational counting, or correctly attaching a numerical name to each item in a set of objects
- Understand number equality in spite of perceptual differences in the volume of the sets of objects being counted; e.g., eight pennies versus eight teddy bears.
- Understand that the number does not change in spite of changes in the configuration of objects counted (number constancy).
- Estimate the number of objects in a small set without counting.
- Use ordinal numbers to represent first, second, third.
- Represent numbers and quantity graphically using symbols, charts, and graphs.
- Acquire temporal concepts, or the sense of time as a continuum that includes the past, present, and future.
- Understand spatial concepts, or how objects and people occupy space and relate to one another in space.
- Be able to conserve number; for example, that the number of objects in each set remains the same (equal) even if the sets look different (are configured differently), i.e, conservation.
- Measure and compare two or more objects and use language to describe comparative measurement: e.g., small, medium, large; hotter/colder; longer/shorter.
- Use standard measuring devices such as rulers, tape measures, and measuring cups and non-standard measures such as straws and footsteps to measure and compare.

Early childhood education is obligated to provide systematic opportunities for children to develop the logical concepts they are developmentally ready to learn. But some ECEs fear that expecting young children to develop logical concepts puts an unrealistic burden on preschoolers and inhibits the spontaneous nature of play. As with all decisions related to when to introduce challenges for children in their play and how to decide what activities to provide, we are guided by children's developmental progress and their interests. The Quiet Thinking centre always includes play materials for children to match, sort, count, order, and name, factors that ensure their incidental learning about the relationships among things. ECEs introduce more challenging play activities related to seriation, quantity, equality, and number constancy, for example, once they have assessed a child's readiness for learning concepts. When children experience inevitable hurdles in their play with these activities, scaffolding is useful because it helps children over these hurdles and safeguards the child's initiative and natural disposition for progress in learning. Successful scaffolding depends on the ECE's skill in supporting the child's efforts to learn in a planned play environment and in helping her surmount the difficulties she encounters by asking key questions at the right time or drawing attention to a relationship that she may have missed on her own.

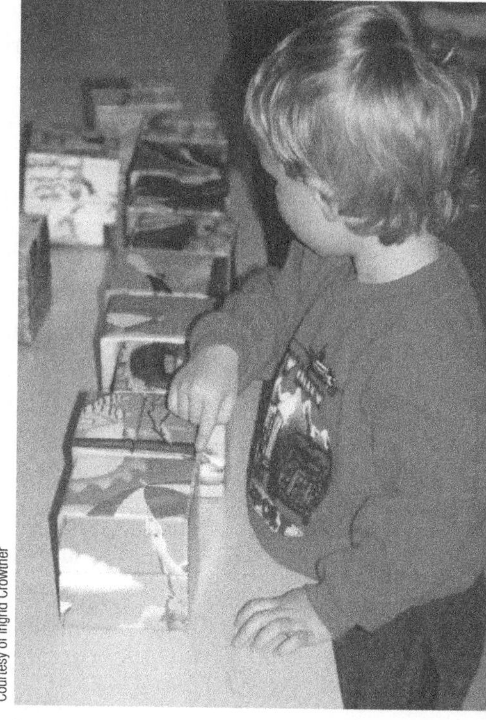
Courtesy of Ingrid Crowther

Problem solving

Children require opportunities in various learning contexts to form relationships among objects in many ways, such as by manipulating, combining, separating, and classifying objects through active, physical play with modular materials, natural materials, specialized kits and puzzles, and free-form materials and modular materials normally found in the Quiet Thinking centre. Children may also benefit from using computer software to help them acquire logical-mathematical understanding. Many of the concepts children are exposed to in their play with concrete materials are addressed by software packages that provide another medium for exploration, manipulation of the symbols onscreen, and enhanced understanding. Play with concrete materials to develop logical concepts may be reinforced in the Project centre (Chapter 18) with computer software that promotes understanding of logical concepts in two dimensions instead of three.

The provision of a well-equipped learning centre that encourages play with materials that allow children to uncover concepts by seeing relationships among things is a first step toward helping them understand logical concepts. For example, children understand fairly early the concept of *more* by seeing that there are many more objects in one set than in the other set. It is important for ECEs to understand their role once the environment has been set; it is not enough to simply set up the materials and leave the area. When children continue to be dependent on what they perceive, ECEs can ask questions, such as "Why do you think that I am seeing something different?" or "Come over here with me to see what I see" (Ormrod, 2006). Being present in the learning centre when children encounter an obstacle allows the ECE to step in and help the child resolve the problem. For example, when a child attempts to follow a pattern using the Cuisenaire rods, the ECE can break the learning down to the basic steps and have the child focus on the order in which the coloured rods appear in the model provided.

The Number and Math Play Station

How you equip the math play station depends on the concepts you want children to achieve and what methods you will depend on to facilitate their learning. Because concept learning develops on each child's individual schedule, the principles of engagement are similar to those for literacy learning. The expectation is that children will interact individually with the materials; their play will be focused; and ECEs will support children in choosing activities appropriate for their level, in beginning the activities, in seeking help to overcome obstacles and avoid distractions, and in finishing the activities. The materials available to children in this play station contain tasks and challenges that guide children toward an understanding of the concept.

Seriation sets, for example, are usually structured to encourage children, over time, to work from a common baseline; classification kits encourage children to find and define the common criteria for sets or groups starting with concrete, visible criteria, and gradually moving to more abstract criteria that define the group.

The Steps in Learning the Concept of Number

Children must acquire the concept of number before they are able to understand the meaning of arithmetical operations, such as addition, subtraction, multiplication, and division. Mathematical problem solving using numbers and other symbols also depends on a solid foundation in number concept. Number is a form of logical-mathematical knowledge that requires an understanding of relationships, classes or sets, order, quantity, equality, and constancy. The concepts of classification (sorting into sets or groups) and of order (including **temporal order**, **spatial order**, and seriation, or order by length) are closely related to number concept. Before children are ready to learn these concepts, however, we see them pass through the early stages of concept learning, and some of these, including understanding the social meaning of number, are largely acquired in social contexts, through small-group experiences. Examples include drawing children's attention to the use of numbers for addresses on streets, for special dates in a year, and for birthdays.

Physical knowledge of numbers involves children's early experiences with the sight and sound of number symbols. They see numbers pasted up on the display board, they feel the number symbols hanging from the number tree, they sing songs with their playmates about numbers during group time—"One little, two little, three little chickadees"—and they recite finger plays and rhymes using numbers—"One, two, buckle my shoe." Even a two-year-old can happily recite 1, 2, 3, 4, 5, in order, much to the delight of her parents, who are sure their child is a mathematical genius! Before children begin to learn about the logical nature of numbers, which leads to number concept, they learn to recognize numbers, to recite and chant numbers, and to feel the shape of number symbols by copying number symbols on sand trays or tracing the outline of a number symbol with a textured sandpaper surface. Recognizing the sight and sound of numbers involves sensory learning, which is followed by social learning experiences that are referred to as the **social-conventional knowledge of number**, sometimes called number sense and knowing the meaning of numbers.

As in learning all types of concepts, it is easiest for children to first experience the concept of number in a physical-sensory way and then in a social context. These steps precede the logical-mathematical steps involved in learning number concept. Children's earliest experience with numbers usually involves becoming socialized to a world that includes understanding the diverse roles that numbers play in our daily lives. When programs are rich with opportunities for children to garden, to cook, and to get out into the community, they see many instances in which numbers are used, on signs, addresses, and price tags. When ECEs draw attention to the presence of numbers in cooking recipes, ages, addresses, sizes, weights, distances, speeds, telephone numbers, prices, using money, and telling time and reading timetables, they are sensitizing children to the presence and the meaning of numbers in all aspects of life. Certain numbers are milestone years in people's lives, and certain dates are associated with festive occasions and traditional holidays. Social-conventional knowledge about numbers makes children aware that numbers have social and cultural meaning.

The Creation of All Kinds of Relationships

Many open-ended, exploratory play experiences that are not directly related to numbers but that motivate children to learn concepts and to create mental relationships between things precede early number concept. For example, when children spontaneously sort objects into groups or collections by recognizing common properties, they begin to understand the notion of set. Set is a fundamental idea in mathematics that usually precedes the ability to quantify. As children notice relationships between objects they are comparing, matching, joining, and dividing, they develop their earliest understandings of mathematical operations (Donaldson, 1978). As they create relationships between objects based on order—for example, in order of shape, or of size from biggest to smallest—they learn about the many kinds of relationships that exist among things in the environment. From early experiences of sorting, making sets, and **ordering** objects, children begin to integrate the notions of pattern and structure that are essential to understanding mathematics. Number concept depends on the child's ability to form relationships among things based on order and classification criteria. When children understand such relationships as same-different, more-less, or big-bigger-biggest, they are usually able to understand the logical significance of numbers. Children need plenty of opportunities to match objects according to a variety of criteria to understand the diverse variables on which things or ideas may be grouped in a set.

Ordering

Ordering is a more complicated form of comparing based on a particular relationship between two objects. To order a set of objects involves creating a relationship between an object and the set of objects to which it is being related. Ordering begins to develop during the sensorimotor period when children play with nesting and stacking materials. Children need to experience ordering by size (seriation), pattern (spatial order), time (temporal order), absolute number (numerical order—1, 2, 3, etc.), and relative number (ordinal numbers—first, second, third, etc.).

Children use play materials such as stacking and nesting sets, Cuisenaire rods, and sequencing and seriation kits to practise making a set in a given order. Children learn order by following a model; by extending a pattern or order; by filling in gaps in an ordered set; and by creating an order for a set of objects with ordinal properties, such as length, time, and size. Before asking them to order numbers, ECEs should ensure that children are able to order objects successfully.

Focused play

SERIATION

Seriation is an arrangement of objects based on graduated order. Ordered sets of objects are sets in which the gradations, or differences in size, between each object in the series and the ones next to it are equal; all the objects in the set are needed to help children grasp this logical concept. Cuisenaire rods, measuring cups, nesting blocks, dolls, eggs, or barrels are based on multiples of one basic unit of measurement. They can be used to help children learn to seriate if they are placed in a graduated order from smallest to largest, or vice versa. The essential problem for children to solve when seriating is "What comes next in the series?"

When children are learning to seriate a set of objects, they usually experiment using trial and error and may start by placing objects at each end and moving toward the middle, fitting the middle two in last. As children progress in their understanding of the seriation concept, they will be able to order by moving in one direction and by planning. Frequently, children understand the concept of building steps and stairs but fail to account for the common base line that will ensure that each object in the ordered series is one graduated size larger or smaller than the previous one. Eventually, children should evolve a plan for their ordering and proceed systematically, without having to make any alterations in the order as they proceed. When children have learned to seriate one whole set of objects by moving in one direction only, without hesitation, they are ready to double seriate. This final step involves placing two sets of objects in ordered sets using **one-to-one correspondence**, and following a systematic plan. One-to-one correspondence will be addressed later in this chapter (see Figure 17–1).

SPATIAL ORDER/TOPOLOGY

Spatial ordering refers to placing objects in a certain order by shape, usually by making or following patterns and by creating equal sets using one-to-one correspondence. Young children are interested in the topological properties of shapes in space and should be encouraged to draw and arrange shapes in different ways (Sime, 1973). (See Figure 17-2, p. 322.) **Topology** is the study of where objects are located in relation to one another and that shape and length may be altered without affecting the figure's properties (Kennedy, Tipps, & Johnson, 2008). Preoperational children are more interested in the topological properties of space than they are in the **Euclidean properties**, which define specific geometric shapes in standard ways and which are learned later (Laurendeau & Pinard, 1968). Forming relationships based on the spatial configuration and order of objects helps children develop an understanding of distance (near-far), part-whole (part of-not part of), position (before-after), and boundary (inside-outside).

TEMPORAL ORDER

Temporal order refers to the order in which events take place. Sequencing activities often addresses temporal ordering concepts with a set of cards that contain a series of pictures related to a familiar ongoing event or to a process that occurs over time. For example, sequenced cards may represent the series of events involved in getting up in the morning, having breakfast, going to school, coming home, having dinner, and going to bed; or of planting a seed, weeding the garden, seeing the plant grow, picking the vegetable, and eating it. Encouraging children to associate specific times of the day with daily events they can recognize, such as going home from school, having dinner, and going to bed, helps them understand the passing of time (Whitin, 1994). Children understand temporal order usually before they begin to tell time. Regular daily routines help children understand the temporal order of the day's events to which they can eventually attach specific times of day.

NUMERICAL ORDER

Children learn to recognize the sight and sound of number symbols very early. Their recognition of the **numerical order** of number symbols—1, 2, 3, 4, 5—is largely socially transmitted through songs, finger plays, rhymes, and activities. Children usually understand and recite the numerical order of number symbols long before they are able to understand what each number represents in terms of quantity. Counting by one number at a time, and then by 10s and by 5s, becomes

EARLY STAGES OF SERIATION

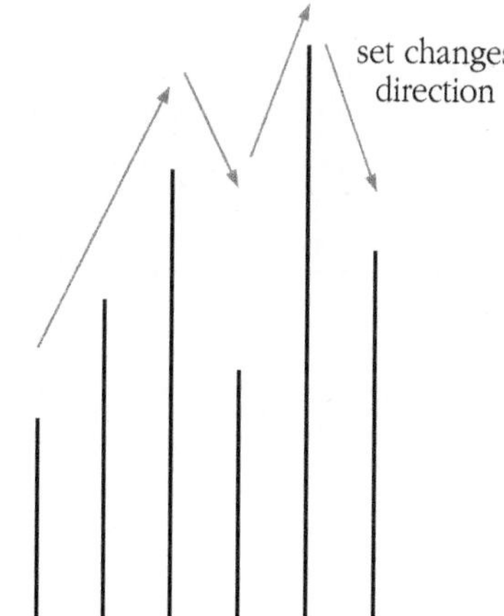

random vertical placement of rods on a table

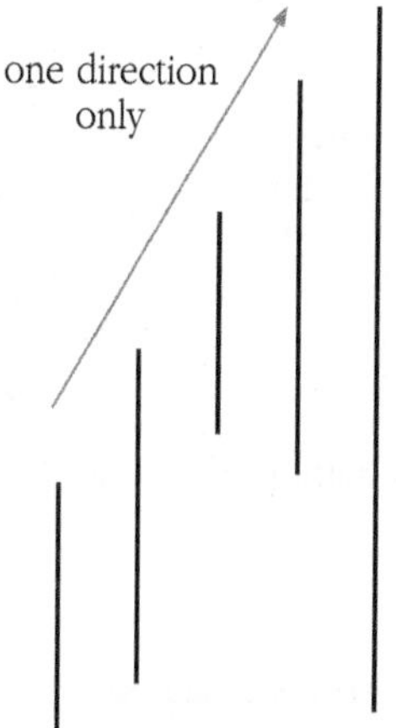

moving of rods creates staircase pattern of progression but omits understanding of common baseline

LATER STAGES OF SERIATION

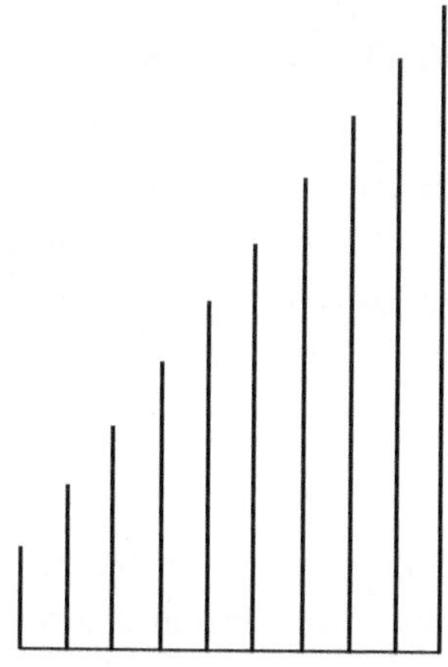

ordering by length in one direction only, respecting the equal gradations that should exist between each successive item in a series with a common baseline

double seriation

Figure 17–1
Stages of seriation

Source: Cruikshank, Fitzgerald, and Jensen (1980).*

a rote learning skill in which children often learn the words in the correct order as if singing the words to a favourite song.

ORDINAL NUMBER

Children understand ordinal number through physical experiences, such as lining up and taking turns in organized physical activities and board games. The ability to form relationships based on which comes first, second, third, fourth, and so on in

*From: Cruikshank, Fitzgerald, and Jenson, *Young Children Learning Mathematics.* (Boston: Allyn and Bacon, 1980). Reprinted with permission from Pearson Education, Inc.

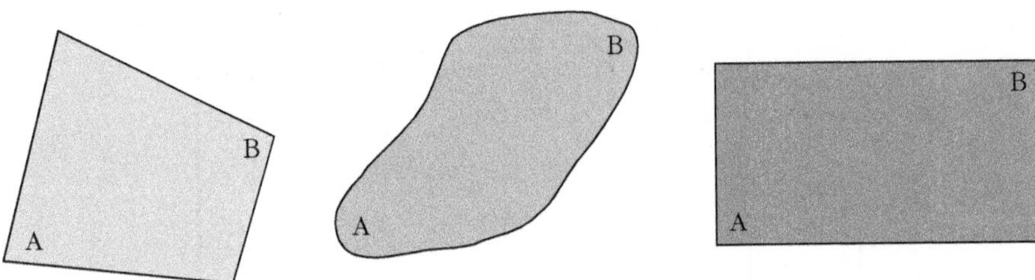

altering shapes without affecting the figure's properties of being open or closed

Figure 17–2
Topology
Source: Cruikshank, Fitzgerald, and Jensen (1980).*

a series is generally acquired through active involvement in real-life situations from an early age. The ability to relate the physical knowledge of ordinal number to an understanding of the concept of order by number develops at the same time that children are learning to count, to understand notions of quantity, and to appreciate the concepts of greater than and less than.

Ordering Patterns and Sequences with Objects

Ordering by establishing sets of objects according to a specific pattern, such as circle, square, triangle, or rectangle, and repeating the pattern is another form of ordering by pattern or visual characteristics. Similarly, children learn to order by lengths or sizes of objects and by sounds and tones from softest to loudest and from the bottom of the musical scale to the top of the scale.

Classification

Classification involves putting objects into groups according to similar attributes. Either the ECE or the children may decide on these attributes. Classification is a form of sorting by creating a set based on a criterion common to all the objects in the set. The common criterion may be concrete and observable, such as colour, shape, or size; it may be knowledge-based, such as nocturnal versus diurnal animals; or it may be subjective or abstract, such as things that I like/do not like, things that are beautiful/ugly, situations that are safe/dangerous, or things that magnets attract versus things they don't attract.

Children's ability to classify progresses from simple sorting activities, such as sorting according to one attribute (grouping the large teddy bears and the small teddy bears), to sorting according to two or three attributes (separating the small, grey teddy bears from the large, brown teddy bears). Initially, children sort objects using their senses, so that colour, shape, and size become the earliest categories, followed by objects of different groupings of properties, such as plastic, wood, metal, paper, and fabric. These might be followed by sorting according to texture, decorations, and patterns. Sorting by function provides other criteria, such as things that we use to clean, to fix things, to write with, and to store things. Objects with concrete, observable characteristics that

*From: From: Cruikshank, Fitzgerald, and Jenson, *Young Children Learning Mathematics*. (Boston: Allyn and Bacon, 1980). Reprinted with permission from Pearson Education, Inc.

distinguish one set from another are easiest to sort, followed by those that can be distinguished based on knowledge, such as the bedroom furniture versus the living room furniture. Forming sets based on abstract criteria (e.g., happy/funny/silly, or more abstract, such as things that are kind and things that are cruel) and forming subsets (i.e., creating hierarchies of classes, such as food/fruit/citrus/oranges) are the most challenging classification tasks for children. As children grasp the concept of classification and move beyond the prescribed categories suggested by the materials in the collection, children are ready to sort random sets of objects, ensuring that all objects become part of a category, and the children themselves define the criteria for each category.

When children are learning to classify, it is important for them to follow some key principles. Often the ECE has to point out these principles after allowing the children to play and to practise sorting using their own methods. In addition to understanding that all objects in a set must have at least one common, unifying characteristic, children have to learn that the same characteristic must apply to all objects put into that set and that unrelated characteristics should be ignored. As they become more experienced, children learn that all available objects to be sorted must be included in one of the groups being made and that no object can remain unclassified. Eventually, children understand that the classes in the classification system should not overlap; that is, no member of the set to be sorted should fit into more than one of the classes (see Figure 17–3).

Number Concept

Once children have had experience ordering and classifying sets of objects, they are more likely to understand concepts related to the logical nature of numbers. Learning number concept is different from acquiring social knowledge about numbers, even though children will have been exposed to activities and everyday living experiences that introduce them to the world of numbers (Kamii, 1982). As in learning other concepts, children must construct the relationships related to understanding number concept for themselves, largely through their active interaction with concrete objects.

An early understanding of number concept starts when the child attempts to put objects in order, using size or temporal order as the criterion, and to create groupings or sets of objects according to specific criteria (i.e., classification). We have seen that concepts of order and set are related to number concept and are achieved through children's self-directed explorations of specific-purpose materials, such as graduated cylinders, rods, or stacking toys, and through sorting activities with buttons, foods, miniature replicas of animals, and sets of vehicles. The ability to sort objects begins both with recognizing similarities and differences and with matching one object to another based on some observable criterion. This step is usually followed by sorting according to a knowledge-based criterion, such as grouping all the spoons together and all the cutting instruments together. About the same time, children learn to match one cup to one saucer, one knife to one fork, one egg to one eggcup, and one hat to each doll. At this stage, they are ready for one-to-one correspondence activities.

One-to-One Correspondence

One-to-one correspondence is the ability to match each object in set B to an object in set A when the numbers of objects in each set are the same. When children place an egg in each section of the egg carton, give a spoon to each doll, and hand a cup

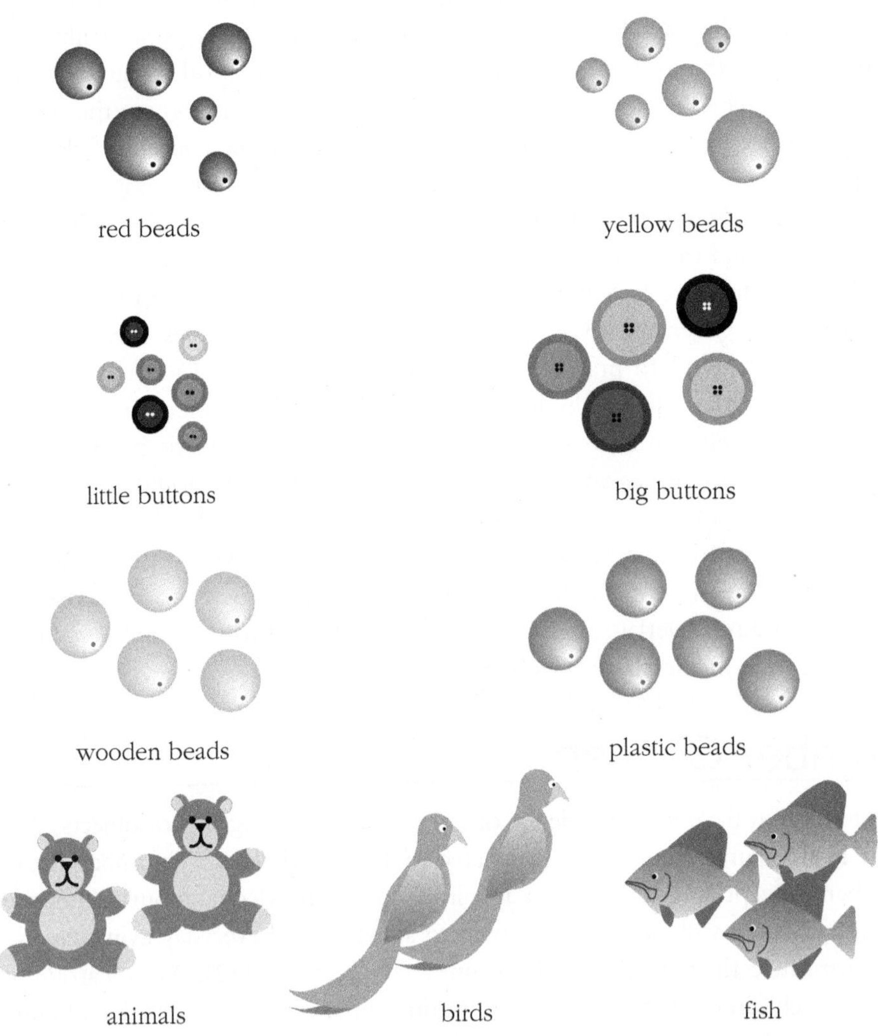

Figure 17–3
Classification

to each child in the circle, they are learning the pairing of one member of set A with one member of set B. After considerable practice with this kind of simple matching, children begin to grasp the idea that the number of objects in set A is the same as the number in set B simply by looking at the configuration of the sets. Similarly, they begin to learn that one-to-one correspondence is absent if they have some objects left over in set A after they have finished matching objects from set A with those in set B. Having some objects left over in set A is visual proof that set A is larger than set B (see Figure 17–4). Thus, children acquire an understanding of what makes sets equal in size.

Children acquire these understandings through self-directed play with materials the ECE has carefully selected and set up in the environment. At this stage, children are simply gaining the notion of the creation of sets through one-to-one correspondence (Donaldson, 1978). Similarly, when children play with groups of objects by sorting them into sets having a common property, such as colour, size, shape, or social meaning, they are adding to their understanding of a set as a group of objects, each of which has a common attribute. As stated earlier, one-to-one cor-

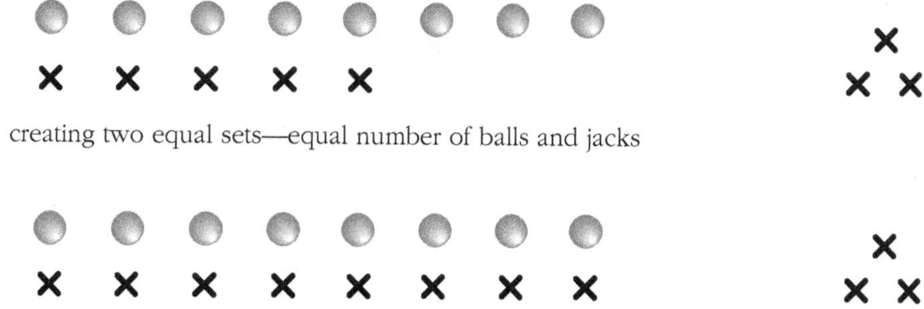

creating two equal sets—equal number of balls and jacks

unequal sets—more jacks than balls

Figure 17–4
One-to-one correspondence

respondence, seriation, and classification activities are essential to the development of number concept before children are able to count meaningfully, to quantify, and to understand number equality.

Counting Objects in a Set

Once children form sets using one-to-one correspondence without hesitation, they can begin counting the number of objects in each set, usually by pointing with their index fingers to each object in turn in the set. This action is, in itself, a form of one-to-one correspondence, as the children have to practise pointing the index finger only once to each object in turn in the series. The idea is that each object, as the child progresses in the series, is one more than the previous object. At this stage, one-to-one correspondence moves from a simple matching activity to an early understanding of quantity. At the same time, counting as part of rhyme or song, or the simple recitation of numbers, changes to counting with some understanding of the mathematical significance of numbers. The child, at this stage, is beginning to attach number symbols used in counting to objects in a set, and to compare the number of objects in one set to the number of objects in the second set. When children begin to match and to compare equal sets of objects arranged in one-to-one correspondence, they are beginning to understand the mathematical value of numbers and notions related to equality.

Children may be encouraged to count objects in a series when they have reached the stage of learning about the equality of sets and the concept of quantity. It is always easier for children to count objects that are physically ordered, for young children will not readily order the objects mentally in their heads. Sometimes, even the physical ordering of objects in a row will not prevent skip counting (see Figure 17–5). Frequently, children will double count objects in a group unless the objects are physically ordered in a row (see Figure 17–6).

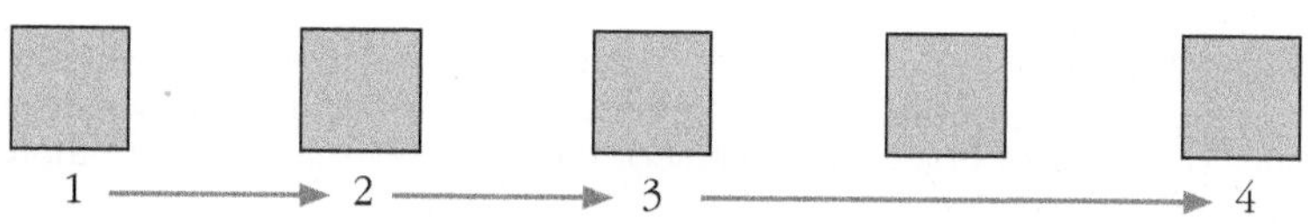

Figure 17–5
Skip counting

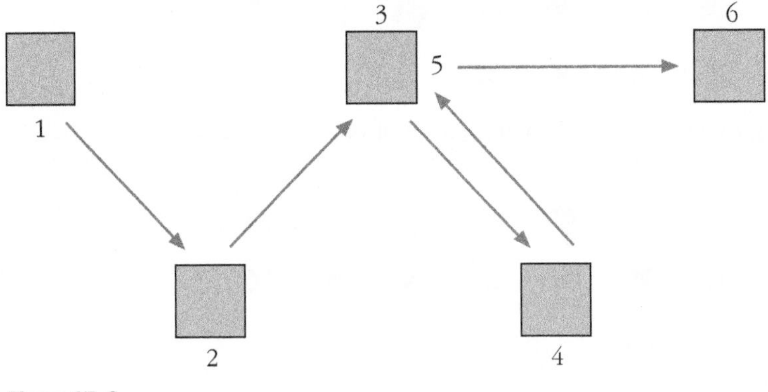

Figure 17–6
Double counting

When children are learning the concept of quantity, they frequently assume that the quantity of objects in a set changes when the objects in the set change. For example, children will count a set of pennies and find that there are eight, and then count a corresponding set of eight balls placed next to them in one-to-one correspondence and find that there are eight (see Figure 17–7). When asked, however, if there are more balls or more pennies, the child will say that there are more balls. Children who are still perceptually bound in the preoperational stage will focus on the size of the balls, which is so much larger than that of the pennies. At this stage, children still believe that number depends on size because size is perceptually apparent.

Number Constancy

When children understand that numbers remain the same regardless of the properties of the objects being counted, and that the quality of *fiveness* or *eightness* remains the same no matter what is being counted, they begin to understand the constancy of numbers. **Number constancy** means that the quality of *eightness*, *oneness*, or *fiveness* remains constant in spite of the properties (e.g., size, shape, texture, and medium) of the objects being counted. To ensure that children understand the constancy of number, at least eight objects should be included in a set to prevent visual estimation of the number of objects to be counted (Kamii, 1982); see Figure 17–8.

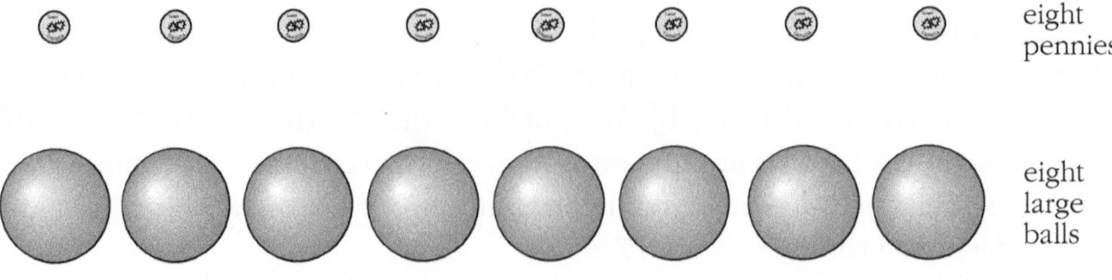

Children may count the number of objects in each set correctly. When asked whether there are more pennies or more balls, if they are focusing only on the perceptual characteristics (i.e., size of objects in each set), they will say that there are more balls than pennies.

Figure 17–7
Understanding quantity (objects in two sets are perceptually different from each other)

The child says there are the same number of kittens as there are pennies.

Figure 17–8
Number constancy

Conservation of Number

Conservation of number involves understanding that the quantity or number of objects in a set remains the same in spite of transformations or changes in the configuration of the set (Piaget, 1969). Preoperational children are unable to conserve, largely because their ability to think and to know depends on their senses, as in, "What I see is what I believe."

As mentioned earlier, children often are confused by differences in the configuration of sets of objects they are counting. For example, when young children count, in turn, a long row of eight pennies and a small vertical stack of eight pennies, they will establish that there are eight pennies in each set. When asked, however, whether the number of pennies in the row or in the stack is the same or whether there are more in one set, they will reply that there are more pennies in the row. Children focus on the visual dimensions of the long row and rely on their perceptions of the physical boundaries of the set to make this judgment, rather than on what they know. Only when they are certain that quantity is independent of the size or configuration of objects in each set being counted are children able to conserve number. When they can retain the idea that the number of pennies in both the row and the stack are the same, in spite of differences in the configuration of each set, they have achieved number concept (see Figure 17–9).

Play Materials to Promote Number Concept

Children develop number concept through their freely chosen play with things, usually modular materials they can order, sort, arrange, count, and quantify. The Quiet Thinking centre should provide a wide variety of modular materials that promote the development of number concept, such as pegs and pegboards, bingo chips, Cuisenaire rods, attribute blocks, stacking and nesting blocks, Unifix

The child says that there are the same number of pennies in each set.

Figure 17–9
Conservation of number

(interlocking sets), pattern blocks, people pieces, centimetre cubes, colour cubes, counting chips, and parquetry tiles. The key to helping children learn number concept using these materials lies in ECEs' skilled observations of their levels of understanding of number. ECEs then carefully select and set up materials to promote children's progress to the next stage. Observing children as they play provides insight into when encouragement, support, and coaching are needed to facilitate the acquisition of a more mature understanding of numbers that builds on what they already know.

Equipment, Materials, and Supplies

MATERIALS FOR NUMBER AND MATH LEARNING

Charlesworth (2005, p. 363) recommends that materials for math learning should be "sturdy and versatile ... fit the outcomes selected ... and fit the developmental levels of the children."

Equipment: rectangular table with a chair at each end to encourage individual work, magnetic board with numbers, chalkboard, and easel

Materials: colour counters; seriation kits; sequencing sets; Cuisenaire rods and a rod rack; tangrams; dominoes; abaci; classification sets with clearly defined similarities, and those with more abstract likenesses; visual calculator; magnetic number symbols; magnetic fraction bars; play money/coin sets and cash registers; clocks; geometric sets; pocket charts; calendars; centimetre cubes; Unifix blocks; base 10 blocks; magnifying lens; measuring cups and beakers; salt or sand trays; felt number symbols; mathematics-related Workjobs; Checkers and other board games with numbers and counters; rulers and tape measures; and dice

Supplies: activity books with numbers, crayons, pencils, chalk, pens, felt-tipped pens, scissors, cut-outs of numbers, unlined paper and centimetre graph paper, crayons matching the colours of the Cuisenaire rods, index cards, construction paper, and masking tape

Activities to Promote Logical Concepts

Many activities to promote logical concepts may be provided to children at least two years old who are no longer putting play materials into their mouths; the idea is to increase the complexity of the tasks as children make progress. Several of these activities may be planned using Cuisenaire rods. Activities with Cuisenaire rods start by encouraging children to handle and explore the properties of the rods—they stack, form patterns, seriate; children can use them for measuring, for comparing, for counting, for adding and subtracting, for seeing inequalities and equalities. Davidson (1977) recommends that they be used in the following ways with preschoolers: exploring, building, making trains, making flat designs and patterns, and building a staircase. They teach such concepts as awareness of attributes and properties, three-dimensional and two-dimensional representations, association of colour with rods and lengths, one-to-one correspondence, counting, comparing equal and unequal, seriation, classification, and simple addition and subtraction. These are excellent hands-on materials for teaching logical concepts and they are aesthetically appealing, wonderful for little hands to hold, and exceptionally versatile.

ORDER

1. Introduce children to the task of double seriation by placing two sets of objects on the table and encouraging children to make two sets of seriated objects. Children first seriate one set and then seriate a second set, using one-to-one correspondence and estimating the order in which objects will be placed to create two seriated sets.
2. Provide a set of ordered objects for a child to seriate at a table and then add additional objects and encourage the child to extend the order. If a pattern is discernible in the ordered set—for example, a colour or shape pattern—encourage children to extend the order of the set by repeating the pattern.
3. Provide a set of ordered materials with some gaps in the order and encourage children to fill in the gaps.
4. Provide Cuisenaire rods for a child to build a staircase or follow a pattern model.

CLASSIFICATION

1. Set up sets of bingo chips or buttons for children to classify based on two observable criteria, such as colour and shape. All the red round objects and all the square yellow objects are, therefore, separated. Ensure that all objects to be sorted fit both criteria for one or the other set.
2. Encourage children to sort the cups, saucers, forks, and spoons that have been borrowed from the Daily Living centre (or set up the same activity in that centre).
3. Provide objects for which the sorting criteria may be more abstract or subjective, such as beautiful/ugly things; useful/not useful things; safe/dangerous things; happy/sad things; things you do when you are playing/working.
4. Wooden and plastic beads: sort beads by colour, size, and shape.

NUMBER (PHYSICAL AND SOCIAL KNOWLEDGE)

1. Sing number songs and recite number rhymes together.
2. Play Number I Spy in the classroom by requiring children to spy a number symbol somewhere in the learning environment.
3. Set up puzzles with number symbols.
4. Set up a magnetic board and magnetic number symbols for children to play with.

NUMBER CONCEPT

1. Set up specific-purpose activities designed to promote one-to-one correspondence, such as sets of eggs and eggcups, dolls and hats, cups and saucers, cars and garages, and stamps and envelopes, and encourage children to make two equal sets.
2. Practise counting with small groups of children, the two equal sets of objects that children have created using one-to-one correspondence. Example: place one set of Cuisenaire rods horizontally and the other vertically and have the children tell you which set has more rods. Then count the rods with the children. Ask the question again.

3. Using the flannelboard, felt number symbols, and felt objects, work with a small group of children to create sets of objects representing the number symbol for each set.
4. Provide Cuisenaire rods and have the children guess the number of units in each rod; count the rods; link the length of each rod to a colour.

Summary

Helping children acquire logical concepts before they enter grade one is a higher-order teaching skill that should be achieved by ECEs. This teaching skill tests ECEs' command of the materials in the play environment and their ability to use them effectively in the Quiet Thinking centre, and other learning centres, to help children uncover logical concepts for themselves as they play. It is not enough to teach only the social-conventional meanings of numbers and to count by rote or to ask children to simply recognize the number symbols. By the time children start grade one, they should be capable of performing simple mathematical operations that they understand, by virtue of their regular and sustained experience with play materials that address ordering, seriation, classification, number constancy, and conservation of number. Effective teaching of logical concepts relies on setting up the learning centre strategically and providing materials that guide children sequentially through the steps involved in understanding logical concepts. Careful setting up of the materials allows ECEs to closely observe what children are doing with the materials and whether or not they seem to understand the concept. Skilful questioning of children about their play with the materials set up in the learning centre reveals children's learning level and the obstacles they may be encountering, which then allows ECEs to try different sets of materials that promote the same concept but in another way. This chapter provides a foundation for activities and projects that take place in the Project centre and the Science Discovery centre, which are addressed in the following chapters.

LEARNING ACTIVITIES

1. Choose eight learning activities from the suggestions provided that promote seriation, classification, and number concept. Write activity cards following the format provided in Chapter 10.
2. Invent one more activity for each of the four main developmental objectives (i.e., ordering, seriation, classification, and number concept) and write an activity card for each new activity you have planned.
3. In your field placement, set up a table for two children to practise classifying sets of objects. Use manipulative and modular play materials that provide clear messages to children about what they should do with them. Write Activity Cards for your activities.
4. Make Workjobs that address concepts related to double seriation, classification according to two or more criteria, number concepts, and science concepts.

Store each of your Workjobs activities in its own box and label each box with a picture showing how to use the materials. Plan a workshop to engage parents in making Workjobs to increase the program's inventory of specific-purpose play materials. (Workjobs activities are then stored on shelves marked with pictures for children to put them back where they found them. Workjobs manuals may be obtained from www.amazon.com.)

18 The Project Centre

"One test of the correctness of educational procedure is the happiness of the child."

—Maria Montessori

Before Reading This Chapter, Have You

- reflected on the spontaneous projects you liked to work on as a child and what you learned from them?
- observed children playing with computers and other technologies?
- examined various technologies and products for children to determine their developmental appropriateness and play value?
- observed children as they negotiate their tasks and roles in projects?
- noted whether or not children, together and individually, achieve their goals for the project?

Outcomes

After reading and understanding this chapter, you should be able to:

- discuss issues related to the use of technologies in early childhood education programs;
- determine your own needs for professional development related to the appropriate use of technologies in programs for young children;
- evolve your approach to using technologies in early childhood programs;
- create a Project centre as a playroom "hub" for planning and pursuing projects;
- set up play stations (e.g., an office area, viewing station, and listening table); and
- plan projects involving several stages and the appropriate use of technologies.

The Impact of Technologies on Early Childhood Education

The belief that children are active learners who construct their knowledge and understanding of the world through play in the concrete world is a cornerstone of early childhood education. This fundamental value is central to this chapter, which addresses children's use of technologies, especially in the context of projects. This chapter begins with a discussion of technologies and children. The recent position statement published by the National Association for the Education of Young Children (NAEYC) entitled "Technology in Early Childhood Programs Serving Children from Birth to Age 8" (2011) is a key resource in the discussion of whether, when, why, and how technologies may be used safely and effectively with young children. The position statement recommends that we be "intentional" with respect to using technologies in early childhood programs, advice that requires consideration of whether the goals and outcomes of programs can be achieved more easily using non-digital materials or whether the technology extends development in ways not possible otherwise (NAEYC, 2011). There is considerable affirmation elsewhere that technology should supplement but not replace first-hand experiences and interactions (O'Hara, 2008).

The integration of advanced technologies into mainstream culture and everyday tasks has made it easier for early childhood programs to become more individualized and accountable. Computers facilitate the storage and maintenance of accurate, up-to-date records about children and the program; quick calculations; virtual experimentation with various programming and environmental design scenarios; and the assessment of children's developmental progress. When used as a tool to help ECEs become more purposeful in their planning and record keeping and to provide new ways for children to demonstrate what they know and understand, technology enhances the early childhood program in ways that were not anticipated decades ago. Technology and social media improve communication with parents, help them feel engaged with their child's program, facilitate regular updates on their child's progress, and empower parents to set responsible limits on screen time in the home (NAEYC, 2011). Serious questions are being raised, however, about the impact of technologies on the nature and quality of children's play: Do the benefits of technology outweigh the potential risks? Are wireless networks safe? Are software products programming the child's young brain? These questions should be researched and debated further.

The Cultural Influences of Computers and Other Technologies

Since the first edition of *Empowering Children* was published in 1993, computers have had an increasingly pervasive influence on our daily lives. Canada and other developed nations have nearly completed a transition from the industrial age to the information age, which social analysts say began in 1994. We seldom question the value and safety of computers for adults, but, increasingly, research on young children's use of computers is producing some cautionary results that suggest that computers may have the capacity to rewire the brain of the young child, reduce attention span, and undermine the normal cognitive development patterns (Greenfield, 2009; Healy, 1998; Sigman, 2008). There is evidence that young children's use of the computer may also pose a risk for the child's developing visual abilities (Maynard, 2010). Others acknowledge the significant benefits of computers to young children's learning but caution that they should be used with discretion only for children older than three (Haugland, 2000; McCarrick, 2005). A study by the U.S. Congress (1995) found that computers are too often used in developmentally inappropriate ways, as drills and repetitive instructional games, and therefore defeat the purpose of play-based early learning programs. Given the current debate, *Empowering Children*, fifth edition, approaches with caution the many issues related to children's growing use of technology, especially those that may alter their play preferences and habits. Guernsey (2010) proposes three principles that frame this discussion of technologies and young children:

1. Consider technology as a resource for exposing children to new content and less as a piece of hardware for practising technical skills.
2. Embed discussions about the proper use of technology into ECE training and professional development programs.
3. Ensure that technology does not supplant (hands-on, interactive) play activities with concrete, malleable, responsive, three-dimensional materials.

What the Literature Says about Computers in Early Childhood Education

Since the publication of Seymour Papert's *Mindstorms* (1980), debate has broadened from questions about whether computers serve children any better than their interactions with the concrete world to questions about the impact of technologies on the brain and development. In 1984, Sherry Turkle claimed that computers open up and extend children's thinking just as various kinds of play with concrete materials produce different modes of thinking. Turkle (2011) now writes that technologies are increasingly isolating us from each other and may be instilling a need for constant support and an inability to be alone. Clearly, more has been learned about the impact of technologies on the human mind and emotions. Historically, there have always been questions about the impact of technologies on young children.

In the 1980s, experts believed that children's use of computers should be examined critically in terms of their potential benefits and hazards before being introduced into early childhood classrooms (Hunka, 1987; Ragsdale, 1987; Sullivan, 1985). Burg (1984, p. 30) suggested that computers, like all educational tools were "value-neutral ... they can be used to promote divergent thinking or conformity, freedom or restriction, self-confidence or fear." Others found that, used effectively, computers can address visual, auditory, and kinetic abilities; promote awareness of cause and effect; and encourage children to explore relationships and associations between objects and events (Shade, 1985).

In the 1990s, the Internet and multimedia allowed for electronic exploration of what children could find out in the world of cyberspace. Van Hoorn et al. (1993) advocated using the computer as both a tool and a tutee; both functions put children in control of their play. Haugland (1999) found that three- to four-year-olds who use computers as partners in the context of learning activities made significantly greater developmental gains when compared with children who did not have access to computers, and they appear to influence children's development of memory, dexterity, problem solving, abstraction, and conceptual understanding. Computers were also used effectively to stimulate divergent thinking and creativity and to improve language, and some evidence suggested that computer use in projects can be a powerful agent of learning for children who are learning a second language (Christian, 1994).

Papert (1998) emphasized that, when used appropriately, computers provide concrete experiences, provide children free access and control of the learning experience, encourage ECEs and children to learn together, support peer tutoring, and foster the exploration of ideas. Tapscott (1998) argued that computers give children control over their learning environment, allowing them to proceed at their own speed, revisit challenging tasks, and repeat or find what they might have missed along the way. Haugland (2000) asserted that computers should be used differently with three- and four-year-olds than with children in kindergarten and the primary grades.

In the first decade of this century, experts probed ways in which computers and other technologies might be used to enhance children's thinking, conceptual understanding, and problem solving. Some research found, instead, that extensive computer use by young children might be closing certain circuits of the brain, which go unused. Concerns were raised that early exposure to computers may be shortening children's attention spans and making it harder for children to focus on books, which are not as flashy and fast-paced (Gyre, 2011). The views that children use computers to represent what they know rather than as information-gathering tools; that computers encourage children to think through learning challenges; and, that computers are used by children as a partner in learning represented the next wave in constructivist approaches to using technology in the classroom (Jonassen et al., 2003). Today, some experts acknowledge that there are issues related to young children's use of computers, but many believe that the benefits outweigh the risks, especially when children use them to support their projects. "When they are used to enhance children's investigations and representations, they can be not only very appropriate but also highly motivating to young children and empower them to take even more control of their learning in project work" (Helm & Katz, 2011, pp. 107–108).

The new culture of technology in the classroom relies on technology as a partner in the learning process because, as noted by Jonassen, Howland, Moore, & Marra (2003), children "do not learn from technology, they learn from thinking" (Jonassen et al., 2003, pp. 11–15). They propose that "meaningful learning will result when technologies engage learners in: knowledge construction, not reproduction; conversation, not reception; articulation, not repetition; collaboration, not competition; reflection, not prescription." Demands on children and adults to develop higher-level intellectual skills are increasing, and evidence suggests that technologies can support children's inquiry, facilitate their recording and representing of what they have learned, and encourage experimentation and hypothesizing of outcomes (Prairie, 2005).

Convincing investigation by developmental psychologists also suggests that computers help to prolong the particularly rich period of representational thinking and creativity beyond early childhood. Later, in primary school, language and literacy skills tend to dominate cognitive activity and replace the younger child's natural tendency to communicate through drawings and images. The left hemisphere is primarily dedicated to language and to intuitive functioning, whereas the right hemisphere processes visual and spatial cues. When used appropriately, computers appear to enable children to represent visually, creatively, and pictorially what they know and think instead of always relying on language and text to communicate what they have understood and felt well into the primary school years.

Screen Time

There is sufficient evidence describing the potential risks associated with computers and other screen technologies, including television, on young children's minds and development that this textbook recommends placing significant limits on children's use of technologies. This principle is especially important for children who do not yet demonstrate the required "executive function abilities" for using computers appropriately. **Executive function** abilities manage attention, emotions, and behaviours in order to reach goals and involve the ability to integrate feelings and thinking that enable us to "reflect, analyze, plan and evaluate" (Galinsky, 2010, p. 4). Executive functions include **working memory** (keeping a number of things in mind in order to complete a task), **cognitive flexibility** (shifting attention between two competing tasks), and **inhibition** (refrain from performing an action if it is not needed for the task and inhibiting an early response in order to investigate further) (Galinsky, 2010). The executive functions allow us not only to know but also to use what we know, and they are useful predictors of achievement (Diamond, 2006). Executive functions are an important factor in projects, especially those with several stages and units of activities.

The figures showing the time young children spend either watching television or on a computer are alarming: 59 percent of children under age two watch television for an average of two hours per day; 70 percent of American children under age four have used a computer (http://www.screensmart.ca/early_years). We know that infants and young children develop and learn through their interaction with concrete objects in the environment and that they should spend the lion's share of their day in play activities in the three-dimensional world. Television does not respond to children's actions and does little to influence development or learning. Researchers have found that television watching in early childhood correlates with brain problems and children's use of other electronic devices, (e.g., videos and computer games), rewires the brain and appears to increase the incidence of attention deficit disorder (ADD) (Doidge, 2007). Recent research correlates with the earlier work of Marshall McLuhan, a Canadian expert on communications, who found that each medium reorganizes the mind in its own way and changes the balance of an individual's senses, increasing some at the expense of others; the consequences of these reorganizations are far more significant than the impact of the content or message (Doidge, 2007, p. 308).

David Elkind (2007) urged that preschool and kindergarten children should not engage in any screen activity for longer than a half hour per day and that children should be encouraged to interact socially while using computers. The Canadian Pediatric Society recommends no screen time for children under age two; limit screen time for children older than age three, that is, one hour of quality educational viewing daily; tune in only to educational shows that help build vocabulary and symbol recognition; and choose shows that encourage imaginary play and role play. Because most children inevitably watch television in their homes, television should not be included in the early childhood program.

Using Technologies to Support Projects in Early Childhood Education

ECEs should reflect carefully on how they will integrate technologies, especially computers, into the projects that emerge from children's play. A balanced approach ensures that children's use of technologies emphasizes the ways in which they use them to access information, to express ideas and feelings, to communicate, to find answers to questions, and to solve problems they encounter in their play and projects. Helm & Katz (2011) found that the most frequently used technologies for project work are the digital camera, scanner, and photocopier. Some programs have access to interactive whiteboards, document cameras (docucams), and digital microscopes that enable deeper exploration of projects. Older technologies such as overhead projectors and transparencies are frequently used for such projects as making murals. Technological tools are often more mysterious initially to ECEs than they are to children who figure them out quickly and often teach adults how to use them. When used to enhance children's projects, technologies are useful tools that "empower (children) to take even more control of their learning" (Helm & Katz, 2011, p. 108). Katz (1994) has always given computers a meaningful role to play in the context of children's projects. Computers and other technologies have features relevant to children's projects, such as *speed,* which makes processes happen quickly; *automation,* which transforms formerly tedious tasks into effortless operations; *capacity* to store and retrieve large amounts of information; *access* to diverse materials from a wide range of resources; *provisionality,* which is the ability to change content; and *interactivity* that allows the user to respond repeatedly to input (Kennewell & Beauchamp, 2007). Beauchamp (2010) recommends that ECEs match the special features of the technology they will use for an activity with the purpose of the activity and not use it simply for its own sake.

Project Learning

The early origins of the project approach in ECE were outlined in Chapter 8. Katz (1994, p. 1) defined a project as "an in-depth investigation of a topic worth learning more about. The investigation is usually undertaken by a small group of children within a class, sometimes by a whole class, and occasionally by an individual child. The key feature of a project is that it is a research effort deliberately focused on finding answers to questions about a topic posed either by the children, the ECE, or the ECE working with the children." When the project approach fully respects children's play, the best features of both worlds are integrated. We know that children need unfettered play in an environment rich in resources for play and opportunities for exploration, finding and embracing challenges, and discovery. The challenge for ECEs is to learn "how to support and not crush children's curiosity and natural dispositions to learn, and yet still achieve curriculum goals" (Helm & Katz, 2011, p. 13). When children identify what they want to explore and investigate in their projects, assemble their resources for the project, and define their own goals, projects become another medium for play. Because many projects for children involve in-depth investigation of worthwhile topics that interest them, children's "research" often focuses on finding answers to questions.

Projects usually involve a small group of children, a whole class, or, occasionally, an individual child working with the ECE, so that the research tasks may be shared. Projects encourage the development of habits of mind related to thinking and learning-to-learn during the early years: these include making sense of experience; analyzing, hypothesizing, synthesizing; predicting and making predictions; finding things out; learning how to be accurate; grasping the consequences of actions; persisting in seeking solutions to problems; and speculating about cause-and-effect relationships (Helm & Katz, 2011, p. 4). All of these skills are necessary for successful academic learning later on, but they are also practical skills that are relevant, lifelong, for daily living.

A Project centre serves as a place where projects that originate in any other learning centre, or outdoors, are developed and come together. For example, children may need access to various technologies and other tools to conduct research on insects, to compile a book of drawings, to print a newsletter for their parents, or to model collages with shapes on the two-dimensional screen that they have created with three-dimensional blocks. Computers, printers, copiers, scanners, cameras, and small items such as scissors, clips, brads, and paper covers (office supplies) are tools for projects that may involve science, art, literacy, and role play. Children can make lists of things they need to do or make at the computer. For example, planning a garden usually involves a design stage in which children graphically represent the shape of the garden, identify the tools they need, and draw reminders about how to look after the garden. Digital cameras allow children to photograph their projects as a visible record of what they have achieved together. Where space allows, a large, low circular or semicircular table located in the Project centre is useful for children to lay out materials, work on and assemble projects, and find easy access to the tools they need.

In the past, projects were often regarded as too advanced and inappropriate for young children under age five, but experience has proven otherwise. In fact, Helm & Katz (2011, p. 108) believe that projects are particularly beneficial for children living in poverty who need access to tools that help them acquire skills, take risks, and learn new approaches to learning, and for children with special needs. Projects encourage children and their teachers to collaborate and contribute to the project; they are based on interests and tasks that the children have identified; they provide variety so that children in small groups can be involved in different pursuits; and the emphasis on documenting the project stages and experiences encourages children to express themselves clearly and purposefully (Helm & Katz, 2011, p. 108). Projects have also proven helpful for children who are second-language learners because they are naturally inclusive activities that carve out a role for all players (Christian, 1994).

The Relationship among Technologies, Projects, and Child Development

Social Development

Computers may serve social development goals by encouraging the shy child who does not respond well to group activities and by drawing out the quiet, passive child who may emerge as a leader in the Project centre (Beaty & Tucker, 1987). Children gain by listening to and seeing the ideas and actions of others take shape within the projects—ideas and behaviours that they may imitate in future projects. During debriefing sessions with the ECE once the project or a phase of it has been completed, children learn to respect and offer supportive comments for the contributions of each child in the group. The social skills they acquire through participating in projects teach social attitudes and behaviours that will last a lifetime. Projects require children to cooperate and help each other, to provide ideas that contribute to the project, and to communicate. Children learn to accept alternative ideas that may not have occurred to them, to give credit and recognition to others for their contributions, and to be fair to those who disagree with them (Helm & Katz, 2011). Children also learn to compare themselves to others and gain self-knowledge as they experience that they have particular strengths to offer while others have their unique strengths.

Physical Development

Some specialized software addresses physical perceptual skills, such as **visual discrimination, ocular motor skills, spatial concepts, figure–ground relationships,** and auditory skills. (See Appendix A, p. 466, for an expanded list of the physical perceptual skills.) Children practise fine-motor skills by colouring, drawing, or playing games using a joystick or a mouse. Software that addresses these skills may provide helpful repetition for the child who is experiencing perceptual difficulties and other physical delays.

Emotional Development

Projects provide many opportunities for children to develop emotional skills. When children are encouraged to use technologies to help with their project ideas or to put their ideas into a recognizable form, self-regulation is a key requirement. The executive functioning abilities, including the ability to change and control their own behaviours, are a crucial prerequisite to children's success in any endeavour worth doing and also in their ability to use computers successfully (Lauricella, Barr, & Calvert, 2008). For example, when they encounter a camera that no longer works or that they don't know how to operate, children learn to ask for help, to be patient as they wait for a resolution, and to recognize the power of persistence when a peer or adult tries several ways to solve the problem and eventually succeeds. Project-based play demands that children accept their position as one member of a larger group that includes children whose interests may be different than their own. Projects also provide an opportunity for children to value the contributions of others. Empathy is required when another child feels left out or is unable to play a principal role, and children should be encouraged to help others feel included and important to the project.

Cognitive Development

Computer software for children provides practice with the executive functions, such as decision making and logical thinking, by encouraging children to choose from a variety of alternatives and to make clear choices of one path or one menu item. The software may provide onscreen encouragement of children's mastery of tasks, which motivates them to proceed to the next level. Whether learning collaboratively at the computer or individually, the computer facilitates the development of learning-to-learn skills and guides children's goal-directed behaviour, which develops rapidly in early childhood (Hughes, 2002). As mentioned earlier, for children to experience success as they play with the computer, early demonstration of the executive functions —working memory, inhibition, and shifting attention between two competing tasks (Galinsky, 2010) is an important prerequisite.

Organization and Design of the Project Centre

The Project centre contains equipment, materials, and supplies for investigation, inquiry, communication, listening, viewing, documenting and reporting, creating and inventing, publishing, and photographing. The various play stations in this centre may include a listening table, a viewing area, an office/desk area, a computer table and chairs, and a work table for projects, which serves as potential play space (see Figure 18–1).

Equipment, Materials, and Supplies

- **Equipment:** computer table, desk, chairs and table, listening table, large table for working on projects (where space allows), storage shelves for old typewriter, desktop or laptop computers, mobile devices, video camcorder, multimedia player, interactive whiteboard, tablets, ebooks, colour printer, software applications, film projector, filmstrip and overhead projector and transparencies, telephone, digital audio recorder, headphones, record player, magnifiers, photocopier, scanner, transparency projectors, light tables, digital cameras, and bulletin boards
- **Materials**: slides in slide holders, View-Master, notebooks, hole punch, binders, file folders, and other office materials
- **Supplies**: printer paper, writing paper and envelopes, index cards, graph paper, plain paper, pencils, paper clips, stapler, scissors, tape, diskettes, erasers, gluestick, self-adhesive notes, and markers

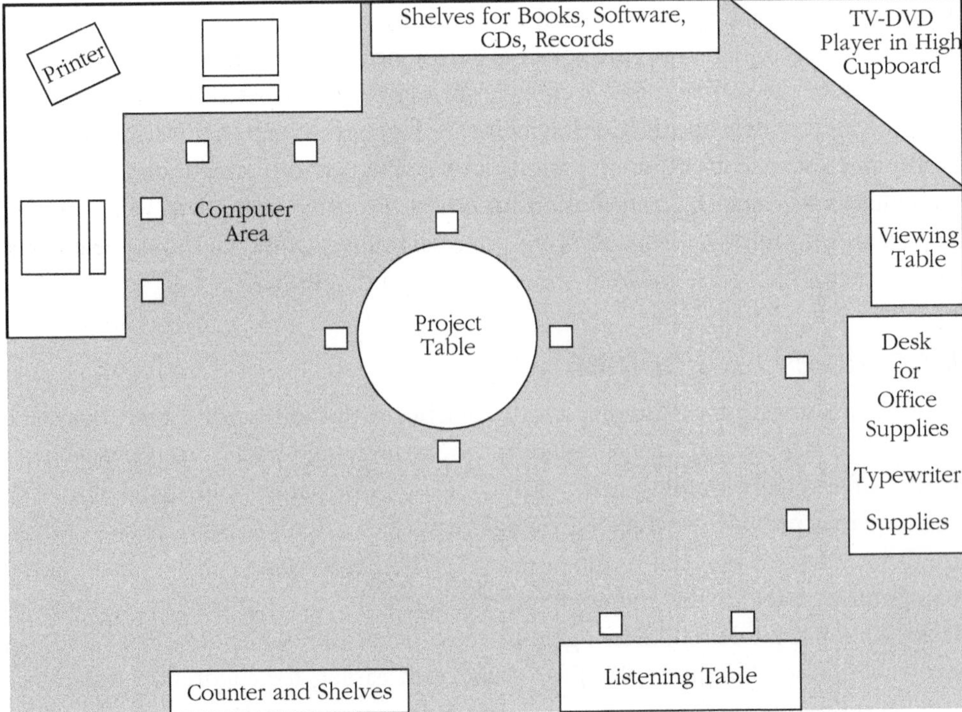

Figure 18–1
The Project centre

Locating the Project Centre

The Project centre is usually located near a quiet area, well away from messy play, and with sufficient space for children to work individually and in small groups. By placing the Project centre near the Quiet Thinking centre, children are encouraged to use the technologies and office materials to complement the perceptual and conceptual learning occurring as children play nearby with specific-purpose and modular materials. When the Project centre is close to the Science Discovery centre, it is handy for children to access information on the Internet to help with their science projects. The location of the Project centre should allow children to move easily from play with modular and specific-purpose kits, to computers and other technologies where they can apply learning gained from play with three-dimensional materials. Some software applications replicate, in two-dimensional or three-dimensional form on the screen, images similar to those that children have experienced with concrete materials. Others use movable building blocks on the screen or the shape configurations in puzzles or let children manipulate shapes and symbols. The Project centre provides opportunities for children to transfer drawing, painting, and design problems they have solved using graphic materials in the Creative Arts centre to drawing and painting programs on the computer. This learning centre should be easily accessible to children who want to use the technologies and office materials to assist their work on projects started in other centres.

Play Stations in the Project Centre

Listening Table

A **listening table** may be located in the Project centre for use in projects related to taping music for a show or parade, conducting interviews for a "program," or creating and recording a story. The listening table and audio equipment should be portable so that, alternatively, they may be located in the Quiet Thinking centre where children can avoid distractions when there is a busy project going on in the Project centre. The number of chairs for children at the table should correspond to the number of headsets available for the tape recorder or record player: two or three headsets at the table at a time usually suffice. CDs and book-CD sets should be stored beside the listening table for easy access by children. Audio recorders encourage children to interview each other about activities or projects they are engaged in and to listen to what they record. A listening table might also house a radio (with or without headphones); a CD and/or MP 3 player; and, perhaps, a record player for playing "old favourite" children's songs.

The listening table promotes auditory discrimination abilities, receptive and expressive language, and enjoyment of recorded music. It also provides respite from the auditory stimuli in the learning environment, as the headsets temporarily separate the child from the playroom noise. At the listening table, children learn how to operate electronic equipment and are soon adept. The ability to use technologies encourages children's feelings of mastery and control over their environment and enhances their self-esteem when they are able to show another child or an ECE how to use a technology. A listening table in the Project centre emphasizes the development of perceptual and manipulative skills and cognitive abilities, and complements activities with similar performance objectives located in the Quiet Thinking centre.

The listening table also recognizes the importance of listening, provides time to be relatively passive and to appreciate the variety of sounds, and provides a quiet space to choose what to listen to and how to focus.

Recorded stories on CDs with verbal instructions to children about when to turn the page, when to sing along, and what to say in response to recorded questions—are helpful additions to the listening table. Children enjoy recording their own stories, and ECEs may record a sociodramatic play episode or sociodrama they produce. CDs that offer stories, rhymes, and songs to promote language skills as well as the development of music appreciation and listening abilities may be stored at the listening table. It is best to separate the listening table and the music area, as there is bound to be conflict between children who are there to listen and those who are there to move to the sounds of the music or to engage in active role play. The musical instruments are best located in an area with space for children to move to the music, and the listening table is more effective in a quiet area that is more task-oriented. When recorded music is needed for movement activities, the ECE may move the CD player from the Project centre to the Active Role Play centre.

Selecting CDs for the listening table should use development as a guide. Many children's CDs are designed to promote specific auditory discrimination abilities, such as *Peter and the Wolf*, which helps children recognize the sounds of instruments in the orchestra. Children today need frequent planned experiences and practice in listening to stories without the accompanying visual stimuli, as these listening experiences foster imagination and "seeing with the mind's eye." Recorded stories with instructions to children about when to perform a physical action, without the visual accompaniment, hone children's listening skills.

Viewing Area

Children are bombarded with television and videos in their homes, much of questionable quality and educational merit, but they do learn from well-produced television programs that challenge their imaginations, moral development, memory skills, and thinking abilities. *Sesame Street* is one example, as are some Canadian-directed television series, such as *Toot and Puddle*, *It's a Big Big World*, and *Mr. Moon*, which challenge children's perceptual skills and deliver strong pro-social messages about empathy and moral judgment. *As a general rule, however, television should remain a home-based technology and should not be imported into the early childhood program.*

A table or a wide shelf may contain handheld viewing materials, such as a View-Master and a transparency viewer. With so many sophisticated technological devices available, we forget the simple pleasures children derive from a View-Master, which does not qualify as technology but offers a pleasing contrast. Old View-Masters are sometimes found at garage sales, while new ones may be obtained through the Fisher-Price website. A filmstrip projector and a small screen serve a similar purpose, and children can easily operate the projector after some instruction and demonstration. When children have access to a range of mechanical, electrical, and technological devices that they can be taught to operate, they feel an enhanced sense of control over their environment. The viewing area might also include a range of kaleidoscopes to complement the three-dimensional materials in other learning centres.

Digital cameras make it easy to retain records of children's activities, particularly to document stages in their projects and finished products. Giving children access to a camera to record images they see provides a window to help us understand what interests them. The people, places, things, and events they capture with a camera reveal much about their perspective of the environment and what they believe is entertaining to others. Children often surprise us with their success in recording an event on camera, creating sets and puppet characters to make an animated film and assisting with the editing. The production of an animated film can interest children over many weeks for each facet of the production, from composing the plot and script, making the sets and puppet characters, and rehearsing the action, to filming, editing, and then promoting their production to parents and other children. Programs are increasingly using interactive whiteboards, docucams, and digital cameras in their investigative projects, as well as soft technologies such as overhead projectors and transparencies. These technologies enhance "not just documentation of project experiences, but also study and investigation by children" (Helm & Katz, 2011, p. 107).

Office Area

Projects that originate in any of the learning centres may be mapped out in the office play station during the planning and reporting stages. The Project centre should contain a desk or table for an old typewriter and a desk for "writing" stocked with office supplies such as paper clips, brads, used envelopes and notepads, stamps, stamp pads, and other office gadgets. This play station provides an environment for sociodramatic play that replicates the home or corporate office where their parents may work and an opportunity for children to develop a range of manipulative, fine motor, perceptual, expressive language, and coordination skills. Some children have experienced farm offices equipped with files of records on livestock, invoices, and photographs of farm equipment and livestock. An office play station introduces children to the varied world of work and addresses literacy skills: the use of letter symbols; the creation of signs, messages, and memos; and the production of letters, stories, and newsletters. A bulletin board, where children can tack messages, mount posters, and display the creations they have made on the computer adds to the emphasis on literacy skills in the office area. Because our society values literacy and verbal and written communication using a variety of production instruments, children readily identify with the play opportunities in the office area.

ACTIVITIES FOR THE OFFICE AREA FOR CHILDREN AGES FOUR TO SIX

1. Set up a publishing company by providing a desk with paper, binders, paper clips, crayons, and pencils, and encourage children to make books out of the graphics they have created at the computer or the typewriter. Children may add art productions from the Creative Arts centre to their books.
2. Encourage children to produce their own messages by copying a poster hung on the wall or by replicating a set of instructions or symbols using a typewriter or a computer graphics program. Help them print out their own productions.
3. Suggest children make "mail" for a post office super unit by stuffing, addressing, and stamping envelopes.

Computer Area

Beaty and Tucker (1987) recommended placing computers and a printer in a sectioned area where distractions are minimized, against a wall, and away from direct sunlight to prevent glare. An electrical outlet should be close by, with a power surge suppressor bar for the computers, the printer, and, possibly, the auxiliary lighting. Because computers and printers are sensitive to heat and dust, they should be placed away from heat sources, chalkboards, and dusty carpets, and desktop models should be covered with dust covers when not in use. Independent use of the computers should be encouraged, but ECEs should clarify and consistently reinforce three rules: (1) do not bring liquids or food into the computer area; (2) use only fingers on the devices; and (3) come to the computers with clean hands.

The computer area, preferably with two computers, monitors, keyboards, printer, and peripherals such as a child's keyboard, drawing pad, and mouse, is a key feature of the Project centre. Two or more chairs should be placed in front of each computer, which should be placed at right angles to each other in one of corner of the learning centre so that children cooperate, help each other, discuss the software, and solve problems together (Davidson, 1989). This arrangement conveys the message that computer play is a social experience as well as a learning time. Children are encouraged to cooperate in solving puzzles and to reach a consensus, perhaps by voting, before the next key is pressed. A strategy for groups of three or more is for one child to operate the keyboard and mouse and for the remaining children to collaborate in solving the puzzle or playing a game.

Children work more easily at the computer if it has a special keyboard with larger letter and number symbols. Drawing software applications promotes eye–hand coordination, manipulative abilities, and fine motor skills and provides another medium for children to represent what they are thinking. When children use word processors they learn letter and number symbols while producing letters, memoranda, notes, and stories that originate in their sociodramatic play. If funds allow for a laptop computer, it can be moved into any learning centre as needed; this provides opportunities to integrate the computer as a tool to facilitate projects that originate in any learning centre that call for planning, research on the Internet, communication with children who may be in other countries, documentation, and reporting.

The computer area should provide shelves close to the computers for software packages, manuals, and reference items for children and adults. A bulletin board on the wall of the Project centre near the computer displays instructions for the use of the computer, as well as graphics that children have made using the computer. Bulletin boards also display reports or diagrams, list tasks and responsibilities, identify project participants, and post newsletters and other children's publications. A nearby cupboard stores CDs; dust-free cloths for dusting furniture and equipment surfaces; extra ink cartridges; paper; and accessories, such as stickers, file cases, and CD envelopes.

Use computers in developmentally appropriate ways.

Developmentally appropriate use of computers and other technologies promotes the transfer of learning to and from other learning centres. Computers should enhance development rather than structure learning. Useful applications allow children to manage their own learning and to reflect on the results of their actions; they also permit them to revise their plans and actions. Applications that do not allow children to execute their own conceptual plan create conflict and disappointment and should be avoided (Burns, Goin, & Donlon, 1990).

Applications and software should assume the role of the adult and, therefore, should be flexible enough to accommodate incorrect responses. Feedback should vary according to children's responses and should encourage children to revise or correct their responses. Content should be sequenced from simple to more complex concepts and build on previous learning; permit choice and active problem solving; and facilitate the discovery of concepts by allowing the child to manipulate pictures on the screen. To explore relationships, children need to be able to change the configuration of screen images. Above all, software should be easy to use, colourful, and clear, and it should promote positive values; violent, vulgar, and mindless content is unacceptable. Aesthetic quality greatly affects the overall appeal of software for children and should be an important criterion in its selection, just as it is for children's books. Software applications that encourage children to collaborate in solving a puzzle, finding solutions to problems, and creating something new optimize the effectiveness of computers in promoting collaborative learning.

CHOOSING DEVELOPMENTALLY APPROPRIATE SOFTWARE

Essa (2011, p. 10) adapted criteria originated by Haugland and Shade (1990) for choosing developmentally appropriate software:

1. *Age appropriateness:* Concepts and methods the software presents have realistic expectations of young children.
2. *Child control:* Children, not the computer, decide on the flow and direction of the activity.
3. *Clear instructions:* Verbal or graphic directions are simple and precise, and written instructions are easy to read.
4. *Expanding complexity:* Software begins with a child's current skills and builds skills in a realistic learning sequence.
5. *Independence:* Children use the computer and software with a minimum amount of adult supervision.
6. *Process orientation:* Children are engaged by exploring and discovering on the computer so that extrinsic rewards are unnecessary, and the essential features of play are maintained, such as freedom to choose, making decisions, deciding when to start and finish.
7. *Real-world model:* Software objects are reliable models of the world.
8. *Technical features:* Software has colourful, uncluttered, animated, and realistic graphics; realistic sound effects; and minimal waiting times.
9. *Trial and error:* Software provides unlimited opportunity for creative problem solving, exploring alternatives, and correcting their own errors.
10. *Transformations:* Children are able to change objects and situations, ask "what if" questions, and see the effects of their actions.

Computer-Supported Projects for Children with Special Needs

Projects using computers are particularly helpful for exceptional children, as they allow them to play a significant role. Children with physical disabilities, for example, might become the record-keepers or the graphic artists drawing the diagrams. Projects encourage children with special needs to participate fully in the life of the playroom and achieve the outcomes in their individual educational plan (IEP) (Helm & Beneke, 2003). Children with disabilities exhibit high motivation and are integrated more effectively in programs that include the use of computers, especially when they are used for projects. Edmiaston (1998) noted that projects should be collaborative for children and ECEs; based on children's interests and shape the experiences to their

Learning with computers

needs; allow for children to do different things within the project; and encourage children to document their project experiences to emphasize their own roles and contributions. Burg (1984) found that children who have problems with language, fine motor skills, and socialization made significant gains through play at a computer. In some instances, play at a computer reduces the effects of disabilities by accommodating the disability and by permitting children to perform certain tasks and operations independently. As well, voice synthesizers and word processors greatly enhance opportunities for language and for communication. The child with physical disabilities may use a computer to turn on the television, answer the telephone, or perform other tasks previously impossible for him.

Computers respond to children's actions on them, are always patient, and may well be the most important improvement in the education of children with disabilities (Behrmann & Levy, 1986). Well-chosen software provides immediate feedback to children. The responsiveness of the computer to children's actions on it gives them a sense of control and mastery and boosts their emotional security, which helps them meet learning challenges presented by the computer. Even researchers who are skeptical about the generalized use of computers with children under age seven tend to acknowledge their usefulness for children with certain disabilities (Healy, 1998). Evidence shows that the use of technologies and applications, i.e., "apps," in programs for all children reduces the digital divide that would otherwise have a negative impact on children with disabilities and also on children from homes without a computer (NAEYC, 2011).

PROJECTS THAT ENCOURAGE CHILDREN TO USE COMPUTERS

1. Plan a garden, using the computer, by drawing the garden and identifying what would be planted in each section. Include pathways or stepping stones in the garden; keep records of seeds and plants purchased, dates they were sown and harvested, and the crop yielded from each patch; and create photos of produce or flowers.
2. Create a favourite recipe book by asking parents to provide recipes for their children's favourite foods. The children use the computer to illustrate the pages, design the cover page, bind the book with laces or brads, and store a copy of the book on the computer for later revisions.
3. Keep records of a project to investigate the characteristics of various types of trees in the neighbourhood. Create a table to compare the trees on a set of descriptive criteria, such as texture of bark, height, size, and shape of leaves or needles; alignment of the branches; whether it has blossoms or seed pods or not; and whether it provides shade or not.
4. Create a program newsletter in the office area, using the computer and printer to add children's drawings, project reports, photos, stories they have created, new songs they have learned, and new outdoor games they have played.
5. Maintain a photo and drawing record of fieldtrips taken by the children to interesting places in the community and children's responses to the

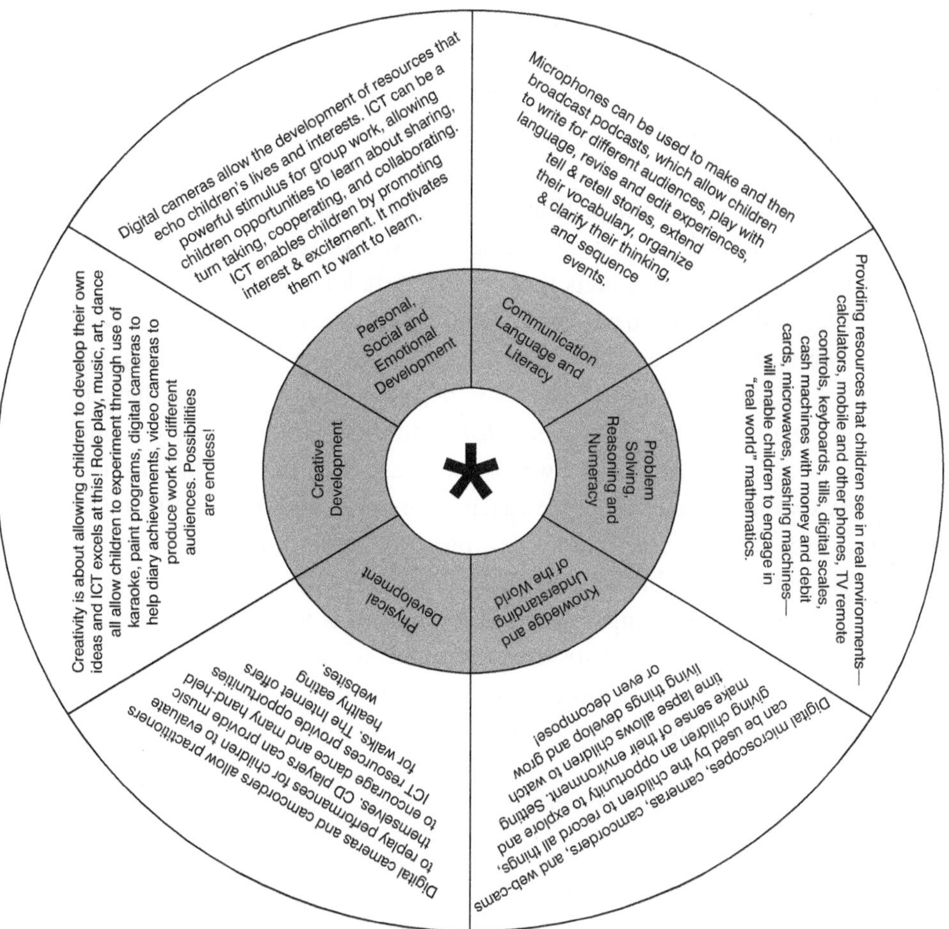

Figure 18–2
How Technology Can Be Integrated into Development and Learning

Source: Tyler, L. (2010). "21st Century Digital Technology and Children's Learning," in M. Reed & N. Canning (Eds). *Reflective Practice in the Early Years* (pp. 44–51). London, UK: Sage.*

experience. After each trip, talk with children about what interested them most, project ideas the trip may have generated, and people they met.

6. Build a website for the program with the children. Explore websites to search for ideas to use in building the website. Discuss the purpose of the website.
7. Create a poetry website to which children can contribute their rhymes, poems, and stories.

Using the Internet to Foster Individual and Collaborative Project Learning

Information technologies have the potential to engage children in active, constructive, intentional, authentic, and cooperative learning (Jonassen et al., 2003). We know that digital literacy is essential in the 21st century, and the Internet is an effective means to encourage collaboration and to connect children to each other within their communities and throughout the world. The Internet challenges children to look for, analyze, and compare information; evaluate what they find; apply information; define their goals; and create symbols, images, and documents that represent their learning. Information technologies act as a *participant* in interaction for children who play with electronic tools; as the *object* of interaction as in the case of a video clip, or as a *tool* for interaction when children send electronic messages through their portable digital screens (DS) or computer or write on an interactive whiteboard (Beauchamp & Kennewell, 2008). Jonassen et al. (2003, p. 47) recommend the thoughtful use of WebQuests to encourage children to gather, analyze, and synthesize information, which implies that they "incorporate cooperative learning, consider multiple perspectives, analyze and synthesize information, and create original products that demonstrate knowledge gained." ECEs may, for example, design WebQuests that promote children's thinking and collaborative investigation and realize a result related to the goal. For example, following a trip to the local children's museum, an ECE might plan a WebQuest that challenges children to investigate other museums for children. Many of these museums, such as the Exploratorium (http://www.exploratorium.edu) in San Francisco, Kidspark (http://www.ontariosciencecentre.ca) in Toronto, and the Boston Children's Museum (http://www.bostonkids.org), provide detailed information on websites about their featured exhibits. Virtual fieldtrips to these and other sites provide children with interactive learning opportunities and ideas for projects, using the websites as resources. Virtual fieldtrips have the added advantage that they are safe; easily accessible for all children, including those with disabilities; allow for exploration at the child's pace; and ensure that children are obtaining information from experts.

SUMMARY OF PRINCIPLES FOR USING TECHNOLOGIES IN EARLY CHILDHOOD EDUCATION

1. Locate computers in classrooms to optimize children's social learning, collaboration, and cooperation on projects.
2. Because computers have the potential to extend children's reliance on visual imaging and creative and representational thinking, use computers as instruments for promoting self-expression, divergent thinking, inquiry, problem solving, documenting, reporting, spatial reasoning, and representation.
3. Select software applications that give the child control over the software and allow for the transfer of learning from other media to the computer, and vice versa.
4. Promote a playful approach to the use of technologies to enhance children's fun, social interaction, curiosity, and discovery.
5. Use computers in projects to solve problems, answer questions, and think logically, not as teaching machines that lead to predefined structures of thought.
6. Ensure that computers encourage children to collaborate, and that they equalize and democratize learning opportunities for children of all cultural and socioeconomic groups and those with disabilities.

Summary

The Project centre is a hub in the playroom because it can be used effectively to support play and learning in all centres; it is a focal point for work on projects. Children are growing up in a world where technologies are taken for granted; therefore, today's children adapt effortlessly to the use of technologies and regard them as everyday tools to help them do things. It is the adults who often have to learn new skills for using technologies effectively with children and to ensure that they are used in developmentally appropriate ways. The Project centre provides space to locate various technologies that children may use constructively in their play in other centres, such as to support their creative productions in the Creative Arts centre, and to facilitate their problem solving and documentation of science projects. The Project centre allows children to escape from the intense activity of other centres. This centre may become a resource hub that children can raid for tools to enhance activities in other centres or as a place to which they may bring their projects to put them together, enter them onto the computer, or solve a problem using a software program. It is a centre where children can play quietly, alone or in groups, with software applications that address skills related to logical concepts and literacy development. Computers are the centrepiece of the Project centre, but other technologies are also present to assist play and learning, such as cameras, projectors, typewriters, audio recorders, photocopiers, scanners, and low-technology devices. When space allows, this centre is a prime location for expansive projects of some duration, where children may spread their work and leave it out.

LEARNING ACTIVITIES

1. After reading this chapter, develop a set of principles to guide your teaching and your use of various technologies to help children learn to think, plan and implement projects, create, communicate, document, solve problems, and display their works.
2. Identify areas where you need to develop technological literacy in order to plan and implement a curriculum and activities that use technologies to promote creative thinking and problem solving skills. State your learning needs as learning outcomes and include the resources you need to consult in order to use technologies effectively with young children. Work on this task with your colleagues to compare notes on learning needs and to prepare a professional development plan to keep in your journal.
3. Visit garage sales, bazaars, and auction sales to find materials for the viewing area (e.g., old View-Master reels, opera glasses and binoculars, kaleidoscopes, photographs and transparencies, and hand-held projectors for slides). Build a viewing area prop box.
4. Visit your local computer store to research educational software applications for young children. List the software companies that produce developmentally appropriate tools for active learning. Decide which software applications are most effective in promoting children's creative thinking, encouraging the children to collaborate and assume control of their learning, and teaching them to document and report what they are doing and have completed.
5. Create a project plan for a multiphase project for children. Your objectives for the project should reflect the principles you have adopted for using technologies with children. Write activity cards for each of the steps in the project. Describe the teaching approach for getting children started on the project and for helping them participate in planning the various steps; set goals; and assemble the materials needed.
6. Generate a list of projects with several stages that would be completed over time by a group of children. Describe the main tasks and skills involved in the projects you list. Write activity cards for each of the discrete activities included as parts of each project.

Section VI
Creative Play

Section VI addresses the following topics:

- the definition of creativity
- the relationship between play and creative pursuits
- developmental stages in creativity and drawing
- creative expression and representation using clay, fabric, wood, and unit blocks
- aesthetic development and appreciation of the visual arts
- unit blocks as creative-constructive play materials
- unit blocks as play materials that convey mathematical concepts
- the use, storage, and protection of unit blocks

Equipping young children to become "autonomous and active creators of the future" is a key purpose of early childhood education (Wright, 2010, p. 10). One reason for optimizing creative development in the early years is that, after age seven, significant aspects of children's inclination for fantasy play, imagination, and risk taking, as well as the ability to think in symbols, become dominated by the more orderly, rule-bound requirements of academic schooling. Protecting children's right and need to express themselves without reining them in and constructing rules and boundaries for their creativity is as important as protecting their right to play. A curriculum to sustain children's creativity during the early years and past age seven should "encourage critical thinking rather than knowledge acquisition, problem-solving skills rather than familiarity with past problems, openness to change rather than commitment to a set of ideas and institutions" (Egan, 1999, p. 78).

Exposure to a wide range of creative materials and opportunities for exploring their properties can enhance children's reliance on the right hemisphere of the brain, which governs visual and spatial tasks (Ormrod, 2006). Early childhood is a time to help children link what is beautiful and artistically valid, link their feelings of wonder at the beauty and precision of nature, and link their sense of balance and symmetry. It is a time to encourage children's ability to represent what they perceive and understand through three-dimensional and two-dimensional media, and through their minds, bodies, and hands.

Two learning centres are prominent in helping children explore materials for the purpose of expressing what they feel, creating something unique, and understanding some universal principles related to perspective, balance, and harmony. The art and modular materials in the Creative Arts and Unit Blocks learning centres are largely abstract tools that encourage children to express themselves, use materials in ways that are interesting and pleasing to them, and explore their properties. They allow children to experiment with art as a medium for self-expression and representation when words fail to communicate what they feel most deeply. The Creative Arts and Unit Blocks centres encourage children's exploration with the tools and supplies needed to experiment, plan, and execute creations that have meaning for them. Children develop a sense of purpose and inner discipline through their unencumbered use of the flexible, divergent materials in these two learning centres, which invite them to represent what they know and understand.

Chapter 19 addresses creative play using surface-diffusible, continuous materials typically found in the art area, as well as other creative arts, such as sewing, moulding with clay, and woodworking. Chapter 20 focuses on unit blocks, which are abstract materials that encourage creative construction; foster children's symbolic and representational thinking skills; and, given the mathematical precision of unit blocks, promote children's recognition of the relationship of parts to the whole and other logical thinking skills.

19 The Creative Arts Centre

"All great artists and thinkers [are] great workers, indefatigable not only in inventing, but also in rejecting, sifting, transforming, ordering."

—FRIEDRICH NIETZSCHE (1878)

BEFORE READING THIS CHAPTER, HAVE YOU

- observed children playing with creative arts materials?
- studied a range of children's artistic productions from age two to age six and tried to discern the developmental progression of their artistry?
- recognized similarities in young children's choices of subjects for their art and in their depictions of people, animals, and other subjects familiar to them?

OUTCOMES

After reading and understanding this chapter, you should be able to

- explain the importance of creative development in early childhood;
- enable children to explore and represent through the visual arts, experimenting with various creative materials in order to understand their unique properties and their usefulness as tools for self-expression and representation;
- link the developmental stages of children's art with appropriate art activities;
- foster children's aesthetic development and appreciation of the variety of ways of representing beauty and conveying meaning among many cultures;
- encourage children to plan their artistic creations and to choose materials for executing their plan; and
- design and set up the Creative Arts centre, including play stations for drawing, painting, messy and dry art, moulding clay, woodworking, and sewing.

What Is Creativity?

Creativity involves perceiving things in new ways, thinking unconventionally, forming unique combinations, and representing an original idea or insight (Schirrmacher, 1988). Wright (2010, p. 3) claims that creativity is both a cognitive trait and a personality trait, and she lists several personal qualities related to creativity: valuing creativity, originality, independence, risk taking, ability to reframe problems, energy, curiosity, attraction to complexity, artistry, open-mindedness, desire for time alone, perceptiveness, concentration, humour, and possession of childlike qualities. Gardner (1983, 1993) claimed that there are many ways to be creative and that people are not necessarily creative in all domains. Some are creative thinkers and writers; others, like architects, are spatially creative; visual artists employ the artistic media of paint, pastel, pencil, fabric, and wood in creating original representations of the world as they see it; still others are creative musicians, orators, athletes, or dancers.

Whatever the creative endeavour, experts appear to agree that the creative impulses are closely related to the mature thinking styles of visualization, imagination, experimentation, analogical and metaphorical thinking, logical thinking, prediction of outcomes, analysis, synthesis, and evaluation (Wright, 2010, p. 3). Wright (2010) makes connections between thinking styles and the ability to execute and represent an original idea or concept. MacKinnon (1971) believed that creative behaviour involves having original or unusual ideas that bear some relationship to authentic situations or goals, and planning, thinking through, and sustaining the ideas until some outcome occurs. Certainly, there is agreement that creativity is not a flash of inspiration that emerges from mindless experimentation or dabbling, but, rather, it is a deliberate, purposeful activity directed toward representing an idea or insight using a creative medium. *Creativity is more closely associated with disciplined habits of mind and skilled, knowledgeable use of materials than with spontaneous and inspired insights.*

Creativity and Play

Facilitating children's creative development follows many of the guidelines for facilitating play. Children should choose when and how they will play, in an environment rich in resources and opportunities for meaningful creative play, under the watchful eyes of adults who guide, sometimes question and challenge, respond to children, and intervene when play is stalled or the children request help. According to Owen (2010, p. 192), there are two ways to stifle creativity in young children: one is to say no to everything they suggest or are curious to try, and the other is to say yes to everything they suggest, to remove all boundaries, accept everything, tell them their ideas are just fine, and never ask for any changes. Enhancing children's natural creativity calls for the utmost authenticity in the way we respond to their inclinations to represent what they feel, experience, and want to say. Creativity is a precious orientation that "is about offering time and space to understand and experience the processes involved—which need personal qualities of application, struggle and testing, alongside the social qualities of cooperation, collaboration and mutual criticism" (Owen, 2010, pp. 192–193).

Creative activity in the early years should expose children to free play with art materials and media, so that they learn to use artistic tools to represent their world as they see it. Young children do not yet have the artistic skills, discipline, ability to plan and follow through, and perspective required to fashion an artistic product that will make a significant impact. They are at a stage, however, when they are able to express themselves freely, acquire knowledge of materials and techniques, and develop their sensory abilities for later creative achievement. Gardner (1989) suggested that young children have a *first draft* sense of what it means to draw a picture, tell a story, or invent a song—a sense that should be encouraged. Children need opportunities to use open-ended materials to express feelings, perceptions, and individuality. Childhood is a time to develop confidence in one's own perspectives and a lifelong appreciation for the value of the visual arts to represent what words alone cannot convey. The early years are a time for children to play at being artists, play with various artistic media, and be exposed to a wide range of experiences that feed their imaginations and stir their creative impulses.

The Creative Arts Centre

The Creative Arts centre is where children are encouraged to nurture their senses, explore beauty in its various forms, and experiment with a range of materials for expressing what they perceive and feel. *It is not a place to put art materials in service of the development of literacy skills or other academic skills development.* Not everything that occurs in the Creative Arts centre is creative, however. Nor is creative exploration confined to this learning centre; creative activity can and should occur in all learning centres. The Creative Arts centre should motivate children to express themselves with a range of art materials and to develop a *creative orientation* (Gardner, 1989).

Creative exploration and experimentation occur whenever children are able to use materials, media, and their own bodies to represent something they know or feel. A well-planned Creative Arts centre fosters creative explorations using **graphic materials** of many kinds: malleable substances such as clay and papier mâché; paint; brushes and pencils; and other media, including **collage**, paste, fabric, wood, and cardboard. In experimenting with art materials, such as dipping their brushes and putting endless blobs of paint on the paper, children are exploring the properties of the brushes, paint, and paper rather than being creative. This type of exploration is an essential stage in learning how to use materials creatively and in testing their potential in a variety of artistic contexts. As children gain confidence in their use of materials, they should be encouraged to choose materials selectively, with a plan in mind, ensuring that their choice of materials matches their plan as closely as possible. Children will seldom tire of having unrestricted access to basic art materials and supplies that leave them in charge of planning and executing what they feel, perceive, and imagine in their own minds.

Aesthetic Development

Aesthetic development refers to the child's emerging sense of what is beautiful and artistically valid, and is closely related to a feeling of wonder. "It is a sensibility that uses imagination as well as the five senses" (Mayesky, 1997, p. 26). As they gain an aesthetic sense, children become aware of the beauty of the environment and sensitive to the relationship between beauty in its various forms and the emotional responses these forms elicit in all of us. Beauty is culturally determined and may be expressed in many ways through music, art, dance, and drama. Children's ability to appreciate beauty in many forms is closely related to their spiritual development. For this reason, aesthetic environments for children should include beautiful things arranged in appealing ways, which reflect the natural environment, have interesting colour and shape combinations, and are artistic representations of aspects of daily life with which children can identify. This is why it is important to include the cultural and artistic works important to the diverse cultures of the children in the group. Care should be taken to choose play materials that are well crafted and pleasing to the senses of touch and sight. Increasingly, the beautiful works of First Nations and Inuit artists appear in Canadian ECE programs, a practice that should be encouraged by accessing the rich array available through virtual galleries. Children's aesthetic development may be nurtured in many simple ways, from displaying art at children's eye level in the hallways and entrances to placing display cases in strategic places; by adding seasonal flowers, fruit, and plant arrangements to the rooms where children play; and by incorporating art, music, dance, and drama into all aspects of the program. A gallery of children's art perhaps at the entrance to the centre or school, allows visitors to admire children's productions.

Aesthetic appreciation is also a taste for quality and an appreciation of harmony in art that develops most readily in a creative climate. Aesthetics are important throughout the whole learning environment but especially in the Creative Arts centre. The artistic creations of children should decorate the bulletin boards and walls. The Creative Arts centre is not a place to hang posters of characters from Disneyland or from popular TV programs. Cute models of popular artifacts, such as Easter bunnies with bows, decorated turkeys, and cartoons of characters from television, are out of place and inappropriate. Displaying adults' versions of what an art activity such as a valentine or jack-o'-lantern should resemble defeats the purpose of the art program. Children do not need contrived ideas to enjoy and find meaning in the art area. For children, self-expression through art is a serious business, not a superficial, casual enterprise designed to entertain.

Gardner (1999) referred to aesthetic development as a *key understanding* that allows us to discriminate between beautiful and not beautiful and to understand the difference between artistic worth and kitsch. Early art education should help children appreciate art and aesthetics by exposing them to great works of art of many cultures and sharpening their sensitivity to beauty and quality (Schiller, 1995). There are many ways of achieving this goal, including taking children to visit art collections in public galleries and art exhibits. Galleries often make their collections accessible to children to help them understand and interpret art and artistry through hands-on programs created and staffed by experts. Increasingly, art galleries, museums, and science centres provide virtual galleries that can be accessed via the Internet; these bring the images of great works of art and other creative exhibits to anyone who can't visit in person. Another way is to bring reproductions of great works of art into the learning environment. ECEs positively influence children's aesthetic sense when they talk to children about their art, encourage them to name and describe their creations to other children, and display their productions prominently in the classroom. Examples should be preserved in children's portfolios to display the progression in their perspectives on their world and their skill with art materials.

When beautiful surroundings and art, music, and drama are integral parts of the children's day, every day, they not only tune their aesthetic sensibilities, but they also learn ways to express their innermost feelings, ideas, and interests in a wide range of constructive ways. A beautiful school environment becomes a haven for children who live their lives in mundane, crowded surroundings, including inner-city environments, where they cannot see the trees and open sky from their homes. Beautiful environments should reflect the colours of a Canadian autumn in natural leaf bouquets, import the green colours of spring through the arrangement of plants, and capture the reflection of sunshine on snow by using mirrors to reflect the winter scene outdoors. Art enhances the quality of life for children because it helps them engage in abstraction and use symbols in ways that contribute to various types of literacy (Sluss, 2005). In a natural environment, children are encouraged to see beyond the material, functional parts of their world and they develop *vision*, including a sense that the world is wonderful. The Creative Arts centre is an environment that has the potential to transport children to a mindset that lies beyond the concrete and rational. In such an environment, children learn that art appreciation has value for its own sake, not the least of which is to add meaning, hope and depth to our experience of life.

Programs that address many aspects of aesthetic development have also discovered meaningful ways to respect and recognize cultural diversity. When parents are encouraged to contribute music—songs, instruments, dance—of their culture and help ECEs integrate them into the program, parents feel that their values and the artistic symbols of their culture are validated. Local galleries often display art unique to the diverse culture of the local environment. Children become skilled at linking various art media, cultural icons, and chosen subjects to a specific cultural community.

The careful arrangement of artwork; the storage of supplies and materials in neat cubicles; and the maintenance of instruments, paper, paste, wood, fabric, and other supplies in clean, neat condition are also priorities for an aesthetically pleasing environment. This approach also teaches respect for the tools used for artistic self-expression. Old supplies, such as stubby crayons, frayed brushes, and paint-caked paint pots, should be discarded. Furniture should ideally be in neutral colours and preferably wooden, sturdy, and easy to clean. Displaying natural things gathered from outdoors, such as driftwood, pine cones, or pink granite rocks, adds to the aesthetic quality of the creative area and fosters children's appreciation of the beauty found in nature that lies close to home.

Developmental Stages of Children's Art

Most adults retain only a fraction of their childhood creative impulses, perceptual sensitivities, and unique ways of viewing the world. What happens to these creative behaviours in the growing years? Artistic endeavours in the visual arts are largely right-hemisphere activities that capitalize on visualization abilities; spatial awareness; spatial reasoning skills; and the retention of visual patterns, such as geometric designs, graphs, and diagrams (Rubenzer, 1984). Children's artistic development passes through distinct stages. Montessori (1949) described the years from two to four as a *sensitive period* for painting, drawing, and other artistic activity. She believed that young children could more easily achieve self-expression through mastering the tools and skills involved in art than through writing or movement. The key to using art as a medium for child development, according to Montessori, lies in providing the materials children need to concretely express their individuality and abstract understanding or perspective. Kellogg (1969) saw children's art as proof of the human being's quest for order and balance. At each stage, children respond to the order they see in the shapes they depict. Although Kellogg (1969) proposed that the shapes created by children at each stage are universal and occur in every culture, Gardner (1989) believed that there are significant cultural differences in the characteristics of children's artistic and graphic development at similar ages and stages. Lowenfelt and Brittain (1987) saw that the stages of children's graphic development tend to correspond with Piaget's cognitive developmental stages; they documented the stages of children's graphic development from 18 months to nine years. Table 19–1 shows the stages from 18 months to seven years and demonstrates that the period from age five to seven is an especially rich creative period in which children understand that they are able to represent graphically what they know or remember, which is consistent with the development of operational thinking. By age seven or eight, much of the creativity that arises from children's visual thinking has decreased, as the right and left hemispheres of the brain have become increasingly defined. As the functioning of the left hemisphere, which controls verbal and abstract thought, increases during the school years, the visual thinking of the right hemisphere becomes less useful and loses its impact. Researchers of creativity in young children have seen a corresponding dramatic decrease at this stage in the child's creative abilities (Gardner, 1980). At this point in the child's development, as mentioned in Chapter 18, computer graphics and drawing tools may be useful instruments for extending and enhancing visual thinking, creative impulses, and the visual imagination well into middle childhood.

The final stage of graphic development in early childhood occurs from about the ages of seven to nine years and is called the **schematic stage**. Because this stage corresponds with children's intense preoccupation with learning to read, with performing numerical operations using rules, and with acquiring factual information, much of the exuberance and freedom evident in children's earlier graphic work begins to fade. Graphic work becomes increasingly a matter of faithfully reproducing forms—of realistically depicting what is seen (Gardner, 1982). As children enter the concrete operational period, when they become more objective and increasingly able to think and solve problems in the absence of concrete objects, their drawings become more objective and literal and less impressionistic. This early operational stage is a period when children may be introduced to activities that rely on specialized skills and the ability to follow steps in an orderly sequence, as required in making creations out of papier mâché, clay, or fabric (Koster, 2005). Children tend to produce fewer drawings and three-dimensional creations with clay and blocks at this stage and are dissatisfied when their productions do not sufficiently represent real life.

TABLE 19–1

STAGES OF GRAPHIC DEVELOPMENT IN EARLY CHILDHOOD FROM 18 MONTHS TO 7 YEARS

Age	Stage	Behaviours	Intentions
18–24 months	disordered scribbling	awkward, random movement of crayon or pencil on paper; holds crayon in tight fist; does not lift crayon or pencil from the paper; child enjoys the kinesthetic experience of scribbling	sensorimotor exploration; to explore properties of crayon and paper along with the movements of the arm and the hand
24–36 months	controlled scribbling	greater control over hand and eye movements; lighter grasp of the crayon or marker; uses motion of the wrist; respect for the boundaries of paper or chalkboard or easel; more awareness of the marks he is making; lifts the brush or crayon frequently to switch colours or to vary the intensity or direction of the brush stroke or crayon lines; draws an animal and mimics the sound; spatial relationships are evident, e.g., juxtaposing two circles—a smaller one for the head and a larger circle for the body	more purposeful; repetitive actions to try different ways to produce an image
3–5 years	pre-schematic stage	representational drawing appears; draws a dog with 4 legs, 2 eyes, and 1 tail; focus at first from the top down; names the scribbles; greater skill in manipulating the graphic materials; fine motor skills and visual perceptual skills are more mature; uses symbols to represent absent objects or events he remembers; memory increases, allowing him to maintain an idea or image of what he wants to capture; geometric forms appear; more knowledgeable interpretation of unique characteristics, physical and cultural, of what he is representing, as in drawing a house with a chimney, veranda, and a car.	child does not mind if adults cannot recognize his drawings; child draws to please himself; tries to interpret what he does; tries to make brush strokes and crayons do what he wants them to do; tries to express what he wants to say or what he feels; attempts to capture and name image; assigns meaning to the image he produces
5–7 years	pre-schematic stage continues	sharp, harmonious perceptions; keen expressive urges; willing to take risks; curious; improved graphic capabilities; enthusiastic, with a drive to express self; vivid imagination; can create images without reference to a model, but too soon to expect original insights or the solving of new problems	tries to represent graphically what he knows or remembers; tries to execute drawings, paintings, and other artistic works that are recognizable; produces images of what is meaningful to him and what he understands

Source: Adapted from V. Lowenfeld and W.L. Brittain (1987). *Creative and Mental Growth* (6th ed.). New York, NY: Macmillan.

Drawing

Drawing is a powerful tool children use for making meaning. Just as building with blocks, making music, and creating patterns are play-based in early childhood, so drawing must be playful in order for children to be motivated, willing to take risks, and fully engaged (Ring, 2010, p. 14). Children draw before they can read and write, but their drawing strengthens their later reading, numeracy, and understanding—and composing through art, like play, is also a function of affective and social development (Wright, 2010, p. 7). Although many of the images children draw at this stage are crude versions of the real world, and their representations of people are distorted, they are very real for children, who have no difficulty assigning a name, a purpose, and a context to their creations. At this stage, "graphic work is truly visible thinking" (Goodnow, 1982, p. 145). Through their drawing and other art forms, children are actively constructing their understanding of themselves and their environments (Wright, 2010, p. 7). Because children are still egocentric during the early pre-schematic stage (three and a half to five years) and see the world from a unique perspective, their own representations of the real world are satisfying to them, and they do not demand that adults find their drawings immediately recognizable. When children are permitted to draw without being rule-bound, their process of drawing brings shape and order to their experience in a purposeful way, and their drawings tend to define reality as they see it rather than passively reflecting reality (Cox, 2005, p. 124). By using the symbol systems of drawing, children manipulate images and concepts familiar to them and to other children who share their unique early childhood artistic "culture." Familiar symbols such as squares, circles, and rectangles combined into "houses," with the sun in one corner, for example, are discernible through children's art that speaks a language all its own and allows children to explore and discover the "hidden principles" that govern human life and the universe (Wright, 2010, p. 9). As children's perceptual skills develop, so do their "seeing skills," and just as they learn to read, they learn to draw (Edwards, 1986). It is the role of ECEs to keep children's desire to draw and to represent their world symbolically alive and lively and to avoid any attempt to mould it into adult-perceived patterns and conventions. Once again, we may learn from the words of an artist who could foresee today's urgent need for creativity and invention:

> Through learning to draw perceived objects or persons, you can learn new ways of seeing that guide strategies in creative thinking and problem solving just as, through learning to read, you acquire verbal knowledge and learn the strategies of local, analytical thought. Using the two modes together, you can learn to think more productively, whatever your creative goals may be. The products of your creative responses to the world will be uniquely your own, your mark on the world. And you will have taken a giant step toward attaining a *modern* brain. For in the years ahead, I believe that perceptual skills combined with verbal skills will be viewed as the basic necessities for creative human thought. (Edwards, 1986, p. 8)

The Role of Art in Early Childhood Education

"Art has the role in education of helping children become more themselves instead of more like everyone else" (Clemens, 1991, p. 4). We have seen that art education is an important vehicle for cultural awareness when cultures are represented in the learning environment together with the tools children need to explore various cultural art forms, such as woven baskets, tapestries, batiks, and soapstone carvings. Katz and Chard (2000) propose four principal learning goals for art education: (1) knowledge

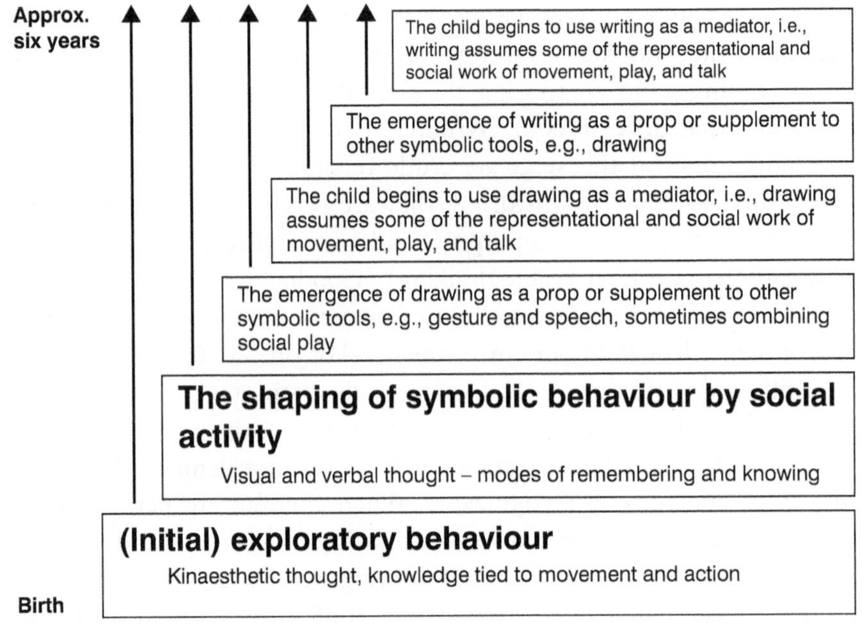

Figure 19–1

The situated nature of drawing within a continuum of children's use of symbol systems

Source: Ring (2003), developed from Dyson (1993).*

of materials and art elements; (2) dispositions to create and think like an artist; (3) feeling and aesthetic responses to the world around them; and (4) skills development that occurs as children learn more about the use of specific materials and are able to discuss what they have created. Creative arts equip young children to become autonomous and active "creators of the future" by encouraging adaptability, imagination, fantasy, sensitivity, decision making, resilience, empathy, an interest in other cultures, communications, problems solving, and lateral thinking (Wright, 2010, p. 10).

Children need an abundance of reliable, high-quality, and **divergent materials** and supplies. The simplest, the most basic, and the easiest to use art materials and supplies are the best. ECEs assume responsibility for selecting and setting up materials; ensuring materials are clean, functional, and in good condition; and encouraging children to appreciate the process in which they are involved, as well as the results of their own efforts and those of others. The ECE has to manage the materials and display children's artistic creations, treating them with the respect they deserve rather than piling them hurriedly on a shelf. The principal role of the ECE in early childhood artistic endeavours is to ensure that children have access to "safe, exciting art supplies, comfortable surroundings, ample space, and time to explore" (Koster, 2005, p. 30). They also need opportunities to be successful and to think like artists. It is not the role of the adult to evaluate the quality of a particular work of art; this approach sends messages to children that it is important to produce art that will please the adult. ECEs should avoid setting a standard for children to emulate or encouraging them to produce something that will please them. An effective strategy is to express interest in what the child is doing, perhaps by commenting on something factual about the artwork (e.g., "The black shows up nicely against the white background" or "I see you've used three colours this time") rather than by expressing an opinion. ECEs who share their feelings about beauty and art with children and who demonstrate

*In *Play and Learning in the Early Years*. Edited by Pat Broadhead, Justine Howard, and Elizabeth Wood. 2010. Sage Publications Ltd. Reprinted with permission from Dr K. Ring and IntellectBooks.

enthusiasm when using art materials to represent meaning are conveying a valuing of art as an important means of self-expression. "It is in the activity of the young child—his preconscious sense of form, his willingness to explore and to solve problems that arise, his capacity to take risks, his affective needs that must be worked out in a symbolic realm—that we find the crucial seeds of the greatest artistic achievements" (Gardner, 1980, p. 269).

Why Product-Based Art Has No Place in Early Childhood Education

Above all, art activities for young children should challenge and stimulate children, not waste their talents by imposing trivial, frivolous, and boring crafts and copying exercises (Katz, 1994). Copying is an unacceptable practice in early childhood education because it fails to promote creativity and discourages children who perceive that they can never live up to the standard the adult has set. Many children stop drawing for this reason. Copying substitutes someone else's representation of an idea or an image to suit someone else's preference and undermines the child's capacity to express what she feels or sees in her own way.

For decades, ECEs have been aware of the importance of process in creative arts and cautioned against using the cut-and-paste type of art more appropriately labelled as busy work. It is surprising that, after so many years of emphasizing the value of children's free exploration of art materials, we still see so many programs where copy-and-paste activities and crafts are deemed to be creative art activities. **Crafts** include activities that ask children to paste ears on paper bunnies or cutouts of faces on pumpkins, for example, or to cut out a model drawn by an ECE on construction paper and match cutout eyes, nose, and mouths to circles. If they are to be used at all, crafts belong at the tables provided for scissors and paper, where the desired outcome is practise for children in using scissors, glue, markers, or crayons and following a pattern. Crafts do not belong in the Creative Arts centre; in fact, one wonders at the value of crafts in any part of the early learning environment when other activities are better suited to practising the fine motor and visual-perceptual skills.

The fact that we still see so much mindless product art in programs undermines the professional status of the work we do and the values our profession represents.

Locating the Creative Arts Centre

Placing the Creative Arts centre close to the Science Discovery centre makes sense, as many of the play and learning experiences available in each centre are complementary. For example, children may want to borrow the naturally occurring substances and items in science collections for their collages or posters. Experimentation with clay in the Creative Arts centre and playing with wet sand in the Science Discovery centre address similar understandings about texture and about the effects of adding water, compacting, moulding, and leaving the clay or sand to dry. These centres are also compatible with the creative intention of the Unit Blocks centre, which may be located nearby. A natural light source is an important feature of the Creative Arts centre, so that children can hold up their works of art to the light to test colour, density of paint, and the transparency of the fabric or paper creations. Natural light also enhances the colour of paint, fabric, and other supplies, avoids the colour distortion caused by artificial light, and enables children to have a clearer vision of the materials they choose to create their work of art.

Organization and Design of the Creative Arts Centre

The Creative Arts centre includes the art area, with easels and tables, the wood construction table, the clay stand, and the sewing table (see Figure 19–2). Although supplies and materials should be neatly arranged and accessible to children, tidiness is not a priority here because of the nature of the play behaviours, which encourage creativity in physical, sensory, emotional, and cognitive experiences. Like the Science Discovery centre, this centre functions better when it has easy access to a water source and tile floors that are easy to mop.

Equipment, Materials, and Supplies

- **Equipment**: easels, storage shelves, drying rack, paper storage rack, two art tables and four to six chairs per table, woodworking bench and stools, and a sewing table and chairs; if space exists, a large table for large creative projects like posters and murals is ideal

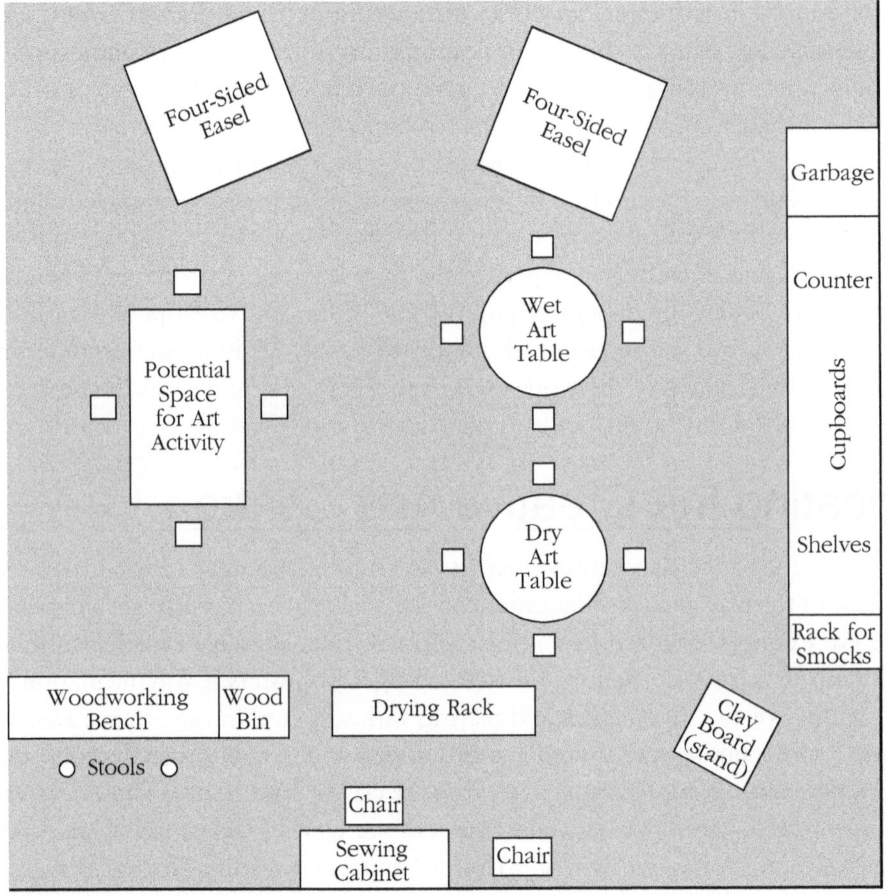

Figure 19–2
The Creative Arts centre

- **Materials**: hammer, saw, vise grips, clamps, softwood scraps, nails with large heads, screwdrivers, screws, brace and bit, pliers, planes, levels, safety goggles, files, crowbars, spools, brushes, scissors, paste paddles, sewing kit, needles, thimbles, embroidery hoops, knitting basket, sewing cards, straws, knife pallets, sponges, paint brushes of several sizes and textures
- **Supplies**: sandpaper, paints of many kinds, glue, paste, tape, collage supplies, aluminum foil, paper towels, paper plates, paper cups, wooden stirring sticks, powdered alum, glycerine, wool, thread, rubber bands, masking tape, egg cartons, soap, brads, paper clips, clothes pegs, thumbtacks, cardboard boxes, straight pins, wax paper, straws, tongue depressors, pipe cleaners, fingerpaints, clay, glitter, burlap, fabric pieces, cotton balls, cotton swabs, sponges, assorted papers (crepe paper, cellophane, tissue paper, Bristol board, cardboard, corrugated cardboard, construction paper, newsprint, computer paper, shiny paper, poster paper, gummed stars and stickers, tracing paper, wallpaper, and onionskin), paint cans, soap flakes, cornstarch, liquid soap, tempera paints, water paints, heavy-gauge plastic, wallpaper paste, sticky paper, crayons, markers, chalk, charcoal, pencils, erasers, rulers, oil pastels, fabric crayons, pencil crayons, paste containers, rubber cement, and fabric and wood glue

Play Stations in the Creative Arts Centre

The Creative Arts centre is composed of the art area, which includes several play stations for messy art and dry art at tables, and easel drawing and painting. This learning centre also houses the table or marble slab where children use clay to fashion their artistic creations, use fabric and sewing supplies at the sewing table, and engage in woodworking at the wood construction table.

Art Area

The art area is the most important part of the Creative Arts centre and usually occupies the lion's share of the space. The art area appeals to children because they are interested in graphic activity that uses a wide range of media for scribbling, drawing, painting, pasting, moulding, sculpting, sewing, and woodworking. Art materials should be organized and available for children to use independently and then return them to their proper place (Koster, 2005).

DRAWING AND PAINTING

Most children endlessly enjoy opportunities to express themselves with brushes, paint, and paper. The pleasure and the chance for self-expression afforded by painting make it important that the easels always be available with paint, clean brushes, and fresh paper. The easels are the centrepiece of the art area, where children may experiment with brushes of various sizes, mixing paint, painting on paper of various sizes and textures, and using different types of paint, from pre-mixed pots to tempera paints that they mix themselves using water. Children's artwork varies depending on whether it is executed while sitting at a table or standing or kneeling at an easel. The angle and height of the easel will influence the nature of their work. For this reason, different types of easels in the art area add variety to the type of exploration and production in which children can engage (see Figure 19–3) and the types of social interactions that occur.

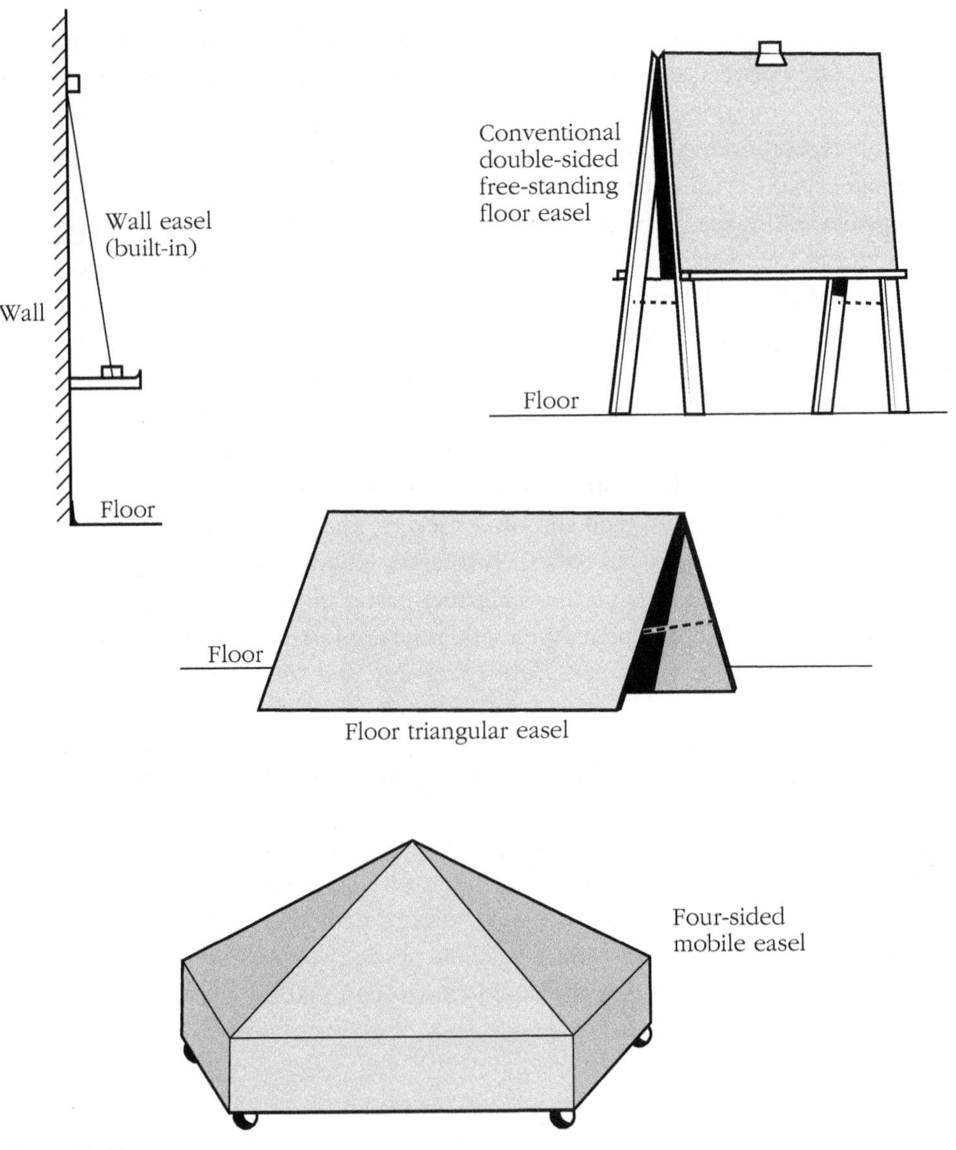

Figure 19–3
Four types of easel

Conventional double-sided easels allow freedom of movement and privacy for children to execute their own painting without interruption from someone painting beside them, while wall easels are stable and, when placed side by side on a wall, allow social interaction between children as they paint. Makeshift easels, in which a triangular-shaped tunnel sits on the floor to provide surface area for two children to paint opposite each other, allow children a broader perspective on their painting than do conventional easels or those built into the wall (Lasky & Mukerji, 1980). Children also enjoy painting on large sheets of paper tacked to a movable frame on the floor or taped directly onto the floor. Painting on paper on the floor facilitates cooperative creative endeavours, such as painting murals.

The art area close to the easels should include a drying rack where children can hang their productions to dry and space for them to mount their productions on a display board or wall, preferably using frames that enhance their artwork. It is important, however, for ECEs to emphasize that the *process* is more interesting and developmentally appropriate than the *product* for children. The importance of process is obvious when we observe the absorption children exhibit in making brush strokes of just the right width and height, choosing just the right colour to represent their images, and trying to fill a special spot on the page with a particular configuration of strokes. As we examine children's art, much is revealed to us about children's thought processes, interests, anxieties, and dreams.

The art area promotes physical development, particularly fine motor skills, perceptual acuity, eye–hand coordination, manipulative abilities, and body awareness. Children practise controlling their movements and moving laterally as they struggle to hold the paper steady with one hand while cutting deliberately and evenly with the other. At the easel, children often sway to the movement of the brush and reach on tiptoe to paint sky and clouds at the top of the easel. In their drawing, children are often preoccupied as they try to faithfully reproduce their perception of an object they are trying to depict. The goal seems to be to *draw to learn* rather than to *learn to draw*, as if drawing somehow sharpens a child's perceptions of something in their environment (Edwards, Gandini, & Forman, 1998). The watchword of the art area is *simplicity*. It is an area for children to make their own choices of basic art materials and to execute their own plans. *Children tend to represent what they know, more than what they see.* This understanding makes presenting models for children to follow or precutting art materials for them to assemble a futile activity for children.

MESSY ART AND DRY ART TABLES

Dry art activities include collage; drawing with markers, crayons, or chalk; and activities in which children draw and cut their own patterns and outlines. Messy art activities include pasting, fingerpainting, and papier mâché creations. Two kinds of artistic endeavours may be assigned to the two tables commonly found in the art area; one table is for the messy art activities, and the other is for the dry art. The activities planned for each table should reflect a developmental approach based on the physical experiences, concepts, thinking styles, and emotional outlets that art activities have the potential to address. Another approach is to regard the two art tables as potential spaces, for example, one to serve children's readiness for expressive materials such as fingerpaint and another to provide practice in cutting with scissors, pasting, and creating a collage.

Drawing and painting at tables with tools other than brushes add to the range of graphic experiences available to children. Felt-tipped markers, crayons, straws, chalk, charcoal, and other instruments are interesting for children to explore with papers of different textures and weight. Drawing with crayons on sandpaper and using felt-tipped markers on blotting paper, coloured chalk on construction paper, and thick paint and paste paddles on cardboard further promote exploration of the sensory and graphic qualities of a range of materials, textures, and consistencies. Even natural products, such as flowers, leaves, soft rocks, and natural clay, can be used as implements to make an imprint on cardboard (McArdle & Barker, 1990).

Messy art

The tools for painting should be varied so that children can experiment with knife pallets, paddles, paint rollers, toothbrushes, sponge brushes, and shaving brushes. Various papers should be available for painting and collage, such as construction paper, newsprint, wallpaper, manila paper, shiny paper for fingerpainting, corrugated paper, parchment, and wax paper. Children also enjoy painting on fabric pieces such as satin, canvas, burlap, and felt. Needless to say, the varied and plentiful materials that should be available for children in the art area call for storage space where materials and tools may be displayed neatly and kept clean. Ideally, storage units in the art area will be mobile, with shelves or drawers on wheels with fitted places to hold the tools, papers, and paints that are needed.

CLAY

Clay is an underestimated art material that promotes children's self-expression and representational thinking using a plastic medium. It is relaxing and sensuous for children as it responds to their kneading and moulding. In this way, clay is a truly responsive medium that reacts immediately to children's actions on it. When natural clay is introduced, children need close supervision by adults, who encourage them to appreciate the physical properties of the clay. Later, a visit to a local potter is an interesting way to help children understand the power of clay to represent an idea and to produce a functional product that is also beautiful and unique. Clay is a particularly stimulating medium for fostering children's representational thinking, as it is infinitely responsive, forgiving, and evocative.

The contribution of clay to children's development of cognitive concepts should not be ignored. Moulding clay into shapes and representations of various sizes teaches children about the concepts of quantity and conservation; that is, they become aware that although the clay may change in shape and appearance, the amount of clay remains the same as long as they have neither added nor subtracted from the original lump. As children shape and reshape the clay into parts of various sizes and roll it back together again, they learn that changes in appearance do not affect the quantity and that appearances can be deceiving (Hughes, 1995).

ECEs sometimes make excuses for not providing clay because of their intolerance of its messiness, because it demands careful preparation before children can use it, and because the cleanup tasks involved are time-consuming. Some children react negatively to getting their hands dirty, and asthmatic children may react to the fine dust clay may generate when dry, so care has to be taken to ensure that it is introduced slowly and never used where food might be served. We used to be able to take children on excursions to dig their own clay, but these days we need to be certain that natural clay is extracted only from areas where there is no risk of toxic contamination from agricultural pesticides or other toxic agents in the soil.

Most natural clay is sold in large, semimoist lumps and has to be prepared using the printed instructions. Powdered or dry mixes should be avoided. Virtually no substitute exists for the sensory qualities, transformational potential, and responsiveness of natural clay, and although children love the texture of dough, it is primarily a sensory material that belongs in the Daily Living centre where it serves as a prop for pretend play.

As they do with unit blocks, children develop skills in using clay over time and with practice. Children first explore clay in a sensorimotor fashion by pounding, kneading, and pinching. Then they master the substance by making balls, clay "worms," and coils, followed by two-dimensional figures pounded and laid out flat on the board or table. Later, they may move on to three-dimensional representation. Children may work alone or with other children at a table or on a marble slab that retains its cool temperature and preserves the texture and consistency of the clay for a longer period. A ball of clay about the size of a grapefruit is recommended for each child. Children should always wear vinyl or plastic aprons or smocks that are easily wiped clean, and they should have access to a deep sink where they can clean their hands and arms themselves.

The responsive qualities of clay surpass those of paints and brushes. Koster (1999) refers to clay as ***nature's magical mind*** because of its unique responsiveness to human touch. Clay responds immediately to the child's hands, often erasing completely any segment of what was formerly there. In painting, which is also a responsive medium, children make frequent modifications to their work, but what is there can never be completely erased. Often, instead of continuing with a work they have started, they will simply discard their first attempt at a painting and start afresh. With clay, children have the option of returning to the lump of clay with which they began. In this way, clay is a more flexible medium than paint, as clay encourages children to entertain new ideas.

The usefulness of clay as a responsive, creative substance reinforces the importance of process in children's artistic endeavours. The clay productions of children are less important than the child's physical, cognitive, and affective involvement in the act of transforming the clay. For this reason, it is not essential for the productions of children to be fired or preserved in any way, certainly not at the stage when children are using clay mostly as a medium for exploration and simple transformation (Clemens, 1991). As children become more skilled in using clay to represent, three-dimensionally, their view of reality, there may be some value in preserving the product, especially if doing so pleases the child. Until this stage is reached, however, the clay with which children have been working should be returned to its airtight container and treated with water to restore its malleable qualities until the next use.

Wood Construction Area

Wood is a versatile material, with its soft texture, lustre, unique smell, and the interesting sound it makes when pieces are knocked together. The early years are a time to become acquainted with the many attractions of wood, and working with it introduces children to the value and the fragility of our trees and forests. Children who learn to enjoy wood when they are young will relate more readily to the urgency of protecting our forests and reforesting harvested areas. Woodworking introduces children to an important resource in our society; it is a part of the Canadian heritage, with which children should identify from an early age, including children and their families from cultures for whom Canada's trees and forests hold infinite appeal and mystery.

The sensory pleasures of working with wood as well as posing physical challenge, make wood a growth-enhancing medium for young children. The best woods to work with are soft woods such as pine, cedar, and balsa, which are sufficiently porous for children to be able to hammer nails into and light enough to hold together when glued. High-quality tools and supplies, including wood glue, sandpaper, nails, and screws, are needed for wood construction. The woodworking area is also used for box construction, sometimes called cardboard carpentry, and is a favourite learning centre for longer projects (Huber, 1999). The presence of a lifelike but child-sized workbench specially designed for children's woodworking makes the area more appealing to children, as does the presence of real tools.

Woodworking

Preschool and kindergarten children are able to use well-made adult tools, as long as an adult supervises them, ensures that children know the rules of safety, and provides as safe an environment as possible. Electrically powered tools are inappropriate, but children can be shown how to use lightweight claw hammers with large-head nails, manual drills, backsaws, clamps, and screwdrivers. ECEs should demonstrate and explain how the tools should be held and used, and watch children carefully at the beginning to ensure they have mastered the basics. Children should hold hammers about eight centimetres from the end of the hammer and should keep their eyes on the top of the tee or nail being hammered. ECEs should encourage them to tap lightly and slowly at first until the nail has been started, then to remove the hand that has been holding the nail steady and tap with greater force. Sometimes, ECEs may start the nail for them, letting the child take over once the nail no longer has to be steadied by hand. Using a wrist movement rather than the whole arm facilitates greater accuracy and more control over the hammer. ECEs should provide a mitre box to steady the wood board while children saw. Use clamps to hold the wood pieces firmly to the workbench. Children may also use manual hand drills to make holes in softwood pieces before hammering in nails or inserting screws.

ECEs may introduce the use of hammers, saws, and drills by giving children practice in hammering and sawing on a large dead tree stump in the playground. By the time they have had practice outdoors, they are usually ready for more intricate work at the workbench. When children engage in wood construction using tools, they should wear safety goggles or glasses. Valuable junk may also be introduced into the wood construction area to stimulate creativity and to promote recycling practices. The tops of frozen orange juice cans and metal screw tops from jam jars and juice bottles make interesting wheels for wooden vehicles and are easily hammered. Small scraps of wood, wood shavings, and even strips of bark can decorate wooden creations. Important supplies for the wood area include a range of sizes of wood pieces (preferably softwood), chunks and strips of polystyrene, wood scraps, recycled materials, paste and wood glue, and cardboard boxes and pieces. For four- to six-year-olds, ECEs may add woodworking tools, hammers, nails with large heads, screws, and screwdrivers.

The main reason for setting the workbench, wood, boxes, cardboard, recycled materials, polystyrene, and glue apart from the art area in the Creative Arts centre is to differentiate wood and cardboard from other art media. The play in this area also involves constructing, fitting, and assembling (rather than freely expressing with continuous and **surface-diffusible materials**, such as paints, crayons, chalk, and markers). Also, the wood and box construction area is dedicated primarily to creating three-dimensional productions, in contrast to the art area, which focuses on producing two-dimensional paintings, collage, and drawings.

BOX CONSTRUCTION

Box construction or cardboard carpentry addresses a multitude of perceptual and physical skills but also promotes spatial reasoning abilities. In this area, children can experience firsthand the usefulness of recycling because discarded packaging, boxes, cartons, and electrical tape (duct tape) are the principal supplies. Although the workbench with a drawer and a shelf for tools and supplies is the centre of the wood and box construction area, space around the workbench, a low counter or another table as a potential play space, makes a useful work surface for engaging in box construction. When large packing boxes are used, children can just as easily work on the floor. Placing a plastic sheet on the floor under the box structure prevents glue from sticking to the floor. ECEs often find that box construction using colourful duct tape is more efficient than using white glue, as the children's creations can be used and decorated immediately, without having to wait for glue to dry. On the other hand, as children become more experienced with wood construction, they should be encouraged to engage in projects over several days or weeks, and in these instances quick-drying glued wood is less interesting than the use of fasteners, nails, or screws to hold their wood construction in place. The woodworking play station is a favourite place for significant projects, particularly when children can leave out their partly completed work until they return to it another day.

ACTIVITIES FOR THE WOOD CONSTRUCTION AREA FOR CHILDREN AGES THREE TO SIX

1. Provide mallets or light hammers, golf tees, and chunks of polystyrene and let children practise hammering golf tees into the polystyrene.
2. Have children make boats to sail in the water table with small pieces of balsa wood, woodcarving tools, string, and fabric pieces.
3. Set up wooden packing crates and paste and let children make their own three-dimensional creations. Once their products have dried, they may want to take them to the art area to paint and decorate them.
4. Set up pieces of pinewood strips with the hammers and nails, and let children explore the materials and tools by hammering and joining pieces of wood together.

Sewing Table and Textile Art Area

A sewing area introduces children to the pleasures of exploring and creating with fabric and yarns, a medium that has properties different from those of wood, cardboard, paper, and paint. This play station acknowledges the importance that European and Chinese cultures in particular place on children's development of fine motor skills and aesthetic sense with needlework, sewing, weaving, and quilting. Like wood, fabric has soothing and aesthetically appealing qualities that children are able to appreciate when they are introduced to fabric's expressive properties. Fabric decorations; pretty placemats; hand-sewn wall hangings and curtains; and bright, patterned cushion covers in the learning centre add to the warmth and friendliness of the setting. When children help to make these items, they feel pride in the surroundings they have helped to create.

Children should be introduced to fabric, weaving, and sewing supplies gradually and with a view to exploring their properties and responsiveness in a variety of ways. Children can cut out squares, match fabrics of similar patterns and textures, glue fabric pieces together, test the strength and opaqueness of fabric, and even paint or dye the fabric long before they ever start working with a needle and thread. Creating quilts by pasting fabric squares on large paper or cardboard is a simple way to introduce children to the concept of quilting. Often children begin to sew with

Sewing table

laces and sewing cards and then practise sewing large buttons on patches of stiff fabric that are easy to hold. Bead stringing is an early activity that enables children to learn the skills associated with hand sewing.

ECEs can also introduce children to sewing by providing needles, thread, and polystyrene pieces or popcorn for them to string. Simple embroidery activities with printed cotton hopsacking, large needles, wool or thread, and an embroidery hoop to hold the fabric firmly in place are interesting ways for children to begin sewing with a thread and needle. In Scandinavian countries, a sewing machine is often part of the learning environment so that the ECE can sew while the children are occupied with their own sewing projects. The adult's involvement with this activity provides an interesting model for children to imitate, especially if she is making something that everyone can enjoy. The sewing table is another play station that lends itself to projects, such as quilt-making, weaving, and fabric collages, which are developed collaboratively over time.

ACTIVITIES FOR THE SEWING TABLE AND TEXTILE ART AREA FOR CHILDREN AGES TWO TO FOUR

1. Set up large needles, thread, and polystyrene or popcorn pieces for children to string to make decorations for a winter tree—a branch in the classroom on which to hang winter decorations.
2. Have children practise lacing leather or plastic strips through holes punched in leather pieces to make pouches or folding cases. Lacing kits may be used.
3. Cut remnants of pretty fabrics into attractive, brightly coloured, and patterned squares of fabric and have children arrange them on large sheets of kraft paper to make a quilt by pasting the fabric pieces on the paper.
4. Provide children with swatches of cloth in many colours and patterns and encourage them to cut out shapes and squares with scissors. The stiffer the cloth, the easier it is for children to hold the cloth while they cut.

ACTIVITIES FOR THE SEWING TABLE AND TEXTILE ART AREA FOR CHILDREN AGES FOUR TO SIX

1. Have children practise sewing buttons with large holes onto pieces of felt, canvas, or heavy cotton using darning needles and wool or heavy-gauge thread.
2. Have children participate in making curtains for the windows. This is a long-term project with several steps. Purchase natural cotton hopsacking in a bolt large enough to create café-style curtains, which are the easiest to make.
3. Collect long grasses, reeds, straw, strips of paper, and balls of string and yarn, and let children explore various ways of weaving these materials to form a wall hanging.
4. Visit a store that sells quilts. Point out to children the various patterns, colours, and textures of the quilts. Have the children try to replicate on construction paper the quilt patterns they saw at the store.

5. Have children cut out quilt squares of cloth in standard sizes from multi-coloured fabric in many patterns. Encourage children to experiment with the arrangement of the squares to make a quilt design. Then provide the children with large needles and thread to stitch the quilt pieces together.

Summary

The Creative Arts centre should be dedicated to fostering children's aesthetic development and their ability to express what they remember, think, or feel, using a wide range of creative materials. This centre should not be used to foster literacy or numeracy. When the Creative Arts centre transports children to a world beyond the functional, mundane surroundings of the world they sometimes inhabit, children develop *vision*, or the ability to see beyond their immediate context to a world that inspires and allows freedom to wonder, imagine, experiment, and express their feelings and aspirations. This centre provides play stations that invite children to experiment with a wide range of creative media, including paints, clay, wood, fabric, cardboard, and many graphic materials. Children are encouraged to practise using the creative media found in the centre and to represent events they have witnessed and remember, things they have seen, and ideas they have gathered through play elsewhere. *ECEs should steadfastly avoid activities that involve precut materials or models that children are asked to copy, and there is no place in this centre for cartoon figures or Disney-like characters that represent an unreal pop-culture world.* The Creative Arts centre offers an environment that should mirror the beauty of our Canadian landscape and the arts of our people in order to foster pride in our culture and the bountiful spaces we inhabit. It is also a centre that should import the beautiful art and artistry of the cultures represented by the children in the program that are a reflection of environments they recognize and appreciate. Space should be provided in the Creative Arts centre for children to display their own works of art.

Learning Activities

1. Observe children playing in the Creative Arts centre. Does the overall environment in the program foster children's appreciation of works of art? Is children's art prominently displayed? Is art from various cultures displayed? Do ECEs interact effectively with children to acknowledge their efforts, demonstrate interest in their productions, and engage them in conversation about various aspects of their artwork? Report on your observations.
2. In a group or individually, build a list of ideas and resources for promoting children's interest in art. Include in your list the types of art you will display, including various cultural selections, and research each piece so that you are able to talk knowledgeably about the works displayed. Build a file containing examples of reproductions, prints, and slides of various works of art to display.
3. Choose two activities from the woodworking area and two from the sewing and textile art area. Write activity cards for each of these activities.
4. Write an activity card for implementing a box construction project with preschool or kindergarten children. Be sure to carefully specify the resources and

tools children will need to create a box construction. More than one activity card may be needed to indicate the sequence of activities that might involved in the project.

5. In groups, visit local art galleries to determine their learning potential for a fieldtrip. Prepare a report describing the features of the gallery, the nature of the art displayed, its potential interest to children, the goals of a field visit to the gallery, and the potential outcomes for children's aesthetic development.
6. Plan a fieldtrip to a local art gallery with the children or research websites of galleries and museums for virtual visits.

20 The Unit Blocks Centre

"Play, then, is far from a trivial pursuit. It is where we stretch our empathic consciousness and learn to become truly human."

—Jeremy Rifkin, *The Empathic Civilization* (2009)

Before Reading This Chapter, Have You

- played with unit blocks in order to better understand their properties and play potential?
- observed children playing with unit blocks and taken note of the environment in which they are located and how play with the blocks is protected?

Outcomes

After reading and understanding this chapter, you should be able to

- trace the evolution of unit blocks as a vehicle for development and learning through play;
- understand the characteristics of unit blocks and their abstract accessories;
- locate and organize the Unit Blocks centre and appropriate storage shelves;
- explain how children's play changes if lifelike (non-abstract) accessories are added to unit blocks;
- describe the developmental stages in block play; and
- facilitate children's play with unit blocks to enhance representational thinking.

The Importance of Unit Blocks as Play and Learning Materials

Blocks are, arguably, the most important play and learning materials for children. They remain a classic fixture in early learning environments, since the 19th-century kindergartens of Friedrich Froebel (1782–1852) because they provide rich opportunities for play that addresses all developmental domains. All cultures have some form of blocks for children, and blocks have been present in children's play for hundreds of years. Blocks take shape according to children's actions on them. As the blocks respond, they, in turn, elicit further action from the child. All types of blocks are highly responsive and dynamic play materials. Unit blocks have special advantages in that they are mathematically precise, large enough to create clear representations, impressive in size and proportion, and handsome to look at (see Figure 20–1).

This chapter emphasizes the role of unit blocks for development in all domains and the importance of creating a learning centre especially dedicated to play with unit blocks. The richness of block play for young children should not be underestimated; instead, programs should make space for unit blocks a priority and allocate funds for purchasing at least two sets. The longevity of unit blocks as play materials

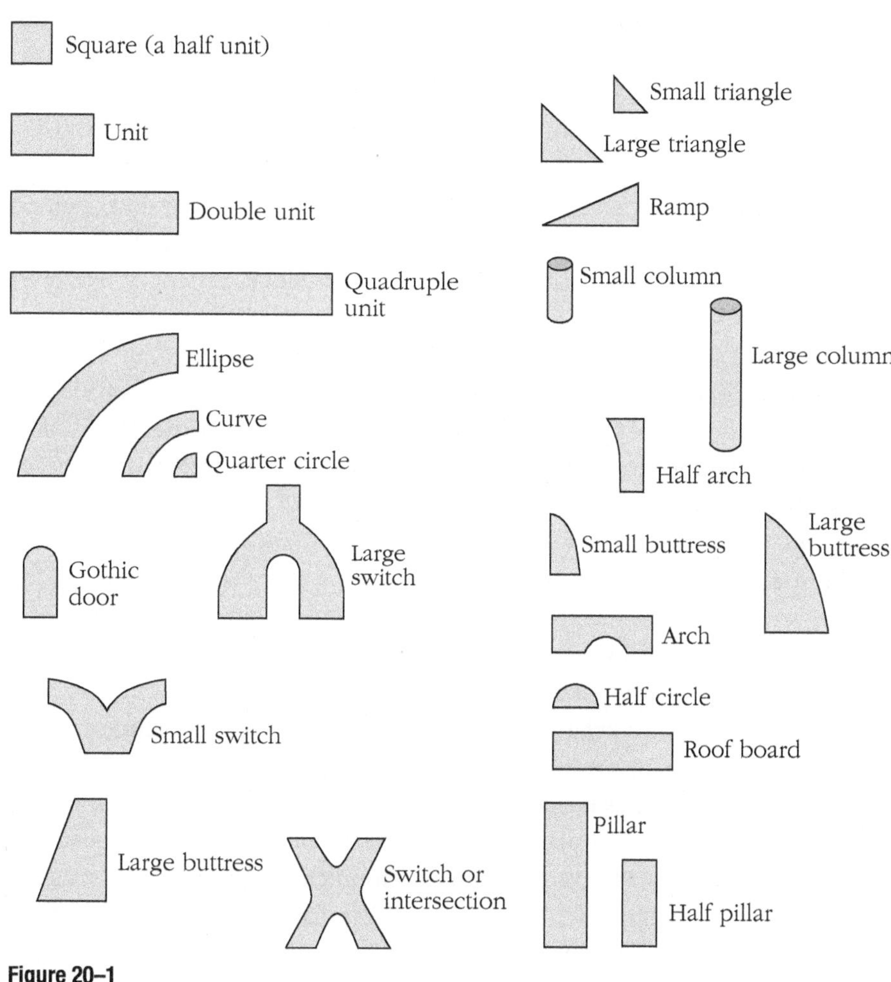

Figure 20–1
Unit blocks

over more than 100 years is sufficient evidence to convince programs of their importance to children's development.

To understand the play value of unit blocks, ECEs need opportunities to play with them and see for themselves. Although there are many types of blocks that enhance play and learning, unit blocks are unique because of their potential to promote representational thinking, abstract thinking, scientific inquiry, spatial and mathematical skills, social abilities, strength, balance and symmetry, fine motor skills development, visual perception, eye–hand coordination, hand control, language development, and logical-mathematical thinking and numeracy. As creative play materials that challenge children's ability to imagine, visualize, and engage in divergent thinking, unit blocks are exceptional.

A Brief History of Blocks as Play Materials

Friedrich Froebel is usually acknowledged as the first educator to invent blocks to help children learn in an educational setting, although the use of blocks for learning can be traced back as far as John Locke, in the 17th century, who is credited with the origin of the classic alphabet blocks with letters on all sides. Froebel's *Gifts and Occupations* (1887) provided the early curriculum for children's open-ended exploration and play with a range of materials, which helped children discover concepts, order, and unity through relatively prescriptive play with the materials. Within Froebel's *Gifts and Occupations* system, Gifts 2 to 6 were composed of various sets of blocks that were undecorated and modular and rather prescriptive in design (Weber, 1984).

American educator Patty Smith Hill (1868–1946), who was director of the department of kindergarten and grade one education at Columbia's Teachers College in New York, invented a new system of blocks that promoted free play and open-ended discovery; they were much larger than the Froebelian blocks and less prescriptive than the Gifts and Occupations. The Smith Hill blocks fastened together with pegs, holes, and grooves, and thereby removed the challenge of experimenting with balance and stability. It was Caroline Pratt (1867–1954) who, in 1914, modified Smith Hill's blocks to create the unit blocks system, which are smaller and of standard proportions, to promote mathematical concepts. In the 1930s, Harriet Johnson described the seven stages of block play following intensive observations of children playing with unit blocks (Weber, 1984).

Since the 1950s, many new types of blocks have appeared on the scene that range from abstract to highly intricate replications of bricks, some interlocking, some abstract, and of many shapes and sizes. The most known and coveted of these may be the Lego blocks designed in Denmark and used the world over by children to create lifelike replications of familiar structures. Over time, Lego blocks have evolved from simple, interlocking cubes or rectangular pieces to include accessories, battery-operated mechanisms to allow for propulsion, and elaborate configurations immediately recognizable as helicopter parts, train engine pieces, robots, and spaceship parts. Lego blocks are valuable play materials, but they are no substitute for unit blocks because they address different developmental skills and play styles. Lego blocks are aesthetically beautiful and easy to manipulate, but they do not challenge the child's representational thinking, spatial skills, and creative abilities to nearly the same extent as the more abstract unit blocks.

The Practicality of Unit Blocks as Play Materials

Typically, programs cite the cost of unit blocks as a reason for using substitutes. Yet, when we understand that children play with unit blocks from infancy through to grade three, and often beyond, their cost–benefit ratio for toddler, preschool, kindergarten, and after-school programs becomes obvious. Unit blocks grow with the child over many years. Children under the age of 18 months usually play with blocks one at a time, and they only gradually begin to stack blocks or put them in a row by the age of two. Blocks respond to children's exploratory play during the sensorimotor period, when children delight in their sound, texture, and stacking properties as they rap them together to make a sound, feel the softness of the wood with their fingers, and run a block along the floor like a truck. As children enter the preoperational period, they build vertical towers of blocks and then begin to connect vertical constructions to horizontal constructions. At three, children begin to make enclosures and patterns, and, at this stage, they are more interested in the properties of the blocks themselves than in representing real-world structures. Closer to four, children build two-dimensional structures that are more authentic representations of houses and buildings, and they decorate their creations before they build complex structures that represent recognizable structures in the real world. By age five, children are building three-dimensional structures, naming what they create that typically represents a structure in the real world, and are elaborating and adding detail to their structures in order to make them more life-like. From ages six to nine and older, children who have played with unit blocks for years are able to innovate and surprise us with complex structures that are masterful, evocative representations of balance, symmetry, detail, and realism. As play materials, unit blocks are amazingly versatile in terms of their age appropriateness for children from 18 months to well into the school-age years. *Therefore, they are one of the best long-term investments in children's play that programs and families can make.*

The key to play with unit blocks is to encourage children to use the blocks alone and not combine them with other play materials or detailed accessories, such as dump trucks or Fisher-Price items. Blocks can be manipulated in two- and three-dimensional configurations. The abstract nature of the unit blocks contributes to children's ability to hold on to their inner vision and assign meaning to an abstract structure. Used in this way, unit blocks are unique materials that assume the identity a child wants to assign. Children are challenged to configure the blocks to represent something that looks real to them, or they can manipulate the block formations to create unusual patterns and structures and experiment with symmetrical design. Creative materials are, by definition, open-ended, divergent, abstract in design, freeform, and responsive to one's actions on them—all characteristics that ensure that unit blocks are a most treasured type of creative play material. Block constructions fit the general criteria that apply to creative productions; that is, the child conceives the production as a work of art, creates the work for an audience that includes his peers and teachers, and represents his own idea in the construction (Gelfer, 1990). As a three-dimensional artistic medium, unit blocks play an essential role in creative development, along with clay, other plastic media, paint, and wood (Gardner, 1980).

Why Unit Blocks Should Not Be Combined with Other Play Materials

The use of unit blocks with other play materials is often debated in ECE. The play value and uses of unit blocks are not well understood these days as they compete with many commercial play materials. It is useful to remember the design and purpose as conceived by Caroline Pratt, which were predicated on the unique symbolic and representational quality of play with unit blocks. She believed that unit blocks should be used by themselves with only the abstract, wooden accessories that accompany the sets; when these accessories are added to complement children's block structures, children are challenged to assign their own meaning and vision to them.

Play with unit blocks alone involves highly imaginative symbolic play, as these abstract materials take on whatever characteristics or functions children assign to them. Children should be given time to experience and master the special properties of unit blocks and to build on their abstract nature by envisioning in their minds what they want the unit blocks to represent. The abstract wooden accessories that come with sets are compatible with the purity and proportion of the unit block sets and enhance the symbolic and, later, the representational nature of children's play with the blocks. An elaborate unit block structure, using the abstract accessories, may represent a space station, for example, with each child agreeing on what the accessories represent. Eventually, they may turn their space station into a super unit of play with the abstract structure as the centrepiece. At this advanced point in their play, children may request or seek out for themselves the more lifelike artifact materials and add them to their structure.

ECEs have to decide at the outset what kind of play they want to foster in the Unit Blocks centre. Those who want to preserve the abstract quality of the play materials and to challenge children's symbolic and representational thinking will discourage children's adding Tonka trucks, Matchbox cars, Fisher-Price people, or other lifelike miniatures to their unit block structures. The stark realism of miniature domestic and farm animals, vehicles, and dollhouses, for example, alters the quality of play with the abstract forms of the unit blocks and their crude wooden accessories. When children build a structure with unit blocks, label it an airport, and then import an airplane and helicopter, and add Matchbox cars to put in the parking lot, their play loses much of its representational value. That does not diminish the value of the role play, but it does remove the creative thinking and imaginary challenges presented by the abstract blocks and accessories.

Once realistic accessories are used with the unit blocks, and play in the Unit Blocks centre becomes focused on role play, the level of engagement of the child changes from envisioning the structure in his mind and choosing blocks to represent his vision. The unit blocks become the background and setting for role play rather than the foreground and central purpose of the symbolic play episode. There is nothing inherently wrong with this; it is, however, a professional issue related to knowing what kind of play you want to encourage in the Unit Blocks centre, exploiting the precious abstract quality of play with unit blocks, and ensuring that the *tools of our trade* are used skilfully, knowledgeably, and for the optimum purpose intended by the materials themselves. ECEs should refrain from prematurely setting up props and artifacts borrowed from other learning centres so as to ensure that children experience the full play value of the unit blocks. Lifelike artifacts should not be introduced unless children ask for them, as they distract children from important types of play and exploration with the unit blocks and abstract accessories alone. Certainly, the lifelike accessories should not be stored in the Unit Blocks centre. ECEs have to establish some clear limits regarding play with unit blocks. For obvious reasons, creative arts supplies such as surface-diffusible materials should not be permitted in the Unit Blocks centre, where they may disfigure the blocks. At advanced stages in their play with unit blocks, children may, however, bring cardboard, scarves, or blankets to the centre when they want to decorate their unit block structures.

Types of Blocks

Blocks come in several forms, sizes, and configurations. Hollow wooden blocks are usually found in the Active Role Play centre, where play with hollow blocks is addressed (Chapter 13). Although hollow blocks were also designed by Caroline Pratt, they serve very different play and developmental purposes than unit blocks and should not be combined with the unit blocks. The hollow blocks should be available to children in the Active Role Play areas and outdoors in fine weather. Tabletop building blocks are often found in the Quiet Thinking centre. There are interlocking tabletop blocks, including Lego in various configurations; foam rubber building blocks for infants; and plastic blocks for toddlers, including the familiar Canadian Mega Bloks. Tinkertoy construction sets and Lincoln Logs promote some of the same types of construction play, but because they are more lifelike reproductions of recognizable things, play with them does not offer the same abstract representational potential. Software packages are also available that promote play with block configurations on the screen. Although the play potential of all kinds of blocks is significant, unit blocks are the most abstract and creative block materials, and, therefore, they deserve their own learning centre, where their developmental potential for young children may be optimized.

Although this textbook recommends that unit blocks be located in the creative play zone, close to the Creative Arts centre, unit blocks may also be juxtaposed with almost any other centre for equally valid reasons. The rationale for locating them in the creative play zone is based in the belief that play with unit blocks is a stimulus for children's symbolic, representational, and divergent thinking when they are used alone, that is, without the addition of lifelike accessories. Children should be encouraged to practise and experiment often and for considerable periods of time with the properties and potential of unit blocks. Ideally, children's unit block structures should be left out for extended timeframes so that children can return to them. It is the abstract nature of unit blocks that challenges children to attribute meaning to their block structures and that engages the child creatively in visioning his product. Children plan which blocks to use, learning about symmetry and design and making do with simple, unadorned objects to execute a plan and simulate a vision of what they want to represent. When their block structure emerges as a close enough version of their inner vision, for example, of a spaceship, or an oil rig, or a playhouse, the rest is left to the children's imagination to fill in the gaps.

While using unit blocks to represent and fashion a product, the child is engaging in play that is as creative as play with clay, with paint, or with wood or fabric. The child begins with an open space on the carpeted floor and, from there, envisions his creation; plans his approach; adjusts his vision; and fashions his structure using these plain, abstract, open-ended materials. It is not surprising that Frank Lloyd Wright attributed his early play with blocks to the seeding of his talent as America's greatest architect; he later praised the vision of his mother, Anne Wright, in providing him with sets of Froebel's blocks (Wellhousen & Kieff, 2001). More recently, engineering and architectural firms are finding that younger employees may be able to handle complex theoretical and mathematical equations, but they are less adept at finding innovative solutions to practical problems, a factor attributed to their lack of play experience building, taking things apart, and putting them back together (Brown, 2010). If we accept that true creativity often emerges from disciplined thinking and a fusion of **spatial skills**, **sensory acuity**, ability to attend, risk taking, emotional engagement, and resourcefulness—rather than spectacular moments of revelation and extraordinary insight—we will better appreciate the value of unit blocks as a rich resource for creative development in young children.

Characteristics of Unit Blocks

Unit blocks are precise materials that are abstract in form, well proportioned, smooth to the touch, and compact to hold; they are the perfect three-dimensional medium for children's experimentation in creating modular structures to represent what they know and understand about their world. Their abstract design challenges a child to think abstractly about what she wants to create and to fashion a product with these abstract shapes that represents what the child wants them to become instead of following the manufacturer's idea of what children usually want to build. Unit blocks have beauty, precision, texture, weight, and sound—physical characteristics that make them endlessly interesting objects of children's sensorimotor exploration. Most unit blocks are made of solid blocks of hardwood, usually birch or alder, which have been finely sanded and polished to a natural lustre, with a unique smell, texture, and warmth. Beautifully crafted unit blocks that are well maintained and treated with respect add to the overall aesthetic quality of the learning environment, in which they should assume a prominent place.

Unit blocks come in sets of approximately 750 blocks; they also may be purchased in half-sets or individually. Toddlers do well with a half-set or a full set, whereas preschoolers and kindergarten children should have access to greater play and learning possibilities with at least two full sets of blocks. Sets contain blocks of different shapes, which are designed for special purposes. The units are multiples of the basic unit. A basic unit measures 14 centimetres by 7 centimetres by 3.5 centimetres; each multiple increases in length only to the maximum size, which is a quadruple unit, of 55.5 centimetres long. Other blocks in a set include pillars (14 centimetres by 3.5 centimetres or 7 centimetres), cylinders (14 centimetres by 3.5 centimetres or 7 centimetres), curves (3.5 centimetres or 7 centimetres by 23 centimetres), arches (3.5 centimetres by 7 centimetres by 28 centimetres), and hardwood planks.

Unit Blocks and Development through Play

Unit blocks are far too valuable to be stored out of children's reach or to be brought out only occasionally. ECEs are sometimes inclined to restrict children's play with unit blocks because of the mess they create, but this thinking underestimates children's ability to tidy them up. Treating unit blocks as materials to be used only on special occasions reveals a lack of understanding of the developmental potential of these materials to further children's cognitive and creative thinking abilities. Unit blocks address performance objectives in the cognitive, physical, social, and emotional domains, and, therefore, they should be available for play at all times.

Unit blocks help children understand mathematical concepts of **unit iteration, subdivision**, and measurement. Unit iteration means that a number of parts can be combined to make a whole; for example, 100 centimetres of distance put together make a 1-metre unit. Subdivision is the mental ability to separate a larger unit into smaller segments; for instance, a hopscotch court can be divided into several smaller units. The mathematical concept of equivalency means that one space divided into several component units corresponds to another space of the same size that is subdivided into a different number of units. Children learn, for example, that the amount of space in an enclosure remains the same regardless of how many units it is subdivided into (Hughes, 1995). Children learn about balance when they stack blocks one on top of the other. They also learn about logical classification as they compare blocks based on their similar dimensions and about shapes as they sort the blocks and return them to the appropriate spots on the storage shelves. Children learn to create **horizontal and vertical grid patterns** to enclose space. They learn to contemplate position and direction in space from a number of perspectives. Few other play materials provide richer learning experience for cognitive development than unit blocks when they are used alone (Hirsch, 1996). Once a unit block structure has been created by the children and has been identified and named, play with the completed structure may be enhanced by adding dramatic play props and play clothes to facilitate sociodramatic play, thereby extending the lifespan of the unit block structure for as long as the play episode endures.

As agents of social learning, unit blocks allow for solitary, parallel, cooperative, and collaborative play endeavours. Rogers (1985) claimed that unit blocks facilitate children's movement from socially isolated play to increasingly higher levels of **social integration**. Blocks foster prosocial behaviour in children, whose collaborative creative-constructive play behaviours are often more evident in block play than in other play environments. Social skills such as sharing, requesting, explaining, helping, cooperating, and partnering are predictable outcomes of block play, especially at the representational stage. As they become increasingly sophisticated "players" with unit blocks, children regularly consult one another, contributing their own ideas and gaining insights into the plan another child has in mind; this challenges them to take a perspective other than their own. Self-regulation improves as children learn to wait their turn to add to or change a structure and are challenged to be patient and to explain clearly why their idea has advantages. In fact, self-regulation is usually a requirement in order for a child to remain a member of the group that is creating a structure (Anderson, 2010, p. 55). Language usually flows during these play periods as children communicate their plans, describe their structures, and negotiate changes or additions to their plans. Play with unit blocks also engages children in scientific inquiry as they explore dimensions, friction, stability and balance, speed, distance, and measurement (see further discussion on p. 387. Hirsch (1984; 1996) has described the stages that children pass through in their block play (see Figure 20–2).

Handling and Manipulating Blocks

Toddlers enjoy carrying blocks around, handling them, and sliding them together. Johnson (1933) referred to this as the *carrying* stage. At this sensorimotor stage in block play, children are simply discovering the properties of blocks, without building with them or using them for a purpose. Practice play may occur as a child

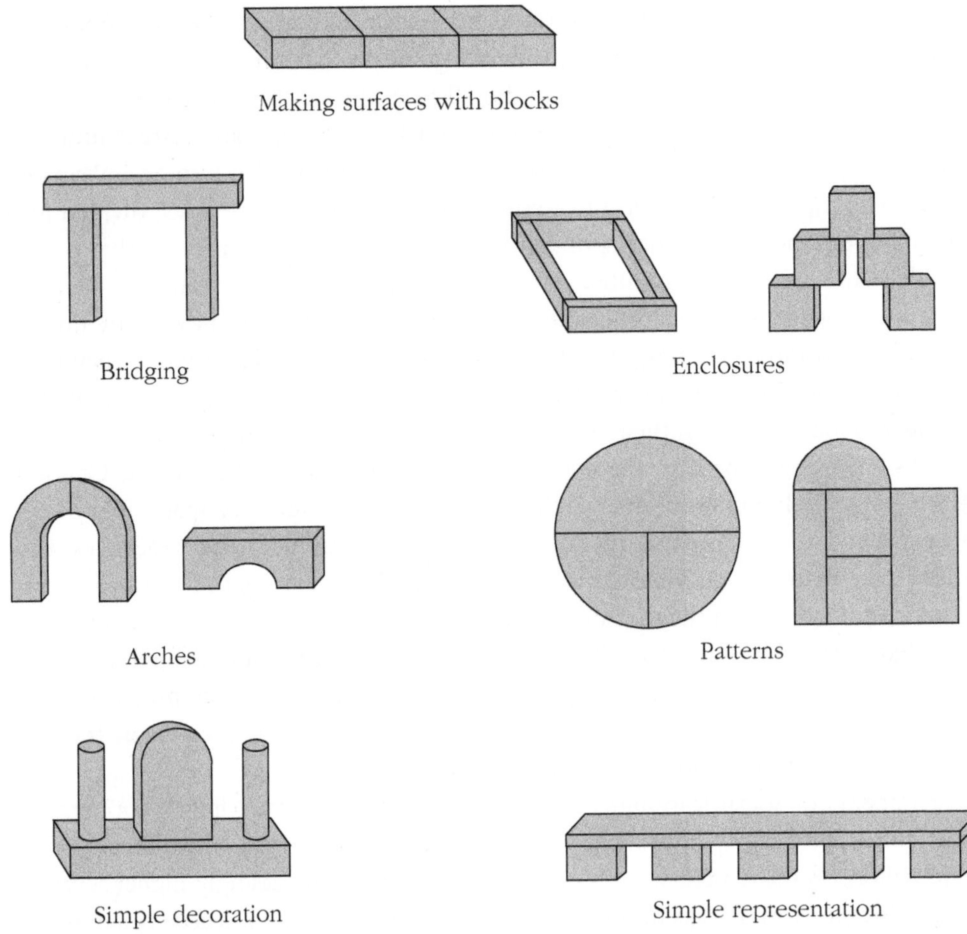

Figure 20–2
Developmental progression of play with unit blocks

knocks two blocks together or slides one along the floor repeatedly, but productive play has not yet appeared. This stage of block play is often compared to the early scribbling stage in children's drawing. For toddlers, one set of unit blocks alone is sufficient to explore the materials in a sensorimotor way by stacking them, making towers, bridging the towers, rubbing and knocking the blocks against one another, sliding them, and examining them from many perspectives. During the first three years, unit blocks are largely sensorimotor play materials that also promote the toddler's motor and manipulative abilities.

Toddlers begin to place blocks beside one another in a purposeful way before they stack three or four blocks one on top of the other (Reifel, 1984). Johnson (1933) refers to this stage as *stacking* when children discover they can balance one block on another. They also may fill a container with small blocks and try to lift the container. Eventually, toddlers make a small tower by stacking blocks, and they arrange the blocks in rows. More rows and piles of blocks appear about age three. Shortly thereafter, children learn to place blocks in compact, interlocking squares to make extended surfaces.

Bridging

The ability to bridge by placing two blocks vertically and one horizontally signals a significant step in the child's cognition, as the task requires planning, predicting, estimating, and using trial and error (Hirsch, 1984). The ability to place the vertical blocks at a necessary distance from each other so that a third block can bridge the space between them is an important developmental achievement and deserves recognition. Once children have grasped the concept of bridging and have practised it repeatedly, they will often build bridges on top of bridges and connect bridges horizontally as well.

Enclosures

In their simplest form, enclosures are four blocks placed so they touch and form an enclosed space. At this stage, children have grasped the concept of using blocks purposefully, and they eventually connect enclosures to one another creating a series of connected *rooms*, usually with no opening between each room. Later in this stage, children will use arches to designate an enclosure with an entry point from one enclosure to the next. It is possible to observe the rudiments of purposeful play and planning at this stage as children appear to struggle with the materials in order to use them to execute their own intentions.

Patterns

Eventually, children begin to connect enclosures and to create elaborate patterns of squares, rectangles, triangles, and pentagons as more and more blocks are used. This is the stage when children's play with unit blocks shows signs that they appreciate the concept of symmetry and balance as they experiment with the triangles, arches, switches, intersections, curves, and buttresses to create intricate designs that achieve a symmetry and visual connection among the various elements. Often as early as three years of age, children begin to use blocks as symbols and begin to attach meanings, such as "This is my house," to their block structures. In the pattern period, block building remains largely horizontal, with most blocks spread out along the floor in an ever expanding array of connecting shapes. At this stage, children may begin to use the accessories and the more specialized unit blocks, such as cylinders, pillars, arches, ramps, gothic doors, switches, buttresses, curves, and quarter circles, to decorate their horizontal structures. Johnson (1933) refers to this stage as *decoration,* when children experiment with a wider array of the shapes. At this point, structures gain symmetry and take on realistic configurations, and children may begin to name their structures; however, the focus of their play appears to be much more on the "rhythmic and intentional ... physical act of block placement, such as placing one to the left, right, front, and then back of the structure" (Wellhousen & Kieff, 2001, p. 51). We see the beginning of their representational use of the unit blocks as children begin to build vertically and to replicate buildings that are recognizable and can be identified and named by the children.

Unit blocks enclosures and towers

Representation

Once children begin to name their structures, their block building generally becomes more vertical and three-dimensional. The structures may assume forms that are more lifelike. A child may call his structure a condominium or a galleria and may practise using new words in the process of representing something he has remembered. Children are usually four to five years of age before their structures begin to symbolize real-world structures, but the age at which children achieve representational play with unit blocks depends very much on how much access they have had to these materials and what kinds of play ECEs encourage with these blocks. In the early stages, children often name their products even though they may bear little resemblance to the actual object they name.

In the later representational stage, children often announce what they are going to build with the blocks and seek the resources they need to execute the rudiments of a plan. Their products are usually recognizable as train tracks, garages to park cars, houses with doors and windows, and other structures that demonstrate their integration of everyday living concepts and social-conventional knowledge with their block play. As their representations become more lifelike, children often seek accessories from other learning centres in the classroom so they can engage in dramatic or sociodramatic play with their block structures as a backdrop. It is at this stage that ECEs may find that the introduction of lifelike accessories is beneficial, as children have struggled with the abstract materials to the point whereby they are able to create structures that meet their own vision and standards of perfection for their dramatic play episodes. This stage usually coincides with the kindergarten years, which underlines the importance of including a Unit Blocks centre in all kindergarten classrooms. Wellhousen and Kieff (2001) concluded that observing children using their own block structures for their pretend play provides ECEs with another opportunity to understand how children view their worlds. It is also possible to form some judgments about the extent to which children are able to use abstract materials to represent their worlds, which is also a key indicator of their cognitive and creative development, and their aesthetic sense.

As their play with unit blocks progresses, children revert to previous stages. They repeat skills already learned, such as stacking, bridging, enclosing, patterning, and decorating, and they elaborate on some of the basic configurations. Children are usually between the ages of five and seven before they are able to relate the interior space of an enclosure (or room) to its contents, that is, to place blocks representing furniture inside a room and differentiate each piece. Even later, about the age of seven, children begin to coordinate external features of the structure, such as driveways, garages, streets, and trees, with the structure itself (Reifel, 1984). At this point in the course of mature, creative-constructive play, children often build and use their own block structures as props to elaborate and extend sociodramatic play.

© Nancy P. Alexander / PhotoEdit

Representation with unit blocks

Facilitating Play with Unit Blocks

Play with unit blocks is largely initiated and directed by the children. The ECE's principal role is to ensure that the environment and schedule maximize children's uninterrupted play with the blocks and to encourage the children to identify and name their structures and use the abstract accessories that accompany unit blocks to enhance their structures. ECEs supervise the Unit Blocks centre to support, encourage, question, express interest, and observe and record children's play with the unit blocks. They expand children's planning and problem solving by asking questions at the right time and by making suggestions when things seem to be at a standstill. Asking questions such as "Are you trying to make your building higher?" and offering comments such as "Your structure reminds me of the new arena," lets children know that you are interested in their structures and that you consider their play to be important. When children want to leave their block building and move to another area, the ECE may have to find a way to preserve what they have completed to date, perhaps by closing off the learning centre temporarily or asking another group of children to play and build in another part of the Unit Blocks centre or playroom. ECEs should encourage concept development by using words that encourage children to reflect on the dimensions and size of their structure, the juxtapositions of various parts of the structure, the distance of one tower or chimney from another, and to focus attention on concepts of tall, wide, high, middle or centre, in front of or behind, underneath, opposite, and other spatial terms. Block play is rich in the development of language skills, especially when ECEs help children find the right words to describe their structure while pointing out its features and using words such as *spire*, *buttress*, *support beam*, *incline*, *symmetrical*, and so on. After taking a fieldtrip to a construction site, or to a downtown public building such as a museum or gallery, ECEs are wise to encourage children to use the unit blocks to replicate the building they visited; this practice also provides an opportunity to revisit the new words they learned during the fieldtrip.

When children are encouraged to play with unit blocks that are always accessible to them, they generally make progress in their block play. Repetitive practice play is usually a signal that children need help and encouragement to move to the next step with the materials. Hanging attractive posters of block structures and tacking photographs of children's block constructions on the bulletin board in the Unit Blocks centre will motivate children toward new heights in their block play. Digital photography allows ECEs to easily preserve the structures children create so they can revisit their structures and make changes based on new understanding and experiences, and they can also show off their products to their parents. Photographs of their work also help instil in children a sense of achievement and appreciation of their own creative endeavours. As with clay, however, the productions are less important than the process involved. There are times, especially for older preschoolers and kindergarten children, when it is more important than at other times to capture their more elaborate structures in a photograph and perhaps have it developed as a poster-sized print for the wall (Clemens, 1991).

ECEs often wonder how to stimulate interest in block play among children who do not readily choose to play in this area. Reading a story about a building or looking at a picturebook or photographs from the picture file will sometimes be enough to spark an idea in a child who has had sensorimotor experience with blocks and is beginning to understand their creative potential. No matter how ECEs try, some children, often girls, seem reticent about playing with blocks. It may be useful to intervene by asking the *regulars* to play somewhere else for a while so that the more reluctant or timid children may benefit from the play and learning opportunities afforded by unit blocks. Pairing a timid child with an experienced block builder can sometimes generate interest in a child who could not get started without some encouragement and coaching from another child. This is also a useful strategy to integrate a child who is new to the centre or who does not speak the primary language of the centre into active participation in the program. For example, in a primarily English-speaking child-care centre, pairing a non-English-speaking child with a regular in the Unit Blocks centre encourages play that is not dependent on language but does call for interaction, cooperation, collaboration, gestures, and a helping relationship. In a context such as this, the child who is new to the centre, or who is learning English, can learn new words and phrases while involved in active play with the blocks and not feel diminished or intimidated because of her lack of command of English words.

Children should take from the shelves only the blocks with which they intend to play, and they should build slightly away from the shelves so they do not prevent other children from reaching for stored blocks. The ECE should clarify the protocol for block play and restate it as often as necessary to promote care and respect for these materials and for the play of others. Actively discouraging hoarding blocks, knocking down structures, dropping or throwing blocks, banging them together, stepping or sitting on blocks unnecessarily, and touching another child's building structure is another important teaching responsibility in this learning centre (Cartwright, 1988). Children generally become so absorbed in their block play that a warning about 10 minutes before they need to tidy up is necessary to allow them to complete their structures to their satisfaction and to disengage themselves gradually from what may have been an intense play experience.

Exploring the Mathematical Relationships of Unit Blocks

Unit blocks not only contribute to creative development and symbolic and representational thinking, but they also are important tools for helping children develop logical mathematical concepts such as number, class, order, and conservation. Play with unit blocks encourages children to develop physical knowledge of objects, such as size, shape, weight, density, and volume. Unit blocks are mathematically precise, as the various blocks are multiples or fractions of basic units. ECEs may encourage children to note the half–whole and quarter–half–whole relationships of units and half-units, and of half-circles, and quarter-circles. Children will learn through experimentation that it takes two half-units to make a whole unit and that four unit blocks equal the length of a quadruple unit. Mathematical relationships may be reinforced by encouraging children to stack blocks on shelves that have painted outlines designating which blocks are to be placed in that spot. This practice draws attention to size relationships, which children readily see when they try to place a half-unit inside a painted outline for a unit and find that the dimensions are not the same.

As children become acquainted with the physical knowledge of the blocks, they also learn to count, measure, sort, classify, identify shapes, create and identify equivalencies, and understand **part–whole relationships**. Increased familiarity with the relationships between quarter-units, half-units, and whole units leads children naturally toward the concept of fractions. As children count the long planks and the half-units, and find that five long planks and five half-units both represent the concept of *fiveness*, they develop the ability to conserve, which involves relying on what they know to be true instead of focusing on the perceptual dimension of length. Blocks also provide children with opportunities to organize materials according to categories, such as shapes, sizes, or function, and to sort the blocks according to classes that the child has named. Children's gradual understanding of these concepts through their concrete manipulation of the unit blocks adds to the importance of making unit blocks readily accessible at all times.

Unit Blocks and Scientific Inquiry: An Example

Scientific inquiry with young children is addressed in Chapter 21. Several science principles may also be addressed in the Unit Blocks centre. The viability of this centre for certain investigations in science encourages ECEs to add some abstract materials to the unit blocks. That is, in fact, recommended by Zan and Geiken (2010), who use wooden ramps and pathways to demonstrate what happens with inclined planes and investigations involving force and motion. Providing children with opportunities to investigate is an important purpose of the Science Discovery centre, but investigation may occur in any learning centre when children try out different ideas and modify their actions on materials to produce different results.

Zan and Geiken (2010, pp. 14–16) make the following suggestions for the ramps and pathways activities.

1. First, play with the materials yourself in order to understand their learning potential.
2. Encourage children to keep trying out their ideas.
3. Observe children closely to assess how they think and reason. Question or comment, but do not correct the children or provide answers to their dilemmas. Encourage them to see that there are no right or wrong answers.
4. Intervene to facilitate their reasoning and to help correct any misperceptions they may have.
5. Encourage children to work in groups and share their experiences to ensure that scientific investigation is a social activity in which children help each other.
6. Encourage the children to draw and write about their structures.

To investigate various principles of physics using ramps and pathways, the authors recommend adding wooden cove moulding to the Unit Blocks centre when children are ready to engage in play with these materials. They recommend using marbles of various sizes to compare the speed and distance of the larger and smaller marbles on the ramps. Moulding should be 1¾ inches (4.5 centimetres) wide, in one-(30 centimetre), two- (60 centimetre), and three-foot (90 centimetre) lengths, with at least eight pieces in each length. Four-foot (120 centimetre) lengths may be added where space allows, but play with ramps and pathways could move out into hallways or outdoors when added space is needed. To investigate the impact of inclines on motion, speed, and distance, various objects that do not roll or that roll differently, such as oval objects, spools, steel marbles, are helpful. Children use unit blocks to prop up the ramps to change the speed and motion of objects as they roll, and they experiment with trying to move an object without touching it, and with how to make a marble turn a corner (Zan & Geiken, 2010, p. 14).

Unit Blocks and Literacy Development

The Unit Blocks centre is a rich environment for children to use and hear new words, which they associate with their active manipulation of the blocks. The unit blocks also provide a stimulus for children to use language and to speak fluently

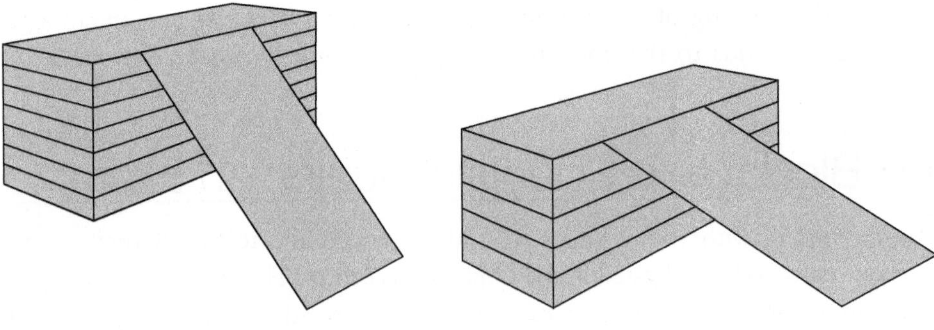

Figure 20–3
Ramps propped up with unit blocks

while occupied in the physical task of building with blocks. Wellhousen and Kieff (2001, p. 92) observed that children "playing with blocks had greater verbal fluency (number of words spoken), used significantly more communication units (complete sentences), and produced more vocabulary diversity (number of different words) than children in the housekeeping center." They concluded that block play is a key environment in which to foster children's language development. Because blocks are abstract symbolic materials that can assume any meaning the child assigns, play with blocks leads children naturally toward an understanding of symbols of all kinds, including the use of letters to represent sounds and of words to represent things and communicate thoughts. Play with unit blocks also exposes children to visual-perceptual skills, such as detecting figure from ground, and shape discrimination, skills related to reading.

Unit Blocks and Physical Development

Anyone who has observed children playing with unit blocks can see how physically active they are as they engage with the blocks—standing up, sitting, stretching, lifting, and putting away. As children try to gain a perspective of their block structure, they change position, lie down, kneel, stand and stretch, and sometimes try to fit themselves inside the structure. Although not as physically challenging as play with hollow blocks, unit blocks rely heavily on eye–hand coordination, perceptual skills, hand control, balance, agility, and stretching.

Unit Blocks and Social-Emotional Development

During the early stages of block play, children are usually preoccupied with their individual physical exploration of the blocks. Later, they begin to build bridges sitting side by side in parallel play, and eventually they begin to cooperate by sharing the same set of blocks and, occasionally, borrowing blocks from each other for their structures. Children talk about their structures and about what they are doing now and what will happen next. Block play provides plenty of practice time for children to share space and blocks, communicate, and wait patiently. Collaboration encourages children to help and depend on each other, to plan collaboratively, to share and take turns, to defer to the better ideas of another child, to practise self-control, and to take initiative. Sometimes, block play may provide a physical and emotional outlet for a child who is experiencing stressful circumstances. The satisfaction they feel seeing a product take shape, based on their plan or vision, provides a sense of empowerment over their environment and hope and solace in the face of negative experiences. Block play also gives children the opportunity to create an environment with the blocks that allows them to express feelings, feel satisfaction, and to temporarily shut out the rest of the world while they are immersed in their block play.

Unit Blocks in Inclusive Settings

Wellhousen and Kieff (2001, p. 158) state that "block play is an important addition to inclusive settings because it provides sensory-rich opportunities for children to explore their physical environment, initiate and sustain social play, and form mental representations while working with children with differing abilities." The inclusive climate created in the Unit Blocks centre sets a pattern for play in all centres. Effort should be made to include children with special needs, while recognizing that the skills and understanding they acquire from play in this learning centre may differ from the child who does not face physical or intellectual challenges. It is also wise to assume that the child with special needs may play with the unit blocks for shorter periods of time and that, although they may play happily alongside other children, they may find it difficult to be fully integrated into the planning and execution of the structures envisaged by more experienced block players. As always, the ECE should find ways to support the block play of the child with special needs to ensure that this play material contributes to the child's overall development.

Frequently, finding sufficient space to accommodate the child with physical needs in the Unit Blocks centre is the first challenge to be addressed. Accessibility to the blocks on the shelves may be another challenge. Some experts recommend reserving a specific space where the child with special needs may play with blocks and be less distracted by the play of other children, which can become noisy and boisterous. Sometimes, the unit blocks may be raised onto a table for easier reach by a child who is seated on the floor. ECEs often have to teach children how to play with the materials in the centre and to physically guide the child to the centre and help her access materials and settle to some active exploration and play. It is also useful to point out to the child the play that the other children are engaged in, as a way of motivating the child to imitate their actions and to set her own goals. With experience in the Unit Blocks centre, the child with special needs may become ready for inclusion with the other children, once he has mastered the basic skills using the materials. It is usually important to select carefully the group with whom the child with special needs is to be integrated. Often, he has to be encouraged to play in the Unit Blocks centre so as to benefit from the richness of play with these abstract materials, as well as from the friendship and closeness that evolves when children collaborate in planning and executing a plan using the unit blocks.

Locating the Unit Blocks Centre

Whatever rationale is used for locating the Unit Blocks centre, there must be an adequate amount of sheltered space and a protected location that does justice to their exceptional play value. Assigning unit blocks to a specific location relative to other learning centres is a challenge because they appear to be compatible with most learning centres, depending on the developmental levels of the children in the program.

When they are located in the Creative Discovery zone, unit blocks complement the abstract thinking and representational thinking, and creative, cognitive, expressive, and physical objectives addressed there. When they are within easy reach of the Daily Living centre, children may be tempted to use them as props for their dramatic and sociodramatic play. Some ECEs locate them close to, but not in, the Active Role Play centre, in order to promote the transfer of learning from the larger and more primitive hollow blocks. This approach sees play with unit blocks and hollow blocks as similar and complementary, but as was noted above, the unit blocks and the hollow blocks are, in fact, unique and different media for play. Placing unit blocks close to the Science Discovery centre may further children's exploration of the mathematical and physical relationships of unit blocks and also the physics involved in exploring planes and ramps. In this context, unit blocks provide another medium for comparing, ordering, estimating, and predicting, as well as for performing simple arithmetical operations, such as adding and subtracting, and developing a basic understanding of fractions. Similar arguments may be made for putting unit blocks near the tabletop activities in the Quiet Thinking centre, which also address number concept, ordering, and measurement.

Because unit blocks are primarily creative materials that promote symbolic thinking, representation, planning, problem solving, and original thinking, they may be best located close to the creative, discovery-oriented learning centres. Wherever the unit blocks are located, it is important that enough space is provided to accommodate children's elaborate constructions and to ensure that there is sufficient space to accommodate children with special needs.

The most difficult space issue to address, however, is often one of where to locate a Unit Blocks centre when space is at a premium—a situation that is all too common. Several points are relevant here; one is that the Unit Blocks centre does not have to be large as long as it is bounded on three sides with storage shelves. When children's play expands, ECEs may allow children to spread into hallways dedicated as temporary play areas, or they may move the unit blocks to a large, unused area of a gymnasium or other room where children's play can be supervised. *Space requirements should not be used as a reason not to include Unit Blocks as a learning centre. Ideally, this learning centre should always be available to children—even if it means taking space from other learning centres.*

Organization and Design of the Unit Blocks Centre

The Unit Blocks centre should consist of a space large enough to accommodate at least four children playing cooperatively, associatively, or solitarily (see Figure 20–4). Cartwright (1988) recommends a minimum of 3 metres by 3.5 metres for up to eight children. The learning centre should have expandable sides to allow the ECE

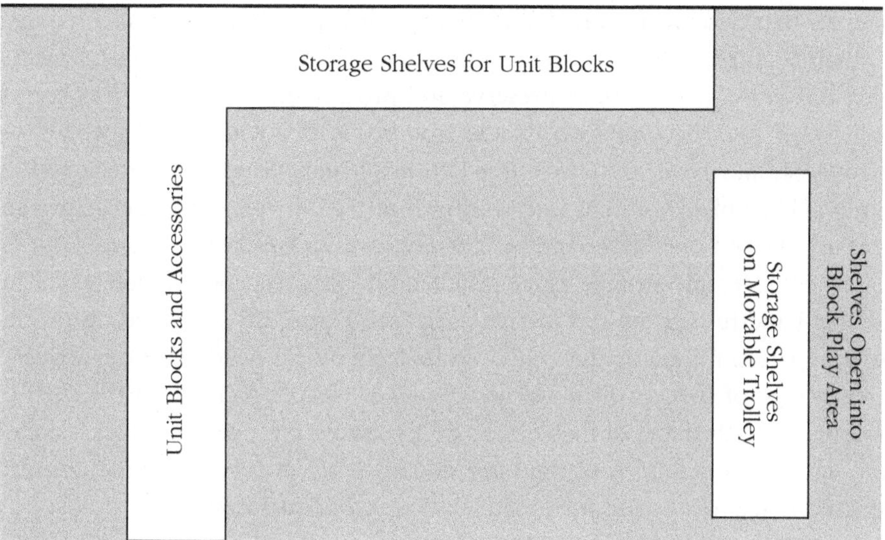

Figure 20–4
The Unit Blocks centre

the freedom to enlarge the area, so that when there are more children than usual, they can still play cooperatively. The Unit Blocks centre should be enclosed on three sides to encourage, over time, the child's vertical building with blocks and to define the unit block play area clearly. Dividers or storage units surrounding the block play area should be low enough for ECEs to observe block play easily. Unit blocks should not spill over into pathways or into the play spaces of other learning centres. They should be well away from high-traffic areas and near neat, clean, relatively quiet activities. They also should be in an area where children are able to avoid other distractions and concentrate on their play.

Unit blocks are best located on a carpeted floor, where cushions may be provided for children to sit on or lean on as they play. An unpatterned, smooth, taut, densely woven carpet with a foam underpad is best. The carpet should be kept clean and vacuumed daily. Avoid using carpets with pre-printed tracks and roadways for children to run their trucks and cars along; these carpets may be appropriate in the Active Role Play centre, where the trucks and cars are stored, but not in the Unit Blocks centre. It is important to ensure that there are enough unit blocks to accommodate the number of children who are permitted to play in the learning centre at one time. One set of unit blocks is only enough for toddlers; two sets are usually a minimum, especially for children who are three years of age and older.

Equipment and Materials

- **Equipment:** shelves for two sets of unit blocks and shelves for abstract wooden accessories
- **Materials:** two sets of unit blocks and abstract wooden accessories designed for play with unit blocks, such as abstract trees, house shapes, and posts for signs

Storage

Unit blocks should be stored separately from hollow blocks and all other types of blocks. They need to be protected from the elements; therefore, storing them for access to children outdoors is not a good idea. These are valuable indoor play materials that deserve a protected place of their own. Unit blocks also require regular maintenance, such as cleaning and sanding when splinters or chips develop, and polishing with a paste wax to preserve and protect the wood and help keep them clean. When they become dirty, blocks may be cleaned with a mild soap and water, but they should never soak in water because it penetrates the surface and causes warping. Unit blocks should not be stored in bins, boxes, or baskets; they should be neatly stacked on shelves and matched according to size and shape. Unit blocks require considerable storage space. Shelf units must be approximately 1.3 metres wide by 1 metre high by 0.3 metres deep (see Figure 20–5). Dividing the shelves into compartments encourages children to stack blocks neatly in the spaces allotted for each type of block, which are designated by shapes painted on the shelf corresponding to each shape of unit block. ECEs should arrange unit blocks so that the same sizes are together, with the long side in view. The centre should also provide sheltered space for the proportionate abstract wooden accessories.

Tidying Up the Unit Blocks Centre

When playtime is over, ECEs should model appropriate tidying up behaviours and encourage the children's involvement in tidying up. Children are not usually ready to assume this rather challenging task by themselves until they are familiar with the routine, and they need the help of adults to ensure the appropriate care and replacement of the blocks on the shelves. Shape recognition, classification skills, task orientation, ordering abilities, comparison recognition (such as same-different, larger-smaller), and manipulative abilities are among the many developmental skills involved in the cleanup process, which is, in itself, a valuable learning activity. The completion of the cleanup process contributes to children's satisfaction with the

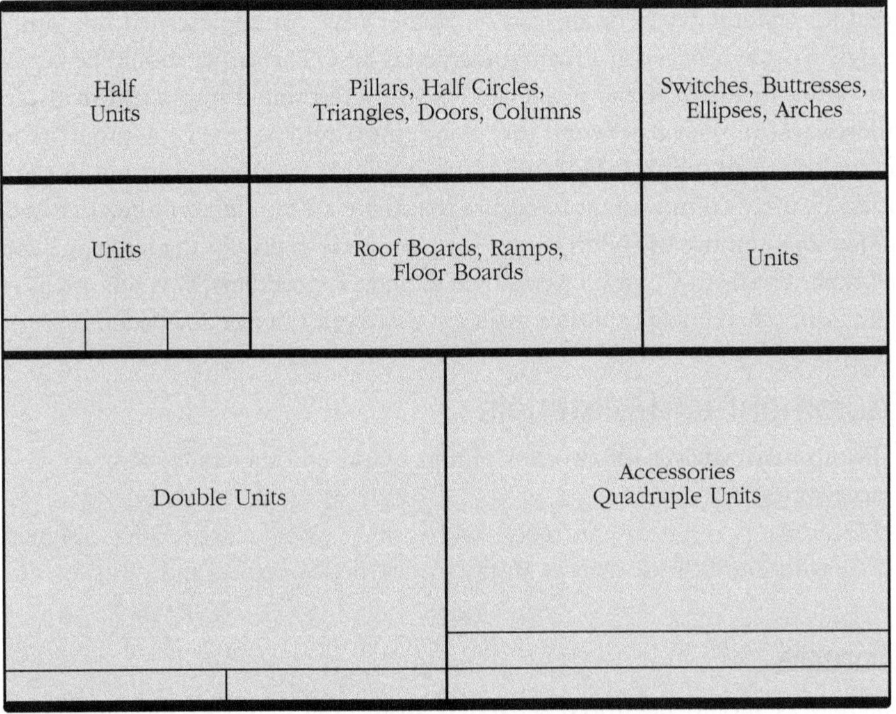

Figure 20–5
A Unit Block storage unit

total play experience and teaches them that to finish well is as important as starting well, an important learning-to-learn skill. Too much emphasis on the need for neatness in the Unit Blocks centre, however, might discourage children from regular play there. Children who want to keep their structure standing to resume play with it later should be allowed to do so when space permits. This practice encourages children to return to their play after an interruption and affirms the value of their play, including the planning that goes into it.

Summary

Unit blocks were designed by Caroline Pratt about a century ago as play materials that allow children to express their intrinsic motivations to test, try out, discover, and invent. Their design was purposefully abstract so that the blocks themselves, and the structures that children built with them, could become what the child intended and encourage the child to use the blocks as symbols of the idea or vision that he holds in his mind. In this way, unit blocks were envisaged by Pratt and by others as play materials that would promote children's abstract thinking and creativity. The simplicity and mathematical precision of unit blocks rely on children's imagination and ingenuity to create something new that represents what children see in their mind's eye. Today's marketplace is replete with exact miniature replicas of pop-culture idols, building materials for children, and technologies that enable children to create, almost instantaneously, models of the real world by fastening together pieces that match and following someone else's visual pattern and outcome. No one would argue that there is no play value in some of the intricate models that children have access to today, but it is a fact that the type of play and creativity that is addressed in working with miniature models of real life things is vastly different from play with abstract blocks that have no inherent structure or outcome in mind. Unit blocks themselves, and the environment in which they are properly placed, call upon children, first, to experiment with the play potential and spatial learning inherent in the blocks, to envisage what their abstract structures might become, and then to represent that vision using the unit blocks.

This chapter emphasizes the importance of providing a separate learning centre for play with unit blocks and the abstract wooden accessories designed to accompany them. The rationale here favours encouraging children to play only with the unit blocks, and not to mix other building materials or artifacts, such as trucks and cars, with them, at least until the child has learned how to create elaborate structures with unit blocks alone that he has fashioned out of his mind's eye.

Learning Activities

1. ECEs need to experience close physical contact with unit blocks to appreciate the aesthetic quality of this play material, as well as its rich play potential. With a group of peers, plan a unit block play workshop, in which all members of the group go through the various stages in block play and explore their potential as building materials. (Professors may refer to the Instructor's Manual for more detail on how to organize unit blocks workshops.)

2. Observe children's play with the unit blocks. Include in your report the play styles you observe, the social contexts of children's play, the role of language in their play, and the role the ECE plays in facilitating children's development as they play with the blocks.
3. Formulate your own approach to children's play with unit blocks based on what you have read and what you have observed in children's play with unit blocks.
4. Visit a preschool program or kindergarten that has a Unit Blocks centre. Observe children's play with the unit blocks, commenting on the stages of block play that you have observed and the role of the ECE in this learning centre. Make suggestions for improving the quality of the Unit Blocks learning centre, by changing the nature of the play, by improving the ECEs effectiveness in facilitating play, or by changing the location and organization of the Unit Blocks centre.
5. Test your understanding of how children develop representational thinking by observing and documenting children's sustained play as they create their own version of a structure they have planned and then executed. Take photos of their structure and include your notes and the photos in your journal.

Section VII

Active Learning in the Natural World

Section VII addresses the following topics:

- the goals of science education and *sciencing* with young children
- the importance of children's contact with nature
- science projects for young children
- gardening as a science project and as a way of life
- playground history and philosophy
- outdoor play and child development
- the impact of outdoor play on children's physical and mental health
- playground safety and zones for play
- outdoor curriculum for all seasons

Section VII discusses children's exploration, play, and learning in contact with nature and natural phenomena, both indoors in the Science Discovery centre and outdoors in the playground. The majority of Canadian children today live in urban environments where their contact with nature and their freedom to explore outdoors are limited by the time pressures of families and by concerns about environmental and safety factors. Preschools and kindergartens create daily opportunities for children to play outdoors, but freedom to explore natural environments is not generally available to centres and schools. We are seeing the impact on children's physical and mental health of "nature deficit disorder" (Louv, 2008). Even in a vast nation like ours, Canadian children are increasingly isolated from nature; they may have infrequent, structured contact with nature, but too many children never experience the freedom, joy, and connection with nature that accompanies daily, spontaneous play and exploration outdoors. In the past, intense physical activity was a regular feature of children's days as they played with abandon in their neighbourhoods, which included open spaces and lots of places for rough-and-tumble play and to run and climb in natural environments. Children's need for regular, spontaneous, and planned physical activity is an urgent priority for programs given the alarming increase in childhood symptoms that predispose children to obesity, heart ailments, diabetes, and other illnesses in adulthood.

21 The Science Discovery Centre

"The natural world is the ultimate web, and essential to the emotional health of children."

—Richard Louv, *Childhood's Future* (1991)

Before Reading This Chapter, Have You

- observed children's play outdoors in natural settings?
- considered your own approach to science and discovery learning?
- reflected on your own physical play outdoors as a child?

Outcomes

After reading and understanding this chapter, you should be able to

- explain the goals of science education for young children: scientific inquiry skills, physical science concepts, and understanding that living organisms require basic ingredients in order to survive;
- foster in children a sense of wonder about nature that contributes to their spiritual development and mental health;
- outline a repertoire of science and environmental studies projects for young children;
- locate, organize, and design the Science Discovery centre;
- set up play stations: exploring table, water play, sand play, nature corner, and resource table;
- plan, prepare, maintain, harvest, and tidy up gardens with young children; and
- create prop boxes and resource kits for science activities and projects.

Sciencing with Young Children

The word *science* comes from the Latin *scire*, meaning to know, and *scientia*, meaning a state of knowing usually acquired from systematic observation, study, and experimentation. Although the word *science* is a noun, not an action word (verb), the gerund ***sciencing*** captures the idea that, in science education, the child is in active pursuit of knowing and finding meaning through play and hands-on exploration of objects and phenomena in the environment. The concept of sciencing transfers a static curriculum into an exciting process of learning through discovery and active exploration (Zeimer, 1987). Science in early childhood education helps children *know* through their physical and sensory interaction with concrete objects and their observation of phenomena. Children explore, formulate plans, ask questions, consider possibilities, evolve and follow strategies, and communicate results in the Science Discovery centre in much the same process-oriented way in which they engage in creative endeavours in the Creative Arts and Unit Blocks centres.

With young children, science implies encouraging them to be curious, ask questions, and solve problems. "Science is observing, questioning, wondering, testing, guessing, recording findings—it is not being told facts about science-related subjects" (Perry & Rifkin, 1992, p. 11). Through their play with substances, objects, and elements that respond to their actions, children discover and experience the relationships that exist in the natural and physical world, such as categories of animals and plants, part–whole relationships, cause-and-effect relationships, and action and reaction phenomena. In this sense, early science education is constructivist education. Children develop their abilities to take perspectives, consider variables, organize their actions, and observe results, all of which contribute to their development. The purpose of science in early childhood is to allow children to explore objects in an atmosphere of experimentation and to define problems, ask questions, and pursue answers as they encounter them in their play (DeVries & Kohlberg, 1987). It is important to develop in children a predisposition for inquiry and scientific thinking, as well as respect for nature, which is only possible when children have regular access to natural surroundings. A key component of the science curriculum is the gardening program, which, in many regions of Canada, may be carried out over at least three seasons of the year.

The physical and natural world is full of exciting phenomena to explore with young children. Spending precious time performing experiments that produce mysterious chemical reactions, or trying to convey the principles of electricity to young children, does not lead to meaningful learning because children have not yet acquired the perceptual and conceptual frameworks they need to understand abstract scientific phenomena they cannot see. For this reason, subjects that address magnetism, matter and energy, planets, weather cycles, day and night, and electricity are inappropriate science topics for early childhood education (Kamii & DeVries, 1993; Smith, 1987).

The best science activities are those that appeal directly to the senses and those that raise children's ecological awareness of phenomena they can observe. As noted by Charlesworth and Lind (2010, p. 77), children's readiness for science depends on their experience with science inquiry and on their process skills, such as comparing, classifying, and measuring. They recommend that four- and five-year-olds "begin with simple versions of intermediate process skills such as making a reasonable guess about a physical change, as in, 'what will happen if?'" and gather and organize simple data (Charlesworth & Lind, 2010, p. 77).

Children need to be active participants in sciencing as a process of discovery. DeVries and Kohlberg (1987) suggested two criteria for selecting good physical knowledge activities. The activity should allow children to (1) act on objects and observe their reactions and (2) act on objects to produce a desired result. The best activities are those in which the physical **transformations** that occur in nature are observable to the child. So many learning opportunities meet these criteria that young children could spend all their time on sciencing activities alone. Our knowledge of how children think and view reality is the framework from which a science curriculum and specific science activities for young children should emerge (Smith, 1989). Planning appropriate science experiences requires knowledge of children's cognitive thinking styles. Natural science explorations are the best activities because children can touch, see, hear, feel, taste, and smell the conditions, transformations, and outcomes they are investigating. Children tend to believe that phenomena they cannot observe directly must be magic, and it is not the purpose of early science experiences to contribute to magical thinking in young children. The natural environment (and naturally occurring things) close to the child is the best place for learning to read, write, and make sense of the world (Twiest & Kupetz, 2000).

The Goals of Science Education for Young Children

Young children are born scientists who have a wonderful curiosity and eagerness to explore as soon as they can crawl: using their explorations and discoveries as a starting point, they pursue their own goals. Creative thinking is closely related to scientific investigation, **hypothesizing**, and problem solving, which encourage children to see things from a number of perspectives, to ask questions before making unqualified statements of fact, and to compare and contrast what they investigate with things and phenomena. It is an exercise in dealing with detail, balancing numerous facts in order to come up with answers or conclusions, and risk taking in the sense that one does not know where the investigation will lead. In this way, creative thinking resembles the scientific method, which provides a disciplined approach to defining and solving novel problems. Creative play involves the ability to plan and think creatively, sometimes alone, sometimes with others, to achieve an end result close to the goal the child envisioned at the beginning. Children play creatively when they feel psychologically safe, free to experiment, and able to express themselves; in supportive, affective environments, children make discoveries that permit them to see everyday phenomena and events in new contexts and from unique perspectives.

It doesn't matter what activities we pursue to spark children's interest in science; what matters is that they eventually learn to think scientifically (Gardner, 1999). To achieve these goals, ECEs have to respect children as emerging scientists, follow children's scientific interests, show enthusiasm for investigation and discovery themselves, and build on children's existing understanding of nature and phenomena. Many science projects emerge from children's natural inquisitiveness. The Science Discovery centre should support open-ended inquiry, foster discovery, promote respect for life, and celebrate a sense of wonder (Ross, 2000). Exploring and observing, comparing and classifying, questioning, investigating, analyzing, predicting, testing, experimenting, inferring, reaching conclusions, documenting, and communicating are skills related to sciencing. Observing properties, such as size, weight, shape, colour, texture, and temperature, and learning that all living organisms, including children, have basic needs that must be met in order to survive are appropriate science activities (Seefeldt, 2005).

Perhaps the most important goal of science education for young children is to foster in all of their explorations and activities a respect for the natural environment. The science/discovery curriculum for young children should start with the self and one's interdependency with the natural environment and other living things. Children are quick to identify with animals and insects; they form relationships with trees and bushes in the natural environments they experience daily; and they learn very early to appreciate their need to adapt to changing natural and seasonal circumstances and events. Instilling in young children a profound appreciation for the natural environment and its strengths and vulnerabilities, and for our individual responsibility to protect the space we inhabit on this planet, are among the most important goals we have in early childhood education.

Exploring and Observing

Beauchamp (2010, p. 170) states that "exploration and investigation form the beginning of scientific inquiry.... Young children need opportunities to explore materials and objects in many different contexts." "The essence of all science is observation" (Martin, 2001, p. 37). Observation leads to questions to be asked, motivates us to find answers to important questions, and enables us to form conclusions based on the information we gain from our observations. Sometimes, children are able to formulate conclusions that might be generalized to other, similar events or phenomena. Exploring is largely an open-ended, sensory activity in which any outcome, if there is one, is unpredictable. Exploring usually implies physical action of some kind, freedom to move wherever and however we want (within safe limits), and an absence of specific objectives or tasks. Children need plenty of time and opportunity to explore. Opportunities to explore the environment on outings allow children to experience natural phenomena, to anticipate and enjoy the changing seasons, and to appreciate the diversity of nature. Exploring occurs in the Science Discovery centre; a wide range of things from nature for children to touch, feel, taste, smell, and hear—and methods and tools to report and document what their senses reveal to them—should be available to children. This centre should help children *see clearly* and notice detail when they explore a rich array of materials. And activities should provide opportunities to classify the materials they investigate according to many criteria that they record.

THINGS TO EXPLORE IN THE SCIENCE DISCOVERY CENTRE

Rocks, semiprecious and everyday stones, leaves and bark from different trees, different types of wood, sand of many different colours and textures, leather, seashells, pine cones and acorns of a variety of shapes and sizes, fabrics in various textures and weaves, grasses, weeds

One way to facilitate exploration is to involve children actively in planning what they want to explore and find out (Beauchamp, 2010, p. 170). Sometimes when children explore, they come to new discoveries that may be demonstrable, like a fact, or intangible, like a sensation or an idea. Exploring does not always lead to discovery, but when it does, the child is motivated to keep exploring. The Science Discovery centre should be set up to increase the likelihood that exploring will lead to meaningful discovery. Children should be encouraged to document what they discover by using charts in which they classify the objects according to a number of simple criteria.

Beginning a science program with a rich sensory program that involves all kinds of naturally occurring substances and things from nature is a gentle first step that allows ECEs to gain confidence in their own understanding of science. Sensory activities can be planned for the wet and dry sand tables, the water play area, the exploring table, and the nature corner. Children love to explore the shine of new spring poplar leaves, the roughness of tree bark, the softness of fur and feathers, the sharpness of burrs and thistles; to smell the sweet fragrance of flowers; to taste the delights of maple sugar and arrowroot; and to hear the sounds of sand, rice, and pebbles in tin sound cans. Sensory activities inevitably lead children to matching, sorting, and classifying according to their sensory perceptions of these items. They learn, for example, to differentiate various samples of wood as denser, heavier, lighter, softer, more textured, grainier, splintery, sweet smelling or acrid, and dry or oozing gum.

Questioning and Inquiry

"Inquiry is investigating to gather information" (Ogu & Schmidt, 2009, p. 12). Systematic observation of living and inanimate things in the environment inevitably leads children to questions such as "Why do bubbles form and what's inside them" or "Why do the rocks sink and the corks float?" Children's questions lead to further observations and experiments designed to help them find answers to their own questions. For example, preschool children are often fascinated by what's inside naturally occurring things such as milkweed pods, nutshells, a pomegranate, cocoons, and birds' nests (which have been duly sanitized). A potential play area, such as a table or countertop, provides space where more intensive investigations may take place that arise from children's observations and questions. This inquiry centre is best placed close to the exploring table, where children are encouraged to investigate further something that attracts their interest and raises questions. This is emergent curriculum at its best, when the materials provided at the inquiry centre are stocked with items from the exploring table that invite children's curiosity.

Comparing and Classifying

Classification is the skill of being able to construct logical groups according to one or more criteria; this skill is central to mathematics and science. It involves *joining* and *separating*, which precedes arithmetical operations such as adding and subtracting, as children first need to put together and join groups (addition) and then they need to separate a group into smaller groups (subtraction) (Lind, 2005). Classification begins with simple matching activities according to their obvious likenesses, such as colour, size, and shape. As more objects are added, children begin to see likenesses not readily apparent to adults, such as *these are all the pointy things, and these are the soft things* (sensory criteria), instead of *these are objects used in cooking, and these are objects used in gardening* (knowledge criteria). Children need opportunities to classify because the ability to see likenesses, patterns, common functions, and abstract similarities and associations lies at the heart of divergent thinking, which fosters creativity and invention.

Children should be encouraged to collect interesting things they see when they are outdoors and sort them according to the criteria that they determine. Other resources are useful as well. The picture file of animals and their **habitats** at the resource table, for example, provides interesting classification challenges for children from sorting according to habitat, and then classifying animals according to mammals, reptiles, and amphibians. The same can be encouraged for photos of different trees and plants. Or of insects that have wings and fly, and those that live in trees (or in the ground or in crevices), and those that have legs, and those with antennae. Various foods can be classified according to their colour, or whether they are fruits, vegetables, grains, or meats, which can lead to interesting discussions about foods common to the cultures represented in the program. Plants can also be sorted according to colour, leaf sizes, and shape, and according to their stems, fruits or blossoms, and seeds. Children who have plenty of experience classifying a wide range of objects develop skills related to scientific thinking, such as observation, analysis, and divergent thinking.

Objects and activities for comparing and classifying may also be found in the inanimate world; for example, in various types of implements, tools, and machinery. Children like to explore and take apart simple machines or engines and to classify parts that spin, parts that make sounds, parts that roll, and parts that connect or snap together. Children develop their concept of part–whole relationships and understand that things, people, animals, and machines and tools all have parts that make up the total package. Experiences with parts and wholes lead to understanding that the whole is usually no more than the sum of all its parts (Lind, 2005).

Measuring

Exploring leads to opportunities for children to measure and compare objects according to length, width, volume, weight, and time; taking measurements leads children to develop more sophisticated criteria for classifying things. The Science Discovery centre should provide many tools for measuring, including tape measures made from simple strings and cloth, and metal tapes, metre sticks, and rulers to measure distance, length, width, height, depth and volume; balance and electronic scales to measure weight; hourglasses and clocks with second hands to measure time; beakers, measuring cups and spoons to measure volume; and thermometers to measure temperature. Preschool children can even begin the process of measuring time by comparing time sequence to the order in which events occur. A good place to begin measurement activities is by encouraging children to measure themselves and each other and to compare sizes and shapes.

Measuring activities introduce children to the process of recording and interpreting data and using simple graphs to display the information they collect about the things they measure. Simple graphs can be constructed initially by using tabletop blocks of three or more colours, with each block standing for one item, and building each set according to the number of like items in a collection or set. For example, children can make a graph using blocks of several colours, each block representing one of the children in the group. The graphs they construct may stand for the number of children who have brown eyes and another for the children with blue or grey eyes. A graph might be constructed to depict the number of trees with leaves and those with needles that they have seen in the park (Figure 21-1). Graphs can show the number of children with birthdays in each month of the year. Graphs constructed by children can also prove their usefulness when they help children make decisions about where to go on a fieldtrip by adding a block to one stack for each child who wants to visit the zoo and another to a different stack for each child who wants to go to the wading pool in the park.

Testing and Experimenting

Science uses several methods of investigation, and testing is one method appropriate for young children (Forman, 2010). When children gather information about things, people, plants, and animals in the environment, they usually want to find some meaning

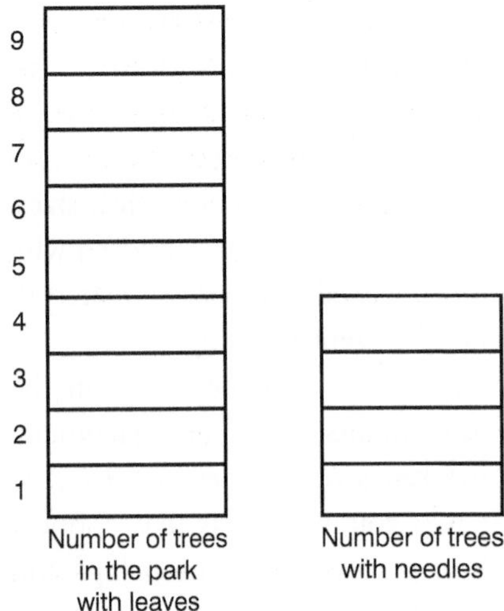

Figure 21–1
Diagram showing simple graph using unit blocks

in the data they collect. Older children usually make inferences based on what they know as opposed to what they see. Preoperational children often want to learn more about what they perceive through their senses by going through a process of testing and experimenting. Preschool and kindergarten children need the observable proof before they can begin to predict and infer based on data they have collected.

Experimenting is the scientific process in which we investigate the effect of changing one variable on the change in a different variable. Experiments are more meaningful when young children observe directly the change or factors that contribute to the phenomenon they are testing. For example, a sinking and floating activity at the water table, whereby children experiment with heavy and light objects that sink or float, provides observable information that can be verified by using the scales to measure weight. Children can see for themselves that weight matters more than size in sinking and floating and that density, or what's inside the object, also accounts for the sinking and floating capacities of various objects. Similarly, children learn about the relationship between speed and incline by testing objects on ramps of different inclines. They pursue what happens when heavier objects are rolled down a ramp as opposed to lighter objects, and they begin to develop a sense of the relationships among distance, speed, weight, and incline.

In testing and experimenting, children should be encouraged to test more than once to prove the relationship among the factors they are testing. Children learn that one trial is not usually enough and that two or three trials will produce a more reliable result. In the testing and experimenting stage, it is wise to introduce the concept of recording the results of each trial to learn the value of keeping track of what one sees and then examining the results of the record keeping so that children can be sure of the relationships they find.

Problem Solving

Perhaps the first phase of early scientific thinking occurs when a child treats a situation as a problem; the problem, as framed by the child, determines the strategy that the child uses to solve the problem (Forman, 2010, p. 2). Scientific investigation, especially the testing and experimenting stage, often involves finding ways to overcome obstacles and solve problems in order to achieve a result. Genuine opportunities to solve problems occur most readily in the context of projects that take place over time and involve several sequential steps. The best projects for young children are those with built-in opportunities for problem solving, some of which may be generated by the children. Curiosity is usually the driving force behind problem solving, which is also motivated by an interest in finding out (Lind, 2005, p. 34).

Gillis and Hardacre (1993) identified several steps in problem solving: identify a problem and define it; formulate a question to clarify the problem; find a range of possible ways to answer the question; gather information about the problem and the various solutions; assemble the information gathered to determine which solutions seem to work best; implement the solution; form conclusions; evaluate the conclusions to determine their effectiveness in answering the question and solving the problem. Problem solving may be called creative when one or more of the following conditions are satisfied: the outcome of the thinking has novelty and value; the thinking is unconventional and departs from traditional beliefs or paradigms; the creative product or the right answer to the problem requires time, motivation, and persistence; and the process of posing and defining the question or problem is part of the creative endeavour (Newell, Shaw, & Simon, 1962).

Creativity and problem-solving abilities have much in common. Problem solving uses critical-thinking skills, which lead to further questioning and hypothesizing, rather than to representing an original idea or insight. Problem solving is more cognitive in nature than is creativity and often involves all three developmental domains acting together (Gardner, 1982). The project approach, involving children in sustained endeavours with numerous steps, is uniquely suited to the development of problem solving skills in the Science Discovery centre.

EXAMPLE

Children were comparing the colour and shine of pennies at the Exploring Table. They took the darkened pennies to the sink and washed them with soap and water. They could not make the tarnished pennies shine. They said they wanted to find out what they could use to make the dark pennies shine again. They tested various methods: brushing them, soaking them, cleaning them with lemon juice, cleaning them with baking soda, cleaning them with salt and vinegar, etc. The children recorded their results and then suggested reasons why the salt and vinegar worked best.

Documenting and Reporting in Science Projects

When children are involved in meaningful projects, they are proud of their work and want to preserve elements of it to show parents and others. A plan, a process, and instruments that children can use to document their progress at each stage and report on its results should be built in to projects. Documenting a project encourages children to reflect on what they have done, the tasks they have left, the successes they have had, and what they might do differently. The challenge is to design tools and procedures that allow children to do their own documentation. Many tools for documentation and reporting are graphic in nature, include photographs and drawings, and rely on pictorial charts and graphs that can be constructed by the children using concrete objects. Prairie (2005) advised that the project should be documented as a story that unfolds in the classroom, with the details presented in story, narration, photos, and

Hands-on learning

drawings. The computers in the Project centre become useful tools for creating charts on which children can record check marks, or draw symbols to represent, for example, the days when their flowers bloomed or their plants poked through the ground. The documentation and reporting stage in a project promotes communication skills and appreciation of language and other forms of representation. Communicating what one has done and what the results were is a key component of the inquiry process and allows children to share what they have achieved (Prairie, 2005).

Spiritual Development in the Science Discovery Centre

A goal of science education is to help young children understand the cycles of life, growth, and death. We have seen that an important task of early childhood is to build a rich inner life, through spontaneous experiences with nature and naturally occurring objects in the environment (Bettelheim, 1987b). The development of a sense of the interconnectedness and interdependence of all living things is a goal that guides the choice of science activities and projects. "Direct contact with nature provides experiences for children with living things and parts of the environment that are self-sustaining. … Although providing all … types of experiences that connect children with nature are beneficial, it is the direct contact experiences that are critical because these experiences are disappearing from children's lives" (Helm & Katz, 2011, p. 8). Books and videos or indirect experiences involving going to parks and zoos where nature is groomed and controlled do not have the same impact.

Children have the capacity to wonder, to feel a sense of awe, and to be moved by mysterious and spiritual events. Children think about abstract questions of a spiritual nature, and they ponder questions of life and death, but children also possess astounding insight about natural phenomena (Coles, 1990). The child whose pet has just died and who can say, "He was a happy dog when he lived with us and I'll always remember him" demonstrates some understanding of the mortality of all living things, as well as a sense of what matters in life. The science curriculum that focuses on the whole life cycle and its generational sequence helps children begin to understand life, death, and the connection between them. Coping with death depends on first knowing what *dead* means. A basic concept of death is best grasped, not when a loved one dies, but in situations of minimal emotional significance, such as with dead insects or worms. Plants provide the most prevalent, accessible, and emotionally neutral opportunities to learn about life and death (Furman, 1990, pp. 16–17).

By exploring natural phenomena, children further their curiosity; whet their appetites for problem solving; kindle a sense of awe and wonder at the mysteries, beauty, and surprises of nature; and fuel their confidence and self-worth. These capacities and feelings arise from a sense of connectedness with nature. A deep-seated sense that the world is a wonderful place is surely one of the most abiding gifts that a science program can offer to young children. Science in this sense has little to do with the complex, abstract mathematical formulas and problems many of us associate with the term, and everything to do with fostering self-worth, respect for life, a love of nature, and the sense of being connected to something larger than oneself. In this kind of psychological environment, children gain a fundamental concern for the health of the environment and for the protection and replenishment of natural resources, as well as a powerful boost for their mental health. A Science Discovery centre designed to promote children's spiritual connectedness with the world of nature and with all living things will reduce fear of the unknown and foster a sense of the basic harmony that exists in the physical and natural world (Holt, 1989).

Physical Science

Physical science experiences for preschool and kindergarten should include activities in which children are able to perceive or observe directly the changes that occur as a result of their own actions on them (Kamii & DeVries, 1993). Prairie (2005) recommended physical science activities in which the child produces movements by her own actions; varies her actions to affect the outcome; observes the action of the object; and experiences immediately the effect of her actions. Activities that fall into one or more of these categories are those involving the use of inclined planes, pendulums, and pulleys; taking apart and putting together or repairing simple mechanical devices; using water as a force; and using wood and other building products. Experiences with electricity, magnetism, and chemical reactions that cannot be observed directly are not appropriate because they do not fit the criteria recommended.

Science Projects

When we tackle science from a child's perspective, a rich new world of challenge and discovery opens up. Science is not a subject to be explored piecemeal, with a volcano experiment here, a seed planting activity there, a shell sorting activity somewhere else, and a water pressure experiment at another time and place. To have meaning for children, science activities should be planned, coherent, and integrated as part of a larger plan or project with several phases. The activities should be sequenced from physical, sensory, exploratory play, toward making comparisons, seeing cause and effect, testing and measuring, accumulating factual information through observation, and documenting and reporting the results. Science projects should promote curiosity, inquiry, exploration, discovery, and positive attitudes. ECEs choose with the children a topic to investigate over time and then plan several exploratory activities sequenced from simple to complex, and from concrete to abstract. Even if only two or three topics are addressed in a school year, children gain more meaningful learning from integrated, long-term investigations. A series of activities that focus on physical learning about a particular element, such as water, or gathering knowledge about animal classes, or learning about the human body through body awareness activities, is more meaningful and lasting than an assortment of activities that address a list of unrelated topics. Children need time to acquire physical knowledge, to link causes and effects through hands-on experience, to chart progress and change, to observe transformations and outcomes, and to reflect and report what they have observed.

Choosing Topics and Projects for Science with Young Children

Many scientists today are preoccupied with environmental concerns. Age-appropriate science projects that concern natural events that may be close to children, such as extreme weather events and geographic changes, help children make sense of issues that concern adults. It is important to introduce environmental projects that emphasize the positive and reinforce the natural forces, elements, and species that society should strive to protect. Projects that have to do with studying species in danger of extinction in our own part of the world; investigating the properties of water and its effect on soil, plants, and trees; or building protective barriers to shield a garden from wind or a sandbox from intense sunlight are concrete ways to help children understand the influence of changing climate. Science activities and projects with children over time produce learning that crosses many subject disciplines (Fromberg, 1995).

A science program for young children that focuses on **natural science** activities will be full of new learning, and not remote and mysterious, as it once was in schools. Natural science (earth and plant science), ecology and the study of the **ecosystems** that support life, environmental science, physical science, and **life science** are appropriate science topics for early childhood education. Science exploration begins with the child's own body, family, home, neighbourhood, and community, and gradually encompasses and moves beyond the child's daily life experience. Holt's (1989) **distance-from-self criterion** implies that the science experiences should begin close to children's daily reality and move farther from the child as development proceeds. Thus, children in Canada will learn about themselves, their pets, domestic animals and plants, and naturally occurring elements in their own environments before they

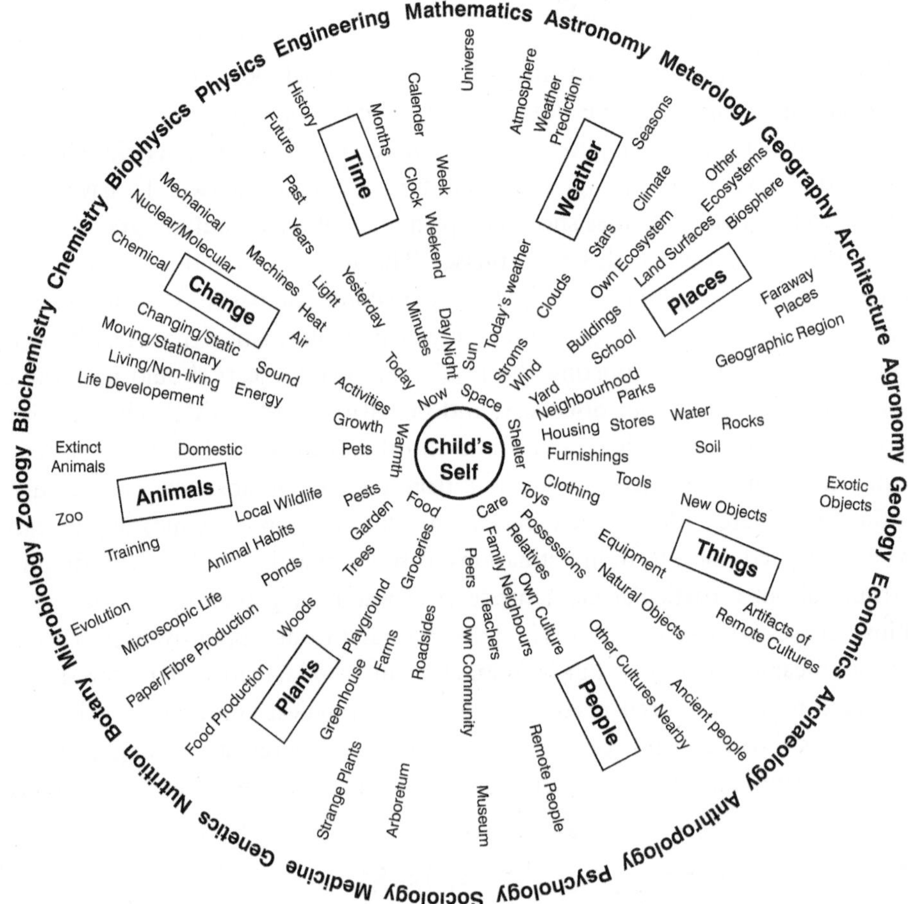

Figure 21–2
Distance-from-self criterion

Source: From Holt, B.G. (1989), *Science with Young Children* (rev. ed.). Washington, D.C.: National Association for the Education of Young Children. p. 119.*

*Reprinted with permission from the National Association for the Education of Young Children (NAEYC). www.naeyc.org

learn about camels, deserts, elephants, or jungles. Dinosaur activities are far too remote in time and place for the child to understand their scientific relevance and are best reserved for other learning centres. For young children, dinosaurs are fantastical creatures that appeal to their sense of wonder and **magical thinking** and add to their perception of the world as a place of mystery, intrigue, and scariness. They should not be treated as a category for investigation in the same way that exploring animal habitats or their eating and sleeping habits is. We know that dinosaurs interest young children, but pictures and models of dinosaurs belong in the learning centres where children engage in fantasy play, not in the Science Discovery centre.

Locating the Science Discovery Centre

The Science Discovery Centre is located near natural light, close to a water source, and on tiled floors, which, when spills occur, can easily be mopped. It should be close to the Creative Arts and the Unit Blocks centres to complement the exploration, discovery, problem solving, and creative play that occur in all three centres. Practical considerations provide many reasons for juxtaposing these centres. The Creative Arts centre encourages exploration of a wide variety of artistic media and materials. The Science Discovery centre provides water, sand, and other naturally occurring substances at the science tables, as well as tools for measuring, sifting, pouring, observing, investigating, and inventing.

Children often like to borrow natural substances and items from science collections for their collage or posters. Experimentation with clay in the Creative Arts centre and with wet sand in the Science Discovery centre addresses similar understandings about texture, the effects of adding water to a substance, compacting, moulding, and drying. Children explore the concepts of size, shape, texture, consistency, **mass**, and space when they draw, paint, carve, make structures out of boxes, and sew. Children also explore these concepts by using water, sand, leaves, bark, shells, nuts, and soils at the science tables. Both areas facilitate sensorimotor, fine motor, and perceptual motor development. Transfer of learning occurs when adjacent learning centres complement each other.

Organization and Design of the Science Discovery Centre

A Science Discovery centre should include things from the nonliving world, such as water, pulleys, and machines, and some things from the living world, such as plants, seeds, and insects. As well, this centre should contain objects to compare, sort, and put in order, tools for measuring and weighing, plenty of paper, and crayons or pencils for recording (Fromberg, 1995). A laptop computer may be a valuable tool here. The centre may accommodate an exploring table, a water and sand area, a nature corner, and a resource table (see Figure 21–3).

Equipment, Materials, and Supplies

- **Equipment:** sand tables (dry sand, wet sand), water table, shelf for materials, theme table and chairs, exploring table and chairs that may double as space for science projects, table or shelves for pet cages, and plants

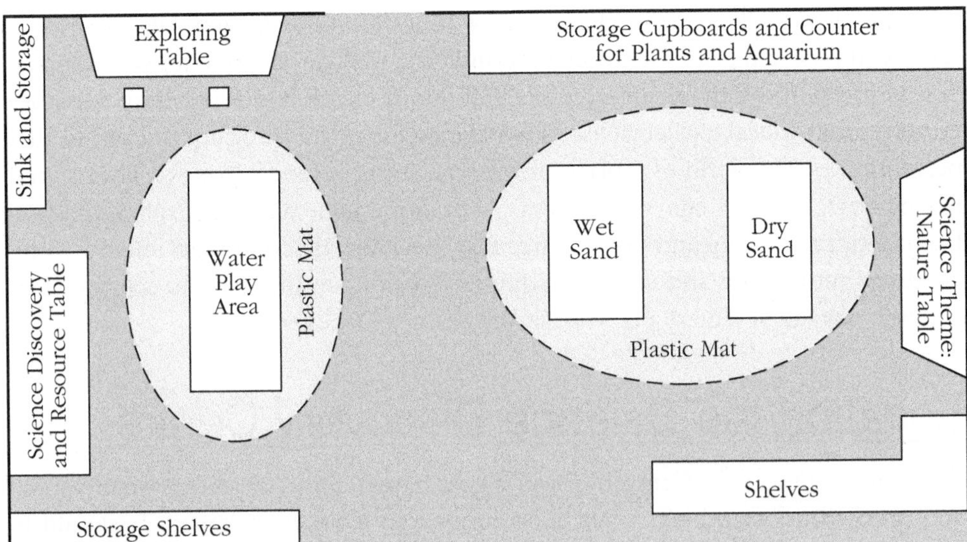

Figure 21–3
Science Discovery centre

- **Materials:** plastic beakers, measuring cups, pails, shovels, sifters, funnels, small vehicles, miniature people, animal sets, rakes and hoes, moulds and cookie cutters, sprinkler can, pet cages, plants, aquarium, balance, magnifying glasses, prisms, thermometer, microscope, flashlight, magnets, watering can, terrarium, potting materials, cooking utensils, aprons, eggbeater, sieve, sponges and mop, bowls of assorted sizes, siphons, plastic tubing, floating and sinking kits, bubble kits, water pump, water wheel, cables, pulleys, ropes, shell collections, rock collections, sand and soil collections, leaf collections, bark collections, science resource books, science picture file, posters, baskets, rags, rulers, and measuring tapes
- **Supplies:** liquid soap, food colouring, paper towels, cloth towels, straws, sand, pet food, fish food, potting soil, baggies, twist ties, tongue depressors, craft sticks, reusable cloths, and cotton cloths

Play Stations in the Science Discovery Centre

Exploring Table

The exploring table allows children to transfer the learning they are acquiring about numbers to activities involving measurement, volume, weight, and space. The exploring table addresses logical skills and concepts as children feel, transform, act on, examine, observe, describe, and record using non-numeric forms of measurement. The exploring table should provide tools that enhance observation and examination, such as magnifying glasses, string, and balances.

Children like to touch and inspect interesting objects, especially the natural kind found outdoors. The more specimens, artifacts, naturally occurring objects, and collections children and ECEs can bring inside, the more the playroom becomes a microcosm of the world outside. Locating the exploring table close to storage shelves and cupboards allows easy access to many items that will be useful for displays, activities, and projects. Stored items should include implements for exploring, such as the measuring tools, a timer, magnifying glasses, a small microscope, tweezers, tongue depressors, prisms, bowls, sponges, reusable cloths and cotton cloths, baskets for collections, a compass, binoculars, transparent plastic jars and small glass containers, baggies for carrying and storing treasures, a flashlight, string, tape, paper, pencils, notepads, and a mirror. Mechanical items to explore include pulleys, levers, gears, weights, simple clocks, old radios, and kitchen implements such as manual egg beaters, sieves, and strainers. A potential space, perhaps an added table, provides space for a small group of children who are engaged in a science project.

MEASURING AND COMPARING

Measurement involves comparing the physical properties of objects and finding relationships between them based on their properties, and then using numbers to describe how the objects can be compared based on the same characteristics. Discovering the physical properties of objects is closely related to understanding concepts related to number, such as order, quantity, and constancy. In an exploring curriculum, young children profit from learning opportunities related to length, area, volume, and weight. Understanding properties such as mass and temperature usually develops later, during the concrete operational period, along with the concepts of time, speed, pressure, and distance.

What young children experience through physical manipulation of things, they understand. Measurement begins with physical experience long before children can understand and use standardized units. Comparing the properties of objects to discover relationships among them helps children develop concepts related to basic measurement. Children pass through stages in developing their understanding of measurement from the sensorimotor stage, which involves exploring things and substances physically, such as by pouring, stacking, and combining, to the next stage, when children compare objects and discover the concepts of bigger-smaller, greater than and less than, longer-shorter, and heavier-lighter by using direct comparisons. Objects placed close to one another make direct comparisons of specific properties easier (Cruikshank et al., 1980). The sand and water tables, as well as the exploring table, facilitate development at these two stages.

Toward the end of the preoperational period, children use arbitrary units, such as a pencil, a piece of string, a length of cardboard, a cup, or a pot, as units of measurement. This type of measurement involves indirect comparison using the selected arbitrary unit as the standard against which all objects are compared. Children seek to determine how many string lengths or how many potfuls there are in whatever is being measured. The ability to use standard units of measurement, such as centimetres and grams, does not occur until the child has acquired the ability to conserve number, length, and volume, which is a characteristic of concrete operational thought (Charlesworth & Radeloff, 1991).

PLANNING ACTIVITIES FOR THE EXPLORING TABLE

The exploring table promotes the acquisition of physical knowledge in activities that often involve the movement of objects and changes in objects. Children act on these objects and observe how the objects respond to their actions. Physical activities should allow children to cause a specific response by their own actions and then change their actions to monitor the changes in response. It is necessary that children see the reaction and that it occurs immediately after the child's action (DeVries & Kohlberg, 1987).

Longer-term investigations that lead to in-depth exploration and to the acquisition of physical knowledge are more effective than short-term, unrelated activities that do little to further children's understanding of scientific phenomena. Simple, sequenced, observable activities related to a single area of investigation give children a chance to discover properties, reactions, and transformations using a variety of materials and methods. Children learn the causes of specific observable events and transformations by observing the consistency of the reactions and responses of materials under certain conditions. Science activities should do more than simply lead children to discover the immediate effects of their actions on objects or substances, and science units should focus on aspects of physical knowledge that encourage children to be aware of how their actions, over time, consciously bring about change or transformation (Forman & Kuschner, 1983).

ACTIVITIES AT THE EXPLORING TABLE FOR CHILDREN AGES THREE TO SIX

1. For younger children, provide objects of geometric shapes to measure and compare, for instance, a ball, an orange, a book, a triangle, a stop sign, a ping-pong ball, and a clockface. Provide lengths of string for children to measure dimensions at various points on the object.
2. Provide a balance and encourage children to weigh many of the objects previously measured. Ask them to predict which of the measured objects will be heaviest. Encourage older children to chart their findings. Ask children to predict which objects will sink/float.
3. Place carrot tops in plastic cups with water in the bottom of the cups and encourage children to chart the growth of the carrot tops by measuring them periodically with a length of string. Encourage the children to maintain the water level.
4. Provide substances that are dry and substances that are wet (e.g., dry sand and wet sand, dry cloths and wet cloths, dry sponges and wet sponges) and encourage children to predict which ones will be heavier and lighter. Children test their hypotheses by weighing each object.
5. Explore together a variety of objects that move in different ways: on wheels, with or without motors, through water, on sand or earth, and in the air.
6. Bring to the exploring table interesting things from nature for children to explore visually, using magnifying glasses or microscopes, or by touch and smell, such as samples of sand from beaches all over the world, strange pebbles or rocks, seashells, and plant matter from various herbs.

Water and Sand Area

The water and sand tables are the centrepieces of the Science Discovery centre. They are often located in the middle of the learning centre on a sheet of plastic that catches spilled sand and water. Placing them close together facilitates the transfer of learning gained in one medium to the other medium. Water and sand hold a special attraction for young children because these sensory media offer endless opportunities for surprise and for feelings of success. In sand and water, children observe how their actions cause the substances to react and transform under specific observable conditions. Sand and water tables are dynamic contexts for learning through play.

WATER PLAY TABLE

Water play

Water has always been a therapeutic element in which children tend to lose themselves to the pleasures of sensory exploration. This element provides infinite delight, as it transforms and responds to a range of stimuli. A clear plastic table on four legs with rolling casters makes the water and the objects in it visible from all sides and from above and below. The table should be placed close enough to a cupboard or shelves to fetch various materials and measuring devices to use in experimenting with the properties of water.

Water is close to the child's daily life experience. It has infinite potential for transformation under various circumstances. For example, splashing produces bubbles; adding food colouring changes the colour of the water; certain substances dissolve in water; some substances take on new properties in water, such as wetness, smoothness, a different texture, and a thinness in consistency; water takes the shape of the container into which it is poured; and water can remove all traces of some substances from objects. These reactions and transformations are just a few examples of the observable properties of water that children can investigate through their play. Water offers children the opportunity to ask their own questions, ponder a multitude of what-if questions, experiment and find observable answers through their own investigations, and alter their thinking about concepts such as conservation of volume, mass, and weight. (See Figure 9-4, p. 177.)

Because water is a sensory medium with recognized therapeutic value for its soothing, calming influence on children, some recommend that a water table should be located close to other learning centres that address emotional objectives, such as the Daily Living or Creative Arts centre. The sensory pleasure of splashing, creating bubbles, pouring, and making currents can transport an anxious child into a more serene world. Children will generally remain with water play for significant periods of time and leave feeling more relaxed. In using this medium, children also develop eye–hand coordination abilities, fine motor and manipulative skills, and heightened perceptual awareness. The child's fascination with water may be partly explained by the responsiveness of the element to the child's actions on it and by its capacity to change under certain observable conditions. Water play is most compatible with the exploratory, experimental atmosphere of the Science Discovery centre, in which children ask their own questions, find answers through their own investigations, and learn to predict outcomes and to monitor causes and effects.

Effective water play depends on careful selection of materials that promote specific kinds of learning. Water play as a medium for investigating specific properties of objects is not achieved by providing a random assortment of plastic toys at the water table; this practice ensures that children's play becomes random and undirected. Setting out materials that lead children to ask questions and explore promotes physical knowledge of the properties of water. Investigating the properties of water calls for jugs, pails, pitchers, scoops, beakers, measuring cups, plastic tubing, a handheld water pump, funnels, siphons, squeeze bottles, watering cans, spray containers, plastic syringes, eyedroppers, sponges, corks, polystyrene, and light pieces of wood (but not all together at the same time). The measuring items might be provided for children to explore volume and size, while the corks, polystyrene, and light pieces of wood help them to explore buoyancy, and the funnels, siphons, squeeze bottles, and syringes can be supplied when exploring water and air pressure. Large and small objects that will sink, such as ball bearings, marbles, buttons, and kitchen utensils, are useful together, as are plastic containers of the same volume but in different shapes.

Requiring children to wear plastic aprons at the water table provides cues about the number of children who can play at the table at one time, protects clothing, and adds to the child's sense of freedom and ability to explore. Providing sponges for children to mop up their own spills makes them independent and responsible for their own actions, a duty children generally accept. Children should also wash their hands before and after using the water table.

ACTIVITIES AT THE WATER PLAY TABLE FOR CHILDREN AGES TWO TO FOUR

1. Have children practise pouring, emptying, filling, comparing, making currents in the water, and directing water into small openings. Initially, provide pitchers, measuring cups, pails, and measured plastic containers. As children develop pouring skills, add jars with small openings, funnels, watering cans, siphons, syringes, and droppers.
2. Wash objects (e.g., plastic materials that need to be cleaned) in sudsy water so that children may observe the cleansing properties of water and soap. Provide a pail of water with a siphon beside the water table for children to rinse the materials, and provide tea towels for children to cooperate in drying and putting them away.
3. Add rocks and other naturally occurring objects, such as seaweed, shells, sand, and sea salt, to the water table for children to explore what happens to things when they are immersed in water. Objects change colour and texture, disperse, and dissolve.

ACTIVITIES AT THE WATER TABLE FOR CHILDREN AGES FOUR TO SIX

1. Provide containers and plastic tubing for children to experiment with draining from one container to another, moving water in tubes using a reservoir, moving water through tubes of various configurations, and squirting water from tubes (DeVries et al., 2003).
2. Encourage children to explore the effect of heating water. Does water dissolve sugar faster when water is heated?
3. Hypothesize what will happen when different liquids are added to water. Gather liquid soap, corn syrup, cooking oil, and vinegar, along with clear plastic containers to scoop out water into the container before adding the new substance. Ask children to predict whether each will mix with the water or form pockets on top of the water. Dump mixtures into a pail after each trial.

SAND PLAY TABLE

For children older than three-and-a-half years, the juxtaposition of sand and water tables allows them to transfer learning from one table to the other and to observe the transformation of the sand when it is wet. Children should not add sand to the water table, however, as sand sinks to the bottom and the water would have to be carefully strained from the water tub to prevent sand from going down the drain. Children should wear aprons and should wash their hands before and after using the sand table.

The different properties of wet sand and dry sand promote greater understanding of the substance and encourage a broader range of play. Wet sand is ideal for promoting physical knowledge through dramatic play and testing play. Introducing small figures of people, trucks, cars, and other props encourages children to cooperate in creating a sand replica of a road system, fort, or castle, like children might do at the beach. The malleable properties of wet sand make building road systems, dams, and bridges feasible. Digging, piling, moulding, and compacting are much easier with wet sand.

Dry sand pours more easily than wet sand and is, therefore, more suitable for play with materials that promote pouring, measuring, comparing, sifting, and stirring. Colanders, sifters, sieves, plastic shaker bottles or cans, baking pans, scoops, spoons, shovels, pails, sand moulds, cookie cutters, measuring containers, handheld garden tools, and plant pots provide the flexibility children need to explore the various properties of wet and dry sand.

ACTIVITIES AT THE SAND PLAY TABLE FOR CHILDREN AGES TWO TO FOUR

1. Set up measured containers of different shapes and sizes in the dry sand table and encourage children to fill, compare, weigh, pour, and sift the sand.
2. Add plastic farm animals, a barn, miniature farm machinery, and fences to the dry sand and let children create a farm scene.
3. At the wet sand table, encourage children to make pathways in the sand to create a maze for their cars or marbles to travel through.

Nature Corner

In bringing science to young children, ECEs should model and teach values that promote respect for the environment, appreciation for nature and for naturally occurring objects, a sense of the interdependence of all living things, and a conservationist attitude toward using and replenishing natural resources. The nature corner includes specimens from the outdoors, including plants and pets; facilities and implements for recreating outdoor life indoors, such as terrariums and aquariums, plant and grow kits, and handheld planting tools; and materials for making and maintaining collections of naturally occurring objects. In addition, the nature corner has supplies for cleaning and feeding pets and for making nature trips (baskets, baggies, small bottles, and plastic containers to hold specimens and plastic gloves). It contains, as well, materials for examining nature, such as a microscope, magnifying glasses, binoculars, and brushes of various sizes. The nature corner should be located close to the resource table, where resource books, albums, picture files, posters, and science-related magazines are kept.

ECOLOGY

Ecology is the study of the relationships between living things and their environments. The nature corner should include activities related to the study of ecosystems so that children can observe the interactions between living things and the settings that sustain them. Children need to develop a lifestyle compatible with nature and understand the impact nature has on their daily lives. Young children benefit from activities in which they can observe living things in their natural habitat; for example, watching plants in a terrarium, fish in an aquarium, and ants in earth. Ecological experiences help children understand the interdependence of all living things. When planning these learning opportunities, ECEs need to understand how children perceive the ecosystem, what features interest them, and what relationships they understand. When a child observes a frog in a pond, the frog is the focus of his attention, and what the frog eats and how the frog responds to external sounds and sensations are of particular interest to him. These are the first steps toward understanding the frog's ecosystem. Children relate the frog's habitat to what they already know about the frog's needs for nourishment and how it protects itself, as well as to what they know about other ecosystems. Children should be able to explore the interrelationships of living things by creating ecosystems in jars, a terrarium, and a fish tank. When children are aware of how living things depend on one another for survival, they understand the need to protect resources that preserve the balance necessary to sustain existing plants and animals. Ecological understanding is promoted when related experiences are added to what is already known and familiar to the child.

CONSERVATION

A natural science curriculum should help children develop conservationist attitudes, which respect and preserve precious natural resources. Children need to know how to use natural resources properly, and how to replace what we take away from our environment. When children develop conservationist values early in life, these values will likely have a lifelong influence on their everyday habits. Conservation activities should focus on concrete knowledge and on social conventions that children can relate to, such as recognizing natural resources, knowing what we need to live, using only what we need, and knowing what kinds of polluting conditions endanger the natural resources. Most early childhood programs have adopted recycling programs as one way of sensitizing children to the importance of preserving natural resources and preventing waste and pollution. A conservationist curriculum encourages children to respect and value the products of nature and to appreciate all living things.

ORGANIZATION OF THE NATURE CORNER

The nature corner should consist of a table with three or four chairs, some shelves, and a cupboard for storing a vast array of materials and supplies. This area is dedicated to developing conservationist skills and provides close contact with living things and earth. Maintenance and repair materials, such as sponges, soft cloths, soap, vinegar, and other safe cleaning agents; tape, paste, or wood glue; and brushes for cleaning and shining, all foster values related to preserving resources, tools, materials, and supplies. The storage cupboard should have space for storing collections of rock specimens, different sands from many locations, shells, bottles of different types of soil, leaf collections, and other specimen collections that children may have gathered and assembled themselves. The exploring table may also display hardy specimens borrowed from local museums to promote hands-on exploration of things, rather than observation.

ACTIVITIES IN THE NATURE CORNER FOR CHILDREN AGES THREE AND FOUR

1. Set up a planting activity with small pots, potting soil, peat moss, hand tools, bulbs, and seeds. Encourage each child to plant a bulb and some grass seed in two separate pots. Place the planted pots on a windowsill.
2. Let children sort collections of naturally occurring objects, such as seashells, nutshells, pretty stones and rocks, and samples of various kinds of bark, according to criteria that they identify.

3. In flats with prepared potting soil, help children start seeds for small vegetable and flower plants that will be ready for planting in the garden patch outdoors in the spring. Try sure-fire crops initially, such as radishes, marigolds, snap-dragons, and lettuce, and then move on to more demanding planting projects using tomato, bean, and pepper seeds.

ACTIVITIES IN THE NATURE CORNER FOR CHILDREN AGES FOUR TO SIX

1. Set up an aquarium with the children, using stones, gravel, plants, and the food necessary to sustain fish. Show children how to care for the fish by keeping the aquarium clean and by aerating the water. Ensure that you do not add more than two or three fish and use a guide to setting up an aquarium.
2. Have children contribute containers of sand from vacation spots they visit with their families. Build and label a collection of various kinds of sand from different areas. Children will be interested in the wide variation of textures and colours in sand.
3. Have children identify classes and subclasses of foods in pictures to promote understanding of the importance of a variety of foods to maintain health and vigour.
4. Set up a terrarium with the children using any large glass container, such as old aquariums. Plants that grow well in a terrarium include small ferns and mosses, although children may select leafy perennials that stay green all year long. Place the terrarium in a well-lit location near a window and teach the children to water it sparingly during the early weeks.

Gardening as a Science Project

Creating a garden with children is an enriching, developmentally appropriate science project that may lead to many spinoff projects year-round. In climates where gardening outdoors is possible for only four to six months a year, planning the garden, researching the various seeds to purchase for planting in the spring, starting seeds indoors in flats, making a scarecrow, and preparing tools and materials for gardening are just a few of the ways to extend the gardening season and its opportunities for learning. Gardening with children enhances their spiritual development, heightens their sense of wonder, and puts them in touch with the earth. Garden projects also lead children to extended investigations of soil, plants, and bugs.

Child Development in the Garden

Gardening enriches the soul and provides many learning opportunities in all developmental domains. Although it requires adult supervision and is usually undertaken in groups, gardening also provides occasions for children to work independently. Children's understanding of the concept of time is enhanced by visible seasonal markers, such as the sprouting of seeds, the ripening of vegetables, and the clearing of the earth at the season's end. Making seeds grow and watching the stages gardens pass through are activities that allow children to observe signs of life, which instil in them a sense of wonder at the regularity of nature. Children acquire factual knowledge about plants, pest control, and life cycles from gardening projects. They practise physical abilities and coordination skills from planting through to harvesting and fall cleanup. Gardening projects enhance vocabulary and

Planting a garden beside the playhouse

language, as well as fluency, memory, time concepts, problem solving, and attending skills. Number concepts, volume, and measurement are understood in concrete ways when children try to gauge the amount of water plants will need, the distance apart to place rows of seeds, and the number of seeds they will need for a row. Gardening also provides an authentic context in which children can create patterns, estimate probabilities, make predictions, and chart the order and timing of events, such as planting, sprouting, and harvesting (Hinnant, 1999). All stages of garden projects provide children with observable results for their efforts. Perhaps most important of all, gardening from an early age becomes embedded in children's memories of early childhood and often lays the foundation for lifelong interest in growing things and in creating beautiful spaces outdoors.

Locating a Garden

The first step in the planning process is to find a suitable location for the garden and to draw a plan. ECEs may decide to concentrate gardening activities and plants in one area of the playground or to locate smaller garden plots throughout the playground in various zones. If the planters are mobile, they can be moved to accommodate other activities or changes in the intensity of the sunlight. If the decision is to set aside one plot for the garden, it is best to start with a small, manageable patch of ground and to cultivate it well, rather than to set aside more space than one adult can handle with a group of children. A patch of two metres square is large enough to prepare and tend during the first year of a garden project. A spot that has good topsoil, is large enough to accommodate a group of about eight children and an ECE working together, and is located near a water source and in a sunny area meets the most important specifications. In most Canadian climates, southeasterly exposure maximizes the amount of sunshine the garden will receive. To make the gardening area more inclusive, particularly for children in wheelchairs, Caples (1996) suggests raising the garden beds to ensure that plants are within reach of a child with physical disabilities, as well as to protect the plants and make them more visible to children.

Planning the Garden

Planning a garden makes an excellent project for the waning days of winter, when children may start seeds in flats and place them on sunny windowsills or under grow lights. The planning stages help children acquire a basic familiarity with seeds, soil, and the names of vegetables and other plants. Children also learn how to use tools and supplies for gardening during the indoor gardening phase. Many preparatory activities, which increase children's anticipation of the garden, occur during the early spring months, including introducing new words and plant names, and establishing protocols for planting, maintaining, and harvesting the garden. Children can explore seed catalogues and gardening magazines, collect posters, draw pictures, make tags for sticks to use as markers for rows, plan and build a scarecrow, examine seeds, and make a scrapbook for photographs and drawings that document the stages in the garden project from beginning to end.

Purchasing tools and supplies provides an occasion for fieldtrips to the local garden centre. The area selected for the garden has to be cleared, filled with good topsoil, and fertilized. A border to separate the garden from adjoining play areas has to be built. When the children's families are included in creating the garden, with its diverse stages and tasks, it becomes a cooperative endeavour in which everyone has a role. When families help with planning, maintaining and harvesting the garden with the children and ECEs they develop a sense of community and ownership that is especially meaningful for families living in high-density residential areas.

PLANTING AND MAINTENANCE TASKS

The arrival of a load of topsoil in early spring is an occasion to get the child-sized spades and rakes out of the storage cupboard and let the children participate in scooping new soil into the garden patch. Once the soil has been prepared, children can help to loosen the soil with a rake, lay strings to mark the row, create rows with a hoe, and start sowing the seeds. Rubber gloves should be worn when handling seeds to protect hands from the toxic coating on some seeds. Preschool and kindergarten children are usually excited by the *real work* involved in watering, weeding, and staking tasks. At each stage in the development of the garden, photographs should record the children's accomplishments.

HARVESTING AND CLEANUP

From the earliest harvesting of crops such as radishes, onion sets, and lettuce, to the later zucchini and pumpkins, children take pride in being able to take produce home for their families and to enjoy raw vegetables at snacktime. Having a compost area promotes recycling and conservationist attitudes. Children also can participate in removing old plants from the garden and placing them in the compost bin, removing stakes and markers, and turning the soil. Deadheading faded blooms is another task that children can undertake. The many excellent books on gardening with children make wonderful additions to the resource table, especially during the planning stages.

INVOLVING FAMILIES IN THE GARDENING PROJECT

So many families live in densely populated urban areas where gardening, if it is carried out at all, is often confined to pots on apartment balconies. Time is also a factor for young families, where essential family chores leave no time to garden. Families will frequently find time, however, to participate in the spring cleanup and planting days organized by the program, at harvest time when the crops are picked and distributed by proud children, and at the end of the season for the fall cleanup. These occasions allow families to make a contribution, form a community network, and contribute gardening ideas from their own culture. Many friendships may be formed by families brought together by the opportunity to engage in the garden project.

GARDENING MATERIALS AND SUPPLIES

- **Equipment:** hose and tap or pump; water sprinkler; wheelbarrow; and large bins for cuttings and weeds
- **Materials:** rakes, spades, hoes, hand shovels, and claws; gardening gloves and rubber gloves; bags and baskets; sprinkler; watering cans; seed packets; flats for seeds; markers and wooden stakes

- **Supplies:** peat moss; sterilized manure and other organic fertilizers; string and rope; old clothes (for a scarecrow); peat pots and starter kits; and gardening books

Resource Table

The Science Discovery centre needs a place where resource materials, such as science and gardening books, field guides, picture files, nature and science posters, and specimens and collections borrowed from museums, are stored for children's activities and projects. It is helpful to have shelves close to the resource table to store books, files, and specimens because only a few of each may be displayed on the table at a time. Children enjoy space at this table to pore over books and picture files when they are seeking information and ideas or are merely browsing. Near the resource table can be a good location for storing prop boxes that hold collections of objects to explore, use for projects, or use as props for play in another centre.

Science picture files are an endless source of delight to children when they have been carefully selected, mounted, and filed. Beautiful photos of a range of scientific phenomena and resources introduce children to a world beyond their immediate environment. They provide unique perspectives from which children can view photos of everyday things in the natural world. Children enjoy small picture files on index cards—stored in shoebox files or in metal recipe boxes—which they can hold easily and spread out before them. Large pictures mounted on construction paper may be hung in the Science Discovery centre to provide ideas and guidance when children embark on specific projects. Prop boxes containing materials for specific science-related projects and *junk boxes* containing objects that have been gathered from various sources and sorted into containers may also be stored near the resource table.

Field guides, especially books of pictures identifying birds, plants, trees, rocks, and shells, are particularly useful for children to consult when they want to see a picture of the specimen or the collection of naturally occurring objects that they have just sorted or mounted on cardboard. Local museums often loan specimens such as butterfly and insect collections, birds, and stuffed animals mounted in glass cases. Specimens such as birds' nests, beehives, wasps' nests, and snake skins make fascinating objects that children may handle gently to investigate their composition and texture.

ACTIVITIES AT THE RESOURCE TABLE FOR CHILDREN AGES FOUR TO SIX

1. Suggest possibilities for projects, such as making feeders for birds, making birds' nests, creating a poster of pretty leaves, learning about animal habitats, or making paper. Encourage children to search the resource books and picture files for ideas of what they would like to do. Discuss what they will need to undertake the project.
2. Leave the field guides to birds on the table for children to look up species that come to the bird feeders in the playground.
3. Set out gluesticks, paste, construction paper, markers, and nature magazines or old calendars and let children create their own picture file or add to the existing one.

Summary

The word *sciencing* is used to describe children's active investigations of things and phenomena in their environment that they can experience through their senses. Active, sensory exploration of a wide range of naturally occurring materials and hands-on testing and experimentation related to cause-and-effect relationships that children can observe build a solid foundation for later science education related to more abstract concepts. Science with young children should foster curiosity, wonder, experimentation, and the habit of checking answers and discoveries and documenting what one finds. Early childhood science curriculum provides opportunities for children to learn skills related to exploring and observing, questioning and inquiry, comparing and classifying, measuring, testing and experimenting, problem solving, and documenting and reporting. Topics and projects for science with young children are those that offer experiences in which the particular characteristics, changes, and phenomena are directly observable, such as earth and plant science; ecology and the ecosystems that support some life forms; environmental science, especially topics related to conservation and respect for resources and the environment; physical science topics involving experiments with water, sand, and shadows that children can observe directly; and life science issues, such as factors that affect our bodies and make them grow and stay healthy. The Science Discovery centre is a prime area for projects that extend over time and involve independent steps that lead sequentially toward greater understanding. There are many excellent resource books that describe the steps involved in science activities and experiments that are developmentally appropriate for children age six and under.

Learning Activities

1. Using this book as a guide, build a project web of activities for two science projects that would be developmentally appropriate for four- and five-year-olds.
2. Winter provides many opportunities for science discovery projects. Plan a series of winter science activities using activity cards, such as activities that encourage children to investigate the properties of snow, explore animal tracks in the snow, and create a booklet of animal track drawings.
3. Choose two activities from the lists provided for the water play table, sand play table, and nature corner. Write activity cards for each of these activities.
4. Create a prop box for a science project and another prop box for a theme-related science display at the resource table. Begin by listing the props you will put in your prop boxes. Then choose or make a sturdy box or container and label the prop box. Assemble materials and supplies for each prop box.
5. Consult book store shelves and catalogues for resource books to add to the Resource Table collection. List the titles, publishers, and content summaries in your journal.

22 Outdoor Play: Playgrounds for Learning

"Children love the natural world.... [they] start to empathize with nature, and by intimately exploring their own outdoor space, they begin to develop a broader sense of caring for the natural world beyond their playground."

—EVERGREEN CANADA, *SMALL WONDERS* (2004)

BEFORE READING THIS CHAPTER, HAVE YOU

- visited community and centre-based or school-based playgrounds and observed children's play and the design of the playgrounds?
- recalled how you played and what you gained from outdoor play as a child?

OUTCOMES

After reading and understanding this chapter, you should be able to

- explain the health, physical, and spiritual benefits of outdoor play;
- outline the evolution of playground design;
- locate and design playground space for young children;
- describe the central features of playground design to facilitate children's physical, social, emotional, and cognitive development;
- apply safety considerations related to playground planning and maintenance in the design of a playground while ensuring freedom for healthy risk taking;
- facilitate children's physical development outdoors; and
- adapt outdoor space and play areas for the child with special needs.

Historical Background

Playgrounds are about the only spaces created in communities specifically for children (Yeo, 2001). Public playgrounds, and some that were attached to schools, began to appear in the late 19th century (Esbensen, 1987). During the early 20th century, public playgrounds were mandated for many municipalities and included sandboxes, a swing, a slide, and a climbing frame. In 1943, the Danes created the **adventure playground**, which inhabited spaces left vacant after the bombing of city streets, where an assortment of discarded materials could be used as play and building materials by the children; this meant that its contents and configuration changed as children built and rebuilt their structures (Yeo, 2001). Adventure playgrounds had a brief period of popularity in some North American playgrounds in the mid-20th century and were followed by the similarly brief creative playground of the 1970s. In the 20th century, the Scandinavians brought nature to school by creating natural environments for children to explore within the school property or close by. Garden areas designed and tended by children, and natural areas where they can roam, have only recently been considered a vital component of early childhood education (Warzecha, 2011).

Natural playgrounds bring children close to nature and enhance their spiritual, aesthetic, creative, and intellectual development and foster mental health. This interest is further evidence of the cyclical trends that emerge in playground design. Children's health issues, especially the alarming increase in obesity in young children and the appearance of adult diseases in early childhood, add to demands to improve the play quality and physical challenges of natural playgrounds and to ensure that children play outside for large parts of each day. Children have basic requirements for their outdoor play environments: a place for ***doing***, a place for ***thinking***, a place for ***feeling***, and a place for ***being*** (Titman, 1994). Evergreen Canada (2004, p. 1) has taken up the playground design challenge, which is to find a balance between natural and built features, and proposes four goals: (1) safeguarding and improving children's health and well-being; (2) nurturing early childhood development; (3) increasing the diversity of natural features and play opportunities; and (4) enhancing the use of the outdoors for children's programming. Canadian playground design has pursued the trend to "offer a wide range of open ended play options for children while remaining safe" (www.naturalplaygrounds.ca).

Playground design today has emerged from play theory, child development theory, and the recent preoccupation with children's physical fitness. The 19th-century Froebelian kindergarten promoted physical well-being as integral to children's overall growth, health, and spiritual and psychological development. Froebel's playgrounds fostered a sense of wonder about, and reverence for, nature and the child's innermost emotions. He and others believed that outdoor play would help children vent anxiety, promote self-expression, and provide emotional outlets for children in ways

Use naturally occurring features.

that could not be matched by indoor play. Finally, in this century, there is a recognition that the "overscheduling" of children and little time for spontaneous social play with peers, which happens most freely outdoors, suggests that we are losing "social capital" and, with that loss, the capacity children have to form and maintain healthy relationships and to be empathetic and understanding of others (Perry, 2002).

Late 20th-century playgrounds were treated largely as places where children could run, be active, and let off steam. In the 21st century, the playground is increasingly envisaged as a way to bring children into direct contact with nature (Hammer, 2011). Children have a spiritual and an emotional need to be close to nature and to feel a sense of harmony with the natural world. Their respect for the environment is inherent during the early years. Being able to touch the earth, to enjoy the sensory and aesthetic pleasures of plants and trees, and to appreciate the constantly changing natural environment enhance children's sense of connectedness to the natural world and deepen their spiritual insights. ECEs frequently describe the calming effect that outdoor play in a natural setting has on children who are inclined to **hyperactivity** and **attention deficit**. For years, we have known that movement promotes thinking in early childhood. Great thinkers such as Montessori, Piaget, and Einstein have linked motor development and bodily expression to cognitive development and learning (Pica, 2010). The playgrounds of preschools and kindergartens are increasingly seen, therefore, as places of critical significance for children's physical, mental, social, and spiritual health (Moore, 2000). Respect for the environment evolves from having spontaneous experiences in natural surroundings. Concerns about urban pollution, climate change, depleted forests, and food and water safety add to the need to bring children into regular, unstructured contact with nature to nurture their respect for the preservation of the environment and to develop conservationist attitudes and habits.

Playground Philosophy

Many children today live in highly regulated urban communities, often in condominiums and apartment buildings, and have little spontaneous access to natural settings. Fewer children today can run out the door of their home to a backyard or a safe neighbourhood where they can play until they are hungry and tired. Because parents fear letting their children play freely outdoors without constant supervision, children's experience with the natural world becomes more restricted. Although children in some programs spend about 25 percent of a school day in the playground, ECEs sometimes forget the dynamic learning potential of the outdoor play area. With its opportunities for freedom, exploration, and spontaneity, outdoor play ultimately affects the quality of children's lives; their sensitivity to, and harmony with, nature; their ability to relate positively to others and to empathize, and their spiritual and mental health. The outdoors has many variables that wise adults will not attempt to control, beyond ensuring children's safety and comfort.

As noted by Henniger (1994), outdoor play spaces should provide opportunities for

1. healthy risk taking, including natural objects such as logs and large rocks placed for children to climb up, hills rather than conventional stone or wooden steps, and sturdy wooden poles installed in the ground for climbing to develop upper body strength;

2. graduated challenges, such as encouraging children to move from walking and balancing on logs placed evenly on the ground to walking on suspended bridges that move as they walk;
3. a variety of play styles, which are facilitated in the diverse play areas that make up the playground, such as the vehicle trails; the loose materials area for construction and dramatic play; the sand and water play area for digging, constructing, and pouring; the garden for planning, estimating, predicting, digging and planting, watering, maintaining and harvesting; and
4. manipulation of the materials and equipment found there, including dramatic and sociodramatic play in the playhouse area, building in the loose materials area, cooperative games using equipment in the group activity area, climbing on apparatus such as rope ladders and climbing poles, sliding on hills, and incorporation of bricks, tiles, logs, lumber, rocks, and other types of construction materials into the loose materials and sand play areas.

Foster adventure and dramatic play.

Outdoor play space should respect children's needs for close interaction with naturally occurring phenomena and for the repose and solace that nature offers. Playground design today includes secluded areas where children may retreat from group play to meander, sit and contemplate the rustling of leaves on the trees, or observe other children, and these are essential elements in playgrounds. Being able to escape from the hurly-burly of a typical day reduces stress, replenishes energy, lifts the spirit, and enhances anticipation of the next phase of the day for children—just as it does for adults. Outdoor play experiences become lifelong reference points that generate appreciation of the healing qualities of the outdoor world.

Outdoor Play and Child Development

Outdoor play has the added benefits of greater freedom of movement, the stimulating effect of fresh air, enhanced challenge, and the larger perspectives that foster positive interactions and a wholesome outlook. Developmental program planning is as important outdoors as it is indoors. The organization of the playground into play zones maximizes the learning potential of outdoor play equipment, natural areas, open and private spaces, and playground surfaces—and exploits the inevitable delights of the passing seasons and changing weather. Bringing nature back into the playground may also involve parents in the planning and the actual work of creating garden spaces, planting shrubs and flowers, and creating hilly areas. In Canada, outdoor play space should capitalize on the play potential of the changing seasons, which offer infinite variety and promote understanding of the passage of time. Children can see and feel the alterations in the landscape, plant life, soil, and other surfaces from one season to the next when they spend time outdoors.

Physical Development and Fitness

Outdoor play has traditionally been thought of as a time for children to develop gross motor skills, let off excess energy, build muscles and endurance, and gain control over the movements of their bodies. Changes in bodily appearance, and in their competence as they master new physical skills, are concrete and observable to children. The progress they

© Jim West / PhotoEdit

Activities for outdoor play

make in running faster than before, and in climbing to the top of the structure today that they were fearful of climbing yesterday, provides children with evidence of their growing strength, courage, and ability. The more self-confidence children have in their bodies, the easier it is for them to interact with others; they meet the challenges of group play and team endeavours with a stronger sense of having valuable contributions to make and with less reliance on adults.

Daily life for many children, particularly in urban areas, has deteriorated in recent years as children spend more time indoors watching television, playing with technologies, and engaged in other sedentary activities that are inhibiting connections with peers and adults and damaging in a lasting fashion children's caring capacities and brain development (Perry, 2002). A growing percentage of overweight children lead passive lifestyles and have calorie-laden diets, which predispose them to a lifetime of problems with their weight, illnesses, and underdeveloped fitness levels. Increasingly, the responsibility for providing children with physically active challenges and well-planned fitness programs rests with the early childhood education program. It is the mandate of our profession that programs include planned fitness activities that challenge children's motor coordination and physical fitness, including heart rates, circulatory function, and aerobic capacities. The physical programs should be planned and implemented daily and be based on developmental outcomes sequenced gradually and include activities that specifically address physical outcomes such as fundamental movements, motor coordination, body awareness, sensory-perceptual abilities, physical abilities, and healthy habits and attitudes. Activities should always be play-based and inviting to children (see Appendix B for specific developmental outcomes). Physical programming for young children should not resemble a callisthenics class or an aerobic exercise session; rather, the physical challenges and developmental opportunities should be invisible within the games and play opportunities that are provided every day indoors and outdoors.

Emotional Development

Children's physical growth and increasing competence in using their bodies produce corresponding gains in their self-esteem and self-concept that depend not on direct praise or rewards but on children's observations of their physical competence (Hitz & Driscoll, 1988). Children acquire self-concept and self-esteem through their successful physical experiences in the environment. Praise cannot replace the child's personal experiences of physical competence and pride in accomplishment. Finally succeeding in reaching the top of the rope ladder on one's own steam or bravely jumping from the rock wall into the sand pit provide a much more profound message to the child that she has met a goal, increased her skill, and taken a risk worth taking.

Social Development

Of equal importance is the greater opportunity provided outdoors for children to interact spontaneously with peers and adults, which is fundamental to social development. The quality of children's physical experiences outdoors and indoors influences children's motivation to be active group participants in physical games, exercises, and sports throughout their growing years. In addition to ensuring that the playground provides for spontaneous exploratory play, ECEs should also plan, set up, and lead physical activities in groups. Outdoor play allows more space for large-group activity than does indoor play, and it challenges children socially as they engage in active games and fitness programs.

Large- and small-group activities and individual play encourage social interaction and the development of self-concept as the child becomes aware of others, cooperates, shares space, and takes turns. Outdoor group projects, such as building forts or canals and making and tending gardens, encourage children to collaborate, to rely on one another, to function as team members, and to communicate. Individual opportunities for physical development, and the successes children feel when they have mastered new tasks and physical feats, enable children to participate in social activities that involve physical challenges and, eventually, in team activities, sports, and games. Children know when they are physically capable and observe how they compare to others in terms of their physical prowess. A well-organized playground balances opportunities for individual play and risk taking with socially oriented games and activities. Playgrounds that encourage social interaction and cooperative activities and that also provide private spaces for quiet contemplation and individual exploration are well-balanced outdoor environments that encourage children to appreciate their own company in space secluded from the bustle of the more active play areas.

Creative Development

Using the playground to facilitate creative development does not imply simply bringing the easels, fingerpaint, and workbench outdoors. Playing outside in a natural play space is full of potential for divergent thinking and using naturally occurring objects such as rocks, logs, branches, stones, and wood chips to represent whatever the child imagines. Creating a space for natural loose materials and for construction items such as planks, bricks, tiles, railings, concrete blocks, drainage pipes, and fence posts, for example, allows for creative construction outdoors to complement the indoor unit blocks and hollow blocks. Vertical logs set firmly into the ground tempt children to throw a cover over the logs to make a fort or an undercover crawl space for sociodramatic play or for hiding. A swinging bridge installed near the playhouse or loose materials area may be transformed into a castle gateway. Importing into the area canvass tarpaulins or other coverings encourages children to figure out how they can be used to enhance their play ideas. Tents, tunnels, and railings help children expand their sociodramatic play episodes beyond the capacity of indoor super units, which are usually limited in the amount of space they may occupy.

Creative development outdoors is not confined, however, to the loose materials area. The sand pit promotes divergent thinking and problem solving when the right items are added, such as measuring scoops, a water source, or digging and hauling implements. Creative ECEs find ways to combine loose materials and the sand area to encourage children to plan and develop their own ideas, perhaps based on a story they have read or a field trip they have taken. This is another example of the emergent curriculum at work.

Modular climbing and playhouse equipment that children can construct, take apart, and rearrange themselves allows children to be creative and to develop physical abilities. Although **prefabricated** climbing structures have the advantage of smooth, well-treated surfaces and of dimensions and scales appropriate for children's small sizes, they also restrict the nature of play. Increasingly, playground play structures are more abstract and lend themselves to play that calls on children's imagination and representational thinking skills, urging them to think through divergent ways of making the play structure become whatever they want it to be.

Spiritual Development

Outdoors, a child's mind may wander more, and the child may follow his senses in exploring and experimenting. Sticks, branches, rocks, mud, water, grass, and sand are dependable but also full of sensuous surprises. Pavement, interlocking bricks, and modern play equipment alone fail to address the emotional and spiritual needs of the child to feel close to nature and to be reassured by its beauty, stability, and endless adaptability. Playgrounds where the ground plane is varied rather than flat provide the strongest connections with the natural world and with the child's imagination (Caples, 1996). Touching the earth means having a place to feel and smell the grass, roll around, pull weeds, climb craggy surfaces, plant flowers, observe the changes in the natural features of the earth, and experience the effect of natural elements in all seasons—rain, wind, snow, ice, heat, and cold. Ensuring that children have close encounters with nature is the surest way to develop a sense of wonder and respect for nature's power and ultimate control over our lives. Feeling stretched physically and meeting physical challenges open the spirit to the endless potential of life and the importance of active participation in our world. The open air and the expanded space, as well as the size of the trees and the complexity of the surfaces, contribute to a sense of the environment as powerful and full of the potential to influence our own lives. In the outdoors, children feel smaller but more connected to their environments. This sense of connectedness to the environment promotes mental health, a realistic perspective, and a healthy respect for nature.

Cognitive Development

Children learn through their physical interaction with the environment. Movement triggers language and self-expression and releases chemicals in the body that affect mood and openness to learning. Play that is cognitively challenging for children indoors usually can be repeated or extended in the outdoor environment. Favourite indoor activities that address perceptual, memory, and logical-mathematical objectives can be adapted for outdoor play. Many traditional outdoor activities, such as obstacle courses, construction projects, and games, which challenge the senses and perceptual processes, also address cognitive and physical outcomes. I Spy, follow-the-leader, hopscotch, and strategy games, such as cooperative parachute activities, present many cognitive challenges to children. Open-ended play in the sand and water, building walls and digging holes, promote mathematical concepts and the ability to estimate, predict, compare, problem solve, and evaluate. The variety of problems to be solved outdoors stretches as far as the imagination can reach. Any adult who observes children cooperating in building a fort with fallen leaves, estimating or measuring the distance between the ball and a hoop, and figuring out how to get from here to there without going through the mud will attest to the variety of thinking skills challenged by the natural world's endless variations. The less structured and rule-bound the playground, the greater the opportunities for exploration, discovery, resourcefulness, use of the imagination, voluntary attending to the task at hand, communication, inductive and deductive thinking, representation, creative problem solving, and self-expression—all prerequisites to healthy cognitive growth.

Howard Gardner (2000) identified three intelligences closely connected to movement and outdoor play experiences. Naturalistic intelligence, which includes sensitivity to one's environment, is influenced by children's exposure to natural surroundings and the things in it—plants, trees, earth, and lots of space. Kinaesthetic intelligence allows children to use their bodies to influence or affect others, solve problems, and compete physically. Spatial intelligence is the ability to orient oneself in space and manage body movements within external constraints. The well-designed playground optimizes children's opportunities to develop intelligences in all domains.

Developing skills through play

Language Development

Language flows more fluently when the child is performing a physical activity. In the freer environment of the outdoors, children who seldom speak indoors may lose their inhibitions and become quite verbal. Even less verbal children often engage in rich, fluid monologues while attempting to unravel obstacles encountered, for example, when making a tent or filling a channel in the sandbox with water to sail small boats. The freedom, space, and sensory ambience of the outdoors are sufficient to trigger language often subdued by structure and closer living quarters indoors. The endless variety outdoors contributes to vocabulary development, and the freedom and open space reduce timidity and promote communication and self-expression. The outdoor environment that is well planned and full of interesting things to do provides plenty for children to talk about and lots of room for wonder, questions, speculation, and hypothesis. I will never forget the experience of observing children playing in the natural playground of the Ryerson Early Learning Centre, when a child playing on a grassy slope yelled to her friends in the playhouse. "Come here quick," she said. "I've found something dead." Four children raced over, and one little boy kneeling close to the carcass of a worm murmured, "What's *dead*?" Imagine the challenge this posed for the nearby ECE, who felt compelled to try to answer that question in simple language.

Safe Outdoor Play in Natural Play Spaces

Freedom, interaction with nature in the playground, and spontaneous exploration depend on preserving the natural features of the playground and on safe play equipment that fits with the natural features. When they know the playground is free of hazards, ECEs are able to facilitate play and learning for children in small groups and to interact with the children rather than always watching for potential accidents.

Legislation in most regions requires daily inspections of playgrounds to ensure that potential hazards are detected before children play outdoors. Programs are required to monitor playground surfaces daily for dangerous protrusions of stones and pieces of wood, foreign objects such as spikes or other building materials, animal contamination, and poor drainage. When inspections are regular and rigorous, the ECE may be free to observe children's play and to extend an interest they demonstrate into a project indoors or outdoors. This is another example of the emergent curriculum at work.

Although children's safety in playgrounds is paramount, the challenge for today's playground designers is to ensure that attention to safety concerns does not diminish the enormous play and learning potential of the natural play space. It is as important to acknowledge the value of risk taking, while managing the risk, as it is to guard against injuries. Children very quickly learn their own tolerance for risk, and they vary as individuals in the amount of physical exertion they are prepared to endure. A skinned knee now and then might be a small price to pay for the thrill of climbing the rock face of the retaining wall and then jumping into the sand pit. Children appreciate the feeling of being trusted to play spontaneously, invent their own play with naturally occurring things outdoors, and explore without stifling constraints. They feel closer to nature when they are allowed to assess its challenges and make their own decisions about how far they will go in their explorations. A valuable part of early learning, particularly in gaining self-knowledge, lies in being permitted to accept the consequences of one's actions and choices in the physical domain.

The National Recreation Association developed the first North American standards for playground apparatus in the United States in 1928; these established a precedent for promoting greater attention to safety concerns in playgrounds. In June 1990, the Canadian Standards Association (CSA) published *A Guideline on Children's Playspaces and Equipment,* which represented the first major attempt in Canada to regulate playground equipment and has since been updated several times. The new CSA standards and guidelines for playgrounds published in 2006 addresses surfacing materials and other playground standards, but creative design is being explored by playground designers. For example, new playgrounds are now using engineered wood fibre and poured-in-place rubber tiles instead of sand and pea gravel surface materials (Warzecha, 2011). The surfacing should be varied in composition, texture, and colour to provide clear boundaries between play zones and to add sensory stimulation, and the varieties should suit the kind of play anticipated in each zone. Hard surfaces should be reserved for entranceways, adult seating areas, and areas under awnings or shelters where children may play out of the rain. Manufacturers are becoming more creative in the provision of safe and durable playground surface materials, and designers are more attentive to the aesthetic and natural features of the environment. (See www.bienenstock@naturalplaygrounds.ca.)

Safe playground design implies that distinct play zones are created, play structures are securely installed, and sufficient equipment and materials are provided to maintain children's interest and to ensure their safety without constant supervision. Once the daily inspection of the playground has been completed, outdoor play should be relaxed and pleasurable. The ECE's primary tasks are to facilitate children's play, respond to individual needs, observe children's play and development, note where new challenges are needed, and interact with children on specific projects and activities and capitalize on the children's ideas and interests that may call for enhancements to the environment.

The presence of an ECE in each play zone is as important outdoors as it is indoors, so that they can focus on facilitating children's play in a circumscribed area. Activities begun indoors, such as water play, may continue outdoors. Seed planting in pots in the Science Discovery centre may continue outdoors with the planting of a garden. Carpentry projects started at the workbench in the Creative Discovery centre may be expanded using the loose materials and greater space available in the playground. Because ECEs need to be actively involved with children in these kinds of activities, they cannot be responsible for supervising the whole playground. When there is any doubt about safety in the playground, some zones should be closed to prevent spreading ECE resources too thinly.

Playground surfaces

Adapting Playgrounds for Children with Special Needs

New standards under the Accessibility for Ontarians with Disabilities Act commit to making public spaces in Ontario, including playgrounds, fully accessible by 2025. Children with physical disabilities and motor impairments need additional physical support in order to use the playground equipment and materials and participate effectively in outdoor play and learning. Raising the beds for flowers and vegetable growing onto planters at waist height for young children enables a child in a wheelchair to plant, maintain, and harvest a garden. Installing tactile markers helps children with visual impairments find their way around equipment and through the playground. If children have hearing impairments, ECEs must remain in the field of vision of these children. Inclusive practice requires ECEs to take an active role in encouraging children to explore the equipment by planning specific activities during the outdoor play period. For example, a game of "follow the leader" around an obstacle course can motivate a child with a disability to challenge his body with new experiences, to master directional concepts, and to practise balance (Caples, 1996, p. 14).

Adult Facilities

In a professional environment, attractive benches, a picnic table, and lawn chairs permit ECEs to engage a group of children in conversation and quiet play, which changes the pace. A spot sheltered from the wind permits ECEs to set up an activity at a picnic table even on cold days A sand pit enclosed on one or two sides by wooden benches provides a useful vantage point for conducting observations and recording ideas for projects and activities. Comfortable adult facilities raise morale, contribute to ECE effectiveness outdoors, and help make the playground an extension of the indoor classroom. The more appealing the outdoor space for everyone, the more time the children will spend outdoors (Esbensen, 1991).

Locating Playgrounds

The decision about where to locate a playground influences all further decisions related to design. Playgrounds should be located immediately beside the centre or school they serve and should be directly accessible from the playroom (Esbensen, 1990). Locating the playground in the lee of the building provides protection from harsh winds, excessive sunlight, and severe cold. Some sunlight for both morning and afternoon play periods extends the time and the regularity with which children are able to play outdoors, especially in colder climates. In inner cities, care should be taken to reduce traffic fumes and noises, protect children's privacy by reducing exposure to public scrutiny, and shield children from harsh winds. Fences are more attractive if constructed of wood or some combination of wood and chain link, always taking care to ensure that erosion of the soil beneath the fence does not leave spaces for children to climb or slide through.

Playgrounds that have a view through a fence to trees and grassy areas enjoy a closer link with the natural world, and the protection of tree barriers. Variations in topography, such as mounds or hills and valleys, a natural water source that can be contained and possibly serve as a sprinkler system in summer, grassy or bushy areas, and sunken levels, add to appeal and interest of the playground. Terrain should be well drained and free of dangerous protrusions and hidden holes. Playgrounds are enhanced by strategically placed planters or flowerbeds and other vegetation that is nontoxic and variable in texture, colour, or shape from season to season.

Excessive sun exposure poses a significant health hazard to children, although children do need some sunshine to maintain vitamin D levels. Playground location should account for the direct sun exposure children will receive, especially during the summer. Wide overhangs from the roof add protection from the sun close to the building, and shade trees or gazebos can be added to shelter areas such as sandboxes and construction areas. In all parts of North America, children should wear washable, brimmed sun hats that tie firmly under the chin when playing outdoors during warm months (Pimento & Kernested, 2004).

Size and Configuration of Playgrounds

The shape, size, and layout of a playground depend on the topography of the land available, the size of the lot on which the centre or school is located, its urban or rural location, and the needs of the children it serves. Guidelines cannot cover all combinations of circumstances, but some general rules of thumb are useful. Playground size should be based on the number of children who will use the playground at one time, the proximity of buildings and traffic, and the number and size of play zones. It is impractical, however, to determine playground size solely by calculating the number of square metres per child. A small playground may foster more social interaction and cooperative play. ECEs find it easier to facilitate play in a densely organized, compact space, but high-density playgrounds effectively reduce the range of play behaviours possible and change the nature of children's interactions. Large, open areas may encourage out-of-bounds behaviour and aimless activity, especially when equipment is placed randomly throughout the available space.

Outdoors as well as indoors, well-planned zones and clear pathways through the space guide children into and out of play zones to minimize interference with play that is underway. Compatible play zones should be grouped together, there should be clear pathways in and out of each zone, and play in one zone should not interfere with play in an adjacent zone. Various playground surfaces define the boundaries of play zones, providing messages about where a certain type of play is to begin and end. Care should be taken to arrange compatible surfaces adjacent to one another. As with the indoor environment, the clear definition of play areas provides cues about the categories and social contexts of play anticipated; these physical and design cues reduce the need for ECEs to intervene and to remind children of rules and expected behaviours. (see Figure 22-1). Experts recommend playground zones for transition, manipulative and creative play, social play, fantasy and sociodramatic play, physical play, and exploration of natural elements; a quiet area, an open area, and an active area; landscaped areas, storage facilities, and adult seating areas (Canadian Institute for Child Health [CICH], 1985; Esbensen, 1987; Walsh, 1988).

Playground Zones

Talbot and Frost (1989) suggested the following design features for playgrounds: variation in size of the playground areas and features of the space; open-ended spaces and abstract shapes that assume any meaning the child assigns; natural elements (earth, fire, air, and water); variation in line quality and shape; sensory stimulation

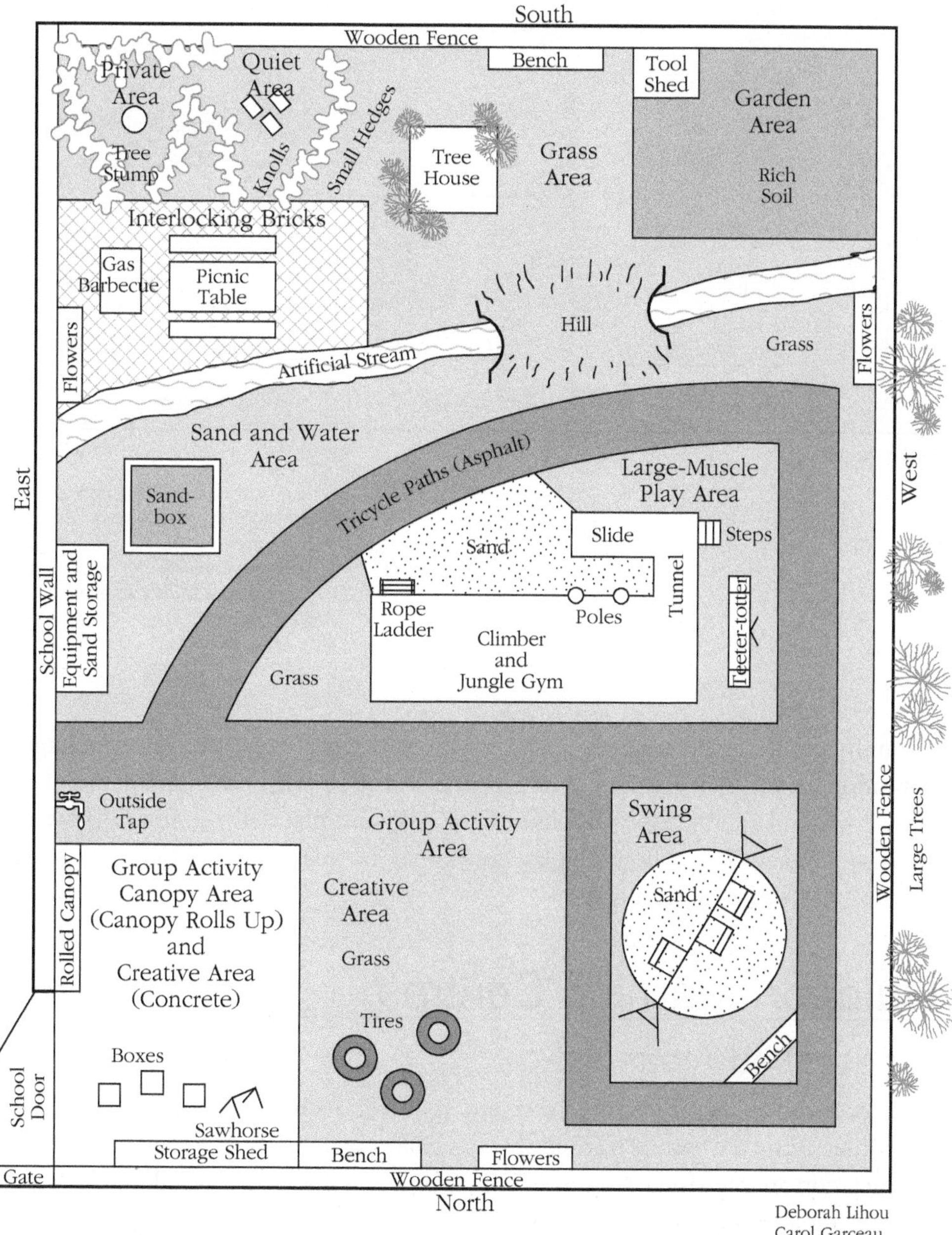

Figure 22–1
Playground design

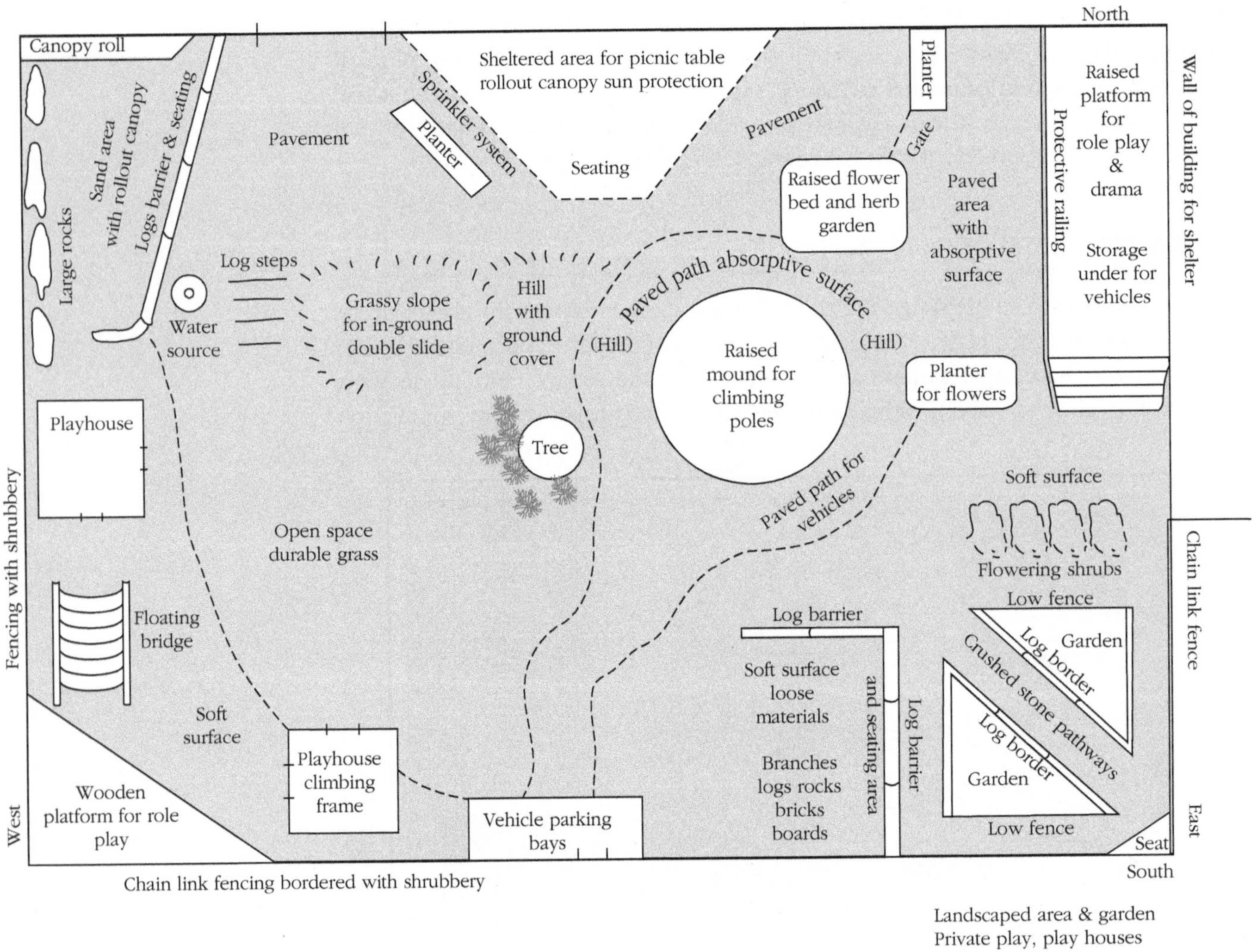

Figure 22–2
Another playground design showing learning centres

through colour, smell, texture, and sound; novelty; mystery; brilliance; juxtaposition of opposites; richness and abundance; connection with other times and places; loose parts and simple tools; the illusion of risk; and places for doing nothing and enjoying privacy. The following play zones may be adapted to incorporate several types of play and social contexts.

Outdoor Learning Centres

Landscaped Areas

Flowers, shrubbery, and trees add aesthetic appeal and a homelike quality to the total environment and are natural features that put children in touch with plant life. Changes in vegetation are the visual markers of the passing seasons that help children anticipate seasonal variations such as frost and snow, buds and flowers, birds and insects, and the changing colours of the leaves and grass. Children form attachments to plants and trees in the environment, and the names of flowers, shrubs, and trees become part of their everyday vocabulary. Landscaped areas encourage children to assume some responsibility for their outdoor environment by maintaining its neat appearance and by removing weeds. Landscaped areas can preserve natural features, such as a small grove of trees for a shady nook, a mound for sliding down in winter, a rocky glen to hide in, or a loamy spot for a vegetable garden. Low wooden fencing, hedges separating play areas, and attractive pathways serve both practical and aesthetic purposes but should not be too dominant. Websites provide design ideas that may be adapted for young children, including www.naturalplaygrounds.ca and www.evergreen.ca.

Private Play Areas

ECEs sometimes focus on children's competence as group members and incorrectly regard a child's need to be alone occasionally as antisocial behaviour. Children need space, however, to remove themselves from the group, especially when they spend their days in group care and schools. Small nooks under a tree, in a grove of low bushes, or behind a storage cupboard, provide children with places where they can be alone for a while. These spots are private enough from the child's perspective, but they should also be visible to the ECE, who can see over the barriers. A little wooden bench or seat on a tree stump adds incentive for the child to remain in the private spot to while away some time. Children need private space and opportunities to just be, and their need to dream, reflect, imagine, and retreat from active playing should be respected (Talbot & Frost, 1989). Adding garden chimes to this area helps to trigger the imagination and to set the space apart from the busy play areas. A private space in the playground may be a place to erect a tent or canopy to enhance the sense of being segregated from the group. Times spent alone in quiet places often spawn ideas and plans, which children may later realize in more active social play. Creative thinking may be nurtured as readily during private moments to reflect and plan, as in the hustle and bustle of the sand area and role play area.

Sand Area

The sand play area should be sheltered from intense sun, out of the wind, and be deep enough for children to use pails, sieves, and scoops and to make puddles and moats around castles. Sand areas should be kept clean, be replenished frequently and inspected daily for signs of domestic animal contamination. Sand areas should be covered at night, but covers should be removed by day to prevent the formation of mould in the sand, particularly in humid climates. A counter or a table placed in the sand area tends to keep sand play inside the area. As the sand play area often becomes a busy place where conflicts may arise, clear limits for play should be established and maintained. Sand should never be thrown, and it should be contained in the sandbox or sand table as much as possible. Locating a playhouse frame, perhaps with a counter and sink, next to the sand area fosters dramatic play and thinking skills, especially for young preschoolers.

Sand play

Sand is most effective outdoors when a water source is nearby; sand needs water to realize its potential as one of nature's most responsive, natural substances. Safe access to water may be facilitated in a number of ways. A simple tap, hose, pump, trickle of a stream, or plastic pool placed adjacent to the sand is all that is needed. Streams have more creative play value than pools because the streams can be dammed, bridged, and used for punting boats and wading in the summer months, and they are safer. When streams are specially constructed, they are easier to control and can be switched on and off easily. Whenever water is added to the playground, ECEs must supervise play constantly, as water is an inherently dangerous element for children. In cold climates, a frozen stream may become a patch of ice for sliding or skating. In fall, the dry basin for the stream collects fallen leaves for building forts.

Loose Materials Area

The outdoors is an ideal place for providing open-ended materials, some naturally occurring and some manufactured. Loose wood or branches, rock piles, a dirt pit, wooden boxes, boards, small ladders, sawhorses, old tires, clotheslines, washtubs, and other props borrowed from indoors facilitate creative-constructive play. The loose materials area may be located at the boundary of a landscaped zone to enclose the piles of odds and ends that are collected. A supply of bricks, some light lumber, logs, leftover patio stones, or interlocking blocks, may provide ideas for a building project. When this area is located close to the sand play, children are able to retrieve items for their building projects with sand and water. A visit to a construction site, followed by play in the sand with loose materials and construction materials such as dump trucks, front-end loaders, and cranes can encourage creative projects over extended periods and offers endless opportunities for divergent thinking, planning, problem solving, and collaboration. This area qualifies as a rich space for creative thinking.

Open Spaces

Open spaces allow large-group play, organized group activities, sociodramatic play on a grand scale, and fantasy play. These areas may be contoured with mounds, slopes, and embankments that can be used differently in each season. Children need space for practising basic fundamental movements, such as running, climbing, jumping, hopping, galloping, rolling, sliding, balancing, and skipping (see Appendix A). The geographical variation in this area provides cues to children about the kinds of active movements that are possible. In summer, hills, mounds, and gullies become places to roll down, climb up, hide in, and jump over and for organized fitness and motor skills programs in the milder months. Open spaces allow children to run, hide, and spread out without the worry of interfering with large equipment or with play in other zones. An open area with a smooth surface permits children to play with balls, hoops, and tricycles as soon as temperatures allow less restrictive clothing. A small frozen rink in winter may provide hours of sliding or, from about three years of age, learning to skate.

Vehicle Trails

Vehicle trails are a favourite feature of most playgrounds; they are even more enticing when they wind through variations in the geography of the playground. Children may transport play materials with wagons and tractors, as long as the vehicles remain on the paved pathways. Clear limits should be set and upheld on the trails. Intersections with STOP and GO signs and signs with directional arrows add interest and constraints that have to be recognized. The surface of this area should be solid enough for wheeled vehicles to move smoothly in damp or dry weather. Gentle inclines make the trails more challenging and fun. Well-configured vehicle trails also lead children from one play zone to another, and, at the same time, define the boundaries of the zones and play areas. Trails that are earth-coloured blend with the natural surroundings, and spongy surface materials absorb impact, reduce injuries, and are pleasing to walk on. Winding trails that twist and turn around the various areas add to the aesthetic appeal of the playground and foster children's imagination.

The typical modular climber made of plastic or wood with many accessories, such as a slide, swing, firefighter's pole, and rope ladder may not be as versatile as a singular apparatus, such as a slide embedded into the ground, a stand-alone swing under a tree, or a series of vertical poles for climbing. For example, a single or double slide set into a hill can also become a means of getting from one area of the playground to another. Large, elaborate playhouses also tend to dominate a playground and reduce the complexity and variety of the play space. Newer trends in playground equipment tend toward apparatus that blends with the natural environment.

Vehicle trails

Double slide set into the hill

Active Play Areas

Playground equipment to promote physical development of the large muscles and motor coordination should address all parts of the child's body, not just the limbs. Moderately sized climbing apparatus, which promote balance and coordination, with ladders, slides, and poles are also obvious choices for hanging by the arms for upper body strength. Slides embedded in a mound of sand for soft landings and a chute with a dropoff that is horizontal to the ground introduce children to height, to the sensation of fast movement, and to risk taking. Single swing seats promote coordination, muscular development, and a sense of freedom and emotional release. Through learning to pump the swing to gain momentum, children develop a sense of the midline of the body. Swings must be located low enough to the ground to permit easy mounting and dismounting by young children. As well, there must be sufficient space to swing and to exit without obstructing pathways or colliding with other children.

Vertical climbing poles

Tree Houses and Playhouses

Playhouses and social and physical play areas built over an impact-absorbing surface material provide opportunities for climbing, balancing, and gaining some security about heights. Most children dream of having a tree house to play in at some time in their early years. Some tree houses may be set in a sturdy tree at a modest height, with easy access by ladder or stairwell. They may also be set on secure wooden frames. In the absence of a tree house, a playhouse on stilts or a house frame also will promote sociodramatic play and language skills. Playhouses should be readily visible but sufficiently removed from quiet play areas to permit children to exercise their imaginations. The same rule about simplicity applies here; more abstract playhouse structures are more conducive to creative role play than elaborate structures loaded with detail that preclude imagination and representational thinking.

An Outdoor Curriculum

Active play is essential for children for large parts of every day and in every season; therefore, the outdoor developmental curriculum design follows the same principles as the indoor curriculum. Appendix A, pages 463–475, provides a list of essential developmental outcomes that should comprise the framework for the outdoor curriculum as it does for the indoor curriculum. Teaching teams should consider together the nature of the play they want children to experience in the outdoor environment and include, every day, occasions for sustained active play outdoors. Developmental outcomes guide the planning of outdoor curriculum and activities that provide stepping stones for children to practise and eventually achieve the outcomes. ECEs observe and assess children's play and their individual developmental progress outdoors in the playground zones just as they would indoors. Some physical development outcomes are more readily fostered in active play areas outdoors. Greater attention may be given, also, to creative and aesthetic development outdoors, as well as to goals that foster children's spiritual development and their sense of wonder about nature and natural phenomena. Although the overall structure of the outdoor curriculum and the indoor curriculum may be the same, the emphases are different in order to capitalize on the additional freedom of movement and variation that is available in most playgrounds.

Winter Play

In some regions of North America, winter presents challenges especially as ECEs try to maximize the amount of time children spend outdoors during long winters. Open spaces and paved areas sheltered from the wind are particularly important during the winter months. Rainy winter weather in some regions poses unique problems with muddy play areas and wet outerwear on a daily basis. Pavement areas that can be kept clear of snow build-up are useful in areas where snow accumulation is heavy. Sturdy vinyl or rubberized outerwear that repels rain effectively and is easily wiped dry is a necessity in some regions. A large roof overhanging a paved or well-drained gravel area permits outdoor play during long rainy periods. Cubbies equipped with open slats for holding rain and snow boots off the floor for easy drying are a great help. Electric drying cupboards where wet snowsuits and nylon shells may be hung to dry quickly make life easier in the many parts of Canada where bulky outerwear is a fact of life for two or three seasons of the year. Children's clothing plays an important role in determining how long and under what conditions children will be able to play outdoors. ECEs need to be warmly dressed themselves, with hoods or hats and warm socks and boots to sustain long periods outdoors, in order to appreciate the infinite possibilities for play and learning outdoors during the winter months. ECEs have a mandate to help children adapt to climate, seasonal variations, and geographical realities, and outdoor environments throughout Canada should be designed with winter in mind, not just spring, summer, and fall. For those lucky enough to live in areas that experience significant snow, children need places to build a slide on a hill for their sleds and carpets, to slide on ice, to make snow forts and sculptures, and open areas to make pathways in the snow, snow people, and snow angels.

Winter provides opportunities for investigating many natural science phenomena, such as wind and air currents, freezing and melting, ice buildup, and **condensation**—and they should be carefully planned. Many creative construction activities are easier with packing snow than with wet sand. Even exploring the various types of snow provides a wealth of concrete, sensory learning for children. Winter is a time to introduce children to sports, including skating, snowshoeing, and skiing. Children as young as three can try bob skates on a patch of ice, pushing a small chair in front of them until they have gained their balance. Plenty of time to simply observe, feel, and explore winter phenomena provides children with endless ideas for art activities in the Creative Arts centre.

Winter offers such interesting play opportunities outside that children in warmer climates are often envious. One January, when visiting a demonstration child-care program in southern Florida, I was surprised to see the walls of the centre decorated with children's drawings of children skating, making snow people, sliding, and snowshoeing. Paper snowflakes decorated the windows. In a corner of one playroom stood a metre-high snowman made of papier mâché and decorated with a red wool scarf, a black hat, and a carrot for his nose. At the time, temperatures there had been in the high 20s (Celsius) for weeks! Stories like this remind us to appreciate the potential of winter play to enrich children's lives and the attraction that snow and wintertime fun have for children in all climatic zones.

Indoor-Outdoor Summer Programs

To use precious summer days to their fullest, ECEs often plan indoor-outdoor programs, bringing whole play stations and a wide range of activities outdoors to paved areas, open spaces, and loose materials areas. Many art activities can be conducted outdoors more easily than inside because of the space available. Fat chalk on wet pavement provides an interesting new medium for children to explore; large paint brushes and pails of water for whitewashing fences, railings, and pavement keep children interested for long periods; hollow blocks used with loose materials allow children to create interesting new structures. Messy activities, such as dyeing, papier mâché, and cardboard construction with leftover appliance boxes and crates, are often easier to manage outdoors. The list of indoor activities that provide interesting new opportunities and effects outdoors grows quickly once ECEs turn their attention to planning for indoor-outdoor play.

Playground Checklist

Safety

- Is the play space located away from dangerous activities or areas, such as entrances to buildings where smokers may congregate?
- Is the space between equipment sufficient to prevent children from colliding with equipment and far enough removed from pathways?
- Do pathways permit vehicle traffic to pass without infringing on play areas?
- Are gradients for vehicle pathways matched to the potential speed of play vehicles?
- Have foreign objects or obstructions been removed from fall zones under and around fixed equipment?
- Are the climbing areas, where children could fall or jump, less than 1.8 metres high?
- Are the fall zones around climbing apparatus able to absorb children's falls? For example, is satisfactory shock-absorbing surface material located beneath raised equipment? If sand or other absorptive material is used under equipment, is it 20 to 25 centimetres deep?
- Is equipment smoothly finished and generally in good repair (no sharp edges, no loose or broken parts, no splinters, flaking paint, frayed ropes, broken parts, protruding nails)?
- Have all worn S-hooks, chains, and bolts been replaced on swings? Are all S-hooks tightly closed?
- Is the end portion of the slide at least 22 to 38 centimetres long?
- If raised above the ground, do slides have large decks and protective handrails at the top?
- Do play structures with closed spaces allow air to circulate sufficiently to control temperature?
- Are all plant materials nontoxic?
- Is most of the play area and interesting equipment well shaded between 10 a.m. and 3 p.m. in summer months?
- Is the playground inspected every day for safety hazards before children play outdoors? Are health hazards from animal contamination minimized (sandbox sand raked or sterilized, hands washed after outdoor play)?
- Is the playground free of areas where standing water or other debris can collect?
- Are wooden play structures and retaining walls preserved with nontoxic materials?
- Are children closely supervised? Can the whole playground be surveyed by ECEs from two or three key vantage points?
- Could a child get caught anywhere? For example, are there any openings in equipment wide enough to trap a child's head?

Contact with Nature

- Does the playground include natural areas with plants, trees, or shrubs and some naturally occurring materials such as wood, rocks, and sand?
- Are the play areas well defined with natural boundaries as much as possible?

- Are there protected areas in the playground where children can play during rainy weather and be out of the sunshine on hot days?
- Does the outdoor environment encourage children to meander, touch, and take in the sensory pleasure of nature?
- Do vehicle riding pathways lead through some natural areas with shrubs and trees?
- Does the equipment blend with the natural features of the environment?
- Does the playground include private play spaces where children can retreat to play alone and still be safe?
- Does the playground include a garden area or planters or smaller beds throughout the playground where children may plant flowers and vegetables?
- Does the playground include equipment that blends with the natural environment to promote balance, upper body development (climbing), motor coordination, moderate risk taking, physical challenge, agility, fitness, and spatial awareness?
- Does the playground have aesthetic appeal based on its natural textures and colours and the location of plant materials and trees?
- Is there adequate space allocated to garden areas, i.e., either one defined area or several smaller spots throughout the playground devoted to planting flowers and vegetables? Are the garden areas defined and protected by small fences or hedges? Is the garden area close to a water source for appropriate irrigation? Are pots or tubs for planting flowers or herbs well secured and away from pathways?

Creative Play

- Does the playground include abstract play structures such as vertical logs embedded in the ground and playhouse frames that encourage sociodramatic play?
- Do the playground zones encourage creative-constructive play with abstract, naturally occurring materials such as sand, rocks, logs, stones, shells, wood chips, and water sources?
- Is there a loose materials area where children can gather and store items collected from field trips to parks and conservation areas, as well as lumber yards and construction sites, that are safe but useful for creative construction activities?
- Is there space for children to store and play with hollow blocks outdoors, close enough to the dramatic play areas to encourage sociodramatic play?
- Does the organization of space in the playground give clear messages to children about the type of play that is encouraged in the area?
- Is there a sufficient number of play spaces in each play zone to accommodate choice for the number of children who are expected to be playing in the area?
- Does the playground include a wooden platform or deck where children can produce skits and drama using props from the playground or from the indoor environment?
- Is there space near a water source to bring clay outdoors to a shady spot?
- Is there a smooth surface area where the easels may be brought out for children to paint outdoors? Are there wall areas with murals that will encourage children to draw and paint?

Source: Adapted from Resource Sheet #32. (1995, Summer) Ottawa, ON: Canadian Child Care Federation.

ACTIVITIES FOR OUTDOOR PLAY IN LANDSCAPED AREAS

1. Plan, design, and maintain a garden of hardy vegetables and flowers. This project can be undertaken during three seasons of the year in most parts of North America and may be started in the early spring with the selection of seeds and the planting of flats, and concluded in the fall with the garden cleanup. Younger preschools may be involved in the early phases of the project and some outdoor garden tasks; older preschoolers and kindergarten children will be able to undertake tasks at all stages in the gardening project.
2. Use props from familiar stories and nursery rhymes in the quiet and private landscaped areas, where a tent or a simple A-frame structure is erected, to stimulate imagination and to foster dramatic and sociodramatic play (for three- to five-year-olds).
3. Plan a barbecue or a picnic lunch with the children that they help prepare. Let them set the picnic table and spread their own condiments on their sandwiches. This type of activity is best conducted in the early spring, before insects, wasps, and flies arrive (for four- to six-year-olds).

ACTIVITIES FOR OUTDOOR PLAY IN OPEN AREAS FOR CHILDREN AGES THREE TO SIX

1. Using the open space and uneven geography of this area, allow children to create snow slides in the winter on the hills for their sleds and carpets. Children love to build tunnels, but they must be closely supervised at all times with two exits and one on top of the tunnel. Open spaces are ideal for building snow people. Snow play is also an excellent time to caution children about the potential hazards of snow.
2. Organize group activities such as follow the leader, activities with balls for catching and throwing games, parachute activities, exercises, and motor skills activities that provide practice in basic movements, such as running, hopping, jumping, galloping, marching, skipping, leaping, swaying, twisting, turning, balancing, bending, and stretching.

ACTIVITIES FOR OUTDOOR PLAY IN OPEN AREAS FOR CHILDREN AGES FOUR TO SIX

1. Build a horizontal snow block house with the children, using simple, connected enclosures and then subdividing the enclosures to make rooms and hallways.
2. Encourage play mirroring. Demonstrate by facing the group and going through a series of moves in slow motion and have the children duplicate the moves. The children then take partners and, facing each other, stand about a metre apart from each other, leaving room between pairs. One child in each pair is the leader and begins moving slowly. The other child is to mirror the leader's actions. After a while, children switch roles. (The game helps promote body awareness, body image, spatial awareness, balance, coordination, directionality, and laterality.)

Playground Equipment List

Large-Muscle

climbing structure or A-frame
crawl-through tunnels
jungle gym
vertical poles embedded in the ground for upper-body climbing, balance, and problem solving
securely suspended rope to climb and swing on
tire or bucket swings
rope ladder
suspended water sprinkler system for summer heat—suspended from support beams holding awnings
firefighter's pole
triangular ladder
slide with 15- to 20-centimetre drop at end
spring-based seesaw
trampoline
ramps for sliding and jumping
floating or suspended bridge
bowling set
snow shovels
baseball bat and ball
large, medium and small-sized balls that bounce
large hoops
punching ball or bag
skipping ropes and hoops
rowboat
small beanbags and target
balance beams or boards that interlock
balance blocks
stilts
pogo stick
skateboards with helmets and shin pads
stationary spring riding animals
horizontal ladder
simple playhouse or house frame
stick horses
tree house
steering wheel on wooden frame
large, hollow, wooden building blocks

Vehicles and Accessories

gas station fuel pump
tricycles
wagons or carts
pedal cars
wheelbarrow
tractor
bicycle pump
hardhats
cargo for wagons and carts

Loose Materials

painted wooden boxes
barrels and kegs
large packing boxes and crates (e.g., appliance cartons)
sawhorses
short wooden ladders
lumber in 1- and 2-metre lengths
rocks and boulders
workbench
softwood supplies
toolkit and tools
tires
logs
tree stump
telephone cable spools
weather-treated, non-toxic large blocks
rope
milk crates
tarpaulins
clothesline and pulleys
large and small paintbrushes
pails
water-soluble paint
old shirts and drop sheets
surplus building materials

Sand and Water

backhoes
buckets
scoops
shovels

sieves
heavy-duty trucks and cars
hose and tap
construction hats
camp stools
fishing rods and nets
tackle box
plastic wading pool
air mattress
diving mask
paddles
small sailing boats
inflatable raft
jugs and plastic pails
funnels and siphons
pup tent
flashlight
sleeping bag
knapsack
tin lunch boxes
canteen
tin pots and pans
saddlebags

Storage and Furniture

storage sheds with locks
benches
picnic table and umbrella
lawn chairs
barbecue or hibachi
firewood and grate
fire pit
prop box

Summary

Children's healthy development depends very much on how much time they can spend being active and playing outdoors in all seasons (Laumann, 2006). In Canadian urban environments, especially, safety and health concerns limit children's spontaneous play outside in their neighbourhoods. Therefore, it is increasingly important for centres and schools to provide outdoor play spaces where children can experience regular contact with nature; become familiar with the natural markers of the changing seasons; and be active, boisterous, and expansive in play in environments that protect them—while at the same time encouraging healthy risk taking. Today's playgrounds are changing and offering more opportunities for contact with nature and the aesthetic pleasure of beautifully designed natural spaces for many types of play. Current playground design trends support indoor-outdoor programming and provide protection from harsh elements so that playtimes can be extended in all seasons and climatic conditions. Play zones accommodate a wide range of categories and social contexts of play, and opportunities for children to escape from the group for quiet, reflective moments.

Most of the principles and practices related to curriculum planning indoors apply to planning outdoor curriculum and it is just as important. Programs must ensure that children are physically active for large parts of every day. Because the time children spend playing outdoors occupies a large share of the day, many of the curriculum's developmental outcomes and objectives should be addressed in outdoor play areas that provide sufficient play places, simple, complex, and super units of play that ensure plenty of choice, and allow ECEs to be engaged with children rather than passively supervise them playing. This chapter emphasizes the importance of playground design that provides zones where specific types of play activities are planned and facilitated.

LEARNING ACTIVITIES

1. Write activity cards related to gardening with young children that promote children's sense of time, task orientation, sensory perceptual skills, concept of measurement, gross motor skills, and eye–hand coordination.
2. Plan a three-season gardening project that begins in late winter and continues to the fall. Include activity cards for planning the garden, choosing supplies and equipment, planting seeds indoors, preparing and planting the garden, maintaining the garden, harvesting, and cleaning up the garden for winter. Ensure that the activities are developmentally appropriate for the younger preschoolers or for the older preschool and kindergarten children.
3. Research local, provincial, and national safety standards for playgrounds. Create a reference file on playground safety guidelines.
4. Draw a scale diagram of an outdoor play area that includes a landscaped area, a garden area, large-muscle play structures, pathways, a sand area, a private area, a loose materials area, open spaces, and vehicle trails. Explain the rationale for your playground design.
5. Plan an outdoor curriculum beginning with clear statements of the developmental outcomes children would be expected to achieve within one year. Include in your curriculum the developmental outcomes, developmental objectives related to each outcome, benchmark activities and/or learning experiences, teaching/learning methods, and assessment tools and methods (which you may cross-reference to other assessment tools you have created).

Section VIII
Empowering Children through Play

Section VIII addresses the following topics:

- articulate a personal philosophy of early childhood education
- determine the values, practices, and standards or outcomes that influence your philosophy
- consider factors related to a philosophical rationale for early childhood education in Canada
- become an advocate for children
- review essential elements of curriculum to promote play and learning:
  - ♦ observe and assess children's developmental levels, needs, and interests
  - ♦ respect individual learning styles

- apply play theory to promote learning
    - select equipment, materials, and supplies
    - plan space
    - design learning centres
    - establish a climate for play, development, and learning
    - design the curriculum framework
    - define developmental outcomes
    - identify developmental objectives
    - plan play activities
    - choose teaching and learning methods
    - evaluate
- exemplary practice

Section VIII summarizes the steps involved in articulating a philosophy of early childhood education and putting the philosophy into practice to promote child development and learning through play. *Empowering Children* emphasizes play theory, the role of the environment, play-based curriculum, and activity and project planning in order to optimize the abundant potential of play to promote healthy development and learning for children from ages two to six. A relevant philosophy respects and integrates the cultural priorities, values, and interests of our diverse Canadian families. A well-articulated philosophy is based on commonly held **values**, proven **practices**, and clearly described developmental standards or **outcomes**. In a period when play is underestimated and threatened in the face of pressures to add academics to preschool and kindergarten curriculums, *children's play must be protected and enhanced because that is how children develop, learn, and fulfill the mandate of early childhood.*

23 Putting Early Childhood Education Philosophy and Theory into Practice

"We do not do the child any disservice by having a clear idea of what types of learning can occur in various play situations. Rather, we add a dimension to play."

—Chris Nash, *The Learning Environment* (1979)

Before Reading This Chapter, Have You

- read all 22 chapters and tested your knowledge and understanding of the book by completing the learning activities at the end of each chapter?
- raised questions and examined your own values, practices, and standards?

Outcomes

After reading and understanding this final chapter, you should be able to

- articulate clearly your own philosophy of early childhood education, including the goals, values, practices, and standards that frame your professional practice;
- state explicitly the importance of play to child health, development, and well-being;
- determine children's developmental stages and readiness for learning based on observations and assessments;
- plan play-based curriculum, activities, learning experiences, and projects;
- document children's progress and achievement related to the developmental outcomes;
- evaluate programs according to children's achievement of the developmental outcomes and their sustained play, interest, and participation; and
- be an advocate for children and for play as the main vehicle for development and learning in early childhood.

Articulating a Philosophy of Early Childhood Education

A well-articulated philosophy of early childhood education is based on commonly held **values**, proven **practices**, and clear developmental **standards** or **outcomes**. Mallory and New (1994, p. 4) cite "a concern regarding the degree of congruence between the values, beliefs, and goals embedded in typical early childhood programs that ultimately affects their inclusiveness and effectiveness." An Ontario research study concluded that "effective early childhood education depends not only on ECE philosophy and practice but on the match between the two; in other words, ECEs' practices are most effective when in accord with their beliefs" (Randall & Pelletier, 1993, p. 95). As reasonable as this statement seems, ECEs know that congruence is difficult to achieve when there are many competing philosophies. A priority for the staff in any early childhood education program is to establish a coherent philosophy based on congruent values and a set of practices that shape and define the program. The standards, often expressed as outcomes, help programs to determine the effectiveness of their practices relative to the stated program philosophy.

An important learning outcome of ECE training programs is to encourage students to formulate a philosophy of early childhood education that will guide their practice. Ontario identified one of the vocational learning outcomes for ECEs as the ability to "apply a personal philosophy of early childhood education within the framework of ethical and professional standards" (College Standards and Accreditation Council, 1996, p. 8). A coherent philosophy is built around standards that are internally consistent. In Canada, this philosophy should include a culturally responsive approach that recognizes and respects the values and practices families bring to the program that are central to children's development and learning (Villegas & Lucas, 2002).

Values

Values are beliefs that motivate behaviour. Appropriate practice in early childhood education is based on the view that children are motivated largely from within. It also assumes that children go through distinct stages but not always in the same sequence or at the same age. Stages may be characterized by specific cognitive styles and other abilities very different from those of an adult. Because development in early childhood is largely grounded in sensory and physical experience, children's knowledge of the world around them depends on the freedom to explore, manipulate, and be physically active through play. Developmental theory values individualized learning, since no two children learn at the same rate, to the same level, or in the same way. Children need freedom to engage in play and learning that is interesting and that matches their individual needs and abilities. Real learning occurs when children integrate new understandings from their concrete play experiences, a process that takes time and patience. Then, they are able to transfer what they have learned to new contexts. *A strong developmental foundation in early childhood promotes higher levels of functioning as adults, a value central to the concept of lifelong learning.* Most important of all, development and learning occur through play when children are fully engaged. Children require an emotionally supportive climate in which their needs are met and they believe that what they do really matters to the adults around them.

Practices

Teaching practices are generally derived from values that guide behaviour and choices. Nine practices associated with development and learning in early childhood follow.

1. Children are free to choose their own play experiences.
2. The environment offers real choices among play alternatives that are meaningful and accessible to children.
3. Play activities and experiences are based on observations of the children to facilitate developmental progress from their present level to a higher level. Unplanned, randomly selected activities that fail to take into account assessments of the individual developmental levels and needs of the children often amount to little more than busy work.
4. ECEs plan a range of play experiences, from simple to complex, beginning with concrete learning challenges in which the skills or concepts to be achieved are clear and observable to the learner. Simple activities are followed by more challenging learning tasks that, in the cognitive domain, for example, move gradually from sensory exploration and physical manipulation to symbolic thinking and representation, and in the physical domain from reflexive movements to the skilled movements children use in sports.
5. A balance of convergent (structured) and divergent (open-ended) activities is provided. Play experiences with specific-purpose materials, such as puzzles and stacking toys, provide built-in cues regarding what is to be done and learned with the materials. The tasks to be accomplished in these structured play experiences are clear to both the ECE and the child. Open-ended activities, such as easel painting, sociodramatic play, and block play, offer opportunities for children to explore materials, invent plans and procedures, try several alternatives, make decisions, and achieve their own outcomes. A balance of individual and group activities that allow for children's unique learning styles is provided.
6. Play equipment, materials, and supplies are organized into well-defined learning centres that provide clear messages about what children are likely to be doing and learning in each learning centre. The environment allows for the transfer of materials from one centre to another and the gathering of equipment, materials, and supplies from a number of learning centres to use in larger projects.
7. The curriculum should include long-term projects comprised of a sequence of activities in which groups of children and ECEs collaborate in order to achieve the desired result and projects which may be undertaken by a child on his own. Projects should be of interest to the children, facilitate inclusion of all children who want to participate, and involve a problem that has multiple avenues to explore (Katz & Chard, 2005). The challenge for ECEs is to encourage children's interest in projects that lead toward their achievement of important goals, such as the ability to link school, home, and community; to identify milestones so that children can mark their progress in stages; and to foster collaborative thinking and problem solving (Helm & Katz, 2011).
8. Ongoing assessment of children's developmental progress references their progress toward the developmental outcomes articulated in the curriculum and the objectives achieved in the activities and projects. ECEs document children's achievement of the developmental objectives and outcomes linked to the curriculum.

9. ECEs are culturally responsive, know about the lives of their children, and use this knowledge to design curriculum that builds on what children recognize and know, stretching them beyond what is familiar to them (Villegas & Lucas, 2002).

Standards or Developmental Outcomes

In early childhood education, standards may be used synonymously with the statement of developmental outcomes, which are complex, verifiable performances that are reliable and based on the integration of several skills, such as the ability to ride a tricycle or to read sentences. Outcomes are linked to the common developmental tasks of early childhood, and achieving them is important in order to progress to the next developmental level. Children's developmental progress is facilitated by their success in play activities, which are sequenced from simple to complex and require progressively higher levels of skill, knowledge, and understanding that may be expressed as developmental objectives. Objectives are often adjusted as a result of repeated observations of children.

ECEs observe children's entering behaviours, document what they observe, monitor the developmental skills they demonstrate as they play, and assess their progress from the point at which the learning process began. Assessment is a sophisticated skill that requires knowledge of child development and well-developed observation and recording skills. Assessment reports and recommendations rely on the ECE's ability to accurately match the child's play in various contexts to the developmental objectives for each child. When children are deemed to have achieved developmental objectives (and outcomes), ECEs may assume that children are making progress. When children fail to demonstrate progress, there is something wrong, either with the climate or the environment or with the match between the planned play activities and the children who are experiencing difficulty or boredom. The same principles apply to children with special needs. Regular and systematic program evaluation strategies that look carefully at all components of the play and learning environment, including the ECEs, will usually reveal problems and weaknesses that can be addressed and overcome. *Promoting developmental progress should not be confused with attempting to accelerate children's development.* Effective developmental programs promote children's progress at their own rate and according to their own learning styles and interests. Evidence that each child is progressing developmentally from the point at which assessment began is what is important. Appendix A provides a sample list of developmental outcomes for early childhood.

Making Decisions and Planning for Play

The usefulness of an educational philosophy lies in its ability to guide decision making, planning, and practice. Facilitating children's development implies an understanding of the developmental tasks of early childhood and of the usual sequence of learning. As well, the creative use of resources and of physical space leads to satisfying play and to positive learning experiences.

In summary, planning for play is based on the following assumptions:

- Play is like food for children; it is essential to their mental and physical health, their development in all domains, and their overall sense of safety and well-being.

- The child should choose play activities from a number of alternatives.
- Flexible play materials and accessible resources are essential to self-expression.
- Adherence to schedules and routines should take second place in daily planning and management to ensure that children's play is central to the program.
- Spiritual development takes place largely in unstructured natural environments, often outdoors, where children have the privacy and individual freedom to explore, physically and cognitively, the things in nature of interest to them.
- Learning through play depends on the quality and the accessibility of a wide range of concrete objects that respond to children's actions on them.
- The environment should provide sufficient space and accessibility for a range of play equipment, materials, and supplies that may be used in flexible ways.
- The environment should offer real choices of play activities and projects in defined learning centres, and in potential play spaces.
- The learning environment should provide messages to children consistent with the ECEs' verbal messages.
- The child's right to privacy should be respected; thus, children should be able to play alone when they choose.
- Some objectives are more readily achieved through individual play.
- Outdoor play every day is essential for children's mental, social, emotional, and physical health.
- Children learn through play outdoors as well as indoors, so both the outdoor and the indoor learning environments should be planned and set up for play. Many activities and projects can be played equally well indoors and outdoors.

A Philosophical Rationale for Early Childhood Education in Canada Revisited

Progressive approaches in the profession recognize our nation's cultural diversity and the pressures on families to prepare their children adequately for success in school and in life. The economic imperatives imposed by competition from other nations, which have had national policy frameworks for universally accessible early childhood programs for several decades, are increasing. Canada lags behind other countries in the provision of a national framework of standards, policies, and public funding for early childhood education. The absence of infrastructure and embedded practices in Canada would allow us to invent new models and practices that fit our aspirations related to economic prosperity, social justice, and culture. Canada needs a national framework for the delivery of *made in Canada* programs for young children that fit with 21st-century realities. On the positive side, we have the advantage of not having to undo or reframe an existing national infrastructure. What we have is, for the most part, a patchwork of uneven services and quality, and *make-do* program models that have been largely locally based. If our nation were to commit to a framework of national standards and policies for early childhood education services for all children, the profession would be better positioned to define its values and create models that address, systematically, our unique challenges. In the absence of a national framework, however, the profession should define the pressing needs out there right now for children, including First Nations children, many of whom are struggling with poverty in a nation that has been identified as one of the richest and most privileged in the world (Organisation for Economic Co-operation and Development [OECD], 2011). Defining the needs and deficits is an important step toward identifying the solutions and becoming informed advocates on behalf of our children. Working with parents and the profession across all provinces and territories, ECEs might articulate collectively what a 21st-century philosophical and practical approach to addressing children's rights, needs, interests, and aspirations looks like in our multicultural Canada.

The notion of the developing child (and the adult he or she might become) should remain a core reference point for a model for early childhood education in Canada. Bloch (2005, p. 423) stated that

> ... we need to open up to new possibilities ... for our own and other people's children, to recognize the interconnectedness of the world, and the necessity for socially, economically, and educationally *just ways* to enhance and provide opportunities for all children and their families.

What might be these *just ways* to enhance opportunities for young children in Canada? Perhaps the human crises we face in Canada provide part of the answer: the unacceptably high percentage of children living in poverty; the alarming incidence of obesity and adult diseases in young children; the alienation of some of our youth; extreme bullying sometimes leading to *kids killing kids*; low literacy rates of Canadians when compared to test results from some other nations; the number of children struggling and then being left behind in classrooms because they do not speak English; and too many children with unidentified special needs. Perhaps a three-pronged approach is worth considering:

1. Assess, acknowledge and address children's mental, emotional, and physical health issues, their detectable cognitive lags and deficits, and their well-being concerns, from birth through adolescence, via the educational system. "Schools should become the centre of the community for families, with support and programs from pregnancy on." (McCain et al, 2011).
2. Promote young children's social adaptation and emotional stability by encouraging them to play creatively and to become *skilled players* with others and individually. Equipping children before age six with the developmental skills in all domains that they need for lifelong learning depends on play-based, culturally relevant, developmental environments and programs governed by legislated national standards that all early childhood programs meet in order to qualify for a licence and public funding.
3. Help children acquire the *habits of mind* that motivate lifelong learning, constructive citizenship, stewardship of the environment and resources, empathy, and social justice. Encourage in children a bias to think globally and act locally. Foster aspirations toward personal success, reflection, and independent and collective action that contribute to effective participation in society.

What Do These *Just Ways* Mean for Early Childhood Education Programs?

Just ways, today, demand recognition of the challenges we face and an acknowledgement that former choices and paths have often failed to recognize how much our cultural and social fabric in Canada has changed in the past two decades. Any lingering beliefs that programs should assimilate children into the values and traditions of a former predominant culture fade fast when confronted with a projection, for example, that more than half the population in some Canadian cities may soon be non-white. A one-size- fits-all early childhood program model will not meet the needs of all children. Canada's commitment to multiculturalism, which provides a unique example to the world, requires our profession to recognize that *mainstream* in Canada means *diverse* in terms of culture, family constellations, family values, educational priorities, sexual orientation, religious affiliation, and child rearing practices. Discussion at many levels in Canada, among people of all cultures and persuasions represented in our population, may determine the central values that should be defined as Canadian (Somerville, 2006). It may be timely to define a moral, social, ethical, and philosophical *education contract* that most people in Canada can subscribe to and actively uphold, leaving room for culturally specific priorities that also protect children's human rights and interests. A consensus might mean that early childhood education would, once again, break new ground for the rest of the education system. The ECE profession would need to describe clearly the national fabric that ECEs are weaving for young children that may ultimately become the pattern for a new Canadian educational and social tapestry.

Steps in Planning the Learning-through-Play Environment and Curriculum

The design of the play and learning environment and the early childhood education curriculum involves seeing the indoor and outdoor classrooms as complex networks of complementary and interdependent parts. This textbook has led the reader through steps intended to foster development and learning through play. The belief is that children acquire the skills, knowledge, understanding, and habits of mind that lead to hope and lifelong learning when they play freely with purpose, enthusiasm and meaning that they largely define for themselves.

Observe and Assess Children's Developmental Levels, Needs, and Interests

Planning environments and programs for young children begins with understanding child development and the particular developmental levels, needs, and interests of the children in the programs. ECEs acquire knowledge of these, largely through regular formal and informal observation and careful record keeping. Through observation, the ECE knows who his children are and how best to make an appropriate fit between the needs of the individual child and the environment in which she plays and learns. Systematic observations, conducted over time, generally reveal children's developmental levels and abilities in all domains. Information from observations is reflected in individual assessment reports for each child. These reports form the basis for planning environments and programs.

Respect Individual Learning Styles

Some children learn better from visual stimuli and need to be able to see a concept demonstrated before they are able to understand. Other children are auditory learners, for whom listening, interpreting, and acting on auditory messages comes easiest. Tactile learners have to touch, feel, and interact physically with things to form concepts that endure. Some children are more inclined to be observers and to be relatively passive in their learning. Many enjoy learning in social contexts by observing, imitating, interacting, and collaborating with others. Other children prefer solitary learning experiences and pursue their own objectives while they play alone, follow their interests, and reach understandings at their own pace. Some learn easily in a quiet, orderly environment where activity and noise are minimal and where they can remain at a task for long periods. Others need plenty of activity, room to move, frequent breaks, and opportunities to change from one activity to another. Activity planning for each learning centre should account for children's individual learning styles. Each child may also employ different learning styles depending on the nature of the task in which he is engaged. Children will generally ask for direction, assistance, and leadership when they need it.

Apply Play Theory to Promote Learning

Understanding play theory, and the role of play as an agent of development and learning, is essential to planning learning environments. Children learn through play that is hands-on and based on sensory exploration, that it is freely chosen, undertaken for its own sake, responsive to their own actions, interesting to them, meaningful, and relevant to their daily lives. The ECE should possess an expert command of the categories and social contexts of play and know how to plan, set up, and implement activities that address a full range of play possibilities. Children play in order to find meaning and to understand. Children learn through play that is motivating, challenging, growth enhancing, healing, and reassuring. Play nourishes and fulfills children as it promotes feelings of success and mastery over the environment. When children experience that they can have a meaningful impact on their surroundings, and that the environment is responsive to their needs and behaviours, they feel valued, effective, and empowered. Knowing that the environment is the third teacher, a key professional skill is to fully comprehend and utilize the learning-through-play potential of the space; configure and design learning centres that support meaningful play activities; provision the learning centres with equipment, materials, and supplies that interest and challenge children; and allocate sufficient play places and time for children to become meaningfully engaged with the materials.

Select Equipment, Materials, and Supplies

Play equipment, materials, and supplies are the tools of the trade for ECEs, who should have an expert grasp of their play and learning potential. A child-centred learning environment means that the equipment is child-sized, play materials are accessible to children, and there is enough space to play with materials without intrusion from other activities. Play materials are the contents of the environment, and they may be set up as simple, complex, or super units defined according to the capacity of the unit to interest children for a period of time and the number of children who would normally play with the unit. Variety in the play and learning environment relates to the categories and contexts of play that each unit of play invites.

Plan Space

Organized play space provides nonverbal messages to children about the types of play and behaviour encouraged in each part of the environment. When space is well planned, children can be more independent and self-directed in their play and spend less time guessing what is expected of them or trying to decipher choices that are not obvious.

ECEs have to know the legal space requirements with respect to the relationship between the contents of the play space and the amount of space available. Space planning should provide directional pathways, which guide behaviour and movement from one learning centre to another. Juxtaposing learning centres that are complementary and creating zones or groupings of learning centres and play stations that involve similar categories of play provide cues to children about what they are to do and learn in each part of the learning environment.

Pathways should lead children into and out of learning centres, and all centres should be accessible from the main pathways. No pathway should flow through an area designated as play space for any piece of equipment. Pathways should go around learning centres, not through them. Dead space is a trouble spot where children tend to lose their motivation for play and become confused about what is expected of them. Densely organized space promotes a high level of social and interactive play; loosely organized space encourages individual and small-group play directed toward projects and activities.

Assuming roles

Design Learning Centres

Learning centres provide the framework for play and learning in the environment, and they are organized and located so as to complement one another. Each learning centre emphasizes particular categories of play; learning centres that promote similar play styles should be placed close to each other to encourage children to transfer the learning and skills acquired in one centre to another nearby centre. The thoughtful juxtaposition of centres with similar goals and play styles also allows for organization of the environment according to the criteria of messy/tidy, noisy/quiet, active/passive, and individual/group-oriented play behaviours. The equipment, materials, and supplies in each learning centre influence the categories of play and social contexts that occur there as well as the specific activities that ECEs should plan and set up for that centre.

When there is no rational plan for the location of learning centres, children have to rely heavily on adult direction and intervention. A high level of adult involvement in guiding, intervening, and leading children's play activities reduces children's freedom and ability to be self-directed. Well-planned learning centres provide non-verbal cues to children about the behaviour expected in the learning centre. ECEs should match equipment, play materials, and supplies to the developmental priorities of each learning centre. To make effective matches, ECEs have to know the play and learning potential inherent in each play material. Knowing the tools of the trade in the ECE profession means knowing the purpose, value, function, and inherent learning in all play materials. ECEs need a keen sense of the time it takes for children to explore materials fully and to master their inherent learning potential. This understanding helps ECEs gauge how long to leave materials and activities set up in a learning centre.

Establish a Climate for Play, Development, and Learning

Children learn when they feel psychologically safe and physically comfortable. Their psychological health depends on their physical well-being and on their sense of being nurtured, valued, and protected. Children need to know that what they do *really matters* to the adults in their lives (Katz, 1974). When they are anxious, afraid, hungry, unloved, abused, tired, suffering from low self-esteem, or unwell, children do not have the courage or the initiative to take risks, lose themselves in absorbing activity, or choose or follow through on tasks and challenges. Play demands children's full attention, interest, and willingness to let go. When children lack these basic capacities and a sense of wholeness and safety in their lives, it is difficult to help them overcome these deterrents to their ability to play.

An important principle in establishing a healthy climate is to ensure that the environment reflects the cultures represented in the population of the centre. This means that cultural priorities and goals, as well as materials and supplies from other cultures, should be well integrated into the environment and daily life of the program. Environments can be designed to promote feelings of effectiveness, self-worth, and mastery in even the most anxious and timid children. ECEs plan activities and experiences that help children overcome some of the emotional, social, and psychological barriers to play. Establishing an emotional climate for play involves being aware of individual needs and capabilities; choosing activities that interest children; recognizing their efforts, however tentative or faltering; and respecting children's feelings and individuality. A healthy and motivating climate for play allows each child the time needed to gain confidence, to reach out, and to tackle new and challenging experiences.

Design the Curriculum Framework

An organized environment for play provides a solid foundation on which to plan and implement the developmental curriculum. Once the components of design, space, contents, and climate are understood, these are connected to the curriculum, which is based on the developmental tasks of early childhood, the priorities of families, the interests of the children, and state-of-the-art practice in early childhood education.

Curriculum design requires that ECEs identify the developmental and learning priorities for the children in the program. In this step, ECEs rely on information about individual children based on their observations and assessment of children's developmental levels and needs; these developmental priorities are reflected in the outcomes toward which the curriculum is directed.

Developmental goals for curriculum reflect the particular priorities of parents and ECEs for the children in the program. Geography, socioeconomic conditions, culture, and social context, among other factors, influence choices of program goals. Today, with so much emphasis on equipping children with the learning-to-learn skills they will need when they start school, building the foundation for learning-to-learn, literacy, and numeracy often assumes a high priority.

DEFINE DEVELOPMENTAL OUTCOMES

Once parents and ECEs have identified the developmental goals that drive a curriculum, ECEs describe the developmental outcomes that children should be able to achieve within a timeframe of perhaps a school year. From the developmental outcomes (Appendix A is a reference point), ECEs derive the developmental objectives and play experiences that guide the sequence of learning that leads toward the achievement of outcomes. Determining the developmental objectives depends on the ECE's understanding of the internal structure of the developmental outcomes—that is, the progressive steps, or bite-sized chunks of development and learning that lead toward the developmental outcome.

IDENTIFY DEVELOPMENTAL OBJECTIVES

Statements of developmental objectives guide activity planning because they describe what children do and practise as they play and, sometimes, the dispositions they need in order to overcome hurdles and challenges. Developmental objectives help ECEs assess the developmental and learning progress children are making and provide clues about other activities that may help children confirm their gains and move on to more complex activities. The statement of "Previous Experience Needed" on activity cards outlines the developmental skills children should have achieved in order to be ready to tackle the new activity.

PLAN PLAY ACTIVITIES

Play activities should address the individual needs and interests of the children. They should be implemented in a learning centre or playground zone where the category of play involved in the activity is compatible with the social contexts of play associated with the learning centre and zone. Activity planning that occurs daily, weekly, and monthly should respond to children's interests and capture events of significance in the environment. It is at this point that the emergent curriculum and the explicit curriculum for play, development and learning converge. *An emergent curriculum and a developmental curriculum framework are interdependent.* The children's present developmental stages, and the progress they need to make to reach the next stages, provide the background of the program; the children's and ECE's interests provide the foreground for planning. It is largely a matter of planning projects and specific activities and setting up environments to accomplish both intentions: achieve developmental outcomes and address children's emerging interests and needs.

Activity cards enable ECEs to think through the activity, what children are likely to do, what they will need in terms of resources, how the activity should be set up, and the previous learning experiences children likely need in order to be able to tackle the activity and make progress. ECEs should break the learning tasks into smaller parts to help children deal with manageable amounts of new learning. An important teaching skill is to understand the internal composition of activities and projects so that play and learning challenges are presented in a rational sequence. A good way to acquire this skill is to make play materials with recycled materials (e.g., Workjobs). The activity card file system is a key teaching tool to help students learn to plan a series of activities that represents the typical sequence in which children acquire skills and understanding. Effective planning involves making knowledgeable matches between developmental objectives and play equipment, materials, and supplies and is largely a matter of understanding and exploiting the play and learning potential of a vast range of concrete objects.

SELECT TEACHING AND LEARNING METHODS

Developmental approaches assume that young children learn through social experience and through interaction individually with concrete objects and experiences in their environment. The more active, sensory-based, hands-on opportunities children have to explore materials and supplies and to learn about the properties and actions of things under a variety of conditions, the more likely they are to build a solid developmental foundation on which later academic learning can build. Inclusive learning environments recognize that children with disabilities often require more intervention in their play and learning to help them over the hurdles posed by their disabilities. It is the ECEs job to ensure that the equipment, materials and supplies used in activities are as accessible as possible to the child with special needs. Developmental programming acknowledges the diversity of play, teaching and learning methods that facilitate progress.

Early childhood is a time for informal education, when children should engage primarily in child-initiated, self-directed activities. The essential characteristics of active, informal methods are that they "inspire children's interest, play, experimentation and cooperation" (DeVries & Kohlberg, 1987, p. 41). Freedom to choose from clear alternatives for play is an essential element of informal pedagogy. The early childhood period is the prime time for building an intellectual foundation of concept formation, habits, skills, and positive attitudes toward discovery and self-directed learning; it is prime time to learn how to learn.

EVALUATE

Evaluation involves gathering information about the value of programs, often to compare programs and make decisions about their adoption, continuation, or elimination. In evaluation, the ECE also collects data about programs to assess their strengths and weaknesses and to determine objectives for improvement and revision. ECEs and administrators should use improvement-oriented (formative) evaluation procedures to monitor the effectiveness of planning and teaching practices in programs, to determine children's participation and progress in the program, to identify weak areas that can be strengthened, to maintain the relevance of programs, and to assist ECEs in understanding their professional roles and improving their performances. There are several popular evaluation systems and kits on the market that may be adapted by ECEs to help them evaluate their programs. ECEs often find that they need to add evaluation criteria to a standardized tool, particularly criteria related to teacher–child interactions; teaching and learning methods; and the range of play styles, types, and contexts of play encouraged in the curriculum, activities, and projects provided.

People sometimes mistakenly associate evaluation with the threat of criticism. They fear that evaluation will expose the weak elements in organizations, programs, and strategies in order to eliminate programs or reassign people. In the past two decades, evaluation has become a sophisticated discipline and has reversed some of the negative connotations previously associated with it. Evaluation is a positive force for renewal, support, and improvement, and evaluation of all components of early childhood education is essential if the profession is to make progress in the interests of children. ECE training programs should instil the confidence to use evaluation tools and to adopt systematic evaluation procedures and instruments. The information gained from the use of program evaluation tools helps ECEs gain a better understanding of what they do; how they do it; and how they can make informed changes in planning and implementing programs that work for children, families, and society.

Evaluation techniques and instruments for ECE programs are still underutilized. The components of program evaluation that should be addressed include activity evaluation, curriculum evaluation, an inventory and analysis of play space and its contents, evaluation of the physical and affective characteristics of the indoor and outdoor play environments, and, most important, evaluation of children's progress related to the developmental outcomes identified in the curriculum. A key evaluation component that needs to be used more pervasively, and on a regular basis, is ECE performance appraisal that emphasizes professional development needs and guides ECEs toward improvements in their skills and knowledge while also recognizing their achievements and contributions.

Exemplary Practice in Early Childhood Education

In Canada, significant distance still lies between the good intentions that prevail in the early childhood profession and present practices. ECEs have to bridge these distances by exercising the will; positive human qualities; and the knowledge, skills, and dispositions needed to meet children's individual needs and to build a strong foundation for their later years. Most ECEs possess the good will and the necessary human qualities of compassion, warmth, nurturance, and dedication. ECEs also need sophisticated, well-honed teaching skills and knowledge of children in order to link research and theory to relevant practice. The challenges we now face, and the need to innovate and develop models specific to our Canadian social and cultural contexts add to the importance of regular, formative ECE performance appraisal leading to professional development.

Summary

This textbook has endeavoured to provide a step-by-step, systematic approach to planning play-based environments and curriculum that will help children build a strong developmental foundation for lifelong learning. *The book highlights the essential role of play to development, learning, and mental and physical health, and the importance of facilitating high-quality, rich, diverse play.* Children are empowered when they achieve their optimal development in all domains. They are more likely to be successful and interested learners as they grow and mature and to feel a heightened sense of control over their own lives and environments. Effective early childhood education plays a crucial role in children's lives, and its influence continues throughout the later childhood years and beyond. It provides the foundation for success in school and for lifelong social adaptation. When children's individual talents are nurtured, they are more likely to become innovators in a world that needs more ingenuity and original thinking. ECEs are essential professionals within the education sector and within society as a whole; they need to be opinion leaders and advocates for children.

Now, and in the future, Canada depends on the optimal development of our children to ensure the stability, prosperity, and integrity of our nation and its citizens in an increasingly competitive world. The degree to which each human being realizes his or her potential is fundamentally related to the holistic development and learning foundations laid during the early years.

Learning Activity

Draft your philosophy of early childhood education referencing the various aspects of philosophy outlined in this chapter. Use the following sections to guide your draft:

1. State your values/beliefs about the role of play in early childhood.
2. Link your values/beliefs about play to the professional and teaching practices you would adopt in your early childhood program.
3. Describe the goals you believe you would prefer for your program and state how you would solicit and act on the goals and priorities of the parents of the children in your program.
4. List and provide a rationale for the developmental and learning expectations you would have for preschool children before they enter formal schooling.
5. Identify developmental outcomes for each developmental domain to which you might assign priority in your program.
6. Explain the approach you would adopt in order to advocate for the important role of play in early childhood and to persuade parents of the centrality of play in early childhood education.

Appendix A

Developmental Outcomes for Children Ages Two to Six

The normal trajectory of child development includes development in all four domains: emotional, social, physical, and cognitive. The following list provides a sample of the developmental outcomes to guide planning for play in early childhood. Developmental outcomes, along with the overarching program goals that are usually selected by ECEs, parents, and other interested persons, form the spine of the curriculum. The list of outcomes and objectives may be used as a reference to guide curriculum and program planning.

Developmental Domains

The domains of development are usually identified by four categories: emotional, social, physical, cognitive. Other domains may include creative, moral, or spiritual development. The developmental domains are intended to capture the central tasks of holistic child development.

Developmental Goals

Developmental goals reflect the interests and priorities of children, their parents, ECEs, and other stakeholders and often determine the particular emphases for a curriculum. Developmental goals may reflect a higher priority for programs, for example, ensuring that children are attuned to their natural environments and are able to survive in harsh climatic and geographic conditions; or, for private programs sponsored by religious organizations, they may reflect the particular religious values and priorities of the families they serve. Other cultural, religious, social-conventional, and knowledge-based goals may also apply. Potential program goals are not included here. The following lists contain generic tasks of child development that are expressed here as developmental outcomes; these are followed by related developmental objectives.

Developmental Outcomes

Developmental outcomes describe clearly the complex, demonstrable, verifiable developmental performances that children are able to demonstrate by the end of a curriculum, usually within a defined period of time. Developmental outcome statements usually begin with "The child has reliably demonstrated ..." and end with a description of what the child has achieved, such as " the ability to skip in a cross-lateral pattern coordinating upper and lower body." The determination that a child has met an outcome is based on observation and assessment of his achievements in play-based activities, play experiences, and projects, and during the normal course of daily routines. Physical outcomes, for example, are sometimes observed and assessed in group games, exercise sessions, and specific activities set up to determine whether children have achieved, for example, the visual and auditory perceptual skills they require in order to begin reading.

Developmental Outcomes and Objectives for the Emotional Domain: Psychological Health and Self-Expression

Developmental Outcome: The child reliably demonstrates Psychological Health: emotional stability and self-expression

DEVELOPMENTAL OBJECTIVES RELATED TO EMOTIONAL STABILITY

forms attachments/bonds
separates from family members successfully for brief periods
trusts others
acts independently
appreciates own achievements
values self (exhibits self-esteem)

DEVELOPMENTAL OBJECTIVES RELATED TO SELF-EXPRESSION

expresses needs verbally
expresses feelings using drama and art media
expresses emotions/feelings verbally
accepts one's own negative feelings
finds acceptable outlets for fear, anger, anxiety, and other powerful negative feelings
clarifies and expresses feelings by using creative play materials, props, etc.

Developmental Outcomes and Objectives for the Social Domain: Social Relationships, Social Perceptions and Behaviours, and Socio-Moral Understanding

Developmental Outcome: The child reliably demonstrates the ability to form Social Relationships: forming interpersonal relationships and interacting with others.

DEVELOPMENTAL OBJECTIVES RELATED TO FORMING INTERPERSONAL RELATIONSHIPS

cares for others/help others
respects others: family members, peers, teachers
initiates contact with others
shows empathy toward others

DEVELOPMENTAL OBJECTIVES RELATED TO INTERACTING WITH OTHERS

interacts successfully with one other child
functions successfully in groups at appropriate times
responds to environmental and social demands appropriately
interacts successfully with others, including adults

Developmental Outcome: The child reliably demonstrates the ability to form relevant Social Perceptions and Behaviours: psychological self-concept and social adaptation

DEVELOPMENTAL OBJECTIVES FOR PSYCHOLOGICAL SELF-CONCEPT

develops authentic concept of self, based on feedback
feels positive about one's gender and gender identity
feels positive about one's ethnic heritage and culture
feels sense of belonging to the group
appreciates humour and fun

DEVELOPMENTAL OBJECTIVES FOR SOCIAL ADAPTATION

understands role in group/social play
demonstrates ease in social situations
imitates remembered events
maintains role in sociodramatic play
respects social norms/rules/conventions
adapts to changing demands

Developmental Outcome: The child reliably demonstrates Socio-Moral Understanding and Behaviour: self-regulation and spiritual development

DEVELOPMENTAL OBJECTIVES RELATED TO SELF-REGULATION

observes limits/rules
considers others
controls/channels emotions appropriately
restrains inappropriate impulses
achieves what one wants in socially acceptable ways
delays gratification
demonstrates empathy for others

DEVELOPMENTAL OBJECTIVES RELATED TO SPIRITUAL DEVELOPMENT

gains a sense of connectedness with the natural environment
expresses wonder at natural phenomena
embraces opportunities for reflection and ask questions about mysterious events
appreciates that some questions do not have obvious answers
understands that each person is connected to many aspects of the natural world
feels a connection to other persons

Developmental Outcomes and Objectives for the Physical Domain: Body Awareness, Basic Fundamental Movements, Sensory-Perceptual Abilities, Spatial Awareness and Kinesthetic Discrimination, Physical Abilities, and Skilled Movements

Developmental Outcome: The child reliably demonstrates Body Awareness: physical self-concept, spatial awareness, laterality, directionality, temporal awareness, and kinesthetic discrimination

DEVELOPMENTAL OBJECTIVES RELATED TO PHYSICAL SELF-CONCEPT

recognizes body parts
names body parts
moves body parts on command (in a song or game)
recognizes differences between one's own body and those of others (e.g., colour of eyes, height, hair colour)
recognizes own individuality and that of others

DEVELOPMENTAL OBJECTIVES RELATED TO SPATIAL AWARENESS

moves body in a confined space
makes body smaller to fit into a small space
projects and controls the body in space without colliding with others
locates objects in space in relation to oneself
locates objects in space without reference to oneself
follows direction and path of objects in space
prints letters and symbols that maintain a consistent direction in space

DEVELOPMENTAL OBJECTIVES RELATED TO LATERALITY

moves both sides of the body simultaneously and equally (bilaterality)
moves each side of the body consecutively, first one side, then the other (alternating laterality)
performs cross-lateral patterns of movement (moves left arm and right leg forward, then right arm, left leg, and so on, in creeping, walking, marching) (cross-laterality)
coordinates one action with one side of the body and a different action with the opposite side (integrated laterality)

DEVELOPMENTAL OBJECTIVES RELATED TO DIRECTIONALITY

moves own body in specific directions or positions
moves objects in specific directions or positions
follows directional signals on command: forward, backward, sideways, left, right
recognizes and follows symbols indicating direction
recognizes and copies correct direction of numbers and letters

DEVELOPMENTAL OBJECTIVES RELATED TO TEMPORAL AWARENESS

moves own body to various tempos, rhythmic patterns, and intensities
sings and claps rhymes
performs simple folk dances
manipulates objects (tossing and catching) to rhythm or music
combines bouncing, tossing, catching, or juggling to music or rhythm

DEVELOPMENTAL OBJECTIVES RELATED TO KINESTHETIC DISCRIMINATION

makes physical adjustments to one's body in the environment
slows down and speeds up on cue
makes physical adjustments to space by crouching, balancing, stretching
turns left or right without toppling
stops quickly
freezes on command

Developmental Outcome: The child reliably demonstrates well-executed Basic Fundamental Movements: locomotor skills, non-locomotor movements, manipulative abilities, and fine motor movements

DEVELOPMENTAL OBJECTIVES RELATED TO LOCOMOTOR SKILLS

crawls
creeps
walks
runs
jumps
hops
gallops
marches
skips
climbs

DEVELOPMENTAL OBJECTIVES RELATED TO NON-LOCOMOTOR MOVEMENTS

bends
curls
stretches
sways
turns
twists
swings
reaches
lifts
pushes
pulls
twirls

DEVELOPMENTAL OBJECTIVES RELATED TO MANIPULATIVE ABILITIES: PROPULSIVE MOVEMENTS AND ABSORPTIVE MOVEMENTS

Propulsive Movements	Absorptive Movements
rolls	catches
throws	traps
kicks	handles ball smoothly
punts	
strikes	
bounces	
volleys	

DEVELOPMENTAL OBJECTIVES RELATED TO FINE MOTOR MOVEMENTS

moves fingers with dexterity
uses pincer movements
controls hand movements
traces
grasps
crushes
arranges objects
shapes and moulds
fills and pours
bends and folds

Developmental Outcome: The child reliably demonstrates Sensory Perceptual Abilities: visual perception, auditory perception, tactile perception, and olfactory perception

DEVELOPMENTAL OBJECTIVES FOR VISUAL PERCEPTION (VISUAL ACUITY)

discriminates form
perceives depth
discriminates figure from ground

DEVELOPMENTAL OBJECTIVES FOR AUDITORY PERCEPTION (AUDITORY ACUITY)

listens actively
discriminates sounds
responds to sounds
integrates movements and commands

DEVELOPMENTAL OBJECTIVES FOR TACTILE PERCEPTION

identifies objects by touching
describes textures and surfaces according to touch

DEVELOPMENTAL OBJECTIVES FOR OLFACTORY PERCEPTION

identifies objects by smell
detects direction from which odour is coming

Developmental Outcome: The child reliably demonstrates Physical Abilities: physical fitness, motor fitness, and healthy habits and attitudes

DEVELOPMENTAL OBJECTIVES FOR PHYSICAL FITNESS

muscular strength—picks up, pushes, pulls objects
muscular endurance—runs, climbs, plays vigorously for extended time
flexibility—moves gracefully and maintains own space without infringing on others
demonstrates cardiovascular endurance
demonstrates circulatory-respiratory endurance

DEVELOPMENTAL OBJECTIVES FOR MOTOR FITNESS

balances while standing, walking, riding vehicle, climbing
gauges speed relative to environment
shows agility in challenging physical tasks
uses power to speed up, climb, throw
coordinates body parts in space and in context

DEVELOPMENTAL OBJECTIVES FOR HEALTHY HABITS AND ATTITUDES

exercises daily
pursues and enjoys physical activity
chooses and eats healthy food
avoids harmful substances

DEVELOPMENTAL OBJECTIVES FOR SKILLED MOVEMENTS

plays games cooperatively
practises sport-related skills: e.g., bouncing balls, dribbling, kicking, aiming, dodging
practises sporting attitudes and team play

Developmental Outcomes and Objectives for the Cognitive Domain: Everyday Living Concepts, Memory, Cognitive-Perceptual Abilities, Learning-to-Learn Skills, Logical Concepts and Thinking Skills, and Language and Literacy

Developmental Outcome: The child reliably demonstrates Knowledge of Everyday Living Concepts: colour, shape, size, space, time, and family relationships

Note: The developmental outcomes and objectives related to this outcome are grouped together because they reflect basic skills and knowledge that young children need in their daily lives. These concepts contain elements of perceptual, language, and logical-thinking skills and concepts that overlap and blur the boundaries between the domains.

DEVELOPMENTAL OBJECTIVES RELATED TO COLOUR CONCEPT

recognizes/perceives colour
matches colour
labels colour
attaches meaning to colour
sorts objects according to colour
discriminates colour groupings (shades, tones, etc.)
sequences colour by shades/tones in one colour group
uses colour to form patterns

DEVELOPMENTAL OBJECTIVES RELATED TO SHAPE CONCEPT

recognizes/perceives shape
matches shapes
labels geometric shapes
attaches meaning to shape
sorts objects according to shape
alters shapes: creates a new shape from another shape
discriminates imbedded shapes
uses shapes to form patterns
alters shape-retaining outlines, boundaries (topology)

DEVELOPMENTAL OBJECTIVES RELATED TO SIZE CONCEPT

recognizes/perceives size
differentiates sizes (big/little, tall/short, etc.)
matches sizes
uses size labels
attaches meaning to size
orders objects by size
sorts objects by size
seriates objects by size
uses labelling words for size (small, medium, large, etc.)
links size to length, width, height
measures objects, record size, make comparisons

DEVELOPMENTAL OBJECTIVES RELATED TO SPACE CONCEPT

differentiates part/whole
puts things together and takes them apart
observes things from different perspectives
knows words related to position (here/there, in/out)
recognizes relative positions (beside, across from, inside)
moves in space
imitates the movements of others
orients self and others in space
knows words related to direction (over/under, around/through)
locates things in the playroom, school, neighbourhood
recognizes representations of things in pictures
recognizes distances between things

creates things in space (using construction materials or other objects such as boxes, furniture, and blankets)
represents and describes things in terms of position and direction

DEVELOPMENTAL OBJECTIVES RELATED TO TIME CONCEPT

remembers the actions of others over time
recalls events not associated with time
recalls events related to past and present
predicts events
places events in the order in which they happened
associates numbers with time (e.g., the clock face)
knows that time passes in constant and measurable units
estimates amount of time a task will take
uses time well (i.e., plans time)
understands relationship between age and time
understands relationships among speed, distance, and time
tells time (six years)

DEVELOPMENTAL OBJECTIVES RELATED TO RECOGNITION OF FAMILY RELATIONSHIPS

knows one's own family members
knows that one's family is important
recognizes similarities among families
recognizes differences among families (e.g., size, culture, habits, customs)
knows that families live in different ways
knows that one has an immediate family and an extended family
recognizes and labels kinship relationships: e.g., brother, aunt, cousin

Developmental Outcome: The child reliably demonstrates Memory: remembering and recalling events and people, things, facts, and concepts

DEVELOPMENTAL OBJECTIVES RELATED TO REMEMBERING AND RECALLING EVENTS AND PEOPLE

remembers familiar routines
recognizes own belongings and storage places (cubbies)
recalls fieldtrip places and experiences
remembers and names others who participated

DEVELOPMENTAL OBJECTIVES RELATED TO REMEMBERING FACTS AND CONCEPTS

remembers and repeats verbal messages
follows verbal instructions
remembers rules and procedures
remembers where things are stored
recalls what was previously seen or heard from memory

DEVELOPMENTAL OBJECTIVES RELATED TO REMEMBERING SEQUENCES AND ORDER

remembers past events in sequence: short-term, then long-term memory
recalls details and events of stories
repeats simple finger plays, songs, and rhymes or poems from memory
counts in order by one's, five's, ten's, and so on
remembers order in line-ups
role plays remembered events from everyday life
maintains social roles in a sociodramatic play context

Developmental Outcome: The child reliably demonstrates Cognitive-Perceptual Abilities: visual, auditory, tactile, and olfactory and gustatory perception

DEVELOPMENTAL OBJECTIVES RELATED TO VISUAL PERCEPTION

identifies/labels objects
discriminates similarities and differences
matches objects according to observable similarities
classifies objects according to observable similarities
recognizes something after seeing only part of it
perceives small details
concentrates on small details in a visual field

DEVELOPMENTAL OBJECTIVES RELATED TO AUDITORY PERCEPTION

identifies/labels sounds
discriminates similarities and differences
matches similar sounds
classifies sounds
recognizes something after hearing only part of it
concentrates on a sound
interprets sounds
identifies direction from which a sound is coming
links what is heard to its source
differentiates between musical sounds
follows sounds to their source
listens actively
follows verbal instructions

DEVELOPMENTAL OBJECTIVES RELATED TO OLFACTORY AND GUSTATORY PERCEPTION

identifies/labels according to touch, smell, taste
discriminates differences/similarities according to touch, smell, taste
matches according to touch, smell, taste
classifies according to touch, smell, taste
labels odours: e.g., fragrant, highly scented, acrid, sour
labels tastes: sweet, sour, bitter
labels textures: rough, smooth, soft, hard

Developmental Outcome: The child reliably demonstrates Learning-to-Learn Skills: task orientation and attending skills

DEVELOPMENTAL OBJECTIVES RELATED TO TASK ORIENTATION

chooses an activity from alternatives
defines the task
begins the activity
follows through/persists/overcomes obstacles
finishes the activity
communicates that one is finished/reports

DEVELOPMENTAL OBJECTIVES RELATED TO ATTENDING SKILLS

delays gratification
exercises self-control
returns to an activity after an interruption
blocks out distractions
uses resources effectively
voluntarily focuses on an activity when requested to do so by the ECE
uses time well; attends to a task for a reasonable period (attention span)

Developmental Outcome: The child reliably demonstrates a repertoire of developmentally appropriate Logical Concepts and Thinking Skills: seriation and ordering, classification, number concept, and problem solving

DEVELOPMENTAL OBJECTIVES RELATED TO SERIATION AND ORDERING

orders by size
orders by temporal sequence
orders by ordinal relationship: first, second, third
seriates items by adhering to common baseline; in one direction only; equal gradations between juxtaposed items in series
doubles seriation of two sets of objects for which there are equal gradations in size between each ordered item in the series

DEVELOPMENTAL OBJECTIVES RELATED TO CLASSIFICATION

Note: All items to be sorted must fit into one of the classes or sets.
sorts according to one observable attribute
sorts according to two observable attributes
sorts according to knowledge-based attribute(s)
sorts according to abstract attribute(s)
sorts according to hierarchies of classes
sorts random objects according to classes the child determines

DEVELOPMENTAL OBJECTIVES RELATED TO NUMBER CONCEPT

knows sight and sound of numbers (recites)
knows social significance (meaning) of number
labels number symbols

creates sets using one-to-one correspondence
recognizes equal sets
counts accurately and meaningfully (understands quantity)
retains constancy of quantity in spite of properties of objects counted (number constancy)
conserves number (knows that number is constant in spite of changes in the configurations of objects)
performs simple arithmetic operations using number, e.g., adds, subtracts

DEVELOPMENTAL OBJECTIVES RELATED TO SOLVING SIMPLE PROBLEMS

links cause and effect
makes comparisons and draws conclusions
anticipates and thinks ahead (plan)
estimates number/amount/comparative sizes
develops creative thinking skills (i.e., originality, flexibility, elaboration)
predicts/estimates probability
tries alternative methods to solve a problem
overcomes obstacles in a task
asks questions; uses resource persons effectively
communicates/reports what one has done

Developmental Outcome: The child reliably demonstrates Language and Literacy Skills: symbol perception; ocular-motor skills; sound perception; receptive language; expressive language; linking language and physical abilities; using language creatively; appreciating language; socialized speech; reading simple words, phrases, and sentences; printing letters, numbers, name, and words

DEVELOPMENTAL OBJECTIVES RELATED TO SYMBOL PERCEPTION (RECOGNIZING AND LABELLING OBJECTS, NUMBERS, ETC.)

recognizes abstract shapes and symbols
discriminates letter symbols
identifies/labels letters
remembers pictures/symbols
reproduces correct directional positioning of letter and number symbols

DEVELOPMENTAL OBJECTIVES RELATED TO OCULAR-MOTOR SKILLS (CONTROLLING THE MOVEMENTS OF THE EYES)

focuses: near/far objects, adjusting focus accordingly (accommodation)
holds eyes steadily on one object in a field and then moves on command to another object (fixation)
follows a moving target with the eyes (pursuit)
moves eyes together in left-to-right direction across a page, poster, or screen in a series of smooth saccades (tracking)
scans a page to pick up an object or a word (e.g., Where's Waldo?)

DEVELOPMENTAL OBJECTIVES RELATED TO SOUND PERCEPTION (LISTENING AND IDENTIFYING SOUNDS)

identifies gross sounds
identifies less obvious sounds/tones
recognizes significant phonemes in words
links sound to its source
differentiates syllables: knows that words are made of distinguishable sounds
claps according to syllables in words
knows that beginning sounds are the first ones we say in a word
knows that ending sounds are the last ones we say in a word
recognizes words with similar beginning and ending sounds
uses words that rhyme (e.g., fish, dish)
imitates sounds

DEVELOPMENTAL OBJECTIVES RELATED TO RECEPTIVE LANGUAGE (LISTENING AND HEARING ACCURATELY)

listens actively/attends
differentiates consonant sounds and blends
understands the speech of others
follows one-, two-, and three-step verbal instructions

DEVELOPMENTAL OBJECTIVES RELATED TO EXPRESSIVE LANGUAGE

labels concrete objects
uses words in correct context (meanings of words)
uses language that others can understand
combines words into sentences
links words and phrases into longer passages
delivers messages accurately
describes events
tells a story

DEVELOPMENTAL OBJECTIVES RELATED TO LINKING LANGUAGE AND PHYSICAL ABILITIES

speaks while physically active (describes actions)
uses words that describe physical actions or sensations
follows verbal instructions in physical activities
represents a verbal instruction physically
pantomimes stories or experiences

DEVELOPMENTAL OBJECTIVES RELATED TO USING LANGUAGE CREATIVELY

uses descriptive words
describes experiences verbally
plays with words: rhymes, nonsense rhymes, riddles
uses words to convince/persuade/influence
recites chants
uses words in song
makes up new words
learns words from other languages

uses words associated with feelings
uses props to enhance and support language
tells stories

DEVELOPMENTAL OBJECTIVES RELATED TO APPRECIATING LANGUAGE

chooses favourite words
finds new words in stories and rhymes
matches similar words according to sound and other properties
repeats favourite stories, rhymes
experiments with other languages and modes of communication (e.g., pantomime)
experiments with creative elements of language (e.g., cacophony, onomatopoeia, alliteration, simile, metaphor)

DEVELOPMENTAL OBJECTIVES RELATED TO SOCIALIZED SPEECH

articulates clearly: pronounce correctly
asks and responds to questions
engages in conversation
observes pragmatics of conversation: speaks in turn, listens to speaker, responds to others

DEVELOPMENTAL OBJECTIVES RELATED TO READING SIMPLE WORDS, PHRASES, AND SENTENCES

recognizes own printed name
recognizes familiar words/names in print
reads simple signs
reads directions in computer software programs
tells stories from illustrations in books
reads simple stories

DEVELOPMENTAL OBJECTIVES RELATED TO PRINTING LETTERS, NUMBERS, NAME, AND WORDS

traces letters, numbers, and other symbols
copies symbols/words on computer screen using mouse or drawing pad
prints own name
prints letters and numbers
prints simple words

Developmental Outcome: The child demonstrates the ability to Think Divergently and to Create

DEVELOPMENTAL OBJECTIVES RELATED TO THINKING DIVERGENTLY

appreciates characteristics that are harmonious and beautiful
tries several ways to solve a problem or find an answer
uses resources effectively: seeks resources from adults, other children, books, and computers
represents objects and events in novel ways

Developmental Outcome: The child demonstrates the ability to Question and Inquire

DEVELOPMENTAL OBJECTIVES RELATED TO QUESTIONING AND INQUIRING

asks "why" questions
looks for alternative ways and answers
seeks new approaches to using materials, resources
asks "what if" questions; hypothesizes what might happen "if"

Developmental Outcome: The child demonstrates the ability to Experiment and Test

DEVELOPMENTAL OBJECTIVES RELATED TO EXPERIMENTING AND TESTING

uses trial and error as method to find answers
asks new questions to get closer to desired answers
seeks alternative solutions to problems
tests solutions and answers to determine accuracy
tests hypotheses in response to the "what if" questions

Appendix B

Learning Environment Audit

Where applicable, answer Y for Yes or N for No in the boxes provided.

1. **Pathways**
   - ☐ Are pathways clear at points of entry?
   - ☐ Are pathways visible from child's eye level?
   - ☐ Are pathways well defined and unobstructed?
   - ☐ Are learning centres separate from one another?
   - ☐ Do pathways reach all learning centres?
   - ☐ Do pathways allow for access to learning centres by children with disabilities?
   - ☐ Do pathways lead children into and out of learning centres?
   - ☐ Are learning centres clearly visible from major pathways?

2. **Use of Space**
   - ☐ Is more than 2/3 of the surface covered (tightly organized space)?
   - ☐ Is less than 1/2 of the surface covered (loosely organized space)?
   - ☐ Is there any dead space (large amount of empty space roughly square or circular in shape without any visible or tangible boundaries)?
   - ☐ Is there enough space around each play unit?
   - ☐ Is there space for a potential unit (empty space surrounded by visible or tangible boundaries)?
   - ☐ Are the three major zones for play clearly visible—e.g., concept learning, role play, creative/discovery?

3. **Location and Design of the Learning Centres**
   - ☐ Have learning centres addressing similar developmental objectives and styles of play been juxtaposed?
   - ☐ Are the learning centres compatible with the intention of the zones for play?
   - ☐ Is there a visible separation between neat and messy learning centres?
   - ☐ Do the space and resources dedicated to each learning centre reflect the goals and developmental outcomes of the program?
   - ☐ Are the limits for play in each learning centre clarified (e.g., using signs or pictures) and understood and observed by children?

4. **Contents of Play Space**

Variety

- ☐ Are all categories/styles and social contexts of play available and facilitated for children in the learning environment?
- ☐ Is there a disproportionate amount of any one kind of thing to do?
- ☐ Does the variety of the play units address the interests and developmental needs of the children individually and collectively?

Complexity

Identify the number of

simple units (? × 1 play place) = ______

complex units (? × 4 play places) = ____

super units (? × 6 or 8 play places) = ____

- ☐ Calculate the total number of play places (i.e., add totals above). ______
- ☐ Identify the number of children usually playing in the learning environment. ______
- ☐ Calculate the complexity of the play and learning environment (i.e., divide the total number of play places by the number of children playing in the learning environment). ____ (Complexity = amount to do per child.)
- ☐ Is the proportion of things to do per child within the ranges deemed acceptable for the age group (i.e., 1–2 years = five to six play places; 3–4 years = three to four play places; 5–6 years = two to three play places)?

Is there a need for:

- ☐ more simple units?
- ☐ more complex units?
- ☐ more super units?

☐ Is there a need to combine units?

How many and what play units can be added to each learning centre to raise the total number of play places?

- ☐ Daily Living ______
- ☐ Active Role Play ______
- ☐ Quiet Thinking ______
- ☐ Science Discovery ______
- ☐ Projects ______
- ☐ Unit Blocks ______
- ☐ Creative Arts ______
- ☐ Total number of additional play units? ______

Calculate revised complexity using this formula: total number of play places divided by number of children normally playing in the learning environment equals the complexity or amount to do per child.

[Complexity = number of play places per child ______]

5. Noise

- ☐ Can noisy and quiet activities take place without disruption?
- ☐ Is the space organized into zones for quiet play and zones for noisy play?
- ☐ Is a washable carpet used in the unit block area?

6. Orderliness

- ☐ Is the space organized so that areas for tidy play and messy play are separate?
- ☐ Is the learning environment simple and easy to maintain?
- ☐ Does the environment convey a sense of order and organization?
- ☐ Are storage units located close to learning centres where supplies and materials will be used?
- ☐ Are materials and supplies visible and accessible to children?
- ☐ Are stored items neatly labelled and numbered to encourage the return of items to their own spots?
- ☐ Do storage units and general organization of space convey the message to children that materials and supplies should be returned to their proper spot so they are ready for use by another child?
- ☐ Does the storage space emphasize the aesthetic quality of the play materials and supplies?
- ☐ Does the environment provide cues as to where materials and supplies should be used (e.g., wet or messy materials stored near tiled floor)?
- ☐ Are there inaccessible storage spaces available for securing certain supplies, unsafe articles, and the ECEs' personal belongings?
- ☐ Is there an effective balance of stationary and mobile storage units?

7. Aesthetic Appeal and Comfort

Aesthetics

- ☐ Does the environment contain a variety of contours, textures, and natural as well as manufactured materials?

- ☐ Is the environment attractive at the child's eye level?
- ☐ Is children's artwork neatly displayed on special bulletin boards at children's eye level?
- ☐ Are beautiful works of artists hung at children's eye level?

Texture

- ☐ Are textured fabrics, seasonal plant and floral arrangements, and other textured furnishings and artifacts (table coverings, curtains, quilts, wall hangings) present or displayed to attract children's attention and develop their aesthetic appreciation?
- ☐ Is washable carpeting used judiciously to soften noise, vary textures, and promote play on the floor?
- ☐ Are natural materials, such as wood, cork, wicker, or cane, used to balance the manufactured building materials?

Colour

- ☐ Are colours used to decorate space?
- ☐ Is colour used to highlight children's work?
- ☐ Are the colours pleasing to the eye and conducive to relaxation in some areas and stimulation in others?
- ☐ Have colours been chosen to influence play and learning behaviour?
- ☐ Does the environment make use of colours familiar to various cultures?

Diversity and Inclusion

- ☐ Does the area provide a relaxed and warm climate for play and learning for all children?
- ☐ Do ECEs try to use common words of the child's home language?
- ☐ Do the learning centres include play materials from various cultures?
- ☐ Does the environment include culturally relevant dress-up clothing, implements, art, decorations, and foods?
- ☐ Is the home language of the children reflected in posters and other print materials in the classroom?
- ☐ Are children encouraged to learn and use words from a language other than English?

Does the space include

- ☐ pictures and artifacts from various cultures all the time?
- ☐ familiar reminders of children's home environments?
- ☐ labels on familiar objects written in the child's home language?

Is the environment

- ☐ efficient and functional?
- ☐ clean?
- ☐ easy to maintain?
- ☐ accessible to all children?

Lighting

- ☐ Has the use of standard fluorescent lighting been reduced as much as possible?
- ☐ Have incandescent and full-spectrum fluorescent lighting been used to ensure higher health, comfort, and aesthetic quality standards?
- ☐ Has lighting been chosen to highlight and enhance the nature of play in specific areas?
- ☐ Is the lighting easy to regulate?
- ☐ Do children have access to windows at their eye level?
- ☐ Are there enough natural light sources?
    - ☐ Is there sufficient natural light in the classroom?
    - ☐ Are the seating areas at tables in the learning centres placed as close as possible to windows to take advantage of natural light?
    - ☐ Do the lighting fixtures enhance the aesthetic quality of the classroom?

8. Play and Learning Climate

- ☐ Is a sociomoral atmosphere that cultivates respect and empathy for others evident in the setting?

- ☐ Do the developmental outcomes and the activities set up for each learning centre appear to be compatible?
- ☐ Does the environment encourage focused play and make it seem important to be involved and to participate?
- ☐ Do the children's play styles and behaviours correspond with the messages intended by the arrangement of play stations, activities and resources available in the learning centres?
- ☐ Does the environment discourage flitting about and mindless roaming?
- ☐ Does the environment promote imaginative play that encourages thoughtfulness, reflection, and wonder?
- ☐ Do the pathways lead to choices of play activities?
- ☐ Is there a balance of areas for individual and group-oriented play?
- ☐ Do the learning centres have an identity of their own (i.e., are they defined by dividers or storage units)?
- ☐ Can children and adults see from one area to another in the playroom, yet still have some privacy?
- ☐ Is there a balance of clearly indicated space for active and quiet play?
- ☐ Are there sufficient workspaces (i.e., tables and chairs) for children to play comfortably either individually or with others?
- ☐ Do the learning centres succeed in organizing equipment, materials, and supplies so children understand what is expected of them in each learning centre?
- ☐ Is the physical environment sufficiently organized and under control, so ECEs can maximize the amount of time they have to observe children and facilitate play and learning (i.e., the closer the number of play places to the number of children playing, the greater the demands on the ECE to intervene and direct children's play)?
- ☐ Does the learning centre provide opportunities for children to make real choices among activities?
    - ☐ Daily Living?
    - ☐ Active Role Play?
    - ☐ Science Discovery?
    - ☐ Quiet Thinking?
    - ☐ Creative Arts?
    - ☐ Projects?
    - ☐ Unit Blocks?

9. Factors to Avoid

- ☐ Is there too much sun?
- ☐ Is there too little natural light?
- ☐ Are the equipment, materials, and supplies broken or shabby?
- ☐ Is the equipment size inappropriate for children?
- ☐ Is the temperature uncomfortable for children at play?
- ☐ Does one bright colour predominate in furniture, flooring, or wall design?

10. Necessary Features

- ☐ Is there easy access to the washrooms?
- ☐ Is there easy access to outdoor play from the indoor playroom?
- ☐ Does the outdoor play area foster close contact between the child and naturally occurring objects such as trees, plants, grass, earth, rocks, and loose materials such as branches, leaves, stones?
- ☐ Are non-toxic plants used to decorate and soften the environment?
- ☐ Are all learning centres visible to ECEs from all areas of the learning environment?

Glossary

accommodation:
(1) the revision that takes place when children alter their existing mental structures to fit what they already know with the new learning or experience that challenges their present understanding; (2) a visual perceptual skill, namely, the ability of the eye to make adjustments to focus on objects at a distance and then objects close at hand, i.e., near–far focusing adjustment.

accountability:
acceptance of one's responsibility for one's choices, decisions, and actions.

action schema:
organized sets of action memories related to physical actions or patterns of actions that are stored in the brain; involves the integration of dynamics (weight, time, flow) and space (size, extension, zone, direction, level, pathways, and patterns).

action schemas:
organized sets of action memories related to physical actions or patterns of actions that are stored in the brain.

activity-centred methods:
direct teaching or supervision by an adult to ensure children's safety and success with the activity, in which a specific outcome is intended.

activity:
an event circumscribed by a time frame, context, or specific setting that includes materials that may be used flexibly or whose use is prescribed. ECEs may plan activities or children may initiate them. Activities address developmental objectives that describe the purposeful nature of the planned activity.

adventure playground:
a playground design that originated in Europe in the 1950s and 1960s and incorporated a "back to nature" focus and discarded building materials that could be used for constructive play.

aerobic capacity:
capacity of the lungs to consume oxygen and increase cardiovascular fitness.

aesthetic appreciation:
a taste for quality and an appreciation of harmony in art that develops most readily in a beautiful environment.

aesthetic development:
an evolving awareness of the beauty of the environment and a sensitivity to the relationship between beauty in its various forms and the emotional responses these forms elicit.

affective climate:
the prevailing emotional and social mood and tone of the environment, usually determined by the degree of healthy interactions, warmth, nurturing, and mutual respect.

affective development:
the social and emotional development of the child.

agility:
ease and grace of physical movement.

artifact:
a product of human art and workmanship, or a reproduction or replica.

assessment reports:
synthesize the information gathered through the assessment process and the analysis of this information, which is then used to make decisions and recommendations contained in the reports.

assessment:
a systematic procedure for gathering and examining evidence of children's developmental progress that relies on observation records, parental input, ECEs perceptions, and other input.

assimilation:
the change that children make in an object, event, or phenomenon to try to fit a new learning experience into existing mental structures.

associative play:
loosely organized play in which children participate in similar activities but do not subordinate their individual interests to those of the group.

attention deficit hyperactivity disorder (ADHD):
a childhood disorder that is applicable only to children who have been diagnosed by professionals as having a persistent attention deficit and hyperactivity for at least six months.

attention deficit:
a condition frequently associated with children with learning disabilities but applicable to any child who has difficulty on a regular basis with staying on task, paying attention, or staying with an activity for a reasonable length of time.

attention span:
the amount of time a child will attend to a task or activity, assuming that it is interesting to the child.

auditory discrimination:
the ability to hear differences and similarities in sounds and tones.

auditory-motor integration:
the ability to move the body according to sounds on command of the auditory stimulus.

authentic assessment:
an assessment of a child's learning based on a comparison to practical and real-world situations; often undertaken in the context of instruction or discovery learning. Outcomes and achievement are measured as closely as possible to the style or the way in which the child learned.

autism:
a severe childhood condition that involves a degree of withdrawal from the world, cognitive impairments, inability to interact in social situations, inappropriate affect, strong need for a predictable environment, and self-stimulation. The concept of a spectrum of autistic behaviour has been developed that describes the degree to which children exhibit autistic behaviours.

autonomy:
ability to carry out a task or a set of tasks independently; ability to follow a set of directions and complete a task with little direct supervision.

axon:
a long fibre that extends from the cell body of the neuron that carries messages away from the cell body to other cells.

back to basics:
a grassroots movement by schools, usually supported by the public, as a result of declining test scores, to return to a basic curriculum with emphasis on reading, writing, and arithmetic and traditional teacher-directed, inputs-based teaching methods.

balance:
a state of bodily equilibrium that includes static balance (maintain one's equilibrium while motionless) and dynamic balance (maintain equilibrium while body is moving).

behavioural science:
the scientific study of human behaviour that dominated the early 20th century; originated with Watson, Thorndike, and Skinner.

behaviourist learning approach:
manipulating the conditions in which teaching is conducted in order to produce prescribed learning that is culturally transmitted; this theoretical school believes that an individual's behaviour is determined by environmental influences that can be modified and managed by controlling external stimuli.

benchmark activities:
activities earmarked in the curriculum as benchmarks and reference points for assessment that allow teachers to determine whether or not children have achieved specific developmental objectives, leading to the outcomes.

benchmarks:
activities or other indicators that describe incremental steps toward the achievement of developmental outcomes.

callisthenics:
gymnastic exercises to achieve bodily fitness and grace of movement.

cardiovascular stamina:
strength and endurance capacities related to the heart and blood vessels.

categories of play:
terms that describe the styles in which children play alone and together and with materials; e.g., functional play, symbolic play, constructive play, games with rules play.

centration:
the tendency of preoperational children to attend to one aspect of a situation/ object to the exclusion of others.

cerebral palsy:
a non-progressive disorder of the central nervous system that affects motor functioning and performance.

child-centred learning:
an educational approach in which the curriculum and the methods for helping children learn are designed and implemented in direct relation to the interests, abilities, stages of development, and needs of individual children.

child-initiated method:
a teaching method that allows children to decide which activities they will be involved in, what materials they will use, and how they will use them.

classical theories:
theories that tried to describe why children play; includes the surplus energy theory, the relaxation theory, the pre-exercise theory, and the recapitulation theory. These theories prevailed in the 17th to late 19th centuries.

classification:
the ability to group objects according to one or more similar attributes that either the teacher or the child defines or selects.

class inclusion:
the understanding that a subordinate class must always be smaller than the super-ordinate class in which it is contained, e.g., cats/animals; food/vegetables.

climate:
the affective (social and emotional) conditions that contribute to the mood or tone prevalent in an environment.

cognitive development:
the child's intellectual and cognitive perceptual development as it relates to processing input.

cognitive developmental theory:
theory that emerged initially from the epistemology of Jean Piaget in the 20th century that investigates children's development of mental structures; the building of intelligence; and knowledge and conceptual understanding related to memory, reasoning, logic, language, perception, symbolic and representational thinking, moral and spiritual understanding, and metacognition.

cognitive flexibility:
a term that describes the executive function of shifting attention between two competing tasks.

cognitive skills:
refers to skills related to cognitive development.

collage materials:
supplies such as small pieces of paper, cloth, wood, foil, and other products used to create a collage.

collage:
a form of art, and the creation of an artistic product, in which various materials are arranged and assembled or glued to a backing; in a broader sense, a collage refers to a collection or grouping involving the juxtaposition of things to create a work of art.

competitive play:
play in which two or more children in a group, or two or more groups of children, compete to win.

complex unit:
a simple play unit with sub-parts, or a juxtaposition of two essentially different play materials, that enables the child to manipulate or improvise. Four play spaces are attributed to a complex unit.

complexity:
the measure of the capacity of the learning environment to keep children interested for a reasonable time. Complexity is calculated by determining the potential of each play unit for active participation by one or more children.

concept formation:
the learning process involved in being able to classify or order ideas or things according to the principles that compose the concept.

concept learning zone:
an area of the playroom that places close together learning centres and play stations that encourage children to play alone and work individually on play activities that require attending skills, concentration, and individual mastery of concepts and skills.

concept:
an idea or an understanding of the relationships that exist among objects, people, or events.

conceptual understanding:
the ability to understand a relationship that exists in the absence of the physical proof or concrete demonstration of the relationship.

concrete operational period:
the developmental stage in which children have the ability to apply simple logic to solve problems, and to perform simple mathematical operations using numerals, by relying on concrete objects. This period applies to children between the ages of seven and eleven or twelve.

concrete operational thought:
thought that involves the ability to reason logically in the presence of the concrete objects; this stage is common among children from ages 7 to 12.

condensation:
the reduction of gas or a solid to a liquid.

configuration:
an arrangement of parts or elements in a particular form or figure; a form or shape resulting from this arrangement.

conservation of number:
the ability to understand that the quantity or number of objects in a set remains the same in spite of transformations or changes in the configuration of the set.

conservation:
the ability to know that changes in the perceptual features of objects do not alter their number, quantity, volume, or equality.

constellations:
a group of associated persons, ideas, or images.

constructive play:
productive play in which children interact with materials in ways that produce results the child intends.

constructivist theory:
theory that children construct their own understanding through active interaction with concrete objects. Planning learning environments and activities for play that build on what children already know facilitates children's understanding and moves them a step further. Children understand a concept when they are able to transfer the learning acquired in one context to another context.

contents:
the play units available within the play space.

continuous materials:
free-form substances, including surface-diffusible types such as earth, sand, clay, and water, that are often used for construction purposes, as in building sand castles.

conventional knowledge:
refers to social-conventional knowledge that is learned largely through cultural transmission and experience in society (see *social-conventional knowledge*).

convergent activities:
refers to play activities that are structured in the sense that the materials involved in the activity lead children to achieve a predetermined outcome; e.g., solving a jigsaw puzzle, assembling a Lego kit, fitting shapes into a formboard.

convergent materials:
materials with similar structural or physiological characteristics under similar environmental conditions; materials that come together from several diverse points toward a common point, conclusion, or opinion.

convergent thinking:
sometimes referred to as nondivergent thinking, it is the ability to think deductively by reasoning from the general to the specific, rather than inductively from the specific to the general.

cooperative games:
games in which the players strive together to achieve a common, shared result; games characterized by sharing, supporting one another, desiring a shared successful outcome.

cooperative play:
group social play involving children with common goals who assume different roles or tasks. Play often persists for a long time and at high levels of complexity.

cortex:
the outer part of the brain, also referred to as the cerebral cortex.

crafts:
activities that involve handiwork and skill based on practice in which a model or a pattern is copied; crafts are differentiated from creative arts, which involve original thinking and composition.

creative development:
an aspect of human development that describes the ability to innovate, be original, create things, and evolve ideas or solve problems in unique ways by using the imagination, focusing on the challenge, and exercising discipline in execution of an idea and a plan.

creative discovery zone:
a zone in the playroom dedicated to learning centres and play stations that promote creative development.

creative-constructive play:
play in which children interact with the play materials for their own purposes, often without any plan or strategy, to produce a specific outcome, usually a product.

creativity:
involves perceiving things in new ways, thinking unconventionally, forming unique combinations, and representing an original idea or insight. It is not a flash of inspiration but a deliberate, purposeful activity directed toward representing an idea or insight using a creative medium.

critical thinking:
the ability to analyze situations and ideas using logic and reasoning skills.

Cuisenaire rods:
precise, metric, colour-coded rods designed by Jean Cuisenaire to help children learn mathematical concepts through informal mathematical experiences and to assist children in transferring intuitive concepts to formal mathematical thinking.

cultural diversity:
a context in which there are individuals whose cultural heritage is different from the mainstream culture and/or different from each other; a multiplicity of cultures coexisting in a larger context.

cultural icon:
an image, a statue, a symbol, or some other object that stands as a representative symbol of something and usually has at least one characteristic in common with that which it represents.

culture:
the ethnicity, racial identity, economic level, family structure, language, religion, and political beliefs that profoundly influence children's development and relationship to the world (NAEYC, 2005).

curriculum design:
the deliberate, informed choice of intentions that include outcomes and objectives, strategies to address the intentions, and ways to determine whether the intentions have been fulfilled.

curriculum framework:
a scheme or structure that organizes the tasks, sequences the steps, suggests strategies, identifies resources needed, and describes the goals and the intended outcomes for a curriculum

curriculum web:
a planning tool that describes graphically the various topics, questions, and activities that may be associated with a broad theme or a subject of inquiry for play and learning

curriculum:
a system of intentions and plans to promote development and learning that is based on an educational philosophy; a formal structure, usually written down, that sets out the relationships among the various curriculum components, such as the goals, outcomes, objectives, activities, resources, methods, assessment, and evaluation.

dead space:
a large amount of empty space roughly square or circular in shape, often in the centre of a room or play area, with no visible boundaries.

decentre:
in cognitive developmental terms, the ability to focus on more than one attribute or property of an object at a time.

decentred pretend:
the ability to entertain multiple perspectives and to see the role and relationship of others to the script or plot of the role play.

decontextualized language:
language pared down to the words themselves, without intonation, gesture, or facial expression; conveys meaning independently of context.

deduction:
reasoning from general concept to specific application.

depth perception:
ability to judge relative distances in three-dimensional space.

developmental curriculum:
a framework for a coherent set of play activities and learning experiences related to the normal tasks of development that articulates the relationships among its various components.

developmental domains:
areas of development dominated by the child's cognitive, physical, social, and emotional capacities.

developmental goals:
long-term intentions or inputs to the curriculum that are derived from assessment reports and the interests and priorities of children, their parents, ECEs, and community stakeholders.

developmental objectives:
short descriptions of observable skills, knowledge, concepts or behaviours that describe the stepping stones that lead children incrementally towards the achievement of developmental outcomes.

developmental outcomes:
statements that describe the desired results to be achieved by children over time based on a curriculum. Outcomes usually describe complex, verifiable performances that are reliable, and that include the integration of several skills, such as the ability to ride a tricycle, skip a rope, or achieve number concept.

developmental skills:
describe the wide range of developmental abilities in all four domains—physical, emotional, social, cognitive—that together describe holistic human development.

developmental tasks:
abilities/skills that children normally acquire at specific stages in their development, such as the ability to focus on the task at hand, to tie their shoelaces, or to coordinate body movements.

developmental theories:
research-driven approaches based on standards or norms typical of normal development that are believed to occur in a sequential manner that is not necessarily age-related.

developmentally appropriate practice (DAP):
a US-based movement that began in 1987 that includes assessing children's

development and learning, designing appropriate curriculum, teaching and facilitating play to enhance development and learning, supporting a caring community of learners, and establishing reciprocal relationships with families.

didactic teaching:
instruction that is structured, circumscribed, and absorbed in details, in that it does not stray from formal rules or literal meanings, sometimes at the expense of wider perspectives.

direct method:
a teaching method normally associated with formal learning that involves teacher-led instruction, teacher-centred or teacher-as-leader techniques, teacher-as-model, or teacher demonstration strategies.

discovery learning:
an approach to learning in which children develop an understanding of concepts or knowledge through first-hand interaction with the environment.

discovery-oriented method:
a teaching method that encourages exploration and hands-on sensory play through manipulation of materials and examination of their properties in order to uncover concepts.

disposition for learning:
an approach to learning that is fuelled by interest, motivation, questioning, curiosity, persistence, resourcefulness, and self-regulation.

disposition:
a general inclination to approach and to think about a task or challenge in a particular way.

distance-from-self criterion:
a criterion first described by Besse Gene Holt that determines the relevance of including science concepts and topics in preschool curriculum according to the relevance of the concept in the daily lives of children; the criterion suggests that topics that are closest to the child in time and space are most readily understood.

divergent activities:
activities that encourage children to try a variety of possible approaches and solutions related to a task or problem and achieve a variety of possible conclusions.

divergent materials:
materials that are flexible in terms of how they are used and what children can achieve with them; e.g., arts materials, blocks, loose materials.

divergent thinking:
the process of proceeding in a variety of directions from a single idea; the ability to see many possible solutions to a problem.

dramatic play area:
this learning centre supports symbolic play, from pretend play to more sophisticated sociodramatic play and sociodrama. It is the area of the playroom that is most like the home environments of young children.

dramatic play:
sustained pretend play in which one child persists in acting out a role using gestures, props, or movement.

duration:
the length of time something takes.

dynamic theories:
modern theories of play, which largely replaced the classical theories in the 20th century and include two main categories: psychoanalytic theories and developmental theories.

dynamics:
the motive forces—physical, social, or moral—affecting behaviour and change in any sphere.

early childhood curriculum:
an outline of the goals, developmental outcomes, and developmental objectives that are determined by ECEs and parents for a group of children, and the related activities, learning experiences, teaching and learning methods, assessment methods, and evaluation.

early primary years:
kindergarten to grade three.

ecological intelligence:
the ability to understand the relationships among living organisms and their physical surroundings.

ecology:
the study of the relationships among living things and the environments in which they exist.

economic performance:
the outcome of activities and analysis related to costs, spending, and revenue in the context of organizations, nations, or other jurisdictions.

ecosystem:
a biological community of interacting organisms and their physical environment.

egocentricity:
state of understanding the self as the centre of all experience, with everything being considered only in relation to the self.

emergent curriculum:
uses the developmental curriculum as the framework for planning programs and assessing and evaluating children's progress; includes activities based on the interests of children and pursues themes and ideas that are negotiated among the ECEs and children.

emergent literacy:
a set of skills, knowledge and attitudes necessary for formal reading and writing and the environment that supports these attributes.

emotional intelligence:
the ability to understand and describe the feelings felt by oneself and by others and to express emotion in appropriate ways.

empathy:
the act of identifying oneself mentally and emotionally with another living being that is related to a feeling of connection with humanity; ability to put oneself mentally in the shoes of another person.

empowering:
to provide or equip with the means, opportunity, permission, and skills needed for independence and self-assertion.

empowerment:
the sense of being equipped and permitted to act independently and make one's own choices.

enactive mode:
a stage of development, usually under the age of 18 months, proposed by psychologist Jerome Bruner, whereby the infant comprehends his world through actions and the senses.

endurance:
muscular or physical endurance is the ability to perform a movement task over an extended period of time as in skipping rope, push-ups, several times in succession.

epistemology:
the branch of philosophy that deals with the nature of knowledge and how we obtain knowledge and understanding.

equilibration:
the motivational factor for learning that occurs as a result of the joint processes of assimilation and accommodation; the attempt to find a balance between one's cognitive schemes and information obtained from the environment; in Piaget's theory, the movement from equilibrium to disequilibrium and back to equilibrium by using one's existing schemes.

equipment:
the furniture, storage containers, and large items of play equipment that are often used to define the boundaries of a learning centre and to denote the type of play that is encouraged there.

equipping:
helping young children develop the abilities they need to function optimally and to gain power over their own actions, choices, and destinies.

Euclidean properties:
the spatial and geometric properties of objects in ordinary experience such as space, size, position, direction, and movement.

evaluation:
the systematic appraisal of the effectiveness of a series of activities, a program, or a curriculum in promoting developmental progress and helping children achieve developmental outcomes.

executive function:
abilities that manage attention, emotions and behaviours in order to reach goals; they involve the ability to integrate feelings and thinking and include working memory, cognitive flexibility, and inhibition.

existential intelligence:
a type of intelligence proposed by Howard Gardner whereby a person is capable of balancing abstract questions related to the larger questions and meaning of life.

experiential learning:
learning by doing, hands-on learning, or learning through experience in authentic contexts.

exploratory methods:
teaching strategies that encourage children to explore with their senses, to touch, engage in hands-on play; similar to discovery-oriented methods.

exploratory play:
play that encourages children to explore with their senses, to manipulate and use their senses to find meaning.

facilitator:
a person whose role is to make something easier for others to do, say, think, or feel.

fantasy play:
a form of symbolic play in which children pretend to be characters and recreate events through dramatic play that they have gathered from stories, television programs, rhymes, and verse.

figure from ground:
a perceptual skill that allows the observer to select a limited number of stimuli from a visual field or mass; in some contexts, the figure and the field may keep changing.

figure–ground relationships:
the relationship between a selected object (the figure) and a visual field or mass (the ground) on which the figure is situated; the relationship may change, as when a bird flies through the sky.

fine motor skills:
the use of the fingers and hands in tasks that require manipulation of objects. These skills may also include hand–eye and foot coordination.

fixation:
ability of both eyes to look simultaneously and accurately from one given target to another.

flexibility:
ability to bend, adapt to circumstance, yield to influence, and change direction.

formal education:
educational setting and prescription for learning that has been most common in grades 4 to 12, which includes formal learning methods associated with the academic approach such as teacher-led instruction, standardized curriculum, testing, and measurement.

formal learning:
learning that usually occurs in the structured contexts of a school and involves the acquisition of knowledge and academic skills; it usually begins when the child is about six or seven.

formative evaluation:
an evaluation approach that emphasizes assessment and constructive feedback that is intended to guide and improve performance.

free play:
play in which children make their own choices and decisions and are free to express their own feelings and representations in play.

free-form materials:
surface-diffusible materials that flow rather than fit together to make the whole.

freedom versus structure debate:
a 20th-century debate between proponents of unfettered "free play" and those who

favoured the introduction of some structured activities in the early childhood play-based curriculum.

functional play:
simple, repetitive movements with or without concrete objects; usually dominant during the sensorimotor period; usually found in the play of infants and toddlers, who explore objects physically, using their senses.

fundamental movements:
these are physical movements that usually involve motor coordination and locomotor and non-locomotor skills.

games-with-rules play:
play in which children begin to accept certain external limitations on their play, such as rules made by someone else. Children also begin to make their own rules and to question existing rules.

gender roles:
conventional expectations of the roles and obligations attributed to males and females.

gender stereotypes:
specific behaviours conventionally attributed to either males or females such as men wear overalls, women cook the meals.

genetic epistemology:
the experimental study of the development of knowledge that was originated by Jean Piaget.

goals:
broad aims that are usually grounded in values and beliefs and lead to actions.

gradation:
a gradual transition from one stage or rank to the next, usually involving uniform steps in grades of size from one item in a series to the next item.

grapheme:
a class of letters representing a unit of sound.

graphic development:
the development of the ability to use and create graphic illustrations using tools, such as pens, crayons, chalk, and pencil.

graphic materials:
tools that are used to create graphic illustrations or representations, such as drawings, signs, outlines, and diagrams using pens, pencils, chalk, paints, and crayons.

graphic representation:
the ability to represent an idea, object, or event using graphic materials.

guide:
an aspect of the teaching role in which the ECE helps the child make the most of the play and learning environment.

habitat:
the natural environment characteristically occupied by an organism.

habits of mind:
a customary way of perceiving and thinking that can be predicted.

hands-on learning:
activity in which children learn largely through their active, physical interaction with concrete objects in the environment.

heredity versus environment controversy:
a 20th-century academic controversy characterized by opposing arguments related to whether the environment or genetic inheritance has the greatest influence on human development

heredity:
the passing on of physical or mental characteristics genetically from one generation to another.

home language:
the language usually spoken in the home of the child.

horizontal and vertical grid patterns:
a framework of spaced parallel bars that are both vertical (at right angles or perpendicular to the plane of the horizon) and horizontal (parallel to the plane of the horizon and at right angles to the vertical).

human capital:
the value or assets of a nation as measured by the competence, integrity, and virtue of its people.

hyperactivity:
higher than normal levels of expected physical activity.

hypothesis:
an educated guess or proposed relationship between events that are either observed or imagined.

iconic mode:
a stage of development, usually between about 18 months and 5 or 6 years, proposed by psychologist Jerome Bruner, whereby the child views the world in concrete images, thereby believing that what she sees must be true and real.

imitative play:
an early form of symbolic play that begins during the first year of life and refers to the child's simple imitation of the parent or other caregiver.

implementation strategies:
the design of environments, the choice of equipment, materials and supplies for play, planned activities, experiences and projects that are linked to the developmental objectives and the outcomes.

inclusive practice:
in narrow terms, the practice of integrating children with special needs into regular classrooms; in broader terms, practice that aims to recognize the rights and interests of all individuals in a group setting irrespective of culture, physical ability, intellect, gender, religion, race, ethnicity, or sexual orientation.

indirect methods:
the facilitation of children's learning through play that uses ECEs as guides and resource persons and relies largely on exploratory, discovery-oriented, and child-initiated teaching strategies.

individual development plan (IDP):
a variation of the individual education plan (IEP); usually includes a written summary of the child's development and interests along with a series of objectives for the child to pursue in a play-based curriculum.

industrial age:
an historical period some define as the period from the Industrial Revolution in the 19th century to the mid-1990s that some see as the beginning of the information age.

informal education:
is an approach to education that was first described by David Elkind that assumes that children learn when they engage in play for its own sake in a well-equipped play environment.

informal learning:
refers to learning that occurs during the sensorimotor and preoperational stages of development in which the child learns through active interaction with concrete objects in the environment and through experience in authentic settings.

information age:
society's current information explosion, resulting from technological advances that began in the mid-1990s.

information processing theory:
a theory of how we encode, store, and retrieve information from the world around us; the view of learning is based on the perceived similarity between the brain and a computer.

inhibition:
an executive function that describes the ability to refrain from performing an action if it is not needed for the task and inhibiting an early response in order to investigate further (Galinsky, 2010, p. 4).

inputs:
information from such sources as assessment reports, parents, children, ECEs, and other stakeholders that provides direction for curriculum in the planning stages.

instrumental approach:
a term used to describe an influence or outcomes that may be achieved through the provision of educational opportunities that are purposeful, so as to have an impact on the learner's knowledge and understanding.

instrumental function of play:
explains the purposeful nature of play activities and the organization of the play environment to promote development and learning.

intelligence:
in a broad sense, the capacity to understand and function in the world and to strategically and resourcefully cope with and adjust to problems and challenges presented. Several theorists have offered various definitions of intelligence. Howard Gardner defines intelligence as the ability to solve problems or to create products that are valued within a particular culture or setting.

intention:
a term sometimes used to refer to the aims or purpose of a curriculum, such as the achievement of outcomes that are clearly described.

interest:
the criterion that determines the extent to which children are motivated to play with the materials and activities or projects.

internal construction of activities:
play materials and activities may be organized so as to challenge the learner, the child, to engage in the learning that is inherent in the particular activity. For example, playing with tall and wide measuring cups in the water table eventually reveals the concept that equal volume does not depend on the height of the container.

interpersonal intelligence:
ability to interact with others and to perceive their moods, motivations and intentions; comfortable in groups and collaborative efforts.

intervention:
a proposed educational, social, or medical strategy or program designed to improve the developmental, academic, psychological, or social status of individuals or a group.

intrapersonal intelligence:
high level of self-knowledge and ability to pursue inner feelings and instincts; preference for working alone and at own pace within one's own space and to one's own ends.

intuitive period:
a time in child development that normally occurs from age four to age seven that is characterized by the pre-logical structure of children's thinking as they gradually move away from reliance on what they perceive through the senses toward the eventual understanding of concepts.

issue:
a situation or conflict to be resolved that contains at least two perspectives or opposing sets of conditions or ways to resolve the matter.

kinaesthetic discrimination:
the ability to use the body to learn about physical capabilities, to develop body awareness, and to move fluidly in space.

kinaesthetic intelligence:
one of the intelligences proposed by Howard Gardner, which describes the person's ability to rely on sensory stimuli to move efficiently in space, to execute skilled movements; a sense of awareness of the position of the voluntary muscles of the body.

laterality:
refers to "sidedness," which is an internal awareness of the symmetry of one's body and of its various sectors; e.g., left and right sides, above and below the body's mid-line.

learn by doing:
an expression used to describe a characteristic of play-based learning that depends on children's active involvement with concrete objects in the environment.

learning centre:
a well-defined area of a playroom or playground, which houses equipment, materials, and supplies that promote specific types and styles of play. The learning centre is an organized yet complex juxtaposition of complementary

and integrated resources for play that is designed to move children further in their development.

learning experiences:
planned or unplanned learning opportunities that are largely open-ended, whereby the outcome of the experience for each child is not predictable or necessarily the same from child to child; examples include fieldtrips, a guest demonstration, attending a concert, or a spontaneous event of some significance.

learning outcomes:
statements that describe the complex verifiable learning that has occurred by the end of a program or curriculum; these statements provide explicit descriptions of what the achievement of the outcome will look like.

learning style:
the approach to learning favoured by a child. For example, children may prefer social learning contexts or solitary learning endeavours, or they may require visual or auditory stimulation, frequent feedback, or considerable independence to learn effectively. Understanding children's learning styles is fundamental to facilitating children's achievement of developmental outcomes.

learning-centred education:
an approach to education that emphasizes the outcomes and results of a learning process rather than the inputs and content to be taught; defines the developmental and learning outcomes to be achieved, describes a range of learning approaches to facilitate the achievement of developmental and learning outcomes, assesses progress toward the outcomes, and verifies the achievement of the outcomes.

learning-to-learn skills:
a term used to describe the skills that are usually necessary for success in academic tasks; i.e., listening, questioning, persisting with challenges, task orientation, and attending—such as ability to return to an activity after an interruption, block out irrelevant stimuli and focus on a task, or delay gratification.

left-brain thinking:
thought that originates in the left hemisphere and governs analytic, logical, temporal, sequential, linear, verbal, abstract, factual, computational, concrete, and practical processes.

life science:
biology and related subjects that have to do with health, well-being, fitness, and adaptation.

linear culture:
culture examined largely on one dimension and which often progresses in a single series of steps or stages.

linguistic intelligence:
sensitivity to the different functions of language including its ability to convince, stimulate, excite, convey information, and entertain.

listening table:
a play station set up to promote children's listening abilities, especially their physical and cognitive auditory perceptual skills; it usually houses audio equipment.

literacy:
refers in a broad sense to the acquisition and use of knowledge and skills that are important within a society; may refer to oral and written language and communication skills, to numerical literacy or numeracy, to cultural literacy, to computer literacy, or to critical literacy.

logical concepts:
abstract knowledge for which the source of understanding lies within the child; conceptual understanding that defines a relationship that is not directly observable, as the source of the concept is inherent in the relationship itself. Understanding logical concepts requires children to make a mental leap from the external, physical, observable realm, and from social-conventional meaning to the realm of concept formation.

logical-mathematical knowledge:
understanding of universal concepts and principles and of the largely abstract relationships that exist between them; e.g., concept of number, equality, conservation; an understanding of what is true, even in the face of apparent contradictions.

loudness:
degree and obtrusiveness of sound.

magical thinking:
describes children's difficulty in distinguishing between fantasy and reality and between the imagined and the real; children are likely to believe that just wishing can make something come true; the tendency to provide a magical explanation for phenomena for which there is no known physical explanation. This type of thinking usually diminishes during adolescence, but it may continue into adulthood.

malleable materials or substances:
soft, pliable substances that can be moulded by the child and that take the shape the child intends. Includes modelling clay, play dough, Plasticene/Play-Doh, and wet sand; sometimes referred to as plastic materials.

manipulative materials:
these materials promote early manipulative play, which includes physical investigation of single objects and patterns in the child's perceptual field followed by play with manipulative materials with two or more objects beyond exploratory handling, such as the assembly of Lego materials, tabletop blocks, beads, and laces.

mass:
the quantity of matter that an object contains.

materials:
the concrete objects that appear in the foreground of the play and learning environment for children to play with, manipulate, explore, and test. Materials take many forms, such as modular, free-form, non-continuous, and surface-diffusible.

maturationist theories:
theories proposed by early developmental psychologists G. Stanley Hall and Arnold Gesell that children develop in largely predictable ways and exhibit behaviours and abilities according to rather universal stages usually linked to ages; theories that development is programmed and influenced more by the individual's genetic endowment (genetic predetermination) than by the environment and learning.

means-ends materials:
specific-purpose materials with an internal structure that guides the direction and outcomes of play. See specific-purpose materials.

melody:
the arrangement of notes in a musical composition to achieve harmony.

mental structures:
theories proposed by Jean Piaget that human adaptation is the result of the organism's construction of mental structures or schemes through the joint processes of assimilation and accommodation leading to equilibration; in early childhood, mental structures are built largely through the child's active interaction with concrete objects in the environment.

metacognition:
the knowledge and ability to think about cognition and thought, an ability which is often linked to "theory of mind."

methods:
the implementation strategies that describe *direct* and *indirect* ways to enhance children's play and to facilitate development and learning through play.

milestone:
a significant stage or event that has been achieved when specific behaviours or skills appear.

modular materials:
materials that have many pieces or multiple units, usually of uniform shapes and sizes, that are made to fit together in specific or general ways.

moral intelligence:
an aspect of intelligence that involves an active superego or conscience and the ability to make choices based on principles of right and wrong.

motivate:
an influence that causes a person to behave in a certain way.

motivation:
a cause or a circumstance that encourages action; the will to move forward.

motor coordination:
the control exercised over the body's muscular movement and the nerves activating it for both fine motor and gross motor movement; may refer to non-locomotor coordination, which involves moving while standing in one place, or to locomotor coordination, which involves movement from one place to another.

motor development:
changes in motor activity toward increasing proficiency; also involves higher level perceptual skills and analysis of visual and auditory input as well as one's ability to organize stimuli.

multiple intelligences:
Howard Gardner's theory that there are nine types of intelligences, which he refers to as "talents," rather than one general factor that governs intelligence.

myelination:
growth of a fatty sheath (myelin) around neurons, enabling faster transmission of messages in the brain.

natural science:
the science of phenomena that originate in nature and the physical world, including the study of plant and animal life, chemistry, physics, geology, biology, botany, and zoology.

naturalistic intelligence:
particular intelligence described by Howard Gardner that has to do with a talent for recognizing patterns in nature and differences among various life forms and natural objects.

nature versus nurture controversy:
a controversy in psychology, particular in the first half of the 20th century, which argued that human development was either influenced largely by genetic inheritance (nature) or by the environment (nurture).

neuron:
cell in the brain or another part of the nervous system that transmits information to other cells.

non-continuous materials:
discrete materials such as blocks or Tinkertoy with measurement prearranged in an imposed standard unit, which may be modular in that pieces fit together to create a product.

non-literal:
attribution of specialized meaning, context, or interpretation to text or words.

number constancy:
the ability to understand that quantity does not change according to the properties of the objects being counted.

number:
an arithmetic value representing quantity that is used in counting and in making calculations; learning the concept of number is a developmental task of early childhood.

numeracy:
the ability to understand and use number in age-appropriate and conventional ways in order to function successfully in society.

numerical order:
the ordering of number symbols, as in 1, 2, 3, and so on.

observation strategies:
tools and practices for observing children at play to learn more about the whole child, to gauge their progress and to determine their interests.

observation:
an organized way of looking at the behaviours and actions of children using specialized tools and methods that will

capture information and data that are as objective as possible.

ocular motor skills:
physical perceptual skills involving the movement, control, and coordination of the eyes, such as fixation, pursuit, accommodation, and tracking.

one-to-one correspondence:
matching two sets of objects when each set contains the same number of objects.

onlooking play:
play in which a child observes children playing but does not physically participate.

onomatopoeia:
words that are formed from a sound associated with the item being named; e.g. buzz, crack.

open education:
a philosophy of education whereby students are encouraged to explore

open-ended materials:
materials with an indefinite amount of learning potential and a maximum amount of flexibility in the ways in which children may use them.

optimal discrepancy:
a term used by Piaget to describe the optimal distance that should exist between something new to be learned and what the child already knows; if there is too much distance between the two, the child may become discouraged and fail to learn.

ordering:
a form of comparing based on a particular relationship in a series between two or more objects based on such criteria as size, colour, weight, time, or another discernible criterion.

ordinal number:
the forming of relationships based on what comes first, second, third, and so on, in a series.

original thinking:
the ability and power to think creatively and to originate or invent something new.

orthodoxies:
a set of beliefs or conventions that are in agreement with what is currently held to be true, especially in religious and philosophical matters.

other first language (OFL):
principal language learned and spoken outside the home; e.g. if home language is Urdu, the OFL in Canada would be English or French.

paradigm:
a way of explaining something or a mode of viewing the world that underlies the theories and methodology of science in a particular period of history; an organized way of viewing an issue or a question.

parallel play:
play in which two children play side by side, each with her own activity, and do not interact, although they may each talk in monologues.

part–whole relationships:
the interaction and relationship of components or elements to the larger item or issue.

pathway:
a broad, elongated, unobstructed space that is visible at children's eye levels and that helps to separate and define learning centres. Pathways lead children into and out of learning centres.

pedagogy:
the science or the study of the techniques and approaches that facilitate learning.

perceptual acuity:
the acuteness or accuracy of the senses: hearing, vision, smell, taste, touch.

phoneme:
letter-sound relationships in words and their letter symbols.

phonology:
the part of language learning that pertains to the production of sound.

physical abilities:
skills associated with physical and motor fitness, such as muscular strength

and endurance, flexibility, cardio-vascular and circulatory-respiratory endurance, balance, speed, agility, power, and coordination.

physical knowledge:
sensory-perceptual learning about the concrete, physical properties of objects. It refers to learning about colour, shape, size, texture, and other observable characteristics of things.

physical science:
a branch of science that deals with inanimate matter and energy as in physics, chemistry, geology, and astronomy.

pitch:
the perceived frequency that is associated with voice quality, such as low and high tones.

pivots:
in role play, a symbol or action or a thing that triggers an extension of the play into a new direction; objects children use to represent something other than the object itself, as in using a block to represent a car.

play places:
term used to designate the number of children who can play at any one time with a simple, complex, or super unit of play; number of children who can be accommodated to play in a given area or in a specific unit of play at a given time.

play station:
an area or equipment within a learning centre dedicated to play with materials that address specific developmental and learning objectives.

play style:
refers to various ways in which children play that are described by the categories of play.

play zone:
designated area of a playroom, classroom, or playground for specific types of play activity, such as active play, creative and discovery play, or quiet play with structured materials.

pluralistic:
the state whereby a number and wide variety of customs and cultural traditions may be tolerated and allowed to be independent, and an acceptance of a diversity of opinions, values, theories, etc., for organizing materials, information, and data.

portfolio:
a system and a framework for storing records, artwork, or data.

potential units:
empty spaces in a play area surrounded by visible or tangible boundaries, to which can be added play equipment and/or materials.

practice play:
an early functional play that is exploratory and usually involves the repetition of physical behaviours that have already been mastered. It is characterized by the infant's sucking on objects, making sounds, gazing, and demonstrating other repetitive, largely sensorimotor behaviours.

practices:
behaviours that are based on a specific set of theories, values, or beliefs; usually recognized as related to a specific theoretical approach.

pragmatics:
the part of language learning that refers to the rules of effective communication in a given context.

praxis:
an accepted practice or custom grounded in theory; the practising of an art or a skill.

prefabricated:
manufactured or made prior to assembly on site; produced in an artificially standardized way.

preoperational period:
a period described by Piaget from approximately age two to age seven that follows the sensorimotor period; thinking depends on the presence of concrete objects.

preoperational thought:
quality of thinking shaped by egocentricity, and "seeing is believing."

pretend play:
play in which children use symbols (words, actions, or other objects) to represent the real world or to practise their own versions of adult behaviours; it is usually simple and somewhat predictable.

productive play:
play in which the outcomes are concrete and increasingly recognizable to adults; play products become more lifelike and recognizable.

program:
play activities and experiences that are planned and implemented which organize and describe the content that is related to the curriculum.

project method:
a teaching approach formulated by William Kilpatrick early in the 20th century that built on the ideas of John Dewey; the project method incorporates manual and motor activities as well as cognitive and aesthetic experiences and is predicated on the construction of a significant plan in some form.

projects:
involve a series of sequenced activities related to the aim of the project and usually requires space to house the project in progress so that children can return to the project after an interruption.

prop boxes:
boxes for storing objects and materials that may be used to set up a super unit that is tied to a specific theme or interest and encourages role play, such as a supermarket, dentist's office, hospital, fire station, etc.

props:
materials that children may use to support their symbolic play, particularly in dramatic and sociodramatic play or sociodrama.

prosthetic devices:
artificial device that replaces a missing body part; can be an artificial organ or part, such as a heart valve or an artificial limb to replace a leg or arm.

psychoanalytic theories:
psychological theory originally described by Sigmund Freud based on his extensive experiments and experience treating patients during the early 20th century; these theories were evolved by the neo-Freudians such as Erik Erikson and Carl Rogers.

pursuit:
an ocular motor skill whereby a child tries to follow a moving target in space without moving the head.

quotient:
the number you get when you divide one number into another number.

reconceptualization:
to reframe or conceptualize differently a body of thought and practice.

reflective practitioner:
a term applied to ECEs and other professionals to describe thoughtful self-analysis of one's own values, performance, perspectives, behaviours.

relationship:
association with another person, thing, or idea.

relevance:
a measure of the extent to which a play material relates to a child's cultural context and life experiences.

repetitive play:
a form of functional play usually involving the repetition of physical behaviours that have already been mastered; sometimes referred to as practice play.

represent:
action that conveys meaning, as in building a house with blocks, role play by a group of children of an event they have experienced, artistic or graphic depiction of an object or experience.

representational play:
a term used by Piaget to describe play that involves the ability to depict an object, person, action, or experience

mentally, even if it is not present in the environment; representation may be realized through role play or constructive play using artistic tools, blocks, or other items.

representational thinking:
involves the ability to represent mentally a remembered or imagined object or action or a series of actions contained in an event that are not perceptually present to the child.

reproductive play:
play in which children represent remembered events, images, and actions. This type of play is increasingly representative of what children understand or want to understand about their environmental experiences.

resource person:
in an early childhood environment, the ECE who responds to children's questions about phenomena or objects, helps them find supplies and materials they need for a project, or joins in their search for new ways of building or making something.

responsive play materials:
materials that respond to the child's actions on them, such as blocks, Lego, modelling clay, puzzles, wet sand, paints, and other artistic supplies.

reversibility:
understanding that an operation can be reversed; ability to return to the original point in thought.

rhyme:
words or syllables that have or end with the same sound as each other; a verse with words at the ends of lines that rhyme with each other.

rhythm:
a harmonious correlation of parts; in music, a pattern of long or short and accented or unaccented parts; in movement, a regular succession of strong and weak elements.

right-brain thinking:
thought that originates in the right hemisphere of the brain and governs intuitive, spontaneous, random, holistic, nonverbal, visual, spatial, sensory, and symbolic processes.

role play zone:
an area of the playroom dedicated to learning centres and play stations that encourage dramatic and sociodramatic play with props that kindle imagination and representational thinking.

rough-and-tumble play:
forms of physically active and boisterous play that sometimes mimic aggression and fighting but are often more closely related to role play.

rule-bound play:
play that is governed by rules, as in games, team sports.

scaffold:
the guidance an adult provides or the questions he asks that enable a child to overcome a hurdle in trying to perform a skill or understand a concept.

scaffolding:
intervention by an adult in a child's learning process that seeks to help a child bridge the gap (optimal discrepancy) that may exist between the skill the child is asked to perform and his or her current level of knowledge and skill.

scanning:
the visual-perceptual task of moving the eyes across a page, usually from left to right, in order to pick out an object or word.

schema, or schemes:
Piagetian term to describe the cognitive structures into which cognitive concepts or mental representations are organized.

schematic stage:
a period beyond infancy when children begin to organize their new cognitive concepts and mental representations into existing schema and are able to depict more realistic representations of what they understand; final stage of graphic development from ages seven to nine years.

sciencing:
a term that captures the idea that in science education the child is in active pursuit of knowledge through hands-on exploration of objects and phenomena in the environment. It transforms a prescribed curriculum into an exciting process of learning through discovery and active exploration.

self-concept:
perceptions and feelings one has about oneself based largely on what others say about them and how the important people in their lives respond to them.

self-control:
conscientiousness; self-discipline; perseverance; able to consider the consequences of actions before acting.

self-esteem:
the respect for and opinion of oneself largely based on one's inner feeling of competence and success in dealing with challenges.

self-regulation:
ability to exercise control over one's impulses without relying on outside intervention; control over behaviour and emotions, and an ability to be self-directed.

semantics:
the part of language learning that addresses the choice of words to convey the intended meaning.

semiotic function:
the ability to use signs and symbols to represent objects or actions, as in pictures, gestures, language, and musical tones.

sensorimotor play:
largely physical and sensory play as children gain control over their movements and gather information by way of the senses. Play involves the child's physical interaction with concrete objects in the environment to discover the physical properties of things.

sensorimotor stage:
Piaget's first stage of development, from birth to about 18 months to two years, in which the infant explores and learns about his world through the senses and develops motor skills. The end of the sensorimotor stage is characterized by the development of object permanence, which is the child's ability to know that objects continue to exist even when they are no longer visible.

sensory acuity:
the accuracy and acuteness of the senses, sometimes referred to as perceptual acuity.

sensory-perceptual skills:
the skills of vision, hearing, taste, smell, and touch.

sequencing:
putting actions and events in order of sequence according to time and a plan.

seriation:
the arrangement of objects based on a graduated order, with a common baseline and equal gradations in the size of successive objects in a series.

set:
a group of objects with at least one common attribute.

shifting attention between two competing tasks:
defined as cognitive flexibility, which is an executive function that enables one to alter one's focus from one task to another without becoming confused.

simple unit:
a play unit with one primary purpose in play; it is generally used by one child at a time for the purpose intended. Simple play units do not usually have subparts; simple units are attributed one play space.

social capital:
refers to the value added to a society whose citizens are educated, aware, productive, involved, and economically secure; refer to *human capital.*

social cognition:
an individual's understanding, ideas, belief systems, etc., of the actions and intentions of others; social cognition forms the basis for our interpersonal interactions in the environment.

social contexts of play:
refers to play that is solitary (child playing alone), parallel (child plays beside another child but doesn't interact), associative

(children participate in a similar activity but do not subordinate their individual interests to those of the group), or cooperative (paired or group social play that involves common goals and tasks to be performed collaboratively).

social integration:
the intermixing of diverse people within a social environment who have been deemed to have the same rights and privileges.

social intelligence:
a term coined by Daniel Goleman to describe the degree of empathy, social cognition, and social facility possessed by an individual that enables one to pick up on social cues and influence others.

social justice:
the commitment of individuals, groups, or a society to the protection and active upholding of the human and political rights, interests, and needs of all who inhabit the larger society.

social-conventional knowledge of number:
the child's ability to understand the social meanings and contexts for the use of number, as for addresses, dates, prices, measurements.

social-conventional knowledge:
facts and information that are socially and culturally transmitted and shared and often arbitrarily assigned, such as rules, proper names, conventions, and customs; factual knowledge that is derived culturally and agreed on by society.

sociocentric:
focusing more on the group than on the self.

sociodrama, or creative drama:
the enactment through play of a story or another dramatic production; it is usually externally motivated, and limitations are imposed on roles and behaviours by the story or by another drama.

sociodramatic play:
play in which two or more children collaborate in dramatizing experiences from their own physical and social environments. It involves representations of remembered events that are common to the children playing. Children assume related roles and follow one another's cues in acting out an event or social context.

sociohistoric theory:
Lev Vygotsky's theory that children actively construct their knowledge and understanding, that language leads thought, and that labelling objects helps children understand concepts. It stresses the importance of the social environment in learning and asserts that children develop concepts and thinking abilities in a social context with the help of teachers, other adults, and peers.

sociomoral:
conventional values and beliefs about acceptable moral conduct within a society.

solitary play:
play in which one child plays alone, although he may be in a room where other children are playing.

space:
in this textbook, this term refers to the physical space available in a playroom for learning centres and play stations and also to the amount of space in each play station that determines the number of children who can play there at one time.

spatial concepts:
abilities to navigate successfully and gracefully in space and to estimate the space needed for self and others to interact and move; also involves understanding of direction and ability to estimate speed, distance, and force.

spatial intelligence:
the ability to notice the details of what one sees and to imagine and manipulate visual objects in one's mind.

spatial ordering:
the arrangement of objects in a certain order by shape, usually by making or following patterns and by creating equal sets using one-to-one correspondence.

spatial skills:
understanding which leads to the skilled ability to make physical adjustments to

the environment such as slowing down, turning, stopping, dodging.

specific-purpose materials:
means-ends materials with an internal structure that often mandates the outcome of play and the steps to be followed to reach it.

spiritual:
things that are not physical but relate to the soul or the human spirit; sensitivity to non-material matters and meanings.

spiritual development:
growing sense of the vital animating essence of a person that is nonphysical; spiritual development may begin with a sense of wonder and a curiosity about all living, natural things and gradually deepens into an exploration of life's larger questions and mysteries.

spiritual intelligence:
the innate need to connect with something larger than ourselves.

spirituality:
an interest and curiosity about matters concerned with the soul or spirit that are often related to natural phenomena.

stamina:
ability to sustain or endure prolonged physical or mental strain.

standards:
objects, qualities, measures, or norms that serve as a basis or example of a principle to which people or things should conform; an objective measure by which accuracy, quality and level of achievement is judged.

station:
refers to a play station or a place in the learning centre set up for a specific activity, such as the exploring table or the water table.

subdivision:
the mental ability to separate a larger unit into smaller segments; for instance, a hopscotch court can be divided into several smaller units.

super unit:
a complex unit that has one or more play materials added to it (i.e., three or more play materials are juxtaposed). Six to eight play spaces may be attributed to super units, which means that they usually occupy a large space and are elaborate.

superhero play:
symbolic play that may be dramatic, sociodramatic, or sociodrama, in which children assume roles associated with fictional, often fantastical, characters from stories or television programs. The superheroes are generally endowed with superhuman qualities, and the play often has a rough-and-tumble quality.

superheroes:
larger-than-life beings, sometimes human and sometimes fantastical, that become for a time the object of children's interest, admiration, and imitation.

supplies:
the consumable items in the play and learning environment that must be replenished frequently.

surface-diffusible materials:
are free-form, essentially two-dimensional materials that can be shaped, with no standard, pre-arranged unit of measurement, such as clay, art materials, wet sand, that are more concerned with how things flow rather than fit together to make the whole, in which the parts run together (are organically integrated) so that they lose some visible identity (Fowler, 1980, p. 172).

symbolic mode:
a stage of development over the age of six proposed by psychologist Jerome Bruner whereby the child knows his world through abstractions and is able to draw from language and thinking to understand abstract ideas and concepts.

symbolic play:
play in which objects and actions are used to represent other objects or actions.

symbolic thinking:
the ability to represent objects and events in the outside world in terms of internal mental entities or symbols. The development of symbolic thinking occurs approximately between the ages of two and four, when children become capable of using one object to stand for another and eventually develop

the ability to use language and number symbols.

synapse:
the junction between two neurons that allows transmission of messages from one to the other.

synaptic pruning:
a process whereby synapses that are inconsistent with typical environmental events and behaviour patterns are eliminated; this process occurs largely in middle childhood and into adolescence.

synaptogenesis:
a process that occurs during the first two years of life when the synapses or connections between neurons are developing rapidly.

syntax:
the part of language learning that involves the rules by which words are put together to form phrases, clauses and sentences.

systems:
considered principles of procedure or classification.

task orientation:
an attending skill that involves choosing and beginning an activity, overcoming obstacles, following through, completing the task, and being able to report that the task is finished.

tasks of early childhood development:
see *developmental tasks.*

teacher demonstration:
a teaching method in which the ECE demonstrates, with or without the help of the child, how to perform a specific movement or skill.

teacher-as-model method:
the ECE performs the actions involved in a game or activity such as Simon Says or hokey pokey or a finger play so that children can imitate his actions.

teacher-directed methods:
planning and teaching strategies in which the ECE decides in advance of the learning experience which objectives will be addressed and how they will be addressed, and guides the implementation of the activity to its anticipated outcome.

temporal order:
the relationship among events according to the order in which they took place.

testing play:
a form of functional play characterized by motor testing, crawling into and out of small places, or challenging one's physical abilities.

thematic play:
symbolic play that pursues a specific subject such as pretending to be a firefighter unravelling a hose, or performing actions related to a song; it may involve sociodrama in which children act out a story or rhyme.

themes:
refer to topics or subjects that may be the focus of projects, explorations, or investigations as in investigating properties of water or animal habitats, and learning about water safety/road safety.

theory of mind:
the ability to think about thought; closely related to empathy, which is children's ability to understand the mental and psychological states (thoughts, feelings, motives) of others and to interpret the behaviours of people who are important in their lives.

third teacher:
refers to the role of the environment in play-based early childhood education in which the organization of physical space and the contents and arrangement of the learning centres guide and motivate the child toward certain kinds of play and learning.

three-dimensional materials:
lifelike representations or whole objects having length, width, and depth, such as an actual apple, a block, or a car.

timbre:
the pattern of overtones of a voice or sound that are whole numbers of octaves above a basic or fundamental frequency; the timbre is a quality which allows us to differentiate one musical instrument

from another, as each has its characteristic overtone pattern.

topology:
the way in which constituent parts are arranged or interrelated; study of space in the context of position or location in which shape or length may be altered without affecting the figures' properties of being open or closed.

tracking:
the ability of the eyes to make a series of long sweeps smoothly across a page, board, or screen, moving slowly or quickly as needed across the page and back again.

transformation:
a dramatic change in the form, outward appearance, or character of something.

transitional literacy:
the learning process children go through in adding another first language to the language they learn and use in the home.

two-dimensional materials:
materials that have length and width but very little depth.

unit iteration:
knowing that a number of parts can be combined to make a whole; for example, 100 centimetres of distance put together make a one-metre unit.

values:
beliefs that are strongly held and form the basis for action and behaviour.

variety:
the potential of the play unit to accommodate different kinds of play activity, such as digging, pouring, building, stacking, and twirling.

virtual:
something that does not really exist but is made by software to appear real from the point of view of the program or user.

visual closure:
an ocular-motor skill related to the visual skills of accommodation, fixation, pursuit, and tracking, all of which influence the ability to read. Eyes must work together and be constantly matched and balanced.

visual discrimination:
the ability of the eyes to receive accurate messages that allow for form discrimination, depth perception, figure-from-ground perception, and ocular motor skills.

visual-spatial intelligence:
the ability to transform and modify initial perceptions, to mentally take a position other than one's own physical position, to recreate aspects of one's visual experience in the absence of the physical stimuli, to orient oneself in a physical context, and to work with graphic depictions of space such as maps, diagrams and geometrical forms.

working memory:
an executive function that involves holding information in one's mind while mentally working with it or updating it, including relating one idea to another, relating what one is reading now to what one just read, and relating what you are learning now to what one learned earlier (Galinsky, 2010, p. 20).

Workjobs:
play activities that are specific-purpose made from recycled materials according to a specified pattern (Baratta-Lorton, 1972, 1979) that help children learn concepts, master skills, and acquire knowledge.

zone of proximal development (ZPD):
describes a range of tasks that a child can perform with the help and guidance of others but cannot yet perform independently.

zones:
see play zones.

References

Abraham, C. (2010, Saturday, October 16). Our time to lead: Failing boys, Part I. *The Globe and Mail*, A16–A17, http://www.theglobeandmail.com/news/national/time-to-lead/failing-boys/failing-boys-and-the-powder-keg-of-sexual-politics/article1758791/.

Ali, M.A. (2005). Effects of migration on parenting capacity of newcomer parents of young children. In V. Pacini-Ketchabaw & A. Pence (Eds.), *Research connections: Supporting children and families* (pp. 135–156). Ottawa, ON: Canadian Child Care Federation.

Allen, K., Paasche, C., Cornell, A., & Engel, M. (1998). *Exceptional children: Inclusion in early childhood programs* (2nd ed.). Toronto, ON: ITP Nelson.

Allen, K.E., Paasche, C., Langford, R., & Nolan, K. (2006). *Inclusion in early childhood programs: Children with exceptionalities* (4th ed.). Toronto, ON: Thomson Nelson.

Almon, J. (2003). The vital role of play in early childhood education. In S. Olfman (Ed.), *All work and no play: How educational reforms are harming our preschoolers* (pp. 17–42). Westport, CT: Praeger.

Anderson, C. (2010). Blocks: A versatile learning tool for yesterday, today and tomorrow. *Young Children, 65*(3), 54–56.

Andrews, J., & Lupart, J. (1993). *The inclusive classroom: Educating exceptional children.* Scarborough, ON: Nelson Canada.

Anselmo, S., & Zinck, R.A. (1987). Computers for young children? Perhaps. *Young Children, 43*(3), 22–27.

Austin, E.M. (1986). Presented at the Annual Conference of the National Association for the Education of Young Children (NAEYC): *Beyond superheroes: Constructive power play in the preschool.* Atlanta, GA: NAEYC.

Baratta-Lorton, M. (1972). *Workjobs.* Menlo Park, CA: Addison-Wesley.

Baratta-Lorton, M. (1979). *Workjobs: Number activities for early childhood.* Menlo Park, CA: Addison-Wesley.

Barone, D.M., Mallette, M.H., & Hong Xu, S. (2005). *Teaching early literacy: Development, assessment and instruction.* New York, NY: Guilford Press.

Baumgartner, J.J., & Buchanan, T. (2010). Supporting each child's spirit. *Young Children, 65*(2), 90–95.

Baumeister, R.F., & Tierney, J. (2011). *Willpower: Rediscovering the greatest human strength.* New York, NY: The Penguin Press.

Beaty, J.J., & Tucker, W.H. (1987). *The computer as a paintbrush: Creative uses for the personal computer in the preschool classroom.* Columbus, OH: Merrill.

Beauchamp, G., & Kennewell, S. (2008). The influence of ICT on the interactivity of teaching, education and information technologies. *Education and Information Technologies, 13*(4), 305–315.

Beauchamp, G. (2010). Knowledge and understanding of the world. In I. Palaiologou (Ed.), *The early years foundation stage: Theory and practice* (pp. 123–137). London, UK: Sage Publications.

Behrmann, M.M., & Levy, S.A. (1986). Computers and special education. In J. Hoot (Ed.), *Computers in early childhood education* (pp. 104–127). Englewood Cliffs, NJ: Prentice-Hall.

Bergen, D. (2002). The role of pretend play in children's cognitive development. *Early Childhood Research and Practice, 4*(1), http://ccrp.html.

Berk, L.E., Mann, T.D., & Ogan, A.T. (2006). Make-believe play: Wellspring for development of self-regulation. In D.G. Singer, R.M. Golinkoff, & K. Hirsch-Pasak, *Play and learning: How play motivates and enhances children's cognitive and social-emotional growth* (pp. 74–100). London, UK: Oxford University Press.

Berk, L.E., & Winsler, A. (1995). *Scaffolding children's learning: Vygotsky and early childhood education.* Washington, DC: National Association for the Education of Young Children.

Berko Gleason, J. (1989). Studying language development. In J. Berko Gleason (Ed.), *The development of language* (2nd ed., pp. 1–34). Columbus, OH: Merrill.

Bernhard, J. (2005). Presented at the Metropolis Conference: *Diversity and inclusion: Consideration for "good care" in early childhood settings in the global era.* Toronto, ON: Metropolis Conference.

Bernhard, J., Hong, S.O., & Fish, J. (2003). Paper presented at the annual Conference of the National Association for the Education of Young Children: *"It never occurred to me!" How knowing family stories can increase teacher-family understanding and support the development of young children and their families.* Chicago, IL: National Association for the Education of Young Children.

Bettelheim, B. (1976). *The uses of enchantment.* New York, NY: Vintage.

Bettelheim, B. (1987a). *A good enough parent.* New York, NY: Random House.

Bettelheim, B. (1987b). The importance of play. *The Atlantic, 262*(3), 35–46.

Bevelier, D., & Neville, H. (2002). Neuroplasticity, developmental. In V.S. Ramachandran (Ed.), *Encyclopedia of the human brain* (Vol. 3). Amsterdam: Academic Press.

Bloch, M. (2005). Making progress: Conceptualizing and reconceptualizing approaches to ECE and child care in the twenty-first century. In J.L. Roopnarine & J.E. Johnson (Eds.), *Approaches to early childhood education* (4th ed., pp. 74–100). Columbus, OH: Pearson Merrill Prentice Hall.

Bodrova, E., & Leong, D.J. (1996). *Tools of the mind: The Vygotskyan approach to early childhood education.* Englewood Cliffs, NJ: Merrill.

Bredekamp, S. (1987). *Developmentally appropriate practice in early childhood programs: Serving children from birth through age 8.* Washington, DC: National Association for the Education of Young Children.

Bredekamp, S. (2004). Play and school readiness in children's play. In E.F. Zigler, D.G. Singer, & S.J. Bishop-Josef (Eds.), *Children's play: The roots of reading* (pp. 159–174). Washington, DC: Zero to Three Press.

British Columbia Ministry of Social Development and Economic Security. (2000). *A better future for British Columbia's kids.* Victoria, BC: British Columbia Ministry of Social Development and Economic Security.

Brizendine, L. (2006). *The female brain.* New York, NY: Morgan Road Books.

Brizendine, L. (2009). *The male brain.* New York, NY: Morgan Road Books.

Broadhead, P., Wood, E., & Howard, J. (2010). Understanding playful learning and playful pedagogies—towards a new research agenda. Conclusion. In P. Broadhead, J. Howard, & E. Wood, *Play and learning in the early years* (pp. 177–185). London, UK: Sage.

Bronfenbrenner, U., & Morris, P. (1998). The ecology of developmental processes. In W. Damon (series ed.) & R.M. Lerner (volume ed.), *Handbook of child psychology: Theoretical models of human development* (5th ed., Vol 1, p. 993). New York, NY: Wiley.

Brooker, L. (2010). Learning to play in a cultural context. In P. Broadhead, J. Howard, & E. Wood, *Play and learning in the early years* (pp. 27–42). London, UK: Sage.

Brown, A.L. (1987). Metacognition, executive control, self-regulation, and other more mysterious mechanisms. In F.E. Weinert & R.H. Kluwe (Eds.), *Metacognition, motivation and understanding* (pp. 65–116). Hillsdale, NJ: Lawrence Erlbaum Associates.

Brown, J., & Fenske, M., with Neporent, L. (2010). *The winner's brain: 8 strategies great minds use to achieve success.* New York, NY: Da Capo Lifelong Press.

Brown, M.H. (2000). Playing: The peace of childhood. *Young Children, 55*(6), 36–37.

Brown, S., with Vaughan, C. (2010). *Play: How it shapes the brain, opens the imagination, and invigorates the soul.* New York, NY: Avery (Penguin).

Bruce, T., & Ockelford, A. (2010). *Understanding symbolic development.* In T. Bruce. Ed. *Early childhood: A guide for students* (2nd ed). London, UK: Sage Publications.

Bruer, J.T. (1999). *The myths of the first three years: A new understanding of early brain development and lifelong learning.* New York, NY: Free Press.

Bruner, J. (1960). *The process of education.* Cambridge, MA: Harvard University Press.

Bruner, J. (1966). *Toward a theory of instruction.* Cambridge, MA: Harvard University Press.

Bruner, J. (1983). *Child's talk: Learning to use language.* New York, NY: W.W. Norton.

Bruner, J. (1986). *Actual minds, possible worlds.* Cambridge, MA: Harvard University Press.

Bruner, J. (1996). *The culture of education.* Cambridge, MA: Harvard University Press.

Bruno, H.E. (2011). Using our brain to stay cool under pressure: The neurobiology of emotional intelligence. *Young Children, 66*(1): 22–27.

Burns, M.S., Goin, L., & Donlon, J.T. (1990). A computer in my room. *Young Children, 45*(1), 62–67.

Butler, A., Gotts, E.E., & Quisenberry, N. (1978). *Play as development.* Columbus, OH: Merrill.

Calfee, R.C., & Hendrick, L.S. (2004). The teacher of beginning reading. In B. Spodek, & O. Saracho, (Eds.), *Contemporary perspectives on language policy and literacy instruction in early childhood education* (pp. 79–109). Greenwich, CT: Information Age Publishing.

Campbell, S. (1984). *Facilities and equipment for day care.* Ottawa, ON: Health and Welfare Canada.

Canada Mortgage and Housing Corporation (CMHC). (1978). *Play spaces for preschoolers.* Ottawa, ON: CMHC.

Canadian Child Care Federation (CCCF). (1995). *Resource Sheet #32.* Ottawa, ON: CCCF.

Canadian Council for Learning. (2011). *The future of learning in Canada.* Ottawa, ON: CCL.

Canadian Institute for Child Health (CICH). (1985). *When child's play is adult business: A consumer guide to safer playspaces.* Ottawa, ON: CICH.

Canadian Standards Association. (2006). *Children's playspaces and equipment.* (CAN/CSA-Z614-06).

Canning, N. (2010). Play in the early years foundation stage. In M. Reed & N. Canning. *Reflective practice in the early years.* London, UK: Sage Publications.

Caples, S.E. (1996). Some guidelines for preschool design. *Young Children, 52*(5), 14–21.

Cappon, Paul. (2010, October 16). Canada: Our time to lead. Failing boys. *The Globe and Mail,* A17.

Carruthers, E., & Worthington, M. (2006). *Children's mathematics, making marks, making meaning* (2nd ed). London, UK: Sage Publications.

Carlsson-Paige, N., & Levin, D.E. (1990). *Who's calling the shots? How to respond effectively to children's fascination with war play and war toys.* Santa Cruz, CA: New Society Publisher.

Cartwright, S. (1988). Play can be the building blocks of learning. *Young Children, 43*(4), 44–47.

Casey, B., & Lippmann, M. (1991). Learning to plan through play. *Young Children, 46*(4), 52–58.

Cass-Beggs, B. (1974). *To listen, to like, to learn.* Toronto, ON: Peter Martin Associates Ltd., 3.

Chambers, B., Patten, M.H., Schaeff, J., & Mau, D.W. (1996). *Let's cooperate.* Toronto, ON: Harcourt Brace.

Charlesworth, R. (2005). *Experiences in math for young children* (5th ed.). Albany, NY: Thomson Delmar Learning.

Charlesworth, R., & Lind, K.K. (2010). *Math and science for young children* (6th ed.). Belmont, CA: Wadsworth Cengage.

Charlesworth, R., & Radeloff, D. (1991). *Experiences in math for young children* (2nd ed.). Albany, NY: Thomson Delmar Learning.

Cherry, C. (1993). *Please don't sit on the kids.* Belmont, CA: Pitman.

Cherry, C., Godwin, D., & Staples, J. (1989). *Is the left brain always right? A guide to whole child development.* Belmont, CA: Fearon.

Chomsky, N. (1972). *Language and mind* (extended ed.). New York, NY: Harcourt Brace.

Chomsky, N. (1980). *Rules and representations.* Oxford, UK: Blackwell.

Christian, D. (1994). *Two way bilingual education: Student learning through two languages.* Santa Cruz, CA: National Center for Research on Cultural Diversity and Second Language Learning.

Christie, J.F., & Johnsen, E.P. (1987). Preschool play. In J.H. Block & N.R. King (Eds.), *School play: A source book* (pp. 109–142) New York, NY: Garland Publishing Inc.

Christie, J.F., & Wardle, F. (1992). How much time is needed for play? *Young Children, 47*(3), 28–32.

Chumak-Horbatsch, R. (2010). Language concerns of immigrant parents: Early childhood practitioners' response. *Journal of the Canadian Association for Young Children, 35*(1), 19–26.

Clemens, S.G. (1991). Art in the classroom: Making every day special. *Young Children, 46*(1), 4–11.

Cleveland, G., & Krashinsky, M. (2004). Discussion paper prepared for the National Conference on Child Care in Canada sponsored by the Canadian Council on Social Development (CCSD): *Financing early learning and child care.* Winnipeg, MB; Ottawa, ON: CCSD.

Cobb, E. (1977). *The ecology of imagination in childhood.* New York, NY: Columbia University Press.

Colbert, C., & Taunton, M. (1992). National Art Education Association (NAEA) briefing paper: *Developmentally appropriate practices for the visual arts education of young children.* Reston, VA: NAEA.

Coles, R. (1990). *The spiritual life of children.* Boston, MA: Houghton-Mifflin.

Coles, R. (1997). *The moral intelligence of children.* New York, NY: Random House.

College Standards and Accreditation Council. (1996). *Program standard: Early childhood education.* Toronto, ON: Ministry of Colleges and Universities.

Conference Board of Canada. (1999). *Employability skills.* Ottawa, ON: Conference Board of Canada.

Cooke, R., Tessier, A., & Armbruster, V. (1987). *Adapting early childhood curricula for children with special needs* (2nd ed.). Columbus, OH: Merrill.

Copple, C.E., & Bredekamp, S. (Eds.). (2009). *Developmentally appropriate practice in early childhood programs serving children from birth through age eight.* Position Statement. Washington, DC: National Association for the Education of Young Children.

Cox, S. (2005). Intention and meaning in young children's drawing. *Journal of Arts and Design Education, 24*(2), 115–125.

Crowther, I. (2003). *Creating effective learning environments.* Toronto, ON: Thomson Nelson.

Cummins, J. (2003). Reading and the bilingual student: Fact and friction. In G.G. Garcia (Ed.), *English learners: Reaching the highest level of English literacy.* Newark, NJ: DE International Reading Association.

Daggett, D. (2005). *Gardeners of Eden: Rediscovering our importance to nature.* Santa Barbara, CA: Thatcher Charitable Trust and Ecoresults.

Darling-Hammond, L. (1996). The right to learn and the advancement of teaching: Research, policy and practice for democratic education. *Educational Researcher, 25*(6), 5–17.

Davidson, J.I. (1989). *Children and computers: Together in the early childhood classroom.* Albany, NY: Delmar Publishing.

Davidson, P.S. (1977). *Ideal book for Cuisenaire rods at the primary level.* New Rochelle, NY: Cuisenaire Co. of America.

Davies, M. (2003). *Movement and dance in early childhood* (2nd ed.). London, UK: Chapman Publishing.

DeBenedet, A., & Cohen, L. (2011). *The art of roughhousing.* Philadelphia, PA: Quirk Books.

Derman-Sparks, L., & Ramsey, P. (2005). A framework for culturally relevant, multicultural, and antibias education in the twenty-first century. In J.L. Roopnarine & J.E. Johnson. (Eds.), *Approaches to early childhood education* (pp. 125–154). Upper Saddle River, NJ: Pearson Education.

DeVries, R. (1997). Piaget's social theory. *Educational Researcher, 26*(2), 4–17.

DeVries, R., & Kohlberg, L. (1987). *Constructive early education: Overview and comparison with other programs.* Washington, DC: National Association for the Education of Young Children.

DeVries, R., Kwak, H.L., & Sales, C. (2002). Experimenting with draining and movement of water in tubes. In R. DeVries (Ed.), *Developing constructivist early childhood curriculum: Practical principles and activities* (pp. 141–163). New York, NY: Teachers College Press, Columbia University.

DeVries, R., & Zan, B. (1994). *Moral classrooms, moral children: Creating a constructivist atmosphere in early education.* New York, NY: Teachers College Press, Columbia University.

DeVries, R., & Zan, B. (1995). Creating a constructivist classroom atmosphere. *Young Children, 51*(1), 4–13.

DeVries, R., Zan, B., Hildebrandt, C., Edmiaston, R., & Sales, C. (2002). *Developing constructivist early childhood curriculum: Practical principles and activities.* New York, NY: Teachers College Press, Columbia University.

Dewey, J. [1916] (1966). *Democracy and education.* New York, NY: Free Press.

Diamond, Adele. (2006). The early development of executive functions. In E. Bralystok and F, I.M. Craik.(Eds.) *Lifespan cognition: Mechanisms of change.* London, UK: Oxford University Press.

Diamond, K.E., Hestenes, L.L., & O'Connor, C.E. (1994). Integrating young children with disabilities in preschool: Problems and promise. Research in review. *Young Children, 49*(2), 68–75.

Doidge, N. (2007). *The brain that changes itself.* New York, NY: Penguin.

Donaldson, M. (1978). *Children's minds.* London, UK: Fontana.

Drolet, D. (2007). Minding the gender gap. *University Affairs,* (October), 9–12.

Duckworth, E. (1991). Twenty-four, forty-two, and I love you: Keeping it complex. *Harvard Educational Review, 61*(1), 1–24.

Duckworth, E. (1987). *The having of wonderful ideas and other essays on teaching and learning.* New York, NY: Teachers College Press, Columbia University.

Dunbar, R. (1996). *Grooming, gossip and the evolution of language.* Cambridge, MA: Harvard University Press.

Dyson, A.H. (1993). From prop to mediator: The changing role of written language in children's symbolic repertoire. In B. Spodek & O.N. Saracho, (Eds.), *Yearbook in early childhood education: Language and literacy in early childhood education* (Vol. 4, pp. 21–41). New York, NY: Teachers College Press.

Edmiaston, R., Dolezal, V., Doolittle, S., Erickson, C., & Merritt, S. (2000). Developing individualized education programs for children in inclusive settings: A developmentally appropriate framework. *Young Children, 55*(4), pp. 36–41.

Edwards, B. (1986). *Drawing on the artist within.* New York, NY: Simon & Schuster.

Edwards, C., Gandini, L., & Forman, G. (1998). *The hundred languages of children: The Reggio Emilia approach to early childhood education: Advanced reflections* (2nd ed.). Greenwich, CT: Ablex Publishing.

Egan, K. (1988). *Primary understanding: Education in early childhood.* New York, NY: Routledge.

Egan, K. (1999). *Children's minds: Talking rabbits and clockwork oranges: Essays on education.* New York, NY: TC Press.

Eliot, L. (1999). *What's going on in there? How the brain and mind develop in the first five years.* New York, NY: Bantam Books.

Eliot, L. (2009). *Pink brain, blue brain: How small differences grow into troublesome gaps and what we can do about it.* Boston, MA: Houghton Mifflin.

Elkind, D. (1976). *Child development and education: A Piagetian perspective.* New York, NY: Oxford University Press.

Elkind, D. (1977). The early years: The vital years. *Journal of the Canadian Association for Young Children, 3*(1), 20–21.

Elkind, D. (1982). *The hurried child: Growing up too fast too soon.* Reading, MA: Addison Wesley.

Elkind, D. (1986). Formal education and early childhood education: An essential difference. *Phi Delta Kappan, 67*(9), 631–636.

Elkind, D. (1987). *Miseducation: Preschoolers at risk.* New York, NY: Knopf.

Elkind, D. (2003). Thanks for the memory: The lasting value of true play. *Young Children, 58*(3), 46–51.

Elkind, D. (2007). *The power of play: Learning what comes naturally.* Cambridge: Perseus Book Group.

Ellswood, R. (1999). Really including diversity in early childhood. *Young Children, 54*(4), 62–66.

Erikson, E. (1963). *Childhood and society* (2nd ed.). New York, NY: Norton.

Esbensen, S.B. (1987). *The early childhood playground: An outdoor classroom.* Ypsilanti, MI: High/Scope Press.

Esbensen, S.B. (1990). Designing the early childhood setting. In I. Doxey (Ed.), *Child care and education: Canadian dimensions* (pp. 178–192). Toronto: Nelson Canada.

Esbensen, S.B. (1991). *Let's play outdoors: Getting back to nature.* Halifax: Child Care Resources.

Essa, E. (2011). *Introduction to early childhood education* (6th ed.), Toronto: Nelson Canada.

Evergreen Canada. (2004). *Small wonders: Designing vibrant natural landscapes for early childhood.* Toronto, ON: Evergreen.

Fein, G. (1985). The affective psychology of play. In C.C. Brown, & A.W. Gottfried (Eds.), *Play interactions: The role of toys and parental involvement in children's development* (pp. 19–28). Skillman, NJ: Johnson & Johnson.

Feez, S. (2010). *Montessori and early childhood.* London, UK: Sage.

Florida, R. (2004). *The rise of the creative class: And how it's transforming work, leisure, community and everyday life.* Boston, MA: Basic Books.

Florida, R. (2010). *The great reset: New ways of living and working drive post-crash prosperity.* New York, NY: Random House.

Forman, G.E., & Kuschner, D.S. (1988). *The child's construction of knowledge: Piaget for teaching children.* Washington, DC: National Association for the Education of Young Children.

Forman, G. (2010). When 2-year-olds and 3-year-olds think like scientists. *Early Childhood Research and Practice, 12*(2), http://ecrp.uiuc.edu/v12n2/forman.html.

Fowke, E. (1969). *Sally go round the sun.* Toronto, ON: McClelland & Stewart.

Fowler, W. (1971). On the value of both play and structure in early education. *Young Children, 27*(1), 24–36.

Fowler, W. (1980). *Infant and child care: A guide to education in group settings.* Boston, MA: Allyn & Bacon.

Fraser, S. (2000). *Authentic childhood: Experiencing Reggio Emilia in the classroom.* Toronto, ON: Thomson Nelson.

Freire, P., & Macedo, D. (1987). *Literacy: Reading the word and the world.* South Hadely, MA: Bergin & Garvey Publishers.

Froebel, F. (1887). *The education of man.* New York, NY: D. Appleton & Co.

Fromberg, D. (1995). *The full day kindergarten: Planning and practicing a dynamic themes curriculum.* New York, NY: Teachers College Press, Columbia University.

Fromberg, D. (2002). *Play and meaning in early childhood education.* New York, NY: Allyn & Bacon.

Frost, J., Wortham, S., & Reifel, S. (2005). *Play and child development.* Upper Saddle River, NJ: Merrill/Prentice Hall.

Furman, E. (1990). Plant a potato: Learn about life (and death). *Young Children, 45*(6), 15–20.

Galinsky, E. (2010). *Mind in the making: The seven essential life skills every child needs.* New York, NY: HarperStudio.

Galizio, C., Stoll, J., Hutchins, P. (2009, July). Exploring the possibilities for learning in natural spaces. *Young Children, 64*(4): 42–48.

Gallenstein, N. (2003). *Creative construction of mathematics and science concepts in early childhood.* Olney, MD: Association for Early Childhood International.

Galvin, E.S. (1994). The joy of seasons: With the children, discover the joys of nature. *Young Children, 49*(4), 4–9.

Garbarino, J. (1989). An ecological perspective on the role of play. In M.N. Bloch & A.D. Pelligrini (Eds.), *The ecological context of children's play.* Norwood, NJ: Ablex.

Gardner, H. (1980). *Artful scribbles: The significance of children's drawings.* New York, NY: Basic Books.

Gardner, H. (1982). *Art, mind and brain.* New York, NY: Basic Books.

Gardner, H. (1983). *Frames of mind.* New York, NY: Basic Books.

Gardner, H. (1989). *To open minds.* New York, NY: Basic Books.

Gardner, H. (1991). *The unschooled mind: How children think and how schools should teach.* New York, NY: Basic Books.

Gardner, H. (1999). *The disciplined mind: What all students should understand.* New York, NY: Simon & Schuster.

Gardner, H. (2000). *Intelligence reframed: Multiple intelligences for the 21st century.* New York, NY: Basic Books.

Gardner, H. (2004). 2004 Introduction: Multiple intelligences after twenty years. In *Frames of mind: The theory of multiple intelligences* (pp. xiii–xxxix). New York, NY: Basic Books.

Gardner, H. (2006). *Five minds for the future.* Cambridge, MA: Harvard Business School Press.

Garvey, C. (1977). *Play.* Cambridge, MA: Harvard University Press.

Gelfer, J. (1990, Summer). Discovering and learning art with blocks. *Day Care and Early Education,* 21–24.

Gillis, J., & Hardacre, J. (1993). Play and problem-solving. In C. Corter & N. Park (Eds.), *What makes kindergarten programs effective?* Toronto, ON: Ministry of Education and Training.

Gilmore, J.B. (1966). Play: A special behavior. In R.N. Haber (Ed.), *Current research in motivation* (pp. 343–355). New York, NY: Holt, Rinehart and Winston.

Ginsberg, H.P., Inoiue, N., & Seo, K.H. (1999). Young children doing mathematics: Observations of everyday activities. In J.V. Copley. (Ed.), *Mathematics in the early years* (pp. 88–99). Washington, DC: National Association for the Education of Young Children.

Ginsberg, H., & Opper, S. (1969). *Piaget's theory of intellectual development: An introduction.* Englewood Cliffs, NJ: Prentice-Hall.

Glazzard, J., & Percival, J. (2010). Assessment for learning. In J. Glazzard, D. Chadwick, J. Percival, & A. Webster, (Eds.), *Assessment for learning in the early years foundation stage* (pp. 1–20). London, UK: Sage.

Glossop, R. (2006). Quoted in M. Gordon, *The roots of empathy: Changing the world child by child* (p. 143). Toronto, ON: Thomas Allen Publishers.

Glossop, R. (2002). Interview. *Link: Roots of Empathy Newsletter, 1*(1), 1.

Gober, S. (2002). *Six simple ways to assess young children.* Albany, NY: Thomson Delmar Learning.

Goleman, D. (1995). *Emotional intelligence.* New York, NY: Bantam.

Goleman, D. (2006). *Social intelligence: The new science of human relationships.* New York, NY: Bantam.

Gonzalez-Mena, J., (2005). *Foundations of early childhood education: Teaching children in a diverse society.* Toronto, ON: McGraw-Hill.

Gordon, M. (2006). *The roots of empathy: Changing the world child by child.* Toronto, ON: Thomas Allen.

Goulet, M. (2001). What is imergent curriculum? In *Resources in early childhood education.* Toronto, ON: General Resources Centre, Ryerson University.

Gowen, J. (1995). Research in review: The early development of symbolic play. *Young Children, 50*(3), 75–84.

Green, M. (2002). *Releasing the imagination.* San Francisco, CA: Jossey-Bass.

Greenberg, P. (1994). How and why to teach all aspects of preschool and kindergarten math naturally, democratically and effectively: For teachers who don't believe in academic programs, who do believe in educational excellence, and who find math boring to the max—part 2. *Young Children, 49*(2), 12–18.

Greenfield, D. (2010). Please touch! A computer adaptive approach for assessing early science. IES 5th Annual Research Conference. June 29.

Greenspan, S. (1997). *The growth of the mind and the endangered origins of intelligence.* Reading, MA: Addison Wesley.

Greenspan, S. (2010). *Great kids: Helping your baby and child develop the 10 essential qualities for a healthy, happy life.* Cambridge, MA: DaCapo Press.

Greenspan, S., & Greenspan, N.T. (2010). *The learning tree: Overcoming learning disabilities from the ground up.* Cambridge, MA: DaCapo Press.

Gross, A.L., & Ortiz, L.W. (1994). Using children's literature to facilitate inclusion in kindergarten and the primary grades. *Young Children, 49*(3), 32–35.

Guernsey, L. (2010). *Into the minds of babes: How screen time affects children from birth to age five.* New York, NY: Basic Books.

Gyre, L. (2011). Advantages and disadvantages of computer technology in preschool. eHow.com. Retrieved from www.eHow.com/about_4779416_advantages-disadvantages-computer-technology-pr.

Hall, E.M., & Dennis, L.A. (1968). *The Hall-Dennis report: Living and learning.* Ontario Provincial Committee of Aims and Objectives of Education in the Schools of Ontario. Toronto, ON.

Hammer, K. (2011, April 26). Kindergarten split classes will "shortchange" students. *The Globe and Mail,* A12.

Hammer, K. (2011, August 31). Why is there so little play in playgrounds? *The Globe and Mail,* A1 & A5.

Haugland, S. (2000). Early childhood classrooms in the 21st century: Using computers to maximize learning. *Young Children, 55*(1), 12–18.

Healy, J. (1998). Computers damage brains of young children. Emaxhealth.com. Retrieved from www.emaxhealth.com/1275computers-damage-brains-youngchildren.

Healy, J. (1998). *Failure to connect: How computers affect our children's minds—for better and worse.* New York, NY: Simon & Schuster.

Healy, J. (2010). *Different learners: Identifying, preventing and treating young children's learning problems.* New York, NY: Simon & Schuster.

Helm, J.H., & Beneke, S., (Eds.) (2003). *The power of projects: Meeting contemporary challenges in early childhood classrooms: Strategies and solutions.* New York, NY: Teachers College Press.

Helm, J.H., Beneke, S., Scranton, P., & Doubet, S. (2003). Responding to children's special needs. In J.H. Helm, & S. Beneke (Eds.), *The power of projects: Meeting contemporary challenges in early childhood classrooms: Strategies and solutions* (pp. 50–63). New York, NY: Teachers College Press.

Helm, J.H., & Katz, L. (2011). *Young investigators: The project approach in the early years.* Washington, DC: NAEYC.

Henniger, M.L. (1994). Planning for outdoor play. *Young Children, 49*(4), 10–15.

Hewitt, K. (2001). Blocks as a tool for learning: Historical and contemporary perspectives. *Young Children, 56*(1), 6–13.

Hiebert, J., & Lefevre, P. (1986). Conceptual and procedural knowledge in mathematics: An introductory analysis. In J. Hiebert, (Ed.), *Conceptual and procedural knowledge: The case of mathematics* (pp. 1–27). Hillsdale, NJ: Lawrence Erlbaum Associates.

Hildebrandt, C., & Zan, B. (2003). Exploring the art and science of musical sounds. In DeVries, R. et al., *Developing constructivist curriculum: Practical principles and activities* (pp. 193–209). New York, NY: Teachers College Press, Columbia University.

Hinnant, H.A. (1999). Growing gardens and mathematicians. *Young Children, 54*(2), 23–26.

Hirsch, E.S. (1996). *The block book* (3rd ed.). Washington, DC: National Association for the Education of Young Children.

Hitz, R., & Driscoll, A. (1988). Praise or encouragement? New insights into praise: Implications for early childhood teachers. *Young Children, 43*(4), 6–13.

Hoffman, M.L. (2000). *Empathy and moral development: Implications for caring and justice.* Cambridge, UK: Cambridge University Press.

Hofmann, R. (1986). Piaget and microcomputer learning environments. *Journal of Learning Disabilities, 19*(3), 181–184.

Hohmann, M., Banet, B., & Weikart, D. (1979). *Young children in action.* Ypsilanti, MI: High/Scope Press.

Holt, B. (1989). *Science with young children* (rev. ed.). Washington, DC: National Association for the Education of Young Children.

Hope, G. (2008). *Thinking and learning through drawing.* London, UK: Sage.

Houle, G.B. (1987). *Learning centres for young children.* West Greenwich, RI: Tot-lot Child Care Products.

Howard, Justine, (2010). Making the most of play in the early years: The importance of children's perceptions. In Broadhead, P., Howard, J., & E. Wood, *Play and learning in the early years* (pp. 145–160). London, UK: Sage.

Howe, C., & Jones, E. (1993). *Engaging children in science.* New York, NY: Macmillan.

Huber, L.K. (1999). Woodworking with young children: You can do it. *Young Children, 54*(6), 32–34.

Hughes, A. & Ellis, S. (1998). *Writing it right: Children writing 3–8.* Glasgow, Scotland: Scottish Consultative Council on Curriculum.

Hughes, F. (1995). *Children, play and development* (2nd ed.). Boston, MA: Allyn and Bacon.

Human Resources Development Canada. (2002). *Knowledge matters: Skills and learning for Canadians.* Ottawa, ON: HRDC.

Hunka, S. (1987). The role of computers in Canadian education. In L.L. Stewin & S.J.H. McCann (Eds.), *Contemporary educational issues: The Canadian mosaic* (pp. 69–81). Toronto, ON: Copp Clark Pitman.

Isaacs, S. (1938). Quoted in "Lecture to National Safety Congress." (1960). *National Froebel Bulletin Foundation, 125.*

Jalongo, M.R., Fennimore, B.S., & Stamp, L.N. (2004). The acquisition of literacy. In B. Spodek & O. Saracho (Eds.), *Contemporary perspectives on language policy and literacy instruction in early childhood education.* Greenwich, CT: Information Age Publishing.

Jambor, T., & Palmer, S.D. (1991). *Playground safety manual.* Birmingham, AL: Injury Prevention Center, University of Alabama.

Jarvis, P. (2010). Born to play: The biocultural roots of rough and tumble play and its impact on young children's learning. In P. Broadhead, J. Howard, & E. Wood, *Play and learning in the early years* (pp. 61–77) London, UK: Sage.

Johnson, J.E., Christie, J.F., & Wardle, F. (2005). *Play, development, and early education.* Boston, MA: Pearson Education.

Johnson, H. (1936). *School begins at two.* New York, NY: New Republic.

Jonassen, D.H., Howland, J., Moore, J., & Marra, R.M. (2003). *Learning to solve problems with technology: A constructivist perspective* (2nd ed.). Columbus, OH: Merrill Prentice Hall.

Jones, E., & Reynolds, G. (1992). *The play's the thing: Teachers' roles in children's play.* New York, NY: Teachers College Press.

Jones, E., & Nimmo, J. (1999). Collaboration, conflict and change: Thoughts on education as provocation. *Young Children, 54*(1), 5–12.

Jones, E., & Nimmo, J. (1994). *Emergent curriculum.* Washington, DC: NAEYC.

Judge, K. & Barish-Wreden, M. (2010, September 7). You'll do better in green: Doctors say nature makes us healthier. *Hamilton Spectator*, http://www.thespec.com/living/healthfitness/article/254023--you-ll-do-better-in-green.

Kagan, J. (1998). *Three seductive ideas.* Cambridge, MA: Harvard University Press.

Kagan, S.L., & Lowenstein, A.E. (2004). School readiness and children's play: Contemporary oxymoron or compatible option? In E.F. Zigler, D.G. Singer, & S.J. Bishop-Josef. (Eds.), *Children's play: The roots of reading* (pp. 59–76). Washington, DC: Zero to Three Press.

Kail, R.V., & Zolner, T. (2005). *Children* (Canadian ed.). Toronto, ON: Pearson Prentice Hall.

Kamerman, S. (2001). *Early childhood education and care: International perspectives.* New York, NY: Institute for Child and Family Policy, Columbia University.

Kamii, C. (1972). An application of Piaget's theory to the conceptualization of a preschool curriculum. In R. Parker (Ed.), *The preschool in action* (pp. 91–131). Boston, MA: Allyn and Bacon.

Kamii, C. (1982). *Number in the preschool.* Washington, DC: National Association for the Education of Young Children.

Kamii, C., & DeClark, G. (1985). *Young children reinvent arithmetic: Implications of Piaget's theory.* New York, NY: Teachers College Press, Columbia University.

Kamii, C., & DeVries, R. (1993). *Physical knowledge in preschool education: Implications of Piaget's theory* (2nd ed.). New York, NY: Teachers College Press.

Karpov, Y.V. (2005). Three- to six-year-olds: Sociodramatic play as the leading activity during early childhood. In *The neo-Vygotskyan approach to child development* (pp. 139–170). Cambridge, UK: Cambridge University Press.

Katz, L. (1974). *Talks with teachers.* Washington, DC: National Association for the Education of Young Children.

Katz, L. (1994). *The project approach.* Champaign, IL: ERIC Clearinghouse on Elementary and Early Childhood Education.

Katz, L., & Chard, S. (1989). *Engaging children's minds: The project approach.* Norwood, NJ: Ablex.

Katz, L.G. (1994). Let's not waste children's minds. *Young Children, 49*(4), 2.

Kellogg, R. (1967). *The psychology of children's art.* New York, NY: Random House.

Kellogg, R. (1969). *Analyzing children's art.* Palo Alto, CA: National Press Books.

Kennedy, L.M., Tipps, S., & Johnson, A. (2008). *Guiding children's learning of mathematics* (11th ed.). Belmont, CA: Thomson Wadsworth.

Kennewell, S., & Beauchamp, G. (2007). The features of interactive whiteboards and their influence on learning. *Learning Media & Technology, 32*(3), 227–241.

Kirn, W., & Cole, W. (2001, April 30). What ever happened to play? *Time,* 38–40.

Kim, J., & Robinson, H.M. (2010). Four steps in becoming familiar with early music standards. *Young Children, 65*(2), 42–47.

Klein, M.D., & Chen, D. (2001). *Working with children from culturally diverse backgrounds.* Albany, NY: Thomson Delmar Learning.

Kostelnik, M.J. (1992). Myths associated with developmentally appropriate programs. *Young Children, 47*(4), 17–23.

Kostelnik, M.J., Whiren, A.P., & Stein, L.C. (1986). Living with He-Man: Managing superhero fantasy play. *Young Children, 41*(3), 3–9.

Koster, J.B. (1999). Clay for little fingers. *Young Children, 54*(2), 18–22.

Koster, J.B. (2005). *Growing artists: Teaching art to young children* (3rd ed.). Albany, NY: Thomson Delmar Learning.

Kotsopoulos, S. (2005). "I do it myself": Are we over-emphasizing independence in early childhood? *Interaction, 19*(3), 23–26.

Kritchevsky, S., Prescott, E., & Walling, L. (1977). *Planning environments for young children: Physical space* (2nd ed.). Washington, DC: National Association for the Education of Young Children.

Kuo, Frances. (2009). Presented at the Annual Meeting of the American Association for the Advancement of Science: *Access to nature is essential to human health.* Chicago, IL: University of Chicago Landscape and Human Health Lab.

Kuschner, D. (1986). *This computer gives you a hard bargain. Is it conflict or frustration when software won't let you change your mind?* Champaign, IL: ERIC Clearinghouse for Early Childhood Education (ERIC Document Reproduction Service No. ED. 279311).

Lambert, E.B., & Clyde, M. (2003). Putting Vygotsky to the test. In D.E. Lytle (Ed.), *Play and educational theory in practice* (pp. 59–67). Westport, CT: Praeger Publishers.

Lasky, L., & Mukerji, R. (1980). *Art: Basic for young children.* Washington, DC: National Association for the Education of Young Children.

Laumann, S. (2006). *Child's play: Rediscovering the joy of play in our families and communities.* Toronto, ON: Random House.

Laurendeau, M., & Pinard, A. (1968). *Les premières notions spatiales de l'enfant.* Montreal, QC: Delachaux and Niestle.

Lauricella, A., Barr, R., & Calvert, S.L. (2008, May 21). Paper presented at the Annual Meeting of the International Communication Association: *Emerging computer skills: Influences of young children's executive functioning abilities and parental scaffolding techniques.* Montreal, QC.

Lazdauskas, H. (1996). Music makes the school go 'round. *Young Children, 51*(5), 22–23.

Leslie, A. (1987). Pretense and representation: The origins of "theory of mind." *Psychological Review 94*: 412–426.

Lesman, A. St. Clair. (2011). How children learn language. *Torch 84*(2), 23–26.

Liberman, J. (1991). *Light medicine of the future.* Santa Fe, NM: Bear & Co. Publishing.

Lind, K.K. (1991). *Exploring science in early childhood: A developmental approach.* Albany, NY: Thomson Delmar Learning.

Lind, K.K. (2005). *Exploring science in early childhood education* (4th ed.). Albany, NY: Thomson Delmar Learning.

Lindauer, S.K. (1987). Montessori education for young children. In J.L. Roopnarine, & J.E. Johnson (Eds.), *Approaches to early childhood education* (pp. 109–26). Columbus, OH: Merrill.

Lipinski, J.M., Nida, R.E., Shade, D.D., & Watson, J.A. (1984). *Competence, gender and preschoolers' freeplay choices when a microcomputer is present in the classroom.* Champaign, IL: ERIC Clearinghouse for Early Childhood Education. (ERIC Document Reproduction Service No. ED. 243609).

Louv, R. (1991). *Childhood's future.* New York, NY. Anchor Books, Doubleday.

Louv, R. (2008). *Last child in the woods: Saving our children from nature-deficit disorder.* Chapel Hill, NC: Algonquin Books of Chapel Hill.

Lovins, L. Hunter, & Cohen, B. (2011). *Climate capitalism: Capitalism in the age of climate change.* New York, NY: Hill and Wang.

Lowenfeld, V., & Brittain, W.L. (1987). *Creative and mental growth* (6th ed.). New York, NY: Macmillan.

MacKinnon, D.W. (1971). Nature and nurture of creative talent. In R. Ripple (Ed.), *Educational psychology: Readings in learning and human abilities.* New York, NY: Harper and Row.

MacNaughton, G. (2003). *Shaping early childhood: Learners, curriculum and contexts.* Berkshire, UK: Open University Press.

Malka, M., & Schulman, S. (1986). Microcomputers in special education: Renewed expectations for solutions to chronic difficulties. *The Exceptional Child, 33*(3), 199–205.

Mallory, B. (1994). Inclusive policy, practice, and theory for young children with developmental differences. In B.L. Mallory and R.S. New (Eds.), *Diversity and developmentally appropriate practices: Challenges for early childhood education.* New York, NY: Teachers College Press.

Mallory, B.L., & New, R.S. (1994). *Diversity and developmentally appropriate practices: Challenges for early childhood education.* New York, NY: Teachers College Press.

Mann, D. (1996). Serious Play. *Teachers College Record, 97*(3), 446–468.

Marjanovic-Shane, A. (2010). A cultural-historical approach to creative education. In Connery, M.C., John-Steiner, V.P., & Marjanovic-Shane, A. (Eds.), *Vygotsky and creativity: A cultural-historical approach to play, meaning-making, and the arts* (Educational Psychology Series, vol. 5, p. 203). New York, NY: Peter Lang.

Martin, D.J. (2001). *Constructing early childhood science.* Albany, NY: Thomson Delmar Learning.

Mayesky, M. (1997). *Creative activities for young children.* Toronto, ON: Thomson Nelson.

Maynard, R. (2010). Computers and young children. *Canadian Children, 35*(1): 15–18.

McArdle, F., & Barker, B. (1990). *What'll I do for art today?* Melbourne, Australia: Thomas Nelson Australia.

McCain, M.N., Mustard, J.M., & McCuaig, K. (2011) *The Early Years Study 3: Making Decisions, Taking Action.* Margaret and Wallace McCain Family Foundation.

McCarrick, K. (2004). Computers and young children. *Pediatrics for Parents, Inc.* October, http://www.pedsforparents.com/articles/2845.shtml.

McCloskey, R. (1969). *Make way for ducklings.* New York, NY: Viking Press.

McCollum, J.A., & Bair, H. (1994). Research in parent-child interaction: Guidance to developmentally appropriate practice for young children with disabilities. In B.L. Mallory, B.L. & R.S. New (Eds.), *Diversity and developmentally appropriate practice: Challenges for early childhood education* (pp. 84–106). New York, NY: Teachers College Press.

McIlroy, A. (2010, May 25). Neuroscience: How poverty shapes the brain—Scientists hope bold new research will help poor kids succeed. *The Globe and Mail,* A1, A6.

McNeill, David. (1992). *Hand and mind: What gestures reveal about thought.* Chicago, IL: University of Chicago Press.

Meaney, M. (2001). Nature, nurture and the disunity of knowledge. *Annals of the New York Academy of Sciences, 935,* 50–61.

Meisels, S. (2000). Personal reflections on testing, teaching and early childhood education. *Young Children, 55*(6), 16–19.

Merzenich, M.M. (2001). Cortical plasticity contributing to child development. In J.L. McLelland & R.S. Siegler (Eds.), *Mechanisms of cognitive development: Behavioral and neural perspectives* (p. 68). Mahwah, NJ: Lawrence Erlbaum Associates.

Mighton, J. (2003). *The myth of ability: Nurturing mathematical talent in every child.* Toronto, ON: House of Anansi Press.

Miller, D.F. (2010). *Positive child guidance* (6th ed.). Belmont, CA: Wadsworth Cengage Learning.

Ministry of Education, Ontario. (2010). *The full-day early-learning-kindergarten program. Draft version.* Toronto, ON.

Moffit, T. (2011). A gradient of childhood self-control predicts health, wealth, and public safety. *National Academy of Sciences (*Proceedings, January), http://www.pnas.org/cgi/doi/10.1073/pnas.

Montessori, M. (1949). *The absorbent mind.* New York, NY: Dell.

Montessori, M. (1964). *The Montessori method.* New York, NY: Schocken.

Moomaw, S. (1984). *Discovering music in early childhood.* Boston, MA: Allyn and Bacon.

Moore, R. (2000). It's time to send nature back to school. *Evergreen, 1*(1), 3.

Moravcik, E. (2000). Music all the livelong day. *Young Children, 55*(4), 27.

Moyles, J. (2010). Foreword. In P. Broadhead, J. Howard, & E. Wood, *Play and learning in the early years* (p. xiii). London, UK: Sage.

Mustard, F. (2004). Presented at Summer Institute on Early Childhood Development: Coping and Competence: *Experience-based brain development in early life and coping skills in adult life.* Toronto, ON: George Brown College.

Mustard, F. (2010, June 4). Interview with Hana Gartner. *The Current.* Toronto, ON: Canadian Broadcasting Corporation.

Music Educators National Conference. (1994). *The school music program: A new vision: The K-12 national standards, pre-K standards, and what they mean to educators.* Reston, VA.

Myers, B.K., & Maurer, K. (1987). Teaching with less talking: Learning centers in the kindergarten. *Young Children, 42*(4), 21.

Nash, C. (1979, 1989). *The learning environment: A practical approach to the education of the three-, four- and five-year-old.* Toronto, ON: Collier Macmillan.

National Association for the Education of Young Children (NAEYC). (1997). *Block play: Building a child's mind.* Washington, DC: NAEYC.

National Association for the Education of Young Children (NAEYC) (2003). Position Statement: *Early childhood curriculum assessment and program evaluation: Building an effective, accountable system in programs.* Washington, DC: NAEYC.

National Association for the Education of Young Children (NAEYC). (2009). Position Statement: *Developmentally appropriate practice in early childhood programs serving children from birth through age eight.* Washington, DC: NAEYC.

National Association for the Education of Young Children (NAEYC). (2011). Position Statement: *Technology in early childhood programs servicing children from birth to age 8.* Washington, DC: NAEYC.

Needham, D. (2010). Problem solving, reasoning and numeracy. In I. Palaiologou (Ed.), *The early years foundation stage: Theory and practice.* (pp. 155). London, UK: Sage Publications.

Neuman, S.B., & Roskos, K.A. (1994). Of scribbles, schemas, and storybooks: Using literacy albums to document young children's literacy growth. *Young Children, 49*(2), 78–85.

New, R. (2005). The Reggio Emilia approach: Provocations and partnerships with U.S. early childhood educators. In J. L. Roopnarine, & J.E. Johnson (Eds.), *Approaches to early childhood education* (4th ed., pp. 314–335). Columbus, OH: Pearson Merrill Prentice Hall.

New, R.S. (1993). Reggio Emilia: Some lessons for U.S. educators. *ERIC Digest.* Urbana, IL: ERIC Clearinghouse on Elementary and Early Childhood Education.

Newell, A., Shaw, J.C., & Simon, H.A. (1962). The processes of creative thinking. In H.E. Gruber, G. Terrell, & M. Wertheimer (Eds.), *Contemporary approaches to creative thinking* (pp. 65–66). New York, NY: Atherton.

Nourot, P.M. (2005). Historical perspectives on early childhood education. In J.L. Roopnarine, & J.E. Johnson. (Eds.) (2005). *Approaches to early childhood education* (4th ed.). Upper Saddle River, NJ: Pearson, Merrill Prentice Hall.

Nourot, P.M., & Van Hoorn, J.L. (1991). Symbolic play in preschool and primary settings. *Young Children, 46*(6), 40–50.

Ogu, U. & Schmidt, R. (2009). Investigating rocks and sand: Addressing multiple learning styles through an inquiry-based approach. *Young Children, 64(*2), 12–18.

O'Hara, M. (2008). Young children, learning and ICT: a case study in the UK maintained sector. *Technology, Pedagogy and Education 17*(1), 29–40.

Olfman, S. (Ed.). (2003). *All work and no play: How educational reforms are harming our preschoolers.* Westport, CT: Praeger Publishers.

Olson, C.P., & Sullivan, E.V. (1987). Beyond the mania: Critical approaches to computers in education. In L.L. Stewin and S.J.H. McCann (Eds.), *Contemporary educational issues: The Canadian mosaic* (pp. 95–106). Toronto, ON: Copp Clark Pitman.

Organisation for Economic Co-operation and Development (OECD). (2001). *Education policy analysis.* Paris, France: OECD.

Organisation for Economic Co-operation and Development (OECD). (2004). *Country note: Canada.* Paris, France: OECD.

Organisation for Economic Co-operation and Development (OECD). (2011). *Your better life index.* Paris, France: OECD.

Ormrod, J.E. (2006). *Educational psychology: Developing learners.* Upper Saddle River, NJ: Pearson Merrill Prentice Hall.

Owen, N. (2010). *Creative development.* In I. Palaiologou (Ed.), *The Early Years Foundation Stage* (pp. 190–209). London, UK: Sage.

Pacini, L.A. (2000). The power of empowerment. *Young Children, 55*(6), 83–85.

Palaiologou, I. & Bangs, M. (2010). Assessment in the early years foundation stage. In I. Palaiologou (Ed.), *The Early Years Foundation Stage* (pp. 53–66). London, UK: Sage.

Palaiologou, I., Walsh, G., Dunphy, E., Lyle, S., Thomas-Williams, J. (2010). The national picture. In I. Palaiologou (Ed.), *The Early Years Foundation Stage.* London, UK: Sage.

Palaiologou, I. (2010). Ed. *The Early Years Foundation Stage.* London, UK: Sage.

Papert, S. (1980). *Mindstorms: Children, computers and powerful ideas.* New York, NY: Basic Books.

Papert, S. (1998, September 1). Technology in schools: To support the system or render it obsolete? *The Atlantic Monthly*, 45–62.

Parten, M. (1933). Social participation among preschool children. *Journal of Abnormal and Social Psychology, 28*, 136–147.

Paley, V.G. (2004). *A child's work: The importance of fantasy play.* Chicago, IL: University of Chicago Press.

Pearlman-Hougie, D. (2010) Fears of parents. Interview. *The Nature of Things.* Canadian Broadcasting Corporation, Sunday, September 5.

Pelligrini, A.D. (1980). The relationship between kindergartners' play and reading, writing, and language achievement. *Psychology in the School, 17,* 530–535.

Pelligrini, A.D. (1984). Children's play and language: Infancy through early childhood. In T.D. Yawkey, & A.D. Pelligrini (Eds.), *Child's play and play therapy* (pp. 45–58). Lancaster, PA: Technomic Publishing.

Pelligrini, A.D. (1991). A longitudinal study of popular and rejected rough-and-tumble play. *Early Education and Development, 2*(3), 205–213.

Pelligrini, A.D., & Boyd, B. (1993). The role of play in early childhood development and education: Issues in definition and function. In B. Spodek (Ed.), *Handbook of research on the education of children* (pp. 105–121). New York, NY: Macmillan.

Penn, H. (2005). *Understanding early childhood: Issues and controversies.* London: Open University Press.

Percival, J. (2010). Values and principles of assessment in the early years foundation stage. In Glazzard, J., Chadwick, D., Webster, A., Percival, J. (Eds.). *Assessment for learning in the early years foundation stage* (pp. 21–41). London, UK: Sage.

Perry, B. (2002). A place for everyone: Nurturing each child's niche. *Early Childhood Today,* November.

Perry, B. (2002). Childhood experience and the expression of genetic potential: What childhood neglect tells us about nature and nurture. *Brain and Mind* (Vol. 3, pp. 79–100). Amsterdam: Kluwer Academic Publishers.

Perry, B. (2010). How sounds become words. http://teacher.scholastic.com/professional/bruceperry/soundsbecomewords.htm.

Perry, B. & Szalavitz, M. (2010). *Born for love: Why empathy is essential and endangered.* Toronto, ON: HarperCollins Canada.

Perry, G., & Rivkin, M. (1992). Teachers and science. *Young Children, 47*(4), 9–16.

Piaget, J. [1926] (1955). *The language and thought of the child.* New York, NY: Meridian Books.

Piaget, J. (1945). *Play, dreams and imitation in childhood.* New York, NY: Norton.

Piaget, J. (1962). *Introduction to causal thinking in the child.* New York, NY: International Universities Press.

Piaget, J. (1969a). *The science of education and the psychology of the child.* New York, NY: Viking.

Piaget, J. & Inhelder, B. (1969b). *The psychology of the child.* New York, NY: Basic Books.

Piaget, J. (1972). *To understand is to invent.* New York, NY: Viking.

Pica, R. (2010). *Experiences in movement: Birth to age 8* (4th ed.). Belmont, CA: Wadsworth Cengage Learning.

Piel, J.A., & Baller, W.A. (1986). Effects of computer assistance on acquisition of Piagetian conceptualization among children of ages two to four. *AEDS Journal, 19*(2–3), 210–215.

Pimento, B., & Kernested, D. (2010). *Healthy foundations in early childhood settings* (4th ed.). Toronto, ON: Nelson Education.

Pinker, S. (2007). The stuff of thought: Language as a window into human nature. London, UK: Viking.

Postman, N. (1982). *The disappearance of childhood.* New York, NY: Delacorte Press.

Prairie, A.P. (2005). *Inquiry into math, science and technology for teaching young children.* Albany, NY: Thomson Delmar Learning.

Prascow, C. (2002). Engaging children's learning through centres in a kindergarten program. *Early Childhood Education, 35*(1), 33–37.

Pratt, D. (1980). *Curriculum design and development.* New York, NY: Harcourt Brace Jovanovich.

Prescott, E. (1994). The physical environment: A powerful regulator of experience. *Child Care Information Exchange, 100*(Nov.–Dec.): 9–15.

Ragsdale, R.G. (1985). Response to Sullivan on Papert's "Mindstorms." *Interchange, 16*(3), 19–36.

Ragsdale, R.G. (1987). Computers in Canada: Communications and curriculum. In L.L. Stewin, & S.J.H. McCann (Eds.), *Contemporary educational issues: The Canadian mosaic* (pp. 82–94). Toronto, ON: Copp Clark Pitman.

Reed, M., & Canning, N. (Eds). (2010). *Reflective practice in the early years.* London, UK: Sage Publications.

Reifel, S. (1984). Block construction: Children's developmental landmarks in representation of space. *Young Children, 42*(42), 61–67.

Resnick, L.B. (1989). Developing mathematical knowledge. *American Psychologist, 44*(2), 162–169.

Resnick, L.B., & Hall, M.W. (1998). Learning organizations for sustainable educational reform. *Daedalus, 127*(4), 89–118.

Richey, D.D., & Wheeler, J.J. (2000). *Inclusive early childhood education.* Albany, NY: Delmar Thomson Learning.

Riel, M. (1985). The computer chronicles newswire: A functional learning environment for acquiring literary skills. *Educational Computing Research, 1*(3), 317–337.

Rifkin, J. (2009). *The empathic civilization: The race to global consciousness in a world in crisis.* New York, NY: Tarcher Penguin.

Ring, K. (2010). Supporting a playful approach to drawing. In P. Broadhead, J. Howard, & E. Wood, *Play and learning in the early years.* London, UK: Sage.

Rogers, C. (1969). *Freedom to learn.* Columbus, OH: Merrill.

Rogers, C.S., & Sawyers, J.K. (1988). *Play in the lives of children.* Washington, DC: National Association for the Education of Young Children.

Rogers-Warren, A.K. (1982). Behavioral ecology in classrooms for young handicapped children. *Topics in Early Childhood Special Education, 2*(1), 21–32.

Roopnarine, J.L., & Johnson, J.E. (2005). *Approaches to early childhood education* (4th ed.). Upper Saddle River, NJ: Pearson Education.

Roskos, K., & Christie J. (2001). Examining the play-literacy interface: A critical review and future directions. *Journal of Early Childhood Literacy, 1*(1) 59–89.

Ross, M.E. (2000). Science their way. *Young Children, 55*(1), 6–13.

Rowan, C. (2010). Virtual child: The terrifying truth about what technology is doing to children. CreateSpace (self-published). Retrieved from www.zoneinproducts.com/virtual-child/.

Rubenzer, R.L. (1984). *Educating the other half: Implications of left/right brain research.* Champaign, IL: ERIC Clearinghouse for Early Childhood Education. (ERIC Document Reproduction Service No. ED.150655).

Rubin, K., Fein, G., & Vandenberg, B. (1983). Play. In P.H. Mussen (series ed.) & E.M. Hetherington (vol. ed.), *Handbook of child psychology: Socialization, personality, and social development* (4th ed., pp. 693–774). New York, NY: Wiley.

Salmon, A. (2010). Tools to enhance young children's thinking. *Young Children, 65* (5): 28–31.

Saltz, R., & Saltz, E. (1986). Pretend play training and its outcomes. In G. Fein, & M. Rivkin (Eds.), *The young child at play: Reviews of research* (Vol. 4, pp. 155–173). Washington, DC: National Association for the Education of Young Children.

Sawyers, J.K., & Rogers, C.S. (1988). *Young children develop through play.* Washington, DC: National Association for the Education of Young Children.

Saxton, M. (2010). *Child language acquisition and development.* London, UK: Sage Publications.

Schaffer, D.R., Wood, E., & Willougby, T. (2002) *Developmental psychology: Childhood and adolescence* (1st Canadian ed.). Toronto, ON: Thomson Nelson.

Schiller, M. (1995). An emergent art curriculum that fosters understanding. *Young Children, 50*(3), 33–38.

Schirrmacher, R. (1988). *Art and creative development for young children.* Albany, NY: Delmar Publishing.

Schreiber, M.E. (1996). Lighting alternatives: Considerations for child care centers. *Young Children, 51*(5), 11–13.

Seefeldt, C. (1995). Art—a serious work. *Young Children, 50*(3), 39–45.

Seefeldt, C. (2005). *How to work with standards in the early childhood classroom.* New York, NY: Teachers College Press.

Segal, M. (2004). The roots and fruits of pretending. In E.F. Zigler, D.G. Singer, & S.J. Bishop-Josef (Eds.), *Children's play: The roots of reading* (pp. 33–49). Washington, DC: Zero to Three Press.

Shade, D.D. (1985). *Will a microcomputer really benefit preschool children? A theoretical examination of computer applications in ECE.* Champaign, IL: ERIC Clearinghouse for Early Childhood Education. (ERIC Document Reproduction Service No. ED. 264951).

Sharna, O. (Ed.). (2003). *All work and no play: How educational reforms are harming our preschoolers.* Westport, CT: Praeger Publishers.

Shenk, D. (2010). *The genius in all of us: Why everything you've been told about genetics, talent and IQ is wrong.* New York, NY: Doubleday.

Sherman, M. & Kay, C.B. (1932). The intelligence of isolated mountain children. *Child Development, 3* (4): 279–290.

Shermis, S. (1974). *Philosophic foundations of education.* New York, NY: Van Nostrand Reinhold.

Shipley, D. (1989). The ecole maternelle. Unpublished paper. Nova Southeastern University.

Shipley, D. (1997). Play for development and for achieving learning outcomes. *Interaction, 11*(1), 18–20.

Shute, N. (2011). For kids, self control factors into future success, http://www.npr.org/2011/02/14/133629477/for-kids-self-control-factors-into-future-success

Siann, G., & Macleod, H. (1986). Computers and children of primary school age: Issues and questions. *British Journal of Educational Technology, 17*(2), 133–144.

Sigman, A. (2008). Computers damage brains of young children. Retrieved from www.emax.Health.com/1275 computers-damage-brains-young-children.

Singer, J.L., & Lythcott, M.A. (2002). Fostering school achievement and creativity through sociodramatic play in the classroom. In *Research in the Schools, 9*(2), 41–50.

Singer, J.L., Plaskon, S.L., & Schweder, A.E. (2003). A role for play in the preschool curriculum. In S. Olfman (Ed.), *All work and no play.* Westport, CT: Praeger Publishers.

Sluss, D.J. (2005). *Supporting play: Birth through age eight.* Albany, NY: Thomson Delmar Learning.

Smilansky, S. (1968). *The effects of sociodramatic play on disadvantaged preschool children.* New York, NY: Wiley.

Smilansky, S. (1971). Can adults facilitate play in children? In S. Arnaud, & N. Curry (Eds.). *Play: The child strives toward self-realization.* Washington, DC: National Association for the Education of Young Children.

Smilansky, S., & Shefatya, L. (1990). *Facilitating play: A medium for promoting cognitive, socio-Emotional and academic development in young children.* Gaithersburg, MD: Psychosocial and Educational Publications.

Smilansky, S. (1992). Pre-conference presentation sponsored by Nova Southeastern University at the Annual Conference of the National Association for the Education of Young Children: *A new model for home/school relationships and the development of responsibility in children.* Washington, DC: National Association for the Education of Young Children.

Smith, R.F. (1987). Theoretical framework for preschool science experiences. *Young Children, 42*(1), 34–40.

Somerville, M. (2006). *The ethical imagination: Journeys of the human spirit (*Massey Lecture Series). Toronto, ON: House of Anansi Press.

Soto, L.D.(1991). Understanding bilingual/bicultural young children. *Research in Review 46*(2), 30–36.

Sperry Smith, S. (2006). *Early childhood mathematics.* Boston, MA: Pearson Allyn & Bacon.

Spodek, B., & Saracho, O. (2003). Historical antecedents of early childhood educational play. In B. Spodek & O. Saracho, *Contemporary Perspectives on Play in Early Childhood Education.* Greenwich, CT: Information Age Publishing.

Statistics Canada. (1999). *Education indicators in Canada: Report of the Pan Canadian Education Indicators Program.* Ottawa, ON: Statistics Canada.

Steffin, S.A. (1986). Using the micro as a weapon: Fighting against convergent thinking. *Childhood Education, 59(2)*, 251–258.

Stephens, K. (1995). *Sciencing: It's here, there, and everywhere.* Redmond, VA: Exchange Press.

Sternberg, R. (1988). *The triarchic mind: A new theory of human intelligence.* New York, NY: Harcourt, Brace, Jovanovich.

Sternberg, R. (2005). Intelligence, competence and expertise. In A.J. Ellikot & C.S. Dweck (Eds.), *Handbook of competence and motivation.* New York, NY: Guildford Publications.

Stipek, D.J. (1982). Work habits begin in preschool. In J.F. Brown (Ed.), *Curriculum planning for young children* (pp. 205–212). Washington, DC: National Association for the Education of Young Children.

Streibel, M.J. (1984). *An analysis of the theoretical foundations for the use of microcomputers in ECE.* Champaign, IL: ERIC Clearinghouse for Early Childhood Education. (ERIC Document Reproduction Service No. ED 248971).

Stuber, G.M. (2007). Centering your classroom: Setting the stage for engaged learners. *Young Children, 62*(7): 1–3.

Sulzby, E., & Teale, W.H. (2003). The development of the young child and the emergence of literacy. In J. Flood, D. Lapp, J.U. Squire, & J. Jensen (Eds.), *Handbook of research on teaching the English language arts* (pp. 300–313). Mahwah, NJ: Lawrence Erlbaum Associates.

Talbot, J., & Frost, J.L. (1989). Magical playscapes. *Childhood Education,* 11–19. (Adapted with permission.)

Tannock, M. (2008). Rough and tumble play: An investigation of the perceptions of educators and young children. *Early Childhood Education Journal, 35*(4), 357–362.

Tapscott, D. (1998). *Growing up digital: The rise of the net generation.* New York, NY: McGraw-Hill.

Teale, W.H., & Sulzby, E. (1989). Emerging literacy: New perspectives. In D.S. Strickland, & L.M. Morrow (Eds.), *Emerging literacy: Young children learn to read and write* (pp. 1–15). Newark, DE: International Reading Association.

Tishman, J.E. & Perkins, D. (1993). Teaching thinking dispositions: From transmission to enculturation. *Theory Into Practice, 32*(3), 147–153.

Tisone, M., & Wismar, B.L. (1985). Microcomputers: How can they be used to enhance creative development? *Journal of Creative Behavior, 19*(2), 97–103.

Tobiassen, D.P., & Gonzalez-Mena, J. (1999). *A place to begin: Working with parents on issues of diversity.* San Francisco, CA: California Tomorrow.

Torrance, P. (1966). *Torrance tests of creative thinking: Norms technical manual research edition.* Princeton, NJ: Personnel Press.

Torrence, M., & Chattin-McNichols, J. (2005). Montessori Education Today. In J.L. Roopnarine, & J.E. Johnson. (Eds.), *Approaches to early childhood education* (4th ed.). Upper Saddle River, NJ: Pearson Merill Prentice Hall. pp. 363–394.

Tovey, H. (2010). Playing on the edge: Perceptions of risk and danger in outdoor play. In P. Broadhead, J. Howard, & E. Wood, *Play and learning in the early years.* London, UK: Sage.

Townsend, M. (2010). Nature-deficit disorder and solastalgia down under. In Louv, R., People in nature. *Psychology Today* (online). Retrieved from www.psychologytoday.com/blog/people-in-nature/201004/nature-deficit-disorder-and-solastalgia-down-under.

Trousdale, A. (2005). Intersections of spirituality, religion and gender in children's literature. *International Journal of Children's Spirituality 10*, 61–79.

Turkle, S. (1984). The intimate machine: Eavesdropping on the secret lives of computers and kids. *Science,* 41–46.

Turkle, S. (2011). *Alone together: Why we expect more from technology and less from each other.* Boston, MA: Basic Books.

Twiest, M.M., & Kupetz, B.N. (2000). Nature, literature and young children: A natural combination. *Young Children, 55*(1), 59–63.

Unger, L. (1998). Mixing business with pleasure. In D. Fromberg & D. Bergen (Eds.), *Play from birth to twelve and beyond: Contexts, perspectives and meanings* (pp. 485–492). New York, NY: Garland Publishing.

Villegas, A.M., & Lucas, T. (2002). Preparing culturally responsive teachers: Rethinking the curriculum. *Journal of Teacher Education. 53*(1), 20–32.

Vinson, B.M. (2001). Fishing and Vygotsky's concept of effective education. *Young Children, 56*(1), 88–89.

Vygotsky, L. (1978). *Mind in society: Development of higher psychological processes.* Cambridge, MA: Harvard University Press.

Walsh, P. (1988). *Early childhood play-grounds: Planning an outside learning environment.* Melbourne, Australia: Martin Educational in association with Robert Andersen and Associates.

Warzecha, M. (2011, July 16). New playground designs aim to be game changers. *The Globe and Mail,* M6.

Watts, D.W. (1991). *Exploring the joy of music.* Richmond Hill, ON: Scholastic Canada.

Weber, E. (1969). *The kindergarten: Its encounter with educational thought in America.* New York, NY: Teachers College Press.

Weber, E. (1984). *Ideas influencing early childhood education: A theoretical analysis.* New York, NY: Teachers College Press, Columbia University.

Weininger, O. (1979). *Play and education.* Springfield, IL: Chas. C. Thomas.

Wellhousen, K., & Kieff, J. (2001). *A constructivist approach to block play in early childhood.* Albany, NY: Delmar Thomson Learning.

Whitebread, D. (2010). Play, metacognition and self-regulation. In P. Broadhead, J. Howard, and E. Wood, *Play and learning in the early years* (pp. 161–176). London, UK: Sage.

Whitehead, M. (2010). *Language and literacy in the early years, 0–7* (4th ed.). London, UK: Sage.

Whitin, D. (1994). Literature and mathematics in preschool and primary: The right connection. *Young Children, 49*(2), 4–11.

Wien, C.A. (2008). *Emergent curriculum in the primary classroom: Interpreting the Reggio Emilia approach in schools.* New York, NY: Teachers College Press.

Wilson, L. (2001). *Partnerships: Families and communities in Canadian early childhood education.* Toronto, ON: Thomson Nelson.

Wing, L.A. (1995). Play is not the work of the child: Young children's perceptions of work and play. *Early Childhood Research Quarterly, 10,* 223–247.

Wolfe, J. (2000). *Learning from the past: Historical voices in early childhood education.* Mayerthorpe, AB: Piney Branch Press.

Wood, E., & Attfield, J. (2005). *Play, learning and the early childhood curriculum.* London, UK: Chapman Publishing.

Wood, E. (2010). *Developing integrated pedagogical approaches to play and learning.* In P. Broadhead, J. Howard, & E. Wood, *Play and learning in the early years.* London, UK: Sage.

Wortham, S.C. (1984). *Organizing instruction in early childhood: A handbook of assessment and activities.* Boston, MA: Allyn and Bacon.

Wright, Robert. (2010). *Multifaceted assessment for early childhood education.* Thousand Oaks, CA: Sage Publications.

Yardley, A. (1988). *Senses and sensitivity* (Young Children Learning Series). Oakville, ON: Rubicon.

Yeo, M. (2001). Playground as pedagogical space. *Early Childhood Education, 34*(2). New York, NY: Human Sciences Press.

Zan, B. & Geikin, R. (2010). Ramps and pathways: Developmentally appropriate intellectually rigorous, and fun physical science. *Young Children, 2*(3), 12–17.

Zeimer, M. (1987). Science and the early childhood curriculum: One thing leads to another. *Young Children, 43*(8), 44–51.

Zigler, E.F., Singer, D.G., & Bishop-Josef, S.J. (Eds.). (2004). *Children's play: The roots of reading.* Washington, DC: Zero to Three Press.

Index

C

D

F

J

K

L

M

N

Q

R

S

T

U